# FLORIDA LAND

Records
*of the*
Tallahassee and
Newnansville
General Land Office
1825-1892

*Alvie L. Davidson*

HERITAGE BOOKS
2008

# HERITAGE BOOKS
*AN IMPRINT OF HERITAGE BOOKS, INC.*

**Books, CDs, and more—Worldwide**

For our listing of thousands of titles see our website
at
www.HeritageBooks.com

Published 2008 by
HERITAGE BOOKS, INC.
Publishing Division
100 Railroad Ave. #104
Westminster, Maryland 21157

Copyright © 1989 Alvie L. Davidson

All rights reserved. No part of this book may be reproduced or transmitted in any form or by any means, electronic or mechanical, including photocopying, recording or by any information storage and retrieval system without written permission from the author, except for the inclusion of brief quotations in a review.

International Standard Book Numbers
Paperbound: 978-1-55613-233-9
Clothbound: 978-0-7884-7457-6

# INTRODUCTION

Between June 2, 1825 and January 20, 1892 many hundreds of claims were made for land in the virgin and unsettled wilderness called Florida. Most of these early pioneers were looking for good farmland or grazing land for their cattle. Others were speculating that the land they were purchasing for as little as $1.25 per acre would some day make them very wealthy. Each had his or her own reason to move southward to the land of swamps, Seminole Indians, alligators, mosquitoes, and a host of other unknown adventures.

Honest and hard-working could be the best description for those early inhabitants of Florida. Most of the land to be settled lay in areas bordered on the North by the Okeefenokee Swamp, on the West by the Gulf of Mexico and its tidal swamps, on the East by the Atlantic Ocean, and on the South by the Everglades and other rivers with adjoining swamps. It took extreme determination and great will power to settle in this land and remain to make it what it is today.

It is not known exactly when the United States government officially opened the federal land offices at Tallahassee and Newnansville (near present Gainesville) but from these Receiver's Receipts it can be determined that the first recorded date was June 2, 1825. These settlers kept passing through these land offices until the last recorded date of January 20, 1892. While compiling this data the authors found information which said that some of the original receipt records were lost during all of the transferring over the years from site to site until a permanent storage place was found. It may never be known how many were lost prior to their final stop in the Bureau of Land Management at Suitland, Maryland.

While examining these files it should be noted that many names of persons who would play an important part in the formation and early history of Florida appear many times. Such names are Edward Carrington Cabell, first United States Representative; David L. Yulee, first United States Senator; William P. DuVal, first Territorial Governor of Florida; and Robert Gamble, noted banker and founder of the famed "Gamble Mansion" in Ellenton, Manatee County, Florida.

It is the hope of the compilers that the material contained herein will be used for furtherance of genealogical research. Many of the documents alluded to herein contain valuable information which might possibly be unavailable from any other source due to burned courthouses or lost documents. Many of the records of the General Land Office reveal such information as marriage dates, birth dates, death dates, place of residences, place of birth, and lists of possible relatives who signed as witnesses on documents.

**Compiler**

Alvie L. Davidson
Dianne H. Davidson
4825 North Galloway Road
Lakeland, Florida 33809

# EXPLANATION

The files referred to in this volume are those of persons who were either purchasing land or receiving land under the Florida Armed Occupation Act of 1842 or the Homestead Act of 1862. By a sampling request of these records it has been found that one of the records used as an example is of John Black, a naturalized citizen from Sweden who presented his naturalization papers to prove his citizenship. He also presented his discharge papers from the U. S. Navy in 1867. Another example is that of George L. Altman in Polk County, Florida, filing for homestead near Fort Meade. The third example is that of Jeremiah Johns, an early settler of Hamilton County, purchasing 40 acres from the General Land Office at Tallahassee.

There is no way of knowing what is contained in any file without requesting a copy of it from the Bureau of Land Management and reviewing all the documents. This is done by writing to: Bureau of Land Management, C/O National Archives Record Center, 8th & Pennsylvania Avenue, N.W., Washington, D.C. 20408. The request must contain the file number, name, and legal description of the land. The Bureau will reply that the file has been found and the cost of the copies will be a said amount. After this fee is paid the copies will be forwarded. This total time elapsed for the search and copying is usually about 5-8 weeks for a single request.

When using this volume to find an ancestor any researcher must keep in mind the many name spelling variations. Some examples are: Rollison for Raulerson; O'Neel for O'Neil; Pelom for Pelham; Standley for Stanley; and Bird for Byrd. Almost any surname (other than common Smith and Brown) has several spelling variations. The names placed into this volume were copied just as they appeared on the document and not corrected.

Some abbreviations were used in compiling this volume.

* Sect. = Section of a Township
* Tp. = Township
* R. = Range
* N = North
* W = West
* S = South
* E = East
* ENE = East by Northeast
* WNW = West by Northwest
* SE = Southeast
* NW = Northwest
* NE = Northeast
* ESE = East by Southeast
* WSW = West by Southwest
* NNW = North by Northwest
* NNE = North by Northeast
* SSE = South by Southeast
* SSW = South by Southwest

In order to better understand how a legal description is read and what it means the compilers suggest a valuable book: THE SOURCE by Arlene Eakle and Johni Cerny (1984 Ancestry Publishing Co. Salt Lake City, UT); Pages 217-254.

Before presenting the final draft of this volume to the publisher it was read and re-read several times for proofing any errors but, as anyone knows, an error can always get past proof readers. If an error is found please pencil it in for future users. Just keep in mind that the compilers are only human.

# DEDICATION

This book is dedicated to
my wife, Dianne Hatcher Davidson,
my daughter, Kimberly Danielle Davidson,
my son, Alan Hatcher Davidson,
and my fantastic Tandy 1000 TX computer.

Without either of these
this work would have been a failure.

# FOREWORD

Florida was the first of the Atlantic Coast colonies to be settled and the last to achieve statehood. A number of factors contributed to the delay, among them a relatively small and unstable population over much of her early history and an erroneous though widespread perception that Florida was simply "a land of swamps, of quagmires, of frogs and alligators and mosquitoes." Many had vigorously opposed the annexation of the territory. One U.S. Congressman predicted that not even the inhabitants of Hell would be willing to immigrate to Florida, and Henry Clay, who should have known better, declared it to be "so loaded and encumbered with land grants" that "scarcely a foot of soil" was left for the United States. This volume listing thousands of federal land transactions in Florida one again proves him wrong, but his was not the last misconception about "the Sunshine State."

Researchers often find it difficult to locate books on Florida's records and resources, and the reason for that is simple: another misconception. Apparently some publishers and many researchers believe that because Florida is relatively young as a state, having achieved statehood more than fifty years after neighboring Georgia, it can be of little genealogical interest outside the current population. Numerous Americans now living in other states but tracing their Florida ancestry back ten generations prove the falsity of that notion, which ignores the fact the St. Augustine was a thriving settlement more than fifty years before the first Mayflower Pilgrim set foot on Plymouth Rock.

Numerous brick walls of long standing in Southern genealogy have toppled when family historians have sought and found "lost" ancestors who sojourned briefly on or relocated permanently to "the long frontier" of peninsular Florida. Especially during the territorial period many less-hardy fledgling Floridians fled home to Georgia or the Carolinas, driven out by the semitropical heat and humidity, a fear of snakes and alligators, or the onslaught of millions of tiny but formidable mosquitoes. Many of the more adventurous stayed for a few years before moving west to Alabama, Texas, or California. Even today, it is estimated that for every two who migrate to Florida another leaves. Descendants of Florida pioneers are found in every state, and one large Australian family traces its line to the 1820's along the Santa Fe River and Alachua County. In the first ten years of the Pioneer Descendant Certificate Program of the Florida State Genealogical Society, more than a thousand descents from ancestors who settled in Florida before statehood on 3 March 1845 have been established, documented, and published—and their numbers increase by several hundred each year.

The hundreds of hours and thousands of dollars invested in a Florida resource of this size and importance give further evidence of increasing recognition that genealogical research in Florida has come of age. The compilers and the publisher have done yeoman service in a most worthy cause.

—Brian E. Michaels, editor, **The Florida Genealogist**;
past president, Florida State Genealogical Society;
member, Florida State Historical Records Advisory Board.

Example No. 1 from EXPLANATION:
#2603 John Black in Hillsborough Co. Homestead Claim

## No. 1.—HOMESTEAD.

Land Office at Gainesville Fla
June 17, 1881.

I, John Black, of Bay View, Hillsboro. Co., Fla. who made Homestead Application No. 7209 for the S ½ of N.E. ¼ Sec. 12, T. 29 S., R. 15 E. do hereby give notice of my intention to make final proof to establish my claim before Wm C Brown Clerk Ct Court at Tampa Florida on the 21st day of July 1881, (Thursday) and that I expect to prove my claim by the following witnesses:

B. C. Youngblood of Bay View
J. M. Moore of Dunedin Hillsborough
H. C. Andrews
J. H. Holmes of County, Florida

John Black
B, (Signature of claimant.)

Land Office at Gainesville Fla
June 17, 1881.

Notice of the above application will be published in the "Guardian" printed at Tampa Fla, which I hereby designate as the newspaper published nearest the land described in said application.

L. A. Barnes
Register.

## United States (viz) of America.

Be it Remembered, That, at the Court of Common Pleas for the City and County of Philadelphia, held at Philadelphia, in the Commonwealth of Pennsylvania, in the United States of America, on the Twentieth day of September in the year of our Lord one thousand eight hundred and Sixty nine John Black a native of Sweden exhibited a petition praying to be admitted to become a Citizen of the United States and it appearing to the said Court that he had declared on oath, before the Prothonotary of this Court on the twenty fifth day of March A.D. 1867 that it was bona fide his intention to become a Citizen of the United States and to renounce forever all allegiance and fidelity to any foreign prince, potentate, state or sovereignty whatsoever and particularly to the King of Sweden of whom he was at that time a Subject And the said John Black having on his solemn oath declared and also made proof thereof agreeably to law, to the satisfaction of the Court, that he had resided one year and upwards within the State of Pennsylvania and within the United States of America upwards of five years immediately preceding his application, and that during that time he had behaved as a man of good moral character, attached to the principles of the Constitution of the United States, and well disposed to the good order and happiness of the same, and having declared on his solemn oath before the said Court that he would support the Constitution of the United States, and that he did absolutely and entirely renounce and abjure all allegiance and fidelity to every foreign prince, potentate, state or sovereignty whatsoever, and particularly to the King of Sweden of whom he was before a subject, And having in all respects complied with the law in regard to Naturalization, thereupon the Court admits the said John Black to become a Citizen of the United States, and orders all the proceeding aforesaid to be recorded by the Prothonotary of the said Court, which was done accordingly.

In Witness Whereof I have hereunto affixed the Seal of the said Court at Philadelphia this twentieth day of September in the year one thousand eight hundred and sixty nine and of the Sovereignty and Independence of the United States of America the Ninety fourth.

(Signed) Fred'k Wilberg

State of Florida } Hillsborough County } ss. I, Wm C Brown Clerk of the Circuit Court for said County, do hereby certify that the foregoing is a true and correct transcript of the original this day exhibited to me by John Black.

Witness my hand and the Seal of said Court at Tampa, County aforesaid this the 2nd day of August A.D. 1881.

Wm C Brown
Clerk

# Honorable Discharge from the United States Navy

Aug 4, 1864

This is to Certify, That No(3) Capt F'cle John Black enlisted Dec 13, 1861 at Philadelphia for three years 38 years of age 5 feet 9 inches high, dark eyes dark hair middy complexion has —— on at ————. As a Testimonial of Fidelity and Obedience is this day Honorably Discharged from the United States Gun Boat "Tahoma" is from the Naval Service of the United States. And, according to the provisions of the second section of the Act approved March 2, 1855 if within three months of this date the above described John Black to present this his Honorable Discharge at any United States Naval Rendezvous, and if found physically qualified, and shall re-enlist for three years or longer, then he shall be entitled to pay during the said three months, equal to that to which he would have been entitled if he had been employed in actual Service.

Approved (Signed) W B Anthony Commanding Officer.
(Signed) Wm H Romaine
Paymaster

Stamped on back

Received
Pay
16
1870
Treasury Dept

(Part of Stamp illegible Clerk)
State of Florida
Hillsborough County } SS W. Brown Clerk of the Circuit Court for said County, do

R

Discharge. Rod 3
This is to certify That No. 8711 John Black
Capt. Foretop, late from U.S.S. "Waco" has
this day been discharged from the U.S. Receiving
Ship "Vermont" and from the naval service.
Dated the 14th, March 1867.
Approved
(Signed) A.G. B. Benham          (Signed) G.W. Hasler
Lt. Com.                                Paymaster.
Com of Officer.

| Name | When Enlisted | Term | Rating | City, Town or Country | Date | Age | Occupation | Eyes | Hair | Comple- |
|------|---------------|------|--------|------------------------|------|-----|-----------|------|------|---------|
| John Black | 1865 1st March | 2 | Capt. Fore | Sweden | | 33 | Mariner 20 | Blue | Brown | Fair |

(Height)
5, 6      (Signed) A.G.B. Benham  Ex Officer.

State of Florida
Hillsborough County } I Wm. C. Brown Clerk of the Circuit Court of said County Do hereby Certify
that the foregoing is a correct transcript of the
original exhibited to me this date by John Black
   Witness my hand and the Seal of said
   Court at Tampa, County aforesaid
   this 2d day of August A.D. 1881.
              Wm. C. Brown
                 Clerk.

[4-369.]

## HOMESTEAD PROOF.—TESTIMONY OF CLAIMANT.

Geo. L. Altman being called as a witness in his own behalf in support of homestead entry No. 1020, for S½ of SW¼ & N½ of SW¼ & NW¼ of SE¼ Sec 30 T 32 S R 25 E, testifies as follows:

Ques. 1.—What is your name—written in full and correctly spelled—your age, and post-office address?

Ans. George Lafayette Altman, my age 22 years last March, Post office Fort Meade Polk Co Fla

Ques. 2.—Are you a native of the United States, or have you been naturalized?

Ans. I am

Ques. 3.—When was your house built on the land and when did you establish actual residence therein? (Describe said house and other improvements which you have placed on the land, giving total value thereof.)

Ans. I bought the improvement, the house was ready built when I established residence in June 1878. Log dwelling, kitchen & out buildings worth about $250.00

Ques. 4.—Of whom does your family consist; and have you and your family resided continuously on the land since first establishing residence thereon? (If unmarried, state the fact.)

Ans. Self, wife & 2 children. & we have resided continuously on the Hd since residence

Ques. 5.—For what period or periods have you been absent from the homestead since making settlement, and for what purpose; and if temporarily absent, did your family reside upon and cultivate the land during such absence?

Ans. My absence has been temporary & family have resided most all the time

Ques. 6.—How much of the land have you cultivated and for how many seasons have you raised crops thereon?

Ans. About 5 acres, 6 seasons raised crops including the present one

Ques. 7.—Are there any indications of coal, salines, or minerals of any kind on the land? (If so, describe what they are, and state whether the land is more valuable for agricultural than for mineral purposes.)

Ans. No indications, more valuable for agriculture

Ques. 8.—Have you ever made any other homestead entry? (If so, describe the same.)

Ans. I have not

Ques. 9.—Have you sold, conveyed, or mortgaged any portion of the land; and if so, to whom and for what purpose?

Ans. I have not

George L. Altman

I HEREBY CERTIFY that the foregoing testimony was read to the claimant before being subscribed, and was sworn to before me this 21" day of April, 1884, and that it was taken in the absence of the circuit judge & no one appeared to contest the said claim.

S. J. Pearce Clk
A B Ferguson DC

Example No. 2 from EXPLANATION:
#4555 George L. Altman's Homestead claim

# HOMESTEAD PROOF.

## Final Affidavit Required of Homestead Claimants.

SECTION 2291 OF THE REVISED STATUTES OF THE UNITED STATES.

I, *Pierce Lafayett Attman*, having made a Homestead entry of the *S½ of SW¼ NE¼ & SW¼ & NW¼ of SE¼* section No. *30* in Township No. *32S* of range No. *25E* subject to entry at *Gainesville Fla* under section No. 2289 of the Revised Statutes, of the United States, do now apply to perfect my claim thereto by virtue of section No. 2291 of the Revised Statutes of the United States; and for that purpose do solemnly *swear* that I am a citizen of the United States; that I have made actual settlement upon and have cultivated said land, having resided thereon since the *3rd* day of *Jan'y*, 18*75* to the present time; that no part of said land has been alienated, except as provided in section 2288 of the Revised Statutes, but that I am the sole bona fide owner as an actual settler; that I will bear true allegiance to the Government of the United States; and further, that I have not heretofore perfected or abandoned an entry made under the homestead laws of the United States.

*George L Altman*

I, *S L Pearce Clk of Ct Ct*, of the Land Office at *Bartow Polk Co Fla*, do hereby certify that the above affidavit was subscribed and sworn to before me this *30"* day of *April*, 1884

and that it is in now taking
in the absence of the *S L Pearce Clk*
Circuit judge Esq. By *A B Ferguson DC*

Example No. 3 from EXPLANATION:
#6872 Jeremiah Johns Purchase of land in Hamilton Co.

**No.** 6872.  **LAND OFFICE,** at Tallahassee March 9 1837

**IT IS HEREBY CERTIFIED,** That, in pursuance of Law, Jeremiah Johns on this day purchased of the *Register* of this Office, the lot or N.W.1/4 S.W.1/4 of section number 15 of range number 15 S+E in township number 1 N. containing 40 acres, at the rate of 1 dollar and 25 cents per acre, amounting to 50 dollars and 13 3/4 cents, for which the said Jeremiah Johns has made payment in full as required by law.

**NOW THEREFORE BE IT KNOWN:** That, on presentation of this certificate to the COMMISSIONER OF THE GENERAL LAND OFFICE, the said Jeremiah Johns shall be entitled to receive a patent for the lot above described.

W. B. Hartley, *Register.*

\* A \*

**2799. ACOCK, Amos**
April 1, 1829, 4 miles N by W Bradfordville, Jackson Co. E 1/2 NW 1/4 Sect. 1 Tp.5 R.10, north and west.

**4574. ACOCK, Amos**
May 13, 1834, 1 1/4 miles W of Greenwood, Jackson Co. SW 1/4 SW 1/4 Sect.36 Tp.6 R.10, north and west. Transferred to **Martin GRAY**, Feb. 4, 1836.

**5210. ACOCK, Isaac**
1/4 mile S of Greenwood in Jackson County, SE 1/4 NW 1/4 Sect. 6 Tp. 5 R. 9, north and west. Transferred to **Elijah Bryan**, Dec. 21, 1836. Sworn before County Clerk **Thomas M. Bush**, Jackson Co.

**2490. ADAMS, Alexander**
Sept. 12, 1828, in Monticello, Jefferson Co. E 1/2 NW 1/4 Sect.30 Tp.2 R.5, north and east.

**4509. ADAMS, Absalom**
Jan. 13, 1834, 2 3/4 miles SSE of Capitola, Jefferson Co. NW 1/4 NE 1/4 Sect.33 Tp.1 R.3, north and east.

**500. ADAMS, Dennis**
June 2, 1825, 1 mile ESE Waukenah, Jefferson Co. W 1/2 SE 1/4 Sect.1 Tp.1 R.4, south and east.

**501. ADAMS, Dennis**
June 2, 1825, 1 mile ESE Waukenah, Jefferson Co. E 1/2 SE 1/4 Sect.2 Tp.1 R.4, south and east.

**520. ADAMS, Dennis**
June 20, 1825, 2 miles SE Waukenah, Jefferson Co. E 1/2 NE 1/4 Sect.11 Tp.1 R.4, south and east.

**701. ADAMS, Dennis**
(Of Fla.) April 16, 1826, 1 mile S Waukenah, Jefferson Co. W 1/2 NE 1/4 Sect.11 Tp.1 R.4, south and east.

**2259. ADAMS, Dennis**
Feb. 16, 1828, 1/4 mile W Jamieson, Gadsden Co. E 1/2 NE 1/4 Sect.12 Tp.3 R.3, north and west. Transferred Nov. 29, 1828 to **Wm. WILLIAMS**.

**2260. ADAMS, Dennis**
Feb. 16, 1828, at Jamieson, Gadsden Co. W 1/2 NW 1/4 Sect.7, Tp.3 R.2, north and west. Transferred Nov. 29, 1828 to **Wm. WILLIAMS**.

**2995. ADAMS, John L.**
Oct. 17, 1854, 2 1/4 miles NNW of McMeekin, Putnam Co. Lot No.17 Sect.18 Tp.10 R.23, south and east. Patent delivered (no date).

**4379. ADAMS, John L.**
June 5, 1856, 2 miles NW of McMeekin, Putnam Co. Lot No.3 Sect.18 Tp.10 R.23, south and east. Excess payment on Entry No. 3178. Patent delivered (no date).

**8452. ADAMS, John W.**
Jan. 15, 1841, 1 mile SSW Chaires, Leon Co. E 1/2 SW 1/4 Sect.34 Tp.1 R.2, north and east.

**856. ADAMS, Kinchen**
March 26, 1851, 1 1/2 miles SW Calvary, Marion Co. N 1/2 NE 1/4 Sect. 9 Tp. 16 R. 21, south and east. Patent delivered Oct. 5, 1874.

**7325. ADAMS, Robert C.**
Feb. 10, 1838, 2 miles W Haywood, Jackson Co. E 1/2 NE 1/4 Sect.31 Tp.6 R.7, north and west.

**7326. ADAMS, Robert C.**
Feb. 10, 1838, 3 miles NNW Haywood, Jackson Co. Lot No. 2 Sect.29 Tp.6 R.7, north and west.

**7928. ADAMS, Robert C.**
March 28, 1839, 1 mile N Haywood, Gadsden Co. W 1/2 NE 1/4 Sect.32 Tp.6 R.7, north and west.

**7180. ADAMS, Robert E.**
Jan. 1, 1838, 2 1/2 miles NNE Haywood, Jackson Co. Lot No. 4 Fractional Sect.29 Tp.6 R.7, north and west.

**1112. ADAMS, Wesley**
(DUP)Feb. 10, 1827, 5 miles NNW Chaires, Leon Co. W 1/2 SW 1/4 Sect. 10 Tp.1 R.2, north and east.

**1113. ADAMS, Wesley**
(DUP) Feb. 10, 1827, 4 miles N Chaires, Leon Co. SE 1/2 Sect. 10 Tp.1 R.2, north and east.

**3417. ADAMS, William**
Feb. 20, 1830, 1/2 mile SW Oakdale, Jackson Co. E 1/2 NW 1/4 Sect.35 Tp.4 R.10, north and west.

**6727. ADAMS, William**
Feb. 1, 1837, 2 miles S by W Myrick, Madison Co. SE 1/4 SW 1/4 Sect.6 Tp.1 R.6, south and east.

**6728. ADAMS, William**
Feb. 1, 1827, 4 miles NNE Lamont,

1

Jefferson Co. NE 1/4 NE 1/4 Sect. 12 Tp.1 R.5, south and east.

**2583. ADDISON, Cassandra**
Mar. 7, 1854, 6 miles E of Saxton, Bradford Co. NE 1/4 SW 1/4 Sect.3 Tp.6 R.21, south and east. Transferred to **John R. ALVARSA**, Sept. 17, 1867. Patent delivered June 9, 1872.

**6186. ADDISON, John**
Dec. 10, 1836, 1/4 mile NW Ocklockonee, Leon Co. NW 1/4 NW 1/4 Sect. 25 Tp.1 R.2, south and west.

**2637. ADKINS, Silas B.**
July 25, 1854, 3 1/4 miles S by W of Hawthorne, Alachua Co. N 1/2 NW 1/4 Sect. 32 Tp.10 R.22, south and east.

**5939. AGIROUS, Jean Baptiste**
Oct.29, 1836, 1 mile SE of Lloyd, Jefferson Co. NE 1/4 SE 1/4 Sect. 26 Tp.1 R.3, north and east.

**7695. AKINS, Seborn C.**
Nov. 18, 1889, 2 miles SW Bushnell, Sumpter Co. SE 1/4 SE 1/4 Sect. 20 NE 1/4 NE 1/4 Sect. 29 Tp.21S R.22E.

**3166. ALBRITON, Asa**
Dec, 21, 1829, 1 1/2 miles SW Wadesboro, Leon Co. W 1/2 NE 1/4 Sect.9 Tp.1 R.3, north and east.

**4768. ALBRITON, Asa**
Jan. 12, 1835, 1 1/4 miles N of Lloyd, Jefferson Co. NE 1/4 NE 1/4 Sect. 9 Tp.1 R.3, north and east.

**5558. ALBRITON, Asa**
Mar. 28, 1836, 1/2 mile SE by S of Wadesboro, Jefferson Co. W 1/2 SE 1/4 Sect. 9 Tp.1 R.3 north and east.

**6365. ALBRITON, Asa**
Dec. 31, 1836, 1 mile NNW Lloyd, Jefferson Co. SE 1/4 NE 1/4 Sect. 9 Tp.1 R.3, north and east.

**110. ALDERMAN, David**
Dec. 21, 1826, 2 miles E Jamieson, Gadsden Co. W 1/2 SW 1/4 Sect. 10 Tp.3 R.2, north and west.

**2055. ALDERMAN, David**
Sept. 9, 1827, 3 miles N Havana, Gadsden Co. W 1/2 SE 1/4 Sect. 10 Tp.3 R.2, north and west.

**6045. ALDERMAN, David**
Nov. 17, 1836, 2 miles ESE Jamieson, Gadsden Co. E 1/2 SW 1/4 Sect. 9 Tp.3 R.2, north and west.

**6125. ALDERMAN, David**
Dec. 2, 1836, 4 miles N Havana, Gadsden Co. E 1/2 SW 1/4 Sect. 10 Tp.3 R.2, north and west.

**6126. ALDERMAN, David**
Dec. 2, 1836, 3 miles N Havana, Gadsden Co. NE 1/4 NE 1/4 and NW 1/4 NE Sect. 15 Tp.3 R.2, north and west.

**3413. ALDERMAN, Isaac N.**
Feb. 16, 1830, 1 1/2 miles E. Hudson, Gadsden Co. W 1/2 NW 1/4 Sect. 26 Tp.3 R.2, north and west.

**3225. ALDERMAN, James**
Jan. 27, 1830, 1 1/2 miles NE Hinson, Gadsden Co. E 1/2 NW 1/4 Sect.15 Tp.3 R.2, north and west. Paid $100 in Scrip No. 29 in favour of **Alex MACOMB**, dated May 30, 1829.

**5351. ALDERMAN, James**
Dec. 18, 1835, 2 1/2 miles E of Iamonia, Leon Co. SW 1/4 NE 1/4 Sect. 15 Tp.3 R.2, north and east.

**8291. ALFORD, Hansford R.**
April 15, 1840, at Jennings, Hamilton Co. E 1/2 NE 1/4 Sect. 11 Tp.2 R.12, north and east.

**8293. ALFORD, Hansford R.**
April 15, 1840, 1/4 mile S Jennings, Hamilton Co. NE 1/4 SE 1/4 Sect. 11 Tp.2 R.12, north and east.

**7508. ALFORD, JANSFORD R.(Hansford ?)**
July 3, 1838, 3 1/2 miles NE Westlake, Hamilton Co. SW 1/4 SE 1/4 Sect.23 Tp.2 R.12, north and east.

**6940. ALFORD, John**
March 25, 1837, c. 1/2 mile S Jennings, Hamilton Co. Lot No.5 Fractional Sect. 12 Tp.2 R.12, north and east.

**5463. ALKMAN, Rebecca**
Feb. 15, 1836, 2 miles SE by S of Chaires, Leon Co. SE 1/4 SE 1/4 Sect. 36 Tp. 1 R.2, north and east. Transferred to **Mary W. NUTTAH**, Jan. 28, 1837.

**2567. ALLBRITTON, Thomas H.**
Mar. 6, 1854, 5 1/2 miles SW of Orange Springs, Marion Co. Lot No. 22 Sect. 31 Tp. 11 R. 23, south and east. Patent delivered Sept. 5, 1856.

**4230. ALLBRITTON, Thomas H.**
Mar. 3, 1856, at Cyril, Alachua Co.

SE 1/4 SE 1/4 Sect. 11 Tp. 8 R. 20, south and east. Patent delivered Aug. 1, 1857.

**556. ALLEN, Andrew Wyatt**
April 20, 1847, 1 1/2 miles SE Watertown, Columbia Co. SW 1/4 SE 1/4 NE 1/4 SW 1/4 Sect. 33 Tp. 3 R.17, south and east.

**2493. ALLEN, ANDREW Y.**
Feb. 24, 1854, at Watertown, Columbia Co. SW 1/4 NW 1/4 Sect. 34 Tp.3 R. 17, south and east. Patent delivered Sept. 5, 1856.

**ALLEN, B. C.** see **Joseph Bunefay #6833**

**46. ALLEN, Ann Amelia**
Nov. 28, 1843, c. 5 miles NE Louise, Bradford Co. SE 1/4 SE 1/4 Sect. 34 Tp. 7 R. 21, south and east.

**5139. Allen, George W.**
Nov. 25, 1859, 1 mile NNE of Rossburg, Suwannee Co. W 1/2 Sect. 32 Tp. 3 R.13, south and east. Patent delivered Sept. 22, 1869.

**5077. ALLEN, John B.**
July 15, 1835, at Concord, Gadsden Co. SW 1/4 SW 1/4 Sect. 18 Tp. 3 R. 1, north and west.

**5997. ALLEN, JOHN B.**
Nov. 10, 1836, 1/4 mile W of Concord, Gadsden Co. SW 1/4 SE 1/4 Sect. 13 Tp. 3 R. 2, north and west.

**6606. ALLEN, Matthew J.**
Jan. 19, 1837, 2 1/4 miles E by S Eridu, Madison Co. W 1/2 SW 1/4 Sect. 15 Tp.2 R.6, south and east.

**ANDREWS, Hercules R. W.**
Joint owner of # 6606

**986. ALLEN, R. C.**
Jan. 22, 1827, 6 miles S Quincy, Gadsden Co. E 1/2 NW 1/4 Sect. 28 Tp. 2 R. 2, north and west. Transferred to **L. H. JONES**, Feb. 12, 1827.

**987. ALLEN, R. C.**
Jan. 22, 1827, 6 miles S Havana, Gadsden Co. W 1/2 NW 1/4 Sect. 28 Tp. 2 R. 2, north and west.

**988. ALLEN, R. C.**
Jan. 22, 1827, 2 miles SE Quincy, Gadsden Co. NE 1/4 Sect. 17 Tp.2 R. 3, north and west. Endorsed to **L. H. JONES** Feb., 1825.

**1068. ALLEN, R. C.**
Feb. 5, 1827, 2 miles NE Wacissa, Jefferson Co. E 1/2 NW 1/4 Sect. 35 Tp.1 R. 4, south and east. Transferred to **Robert GAMBLE**, Feb. 16, 1827.

**1069. ALLEN, R. C.**
Feb. 5, 1827, 5 miles S Waukenah, Jefferson Co. E 1/2 SW 1/4 Sect. 26 Tp. 1 R. 4, south and east. Transferred to **Robt. GAMBLE**, Feb. 16, 1827.

**1188. ALLEN, R. C.**
March 2, 1827, 3 miles NNE Lake Jackson Station, Leon Co. Lot No. 2 Sect. 21 Tp. 2 R. 1, north and west.

**1805. ALLEN, R. C. & Co.**
June 5, 1827, 2 1/2 miles NW Vereen, Wakulla Co. E 1/2 NW 1/4 Sect. 30 Tp. 2 R. 1, south and east.

**2867. ALLEN. R. C.**
July 6, 1829, 1 mile SE Ocheesee, Calhoun Co. Lot No. 3 Sect. 8 Tp. 2 R. 7, north and west.

**2868. ALLEN, R. C.**
July 6, 1829, c. 2 1/2 miles W Roy, Liberty Co. Lot No. 3 Sect. 9 Tp. 2 R. 7, north and west.

**4620. ALLEN, R. C.**
Oct. 13, 1834, 4 3/4 miles E by S of Myrick, Madison Co. E 1/2 SW 1/4 Sect. 6 Tp. 1 R. 8, south and east.

**4622. ALLEN, R. C.**
Oct. 14, 1834, 3/4 mile N of Corey, Leon Co. NE 1/4 SE 1/4 Sect. 20 Tp. 1 R. 2, south and east.

**4623. ALLEN, R. C.**
Oct. 14, 1834, 1 mile NNE of Corey, Leon Co. NW 1/4 SW 1/4 Sect. 21 Tp. 1 R. 2, south and east.

**1070. ALLEN, Richard C. & Co.**
Feb. 5, 1827, 5 miles S Waukenah, Jefferson Co. E 1/2 NE 1/4 Sect. 26 Tp. 1 R. 4, south and east. Transferred to **Robert GAMBLE**, Feb. 16, 1827.

**2912. ALLEN, Richard C.**
July 8, 1829, 1 mile NE Sneads, Jackson Co. E 1/2 SE 1/4 Sect. 25 Tp. 4 R. 7, north and west.

**2923. ALLEN, Richard C.**
July 9, 1829, c. 1/2 mile N Haywood, Jackson Co. Lot No. 2 Sect. 33 Tp. 6 R. 7, north and west.

**2924. ALLEN, Richard C.**
July 9, 1829, c. 1/2 mile N Haywood, Jackson Co. Lot No. 1 Sect. 33 Tp. 6 R. 7, north and west.

**2925. ALLEN, Richard C.**
July 9, 1829, c. 2 miles NNW Hay-

wood, Jackson Co. Lot No. 1 Sect. 29 Tp. 6 R. 7, north and west.

**2926. ALLEN, Richard C.**
July 9, 1829, c. 2 1/2 miles NNW Haywood, Jackson Co. Lot No. 1 Sect. 20 Tp. 6 R. 7, north and west.

**2927. ALLEN, Richard C.**
July 9, 1829, c. 3 miles NNW Haywood, Jackson Co. Lot No. 1 Sect. 19 Tp.6 R. 7, north and west.

**2928. ALLEN, Richard C.**
July 9, 1829, c. 5 miles WNW Haywood, Jackson Co., Lot No. 3 Sect. 18 Tp. 6 R. 7, north and west.

**2929. ALLEN, Richard C.**
July 9, 1829, 1/4 mile SE Butler, Jackson Co., Lot No. 1 Sect. 34 Tp. 5 R. 7, north and west.

**3074. ALLEN, Richard C.**
Oct. 1, 1829, 3 1/2 miles S by W Meridian, Leon Co. E 1/2 NW 1/4 Sect. 1 Tp. 2 R. 1, north and west. Transferred to **Edward SINGLETARY**, (no date).

**3288. ALLEN, Richard C.**
Feb. 11, 1830, 2 1/2 miles N Lamont, Jefferson Co. W 1/2 SW 1/4 Sect. 11 Tp. 1 R. 5, south and east.

**3289. ALLEN, Richard C.**
Feb. 11, 1830, 2 1/2 miles N Lamont, Jefferson Co. E 1/2 SW 1/4 Sect. 11 Tp. 1 R. 5, south and east.

**3290. ALLEN, Richard C.**
Feb. 11, 1830, 2 miles N Lamont, Jefferson Co. W 1/2 NW 1/4 Sect. 14 Tp. 1 R. 5, south and east.

**3291. ALLEN, Richard C.**
Feb. 11, 1830, 2 miles N Lamont, Jefferson Co. E 1/2 NE 1/4 Sect. 15 Tp. 1 R. 5, south and east.

**3292. ALLEN, Richard C.**
Feb. 11, 1839, 2 miles N Lamont, Jefferson Co. E 1/2 SE 1/4 Sect. 10 Tp. 1 R. 5, south and east.

**3396. ALLEN, Richard C.**
Feb. 16, 1830, 1 1/2 mile N Lamont, Jefferson Co. SW 1/4 Sect. 14 Tp. 1 R. 5, south and east.

**4474. ALLEN, Richard C.**
Dec. 14, 1833, 3 miles E of Snead, Gadsden Co. E 1/2 NW 1/4 Sect. 31 Tp. 4 R. 6, north and west.

**6042. ALLEN, Richard C.**
Nov. 17, 1836, c. 1 mile NW Chattahoochee, Jackson Co. N 1/2 Lot No. 3 Fractional Sect. 30 Tp. 4 R. 6, north and west.

**6043. ALLEN, Richard C.**
Nov. 17, 1836, 2 miles W by N Chattahoochee, Jackson Co. SW 1/4 SE 1/4 Sect. 25 Tp. 4 R. 7, north and west.

**6044. ALLEN, Richard C.**
Nov. 17, 1836, 1/2 mile E Snead, Jackson Co. W 1/2 NE 1/4 and E 1/2 NW 1/4 Sect. 36 Tp. 4 R. 7, north and west.

**ALLEN, Richard C.** see **Romeo LEWIS** #6626 & 6627

**4621. ALLEN, W. C.**
Oct. 13, 1834, 6 miles E by S of Myrick, Madison Co. E 1/2 NW 1/4 Sect. 7 Tp. 1 R. 8, south and east.

**2635. ALLIGOOD, Sam'l**
Jan. 17, 1829, at Moody, Leon Co. E 1/2 NW 1/4 Sect. 17 Tp. 2 R. 1, south and east.

**7828. ALLMON, John James**
Jan. 21, 1839, 2 miles SSE Dills, Jefferson Co. SW 1/4 SW 1/4 Sect. 8 Tp. 2 R. 6, north and east.

**8977. ALSOBROOK, Johnson**
Oct. 9, 1846, 1 3/4 miles N Greenwood, Jackson Co. NE 1/4 NE 1/4 Sect. 30 Tp. 6 R. 5, north and west.

**8978. ALSOBROOK, Johnson**
Oct. 9, 1846, 1 3/4 miles N by W Greenwood, Jackson Co. W 1/2 SE 1/4 Sect. 19 Tp. 6 R. 9, north and west.

**4555. ALTMAN, George Lafayette**
May 13, 1884, 2 miles NW Jane Jay, Hardee Co. S 1/2 SW 1/4 NE 1/4 SW 1/4 and NW 1/4 SE 1/4 Sect. 30 Tp. 32S R. 25E.

**5955. ANDERS, Alexander**
Nov. 1, 1836, 2 miles E of Jamieson, Gadsden Co. W 1/2 NE 1/4 Sect. 9 Tp. 3 R. 2, north and west.

**7846. ANDERS, Owen E.**
Feb. 1, 1839, 3/4 mile SE by S Jamieson, Gadsden Co. SE 1/4 SE 1/4 Sect. 8 Tp. 3 R. 2, north and west.

**3706. ANDERS, OWEN E.**
Jan. 23, 1883, 2 miles W Alva, Lee Co. Lots 1, 2 & 3, NE 1/4 SE 1/4 Sect. 24 Tp. 43S, R. 27E.

**6534. ANDERS, Stephen E.**

Jan. 13, 1837, c. 1 1/2 miles SW Meridian, Leon Co. S 1/2 Lot No. 2 Fractional Sect. 25 Tp. 3 R. 1, north and west.

**4327. ANDERSON, David**
Mar. 18, 1833, 2 miles NE Quincy, Gadsden Co. NE 1/4 NW 1/4 Sect. 1 Tp. 2 R. 4, north and east.

**5602. ANDERSON, David**
April 19, 1836, 6 miles W by N of Dills, Jefferson Co. Lot No. 5 Sect. 36 Tp. 3 R. 4, north and east.

**6328. ANDERSON, David**
Dec. 27, 1836, c. 1 mile NE Alma, Jefferson Co. Lot No. 3 Fractional Sect. 25 Tp. 3 R. 4, north and east.

**265. ANDERSON, Duncan**
Jan. 1, 1827, 8 miles NE of Graceville, Jackson Co. E 1/2 NW 1/4 Sect. 20 Tp. 7 R. 12, north and west.

**393. ANDERSON, Duncan**
May 5, 1827, 4 miles NW Campbellton (Ala.?) Jackson Co. W 1/2 NW 1/4 Sect. 20 Tp. 7 R. 12, north and west.

**5857. ANDERSON, Duncan C.**
Sept. 21, 1836, 2 1/4 mile E of Encheehenna, Walton Co. W 1/2 SE 1/4 Sect. 36 Tp. 2 R. 18, north and west. (Note written in red ink across receipt: "Entry changed from Tp. 3 to Tp. 2, see certificate No. 13524." On back of receipt: "See letter to **Hon. E. A. MAXWELL** of March 14, 1854. Change of entry authorized. See letter to the R & R of May 17, 1855.)

**6813. ANDERSON, James H.**
Mar. 1, 1837, 1/2 mile E Drifton, Jefferson Co. E 1/2 NW 1/4 Sect. 17 Tp. 1 R. 5, north and east.

**6814. ANDERSON, James H.**
Mar. 1, 1837, at Drifton, Jefferson Co. SE 1/4 NW 1/4 SW 1/4 NE 1/4 Sect. 18 Tp. 1 R. 5, north and east.

**8411. ANDERSON, James S.**
Oct. 16, 1840, 1 mile SSW Madison, Madison Co. SE 1/4 SW 1/4 Sect. 34 Tp. 1 R. 9, north and east.

**8773. ANDERSON, James S.**
April 17, 1845, 4 miles E Talmouth, Suwannee Co. Lot No. 4 Sect. 35 Tp. 1 R. 11, south and east.

**8775, ANDERSON, James S.**
April 28, 1845, 5 miles E Talmouth, Suwannee Co. Fractional Lot No. 6 SE 1/4 Sect. 34 Tp. 1 R. 11, south and east.

**2649. ANDERSON, John C.**
Jan. 19, 1829, 2 miles SE Eucheanna, Walton Co. E 1/2 SE 1/4 Sect. 3 Tp. 1 R. 18, north and west.

**7412. ANDERSON, John W.**
Mar. 16, 1838, at Madison, Madison Co. W 1/2 NE 1/4 Sect. 34 Tp. 1 R. 9, north and east.

**8431. ANDERSON, John W.**
Dec. 16, 1840, 1 1/2 miles N by W Hawkins, Liberty Co. SW 1/4 NW 1/4 Sect. 29 Tp. 1 R. 6, south and east.

**2615. ANDERSON, Joseph**
Jan. 12, 1829, 2 1/2 miles NNE Alma, Jefferson Co. Lot No. 4 Sect. 24 Tp. 3 R. 4, north and east.

**8418. ANDERSON, Norman**
Nov. 9, 1840, 2 miles SSW Eucheeanna, Walton Co. E 1/2 SW 1/4 Sect. 36 Tp. 2 R. 18, north and west.

**8650. ANDERSON, Norman C.**
March 1, 1844, 1 3/4 miles SSE Eucheeanna, Walton Co. W 1/2 SW 1/4 Sect. 36 Tp. 2 R. 8, north and west.

**5729. ANDERSON, Thomas**
June 24, 1836, 1/4 mile SW of Madison, Madison Co. NW 1/4 NW 1/4 Sect. 33 Tp. 1 R. 9, north and east.

**8409. ANDERSON, Thomas**
Sept. 16, 1840, 1 mile W Madison, Madison Co. SE 1/4 NW 1/4 Sect. 33 Tp. 1 R. 9, north and east.

**8410. ANDERSON, Thomas M.**
Oct. 16, 1840, 1 1/2 miles SW Madison, Madison Co. NW 1/4 SW 1/4 Sect. 33 Tp. 1 R. 9, north and west.

**5540. ANDERSON, Uriah**
Mar. 16, 1836, 3 1/2 miles N of Monticello, Jefferson Co. SW 1/4 SW 1/4 Sect. 1 Tp. 2 R. 4, north and east.

**5966. ANDERSON, Walker**
Nov. 5, 1836, 1/2 mile NNW of Pace Junction, Santa Rosa Co. Lot No. 5 Fractional Sect. 25 Tp. 1 R. 29, north and west. Transferred to **Blake JERNIGAN**, Jan. 31, 1838.

**5967. ANDERSON, Walker**
Nov. 5, 1836, at Hart, Santa Rosa Co. Fract. Sect. 24 Tp. 1 R. 29, north and west. Transferred to **Blake JERNIG-**

AN, Jan. 31, 1838.
**6632. ANDERSON, Walker**
Jan. 23, 1837, just N Pine Barren Station, Escambia Co. Lots No. 1 and 2 Fractional Sect. 15 Tp. 3 R. 3, north and west.
**8595. ANDERSON, William**
July 26, 1843, 2 miles N by W Lake Jackson (town), Leon Co. N 1/2 Lot No. 2 Sect. 36 Tp. 2 R. 2, north and west.
**5813. ANDREWS, Edward**
Jan. 24, 1887, 2 1/2 miles S by W Norfleet, Leon Co. N 1/2 SW 1/4 Sect. 12 Tp. 1S R. 2W.
**4707. ANDREW, F. L.**
Dec. 12, 1834, 2 miles E of Corey, Leon Co. NE 1/4 NW 1/4 Sect. 27 Tp. 1 R. 2, south and east.
**5736. ANDREWS, Hercules R. W.**
June 29, 1836, 1 1/4 miles SE of Octahatchee, Hamilton Co. W 1/2 NE 1/4 Sect. 24 Tp. 1 R. 14, south and east.
**5896. ANDREWS, Hercules R. W**
Oct. 10, 1836, 2 1/2 miles W of Gadsden, Gadsden Co. Lot No. 4 Fract. Sect. 17 Tp. 1 R. 2, north and west.
**6055. ANDREWS, Hercules R. W.**
Nov. 18, 1836, c. 1/2 mile E Parker, Bay Co. Fractional Sect. 30 Tp. 4 R. 13, south and west.
**7621. ANDREW, Thomas J.**
Sept. 3, 1838, 1 mile SSW Genoa, Hamilton Co. SE 1/4 SE 1/4 Sect. 18 Tp. 1 R. 15, south and east.
**ANDREWS, W. see Matthew J. ALLEN**
**2211. ARGYLE, Wm./William**
Jan. 7, 1828, 3 miles NW Capitola, Leon Co. E 1/2 SE 1/4 Sect. 15 Tp. 1 R. 2, north and east.
**2272. ARGYLE, Wm./William**
(Of Fla.) Feb. 22, 1828, 2 1/2 miles N Chaires, Leon Co., E 1/2 NE 1/4 Sect. 15 Tp. 1 R. 2, north and east.
**2336. ARGYLE, Wm./William**
April 1828, 2 1/2 miles NW Capitola, Leon Co. W 1/2 SW 1/4 Sect. 14 Tp. 1 R. 2, north and east.
**2937. ARMISTEAD, John Clayton**
(Of Va.) July 13, 1829, 3 miles NW Greensboro, Gadsden Co. W 1/2 NW 1/4 Sect. 31 Tp.3 R. 5, north and west.

**2938. ARMISTEAD, John Clayton**
July 13, 1829, 2 1/2 miles NW Greensboro, Gadsden Co. NE 1/4 Sect. 31 Tp. 3 R.5, north and west.
**ARMISTEAD, Latinus, see Hector W. BRADEN**
**1754. ARMISTEAD, L. & M. A.**
(DUP) June 4, 1827, at Black Creek, Leon Co. SW 1/4 Sect. 12 Tp.1 R. 2, north and east.
**1992. ARMISTEAD, L. & M. A.**
July 10, 1827, at Drifton, Jefferson Co. West Half Sect. 7 Tp. 1 R. 5, north and east.
**2025. ARMISTEAD, L. & M. A.**
Aug. 13, 1827, just N Drifton, Jefferson Co. W 1/2 NE 1/4 Sect. 7 Tp. 1 R. 5, north and east.
**2026. ARMISTEAD, L. & M. A.**
Aug. 13, 1827, at Drifton, Jefferson Co. W 1/2 SE 1/4 Sect. 7 Tp. 1 R. 5, north and east.
**2027. ARMISTEAD, L. & M. A.**
Aug. 13, 1827, 1/4 mile NE Drifton, Jefferson Co. E 1/2 NE 1/4 Sect. 7 Tp. 1 R. 5, north and east.
**2028. ARMISTEAD, L. & M. A.**
Aug. 13, 1827, 1/2 mile SE Drifton, Jefferson Co. E 1/2 SE 1/4 Sect. 7 Tp. 1 R. 5, north and east.
**414. ARMISTEAD, L. & M. A.**
Sept. 17, 1827, 3 miles N Roy, Gadsden Co. Lot No. 5 Sect. 26 Tp. 3 R. 7, north and west.
**415. ARMISTEAD, L. & M. A.**
(Assignee of **Isaac BROWN**) Sept. 24, 1827, 3 miles N Roy, Gadsden Co. Lot No. 1 fract. Sect. 35 Tp. 3 R. 7, north and west.
**421. ARMISTEAD, L. & M. A.**
(Assignee of **F. CHAMBLISS**) July 24, 1828, 7 miles SSW River Juntion, Gadsden Co. SW 1/4 Sect. 25 Tp. 3 R. 7, north and west.
**2274. ARMISTEAD, L. & M. A.**
Feb. 26, 1828, 6 miles S by W Rover Junction, Gadsden Co. W 1/2 SW 1/4 Sect. 30 Tp. 3 R. 6, north and west.
**2904. ARMISTEAD, L. & M. A.**
July 7, 1829, c. 7 miles WSW Chattahoochee, Jackson Co. Lot No. 3 Sect. 35 Tp. 3 R. 7, north and west.
**2905. ARMISTEAD, L. & M. A.**
July 7, 1829, c. 7 miles WSW Chatta-

hoochee, Jackson Co. E 1/2 SE 1/4 Sect. 25 Tp. 3 R. 7, north and west.

**2906. ARMISTEAD, L. & M. A.**
July 7, 1829, c. 8 miles WSW Chattahoochee, Jackson Co. Lot No. 2 Sect. 35 Tp. 3 R. 7, north and west.

**2907. ARMISTEAD, L. & M. A.**
July 7, 1829, 6 miles S by E Chattahoochee, Jackson Co. E 1/2 NE 1/4 Sect. 36 Tp. 3 R. 7, north and west.

**2952. ARMISTEAD, L. & M. A.**
July 21, 1829, 2 1/2 miles NW Roy, Gadsden Co. Lot No. 4 Sect. 34 Tp. 3 R. 7, north and west.

**416. ARMISTEAD, Latinns**
(Assignee of **Louis BROWN**) Nov. 1, 1827. 5 miles S Snead, Jackson Co. Lot N. 5, Fractional Sect. 26 Tp. 3 R. 7, north and west.

**8714. ARNOLD, AMBROSE**
Oct. 11, 1844, 2 1/4 miles S by E Hardaway, Gadsden Co. SW 1/4 SE 1/4 Sect. 35 Tp.3 R. 5, north and west.

**4954. ASHLEY, Luiz**
July 7, 1834, 2 1/4 miles SSW of Tallahassee, Leon Co. NE 1/4 SE 1/4 Sect. 9 Tp. 1 R. 1, south and west.

**1762. ASHTON, Jno.**
June 4, 1827, 3 miles W by S of Black Creek, Leon Co. W 1/2 NW 1/2 Sect. 15 Tp. 1 R. 2, north and east. Assigned (no date) to **Jno. ASHTON**. (Teste: **T. H. POPE**). Patent issued to **Jno. ASHTON** (no date). Transferred Nov. 1834 to **Kenneth BUNBRY**.

**5757. ASHTON, John**
July 6, 1836, 2 miles SW of Cherrylake(town), Madison Co. NE 1/4 SE 1/4 Sect. 19 Tp. 2 R. 9, north and east.

**362. ASKINS, Samuel G.**
Apr. 24, 1827, 3 miles SW Campbellton, Jackson Co. E 1/2 SW 1/4 Sect. 3 Tp. 6 R. 12, north and west.

**5756. ASTON, John**
July 6, 1836, 3 miles SW of Cherrylake(town), Madison Co. NE 1/4 SE 1/4 Sect. 19 Tp. 2 R. 9, north and east.

**ATCHYESA, Sarah** see **Appleton ROSSETTER**

**1723. ATKINS, S. B.**
February 21, 1853, 1 mile NE of Grove Park, Alachua Co. Lot 1 Sect. 31 Tp. 10 R. 22, south and east.

**6036. ATKINSON, Daniel J.**
November 15, 1836, 2 miles SW Tallahassee, Leon Co. SE 1/4 NE 1/4 Sect. 10 Tp. 1 R. 1, south and west.

**611. ATKINSON, Shadrach**
(Of Georgia) November 9, 1825. 5 miles E Meridian, Leon Co. Lot No. 4 Fractional Sect. 23 Tp. 3 R. 1, north and east.

**612. ATKINSON, Shadrach**
November 9, 1825. 6 miles E Meridian, Leon Co. Lot No. 4 Sect. 24 Tp. 3 R. 1, north and east.

**4676. ATKINSON, Shadrach**
December 4, 1834, 3/4 miles W of Stringer, Leon Co. W 1/2 SW 1/4 Sect. 29 Tp. 3 R. 3, north and east.

**4677. ATKINSON, Shadrach**
December 4, 1834, 2 3/4 miles N of Stringer, Leon Co. SW 1/4 NW 1/4 Sect. 10 Tp. 3 R. 3, north and east.

**4678. ATKINSON, Shadrach**
December 4, 1834, 1 mile N by W of Stringer, Leon Co. SE 1/4 NE 1/4 Sect. 19 Tp. 3 R. 3, north and east.

**4696. ATKINSON, Shadrach**
December 11, 1834, 3/4 mile NW of Copeland, Leon Co. E 1/2 SE 1/4 Sect. 30 Tp. 3 R. 3, north and east.

**7045. ATKINSON, Shadrach**
September 20, 1837, 2 3/4 miles N Quincy, Gadsden Co. SE 1/4 SW 1/4 and SW 1/4 SE 1/4 Sect. 19 Tp. 3 R. 3, north and east.

**7047. ATKINSON, Shadrach**
September 27, 1837, 1 1/4 miles N Copeland, Jefferson Co. W 1/2 SE 1/4 Sect. 20 Tp. 3 R. 3, north and east.

**7056. ATKINSON, Shadrach**
Oct. 6, 1837, 1/2 mile N by W Stringer, Jefferson Co. E 1/2 NE 1/4 Sect. 29 Tp. 3 R. 3, north and east.

**7057. ATKINSON, Shadrach**
Oct. 6, 1837, 1/2 mile NNW Stringer, Jefferson Co. E 1/2 NW 1/4 E 1/2 SW 1/4 Sect. 2 Tp. 3 R. 3 north and east.

**7058. ATKINSON, Shadrach**
Oct. 6, 1837, at Stringer, Jefferson Co. E 1/2 NW 1/4 NW 1/4 NW 1/4 Sect. 28 Tp. 3 R. 3, north and east.

**7450. ATKINSON, Shadrach**
April 12, 1838, 1/4 mile W by N Stringer, Jefferson Co. W 1/2 NE 1/4

Sect. 29 Tp. 3 R. 3, north and east.
**7456. ATKINSON, Shadrach**
April 21, 1838, 2 miles NNW Stringer, Jefferson Co. W 1/2 SW 1/4 Sect. 19 Tp. 3 R. 3, north and east.
**7457. ATKINSON, Shadrach**
April 21, 1838, 1/2 mile E Stringer, Jefferson Co. SW 1/4 SW 1/4 Sect. 27 Tp. 3 R. 3, north and west.
**7458. ATKINSON, Shadrach**
April 21, 1838, 1/4 mile NE Stringer, Jefferson Co. SE 1/4 SE 1/4 Sect. 25 Tp. 3 R. 2, north and east.
**7680. ATKINSON, Shadrach**
Oct. 22, 1838, 3/4 mile N Stringer, Jefferson Co. NW 1/4 NE 1/4 Sect. 21 Tp. 3 R. 3, north and east.
**7681. ATKINSON, Shadrach**
Oct. 22, 1838, 1 mile SE Stringer, Jefferson Co. W 1/2 NW 1/4 Sect. 34 Tp. 13 R. 3, north and east.
**8137. ATKINSON, Shadrach**
Nov. 12, 1839, 4 1/2 miles E Stringer, Jefferson Co. W 1/2 SW 1/4 Sect. 35 Tp. 5 R. 3, north and east.
**8138. ATKINSON, Shadrach**
Nov. 12, 1839, 2 1/2 miles SE Stringer, Jefferson Co. E 1/2 SE 1/4 Sect. 34 Tp. 3 R. 3, north and east.
**3845. ATTAWA, Jessie**
Jan. 13, 1831, 3 miles E Monticello, Jefferson Co. E 1/2 NW 1/4 Sect. 24 Tp. 2 R. 5, north and east.
**5256. AUSTIN, Benjamin F.**
Nov. 7, 1835, 4 1/4 miles W of Felkel, Leon Co. SW 1/4 SE 1/4 Sect. 2 Tp. 2 R. 1, north and east.
**AUSTIN, Thomas I.** co-owner of #5256.
**4318. AUSTIN, William D.**
Mar. 4, 1833, 3 miles NE of Centerville, Leon Co. NE 1/4 NW 1/4 Sect. 8 Tp. 2 R. 2, north and east.
**2501. AVERETT, Abner**
Sept. 23, 1828, 3 miles NNE Midway, Gadsden Co. W 1/2 NE 1/4 Sect. 27 Tp. 2 R. 2, north and west.
**2522. AVERETT, Abner**
Oct. 13, 1828, 3 miles NE Midway, Gadsden Co. E 1/2 NE 1/4 Sect. 27 Tp. 2 R. 2, north and west.
**2538. AVERETT, Wm. H**
Nov. 7, 1828, 2 3/4 miles NW Lake Jackson Station, Leon Co. W 1/2 NW 1/4 Sect. 26 Tp. 2R. 2, north and west.

**6165. AYCOCK, Amos**
Dec. 8, 1836, 5 miles W by N Malone, Jackson Co. E 1/2 NE 1/4 and SW 1/4 NE 1/4 Sect. 32 Tp. 7 R. 10, north and west.

## * B *

**7522. BACON, Henry W.**
July 9, 1838, 3 miles SSW Nash, Jefferson Co. SW 1/4 SE 1/4 Sect. 33 Tp. 1 R. 4, north and east.

**438. BADGER, Harriet**
June 27, 1846, just E Emathia, Marion Co. SW 1/4 NW 1/4 Sect. 11 Tp. 14 R. 20, south and east. Patent delivered July 18, 1857.

**462. BADGER, Harriet**
Sept. 24, 1846, near Emathia, Marion Co. E 1/2 SE 1/4 Sect. 10 and W 1/2 SW 1/4 Sect.11 Tp. 14 R. 20, south and east. Patent delivered July 18, 1857.

**1988. BADGER, James W.**
July 26, 1856, 3/4 mile SSE of Emathla, Marion Co. NW 1/4 NW 1/4 Sect. 11 Tp. 14 R. 20, south and east. Patent delivered July 18, 1857.

**1034. BAGGS, David L.**
(DUP) Jan. 30, 1827, 3 1/2 miles S Havana, Gadsden Co. W 1/2 SW 1/4 Sect. 14 Tp. 2 R. 2, north and west. Signed by **ALLEN, M. F.**, as receiver.

**2271. BAGGS, David S.**
Feb. 21, 1828, 4 miles N Lake Jackson Station, Leon Co. Lot No. 8 Sect. 7 Tp. 2 R. 1, north and west. Co-owners were **Andrew N. JOHNSON** and **Stephen BROWNING** of Fla. Total of 31 acres.

**2605. BAGLEY, Eliza**
Jan. 12, 1829, includes Meadows and Millwood Stations and between and extends 2 1/2 miles west; 4 1/2 sq. miles, Marion Co. N 1/2 NW 1/4 Tp. 13 S. R. 22, east. ( She swore that her house had burned and receipt in it.) Receipt for patent issued by **J. A. LEE**, March 1, 1875.

**4333. BAGGETT, Nicholas**
Mar. 21, 1833, 3/4 mile SW Fentress, Santa Rosa Co. NW 1/4 SE 1/4 Sect. 13 Tp. 3 R. 27, north and west. Transferred to **Eli HORNE**, June 24, 1833.

**3248. BAHAN, John B.**
Feb. 4, 1830, 3 miles NE Milton, Santa Rosa Co. W 1/2 NW 1/4 Sect. 36 Tp. 2 R. 28, north and west.

**5152. BAHAN, John B.**
Sept. 23, 1835, at Roeville, Santa Rosa Co. SE 1/4 SW 1/4 Sect. 24 Tp. 2 R. 28, north and west.

**6141. BAHAN, John B.**
Dec. 5, 1836, 2 miles N by E Milton, Santa Rosa Co. SE 1/4 SW 1/4 and SW 1/4 SE 1/4 Sect. 35 Tp. 2 R. 28, south and west.

**2093. BAILEY, John**
(Of Georgia) Nov. 8, 1827, 5 miles E El Destino, Leon Co. E 1/2 NE 1/4 Sect. 12 Tp. 1 R. 3, south and east.

**3526. BAILEY, William**
May 22, 1830, 1 3/4 miles N Old Town, Dixie Co. E 1/2 NW 1/4 Sect. 2 Tp. 10 R. 13, south and east.

**3600. BAILEY, William**
Sept. 1, 1830, 1 mile W Capps, Jefferson Co. E 1/2 NE 1/4 Sect. 11 Tp. 1 R. 5, south and east.

**3832. BAILEY, William**
Jan. 3, 1831, 1 1/2 miles ENE Lloyd, Jefferson Co. W 1/2 NW 1/4 Sect. 14 Tp. 1 R.3, north and east.

**6443. BAILEY, William**
Jan. 24, 1837, just NW Old Town, Dixie Co. Lot No. 7 Fract. Sect. 12 Tp. 10 R. 13, south and east.

**6667. BAILEY, William**
Jan. 25, 1837, just NE Old Town, Dixie Co. Lots No. 5 and 6, Fract. Sect. 12 Tp. 10 R. 13, south and east.

**6668. BAILEY, William**
Jan. 25, 1837, just N Old Town, Dixie Co. E 1/2 SE 1/4 Sect. 11 Tp. 10 R. 13, south and east.

**6669. BAILEY, William**
Jan. 25, 1837, 1 1/2 miles W Old Town, Dixie Co. W 1/2 NE 1/4, W 1/2 SE 1/4 Sect. 9 Tp. 10 R. 13, south and east.

**6670. BAILEY, William**
Jan. 25, 1837, 2 miles W Old Town, Dixie Co. SW 1/4 Sect. 9 Tp. 10 R. 13, south and east.

**6671. BAILEY, William**
Jan. 25, 1837, 2 miles NNW Old Town, Dixie Co. NE 1/4 Sect. 3 Tp. 10 R. 13, south and east.

**8338. BAILEY, William**
June 12, 1840, 3 miles E by N Dills, Jefferson Co. E 1/2 NE 1/4 Sect. 35 Tp. 3 R. 6, north and east.

**8445. BAILEY, William**

Jan. 4, 1841, 3 1/4 miles E Dills, Jefferson Co. NW 1/4 NE 1/4 Sect. 2 Tp. 2 R. 6, north and east.
**70. BAILEY, William**
Dec. 16, 1844, 1/2 mile SW Ringgold, Hernando Co. E 1/2 SE 1/4 Sect. 11 Tp. 21 R. 18, south and east. Patent delivered Jan. 9, 1855.
**71. BAILEY, William**
Dec. 16, 1844, near Ringgold, Hernando Co. SE and SW quarters Sect.12 Tp. 21 R. 18, south and east.
**72. BAILEY, William**
Dec. 16, 1844, near Ringgold, Hernando Co. E 1/2 NW 1/4 and E 1/2 SE 1/4 and SW 1/4 Sect. 13 Tp. 21 R.18, south and east.
**73. BAILEY, William**
Dec. 16, 1844, 1 mile S Ringgold, Hernando Co. W 1/2 SE 1/4 Sect. 13 Tp. 21 R. 18, south and east.
**74. BAILEY, William**
Dec. 16, 1844, 1/2 mile SW Ringgold, Hernando Co. E 1/2 NE 1/4 Sect. 14 Tp. 21 R. 18, south and east.
**75. BAILEY, William**
Dec. 16, 1844, 1/2 mile SW Ringgold, Hernando Co. W 1/2 NE 1/4 Sect. 14 Tp. 21 R. 18, south and east.
**77. BAILEY, William**
Dec. 16, 1844, 1 mile SW Ringgold, Hernando Co. E 1/2 NE 1/4 Sect. 15 Tp. 21 R. 18, south and east.
**78. BAILEY, William**
Dec. 16, 1844, 1 1/2 miles S Ringgold, Hernando Co. W 1/2 NW 1/4 and W 1/2 SW 1/4 Sect. 21 Tp. 21 R. 18, south and east.
**81. BAILEY, William**
Dec. 16, 1844, 2 1/2 miles SW Ringgold, Hernando Co. W 1/2 NW 1/4 Sect. 26 Tp. 21 R. 18, south and east.
**82. BAILEY, William**
Dec. 16, 1844, 2 miles NE Centralia, Hernando Co. E 1/2 NE 1/4 Sect. 27 Tp. 21 R. 18, south and east.
**2446. BAILEY, William I.**
Feb. 22, 1854, 7 miles N of Brooksville, Hernando Co. W 1/2 NW 1/4 Sect. 13 Tp. 21 R. 18, south and west.
**231. BAILEY, William John**
Dec. 19, 1845, 6 1/2 miles E Tooke Lake, Hernando Co. E 1/2 NE 1/4 Sect. 13 Tp. 22 R. 18, south and east.

**254. BAILEY, William John**
Jan. 6, 1846, c. 1 mile N Bridgeport, Hillsborough Co. Lots No. 5 and 6 Fractional Sect. 22 Tp. 28 R. 16, south and east.
**256. BAILEY, William John**
Jan. 6, 1846, c. 1 mile NW Safety Harbor, Hillsborough Co. NE 1/4 SE 1/4 and No. 2 Fractional Sect. 34 Tp. 28 R. 16, south and east.
**257. BAILEY, William John**
Jan. 6, 1846, at Safety Harbor, Hillsborough Co. Lots No. 1 and 2 Fractional Sect. 3 Tp. 29 R. 16, south and east.
**258. BAILEY, William John**
Jan. 6, 1846, just S of Safety Harbor, Hillsborough Co. Lot No. 3 Fractional Sect. 10 Tp. 29 R. 16, south and east.
**266. BAILEY, William John**
Jan. 7, 1846, c. 4 1/2 miles W Centralia, Hernando Co. W 1/2 SE 1/4 and E 1/2 SW 1/4 Sect. 34 Tp. 21 R. 18, south and east.
**676. BAILEY, William John**
Jan. 23, 1849, 1 mile N Safety Harbor, Hillsborough Co. NE 1/4 NE 1/4 Sect. 33 Tp. 28 R. 16, south and east.
**680. BAILEY, William John**
April 6, 1849, near Dellwood, Hillsborough Co. Lot No. 2 Sect. 10 Tp. 29 R. 16, south and east.
**728. BAILEY, William J.**
April 6, 1850, 2 miles N Oldsmar, Hillsborough Co. N 1/2 NW 1/4 Sect. 12 Tp. 28 R. 16, south and east.
**818. BAILEY, William J.**
Feb. 3, 1851, 2 1/2 miles SE Ringgold, Hernando Co. SW 1/4 SE 1/4 Sect. 26 Tp. 21 R. 18, south and east.
**819. BAILEY, William J.**
Feb. 3, 1851, 4 1/2 miles E Centralia, Hernando Co. E 1/2 SE 1/4 Sect. 35 Tp. 21 R. 18, south and east.
**911. BAILEY, William J.**
July 19, 1851, 6 1/2 miles E Centralia, Hernando Co. NE 1/4 SW 1/4 Sect. 36 Tp. 21 R. 18, south and east.
**116. BAILEY, Wm.**
Dec. 22, 1826, 3 miles N Monticello, Jefferson Co. NW 1/4 Sect. 7 Tp. 2 R. 4, north and east.
**1760. BAILEY, Wm.**
June 4, 1827, 2 1/2 miles NE of Byrd,

Jefferson Co. W 1/2 SW 1/4 Sect. 12 Tp. 1 R. 3, north and east.

**2035. BAILEY, Wm.**
Aug. 15, 1827, in Monticello, Jefferson Co. W 1/2 NW 1/4 Sect. 30 Tp. 2 R. 5, north and east.

**2196. BAILEY, Wm.**
(Of Florida) Dec. 31, 1827, 2 miles NW Braswell Station, Leon Co. W 1/2 NE 1/4 Sect. 7 Tp. 1 R. 4, north and east.

**1629. BAILEY, Wm.**
May 28, 1827, 6 miles NW Monticello, Jefferson Co. Lot No. 2 Fractl. Sect. 17 Tp. 2 R. 4, north and east. Transferred May 29, 1827, to **John G. GAMBLE**.

**3267. BAILEY, Wm.**
Feb. 10, 1830, 3 miles N Lamont, Jefferson Co. W 1/2 SW 1/4 Sect. 2 Tp. 1 R. 5, south and east.

**3268. BAILEY, Wm.**
Feb. 10, 1830, 3 miles N Lamont, Jefferson Co. E 1/2 SW 1/4 Sect. 2 Tp. 1 R. 5, south and east.

**3269. BAILEY, Wm.**
Feb. 10, 1830, 2 1/2 miles SW Lamont, Jefferson Co. E 1/2 NE 1/4 Sect. 4 Tp. 2 R. 5, south and east.

**3270. BAILEY, Wm.**
Feb. 10, 1830, 2 miles SW Lamont, Jefferson Co. W 1/2 NW 1/4 Sect. 3 Tp. 2 R. 5, south and east.

**3271. BAILEY, Wm.**
Feb. 10, 1830, 1/2 mile S Lamont, Jefferson Co. W 1/2 NW 1/4 Sect. 35 Tp. 1 R. 5, south and east.

**3274. BAILEY, Wm.**
Feb. 10, 1830, 3 1/2 miles N Lamont, Jefferson Co. W 1/2 NW 1/4 Sect. 11 Tp. 1 R. 5, south and east.

**3275. BAILEY, Wm.**
Feb. 10, 1830, 3 1/2 miles N Lamont, Jefferson Co. E 1/2 NW 1/4 Sect. 11 Tp. 1 R. 5, south and east.

**3278. BAILEY, Wm.**
Feb. 10, 1830, at Lamont, Jefferson Co. E 1/2 SE 1/4 Sect. 27 Tp. 1 R. 5, south and east.

**3279. BAILEY, Wm.**
Feb. 10, 1830, at Lamont, Jefferson Co. W 1/2 SW 1/4 Sect. 26 Tp. 1 R. 6, south and east.

**3280. BAILEY, Wm.**
Feb. 10, 1830, 2 miles E Lamont, Madison Co. E 1/2 SE 1/4 Sect. 25 Tp. 1 R. 5, south and east.

**3282. BAILEY, Wm.**
Feb. 10, 1830, just S Lamont, Jefferson Co. E 1/2 NW 1/4 Sect. 35 Tp. 1 R. 5, south and east.

**3283. BAILEY, Wm.**
Feb. 10, 1830, 1 mile SE Lamont, Madison Co. E 1/2 NE 1/4 Sect. 35 Tp. 1 R. 5, south and east.

**3386. BAILEY, Wm.**
Feb. 16, 1830, E part of Old Town, Dixie Co. E 1/2 NE 1/4 Sect. 14 Tp. 10 R. 13, south and east.

**3367. BAILEY, Wm.**
Feb. 16, 1830, c. 2 miles NE Old Town, Dixie Co. Lot No. 5 fract. Sect. 1 Tp. 10 R. 13, south and east.

**3368. BAILEY, Wm.**
Feb. 16, 1830, c. 2 miles NE Old Town, Dixie Co. SW 1/4 Sect. 3 Tp. 10 R. 13, south and east.

**3369. BAILEY, Wm.**
Feb. 16, 1830, 2 miles N Old Town, Dixie Co. W 1/2 NE 1/4 Sect. 2 Tp. 10 R. 13, south and east.

**3370. BAILEY, Wm.**
Feb. 16, 1830, 1 1/4 miles NNW Old Town, Dixie Co. W 1/2 SW 1/4 Sect. 2 Tp. 10 R. 13, south and east.

**3371. BAILEY, Wm.**
Feb. 16, 1830, 2 miles N Old Town, Dixie Co. W 1/2 NW 1/4 Sect. 2 Tp. 10 R. 13, south and east.

**3372. BAILEY, Wm.**
Feb. 16, 1830, 2 miles NNW Old Town, Dixie Co. SW 1/4 Sect. 3 Tp. 10 R. 13, south and east.

**3373. BAILEY, Wm.**
Feb. 16, 1830, 1 1/4 miles WNW Old Town, Dixie Co. SW 1/4 Sect. 10 Tp. 10 R. 13, south and east.

**3374. BAILEY, Wm.**
Feb. 16, 1830, 1/2 mile NW Old Town, Dixie Co. W 1/2 SE 1/4 Sect. 10 Tp. 10 R. 13, south and east.

**3375. BAILEY, Wm.**
Feb. 16, 1830, 1 mile W Old Town, Dixie Co. W 1/2 Sect. 15 Tp. 10 R. 13, south and east.

**3387. BAILEY, Wm.**
Feb. 16, 1830, 2 miles NW Old Town, Dixie Co. E 1/2 NE 1/4 Sect. 9 Tp. 10

R. 13, south and east.

**3388. BAILEY, Wm.**
Feb. 16, 1830, 1 1/2 miles W Old Town, Dixie Co. E 1/2 SE 1/4 Sect. 9 Tp. 10 R. 13, south and east.

**3676. BAILEY, Wm.**
Oct. 11, 1830, 2 miles WSW Ashville, Jefferson Co. E 1/2 SW 1/4 Sect. 6 Tp. 2 R. 7, north and east.
See **David THOMAS, Alex WATSON** and **William KERR.**

**3305. BAILEY, Wm. J.**
Feb. 12, 1830, 3 miles E Lloyd, Jefferson Co. E 1/2 NW 1/4 Sect. 19 Tp. 1 R. 4, north and east.

**3376. BAILEY, Wm. J.**
Feb. 16, 1830, c. 2 miles NE Old Town, Dixie Co. Lot No. 3 Fract. Sect. 1 Tp. 10 R. 13, south and east.

**3377. BAILEY, Wm. J.**
Feb. 16, 1830, c. 2 miles NE Old Town Dixie Co. Lot No. 4 Sect. 1 Tp. 10 R. 13, south and east.

**3650. BAILEY, Wm. J.**
Oct. 11, 1830, 3 1/2 miles S Dills, Jefferson Co. W 1/2 NW 1/4 Sect. 30 Tp. 2 R. 6, north and east.

**6415. BAILEY, Wm. J.**
Jan. 4, 1837, 2 miles SE Maysland, Madison Co. E 1/2 NW 1/4 W 1/2 SE 1/4 Sect. 11 Tp. 2 R. 7, north and east.

**6416. BAILEY, Wm. J.**
Jan. 4, 1837, 3/4 mile SE Maysland, Madison Co. E 1/2 NW 1/4, W 1/2 SE 1/4 Sect. 2 Tp. 2 R. 7, north and east.

**6661. BAILEY, Wm. J.**
Jan. 25, 1837, at Greenville, Madison Co. SE 1/4 NW 1/4 Sect. 21 Tp. 1 R. 7, north and east.

**6662. BAILEY, Wm. J.**
Jan. 25, 1837, 1 mile N Hamburg, Madison Co. W 1/2 NW 1/4 Sect. 12 Tp. 2 R. 7, north and east.

**6663. BAILEY, Wm. J.**
Jan. 25, 1837, at Greenville, Madison Co. W 1/2 NW 1/4, W 1/2 NE 1/4 Sect. 21 Tp. 1 R. 7, north and east.

**6664. BAILEY, Wm. J.**
**6665.** Affidavit of **Wm. J. BAILEY** that he had lost these two receipts sworn before **Mathew J. ALLEN**, Receiver, May 30, 1838. NW 1/4 Sect. 10 and W 1/4 SE 1/4 Sect. 3 Tp. 1 R. 7, north and east.

**6664. BAILEY, Wm. J.**
Jan. 25, 1837, just W Spray, Madison Co. NW 1/4 Sect. 10 Tp. 1 R. 7, north and east.

**6665. BAILEY, Wm. J.**
Jan. 25, 1837, at Spray, Madison Co. W 1/2 SE 1/4 Sect. 3 Tp. 1 R. 7, north and east.

**1251. BAILEY, William John**
Mar. 15, 1852, 2 1/2 miles NNW of Norman, Hernando Co. W 1/2 NE Sect. 12 Tp. 22 R. 18, south and east.

**1252. BAILEY, William John**
Mar. 15, 1852, at Dellwood on NW shore of Tampa Bay, Hillsborough Co. Lot No. 1 Sect. 10 and NE 1/4 NE Sect. 9 Tp. 29 R. 16, south and east.

**1331. BAILEY, William John**
May 19, 1852, 1 mile NW by N of Bridgeport on Tampa Bay, Hillsborough Co. W 1/2 SE Sect. 34. Tp. 28 R. 16, south and east.

**1332. BAILEY, William John**
May 19, 1852, at Rock Point, 8 miles NW of Tampa, Hillsborough Co. SE 1/4 NW 1/4, NE 1/4 SW Sect. 9 Tp. 29 R.15, south and east.

**1970. BAILEY, Zachariah**
Patent for above rec'd June 28, 1831 by **Wm. BAILEY** at Register's Office, Tallahassee. Certificate of which was lost or mislaid.. (No description given).

**3993. BAILEY, Zachariah**
June 28, 1831, 4 miles SW Monticello, Jefferson Co. W 1/2 NW 1/4 Sect. 11 Tp. 1 R. 4, north and east.

**6710. BAISDEN, Moses B.**
May 8, 1888, 2 miles W Greer, Pasco Co. N 1/2 SE 1/4 Sect. 20 Tp. 25S R. 21 E.

**7918. BAISDEN, Sarah M.**
Mar. 11, 1839, 1/4 mile W Greenhead, Washington Co. NE 1/4 SE 1/4 Sect. 7 Tp. 1 R. 14, north and east.

**6523. BAKER, Elisha**
Jan. 12, 1837, 2 miles S Jasper, Hamilton Co. NW 1/4 SE 1/4 Sect. 17 Tp. 1 R. 14, north and east.

**7375. BAKER, ELisha**
Mar. 1, 1838, 2 3/4 miles W Marion, Hamilton Co. NE 1/4 SE 1/4 Sect. 17 Tp. 1 R. 14, north and east.

**483. BAKER, George W.**
Oct. 9, 1830, 3 miles W Ashville, Jefferson Co. E 1/2 SW 1/4 Sect. 35 Tp. 3 R. 6, north and east.

**484. BAKER, James**
Oct. 9, 1830, 3 miles W Ashville, Jefferson Co. W 1/2 SW 1/4 Sect. 35 Tp. 3 R. 6, north and east.

**6286. BAKER, James**
June 23, 1897, 1/4 mile Calvary, Marion Co. N 1/2 SW 1/4 and N 1/2 SE 1/4 Sect. 34 Tp. 15S R. 21E.

**602. BAKER, James M. C.**
Oct. 12, 1825, 1 mile NNW El Destino, Leon Co. E 1/2 NE 1/4 Sect. 1 Tp. 1 R. 2, south and east.

**603. BAKER. James M. C.**
Oct. 12, 1825, 1 mile N El Destino, Leon Co. W 1/2 NW 1/4 Sect. 6 Tp. 1 R. 3, south and east.

**798. BAKER, James M. C.**
(Of Florida) Nov. 9, 1826, at Wadesboro, Leon Co. E 1/2 NW 1/4 Sect. 6 Tp. 1 R. 3, south and east.

**341. BAKER, Nicholas**
April 12, 1827, 6 miles ENE Graceville, Jackson Co. E 1/2 SW 1/4 Sect. 27 Tp. 7 R. 12, north and west.

**8467. BAKER, Simmons J.**
Feb. 6, 1841, 1/4 mile N Fairgrounds, Jackson Co. E 1/2 NW 1/4 Sect. 32 Tp. 5 R. 10, north and west.

**7921. BAKER, Starke**
Mar. 14, 1839, 1/2 mile N by E Oak Grove, Okaloosa Co. E 1/2 SW 1/4 Sect. 9 Tp. 5 R. 23, north and west.

**8450. BALEY, Mary**
Jan. 13, 1841, 2 1/2 miles SSE Juniper, Gadsden Co. SW 1/4 SW 1/4 Sect. 27 Tp. 2 R. 5, north and west.

**6035. BALEY, Isham**
Nov. 15, 1836, 1 1/2 miles S by W Darsey, Gadsden Co. SE 1/4 SE 1/4 and SW 1/4 SE 1/4 Sect. 12 Tp. 3 R. 2, north and west. Certified as recorded Oct. 30, 1838, in Clerk's Office of Gadsden Co.,(signed) **John G. GUNN**, Cl'k, by **R. C. LESTER**, D.C.

**8243. BALL, Frederick A.**
Feb. 29, 1840, 3 miles NW Bagdad Junction, Santa Rosa Co. N 1/2 Lot 5 Sect. 3 Tp. 1 R. 28, north and west.

**4716. BALL, Griffin**
Jan. 28, 1858, 3/4 mile S of Dukes, Union Co. S 1/2 of NE 1/4 and N 1/2 of SE 1/4 Sect. 22 Tp. 6 R. 19, south and east. Patent delivered Sept. 8, 1863.

**4878. BALL, Griffin**
Oct. 11, 1858, 1/2 mile NE of Dukes, Union Co. NE 1/4 SE 1/4 Sect. 15 Tp. 6 R. 19, south and east. Patent delivered Sept. 8, 1863.

**4857. BALL, James T.**
Feb. 10, 1835, 1 mile NNE of Octahatchee, Hamilton Co. W 1/2 NW 1/4 Sect. 12 Tp. 2 R. 11, north and east.

**2452. BALLARD, James C.**
Feb. 22, 1854, 1 mile NW of Blitchton, Marion Co. N 1/2 SE 1.4 Sect. 6 and NW 1/4 SW 1/4 Sect. 5 Tp. 14 R. 20, south and east. Transferred to **James CAMPBELL**, Dec. 19,1854.

**3652. BALTZELL, Thomas**
Oct. 11, 1830, 3 1/2 miles W by S Alford, Jackson Co. W 1/2 NE 1/4 Sect. 5 Tp. 3 R. 12, north and west.

**5070. BALTZELL, Thomas**
July 11, 1835, 1/4 mile W of Haywood, Jackson Co. E 1/2 NE 1/4 Sect. 5 Tp. 5 R. 7, north and west.

**5643. BALTZELL, Thomas**
May 2, 1836, 3/4 mile SW of Haywood, Jackson Co. SE 1/4 Sect. 5 Tp. 5 R. 7, north and west.

**5644. BALTZELL, Thomas**
May 2, 1836, 3/4 mile SW of Haywood, Jackson Co. NW 1/4 SW 1/4 Sect. 5 Tp. 5 R. 7, north and west.

**7882. BALTZELL, Thomas**
Feb. 21, 1839, 1/4 mile NW Haywood, Jackson Co. W 1/2 SE 1/4 Sect. 32 Tp. 6 R. 7, north and west.

**6238. BANNINGTON, Perry**
Dec. 17, 1836, 3 miles NE Lamont, Jefferson Co. SW 1/4 SE 1/4 Sect. 13 Tp. 1 R. 5, south and east.

**6239. BANNINGTON, Perry**
Dec. 17, 1836, 1/2 mile NE Drifton, Jefferson Co. W 1/2 NW 1/4 Sect. 8 Tp. 1 R. 5, north and east.

**1138. BANKNIGHT, Jacob**
Jan. 29, 1852, 3 miles SE Adam, Alachua Co. Lot 9 Sect. 3 Lot No. 3 Sect. 10 NE 1/4 NW 1/4 Sect. 9 SE 1/4 SE 1/4 Sect. 4 Tp. 12 R. 18, south and east.

**1451. BANKS, William**
(DUP) May 22, 1827, 1 1/2 miles W Quincy, Gadsden Co. W 1/2 NE 1/4 Sect. 11 Tp. 2 R. 4, north and west.

**1452. BANKS, William**
(DUP) May 22, 1827, 1 mile W Quincy, Gadsden Co. E 1/2 NE 1/4 Sect. 11 Tp. 2 R. 4, north and west.

**1548. BANKS, William**
(DUP) May 24, 1827, 2 miles W Simsville, Jackson Co. E 1/2 SE 1/4 Sect. 11 Tp. 3 R. 10, north and west.

**1549. BANKS, William**
(DUP) May 24, 1827, 3 1/2 miles E Rock Creek, Jackson Co. W 1/2 SE 1/4 Sect. 19 Tp. 3 R. 9, north and west.

**1590. BANKS, William**
(DUP) May 25, 1827, 1/2 mile N Oakdale, Jackson Co. W 1/2 NW 1/4 Sect. 25 Tp. 4 R. 10, north and west.

**1591. BANKS, William**
(DUP) May 25, 1827, at Oakdale, Jackson Co. E 1/2 SE 1/4 Sect. 26 Tp. 4 R. 10, north and west.

**1589. BANKS, W.**
May 25, 1827, at Oakdale, Jackson Co. W 1/2 NW 1/4 Sect. 36 Tp. 4 R. 10, north and west.

**1592. BANKS, W.**
May 25, 1827, 1 1/2 miles E Marianna, Jackson Co. W 1/2 SE 1/4 Sect. 2 Tp. 4 R. 10, north and west.

**1622. BANKS, W. B.**
May 26, 1827, 2 miles S Welchton, Jackson Co. W 1/2 SE 1/4 Sect. 2 Tp. 5 R. 12, north and west. Transferred May 28, 1827, to **Chas. WILLIAMSON**

**1623. BANKS. W. B.**
May 26, 1827, 2 miles S Welchton, Jackson Co. E 1/2 SE 1/4 Sect. 2 Tp. 5 R. 12, north and west. Transferred May 28, 1827, to **Chas. WILLIAMSON**

**2485. BANNERMAN, Charles**
Sept. 8, 1828, 1/4 mile NW Meridian, Leon Co. W 1/2 SW 1/4 Sect. 18 Tp. 3 R. 1, north and east.

**2486. BANNERMAN, Charles**
Sept. 8, 1828, at Meridian, Leon Co. Lot No. 4 Sect. 19 Tp. 3 R. 1, north and east.

**3852. BANNERMAN, Charles**
Jan. 19, 1831, at Meridian, Leon Co. Lot No.3 Sect. 19 Tp. 3 R. 1, north and east.

**5548. BANNERMAN, Charles**
Mar. 19, 1836, 3 1/2 miles E of Concord, Gadsden Co. SE 1/4 SW 1/4 Sect. 18 Tp. 3 R. 1, north and east.

**690. BANNERMAN, John W.**
(Of N.C.) March 15, 1826, 1 mile N Meridian, Leon Co. E 1/2 NW 1/4 Sect. 18 Tp. 3 R. 1, north and east.

**3446. BANNERMAN, Joseph W.**
March 11, 1830, 1 1/2 miles S Wadesboro, Leon Co. W 1/2 NE 1/4 Sect. 18 Tp. 3 R. 1, north and east.

**630. BANNERMAN, Jos. W.**
Dec. 8, 1825, 1/2 mile N Meridian, Leon Co. W 1/2 NW 1/4 Sect. 18 Tp. 3 R. 1, north and east.

**1323. BANNERMAN, J. W.**
May 3, 1827, 1/2 mile N Meridian, Leon Co. E 1/2 SW 1/4 Sect. 18 Tp. 3 R. 1, north and east.

**5893. BARBER, Asa**
Oct. 8, 1836, 2 miles SE of Jamieson, Gadsden Co. W 1/2 NE 1/4 Sect. 17 Tp. 3 R. 2, north and west.

**7962. BARBER, Asa**
May 15, 1839, 1 3/4 miles E Hinson, Gadsden Co. NE 1/4 SE 1/4 Sect. 26 Tp. 3 R. 2, north and west.

**7963. BARBER, Asa**
May 15, 1839, 2 1/4 miles E Hinson, Gadsden Co. NW 1/4 SW 1/4 Sect. 25 Tp. 3 R. 2, north and west.

**951. BARBER, Isaiah**
Sept. 19, 1951, 2 1/2 miles SE Dade City, Pasco Co. NW 1/4 NW 1/4 Sect. 36 and NE 1/4 NE 1/4 Sect. 35 Tp. 24 R. 21, south and east. Patent delivered July 31, 1856.

**7768. BARBER, Jerdin**
Dec. 18, 1838, 1 1/4 miles W by N Concord, Gadsden Co. NW 1/4 NE 1/4 Sect. 14 Tp. 3 R. 2, north and west.

**7978. BARBER, Darias B.**
May 31, 1839, 1 mile E by S Havana, Gadsden Co. NE 1/4 NE 1/4 Sect. 35 Tp. 3 R. 2, north and west.

**5826. BARBER, Jordan**
Sept. 5, 1836, 1 mile NE of Hinson, Gadsden, Co. SE 1/4 NW 1/4 Sect. 22 Tp. 3 R. 2, north and west.

**8225. BARBER, Lawson**
Jan. 17, 1840, 3 miles E by N Hinson, Gadsden Co. SE 1/4 NE 1/4 Sect. 26 Tp. 3 R. 2, north and west.

**220. BARBER, Moses**
Nov. 26, 1845, near MacClenny, Baker Co. NE 1/4 SW 1/4 and SW 1/4 NE 1/4 Sect. 30 Tp. 2 R. 22, south and east.

**5930. BARBER, Solomon**
Oct. 26, 1836, 2 miles S by E of Concord, Leon Co. NW 1/4 SE 1/4 Sect. 30 Tp. 3 R. 1, north and west.

**7760. BARBER, Solomon**
Dec. 15, 1838, 2 miles S by E Concord, Gadsden Co. SW 1/4 SE 1/4 Sect. 30 Tp. 3 R. 1, north and west.

**7793. BARBER, Solomon**
Dec. 4, 1839, 1 1/4 miles W by W Meridian, Leon Co. E 1/2 NW 1/4 Sect. 18 Tp. 3 R. 1, north and west.

**4180. BARBER, William**
June 20, 1832, 1/2 mile S by E of Dorsey, Gadsden Co. NE 1/4 SE 1/4 Sect. 12 Tp. 3 R. 2, north and west.

**7678. BARBER, William**
Oct. 19, 1838, 1 1/4 miles S Darsey, Gadsden Co. W 1/2 SW 1/4 Sect. 12 Tp. 3 R. 2, north and west.

**7765. BARBER, William**
Dec. 18, 1838, 1 3/4 miles NNW Concord,, Gadsden Co. SW 1/4 SE 1/4 Sect. 14 Tp. 3 R. 2, north and west.

**7766. BARBER, William**
Dec. 18, 1838, 1 1/2 miles SSW Concord, Gadsden Co. SW 1/4 NW 1/4 Sect. 13 Tp. 3 R. 2, north and west.

**7772. BARBER, William**
Dec. 20, 1838, 1 mile N by W Meridian, Leon Co. NW 1/4 NW 1/4 Sect. 18 Tp. 3 R. 1, north and west.

**7773. BARBER, William**
Dec. 20, 1838, 1 mile S Darsey, Gadsden Co. SE 1/4 SE 1/4 Sect. 11 Tp. 3 R. 2, north and west.

**2763. BARBER, Wm.**
Feb. 25, 1829, 5 miles NW Havana, Gadsden Co. E 1/2 SW 1/4 Sect. 14 Tp. 3 R. 2, north and west.

**2812. BARBER, Wm.**
April 30, 1829, 4 miles NW Havana, Gadsden Co. W 1/2 NW 1/4 Sect. 20 Tp. 3 R. 2, north and west.

**3181. BARBER, Wm.**
Dec. 25, 1829, 3 miles NNW Havana, Gadsden Co. W 1/2 SW 1/4 Sect. 17 Tp. 3 R. 2, north and west.

**1590. BARCO, Stephen**
Dec. 28, 1852, 6 miles W of Guilford, Union Co. SE 1/4 SE 1/4 Sect. 18 Tp. 5 R. 18, south and east. Patent delivered Feb. 7, 1857.

**2025. BARNES, Cordin**
Aug. 8, 1853, 1 1/2 miles NNW of Ekal, Sumter Co. SE 1/4 NE 1/4 Sect. 20 Tp. 20 R. 22, south and east.

**5365. BARNES, James**
Dec. 28, 1835, 1 mile W by N of Centerville, Leon Co. SW 1/4 NW 1/4 Sect. 23 Tp. 2 R. 1, north and east.

**5366. BARNES, James**
Dec. 28, 1835, 1 mile W by N of Centerville, Leon Co. SE 1/4 NW 1/4 Sect. 23 Tp. 2 R. 1, north and east.

**5367. BARNES, James**
Dec. 28, 1835, 1 mile W by N of Centerville, Leon Co. W 1/2 SW 1/4 Sect. 23 Tp. 2 R. 1, north and east.

**5416. BARNES, James**
Jan. 20, 1836, 1/4 mile NNE of Bradfordville, Leon Co. NW 1/4 NW 1/4 Sect. 23 Tp. 2 R. 1, north and east.

**4475. BARNES, William T.**
Dec. 14, 1833, 5 1/2 miles S by E of Dill, Jefferson Co. NE 1/4 SW 1/4 Sect. 23 Tp. 2 R. 6, north and east.

**4476. BARNES, William T.**
Dec. 14, 1833, 5 1/2 miles SSE of Dill, Jefferson Co. NW 1/4 SE 1/4 Sect. 23 Tp. 2 R. 6, north and east.

**6559. BARNES, William T.**
Jan. 16, 1837, 3/4 mile E Bailey, Madison Co. NW 1/4 Sect. 19 Tp. 2 R. 8, north and east.

**4465. BARNEY, Guilford**
Dec. 2, 1833, at Miccosukee, Leon Co. NE 1/4 NW 1/4 Sect. 8 Tp. 2 R. 3, north and east.

**6463. BARRENTON, Charles**
Jan. 9, 1837, 2 1/2 miles N Monticello, Jefferson Co. E 1/2 NE 1/4 Sect. 7 Tp. 2 R. 5, north and east.

**6464. BARRENTON, Charles**
Jan. 9, 1837, 2 miles SE Alma, Jefferson Co. W 1/2 NW 1/4 Sect. 8 Tp. 2 R. 5, north and east.

**6312. BARRINGTON, Perry**
Dec. 26, 1836, Just E Drifton, Jefferson Co. E 1/2 SW 1/4 Sect. 8 Tp. 1 R. 5, north and east. Patent delivered Feb. 19, 1846 to **W. BEATTY**

**6731. BARRON, Benjamin**
Feb. 3, 1837, 2 miles W Ashville, Jefferson Co. NW 1/4 NW 1/4 Sect. 1 Tp. 2 R. 1, north and east.

**519. BARRON, Benj.**
May 10, 1831, 7 miles NW Copeland, Jefferson Co. NE 1/4 Sect. 34 Tp. 3 R. 6, north and east.

**4996. BARRON, Charles S.**
June 15, 1835, at Pensacola, Escambia Co. Lot No. 4 Sect. 33 Tp. 2 R. 30, south and west.

**4997. BARRON, Charles S.**
June 15, 1835, at Pensacola, Escambia Co. Lot No. 1 Fractional Sect. 52 Tp. 2 R. 30, south and west.

**5002. BARRON, Charles S**
June 16, 1835, 2 1/2 miles SSW of Olive, Escambia Co. Lot No. 6 Fractional Sect. 30 Tp. 1 R. 30, south and west.

**5003. BARRON, Charles S.**
June 16, 1835, 1/2 mile S of Brent, Escambia Co. Fractional Sect. 34 Tp. 1 R. 30, south and west.

**5004. BARRON, Charles S.**
June 16, 1835, 1 1/4 miles SSW of Olive, Escambia Co., Lot No. 5 Fractional Sect. 30 Tp. 1 R. 30, south and west.

**5005. BARRON, Charles S.**
June 16,, 1835, 1 1/4 miles SW of Olive, Escambia Co. Lot No. 2 Sect. 29 Tp. 1 R. 30, south and west.

**5006. BARRON, Charles S.**
June 16, 1835, 1 1/4 miles SW of Olive, Escambia Co. Lot No. 3 Sect. 29 Tp. 1 R. 30, south and west.

**5007. BARRON, Charles S.**
June 16, 1835, 1 1/4 miles SW of Olive, Escambia Co. Lot No. 1 Sect. 29 Tp. 1 R. 30, south and west.

**6652. BARRONTON, Charles**
Jan. 14, 1837, 2 1/2 miles N Monticello, Jefferson Co. NW 1/4 SW 1/4 Sect. 8 Tp. 2 R. 5, north and east.

**6553. BARRONTON, Charles**
Jan.14, 1837, 3 miles N Monticello, Jefferson Co. SE 1/4 SE 1/4 Sect. 6 Tp. 2 R. 5, north and east.

**7330. BARRONTON, Charles**
Feb. 15, 1838, 4 miles N Monticello, Jefferson Co. W 1/2 SE 1/4 Sect. 6 Tp. 2 R. 5, north and east.

**8209. BARROW, Richmond**
Jan. 7, 1840, 1/4 mile SE Oak Grove, Okaloosa Co. SW 1/4 NW 1/4 Sect. 21 Tp. 5 R. 23, north and west.

**BARROW, Reuben N.** see **James KENNEDY, # 4523.**

**4167. BARRY, Nicholas**
Feb. 15, 1856, 2 miles E of Haynesworth, Alachua Co. N 1/2 of Lot No. 2 Sect. 2 Tp. 8 R. 19, south and east.

**4219. BARRY, Nicholas**
Mar. 3, 1856, 1 1/2 miles NNE of Haynesworth, Alachua Co. W 1/2 of SE 1/4 Sect. 35 Tp. 7 R. 19, south and east.

**8570. BARTLETT, Cosam J.**
Jan. 6, 1843, 1 1/2 miles N by E Perkins, Madison Co. NE 1/4 NE 1/4 Sect. 24 Tp. 1 R. 1, south and west. Transferred to **Simon TOWLS**, May 28, 1844.

**547. BASKINS, Jas. J.**
Nov. 15, 1834, 2 miles SSW Chipola, Calhoun Co. SW 1/4 NW 1/4 Sect. 17 Tp. 1 R. 9, north and west. 40 12/100 acres, $50.15. Bills of Central Bank of Florida.

**7369. BASSETT, William**
Mar. 1, 1838, 3 1/2 miles NNE Westlake, Madison Co. SW 1/4 SW 1/4 Sect. 26 Tp. 2 R. 12, north and east.

**7370. BASSETT, William**
Mar. 1, 1838, 3 1/2 miles N by E Westlake, Madison Co. SE 1/4 SE 1/4 Sect. 27 Tp. 2 R. 12, north and east.

**8184. BATES, Henry**
Dec. 21, 1839, 1/4 mile SSE Malone, Jackson Co. SW 1/4 NE 1/4 SE 1/4 NW 1/4 Sect. 8 Tp. 6 R. 9, north and west.

**5494. BATES, James A.**
April 15, 1886, 2 miles SW Orange City Junction, Volusia Co. E 1/2 NE 1/4 Sect. 30 and W 1/2 NW 1/4 Sect. 29 Tp. 18S R. 29E.

**604. BATES, Rebecca**
Dec. 28, 1847, c. 1 mile N Alachua,

Alachua Co. SE 1/4 NE 1/4 Sect.11 Tp. 8 R. 18, south and east. Patent delivered Oct. 20, 1859.

**2367. BATTLE, Amos I.**
May 8, 1828, in Marianna, Jackson Co. NW 1/4 Sect. 11 Tp. 4 R. 10, north and west.

**2368. BATTLE, Amos I.**
May 8, 1828, in Marianna, Jackson Co. SE 1/4 Sect. 11 Tp. 4 R. 10, north and west.

**2369. BATTLE, Amos I.**
May 8, 1828, 1/2 mile E Marianna, Jackson Co. E 1/2 NE 1/4 Sect. 11 Tp. 4 R. 10, north and west.

**2370. BATTLE, Amos I.**
May 8, 1828, 1/2 mile SE Marianna, Jackson Co. W 1/2 SW 1/4 Sect. 11 Tp. 4 R. 10, north and west.

**BATTLE, Isaac L. see John W. LEWIS**

**6858. BAUGH, James**
March 8, 1837, 1 1/2 miles SSW Dills, Jefferson Co. SE 1/4 E 1/2 SW 1/4 Sect. 12 Tp. 2 R. 5, north and east.

**6859. BAUGH, James**
March 8, 1837, 1 mile S Dills, Jefferson Co. W 1/2 SW 1/4 Sect. 7 Tp. 2 R. 6, north and east.

**6860. BAUGH, James**
March 8, 1837, 2 miles S by W Dills, Jefferson Co. W 1/2 NE 1/4 Sect. 13 Tp. 2 R. 5, north and east.

**1147. BAXLEY, Samuel**
Feb. 2, 1852, 1 mile NNW Alachua, Alachua Co. NW 1/4 NW 1/4 Sect. 14 Tp. 8 R. 18, south and east. Patent delivered June 2, 1855

**6213. BAXTER, David**
Dec. 15, 1836, at Ellis, Jackson Co. NW 1/4 SW 1/4 Sect. 10 Tp. 6 R. 10, north and west.

**7911. BAXTER, Israel**
March 5, 1839, 2 1/2 miles SW Ellis, Jackson Co. W 1/2 NW 1/4 Sect. 17 Tp. 6 R. 10, north and west.

**7912. BAXTER, Israel**
Mar. 5, 1839, 3 miles SW Ellis, Jackson Co. E 1/2 NW 1/4 Sect. 20 Tp. 6 R. 25, north and west.

**2809. BAXTER, James O.**
April 25, 1829, 7 miles WNW Greenwood, Jackson Co. W 1/2 SW 1/4 Sect. 29 Tp. 6 R. 10, north and west.

**3087. BAXTER, James O.**
Oct. 21, 1829, 5 miles NW Marianna, Jackson Co. E 1/2 SW 1/4 Sect. 20 Tp. 6 R. 10, north and west.

**8961. BAXTER, James O.**
July 25, 1846, 2 3/4 miles S by W Ellis, Jackson Co. NE 1/4 SE 1/4 Sect. 20 Tp. 6 R. 10, north and west.

**1930. BAXTER, Jas. O.**
June 19, 1827, 5 miles WNW Greenwood, Jackson Co. E 1/2 SE 1/4 Sect. 21 Tp. 6 R. 10, north and west.

**6287. BAXTER, Jas. O.**
Dec. 23, 1836, 6 miles W by N Greenwood, Jackson Co. NW 1/4 Sect. 29 Tp. 6 R. 10, north and west.

**6288. BAXTER, Jas. O.**
Dec. 23, 1836, 6 miles WNW Greenwood, Jackson Co. W 1/2 SE 1/4 Sect. 20 Tp. 6 R. 10, north and west.

See **James PATTERSON #385**

**1067. BAXTER, John**
Feb. 5, 1827, 2 miles SSE Quincy, Gadsden Co. W 1/2 SW 1/4 Sect. 17 Tp. 2 R. 3, north and west.

**2946. BAXTER, Sarah**
July 20, 1829, 7 miles WNW Greenwood, Gadsden Co. W 1/2 NW 1/4 Sect. 20 Tp. 6 R. 10, north and west.

**2308. BEAL, Thomas**
Oct. 28, 1853, 3/4 miles SW of Fort McCoy, Marion Co. SE 1/4 NE 1/4 and E 1/2 SE 1/4 Sect. 9 Tp. 13 R. 23, south and east. Patent delivered July 24, 1857.

**3060. BEARD, I. F.**
Sept. 23, 1829, 1/2 mile SW Copeland, Leon Co. W 1/2 NW 1/4 Sect. 4 Tp. 2 R. 3, north and east.

**5883. BEARD, Israel F.**
Oct. 3, 1836, 1/4 mile SE of Stringer, Jefferson Co. E 1/2 NW 1/4 Sect. 34. Tp. 3 R. 3, north and west.

**6251. BEARD, James B.**
Dec. 20, 1836, 4 miles W by S Alma, Leon Co. E 1/2 NW 1/4 SW 1/2 NE 1/4 Sect. 5 Tp. 2 R. 4, north and east.

**6350. BEARD, James B.**
Dec. 30, 1836, 4 miles W by S Alma, Jefferson Co. E 1/2 NE 1/4 Sect. 6 Tp. 2 R. 4, north and east.

**6351. BEARD, James B.**
Dec. 30, 1836, 4 1/4 miles W by S Alma, Jefferson Co. W 1/2 NW 1/4 Sect. 5 Tp. 2 R. 4, north and east.

**5806. BEASLEY, Abraham**
Aug. 22, 1836, 5 miles E of Norum, Washington Co. SE 1/4 NE 1/4 Sect. 12 Tp. 2 R. 15, north and west.

**6378. BEASLEY, Cornelius**
Jan. 3, 1837, 2 miles NNW Lamont, Jefferson Co. W 1/2 SW 1/4 Sect. 15 Tp. 1 R. 5, south and east.

**4299. BEASLEY, Jarrel**
Mar. 28, 1856, 2 miles NW Silver Springs, Marion Co. SE 1/4 NW 1/4 Sect. 1 Tp. 15 R. 22, south and east.

**340. BEASLEY, John**
April 12, 1827, 4 miles ENE Campbellton, Jackson Co. W 1/2 SE 1/4 Sect. 27 Tp. 7 R. 11, north and west.

**4879. BEAZLEY, Cornelius**
Mar. 4, 1835, 5 1/4 miles E by N of Leonton, Jefferson Co. W 1/2 NW 1/4 Sect. 5 Tp. 2 R. 5, south and west.

**5609. BEAZLEY, Cornelius**
April 20, 1836, 2 1/2 miles NE Monticello, Jefferson Co. SE 1/4 NW 1/4 Sect. 22 Tp. 1 R. 5, south and east.

**5860. BEAZLEY, Cornelius**
Sept. 26, 1836, 4 1/4 miles E by S of Capps, Jefferson Co. W 1/2 NE 1/4 Sect. 11 Tp. 1 R. 5, south and east.

**7786. BEAZLEY, Cornelius**
Dec. 31, 1838, 1/4 mile SE McClellan, Jefferson Co. NW 1/4 SE 1/4 Sect. 15 Tp. 1 R. 5, south and east.

**6498. BEAZLEY, Robert**
Jan. 10, 1837, 2 miles N Lamont, Jefferson Co. SE 1/4 SW 1/4 Sect. 10 Tp. 1 R. 5, south and east.

**7541. BEAZLEY, Robert**
July 18, 1838, 1/4 mile NNW Lamont, Jefferson Co. NE 1/4 SW 1/4 Sect. 22 Tp. 1 R. 5, south and east.

**1672. BECKETT, Edward M.**
Jan. 27, 1853, 3 miles NW of Belleview, Marion Co. SW 1/4 NE 1/4 Sect. 27 Tp. 16 R. 22, south and east. Patent delivered Feb. 1, 1859.

**2250. BECKETT, Edward M.**
Oct. 12, 1853, 2 miles NE of Belleview, Marion Co. NW 1/4 NW 1/4 Sect. 26 Tp. 16 R. 22, south and east. Patent delivered Feb. 1, 1859.

**2251. BECKETT, Edward M.**
Oct. 12, 1853, 2 3/4 miles E of Belleview, Marion Co. N 1/2 NE 1/4 Sect. 27 and W 1/2 NE 1/4 Sect. 34 Tp. 16 R. 22, south and east. Patent delivered Feb. 1, 1859.

**2900. BECKETT, Lucinda**
(Formerly **Lucinda LOVETT**), 1 3/4 miles NE Clearwater, Pinellas Co. N 1/2 SE 1/4 Sect. 1 Tp. 29S R. 15E and NW 1/4 SW 1/4 Sect. 6 Tp. 29S R. 16E. (No date given).

**2964. BEELAND, John**
July 28, 1829, 1/4 mile NW Stringer, Leon Co. E 1/2 SE 1/4 Sect. 20 Tp. 3 R. 3, north and east.

**4932. BEELY, William M.**
April 8, 1835, 4 3/4 miles W by N of Greenwood, Jackson Co. SE 1/4 NW 1/4 Sect. 28 Tp. 6 R. 10, north and west.

**2331. BEESLEY, John**
April 7, 1828, 4 miles NE Campbellton, Jackson Co. W 1/2 SE 1/4 Sect. 21 Tp 7 R. 11, north and west.

**2535. BEESLEY, John**
Oct. 29, 1823, 6 miles ENE Campbellton, Jackson Co. W 1/2 NW 1/4 Sect. 27 Tp. 7 R. 11, north and west.

**2243. BEESLY, John**
(Of Fla.) Feb. 1, 1828, 4 miles ENE Campbellton, Jackson Co. E 1/2 NW 1/4 Sect. 27 Tp. 7 R. 11, north and west.

**4025. BEILING, John W.**
Dec. 21, 1855, 2 miles NE of Providence, Columbia Co. E 1/2 NE 1/4 and NE 1/4 of SE 1/4 Sect. 29 and NW 1/4 of NW 1/4 Sect. 28 Tp. 5 R. 18, south and east.

**1358. BELCHER, Wm.**
May 14, 1827, 2 miles E Quincy, Gadsden Co. W 1/2 SE 1/4 Sect. 4 Tp. 2 R. 3, north and west.

**1910. BELCHER, William**
(DUP) June 13, 1827, 1/2 mile W Miccosukee, Leon Co. W 1/2 NE 1/4 Sect. 8 Tp. 2 R. 3, north and west.

**30. BELCHER, William**
Nov. 1 1826, near Florence, Gadsden Co., NW 1/4 Sect. 9 Tp. 2 R. 3, north and west.

**4704. BELL, Daniel**
Dec. 12, 1834, 3 miles SE of Marion, Hamilton Co. E 1/2 NW 1/4 Sect. 9 Tp. 1 R. 14, north and east.

**4705. BELL, Daniel**
Dec. 12, 1834, 2 miles S by E of

Jasper, Hamilton Co. E 1/2 NE 1/4 Sect. 17 Tp. 1 R. 14, north and east.

**5128. BELL, Daniel**
Aug. 10, 1835, 2 1/2 miles S of Jasper, Hamilton Co. W 1/2 NE 1/4 Sect. 17 Tp. 1 R. 14, north and east.

**5129. BELL, Daniel**
Aug. 10, 1835, 2 miles SE of Jasper, Hamilton Co. NW 1/4 SE 1/4 Sect. 9 Tp. 1 R. 14, north and east.

**6192. BELL, Daniel**
Dec. 12, 1836, 4 miles SW Jasper, Hamilton Co. SW 1/4 SW 1/4 Sect. 11, Tp. 1 R. 13, north and east.

**6817. BELL, Daniel**
March 1, 1837, 3 miles NNW Mariana, Hamilton Co. W 1/2 NW 1/4 W 1/2 SW 1/4 Sect. 24 Tp. 1 R. 13, north and east.

**6934. BELL, Daniel**
March 23, 1837, 2 miles SW Jasper, Hamilton Co. E 1/2 NW 1/4 Sect. 17 Tp. 1 R. 14, north and east.

**7171. BELL, Daniel**
Dec. 27, 1837, 1 1/2 miles SSE Jasper, Hamilton Co. W 1/2 NE 1/4 Sect. 9 Tp. 1 R. 14, north and east.

**7741. BELL, Daniel**
Dec. 1, 1838, 3 3/4 miles N by W Marion, Hamilton Co. E 1/2 NW 1/4 Sect. 24 Tp. 1 R. 13, north and east.

**8380. BELL, Hector**
June 24, 1890, N by W Dicker, Suwannee Co. NW 1/4 NE 1/4 and NE 1/4 NW 1/4 Sect. 32 Tp. 1S R. 13E.

**6193. BELL, James S.**
Dec. 12, 1836, c. 1/2 mile S Belleville, Hamilton Co. Lot No. 6 Fractional Sect. 6 Tp. 2 R. 11, north and east.

**6517. BELL, James S.**
Jan. 10, 1837, c. 1 1/2 miles S Belleville, Madison Co. Lot No. 2 Fract. Sect. 7 Tp. 2 R. 11, north and east.

**7737. BELL, James S.**
Dec. 1 1838, 2 3/4 miles SE Belleville, Hamilton Co. E 1/2 NW 1/4 Sect. 12 Tp. 2 R. 11, north and east.

**7783. BELL, Joseph**
Dec. 27, 1838, 1 mile S Bond, Madison Co. SW 1/4 NW 1/4 Sect. 4 Tp. 2 R. 8, north and east.

**7770. BELL, Larkin**
Dec. 19, 1838, 1 mile N by W Concord, Gadsden Co. SW 1/4 NE 1/4 Sect. 12 Tp. 3 R. 2, north and west.

**8834. BELL, Marmaduke H.**
Nov. 5, 1845, 2 miles SSE Greenwood, Jackson Co. NW 1/4 NW 1/4 Sect. 3 Tp. 5 R. 9, north and west.

**8835. BELL, Marmaduke H.**
Nov. 5, 1845, 2 miles SSE Greenwood, Jackson Co. NE 1/4 NW 1/4 Sect. 3 Tp. 5 R. 9, north and west.

**565. BELL, Wm. A**
March 24, 1835, 1 mile W of Pensacola, Escambia Co. Fractional Sect. 23 Tp. 2 R. 30, south and west.

**487. BELLAME, Abram**
Oct. 8, 1830, 3 miles W Champaign, Madison Co. W 1/2 SW 1/4 Sect. 21 Tp. 1 R. 8, north and east.

**115. (sic) BELLAME, John**
Dec. 22, 1826, 3 miles N Monticello, Jefferson Co. Lot No. 6 Fractional Sect. 7 Tp. 2 R. 4, north and east.

**3630. BELLAME, John**
Oct. 11, 1830, 1 mile E Dills, Jefferson Co. E 1/2 NE 1/4 Sect. 5 Tp. 2 R. 6, north and east.

**3631. BELLAME, John**
Oct. 11, 1830, 1/2 mile E Dills, Jefferson Co. W 1/2 NW 1/4 Sect. 5 Tp. 2 R. 6, north and east.

**3633. BELLAME, John**
Oct. 11, 1830, 2 1/2 miles ESE Dills, Jefferson Co. W 1/2 NE 1/4 Sect. 9 Tp. 2 R. 6, north and east.

**3634. BELLAME, John**
Oct. 11, 1830, 2 miles ESE Dills, Jefferson Co. W 1/2 NW 1/4 Sect. 9 Tp. 2 R. 6, north and east.

**3635. BELLAME, John**
Oct. 11, 1830, 2 1/2 miles SE Dills, Jefferson Co. W 12 SW 1/4 Sect. 9 Tp. 2 R. 6, north and east.

**3636. BELLAME, John**
Oct. 11, 1830, 4 miles ESE Dills, Jefferson Co. E 1/2 SW 1/4 Sect. 10 Tp. 2 R. 6, north and east.

**3637. BELLAME, John**
Oct. 11, 1830, 4 1/2 miles ESE Dills, Jefferson Co. W 1/2 SE 1/4 Sect. 10 Tp. 2 R. 6, north and east.

**3638. BELLAME, John**
Oct. 11, 1830, 5 miles E by S Dills, Jefferson Co. E 1/2 SE 1/4 Sect. 10 Tp.2 R. 6, north and east.

**3639. BELLAME, John**
Oct. 11, 1830, 4 miles SE Dills, Jefferson Co. E 1/2 NE 1/4 Sect. 15 Tp. 2 R. 6, north and east.

**3642. BELLAME, John**
Oct. 11, 1830, 4 1/2 miles SE Dills, Jefferson Co. E 1/2 SW 1/4 Sect. 13 Tp. 2 R. 6, north and east.

**3643. BELLAME, John**
Oct. 11, 1830, 4 3/4 miles SE Dills, Jefferson Co. W 1/2 SE 1/4 Sect. 15 Tp. 2 R. 6, north and east.

**3644. BELLAME, John**
Oct. 11, 1830, 3 3/4 miles SE Dills, Jefferson Co. E 1/2 SE 1/4 Sect. 17 Tp. 2 R. 6, north and east.

**3645. BELLAME, John**
Oct. 11, 1830, 3 miles S Dills, Jefferson Co. E 1/2 NW 1/4 Sect. 19 Tp. 2 R. 6, north and east.

**3646. BELLAME, John**
Oct. 11, 1830, 3 1/2 miles SSE Dills, Jefferson Co. W 1/2 NE 1/4 Sect. 21 Tp. 2 R. 6, north and east.

**3647. BELLAME, John**
Oct. 11, 1830, 3 miles SSE Dills, Jefferson Co. E 1/2 NW 1/4 Sect. 21 Tp. 2 R. 6, north and east.

**3648. BELLAME, John**
Oct. 11, 1830, 3 3/4 miles SSE Dills, Jefferson Co. E 1/2 SW 1/4 Sect. 21 Tp. 2 R. 6, north and east.

**3649. BELLAME, John**
Oct. 11, 1830, 3 1/2 miles SSE Dills, Jefferson Co. E 1/2 NE 1/4 Sect. 22 Tp. 2 R. 6, north and east.

**3687. BELLAME, John**
Oct. 14, 1830, 2 1/2 miles S Champaign, Madison Co. E 1/2 SW 1/4 Sect. 35 Tp. 1 R. 8, north and east.

**3689. BELLAME, John**
Oct. 14, 1830, 2 1/2 miles S Champaign, Madison Co. E 1/2 SE 1/4 Sect. 33 Tp. 1 R. 8, north and east.

**3695. BALLAME, John**
Oct. 14, 1830, 2 miles E by S Champaign, Madison Co. W 1/2 SE 1/4 Sect. 19 Tp. 1 R. 9, north and east.

**3696. BALLAME, John**
Oct. 11, 1830, 2 miles ESE Champaign, Madison Co. E 1/2 NW 1/4 Sect. 30 Tp. 1 R. 9, north and east.

**3697. BELLAME, John**
Oct. 11, 1830, 3 miles W Madison, Madison Co. W 1/2 SW 1/4 Sect. 30 Tp. 1 R. 9, north and east.

**7280. BELLAME, John**
Jan. 30, 1838, 6 1/2 miles SE by S Dills, Jefferson Co. SW 1/4 SE 1/4 Sect. 24 Tp.2 R. 6, north and east.

**4030. BELLAMI, John**
July 16, 1831, 4 1/2 miles SSW of Mears Spur, Gadsden Co. W 1/2 NW 1/4 Sect. 2 Tp. 2 R. 6, north and west.

**4031. BELLAMI, John**
July 16, 1831, 4 1/4 miles SSW of Mears Spur, Gadsden Co. W 1/2 SW 1/4 Sect. 2 Tp. 2 R. 6, north and east.

**5737. BELLAMI, John**
June 29, 1836, 3 miles E by S of Dills, Jefferson Co. E 1/2 SE 1/2 Sect. 8 Tp. 2 R. 6, north and east.

**5738. BELLAMI, John**
June 29, 1836, 2 1/2 miles E of Dills, Jefferson Co. E 1/2 NW 1/4 Sect. 2 Tp. 2 R.6, north and east.

**4019. BELLAMI, William**
July 16, 1831, 2 1/2 miles NNE of Monticello, Jefferson Co. W 1/2 SE 1/4 Sect. 22 Tp. 2 R. 5, north and east.

**4020. BELLAMI, William**
July 16, 1831, 2 3/4 miles NNE of Monticello, Jefferson Co. E 1/2 NE 1/4 Sect. 27 Tp. 2 R. 5, north and east.

**4021. BELLAMI, William**
July 16, 1831, 3 3/4 miles NNE of Monticello, Jefferson Co. W 1/2 NE 1/4 Sect. 27 Tp. 2 R. 5, north and east.

**4022. BELLAMI, William**
July 16, 1831, 3 miles E of Monticello, Jefferson Co. W 1/2 NW 1/4 Sect. 35 Tp. 2 R. 5, north and east.

**1765. BELLAMIE, Abraham(Sr.)**
June 4, 1827, 3 1/2 miles E of Monticello, Jefferson Co. E 1/2 NW 1/4 Sect. 26 Tp. 2 R. 5, north and east.

**1764. BELLAMIE, Jno. (Sr.)**
June 4, 1827, 2 miles S of Monticello, Jefferson Co. E 1/2 NW 1/4 Sect. 6 Tp. 1 R. 5, north and east.

**1766. BELLAMIE, Jno.(Sr.)**
June 4, 1827, 1 mile S of Monticello, Jefferson Co. SW 1/4 Sect. 32 Tp. 2 R. 5, north and east.

**1767. BELLAMIE, Jno. (Sr.)**
June 4, 1827, 2 miles SE of Monticello, Jefferson Co. E 1/2 SE 1/4 Sect. 31 Tp. 2 R. 5, north and east.

**1772. BELLAMIE, Jno. (Sr.)**
(DUP) June 4, 1827, at Drifton, Jefferson Co. SE 1/4 Sect. 6 Tp. 1 R. 5, north and east.

**2139. BELLAMIE, Jno.**
Dec. 12, 1827, 3 miles NNE Moseley Hall, Madison Co. E 1/2 NE 1/4 Sect. 10 Tp. 1 R. 8, south and east.

**2140. BELLAMIE, Jno./John**
Dec. 12, 1827, 3 miles NNE Moseley Hall, Madison Co. W 1/2 NE 1/4 Sect. 10 Tp. 1 R. 8, south and east.

**2141. BELLAMIE, Jno./John**
Dec. 12, 1827, 1 1/2 miles N Moseley Hall, Madison Co. E 1/2 NE 1/4 Sect. 17 Tp.1 R. 8, south and east.

**2142. BELLAMIE, Jno./John**
Dec. 12, 1827, 2 miles N by E Moseley Hall, Madison Co. W 1/2 NE 1/4 Sect. 17 Tp. 1 R. 8, south and east.

**2143. BELLAMIE, Jno./John**
Dec. 12, 1827, 2 miles NNE Moseley Hall, Madison Co. E 1/2 NW 1/4 Sect. 17 Tp. 1 R. 8, south and east.

**2144. BELLAMIE, Jno./John**
Dec. 12, 1827, 2 1/4 miles NNE Moseley Hall, Madison Co. W 1/2 NW 1/4 Sect. 17 Tp.1 R. 8, south and east.

**2307. BELLAMIE, Jno./John**
March 13, 1828, 1 mile NE Moseley Hall, Madison Co. E 1/2 of Sect. 21 Tp. 1 R. 8, south and east.

**2301. BELLAMIE, Jno./John**
March 12, 1828, 1 mile N Moseley Hall, Madison Co. NE 1/4 Sect. 20 Tp. 1 R. 8, south and east.

**2302. BELLAMIE, Jno./John**
March 12, 1828, 2 miles E Moseley Hall, Madison Co. E 1/2 NE 1/4 Sect. 27 Tp. 1 R. 8, south and east.

**2303. Bellamie, Jno./John**
March 12, 1828, 9 miles WSW Madison, Madison Co. E 1/2 SE 1/4 Sect. 9 Tp. 1 R. 8, south and east.

**2304. BELLAMIE, Jno./John**
March 12, 1828, 2 1/2 miles ENE Moseley Hall, Madison Co. W 1/2 SW 1/4 Sect. 23 Tp. 1 R. 8, south and east.

**2305. BELLAMIE, Jno./John**
March 12, 1828, 3 miles NNE Moseley Hall, Madison Co. W 1/2 NW 1/4 Sect. 15 Tp. 1 R. 8, south and east.

**2308. BELLAMIE, Jno./John**
March 13, 1828, 1 1/2 miles NE Moseley Hall, Madison Co. NW 1/4 Sect. 22 Tp. 1 R. 8, south and east.

**2170. BELLAMY, Abram**
(Of Fla.)Dec. 25, 1827, 2 miles N Moseley Hall, Madison Co. SE 1/4 Sect. 17 Tp. 1 R. 8, south and east.

**2171. BELLAMY, Abram**
Dec. 25, 1827, at Moseley Hall, Madison Co. SE 1/4 Sect. 29 Tp. 1 R. 8, south and east.

**8913. BELLAMY, Ann B.**
Feb. 24, 1846, 3 1/2 miles E Everett, Washington Co. E 1/2 SE 1/4 Sect. 11 Tp. 3 R. 13, north and west.

**BELLAMY, Edward C. see Isaac TORT.**

**1761. BELLAMY, Jno./John**
(DUP) June 4, 1827, 3 miles ENE Byrd, Jefferson Co. W 1/2 NE 1/4 Sect. 12 Tp. 1 R. 3, north and east.

**2224. BELLAMY, Jno./John**
(Of Fla.) Jan. 14, 1828, 4 miles NNE Moseley Hall, Madison Co. NW 1/4 Sect. 9 Tp. 1 R. 8, south and east.

**3017. BELLAMY, Jno./John**
Sept. 7, 1829, 1 mile NE Moseley Hall, Madison Co. E 1/2 SE 1/4 Sect. 23 Tp. 1 R. 8, south and east.

**3018. BELLAMY, Jno./John**
Sept. 7, 1829, 2 1/2 miles ENE Moseley Hall, Madison Co. W 1/2 NW 1/4 Sect. 24 Tp. 1 R. 8, south and east.

**3019. BELLAMY, Jno./John**
Sept. 7, 1829, 2 1/2 miles ENE Moseley Hall, Madison Co. W 1/2 NW 1/4 Sect. 24 Tp. 1 R. 8, south and east.

**3020. BELLAMY, Jno./John**
Sept. 7, 1829, 4 1/2 miles ENE Moseley Hall, Madison Co. E 1/2 SE 1/4 Sect. 13 Tp. 1 R. 8, south and east.

**3021. BELLAMY, Jno./John**
Sept. 7, 1829, 5 miles ENE Moseley Hall, Madison Co. W 1/2 SW 1/4 Sect. 18 Tp. 1 R. 9, south and east.

**3022. BELLAMY, Jno./John**
Sept. 7, 1829, 3 miles SW Madison, Madison Co. W 1/2 SW 1/4 Sect. 5 Tp. 1 R. 9, south and east.

**3024. BELLAMY, Jno./John**
Sept. 7, 1829, 5 miles SSW Madison, Madison Co. W 1/2 SW 1/4 Sect. 8

Tp. 1 R. 9, south and east.
**3025. BELLAMY, Jno./John**
Sept. 7, 1829, 4 1/2 miles SSW Madison, Madison Co. W 1/2 NW 1/4 Sect. 8 Tp. 1 R. 9, south and east.
**3658. BELLAMY, Jno./John**
Oct. 5, 1830, just NE Greenville, Madison Co. E 1/2 SE 1/4 Sect. 21 Tp.1 R. 7, north and east.
**3659. BELLAMY, Jno./John**
Oct. 12, 1830, 1/2 mile E Greenville, Madison Co. W 1/2 NW 1/4 Sect. 22 Tp. 1 R. 7, north and east.
**3660. BELLAMY, Jno./John**
Oct. 12, 1830, 1/2 mile SW Greenville, Madison Co. W 1/2 SW 1/4 Sect. 22 Tp. 1 R. 7, north and east.
**3661. BELLAMY, Jno./John**
Oct. 12, 1830, 3 miles E Greenville, Madison Co. W 1/2 NE 1/4 Sect. 24 Tp. 1 R. 7, north and east.
**3662. BELLAMY, Jno./John**
Oct. 12, 1830, 3 miles E by S Greenville, Madison Co. W 1/2 SE 1/4 Sect. 24 Tp. 1 R. 7, north and east.
**3663. BELLAMY, Jno./John**
Oct. 12, 1830, 3 miles E by S Greenville, Madison Co. E 1/2 SE 1/4 Sect. 24 Tp. 1 R. 7, north and east.
**3664. BELLAMY, Jno./John**
Oct. 12, 1830, 3 1/4 miles ESE Greenville, Madison Co. E 1/2 NE 1/4 Sect. 25 Tp. 1 R. 7, north and east.
**3679. BELLAMY, Jno./John**
Oct. 11, 1830, 3 miles W by S Champaign, Madison Co. E 1/2 SE 1/4 Sect. 20 Tp. 1 R. 8, north and east.
**3681. BELLAMY, Jno./John**
Oct. 14, 1830, 1 1/2 miles S Champaign, Madison Co. E 1/2 SW 1/4 Sect. 26 Tp. 1 R. 8, north and east.
**3682. BELLAMY, John**
Oct. 14,1830, 1 1/2 miles S Champaign, Madison Co. W 1/2 SE 1/4 Sect. 26 Tp. 1 R. 8, north and east.
**3683. BELLAMY, John**
Oct. 14, 1830, 2 miles SW Champaign, Madison Co. E 1/2 NW 1/4 Sect. 27 Tp. 1 R. 8, north and east.
**3684. BELLAMY, John**
Oct. 14, 1830, 2 1/2 miles WSW Champaign, Madison Co. W 1/2 NW 1/4 Sect. 28 Tp. 1 R. 8, north and east.
**3686. BELLAMY, John**
Oct. 11, 1830, 2 1/2 miles S by W Champaign, Madison Co. W 1/2 SW 1/4 Sect. 35 Tp. 1 R. 8, north and east.
**3833. BELLAMY, John**
Jan. 5, 1831, 2 miles W Champaign, Madison Co. W 1/2 NW 1/4 Sect. 21 Tp. 1 R. 8, north and east.
**3951. BELLAMY, John**
April 13, 1831, 6 miles SE Dills, Jefferson Co. W 1/2 NW 1/4 Sect. 23 Tp. 2 R. 6, north and east.
**3952. BELLAMY, John**
April 13, 1831, 6 miles SE Dills, Jefferson Co. E 1/2 NW 1/4 Sect. 23 Tp. 2 R. 6, north and east.
**3958. BELLAMY, John**
May 2, 1831, 5 miles WSW Ashville, Jefferson Co. E 1/2 NE 1/4 Sect. 10 Tp. 2 R. 6, north and east.
**6379. BELLAMY, Samuel C.**
Jan. 3, 1837, at Fair Grounds, Jackson Co. E 1/2 SW 1/4 and W 1/2 SE 1/4 Sect. 32 Tp. 5 R. 10, north and west.
**7131. BELLAMY, Samuel C.**
Dec. 7, 1837, 7 miles E by S Welchton, Jackson Co. SW 1/4 Sect. 36 Tp. 6 R. 11, north and west.
**7132. BELLAMY, Samuel C.**
Dec. 7, 1837, 6 miles E by S Welchton, Jackson Co. NE 1/4 Sect. 35 Tp. 6 R. 11, north and west.
**7133. BELLAMY, Samuel C.**
Dec. 7, 1837, 4 miles SW Ellis, Jackson Co. W 1/2 NW 1/4 Sect. 31 Tp. 6 R. 10, north and west.
**4032. BELLAMY, William**
July 16, 1831, 3 miles E by S of Sedalia, Gadsden Co. E 1/2 SW 1/4 Sect. 23 Tp. 2 R. 5, north and east.
**4033. BELLAMY, William**
July 16, 1831, 3 1/2 miles E by S of Sedalia, Gadsden Co. W 1/2 SE 1/4 Sect. 23 Tp. 2 R. 5, north and east.
**6791. BELLAMY, William**
March 1, 1837, 3 1/2 miles E Monticello, Jefferson Co. NE 1/4 NW 1/4 Sect. 35 Tp. 2 R. 5, north and east.
**6792. BELLAMY, William**
Mar. 1, 1837, 4 miles W Monticello, Jefferson Co. W 1/2 NW 1/4 Sect. 25 Tp. 2 R. 5, north and east.
**6793. BELLAMY, William**
Mar. 1, 1837, 3 3/4 miles E Monticello, Jefferson Co. E 1/2 NE 1/4 Sect.

26 Tp. 2 R. 5, north and east.

**8480. BELLAMY, William**
Dec. 29, 1845, 5 miles NW Myrick, Madison Co. NW 1/4 Sect. 27 Tp. 1 R. 6, north and east. This tract was entered by **John MURPHY** and claimed by **William BELLAMY** whose claim was admitted.

**3214. BELLAMY, Wm.**
Jan. 18, 1830, 5 miles E Monticello, Jefferson Co. SE 1/4 Sect. 26 Tp. 2 R. 5, north and east.

**4888. BELLEMAY, John**
Mar. 13, 1835, 4 1/2 miles SE of Dill, Jefferson Co. E 1/2 NW 1/4 Sect. 22 Tp. 2 R. 6, north and east.

**4889. BELLAMAY, John**
Mar. 13, 1835, 4 1/4 miles SE of Dill, Jefferson Co. W 1/2 NE 1/4 Sect. 22 Tp. 2 R. 6, north and east.

**8853. BELSHER, William**
Dec. 12, 1845, 3 3/4 miles E by N Barker, Holmes Co. SE 1/4 SW 1/4 Sect. 17 Tp. 6 R. 16, north and west.

**8854. BELSHER, William**
Dec. 12, 1845, 3 1/2 miles E by N Barker, Holmes Co. SE 1/4 SE 1/4 Sect. 18 Tp. 6 R. 16, north and west.

**883. BELSHER, Wm.**
Jan. 17, 1827, 1 mile E Quincy, Gadsden Co. W 1/2 SW 1/4 Sect. 4 Tp. 2 R. 3, north and west.

**884. BELSHER, Wm.**
Jan. 17, 1827, 1 mile E Quincy, Gadsden Co. E 1/2 SW 1/4 Sect. 4 Tp. 2 R. 3, north and west.

**887. BELSHER, Wm.**
Jan. 17, 1827, 1 mile E Quincy, Gadsden Co. E 1/2 NE 1/4 Sect. 8 Tp. 2 R. 3, north and west.

**3508. BEMBREY, William**
May 8, 1830, 1 1/2 miles SW Bradfordville, Leon Co. E 1/2 NW 1/4 Sect. 28 Tp. 2 R. 1, north and east. Transferred for $150.00 Nov. 29, 1829 to (unknown) Teste: **Daniel FAUST**.

**2204. BENTLEY, Jeremiah**
(Of Fla.) Dec. 31, 1827, 4 miles WNW Alma, Jefferson Co. W 1/2 NW 1/4 Sect. 30 Tp. 3 R. 4, north and east.

**2496. BENTLEY, Jeremiah**
Sect. 17, 1828, 3 1/2 miles E Stringer, Leon Co. E 1/2 SW 1/4 Sect. 30 Tp. 3 R. 4, north and east.

**3213. BENTLEY, Jeremiah**
Jan. 18, 1830, 3 miles E Stringer, Jefferson Co. E 1/2 NE 1/4 Sect. 25 Tp. 3 R. 3, north and east.

**3511. BENTLEY, John**
May 13, 1830, 4 miles E Stringer, Leon Co. W 1/2 SE 1/4 Sect. 30 Tp. 3 R. 4, north and east.

**2122. BERRY, William F.**
Aug. 29, 1853, 1 1/4 miles E of LaCrosse, Alachua Co. SW 1/4 SE 1/4 Sect. 26 Tp. 7 R. 19, south and east. Patent delivered June 13, 1856.

**671. BESSENT, Abraham**
Dec. 27, 1848, 3 miles NW Belmore, Clay Co. NW 1/4 SW 1/4 Sect. 32 Tp. 6 R. 24, south and east. Patent delivered July 7, 1857.

**8554. BETTON, Turbutt Lane**
Sept. 6, 1842, 4 miles NE Marion, Hamilton Co. Lot No. 1 Sect. 23 Tp. 1 R. 14, south and east.

**366. BEVAN, Robert**
April 20, 1846, near Rocky, Levy Co. W 1/2 SE 1/4 and SE 1/4 SE 1/4 Sect. 12 Tp. 13 R. 14, south and east.

**2381. BEVERIDGE, Anna M.**
May 20. 1828. at Marianna, Jackson Co. W 1/2 SE 1/4 Sect. 4 Tp. 4 R. 10, north and west.

**2023. BEFERIDGE, Anna M.**
Aug. 10, 1827, at Marianna, Jackson Co. E 1/2 SE 1/4 Sect. 4 Tp. 4 R. 10, north and west.

**1953. BEVERIDGE, Robert**
June 25, 1827, 1 mile SE Marianna, Jackson Co. W 1/2 SW 1/4 Sect. 3 Tp. 4 R. 10, north and west.

**1954. BEVERIDGE, Robert**
June 25, 1827, 1/2 miles ESE Marianna, Jackson Co. E 1/2 NE 1/4 Sect. 10 Tp. 4 R. 10, north and west.

**690. BEVILL, Granville**
Sept. 11, 1849, 7 1/2 miles W Ft. Drane, Marion Co. SE 1/4 NW 1/4 Sect. 2 Tp. 13 R. 19, south and east.

**693. BEVILL, Granville**
Nov. 15, 1849, 7 1/2 miles W Ft. Drane, Marion Co. NE 1/4 NW 1/4 Sect. 2 Tp. 13 R. 19, south and east.

**4489. BEVILL, John R.**
Jan. 12, 1857, 1/2 mile N of Tioga, Alachua Co. S 1/2 of Lot No. 2 and SE 1/4 of SW 1/4 Sect. 27 and N 1/2

of Lot No. 1 and NE 1/4 of NW 1/4 Sect. 34 Tp. 9 R. 18, south and east.
**5226. BEVILL, John R.**
Mar. 17, 1860, 1 mile NE of Tioga, Alachua Co. S 1/2 Lot No. 1 Sect. 34 Tp. 9 R. 18, south and east. Patent delivered Oct. 8, 1873.
**BIBB, Benjamin S. see GILMER, Wm. B. L.**
**3491. BIMBY, Kenneth**
Apr. 21, 1830, 4 1/2 miles WSW Centerville, Leon Co. E 1/2 SW 1/4 Sect. 33 Tp. 2 R. 1, north and east. Assigned Nov. 1, 1834, to **John C. HALL**, before the Register, **G. W. WARD**, by Geo. T. WARD, Clerk.
**8533. BINDO, David**
Mar. 24, 1842, 1 1/4 miles S by W Concord, Gadsden Co. SW 1/4 SW 1/4 Sect. 19 Tp. 3 R. 1, north and west.
**4185. BINE, Archibald**
July 11, 1832, 3 1/2 miles E of Mount Pleasant, Gadsden Co. SW 1/4 NE 1/4 Sect. 11 Tp. 3 R. 4, north and west.
**4678. BINGHAM, John A.**
Aug. 6, 1884, 1 1/2 miles NW Eagle Lake(town) W of lake, Polk Co. W 1/2 NW 1/4 and Lot No. 1 and 2, E 1/2 NE 1/4 Sect. 2 Tp. 29S and R. 25E.
**92. BINI, John**
Dec. 12,1826, 3 miles W Jamieson Station, Gadsden Co. SE 1/4 Sect. 9 Tp. 3 R. 3, north and west. Transferred Dec. 12, 1826 to L. and **M. A. ARMSTEAD**.
**6236. BIRD, Benjamin F.**
Dec. 17, 1836, 4 miles SW El Destino, Leon Co. SE 1/4 SW 1/4 Sect. 21 Tp. 1 R. 2, south and east.
**4310. BIRD, Daniel**
Feb. 13, 1833, 1 mile NNE of Braswell, Jefferson Co. SE 1/4 NE 1/4 Sect. 10 Tp. 1 R. 4, south and east. Transferred to **Ware G. TUCKER**, May 31, 1841.
**6821. BIRD, Daniel**
Mar. 1, 1827, c. 4 miles WSW Lamont, Jefferson Co. Lot Not. 1 Fractional Sect. 31 Tp. 1 R. 5, south and east. (Note: Joining **APYLES** tract and **BIBB**'s land.)

**6867. BIRD, Daniel**
Mar. 8, 1837, 2 miles SW Lamont, Jefferson Co. E 1/2 NW 1/4 Sect. 33 Tp.1 R. 5, south and east.
**6868. BIRD, Daniel**
Mar. 9, 1837, 1 1/4 miles W Lamont, Jefferson Co. W 1/2 SE 1/4 Sect. 28 Tp. 1 R. 5, south and east.
**4590. BIRD, Dock**
May 28, 1884, 2 1/2 miles NW Laurel Hill, Okaloossa Co. W 1/2 SE 1/4 and SE 1/4 SE 1/4 Sect. 26 Tp. 6N R. 23W.
**4337. BIRD, James**
Mar. 29, 1838, 1 mile W of Champaign, Madison Co. NW 1/4 NE 1/4 Sect. 22 Tp. 1 R. 8, north and east.
**5120. BIRD, James**
July 30, 1835, 6 1/2 miles NNW of Champaign, Madison Co. NW 1/4 NW 1/4 Sect. 17 Tp. 1 R. 8, north and east.
**6115. BIRD, James**
Nov. 30, 1830, 2 miles SSE Cherry Lake Post Office, Madison Co. E 1/2 NW 1/4 Sect. 26 Tp.2 R. 8, north and east.
**6040. BIRD, John**
Nov. 17, 1836, 2 miles E Snead, Jackson Co. NE 1/4 SE 1/4 Sect. 9 Tp. 3 R. 7, north and west.
**6041. BIRD, John**
Nov. 17, 1836, 1 1/2 miles ENE Snead, Jackson Co. NW 1/4 NW 1/4 Sect. 10 Tp. 3 R. 7, north and west.
**6175. BIRD, John**
Dec. 9, 1836, 2 miles SW Snead, Jackson Co. E 1/2 NE 1/4 Sect. 10 Tp. 3 R. 7, north and west.
**7468. BIRD, John**
May 14, 1838, 1 1/4 mile S Snead, Jackson Co. E 1/2 SE 1/4 Sect. 3 Tp. 3 R. 7, north and west.
**7506. BIRD, John**
June 30, 1838, 1 3/4 miles S Snead, Jackson Co. W 1/2 SE 1/4 Sect. 10 Tp. 3 R. 7, south and west.
**5245. BIRD, Sherod**
May 18, 1860, 2 1/2 miles W of Live Oak, Suwannee Co. SE 1/4 SW 1/4 Sect. 20 Tp. 2 R. 13, south and east. Patent delivered Aug. 26, 1869.
**6153. BIRD, Silianus**
Dec. 5, 1836, 1/2 mile NW Cham-

paign, Madison Co. NW 1/4 SW 1/4 Sect. 14 Tp. 1 R. 8, north and east.

**6278. BISHOP, George**
Dec. 22, 1836, 5 miles NNW Aucilla, Jefferson Co. E 1/2 NE 1/4 Sect. 30 Tp. 2 R. 6, north and east.

**2603. BLACK, John**
Aug. 20, 1881, 1 mile NE Clearwater, Pinellas Co. S 1/2 NE 1/4 Sect. 12 Tp. 29S R. 15E.

**4308. BLACK, William**
Feb. 11, 1833, 2 miles SW of Iamonia, Leon Co. NE 1/4 NE 1/4 Sect. 14 Tp. 3 R. 1, north and east.

**477. BLACKBORN, James Christenberry**
Nov. 6, 1846, 1 mile SW Rixford, Suwannee Co. SW 1/4 SE 1/4 Sect. 1 Tp. 2 R. 13, south and east. Patent delivered Nov. 7, 1854.

**5697. BLACKBURN, Elias E.**
June 10, 1836, 4 miles E by N of Stringer, Jefferson Co. W 1/2 SW 1/4 Sect. 29 Tp. 3 R. 4, north and east.

**6088. BLACKBURN, Elias E.**
Nov. 24, 1836, 3 miles WNW Alma, Leon Co. E 1/2 SE 1/4 Sect. 29 Tp. 3 R. 4, north and east.

**6089. BLACKBURN, Elias E.**
Nov. 24, 1836, 3 miles W by N Alma, Leon Co. W 1/2 SW 1/4 Sect. 28 Tp. 3 R. 4, north and east.

**6091. BLACKBURN, Elias E.**
Nov. 24, 1836, 5 miles W by N Alma, Leon Co. E 1/2 SE 1/4 Sect. 30 Tp. 3 R. 4, north and east.

**6519. BLACKBURN, George S.**
Jan. 3, 1837, 4 miles N Monticello, Jefferson Co. SW 1/4 SW 1/4 Sect. 31 Tp. 3 R. 5, north and east.

**4463. BLACKBURN, Neome**
Nov. 19, 1856, 2 miles S of Rixford, Suwannee Co. E 1/2 of NE 1/4 Sect. 13 Tp. 2 R. 13, south and east. Patent delivered Aug. 12, 1863.

**4066. BLACKBURN, William**
Aug. 22, 1831, 1 1/4 miles E of Monticello, Jefferson Co. W 1/2 SW 1/4 Sect. 28, Tp. 2 R. 5, north and east.

**4582. BLACKBURN, William**
June 9, 1834, 5 1/4 miles W by N of Dill, Jefferson Co. NE 1/4 NW 1/4 Sect. 31 Tp. 3 R. 5, north and east.

**4583. BLACKBURN, William**
June 9, 1834, 5 1/2 miles W by N of Dill, Jefferson Co. NW 1/4 NW 1/4 Sect. 31 Tp. 3 R. 5, north and east.

**5015. BLACKBURN, William**
June 27, 1835, 7 1/2 miles E by S of Stringer, Jefferson Co. Lot. 2 Sect. 36 Tp. 3 r. 4, north and east.

**5016. BLACKBURN, William**
June 27, 1836, 5 1/2 miles W by N of Dill, Jefferson Co. SW 1/4 NW 1/4 Sect. 31 Tp. 3 R. 5, north and east.

**5017. BLACKBURN, William**
June 27, 1835, 5 3/4 miles WNW of Dill, Jefferson Co. SE 1/4 NW 1/4 Sect. 31 Tp. 3 R. 5, north and east.

**6244. BLACKBURN, William**
Dec. 19, 1836, just N Alma, Jefferson Co. Lot No. 1 Fractional Sect. 26 Tp 3 R. 4, north and east.

**6245. BLACKBURN, William**
Dec. 19, 1836, 2 miles E Alma, Jefferson Co. W 1/2 SE 1/4 Sect. 31 Tp. 3 R. 5, north and east.

**6246. BLACKBURN, William**
Dec. 19, 1836, c. 1 mile N Alma, Jefferson Co. Fractional Sect. 23 Tp. 3 R. 4, north and east.

**2712. BLACKBURN, Wm.**
Feb. 5, 1829, 1 mile W Monticello, Jefferson Co. E 1/2 NW 1/2 Sect. 25 Tp. 2 R. 4, north and east.

**2766. BLACKBURN, Wm.**
March 2, 1829, 1/2 mile W Monticello, Jefferson Co. W 1/2 NW 1/4 Sect. 25 Tp. 2 R. 4, north and cast.

**2976. BLACKBURN, Wm.**
Aug. 10, 1829, 2 miles NE Alma, Jefferson Co. E 1/2 SW 1/4 Sect. 36 Tp. 3 R. 5, north and east.

**8507. BLACKLEDGE, Edward**
Nov. 8, 1841, 1/2 mile W Lake Jackson, Leon Co. SW 1/4 SE 1/4 Sect. 36 Tp. 2 R. 2, north and west.

**3035. BLACKLEDGE, James**
Sept. 11, 1829, 2 miles NE Capitola, Leon Co. E 1/2 NE 1/4 Sect. 20 Tp. 1 R. 3, south and east.

**3037. BLACKLEDGE, Jas.**
Sept. 12, 1829, 1 mile S Ivan, Wakulla Co. W 1/2 NE 1/4 Sect. 20 Tp. 1 R. 3, south and east.

**6915. BLACKLIDGE, James**
March 15, 1837, 2 miles S by E El Destino, Jefferson Co. NE 1/4 SW

1/4 Sect. 20 Tp. 1 R. 3, south and east.
**6922. BLACKLIDGE, James**
March 18, 1837, 2 1/2 miles SSE El Destino, Jefferson Co. SW 1/4 SE 1/4 Sect. 20 Tp. 1 R. 3, south and east.
**8777. BLACKLIDGE, James**
May 9, 1845, 1/2 mile W by N Lake Jackson(town), Leon Co. SE 1/4 SE 1/4 Sect. 36 Tp. 2 R. 2, north and west.
**8952. BLACKSHEAR, David**
June 17, 1846, 4 miles NNW Dellwood, Jackson Co. S 1/2 SW 1/4 Sect. 10 Tp. 5 R. 9, north and west.
**8953. BLACKSHEAR, David**
June 17, 1846, 5 3/4 miles NNW Dellwood, Jackson Co. E 1/2 NW 1/4 Sect. 15 Tp. 5 R. 9, north and west.
**617, BLACKSHEAR, Lewis**
Feb. 18, 1848, c. 2 miles NE Lake Geneva, Clay Co. NW 1/4 SE 1/4 Sect. 23 Tp. 8 R. 22, south and east.
**1930. BLACKSHEAR, Lewis**
July 8, 1853, 3 1/4 miles SE of S Thenessa, Bradford Co. SW 1/4 SE 1/4 Sect. 23 Tp. 8 R. 22, south and east.
**BLACKWELL, A. B. see LOFTIN, William M.**
**2362. BLAKE, Edwin, L. T.**
Nov. 7, 1853, at Oakton, Putnam Co. Lot No. 13 Sect. 31 Tp. 10 R. 23, south and east.
**3257. BLAKE, Miles**
Feb. 6, 1830, 3 miles W Wadesboro, Leon Co. E 1/2 SE 1/4 Sect. 4 Tp.1 R. 2, north and east.
**4113. BLAKE, Miles**
Dec. 20, 1831, 5 1/2 miles NNW of Perkins, Leon Co. E 1/2 SW 1/4 Sect. 4 Tp. 1 R. 2, north and east.
**4959. BLAKE, Miles**
May 11, 1835, 3 3/4 miles SSE of Miccosukee, Jefferson Co. W 1/2 SW 1/4 Sect. 20 Tp. 2 R. 3, north and east.
**5309. BLEACH, Abraham**
Dec. 5, 1835, 1 mile S of Lloyd, Jefferson Co. NW 1/4 SW 1/4 Sect. 27 Tp. 3 R. 3, north and east.
**5310. BLEACH, Abraham**
Dec. 5, 1835, 5 miles NNW of Lloyd, Jefferson Co. NE 1/4 SE 1/4 Sect. 22 Tp. 3 R. 3, north and east.
**905. BLEACH, John (Sr.)**
July 14, 1851, 1 1/2 miles SW Santos, Marion Co. SE 1/4 SE 1/4 Sect. 14 Tp. 16 R. 22, south and east.
**1131. BLEACH, Wm. or Willis**
Jan. 28, 1852, 2 miles NNE Ocala, Marion Co. S 1/2 SE 1/4 Sect. 5 Tp. 15 R. 22, south and east.
**708. BLITCH, James**
Feb. 2, 1850, 1 mile SW Agnew, Marion Co. SW 1/4 SW 1/4 Sect. 23 and SE 1/4 SE 1/4 Sect. 22 Tp. 15 R. 21, south and east.
**755. BLITCH, John**
Nov. 18, 1850, near Belleview, Marion Co. NE 1/4 NE 1/4 Sect. 23 Tp. 16 R. 22, south and east.
**6142. BLITCH, Keland S.**
Sept. 13, 1887, 1 1/2 miles NE Pinland, Taylor Co. E 1/2 NE 1/4 Sect. 28 and W 1/2 NW 1/4 Sectt. 27 Tp. 5S R. 8E.
**4082. BLOOM, Henry M.**
Jan. 11, 1856, 3 miles SW of Ogden, Columbia Co. SE 1/4 of SW 1/4 Sect. 32 Tp. 3 R. 15, south and east.
**4083. BLOOM, Henry M.**
Jan. 11, 1856, 2 1/4 miles SE of Ogden, Columbia Co. E 1/2 of NE 1/4 Sect. 4 Tp. 4 R. 15, south and east.
**2242. BLOUNT, Cornelius**
Jan. 31, 1828, 3 miles SW Havana, Gadsden Co. W 1/2 SE 1/4 Sect. 8 Rp. 2 R. 2, north and west.
**6009. BLOUNT, Eugene B.**
Aug. 12, 1887, 1 mile NE Tiger Bay, Polk Co. N 1/2 NW 1/4 and SE 1/4 of NW 1/4 and NE 1/4 SW 1/4 Sect. 26 Tp. 31S R. 24E.
**BLOUNT or BLUNT, Redding see KIRKLAND, Moses**
**126. BLOUNT, Willie**
Dec. 23, 1826, 4 miles NW of Aycock Station, Jackson Co. SE 1/4 Sect. 13 Tp. 5 R. 12, north and west.
**4372. BLUCKBIDGE, James**
June 20, 1833, 1 mile NE of Capitola, Jefferson Co. NW 1/4 SE 1/4 Sect. 20 Tp. 1 R. 3, south and east.
**128. BLUE, Daniel**
Feb. 20, 1845, 2 1/2 miles E Pine Mount, Suwannee Co. NE 1/4 SW 1/4 Sect. 4 Tp. 4 R. 14, south and east.
**8027. BLUNT, Cornelius**
Aug. 10, 1839, at Havana, Gadsden

Co. SE 1/4 SE 1/4 Sect. 34 Tp. 3 R. 2, north and west.

**6467. BLUNT, P.**
Jan. 9, 1837, 1 1/2 miles SW Havana, Gadsden Co. SE 1/4 SW 1/4 Sect. 4 Tp. 2 R. 2, north and west.

**6468. BLUNT, P.**
Jan. 9, 1837, in Havana, Gadsden Co. SE 1/4 SW 1/4 Sect. 34 Tp. 3 R. 2, north and west.

**6528. BLUNT, Philip**
Jan. 12, 1837, 2 miles ENE Jamieson, Gadsden Co. E 1/2 NW 1/4 Sect. 3 Tp. 2 R. 2, north and west.

**2813. BOARD, Rachel**
July 11, 1854, 4 1/2 miles SSW of New River, Bradford Co. SE 1/4 SW 1/4 Sect. 21 Tp. 6 R. 20, south and east. Patent delivered Feb. 19, 1857.

**2912. BOARD, Rachel**
Sept. 18, 1854, 2 miles SW of New River, Bradford Co. SW 1/4 SE 1/4 Sect. 21 Tp. 6 R. 20, south and east. Patent delivered Feb. 23, 1857.

**5985. BOATRIGHT, Benjamin, Sr.**
Nov. 8, 1836, 3/4 mile SE of Bond, Madison Co. W 1/2 SE 1/4 Sect. 9 Tp. 2 R. 8, north and east.

**7931. BOATRIGHT, Benjamin**
Mar. 6, 1839, 2 miles NE Ockeesee, Calhoun Co. SW 1/4 NW 1/4 Sect. 14 Tp. 2 R. 8, north and east.

**8100. BOATRIGHT, Benjamin**
Sept. 30, 1839, 6 miles E Alliance Station, Calhoun Co. SW 1/4 SE 1/4 Sect. 10 Tp. 2 R. 8, north and east.

**5861. BOATRIGHT, Bennrik**
Sept. 27, 1836, 3/4 mile SE of Hamburg, Madison Co. NW 1/4 NW 1/4 Sect. 14 Tp. 2 R. 8, north and east.

**5862. BOATRIGHT, Bennrik**
Sept. 27, 1836, 3/4 mile SE by S of Hamburg, Madison Co. E 1/2 SW 1/4 Sect. 11 Tp. 2 R. 8, north and east.

**3829. BOATRIGHT, Chesley I. D.**
Jan. 3, 1831, 5 miles W by N Cherry Lake, Madison Co. W 1/2 SW 1/4 Sect. 2 R. 8, north and east.

**3831. BOATRIGHT, Chesley I. D.**
Jan.3, 1831, 5 miles W by N Cherry Lake, Madison Cc. E 1/2 SW 1/4 Sect. 2 Tp.2 R. 6, north and east.

**6512. BOATRIGHT, Charley**
Jan. 10, 1837, 4 miles S by E Moseley Hall, Madison Co. NE 1/4 SW 1/4 Sect. 15 Tp. 2 R. 8, south and east.

**BOATRIGHT, Chastney see JARMIN, Berry**

**7240. BOATRIGHT, Francis**
Jan. 16, 1838, at Hamburg, Madison Co. SE 1/4 NW 1/4 Sect. 15 Tp. 2 R. 8, north and east.

**4775. BOATWRIGHT, Beniah**
Jan. 14, 1835, 2 miles SE of Bond, Madison Co. E 1/2 SE 1/4 Sect. 10 Tp. 2 R. 8, north and east.

**4776. BOATWRIGHT, Beniah**
Jan. 14, 1835, 2 miles SE of Bond, Madison Co. NW 1/4 SE 1/4 Sect. 10 Tp. 2 R. 8, north and east.

**2057. BOATWRIGHT, Benjamin**
Sept. 9, 1827, 1/2 mile N Bradfordville, Leon Co. W 1/2 SE 1/4 Sect. 15 Tp. 2 R. 1, north and east.

**4536. BOATWRIGHT, Benjamin**
Jan. 29, 1834, 6 miles W by N of Bradfordville, Leon Co. SE 1/4 NE 1/4 Sect. 15 Tp. 2 R. 1, north and east.

**4537. BOATWRIGHT, Benjamin**
Jan. 29, 1834, 6 3/4 miles W by N of Bradfordville, Leon Co. NE 1/4 SE 1/4 Sect. 15 TP. 2 R. 1, north and east.

**5308. BOATWRIGHT, Chesley**
Dec. 5, 1835, 1/2 mile NNE of Hamburg, Madison Co. E 1/2 NW 1/4 Sect. 11 Tp. 2 R. 8, north and east.

**4101. BOATWRIGHT, Chesley J. D.**
Oct. 26, 1831, 3 miles N by W of Champaign, Madison Co. W 1/2 SE 1/4 Sect. 2 Tp. 2 R. 8, north and east.

**5909. BOATWRIGHT, Chesley J. D.**
Oct. 18, 1836, 2 1/2 miles ESE of Bond, Madison Co. NW 1/4 NE 1/4 Sect. 11 Tp. 2 R. 8, north and east.

**4731. BOATWRIGHT, Dawson**
Dec. 22, 1834, 5 1/2 miles W of Bradfordville, Leon Co. NW 1/4 NE 1/4 Sect. 22 Tp. 2 R. 1, north and east.

**4732. BOATWRIGHT, Dawson**
Dec. 22, 1834, 6 1/2 miles N by W of Bradfordville, Leon Co. NE 1/4 SW 1/4 Sect. 15 Tp. 2 R. 1, north and east.

**2959. BOLE, Wm.**
July 27, 1829, 3 miles S by E Fincher, Leon Co. W 1/2 SW 1/4 Sect. 30 Tp. 3 R. 4, north and east.

**6025. BOMBER, Jordan**
Nov. 15, 1836, 2 miles N Havana,

Gadsden Co. NW 1/4 SW 1/4 Sect. 22 Tp. 3 R. 2, north and west.

**6024. BOMBER, William**
Nov. 15, 1836, 2 miles SE Darsey, Gadsden Co. E 1/2 SW 1/4 Sect. 7 Tp. 3 R. 1, north and west.

**8628. BONNELL, John**
Jan. 23, 1844, 10 miles E by N Genoa, Hamilton Co. N 1/2 NE 1/4 Sect. 2 Tp. 1 R. 16, south and east.

**8880. BONNELL, John**
Jan. 24, 1846, 5 miles SSE Miller's Ferry, Washington Co. SE 1/4 NE 1/4 Sect. 2 Tp. 1 R. 16, south and east.

**814. BONNELL, John**
Jan. 25, 1851, 6 miles S by E Benton, Columbia Co. NW 1/4 NE 1/4 Sect. 34 Tp. 1 R. 17, south and east. Patent delivered April 26, 1856.

**884. BOOLEY, Hurbert H.**
Jan. 23, 1851, 1/2 mile W Keysville, Hillsborough Co. S 1/2 SW 1/4 Sect. 9 Tp. 30 R. 22, south and east.

**256. BOORER, E. J.**
Dec. 30, 1826, 14 miles NW of Marianna, Jackson Co. NW 1/4 Sect. 9 Tp. 5 R. 11, north and west.

**6229. BOOTH, Edwin B.**
Dec. 16, 1836, 1/2 mile W Midway, Gadsden Co. W 1/2 SW 1/4 Sect.5 Tp. 1 R. 2, north and west.

**8152. BOOTH, Edwin G.**
Nov. 21, 1839, 3 miles NW Dennett, Hamilton Co. Lot No 3 Sect. 19 Tp. 2 R. 7, north and west.

**8584. BOOTH, Edwin G.**
April 14, 1843, 3 miles W by N Rockbluff, Liberty Co. Lot No. 2 Sect. 20 Tp. 2 R. 7, north and west.
see **Henry D. STONE**

**2234. BORSTIE, F. C.**
Oct. 7, 1853, 1 1/2 miles E of Peacock, Levy Co. E 1/2 NE 1/4 and E 1/2 NW 1/4 and E 1/2 SW 1/4 Sect. 8 Tp 13 R. 19, south and east. Patent delivered Mar. 17, 1858.

**2235. BORSTIE, F. C.**
Oct. 7, 1853, 1 mile E of Peacock, Levy Co. NW 1/4 Sect. 9 Tp. 13 R. 19, south and east. Patent delivered Mar. 17, 1858.

**4153. BOSTON, George W.**
Feb. 11, 1856, 1 1/2 mile NW of Haynesworth, Alachua Co. NE 1/4 of NE 1/4 Sect. 25 Tp. 7 R. 18, south and east.

**4912. BOSTON, George W.**
Dec. 13, 1858, 2 1/4 miles SSE of Santa Fe, Alachua Co. E 1/2 NE 1/4 Sect. 33 Tp. 2 R. 2, north and west.

**5395. BOSTICK, Tristram**
Jan. 12, 1836, 2 1/4 miles SE by S of Littman, Gadsden Co. SW 1/4 NE 1/4 Sect. 14 Tp. 2 R. 3, north and west.

**7415. BOWEN, Daniel**
Mar. 19, 1838, 1 mile S Marion, Hamilton Co. Lot No. 1 Fractional Sect. 7 Tp. 1 R. 14, south and east.

**3869. BOWEN, John D.**
Feb. 2, 1831, 3 miles NW Midway, Gadsden Co. W 1/2 SE 1/4 Sect. 36 Tp. 2 R. 3, north and west. Transferred May 12, 1832, to **Burrell G. PERRY**, "for his use and benefit.

**2375. BOWL, Levi**
May 15, 1828, 3 miles E Copeland, Jefferson Co. E 1/2 NE 1/4 Sect. 36 Tp. 3 R. 3, north and east.

**2084. BOWLES, Jno.**
Oct. 29, 1827, 2 miles E. Stringer, Jefferson Co. W 1/2 NE 1/4 Sect. 36 Tp. 3 R. 3, north and east.

**2083. BOWLS, Wm.**
Oct. 29, 1827, 3 1/2 miles E Stringer, Jefferson Co. E 1/2 SE 1/4 Sect. 25 Tp. 3 R. 3, north and east.

**4567. BOYD, Abram**
April 3, 1834, 1 3/4 miles S by E of Bradfordville, Leon Co. W 1/2 NW 1/4 Sect. 35 Tp. 2 R. 1, north and east.

**1160. BOYD, Henry**
Feb. 9, 1852, 3 miles SE of Lulu, Columbia Co. NE 1/4 SW 1/4 Sect. 3 Tp. 5 R. 18, south and east. Patent delivered Feb. 17, 1860.

**1170. BOYD, Henry**
Feb. 12, 1852, 5 miles W of Guildford, Union Co. SE 1/4 NW 1/4 Sect. 3 Tp. 5 R. 18, south and east. Patent delivered Feb. 17, 1860.

**989. BOYD, Jno./John**
Jan. 22, 1827, 4 miles SW Quincy, Gadsden Co. E 1/2 SW 1/4 Sect. 27 Tp. 2 R. 3, north and west.

**990. BOYD, Jno./John**
Jan. 22, 1827, 4 miles SW Quincy, Gadsden Co. W 1/2 SE 1/4 Sect. 27

Tp. 2 R. 3, north and west.
**991. BOYD, Jno./John**
Jan. 22, 1827, 5 miles SSE Quincy, Gadsden Co. E 1/2 SE 1/4 Sect. 27 Tp. 2 R. 3, north and west.
**862. BOYD, Jno./John**
Jan. 16, 1827, 2 miles NNE Midway, Gadsden Co. W 1/2 SE 1/4 Sect. 28 Tp. 2 R. 2, north and west.
**863. BOYD, Jno./John**
Jan. 16, 1827, 2 miles NNE Midway, Gadsden Co. E 1/2 SE 1/4 Sect. 28 Tp. 2 R. 2, north and west.
**1003. BOYD, Jno./John**
Jan. 25, 1827, 3 miles NNE Midway, Gadsden Co. E 1/2 NE 1/4 Sect. 33 Tp. 2 R. 2, north and west.
**1004. BOYD, John**
Jan. 25, 1827, 2 1/2 miles NNE Midway, Gadsden Co. NW 1/4 Sect. 34 Tp. 2 R. 2, north and west.
**1005. BOYD, John**
Jan. 25, 1827, 3 miles NNE Midway, Gadsden Co. SW 1/4 Sect. 27 Tp. 2 R. 2, north and west.
**2437. BOYD, John**
July 12, 1828, 3 miles SE Miccosukee, Leon Co. W 1/2 NE 1/4 Sect. 27 Tp. 2 R. 3, north and west.
**4436. BOYET, Isaac**
Oct. 15, 1833, 1 mile N by W of Wadesboro, Leon Co. NW 1/4 SE 1/4 Sect. 26 Tp. 2 R. 2, north and east. Transferred to **James L. HART**, Feb. 5, 1836.
**5223. BOYET, Isaac**
Oct. 17, 1835, 8 3/4 miles SE by E of Centerville, Leon Co. NE 1/4 SE 1/4 Sect. 36 Tp. 2 R. 2, north and east. Transferred fo **John L. HART**, Feb. 5, 1836.
**8740. BOYKIN, John A.**
Dec. 14, 1844, at Steaphead, Gadsden Co. NW 1/4 SW 1/4 Sect. 17 Tp. 2 R. 6, north and west.
**8828. BOYKIN, John A.**
Sept. 27, 1845, 1/2 mile E Steaphead, Gadsden Co. SW 1/4 SW 1/4 Sect. 17 Tp. 2 R. 6, north and west.
**8340. BOZEMAN, David**
June 16, 1840, 1/2 mile SW McClellan, Jefferson Co. E 1/2 NE 1/4 Sect. 21 Tp. 1 R. 5, north and east.
**343. BOZLMAN, Chapman**
(Assignee of **Ramsey SCOTT**) April 12, 1827, 3 miles NNE Campbellton, Jackson Co. E 1/2 NW 1/4 Sect. 19 Tp. 7 R. 11, north and west.
**2810. BRACKENRIDGE, Henry**
April 28, 1829, 6 miles SSW DeFuniak Springs, Walton Co. W 1/2 SW 1/4 Sect. 20 Tp. 2 R. 19, north and west.
**3579. BRACKENRIDGE, Henry M.**
July 19, 1830, c. 5 miles SE Pensacola, Escambia Co. (Marked "Land at Deer Point") Lot No. 5 Fractional Sect.4 Tp.3 R. 29, south and west.
**729. BRADEN, Hector/Hector W.**
(Of Fla.) July 25, 1826, 1 mile NW Wadesboro, Leon Co. W 1/2 NE 1/4 Sect. 36 Tp. 2 R. 2, north and east.
**731. BRADEN, Hector/Hector W.**
(Of Fla.) July 28, 1826, 1 mile N Wadesboro, Leon Co. E 1/2 NE 1/4 Sect. 36, Tp. 2 R. 2, north and east.
**743. BRADEN, Hector/Hector W.**
(Of Fla.) Aug. 22, 1826, 2 miles N Wadesboro, Leon Co. W 1/2 SE 1/4 Sect. 25 Tp. 2 R. 2, north and east.
**744. BRADEN, Hector/Hector W.**
(Of Fla.) Aug. 22, 1826, 2 miles N Wadesboro, Leon Co. E 1/2 SW 1/4 Sect. 25 Tp. 2 R. 2, north and east.
**1219. BRADEN, Hector W.**
(DUP) March 20, 1827, 1 1/2 miles NW Wadesboro, Leon Co. E 1/2 NW 1/4 Sect. 36 Tp. 2 R. 2, north and east.
**1770. BRADEN, Hector W.**
(DUP) June 4, 1827, 1/2 mile SW Black Creek, Leon Co. NW 1/4 Sect. 13 Tp. 1 R. 2, north and east.
**1771. BRADEN, Hector W.**
(DUP) June 4, 1827, 1 mile SSW of Black Creek, Leon Co. SW 1/4 Sect. 13 Tp. 1 R. 2, north and east.
**1877. BRADEN, Hector W.**
June 7, 1827, 1/2 mile N Wadesboro, Leon Co. E 1/2 NW 1/4 Sect. 31 Tp. 2 R. 3, north and east.
**2001. BRADEN, Hector W.**
July 17, 1827, at Natural Bridge, Leon Co. W 1/2 NE 1/4 Sect. 29 Tp. 12, R. 2, south and east.
**2003. BRADEN, H. W. and L. ARMISTEAD**
July 20, 1827, at Natural Bridge, Leon Co. W 1/2 SE 1/4 Sect. 29 Tp. 2 R. 2,

south and east.

**2004. BRADEN, H. W. and L. ARMISTEAD**
July 20, 1827, 1/2 mile SW Natural Bridge, Leon Co. SW 1/4 Sect. 29 Tp 2 R. 2, south and east.

**2005. BRADEN, H. W. and L. ARMISTEAD**
July 20, 1827, 3/4 mile S Natural Bridge, Leon Co. E 1/2 NW 1/4 Sect. 32 Tp. 2 R. 2, south and east.

**2006. BRADEN, H. W. and L. ARMISTEAD**
July 20, 1827, 3/4 mile S Natural Bridge, Leon Co. W 1/2 NE 1/4 Sect. 32 Tp. 2 R. 2, south and east.

**2051. BRADEN, Hector W. and Latinus ARMISTEAD**
Sept. 1, 1827, 1/2 mile S Natural Bridge, Leon Co. W 1/2 SE 1/4 Sect. 2 Tp. 2 R. 2, south and east.

**4350. BRADEN, Hector W.**
April 18, 1833, at Cody, Jefferson Co. E 1/2 NE 1/4 Sect. 30 Tp 1 R. 3, south and east.

**4351. BRADEN, Hector W.**
April 18, 1833, at Cody, Jefferson Co. W 1/2 SE 1/4 Sect. 30 Tp. 1 R. 3, south and east.

**4352. BRADEN, Hector W.**
April 18, 1833, 1/2 mile SE of Cody, Jefferson Co. W 1/2 NE 1/4 Sect. 29 Tp. 1 R. 3, south and east.

**4353. BRADEN, Hector W.**
April 18, 1833, 1/2 mile E of Cody, Jefferson Co. NW 1/4 Sect. 29 Tp. 1 R. 3, south and east.

**4354. BRADEN, Hector W.**
April 18, 1833, 3/4 mile SE of Cody, Jefferson Co. SE 1/4 SW 1/4 Sect. 29 Tp. 1 R. 3, south and east.

**4355. BRADEN, Hector W.**
April 18, 1833, 1 mile W of Cay, Jefferson Co. NE 1/4 NW 1/4 Sect. 32 Tp. 1 R. 3, south and east.

**2849. BRADEN, John A.**
July 29, 1854, 2 1/4 miles NNW of Santa Fe, Alachua Co. SW 1/4 Sect. 8 Tp. 7 R. 19, south and east. Patent delivered (no date).

**2850. BRADEN, John A.**
July 29, 1854, 1 mile W of Santa Fe, Alachua Co. N 1/2 NE 1/4 Sect. 18 Tp. 7 R. 19, south and east. Patent delivered (no date).

**4628. BRADFORD, Edward**
Oct. 18, 1834, 2 1/4 miles N by E of Bradfordville, Leon Co. SE 1/4 SW 1/4 Sect. 11 Tp. 2 R. 1, north and eaast.

**4629. BRADFORD, Edward**
Oct. 18, 1834, 1 mile NNE of Bradfordville, Leon Co. NW 1/4 NE 1/4 Sect. 14 Tp. 2 R. 1, north and east.

**4652. BRADFORD, Edward**
Oct. 30, 1834, 1/2 mile N of Bradfordville, Leon Co. SE 1/4 SE 1/4 Sect. 15 Tp. 2 R. 1, north and east.

**4653. BRADFORD, Edward**
Oct. 30, 1834, 3 1/4 miles NNE of Bradfordville, Leon Co. W 1/2 SW 1/4 Sect. 12 Tp. 2 R. 1, north and east.

**4654. BRADFORD, Edward**
Oct. 30, 1834, 1/2 mile N by E of Bradfordville, Leon Co. NE 1/4 NE 1/4 Sect. 15 Tp. 2 R. 1, north and east.

**4995. BRADFORD, Edward**
June 15, 1835, 4 1/2 miles W by N of Bradfordville, Leon Co. W 1/2 SW 1/4 Sect. 14 Tp. 2 R. 1, north and east.

**5158. BRADFORD, Edward**
Sept. 26, 1835, 3/4 mile N of Bradfordville, Leon Co. E 1/2 NE 1/4 Sect. 15 Tp. 2 R. 1, north and east.

**5639. BRADFORD, Edward**
April 30, 1836, 3 miles W of Felkel, Leon Co. NW 1/4 SW 1/4 Sect. 1 Tp. 2 R. 1, north and east.

**5961. BRADFORD, Edward**
Nov. 3, 1836, 1 mile N by W of Centerville, Leon Co. NW 1/4 NW 1/4 Sect. 13 Tp. 2 R. 1, north and east.

**5962. BRADFORD, Edward**
Nov. 3, 1836, 2 1/4 miles N by W of Centerville, Leon Co. W 1/2 NE 1/4 Sect. 11 Tp. 2 R. 1, north and east.

**6313. BRADFORD, Edward**
Dec. 26, 1836, 2 miles NNE Bradfordville, Leon Co. E 1/2 NE 1/4 Sect. 11 Tp. 2 R. 1, north and east.

**6314. BRADFORD, Edward**
Dec. 26, 1836, 1/2 mile NE Bradfordville, Leon Co. E 1/2 SW 1/4 and SW 1/4 NE 1/4 Sect. 14 Tp. 2 R. 1, north and east.

**3640. BRADFORD, Edward**
Dec. 28, 1836, 1 1/2 miles ENE Bradfordville, Leon Co. E 1/2 SE 1/4

Sect. 14 Tp. 2 R. 1, north and east.

**6531. BRADFORD, Edward**
Jan. 13, 1837, 1/2 mile E Bradford, Leon Co. NE 1/4 NW 1/4 Sect. 23 Tp. 2 R. 1, north and east.

**6532. BRADFORD, Edward**
Jan. 13, 1837, 3/4 mile SE Bradfordville, Leon Co. E 1/2 SE 1/2 Sect. 23 Tp. 2 R. 1, north and east.

**6533. BRADFORD, Edward**
Jan. 13, 1837, 3/4 mile E Bradfordville, Leon Co. E 1/2 NE 1/4 Sect. 23 Tp. 2 R. 1, north and east.

**6562. BRADFORD, Edward**
Jan. 15, 1837, at Bradfordville, Leon Co. W 1/2 NE 1/4 Sect. 23 Tp. 2 R. 1, north and east.

**6561. BRADFORD, Edward**
Jan. 16, 1837, 1 mile NE Bradfordville, Leon Co. W 1/2 SE 1/4 Sect 14 Tp. 2 R. 1, north and east. See **Thomas A. BRADFORD, #4649.**

**3836. BRADFORD, Edwin**
Jan. 7, 1831, 1 1/2 miles NE Bradfordville, Leon Co. E 1/2 NW 1/4 Sect. 14 Tp. 2 R. 1, north and east.

**3844. BRADFORD, Edwin**
Jan. 11, 1831, 1 mile NE Bradfordville, Leon Co. W 1/2 SE 1/4 Sect. 11 Tp. 2 R. 1, north and east.

**3220. BRADFORD, Henry B.**
Jan. 20, 1830, 2 miles NNW Centerville, Leon Co. E 1/2 SE 1/4 Sect. 11 Tp. 2 R. 1, north and east.

**3839. BRADFORD, Henry B.**
Jan. 7, 1831, 7 miles NE Tallahassee, Leon Co. W 1/2 SW 1/4 Sect. 27 Tp. 2 R. 1, north and east.

**5117. BRADFORD, Richard H.**
July 28, 1835, 1 1/4 miles W by N of Iomonia, Gadsden Co. SE 1/4 NE 1/4 Sect.14 Tp. 3 R. 1, north and east.

**5169. BRADFORD, Richard H.**
Sept. 29, 1835, 3 1/2 miles W of Iomonia, Leon Co. NE 1/4 NW 1/4 Sect. 14 Tp. 3 R. 1, north and east.

**5596. BRADFORD, Thomas**
April 14, 1836, 6 miles W of Bradfordville, Leon Co. SE 1/4 SW 1/4 Sect. 15 Tp. 2 R. 1, north and east.

**4649. BRADFORD, Thomas A.**
Oct. 26, 1834, 1 1/4 miles N by W of Bradfordville, Leon Co. E 1/2 SW 1/4 Sect. 10 Tp. 2 R. 1, north and east.

Transferred to **R. H. CROWELL.** Transferred to **Edward BRADFORD** (no dates given).

**5515. BRADFORD, Thomas A.**
Mar. 7, 1836, 1 mile N by W of Bradfordville, Leon Co. W 1/2 NW 1/4 Sect. 15 Tp. 2 R. 1, north and east.

**2464. BRADLEY, John**
Aug. 22, 1828, at Welchton, Jackson Co. E 1/2 NE 1/4 Sect. 34 Tp. 6 R. 12, north and west.

**4206. BRADLEY, Moses, Dennis HILLS, Enoch HALL, Amara HAYDEN**

**5006.**
Aug. 25, 1832, 2 miles S of Ellaville, Madison Co. Lot No. 3 Sect. 35 Tp.1 R. 11, south and east.

**587. BRADLEY, Nicholas Meriweather**
Aug. 23, 1847, c. 2 1/2 miles SW Ocala, Marion Co. Lot No 1 and 2 Fractional Sect. 36 and Lot No. 4 Fractional Sect. 25 Tp. 15 R. 21, south and east.

**3863. BRADLEY, R. D.**
Jan. 27, 1831, 4 miles SSE Ashville, Jefferson Co. E 1/2 SE 1/4 Sect. 13 Tp. 2 R. 6, north and east.

**3864. BRADLEY, R. D.**
Jan. 27, 1831, 3 3/4 miles SSE Ashville, Jefferson Co. E 1/2 NE 1/4 Sect. 13 Tp. 2 R. 6, north and east.

**516. BRADLEY, R. D.**
May 2, 1831, 1/2 miles N Ashville, Jefferson Co. W 1/2 NW 1/4 Sect. 33 Tp. 3 R. 7, north and east.

**517. BRADLEY, R. D.**
May 2, 1831, 1 mile NE Ashville, Jefferson Co. E 1/2 NE 1/4 Sect. 32 Tp. 3 R. 7, north and east.

**406. BRADSHAW, Robt. B.**
(Assignee of **Sarah BRANTLY**) May 7, 1827, 2 miles NW Campbellton, Jackson Co. NE 1/4 Sect. 34 Tp. 7 R. 12, north and west. Transferred from **R. BRADSHAW** to **J. DANIEL** (no dates given).

**407. BRADSHAW, Robt. B.**
(Assignee of **Guthry MOORE**) May 7, 1827, 3 miles W Campbellton, Jackson Co. SE 1/4 Sect. 27 Tp. 7 R. 12, north and west. Transferred from **R. B. BRADSHAW** to **J. DANIEL** (no dates given).

**6180. BRADSHAW. Tabitha Quintine**

Sept. 17, 1887, 1 1/2 miles NW Cadillac, Alachua Co. E 1/2 NE 1/4 Sect. 2 Tp. 9S R. 17E.

**6159. BRANCH, Lewis H.**
Dec. 7, 1836, 4 miles NW of Marianna, Jackson Co. SE 1/4 NW 1/4 Sect. 5 Tp.2 R. 1, north and east.

**611. BRANING, George**
Feb. 1, 1848, c. 1 mile NW Middleburg, Clay Co. Lots 7, 8 and 9 Sect. 11 Tp. 5 R. 24, south and east. Patent delivered July 19, 1856.

**675. BRANNING, George**
July 14, 1848, 3 1/2 miles W Rideout, Clay Co. Lots No. 14 and 15 Sect. 3 Tp. 5 R. 24, south and east. Patent delivered July 19, 1856.

**BRANNING, George see James B. COLE, #601**

**642. BRANNING, William**
May 1, 1848, 4 miles NW Belmore, Clay Co. NE 1/4 NE 1/4 Sect. 36 Tp. 6 R. 23, south and east. Patent delivered January 20, 1855.

**776. BRANTLEY** (No first name given)
Dec. 14, 1850, 1 1/2 miles NE Ocala, Marion Co. NE 1/4 SW 1/4 and NW 1/4 SE 1/4 Sect. 9 Tp. 15 R. 22, south and east. Patent delivered June 20, 1857.

**276. BRANTLY, Elbert**
Jan. 1, 1827, 6 miles NW of Marianna, Jackson Co. SW 1/4 Sect. 4 Tp. 5 R. 11, north and west.

**613. BRANZAN, Abner**
(Of Fla.) Nov. 10, 1825, 2 miles E Maxwell's Spur, Leon Co. W 1/2 NW 1/4 Sect. 17 Tp.1 R. 1, south and east.

**7407. BREADEN, John**
Mar. 14, 1838, 4 miles SE by S Dills, Jefferson Co. W 1/2 NW 1/4 Sect. 21 Tp. 2 R. 6, north and east.

**8904. BREADEN, John**
Feb. 16, 1846, 4 miles N by W Monticello, Jefferson Co. W 1/2 NW 1/4 Sect. 12 Tp. 2 R. 4, north and east.

**2655. BRECKENRIDGE, Henry M.**
Jan. 21, 1829, 5 1/2 miles Rock Hill, Walton Co. E 1/2 SE 1/4 Sect. 19 Tp. 2 R. 19, north and west.

**2656. BRECKENRIDGE, Henry M.**
Jan. 21, 1829, 6 1/2 miles SSW DeFuniak Springs, Walton Co. E 1/2 SW 1/4 Sect. 20 Tp. 2 R. 19, north and west.

**3266. BRECKENRIDGE, Henry M.**
Feb. 9, 1830, 5 1/2 miles SW DeFuniak Springs, Walton Co. E 1/2 NW 1/4 Sect. 20 Tp 2 R. 19, north and west.

**5920. BREDEN, John**
Oct. 24, 1836, 2 miles E by S of Redoak, Madison Co. NE 1/4 NW 1/4 Sect. 20 Tp. 2 R. 6, south and east.

**5921. BREDEN, John**
Oct. 24, 1836, 2 1/4 miles E by S of Redoak, Madison Co. W 1/2 NW 1/4 Sect. 21 Tp. 2 R. 6, south and east.

**3456. BRENNAN, Amelia Caroline**
March 15, 1830, 3 miles SSE Bradfordville, Leon Co. W 1/2 NW 1/4 Sect. 32 Tp. 2 R. 1, north and east.

**BRENAN, Eliza see E. B. OVERSTREET, #3080 and 3081**

**BRENNAN, Octavus see Amelia BRENNAN #3456.**

**8336. BRETT, Joseph D.**
June 5, 1840, 5 miles NNE Graceville in Florida. Property in Geneva Co., Alabama. E 1/2 SW 1/4 Sect. 19 Tp. 7 R. 12, north and west.

**4006. BRWER, John M.**
Dec. 17, 1855,(Elbert Co., Ga.) 2 miles W of Hodson, Levy Co. SW 1/4 Sect. 25 and E 1/2 of NE 1/4 and E 1/2 of SE 1/4 Sect. 27 Tp. 12 R. 18, south and east.

**6374. BRICKEL, Gabriel**
Jan.2, 1837, 3 miles WSW Miccosukee, Leon Co. NW 1/4 Sect. 13 Tp.2 R. 2, north and east.

**43. BRIDGMAN, Dan'l**
Nov. 7, 1826, c. 5 miles SW Ellis Post Office, Jackson Co. SE 1/4 Sect. 19 Tp. 6 R. 11, north and west. Transferred Dec. 29, 1826, to **R. C. ALLEN & CO.** by **David THOMAS**, attorney in fact for **Daniel BRIDGMAN.**

**4295. BRIGHAM, Emerald**
Feb. 5, 1833, 5 3/4 miles E of Capitola, Jefferson Co. SW 1/4 SW 1/4 Sect. 25 Tp. 1 R. 3, north and east.

**4296. BRIGHAM, Emerald**
Feb. 5, 1833, 5 1/2 miles E of Capitola, Jefferson Co. NE 1/4 SE 1/4 Sect. 25 Tp.1 R. 3, north and east.

**439. BRIGHT, James**
Dec. 22, 1828, 3 miles NE Miller's Ferry, Washington Co. NW 1/4 Sect.

14 Tp. 2 R. 16, north and west.

**3966. BRIGHT, James**
May 15, 1831, 2 miles SW Norum, Washington Co. E 1/2 SE 1/4 Sect. 14 Tp. 2 R. 16, north and west.

**4073. BRINSON, Cyprian**
Jan. 8, 1856, 3/4 mile S of Rixford, Suwannee Co. E 1/2 of NW 1/4 and E 1/2 of SW 1/4 Sect. 1 Tp. 2 R. 13, south and east.

**342. BRITT, John**
April 12, 1827, 5 miles ESE Campbellton, Jackson Co. SE 1/4 Sect. 9 Tp.6 R. 11, north and west.

**2096. BROCK, Jno. H.**
Nov. 12, 1827, 2 miles ESE Felkel, Leon Co. E 1/2 NE 1/4 Sect. 12 Tp. 2 R. 2, north and east.

**2268. BROCK, Jno. H. COALTER, Jno.**
(Trustee for **Agnes S. B. CABELL**, of Virginia) Feb. 19, 1828, 1 1/2 miles NW Waukenah, Jefferson Co. E 1/2 NE 1/4 Sect. 35 Tp. 1 R. 4, north and east.

**2269. BROCK, Jno. H. COALTER, Jno.**
(Trustee for **Agnes S. B. CABELL**, of Virginia) Feb. 19, 1828, 1 mile NE Waukenah, Jefferson Co. SW 1/4 Sect. 35 Tp. 1 R. 4, north and east.

**4917. BROCK, John H.**
Mar. 31, 1835, 3/4 miles W of Copeland, Leon Co. NE 1/4 NW 1/4 Sect. 7 Tp. 2 R. 3, north and east.

**7754. BROCKETT, Lemuel B.**
Dec. 10, 1838, 2 miles NNW Dills, Jefferson Co. W 1/2 NW 1/4 Sect. 25 Tp. 3 R. 5, north and east.

**7755. BROCKETT, LEMUEL B.**
Dec. 10, 1838, 2 miles N by W Dills, Jefferson Co. E 1/2 NE 1/4 Sect. 26 Tp. 3 R. 5, north and east.

**6955. BRODIE, Wm. H.**
Mar. 25, 1837, 5 miles SE by S Odens, Franklin Co. Lot No. 1 Fractional Sect. 22 Tp. 9 R. 10, south and west.

**6995. BRODIE, Wm. H.**
April 13, 1837, 2 miles SE Indian Pass, Gulf Co. Fractional Sect. 21 Tp. 9 R. 10, south and west.

**6996. BRODIE, Wm. H.**
April 13, 1837, 4 miles SSE Higgins, Gulf Co. Lot No. 2 Fractional Sect. 22 Tp. 9 R. 10, south and west.

**6997. BRODIE, Wm. H.**
April 13, 1837, 4 1/4 miles SE Higgins, Gulf Co. Lots No. 9 and 10, Fractional Sect. 14 Tp. 9 R. 10, south and west.

**6999. BRODIE, Wm. H.**
April 13, 1837, c. 4 miles S by W Higgins, Gulf Co. Lots No. 1, 2 and 7 Fractional Sect. 20 Tp. 9 R. 10, south and west.

**9170. BROOKENS, Robert**
Mar. 23 1891, 2 miles SE Starr, Suwannee Co. S 1/2 SW 1/4 Sect. 4 Tp. 3S R. 13E.

**2074. BROOKER, John G.**
Aug. 19, 1853, 2 miles SW of Waldo, Alachua Co. S 1/2 Lot No. 2 Sect. 30 Tp. 8 R. 20, south and east. Patent delivered June 18, 1857.

**740. BROOKS, Eliza**
May 23, 1850, 5 miles NE Suwannee Valley, Columbia Co. NW 1/4 SW 1/4 Sect. 31 Tp. 1 R. 17, south and east.

**3115. BROOKS, James**
(Of Ga.) Nov. 11, 1829, 5 miles WSW Alma, Leon Co. SW 1/4 Sect. 6 Tp. 2 R. 4, north and east.

**3116. BROOKS, James**
Nov. 11, 1829, 1 miles E Stringer, Leon Co. E 1/2 SW 1/4 Sect. 27 Tp. 3 R. 2, north and east.

**3117. BROOKS, James**
Nov. 11, 1829, 1 1/2 miles Copeland, Leon Co. E 1/2 NE 1/4 Sect. 34 Tp. 3 R. 3, north and east.

**3120. BROOKS, James**
(Of Ga.) Nov. 14, 1829, 1 3/4 miles SE Fincher, Leon Co. W 1/2 SE 1/4 Sect. 98 Tp. 3 R. 3, north and east.

**3121. BROOKS, James**
Nov. 14, 1829, 2 miles WNW Copeland, Leon Co. E 1/2 SW 1/4 Sect. 28 Tp. 3 R. 3, north and east.

**3122. BROOKS, James**
Nov. 14, 1829, 2 1/2 miles E Stringer, Leon Co. SE 1/4 Sect. 26 Tp. 3 R. 3, north and east.

**3243. BROOKS, James**
Feb. 2, 1830, 3 1/2 miles E Copeland, Jefferson Co. E 1/2 SE 1/4 Sect. 36 Tp. 3 R. 3, north and east.

**3875. BROOKS, James**
Feb. 10, 1831, 3 miles E Stringer, Leon

Co. E 1/2 SW 1/4 Sect. 26 Tp. 3 R. 3, north and east.

**628. BROOKS, James**
March 4, 1848, 2 1/2 miles SW Mason, Columbia Co. NE 1/4 NE 1/4 Sect. 6 Tp. 6 R. 17, south and east.

**4882. BROOKS, John M.**
Mar. 7, 1835, 1/4 mile NW Miccosukee, Jefferson Co. SE 1/4 NW 1/4 Sect. 7 Tp. 2 R. 3, north and east.

**757. BROOKS, Robert W.**
Nov. 25, 1850, 4 miles NE Suwannee Valley, Columbia Co. SW 1/4 NW 1/4 and SW 1/4 SW 1/4 Sect. 31 Tp. 1 R. 17, south and east. Patent delivered April 26, 1856.

**187. BROOKS, Robert Wilson**
Oct. 24, 1845, c. 5 miles NE Suwannee Valley, Columbia Co. Lot No. 1 Sect. 36 Tp. 1 R. 16, south and east. Patent delivered Sept. 4, 1858.

**340. BROOKS, Spencer**
March 14, 1846, c. 4 miles W Martin, Marion Co. NE 1/4 SE 1/4 Sect. 14 and NW 1/4 SW 1/4 Sect. 13 Tp. 14 R. 20, south and east. Patent delivered Dec. 4, 1856.

**2712. BROOKS, Wiley**
May 1, 1854, 2 miles SW of Romeo, Marion Co. SW 1/4 SW 1/4 Sect. 11 Tp. 15 R. 18, south and east. Patent delivered July 18, 1857.

**353. BROOKS, Wiley**
April 3, 1846, 4 1/2 miles W Martin, Marion Co. W 1/2 NE 1/4 Sect.14 R. 20, south and east. Patent delivered Dec.4, 1856.

**415. BROOKS, Wiley**
May 15, 1846, 4 1/2 miles SW Martin, Marion Co. W 1/2 SW 1/4 Sect. 14 Tp. 14 R. 20, south and east. Patent delivered Dec. 4, 1856.

**7040. BROWARD, Francis**
Sept. 11, 1837, 9 1/2 miles N by W Belmont, Hamilton Co. Lot No. 2 Fractional Sect. 12 Tp. 2 R. 15, south and east.

**4248. BROWN, Allen R.   BROWN, John T.**
Dec. 7, 1832, 2 3/4 miles SW of Gretna, Gadsden Co. SW 1/4 NW 1/4 Sect. 35 Tp. 3 R. 5, north and east.

**4052. BROWN, Benjamin J.**
Jan. 1, 1856, 2 miles E by N Columbia, Columbia Co. SW 1/4 SE 1/4 N 1/2 SW 1/4 NW 1/4 Sect. 12 Tp. 5 R.16, south and east.

**BROWN, Geo.** see **George Hammond SHARP, #457**

**1738. BROWN, George L.**
Mar. 1, 1853, at Haynesworth, Alachua Co. SW 1/4 of NW 1/4 Sect. 32 Tp. 7 R. 20, south and east. Patent delivered July 4, 1857.

**4164. BROWN, George L.**
Feb. 14, 1856, 1 1/2 miles SSE of Thomasville, Alachua Co. Lot No. 3 Sect. 31 Tp. 7 R. 20, south and east. Patent delivered July 4, 1859.

**5740. BROWN, Hezekiah**
June 30, 1836, 1 mile NNE of Hamburg, Madison Co. W 1/2 NE 1/4 Sect. 14 Tp. 2 R. 8, north and east.

**7223. BROWN, Hezekiah**
Jan. 12, 1838, 1/4 mile E Hamburg, Madison Co. NW 1/4 SE 1/4 Sect. 15 Tp. 2 R. 8, north and east.

**8357. BROWN, Hezekiah**
June 19, 1840, 3 miles E by N Dills, Jefferson Co. E 1/2 NW 1/4 and W 1/2 NE 1/4 Sect. 36 Tp. 3N R. 6E.

**2930. BROWN, Isaac**
July 9, 1829, c. 2 miles S Haywood, Jackson Co. Lot No. 3 Sect. 17 Tp. 5 R. 7, north and west.

**4213. BROWN, James**
Sept. 6, 1832, 6 1/2 miles NNW of Haywood, Jackson Co. SW 1/4 SE 1/4 Sect. 11 Tp. 6 R. 8, north and west.

**4612. BROWN, James**
Sept. 10, 1834, 10 miles E of Bascom, Jackson Co. Lot No. 1 Sect. 12 Tp 6 R. 8, north and west.

**6286. BROWN, James**
Dec. 23, 1836, 5 miles W by N Malone, Jackson Co. NE 1/4 SE 1/4 Sect. 29 Tp. 7 R. 10, north and west.

**3196. BROWN, Jesse D.**
Jan. 1, 1830, 2 miles E by S El Destino, Jefferson Co. E 1/2 SW 1/4 Sect. 9 Tp. 1 R. 3, north and east.

**3866. BROWN, Jesse D.**
Jan. 31. 1831, 3 miles SE Wadesboro, Jefferson Co. W 1/2 SW 1/4 Sect. 9 Tp.1 R. 3, north and east.

**222. BROWN, Jno. B.**
(DUP) Dec. 30, 1826, at Everett, Washington Co. NE 1/4 Sect. 11 Tp. 3

R. 13, north and west.

**1819. BROWN, Jno. B.**
June 5, 1827, 3 miles ESE Everett, Washington Co. W 1/2 SW 1/4 Sect. 14 Tp. 3 R. 13, north and west. Indorsed Nov. 1, 1828, to **Anthony BURNS (BARNS?)**. Indorsed Apr. 20, 1829 to **Robert POTTER**.

**2808. BROWN, Jno. B.**
April 21, 1829, 5 miles WSW Miccosukee, Leon Co. W 1/2 NW 1/4 Sect. 14 Tp. 2 R. 2, north and east.

**2435. BROWN, John**
July 8, 1828, 3 miles ESE Everett, Washington Co. E 1/2 SE 1/4 Sect. 15 Tp. 3 R. 13, north and west. Transferred Nov.1, 1828, to **Anthony BURNES**. Transferred Sept. 5, 1929, to **Myles EVERETT** and his heirs.

**1597. BROWN, John**
Dec. 30, 1852, 3 1/2 miles NE of New River, Bradford Co. E 1/2 NE 1/4 Sect. 9 Tp. 6 R. 21, south and east. Patent delivered Nov. 24, 1856.

**1601. BROWN, John**
Jan. 1, 1853, 4 1/2 miles NE of New River, Bradford Co. SW 1/4 NE 1/4 Sect. 10 Tp. 6 R. 21, south and east. Patent delivered Nov. 24, 1856

**1641. BROWN, John**
Jan. 15, 1853. 3 1/2 miles NNE of New River, Bradford Co. NW 1/4 NE 1/4 and NE 1/4 NW 1/4 Sect. 10 Tp. 6 R. 21, south and east. Patent delivered 1856.

**1642. BROWN, John**
Jan. 15, 1853, 4 miles NE of New River, Bradford Co. NW 1/4 SW 1/4 Sect. 10 Tp. 6 R. 21, south and east.

**3006. BROWN, John B.**
Sept. 3, 1829, 1 mile NE Welchton, Jackson Co. E 1/2 NE 1/4 Sect. 19 Tp. 6 R. 10, north and west.

**7981. BROWN, John B.**
June 1, 1839, 3 1/2 miles NNE Graceville, Jackson Co. E 1/2 NW 1/4 Sect. 30 Tp. 7 R. 12, north and west.

**7985. BROWN, John B.**
June 1, 1839, 3 1/4 miles NNE Graceville, Jackson Co. NE 1/4 SW 1/4 Sect. 30 Tp. 7 R. 12, north and west.

**3607. BROWN, John C.**
Sept. 11, 1830, 4 miles W Miccosukee, Leon Co. W 1/2 SW 1/4 Sect. 11 Tp.2 R. 2, north and east.

**3618. BROWN, John C.**
Sept. 23, 1830. 1 1/2 miles SE Iamonia, Leon Co. E 1/2 SW 1/4 Sect. 20 Tp. 3 R. 2, north and east.

**BROWN, John I.** see **Allen R. BROWN #4248**.

**5144. BROWN, John P.**
Aug. 21, 1835, 3 1/2 miles N by W of Stringer, Leon Co. NW 1/4 SW 1/4 Sect. 5 Tp. 1 R. 3, north and east.

**2194. BROWN, John R.**
Sept. 22, 1853, 1 mile SSE of York, Marion Co. NE 1/4 SE 1/4 Sect. 35 Tp. 15 R. 20, south and east. Patent delivered June 14, 1858.

**5149. BROWN, Leavin**
Aug. 22, 1835, 1 mile SE of Butler, Jackson Co. NW 1/4 NW 1/4 Sect. 4 Tp.4 R. 7, north and west.

**5150. BROWN, Leavin**
Aug. 22, 1835, 1 mile SE of Butler, Jackson Co. NE 1/4 NW 1/4 Sect. 4 Tp. 4 R. 7, north and west.

**4757. BROWN, Nicholas N.**
Jan. 6, 1835, 1/2 mile N of Octahatchee, Hamilton Co. NE 1/4 NW 1/4 Sect. 11 Tp. 2 R. 2, north and east.

**5881. BROWN, Sarah**
Oct. 3, 1836, 1/4 mile E of Felkel, Leon Co. E 1/2 NW 1/4 and W 1/2 NE 1/4 Sect. 3 Tp. 2 R. 2, north and east.

**5882. BROWN, Sarah**
Oct. 3, 1836, 1/4 mile SE of Felkel, Leon Co. SE 1/4 NE 1/4 and NE 1/4 SE 1/4 Sect. 3 Tp. 2 R. 2, north and east.

**1174. BROWN, Thomas**
(DUP) Feb. 25, 1827, 8 miles NNE Lake Jackson Station, Leon Co. Lot No. 7 Sect. 20 Tp. 2 R. 1, north and west.

**1175. BROWN, Thomas**
(DUP) Feb. 25, 1827, 3 miles NNE Lake Jackson Station, Leon Co. Lot No. 3 Sect. 21 Tp. 2 R. 1, north and west.

**1176. BROWN, Thomas**
(DUP) Feb. 25, 1827, 3 miles NNE Lake Jackson Station, Leon Co. Lot No. 4 Sect. 21 Tp. 2 R. 1, north and

west. See **John SAPP**

**5260. BROWN, William**
Nov. 12, 1835, 1 mile N of Braswells, Jefferson Co. SW 1/4 NW 1/4 Sect. 9 Tp. 1 R. 4, south and east.

**1683. BROWNING, David**
Jan. 31, 1853, 3 miles SW of Ellerbe, Union Co. NW 1/4 NE 1/4 Sect. 1 Tp. 5 R. 20, south and east. Patent delivered (no date).

**235. BROWNING, Stephen**
(DUP) Dec. 30, 1826, 2 miles SE Florence, Gadsden Co. NW 1/4 Sect. 11 Tp. 2 R. 2, north and west.

**2394. BROWNLEE, James**
Feb. 20, 1854, 2 1/4 miles NE of Elmwood, Alachua Co. NE 1/4 NW 1/4 and NW 1/4 NE 1/4 Sect. 13 Tp. 13 R. 19, south and east.

**6658. BRUCE, Eliza A.**
Jan. 24, 1837, 2 3/4 miles W Tallahassee, Leon Co. W 1/2 NW 1/4 Sect. 33 Tp. 1 R. 1, north and west. On back, "E. A. BRUCE's Receipt."

**5444. BRUMBLEY, Babtist**
Feb. 6, 1836, 1 1/4 miles NNW of Stringer, Jefferson Co. NW 1/4 SE 1/4 Sect. 19 Tp. 3 R. 3, north and east.

**5445. BRUMBLEY, Babtist**
Feb. 6, 1836, 1 mile NNW of Stringer, Jefferson Co. NE 1/4 SW 1/4 Sect. 19 Tp. 3 R. 3, north and east.

**2598. BRUMBLEY, James**
Jan. 2, 1829, 1 mile SW Moody, Wakulla Co. W 1/2 NE 1/4 Sect. 30 Tp. 2 R. 1, south and east.

**1190. BRUMLEY, Babtiste**
(DUP) March 5, 1827, 1 miles W Stringer, Leon Co. E 1/2 NW 1/4 Sect. 29 Tp. 3 R. 3, north and east.

**2632. BRUMLEY, Babtiste**
Jan. 16, 1829, 2 1/2 miles W Fincher, Leon Co. W 1/2 NW 1/4 Sect. 29 Tp. 3 R. 3, north and east.

**6240. BRUMLEY, Babtiste**
Dec. 19, 1836, 2 miles NW Alma, Leon Co. E 1/2 NW 1/4 Sect.28 Tp. 3 R. 4, north and east.

**8149. BRUMLEY, Babtiste**
Nov. 19, 1839, 3 miles SSE Stringer, Jefferson Co. NE 1/4 NE 1/4 Sect. 20 Tp. 3 R. 4, north and east.

**2545. BRUMLY, Babtiste**
Nov. 16, 1828, 1 mile NW Copeland, Leon Co. E 1/2 SW 1/4 Sect. 29 Tp. 3 R. 3, north and east.

**1812. BRUTON, A.**
June 5, 1827, 2 miles W by N Quincy, Gadsden Co. E 1/2 NE 1/4 Sect. 31 Tp. 3 R. 3, north and west. Transferred March 28, 1828 by Quit-claim Deed to **Duncan FULTON**.(signed **A. BRUTON**). Teste: **Daniel J. BRUTON, N. D. GEIGER**.

**1415. BRUTON, Aquilla**
May 21, 1827, 2 miles N Quincy, Gadsden Co. E 1/2 SE 1/4 Sect. 30 Tp. 3 R. 3, north and west. Transferred to **Duncan FULTON**, by quit-claim deed, on March 23, 1828. Witnesses: **Daniel J. BRUTON** and **N. D. ZEIGLER**.

**8020. BRUTON, Daniel J**
(Of Ga.) Also **George W. BRUTON** and **Nathaniel ZEIGLER**, July 12, 1839, 4 miles N Gretna, Gadsden Co. W 1/2 NW 1/4 Sect. 4 Tp. 3 R.4, north and west.

**BRUTON, George W.** see **Daniel FULTON**

**5498. BRYAN, Edward**
Mar. 2, 1836, 6 miles W of Dellwood, Jackson Co. E 1/2 NW 1/4 Sect. 19 Tp. 5 R. 9, north and west.

**5499. BRYAN, Edward**
Mar. 2, 1836, 5 3/4 miles W of Dellwood, Jackson Co. W 1/2 NE 1/4 Sect. 19 Tp. 5 R. 9, north and west.

**5500. BRYAN, Edward**
Mar. 2, 1836, 6 miles W of Dellwood, Jackson Co. SE 1/4 NE 1/4 Sect. 19 Tp. 5 R. 9, north and west.

**6584. BRYAN, Edward**
Jan. 18, 1837, 3 miles S by E Greenwood, Jackson Co. SE 1/4 SE 1/4 and SW 1/4 SE 1/4 Sect. 17 Tp. 5 R. 9, north and west.

**8189. BRYAN, Edward**
(Of Ga.) Dec. 28, 1839, 1 mile E Dennett, Madison Co. E 1/2 SW 1/4 and E 1/2 NW 1/4 Sect. 36 Tp. 2 R. 7, north and east.

**8190. BRYAN, Edward**
Dec. 28, 1839, 1 1/4 miles E Spray, Madison Co. NW 1/4 Sect. 12 Tp. 1 R. 7, north and east.

**8191. BRYAN, Edward**
Dec. 28, 1839, 2 miles SSE Bailey,

Madison Co. W 1/2 SW 1/4 and E 1/2 SW 1/4 Sect. 19 Tp. 2 R. 8, north and east.

**8192. BRYAN, Edward**
Dec. 28, 1839, 1 mile N by E Spray, Madison Co. E 1/2 NW 1/4 Sect. 2 Tp. 1 R. 7, north and east.

**8193. BRYAN, Edward**
Dec. 28, 1839, 2 miles NNE Spray, Madison Co. E 1/2 NE 1/4 Sect. 2 Tp. 1 R. 7, north and east.

**8194. BRYAN, Edward**
Dec. 28, 1839, 2 1/2 miles SE Dennett, Madison Co. W 1/2 NW 1/4 Sect. 1 Tp. 1 R. 7, north and east.

**8195. BRYAN, Edward**
Dec. 28, 1839, 1 mile SE Bailey, Madison Co. E 1/2 NW 1/4 Sect. 30 Tp. 2 R. 8, north and east.

**8196. BRYAN, Edward**
Dec. 28, 1839, 3/4 mile SE Bailey, Madison Co. SW 1/4 SE 1/4 SE 1/4 SW 1/4 Sect. 19 Tp. 2 R. 8, north and east.

**8197. BRYAN, Edward**
Dec. 28, 1839, 2 miles SW Dennett, Madison Co. E 1/2 SE 1/4 Sect. 35 Tp. 2 R. 7, north and east.

**8708. BRYAN, Edward**
Oct. 4, 1844, 5 miles SSE Greenwood, Jackson Co. N 1/2 SW 1/4 Sect. 10 Tp. 5 R. 9, north and west.
See **Gibson MARTIN, #4580**

**2074. BRYAN, Elijah**
Oct. 5, 1827, 1 1/4 miles S by W Greenwood, Jackson Co. NW 1/4 Sect. 7 Tp. 5 R. 9, north and west.

**3096. BRYAN, Elijah**
Oct. 28, 1829, 2 miles S Greenwood, Jackson Co. E 1/2 SW 1/4 Sect. 7 Tp. 5 R. 9, north and west.

**4554. BRYAN, Elijah**
Feb. 24, 1834, 2 1/2 miles S of Greenwood, Jackson Co. W 1/2 NE 1/4 Sect. 7 Tp. 5 R. 9, north and west.

**4555. BRYAN, Elijah**
Feb. 24, 1834, 5 miles W by N of Dellwood, Jackson Co. NW 1/4 NW 1/4 Sect. 20 Tp. 5 R. 9, north and west.

**4556. BRYAN, Elijah**
Feb. 24, 1834, 5 1/2 miles W by N of Dellwood, Jackson Co. NE 1/4 NE 1/4 Sect. 19 Tp. 5 R. 9, north and west.

**4557. BRYAN, Elijah**
Feb. 24, 1834, 5 3/4 miles NNW of Dellwood, Jackson Co. E 1/2 SW 1/4 Sect. 17 Tp. 5 R. 9, north and west. Transferred to **William BRYAN** Nov. 28, 1835.

**4558. BRYAN, Elijah**
Mar. 13, 1834, 6 miles NNW of Dellwood, Jackson Co. W 1/2 SE 1/4 Sect. 18 Tp. 5 R. 9, north and west.

**4597. BRYAN, Elijah**
July 10, 1834, 1 1/2 miles S of Greenwood, Jackson Co. E 1/2 NE 1/4 Sect. 7 Tp. 5 R. 9, north and west.

**4739. BRYAN, Elijah**
Dec. 23, 1834, 2 miles S of Greenwood, Jackson Co. SE 1/4 Sect. 7 Tp. 5 R. 9, north and west.

**4740. BRYAN, Elijah**
Dec. 23, 1834, 2 1/4 miles S of Greenwood, Jackson Co. SW 1/4 SW 1/4 Sect. 17 Tp. 5 R. 9, north and west.

**5075. BRYAN, Elijah**
July 15, 1835, 6 miles W by N of Dellwood, Jackson Co. NW 1/4 Sect. 18 Tp 5 R. 9, north and west.

**5076. BRYAN, Elijah**
July 15, 1835, 5 3/4 miles W by N of Dellwood, Jackson Co. NW 1/4 NE 1/4 Sect. 18 Tp. 5 R. 9, north and west.

**5559. BRYAN, Elijah**
Mar. 28, 1836, 5 3/4 miles W of Dellwood, Jackson Co. W 1/2 SW 1/4 Sect. 20 Tp. 5 R. 9, north and west.

**5559. BRYAN, Elijah**
Mar. 28, 1836, 6 miles W of Dellwood, Jackson Co. S 1/2 Sect. 19 Tp. 5 R. 9, north and west.

**5581. BRYAN, Elijah**
April 8, 1836, 2 1/2 miles SW by S of Greenwood, Jackson Co. W 1/2 NW 1/4 Sect. 12 Tp. 5 R. 10, north and west.

**5804. BRYAN, Elijah**
Aug. 22, 1836, 4 1/2 miles NNE of Fairgrounds, Jackson Co. SE 1/4 SE 1/4 Sect. 13 Tp.5 R. 10, north and west.

**5879. BRYAN, Elijah**
Oct. 3, 1836, 3/4 mile S of Greenwood, Jackson Co. W 1/2 NW 1/4

and W 1/2 SW 1/4 Sect. 5 Tp. 5 R. 9, north and west.

**5880. BRYAN, Elijah**
Oct. 3, 1836, 1 mile S of Greenwood, Jackson Co. E 1/2 NE 1/4 and E 1/2 SE 1/4 Sect. 6 Tp. 5 R. 9, north and west.

**6315. BRYAN, Elijah**
Dec. 26, 1836, 1/2 mile SE Greenwood, Jackson Co. E 1/2 SW 1/4 and E 1/2 NW 1/4 Sect. 5 Tp. 5 R. 9, north and west.

**8440. BRYAN, Elijah**
Jan. 1, 1841, 1 mile SW San Helena, Leon Co. NE 1/4 SW 1/4 Sect. 19 Tp. 1 R. 1, north and west.

**8737. BRYAN, Elijah**
Dec. 5, 1844, 4 miles NNE Everett, Washington Co. E 1/2 SE 1/4 Sect. 2 Tp.3 R. 13, north and west.
See **Wm. T. DURHAM, #4553**.

**8156. BRYAN, Hardy**
Nov. 28, 1839, 1/4 mile W Dennett, Madison Co. N 1/2 W 1/2 SE 1/4 Sect. 28 Tp. 2 R. 7, north and east.

**8157. BRYAN, Hardy**
Nov. 28, 1839, 1/8 mile S Hamburg, Madison Co. W 1/2 SE 1/4 Sect. 21 Tp. 2 R. 7, north and east.

**8174. BRYAN, Hardy**
Dec. 12, 1839, 1/4 mile SSE Bailey, Madison Co. E 1/2 SE 1/4 Sect. 21 Tp. 2 R. 7, north and east.

**8175. BRYAN, Hardy**
Dec. 12, 1839, 2 miles SE by S Hamburg, Madison Co. W 1/2 SW 1/4 Sect. 22 Tp. 2 R. 7, north and east.

**8188. BRYAN, Hardy**
Dec. 28, 1839, 2 miles NNW Dennett, Madison Co. W 1/2 NE 1/4 Sect. 29 Tp. 2 R. 7, north and east.

**8388. BRYAN, Hardy**
Aug. 17, 1840, at Dennett, Madison Co. N 1/2 SW 1/4 Sect. 27 Tp. 2 R. 7, north and east.

**8389. BRYAN, Hardy**
Aug. 17, 1840, 1 mile N by E Dennett, Madison Co. W 1/2 NW 1/4 Sect. 27 Tp. 2 R. 7, north and east.

**3913. BRYAN, Jacob**
Mar. 11, 1831, 4 miles NNE Aucilla, Jefferson Co. W 1/2 NE 1/4 Sect. 32 Tp. 2 R. 6, north and east.

**240. BRYAN, John**
Dec. 30, 1826, 4 miles W Macon Station, Washington Co. NW 1/4 Sect. 18 Tp. 2 R. 18, north and west.

**2625. BRYAN, John**
Jan. 15, 1829, 4 miles NE Miller's Ferry, Washington Co. E 1/2 SE 1/4 Sect. 11 Tp. 2 R. 16, north and west.
Transferred to **James BRIGHT**, March 11, 1833.

**2626. BRYAN, John**
Jan. 15, 1829, 3 miles ENE Miller's Ferry, Washington Co. W 1/2 SW 1/4 Sect. 12 Tp. 2 R. 16, north and west.
Transferred to **James BRIGHT**, March 11, 1833.

**8706. BRYAN, John**
Oct. 4, 1844, 4 miles W Dellwood, Jackson Co. W 1/2 SW 1/4 Sect. 15 Tp. 5 R. 9, north and west.

**6846. BRYAN, Joseph**
March 7, 1837, 1 1/2 miles SE Facil, Hamilton Co. NE 1/4 SW 1/4 Sect. 35 Tp. 1 R. 15, south and east.

**7206. BRYAN, Joseph**
Jan. 10, 1838, 1 1/2 miles SE Facil, Hamilton Co. SE 1/4 SW 1/4 and NW 1/4 SE 1/4 Sect. 35

**8044. BRYAN, Lewis**
Aug. 17, 1839, 2 miles NNW White Springs, Hamilton Co. N 1/2 Lot No. 4 Sect. 2 Tp. 2 R. 15, south and east.

**6295. BRYAN, Milton J.**
Dec. 24, 1836, 3 miles S by E Jasper, Hamilton Co. SE 1/4 NW 1/4 Sect. 21 Tp.1 R. 14, north and east.

**8881. BRYAN, Milton J.**
Jan. 24, 1846, 8 3/4 miles N by E Facil, Hamilton Co. NE 1/4 Sect. 24 Tp 1 R. 16, south and east.

**250. BRYAN, Moses**
Dec. 30, 1826, 4 miles SE of Havana, Gadsden Co. W 1/2 SE 1/4 Sect. 18 Tp. 2 R. 2, north and west.

**1994. BRYAN, Moses**
(Of Fla) July 1827, 1/2 mile S Helena, Leon Co. W 1/2 SE 1/4 Sect. 20 Tp. 1 R. 1, north and west.

**2240. BRYAN, Moses**
(Of Fla) Jan. 29, 1828, 3 miles WNW Tallahassee, Leon Co. E 1/2 NW 1/4 Sect. 28 Tp. 1 R. 1, north and west.

**2346. BRYAN, Nathan**
April 15, 1828, 3 miles W Alma, Jefferson Co. W 1/2 NE 1/4 Sect. 32

Tp. 3 R. 4, north and east.

**4186. BRYAN, Nathaniel**
July 14, 1832, 1 1/2 miles S of Facil, Hamilton Co. SE 1/4 NE 1/4 Sect. 34 Tp.1 R. 15, south and east.

**6434. BRYAN, Nathaniel**
Jan. 5, 1837, 1/2 mile S Facil, Hamilton Co. NE 1/4 NE 1/4 Sect. 34 Tp. 1 R. 15, south and east.

**6435. BRYAN, Nathaniel**
Jan. 5 1837, 3/4 mile S Facil, Hamilton Co. NW 1/4 SE 1/4 Sect. 34 Tp. 1 R. 15, south and east.

**6436. BRYAN, Nathaniel**
Jan. 5, 1837, 3/4 mile S Facil, Hamilton Co. NE 14 SE 1/4 and SW 1/4 NE 1/4 Sect. 34 Tp. 1 R. 15, south and east.

**6621. BRYAN, Nathaniel**
Jan. 21, 1837, at Facil, Hamilton Co. W 1/2 SE 1/4 Sect. 27 Tp. 1 R. 15, south and east.

**7222. BRYAN, Nathaniel**
Jan. 12, 1838, 1 1/4 miles S Facil, Hamilton Co. E Division of Lot No. 1 Fraction Sect. 3 Tp. 2 R. 15, south and east.

**2416. BRYAN, Nathaniel**
Feb. 21, 1854, 1/2 mile S of Houston, Suwannee Co. SW 1/4 NW 1/4 Sect. 3 Tp. 3 R. 14, south and east. Patent delivered Aug. 19, 1869.

**1057. BRYAN, Nathaniel**
Dec. 23, 1851, 7 miles NE of Bradford, Suwannee Co. Lot 3 Sect. 27 Tp. 5 R. 13, south and east. Patent delivered Feb. 23, 1857.

**3776. BRYAN, Nedham**
Dec. 4, 1830, 3 1/2 miles E Copeland, Leon Co. E 1/2 NE 1/4 Sect. 31 Tp. 3 R. 4, north and east.

**5385. BRYAN, Needham**
Jan. 4, 1836, 3 miles S by W Monticello, Jefferson Co. W 1/2 SE 1/4 Sect. 1 Tp. 1 R. 4, north and east.

**5532. BRYAN, Needham**
Mar. 11, 1836, 1/2 mile E of Drifton, Jefferson Co. E 1/2 SE 1/4 Sect. 12 Tp. 1 R. 4, north and east.

**7391. BRYAN, Philemon**
Mar. 6, 1838, at Facil, Hamilton Co. E 1/2 SW 1/4 Sect. 27, Tp. 1 R. 15, south and east.

**7392. BRYAN, Philemon**
Mar. 6, 1838, 1/4 mile SSW Facil, Hamilton Co. NE 1/4 NW 1/4 Sect. 34 Tp. 1 R. 15, south and east.

**7433. BRYAN, Sanford**
July 2, 1889, 1 3/4 miles N by W Mango, Hillsborough Co. N 1/2 NW 1/4 Sect. 4 Tp. 29S, R. 20E.

**320. BRYAN, Stephen**
Feb. 16, 1846, near Anthony, Marion Co. W 1/2 NE 1/4 and E 1/2 NW 1/4 Sect. 4 Tp. 14 R. 22, south and east. Transferred Jan. 26, 1854 to **Joseph COLD**. Attest: **R. L. NELSON, Stephen BRYAN**, and **E. D. HOWSE**. Patent forwarded Aug. 10, 1855.

**401. BRYAN, Stephen**
May 7, 1846, 1 1/2 miles SE Silver Springs, Marion Co. NE 1/4 NW 1/4 and NW 1/4 NE 1/4 Sect. 9 Tp. 15 R. 23, south and east. Transferred to **Joseph** and **T. W. CALDWELL**, March 16, 1853. "Recorded in the clerk's office in Marion Co., Fla., E Book E on page 592(sic) May 9, 1856." Patent delivered May 12, 1856.

**74. BRYAN, Wm.**
Nov. 27, 1826, c. 2 miles E Glass Post Office, Jackson Co. NW 1/4 Sect. 5 Tp. 3 R. 12, north and west.

**4460. BRYAN, William**
Nov. 22, 1835, at Fentress, Santa Rosa Co. NW 1/4 NE 1/4 Sect. 12 Tp. 3 R. 27, north and west.

**5505. BRYAN, William**
March 2, 1836, 5 miles W of Dellwood, Jackson Co. E 1/2 NE 1/4 Sect. 20 Tp. 5 R. 9, north and west.

**5506. BRYAN, William**
Mar. 2, 1836, 4 3/4 miles W of Dellwood, Jackson Co. NW 1/4 NE 1/4 Sect. 20 Tp. 5 R. 9, north and west.

**5507. BRYAN, William**
Mar. 2, 1836, 5 miles W of Dellwood, Jackson Co. SE 1/4 NW 1/4 Sect. 20 Tp. 5 R. 9, north and west.

**4143. BRYAN, William C.**
Feb. 28, 1832, at Marianna, Jackson Co. W 1/2 NW 1/4 Sect. 4 Tp. 1 R. 10, north and west.

**7015. BRYAN, William C.**
May 24, 1837, 1 1/2 miles NNE Bayhead, Bay Co. NW 1/4 NW 1/4 Sect. 9 Tp. 2 R. 13, south and west.

**2353. BRYAN, Wm.**
April 26, 1828, at San Helena, Leon Co. E 1/2 SE 1/4 Sect. 18 Tp 1 R. 1, north and west.

**3627. BRYAN, Wm.**
Oct. 6, 1830, 1 mile SE Jamieson, Gadsden Co. W 1/2 SW 1/4 Sect. 8 Tp. 3 R. 2, north and west. Bought with Scrip No. 191, issued to **Alex'r MACOMB**, dated May 30, 1829.

**6941. BRYAN, Wm. J.**
March 25, 1837, 1 mile SE Facil, Hamilton Co. SE 1/4 NW 1/4 Sect. 34 Tp. 1 R. 15, south and east.

**2603. BRYANT, David**
Mar. 11, 1854, 2 1/4 miles N by E of Mason, Columbia Co. E 1/2 SW 1/4 Sect. 11 Tp. 5 R. 17, south and east. Patent delivered Oct. 20, 1859.

**2511. BRYANT, John**
Feb. 27, 1854, 3 miles SSE of Mason, Columbia Co. SE 1/4 SE 1/4 Sect. 24 and SE 1/4 NE 1/4 Sect. 25 Tp. 5 R. 17, south and east. Patent delivered Nov. 3, 1856.

**2998. BRYANT, Joseph**
Oct. 17, 1854, 2 1/4 miles N of Mason, Columbia Co. NW 1/4 SE 1/4 Sect. 10 Tp. 5 R. 17, south and east.

**4984. BRYANT, Joseph**
Mar. 14, 1859, 4 miles E of Columbia, Columbia Co. SE 1/4 SW 1/4 and SW 1/4 SE 1/4 Sect. 8 Tp. 5 R. 17, south and east. Patent sent to **W. T. HENRY**, Oswega, Fla., July 28, 1902.

**2191. BRYANT, Langley(Jr.)**
Sept. 21, 1853, 1 3/4 miles NE of Lulu, Columbia Co. SE 1/4 SW 1/4 and NE 1/4 SE 1/4 Sect. 26 Tp. 4 R. 17, south and east.

**2445. BRYANT, Langley (Jr.)**
Feb. 22, 1854, 3 3/4 miles SW of Jefferson, Columbia Co. NE 1/4 NW 1/4 Sect. 35 Tp. 4 R. 17, south and east.

**3135. BRYANT, Needham**
Nov. 26, 1829, 4 miles W Alma, Leon Co. E 1/2 SW 1/4 Sect. 32 Tp. 3 R. 4, north and east.

**1299. BRYANT, Oliver**
Mar. 24, 1852, 1 1/4 miles N of 30 Mile Siding Station, Alachua Co. W 1/2 Lot 4 NW 1/4 Sect. 9 Tp. 8 R. 18, south and east. Patent delivered May 4, 1857.

**2911. BRYANT, Sarah**
Sept. 16, 1854, 4 miles NW of Bass, Columbia Co. SE 1/4 SW 1/4 Sect. 5 Tp. 5 R. 17, south and east. Patent delivered Sept. 20, 1856.

**5069. BRYANT, Sarah**
Aug. 9, 1859, 3 1/2 miles SE of Bass, Columbia Co. NE 1/4 SW 1/4 Sect. 6 Tp. 5 R. 17, south and east.

**1194. BRYANT, Sill Johnson**
Feb. 20, 1852, 1 mile W of Lulu, Columbia Co. SE 1/4 SE 1/4 Sect. 29 Tp. 4 R. 18, south and east. Patent delivered Mar. 4, 1857.

**1588. BRYANT, Sill Johnson**
Dec. 27, 1852, 1 1/4 miles NW of Lulu, Columbia Co. SW 1/4 SE 1/4 Sect. 29 Tp. 4 R. 18, south and east. Patent delivered Mar. 4, 1857.

**2355. BRYANT, Sill Johnson**
Nov. 7, 1853, 4 1/2 miles SSW of Lulu, Columbia Co. SW 1/4 NW 1/4 and NW 1/4 SW 1/4 Sect. 2 Tp. 5 R. 17, south and east. Patent delivered Oct. 20, 1859.

**2789. BRYANT, Silvester (Sr.)**
July 5, 1854, 4 miles E of Hardee Town, Levy Co. NE 1/4 SW 1/4 Sect. 25 Tp. 11 R. 13, south and east.

**1221. BRYANT, Thomas**
Feb. 27, 1852, 3 1/2 miles NE of Mason, Columbia Co. NE 1/4 NE 1/4 Sect. 23 Tp. 5 R. 17, south and east. Patent delivered Feb. 20, 1857.

**2529. BRYANT, Thomas**
Mar. 1, 1854, 2 1/4 miles NE of Mason, Columbia Co. SW 1/4 SW 1/4 Sect. 13 Tp. 5 R. 17, south and east. Patent delivered Oct. 11, 1869.

**1902. BUDDINGTON, Osias(Ozias)**
June 18, 1853, 7 miles NE of Highland, Clay Co. SW 1/4 NE 1/4 Sect. 32 Tp. 4 R. 24, south and east. Patent delivered Dec. 18, 1874.

**2058. BUDDINGTON, Osias**
Aug. 16, 1853, 3/4 mile W of Oxford, Clay Co. NE 1/4 SE 1/4 Sect. 25 Tp. 5 R. 24, south and east. Patent delivered Dec. 18, 1874.

**2059. BUDDINGTON, Osias**
Aug. 16, 1853, 5 1/2 miles NW of Long Branch, Clay Co. SE 1/4 SW 1/4 Sect. 3 and NE 1/4 NW 1/4 Sect.

10 Tp. 6 R. 24, south and east. Patent delivered Dec. 18, 1874.

**1944. BUDDINGTON, Osias**
June 14, 1853, 1 mile N of Oypas, Clay Co. N 1/2 NE 1/4 Sect. 21 Tp. 5 R. 24, south and east. Patent delivered Dec. 18, 1874.

**1923. BUDDINGTON, Osias**
July 5, 1853, 7 miles E of Highland, Clay Co. SE 1/4 NW 1/4 Sect. 32 Tp. 4 R. 24, south and east. Patent delivered Dec. 18, 1874.

**1903. BUDDINGTON, Osias**
June 18, 1853, 6 3/4 miles NE of Highland, Clay Co. SW 1/4 NE 1/4 Sect. 29 Tp. 4 R. 24, south and east. Patent delivered Dec. 18, 1874.

**1945. BUDDINGTON, Osias**
July 14, 1853, 1 1/2 miles SW of Middleburg, Clay Co. SW 1/4 SE 1/4 Sect. 15 Tp. 5 R. 24, south and east. Patent delivered Dec. 18, 1874.

**1946. BUDDINGTON, Osias**
July 14, 1853, 8 miles NW of Rideout, Clay Co. SW 1/4 SE 1/4 Sect. 20 Tp. 4 R. 24, south and east. Patent delivered Dec. 18, 1874.

**1959. BUDDINGTON, Osias**
July 20, 1853, 5 1/2 miles NNW of Long Branch, Clay Co. NE 1/4 Sect. 10 Tp. 6 R. 24, south and east. Patent delivered Dec. 18, 1874.

**1960. BUDDINGTON, Osias**
July 20, 1853, 6 miles NW of Longbranch, Clay Co. W 1/2 SW 1/4 Sect. 2 Tp. 6 R. 24, south and east. Patent delivered Dec. 18, 1874.

**1961. BUDDINGTON, Osias**
July 20, 1853, 4 3/4 miles NW of Longbranch, Clay Co. NW 1/4 NW 1/4 and SW 1/4 SW 1/4 Sect. 11 Tp. 6 R. 24, south and east. Patent delivered Dec. 18, 1874.

**2002. BUDDINGTON, Osias**
Aug. 3, 1853, 9 1/2 miles SW of Rideout, Clay Co. SE 1/4 SE 1/4 Sect. 19 Tp. 4 R. 24, south and east. Patent delivered Dec. 18, 1874.

**2313. BUDDINGTON, Osias**
Oct. 29, 1853, 7 miles NW of Rideout, Clay Co. SW 1/4 SE 1/4 Sect. 19 and NW 1/4 NE 1/4 Sect. 30 Tp. 4 R. 24, south and east. Patent delivered Dec. 18, 1874.

**4692. BUENNITRY, Babtist**
Dec. 10, 1834, 1 mile NNW of Stringer, Leon Co. SW 1/4 SW 1/4 Sect. 20 Tp. 3 R. 3, north and east.

**141. BUIE, Archibald**
Dec. 27, 1827, at Gretha, Gadsden Co. NE 1/4 Sect. 26 Tp. 3 R. 4, north and west.

**1816. BUIE, Archibald**
June 5, 1827, 5 1/2 miles W by N of Quincy, Gadsden Co. E 1/2 SE 1/4 Sect. 11 Tp. 3 R. 4, north and west.

**1815. BUIE, Daniel**
June 5, 1827, 4 miles NNW of Quincy, Gadsden Co. E 1/2 SE 1/4 Sect. 23 Tp. 3 R. 4, north and west.

**4054. BUIE, Daniel**
Aug. 2, 1831, 3 1/4 miles E of Deerhunt, Liberty Co. E 1/2 NW 1/4 Sect. 11 Tp. 3 R. 6, north and west.

**4271. BUIE, Daniel**
Jan. 7, 1833, 3 1/4 miles NE of Mears Spur, Gadsden Co. SW 1/4 NE 1/4 Sect. 2 Tp. 3 R. 6, north and west.

**7465. BUIE, Daniel**
May 5, 1838, 2 1/2 miles E Chattahoochee, Gadsden Co. SE 1/4 NE 1/4 Sect. 2 Tp. 3 R. 6, north and west.

**4246. BUIE, John**
Nov. 19, 1832, 3 3/4 miles SE of Jumper, Gadsden Co. NW 1/4 NW 1/4 Sect. 34 Tp. 2 R. 5, north and west.

**4488. BULAND, John**
Dec. 24, 1833, 1 mile N of Stringer, Leon Co. NW 1/4 SW 1/4 Sect. 21 Tp. 3 R. 3, north and east.

**55. BULL, Larkin**
Nov. 8, 1826, near Lake Jackson Post Office, Gadsden Co. SW 1/4 Sect. 31 Tp. 2 R. 2, north and west. Transferred to **Mathew JONES**, Nov. 8, 1826.

**3062. BULLOCK, Geo.**
Sept. 23, 1829, 4 miles SSE El Destino, Leon Co. W 1/2 SE 1/4 Sect. 21 Tp. 1 R. 3, south and east.

**3911. BUNCH, Andrew**
Mar. 10, 1831, 2 1/2 miles SW Tallahassee, Leon Co. E 1/2 NW 1/4 Sect. 11 Tp. 1 R. 1, south and west.

**6833. BUNEFAY, Joseph**
Mar. 3, 1837, 3 miles S Wallace, Santa Rosa Co. E 1/2 NE 1/4 Sect. 31 Tp. 2 R. 29, north and west. Trans-

ferred Aug. 23, 1837 to **Robert ROBINSON**. Transferred Dec. 25, 1839 to **B. C. ALLEN**. Attest: **Robert ROBINSON** and **C. LOVE**.

**8432. BURDS, David**
Dec. 16, 1840, 2 1/4 miles E by S Hinson, Gadsden Co. SE 1/4 SW 1/4 Sect. 26 Tp. 3 R. 2, north and west.

**4750. BURGESS, Samuel H.**
Dec. 30, 1834, 4 1/2 miles S by E of Wewahitchka, Gulf Co. Lot No. 1 Sect. 17 Tp. 5 R. 9, south and west.

**4751. BURGESS, Samuel H.**
Dec. 30, 1834, 4 3/4 miles S by E of Wewahitchka, Gulf Co. Lot No. 1 Sect. 20 Tp. 5 R. 9, south and west.

**5888. BURGESS, Samuel H**
Oct. 6, 1836, 2 1/4 miles S of Greenwood, Jackson Co. Lot No. 13 Fractional Sect. 18 Tp. 5 R. 9, south and west.

**226. BURKS, James**
Dec. 15, 1845, near Citra, Marion Co. W 1/2 NW 1/4 Sect. 34 Tp. 12 R. 22, south and east.

**319. BURLESON, Daniel Allison**
Feb. 12, 1846, c. 6 miles W Orange Lake, Marion Co. Lots No. 4 and 5 Fractional Sect. 20 Tp. 12 R. 22, south and east. On the back of receipt: "Feb. 13, 1846, **J. PARSON**'s receipt for land."

**458. BURLESON, Daniel Allison**
Sept. 11, 1846, 1 mile E Citra, Marion Co. S 1/2 SW 1/4 Sect. 26 Tp. 12 R. 22, south and east.

**459. BURLESON, Daniel Allison**
Sept. 11, 1846, c. 1 1/2 miles SE Citra, Marion Co. SE 1/4 SE 1/4 Sect. 26 and NE 1/4 NE 1/4 Sect. 35 Tp. 12 R. 22, south and east.

**1991. BURLEY, David**
(DUP) July 7, 1827, c. 5 miles SE Wakulla, Wakulla Co. Lot No. 2 Sect. 18 Tp. 3 R. 2, south and east.

**2448. BURLEY, David**
Aug. 1, 1828, c. 2 miles ENE Newport, Wakulla Co. Lot No. 3 Sect. 18 Tp. 3 R. 2, south and east.

**BURNES, Anthony** see **John BROWN**

**764. BURNETT, Bryan**
Dec. 3, 1850, at Blounts Ferry, Hamilton Co. SE 1/4 Sect. 15 Tp. 2 R. 16, north and east.

**1051. BURNETT, James**
Dec. 19, 1851, 1/2 mile NNE Ayril, Alachua Co. W 1/2 Lots No. 1 and 2 Sect. 1 Tp. 8 R. 19, south and east and Lot No. 7 Sect. 6 Tp. 8 R. 20, south and east.

**6006. BURNETT, Samuel**
Nov. 14, 1836, at San Helena, Leon Co. SW 1/4 SE 1/4 Sect. 17 Tp. 1 R. 1, north and west.

**778. BURNEY, Arthur**
(Of Fla.) Oct. 3, 1826, 1 mile ESE Miccosukee, Leon Co. E 1/2 SE 1/4 Sect. 10 Tp.2 R. 3, north and east.

**1893. BURNEY, Arthur**
June 9, 1827, 1/2 mile E Miccosukee, Leon Co. W 1/2 NE 1/4 Sect. 10 Tp. 2 R. 3, north and east.

**2770. BURNEY, Arthur**
March 5, 1829, 6 miles NE Wadesboro, Leon Co. Lot No. 3 Sect. 14 Tp 2 R. 3, north and east.

**4060. BURNEY, Arthur**
Aug. 11, 1831, 1 1/2 miles E of Capitola, Leon Co. W 1/2 NE 1/4 Sect. 19 Tp.1 R. 3, north and east.

**6368. BURNEY, Arthur**
Dec. 31, 1836, 3 miles NE Wadesboro, Leon Co. W 1/2 SW 1/4 Sect. 28 Tp. 2 R. 3, north and east.

**6369. BURNEY, Arthur**
Dec. 31, 1836, 3 miles NE Wadesboro, Leon Co. E 1/2 NE 1/4 Sect. 32 Tp. 3 R. 2, north and east.

**6370. BURNEY, Arthur**
Dec. 31, 1836, 2 1/2 miles ENE Wadesboro, Leon Co. W 1/2 NW 1/4 Sect. 33 Tp. 2 R. 3, north and east.

**2187. BURNEY, Ellis**
Dec. 31, 1827, 1 mile N Miccosukee, Leon Co. E 1/2 NE 1/4 Sect. 4 Tp. 2 R. 3, north and east.

**2554. BURNEY, Ellis**
Nov. 28, 1828, 1/2 mile S Copeland, Leon Co. W 1/2 NE 1/4 Sect. 4 Tp. 2 R. 3, north and east.

**2772. BURNEY, Guilford**
March 5, 1829, 1/2 mile W Miccosukee, Leon Co. W 1/2 SE 1/4 Sect. 8 Tp. 2 R. 3, north and east.

**6342. BURNEY, Guilford**
Dec. 28, 1836, 1 mile W Miccosukee, Leon Co. NW 1/4 NW 1/4 Sect. 8 Tp. 2 R. 3, north and east.

**2241. BURNEY, Willis**
(Of Fla.) Jan. 31, 1828, 1/2 mile SW Copeland, Leon Co. E 1/2 NE 1/4 Sect. 5 Tp. 2 R. 3, north and east.

**2537. BURNEY, Willis**
Nov. 7, 1828, 1/2 mile W Miccosukee, Leon Co. E 1/2 NE 1/4 Sect. 8 Tp. 2 R. 3, north and east.

**2675. BURNS, Robert**
Jan. 27, 1829, 1 1/2 miles ESE Norum, Washington Co. E 1/2 NE 1/4 Sect. 17 Tp. 2 R. 15, north and west.

**3209. BURT, Oswell E.**
Jan. 8, 1830, 1 mile SSW Monticello, Jefferson Co. E 1/2 SE 1/4 Sect. 36 Tp. 2 R. 4, north and east.

**7998. BUSH, Asbury F.**
June 22, 1839, 3 miles SW Oakdale, Jackson Co. SW 1/4 NE 1/4 Sect. 4 Tp. 3 R. 10, north and west.

**2677. BUSH, Jno.**
Jan. 27, 1829, 4 1/2 miles S Vernon, Washington Co. W 1/2 SW 1/4 Sect. 14 Tp. 2 R. 15, north and west.

**290. BUSH, Jno. W.**
Jan. 1, 1827, 3 miles S Vernon, Washington Co. NE 1/4 Sect. 15 Tp. 2 R. 15, north and west. **86. BUSH, John** Dec. 2, 1826, 1 mile NE Norum Post Office, Washington Co. SE 1/4 Sect. 9 Tp. 2 R. 15, north and west. Transferred to **Jno. W. BUSH**, Dec. 2, 1826

**7627. BUSH, John**
Sept. 7, 1838, 3/4 mile W Marianna, Jackson Co. E 1/2 NW 1/4 Sect. 9 Tp. 4 R. 10, north and west.

**446. BUSH, John**
Dec. 27, 1828, 1 mile E Norum, Washington Co. SE 1/4 Sect. 14 Tp. 2 R. 15, north and west.

**7997. BUSH, John**
(And **James L. FINLEY**) June 22, 1839, 3 1/2 miles SW Oakdale, Jackson Co. W 1/2 SE 1/4 Sect. 4 Tp. 3 R. 10, north and west.

**8483. BUSH, John**
April 19, 1841, 4 1/2 miles W by S Oakdale, Jackson Co. NE 1/4 SE 1/4 Sect. 4 Tp. 3 R. 10, north and west.

**445. BUSH, John W.**
Dec. 21, 1828, 3 miles ESE Norum, Washington Co. W 1/2 NW 1/4 Sect. 15 Tp. 2 R. 15, north and west.

**6724. BUSH, John W.**
Feb. 1, 1837, just SE Marianna, Gadsden Co. W 1/2 NW 1/4 Sect. 9 Tp. 4 R. 10, north and west.

**7949. BUSH, Thomas M.**
May 3, 1839, 4 miles SSE Kynesville, Jackson Co. W 1/2 NE 1/4 E 1/2 SE 1/4 Sect. 27 Tp. 4 R. 11, north and west.

**7950. BUSH, Thomas M.**
May 3, 1839, 3 1/2 miles SSE Kynesville, Jackson Co. SE 1/4 Sect. 22 Tp. 4 R. 11, north and west.

**7968. BUSH, Thomas M.**
May 23, 1839, 6 miles SSW Overstreet, Gulf Co. W 1/2 SW 1/4 Sect. 25 Tp. 6 R. 11, north and west.

**7969. BUSH, Thomas M.**
May 23, 1839, 5 miles N Campbellton, (Jackson Co., Fla) Geneva Co., Ala. E 1/2 NE 1/4 Sect. 19 Tp. 7 R. 12, north and west.

**7970. BUSH, Thomas M.**
May 23, 1839, 6 miles E Welchton, Jackson Co. W 1/2 NE 1/4 E 1/2 SE 1/4 Sect. 26 Tp. 6 R. 11, north and west.

**7971. BUSH, Thomas M.**
May 23, 1839, 7 1/2 miles NNE Welchton, Jackson Co. SW 1/4 W 1/2 NW 1/4 Sect. 24 Tp. 6 R. 11, north and west.

**7972. BUSH, Thomas M.**
May 23, 1839, 6 1/4 miles NNE Welchton, Jackson Co. NE 1/4 E 1/2 SW 1/4 Sect. 23 Tp. 6 R. 11, north and west.

**7973. BUSH, Thomas M.**
May 23, 1839, 6 miles NNE Welchton, Jackson Co. W 1/2 SW 1/4 and SE 1/4 SW 1/4 Sect. 23 Tp. 6 R. 11, north and west.

**7974. BUSH, Thomas M.**
May 23, 1839, 2 miles E Campbellton, Jackson Co. SW 1/4 Sect. 29 Tp. 7 R. 12, north and west.

**7975. BUSH, Thomas M.**
May 23, 1839, 5 mile NE by N Welchton, Jackson Co. SE 1/4 SW 1/4 Sect. 22 Tp. 6 R. 11, north and west.

**8002. BUSH, Thomas M.**
July 1, 1839, 5 1/2 miles NNE Campbellton, Jackson Co. (State line) NW 1/4 Sect. 23 Tp. 7 R. 11, north and

west. The above receipt is ante-dated by 6 months according to the serial No. 8003 being dated Jan. 8, 1839.

**8003? BUSH, Thomas M.**
July 1, 1839, 8 miles NNE Campbellton.(Land is in Houston Co., Ala.) N 1/2 NW 1/4 Sect. 22 TP. 7 R. 11, north and west. See **John REVELS**, duplicate number.

**8004. BUSH, Thomas M.**
July 1, 1839, 3 miles SW Ellis, Jackson Co. W 1/2 NE 1/4 Sect. 18 Tp. 6 R. 10, north and west.

**8005. BUSH, Thomas M.**
July 1, 1839, 2 1/2 miles NW Welchton, Jackson Co. SW 1/4 Sect. 22 Tp. 6 R. 12, north and west.

**8006. BUSH, Thomas M.**
July 1, 1839, 1 3/4 miles SSE Campbellton, Jackson Co. W 1/2 NE 1/4 Sect. 5 Tp. 6 R. 11, north and west.

**8007. BUSH, Thomas M.**
July 1, 1839, 5 1/4 miles W Malone, Jackson Co. E 1/2 NE 1/4 Sect. 31 Tp. 7 R. 10, north and west.

**8008. BUSH, Thomas M.**
July 1, 1839, 3 miles SSE Campbellton, Jackson Co. W 1/2 NW 1/4 Sect. 4 Tp. 6 R. 11, north and west.

**8009. BUSH, Thomas M.**
July 1, 1839, 5 miles E Welchton, Jackson Co. E 1/2 SW 1/4 Sect. 25 Tp. 6 R. 11, north and west.

**8010. BUSH, Thomas M.**
July 1, 1839, 5 miles E by S Campbellton, Jackson Co. E 1/2 NE 1/4 Sect. 2 Tp. 6 R. 11, north and west.

**8011. BUSH, Thomas M.**
July 1, 1839, 6 miles E by S Campbellton, Jackson Co. W 1/2 NW 1/4 SW 1/4 SW 1/4 Sect.1 Tp. 6 R. 11, north and west.

**8034. BUSH, Thomas M.**
Aug. 17, 1839, 2 miles NNW Ellis, Jackson Co. E 1/2 NE 1/4 Sect. 6 Tp. 6 R. 10, north and east.

**8035. BUSH, Thomas M.**
Aug. 17, 1839, 4 miles NNE Campbellton, Jackson Co. SW 1/4 Sect. 32 Tp. 7 R. 11, north and west.

**8036. BUSH, Thomas M.**
Aug. 17, 1839, 3 miles NW Campbellton, Jackson Co. S 1/2 E 1/2 NW 1/4 Sect. 36 Tp. 7 R. 12, north and west.

**8037. BUSH, Thomas M.**
Aug. 17, 1839, at Campbellton, Jackson Co. NE 1/4 E 1/2 NW 1/4 Sect. 6 Tp. 6 R. 11, north and west.

**8038. BUSH, Thomas M.**
Aug. 17, 1839, at Campbellton, Jackson Co. S 1/2 Sect. 31 Tp. 7 R. 11, north and west.

**8040. BUSH, Thomas M.**
Aug. 17, 1839, 1 mile SE by S Campbellton, Jackson Co. E 1/2 NE 1/4 SW 1/4 NW 1/4 Sect. 5 Tp. 6 R. 11, north and west.

**8041. BUSH, Thomas M.**
Aug. 17, 1839, 2 miles NE Jacob, Jackson Co. NE 1/4 Sect. 8 Tp. 6 R. 11, north and west.

**8042. BUSH, Thomas M.**
Aug. 17, 1839, 1 mile SW Oakdale, Jackson Co. NW 1/4 NE 1/4 Sect. 4 Tp. 3 R. 10, north and west.

**5901. BUTLER, Levi**
Oct. 13, 1836, 2 miles NNE of Hinson, Gadsden Co. SW 1/4 NW 1/4 Sect. 25 Tp. 3 R. 2, north and west.

**784. BUTLER, Robert**
(Of Fla.) Oct. 9, 1826, 1/2 mile W Bradfordville, Leon Co. W 1/2 NW 1/4 Sect. 21 Tp. 2 R. 1, north and east.

**8863. BUTLER, Sampson H.**
Dec. 24, 1845, at Dennett, Madison Co. N 1/2 N 1/4 Sect. 34 Tp. 2 R. 7, north and east.

**8864. BUTLER, Sampson H.**
Dec. 24, 1845, 1/4 mile E Dennett, Madison Co. W 1/2 SE 1/4 Sect. 22 Tp. 2 R. 7, north and east.

**8865. BUTLER, Sampson H.**
Dec. 24, 1845, 1/2 mile SW Bailey, Madison Co. W 1/2 SW 1/4 Sect. 23 Tp. 2 R. 7, north and east. **3064. BUTLER, Wm.**
Sept. 25, 1829, 3/4 mile S Jamieson, Gadsden Co. W 1/2 NE 1/4 Sect. 18 Tp. 3 R. 2, north and west. Transferred to **Benjamin CHAPPELL**, Dec. 25, 1829.(H. G. McFARLAND,J. P.)

**6237. BYRD, Isaac F. S. C.**
Dec. 17, 1836, 4 1/2 miles SW El Destino, Leon Co. SW 1/4 SE 1/4 Sect. 21 Tp. 1 R. 2, south and east.

**8. BYRD, JOSE**
Aug. 31, 1826, NW Quincy, Gadsden Co. SE 1/4 Sect. 26 Tp. 3 R. 4, north

and west.(160.25 acres) Transferred to **R. K. CALL**, Aug. 31, 1826. Registered in Gadsden Co. Dec. 11, 1837, **Lorenzo L. SEXTON**, Clerk Co. Court.

**1124. BYRD, Joshua H.**
(DUP) Feb. 14, 1827, 2 miles SSE Miccosukee Station, Leon Co. S 1/2 NW 1/4 Sect. 22 Tp. 2 R. 3, north and east.

**1125. BYRD, Joshua H.**
Feb. 14, 1827, 2 miles ESE Miccosukee Station, Leon Co. Lot No. 5 Sect. 14 Tp. 2 R. 3, north and east.

**2438. BYRD, Nathan**
July 12, 1828, 7 miles NE by E Wadesboro, Leon Co. Lot No. 5 Sect. 23 Tp. 2 R. 3, north and east. (80 acres)

**3507. BYRD, Nathan**
May 7, 1830, at Meridian, Leon Co. W 1/2 NW 1/4 Sect. 19 Tp. 1 R. 3, north and east.

**658. BYRD, Olive**
(Of N. Carolina) Jan. 26, 1826, 5 miles SSE Miccosukee, Leon Co. Lot No. 1 Sect. 23 Tp. 2 R. 3, north and east.

**5286. BYRD, Robert F.**
Nov. 26, 1835, 2 miles NE of Corey, Leon Co. W 1/2 SW 1/4 Sect. 22 Tp. 1 R. 2, south and east.

**4761. BYRD, SARAH E.**
Jan. 9, 1835, 2 miles W by N of Lloyd, Jefferson Co. E 1/2 NE 1/4 Sect. 20 Tp. 2 R. 3, north and east.

**BYRON, Edward** see **James J. TRAMMELL # 4417.**

## * C *

**2235. CABELL, Abram J.**
Jan. 28, 1828, 1/2 mile S Drifton, Jefferson Co. E 1/2 SW 1/4 Sect. 18 Tp. 1 R. 5, north and east.

**2236. CABELL, Abram J.**
Jan. 28, 1828, 1/2 mile SE Drifton, Jefferson Co. SE 1/4 Sect. 18 Tp. 1 R. 5, north and east.

**2237. CABELL, Abram J.**
Jan. 28, 1828, 1 mile S Drifton, Jefferson Co. E 1/2 NW 1/4 Sect. 19 Tp. 1 R. 5, north and east.

**2238. CABELL, Abram J.**
Jan. 28, 1828, 1 1/2 miles S Drifton, Jefferson Co. NE 1/4 Sect. 19 Tp. 1 R. 5, north and east.

**CABELL, Agnes S. B.** see **John H. BROCK** and **John G. GAMBLE**.

**7734. CABELL, Edward C.**
Nov. 29, 1838, at Drifton, Jefferson Co. SE 1/4 NE 1/4 Sect. 18 Tp. 1 R. 5, north and east.

**8963. CABELL, Edward Carrington**
Aug. 4, 1846, 1/4 mile SE Capps, Jefferson Co. W 1/2 SE 1/4 Sect. 1 Tp. 1 R. 4, south and east.

**388. CADE, Robert**
May 4, 1846, c. 4 1/2 miles NE Ocala, Marion Co. SW 1/4 NW 1/4 and NW 1/4 SE 1/4 Sect. 32 Tp. 14 R. 21, south and east.

**3167. CAFTON, John**
Dec. 21, 1829, 1 1/2 miles SW Wadesboro, Leon Co. NW 1/4 Sect. 9 Tp. 1 R. 3, north and east.

**2555. CAIL, John**
Mar. 4, 1854, 2 1/2 miles E of Island Grove, Alachua Co. SE 1/4 SE 1/4 Sect. 11 and Lot No. 10 Sect. 12 Tp. 12 R. 22, south and east.

**4741. CAIN, Daniel A.**
Dec. 23, 1834, 2 miles SSW of Felkel, Leon Co. SE 1/4 NW 1/4 Sect. 8 Tp. 2 R. 2, north and east.

**4742. CAIN, Daniel A.**
Dec. 23, 1834, 1 1/2 miles N of Centerville, Leon Co. SE 1/4 NE 1/4 Sect. 7 Tp. 2 R. 2, north and east.

**1317. CALDWELL, Francis S.**
May 13, 1852, 2 miles NE of Conner, Marion Co. N 1/2 Lot 10 Sect. 25 Tp. 14 R. 23, south and east.

**1152. CALDWELL, Francis Samuel**
Feb. 5, 1852, 2 miles NE of Conner, Marion Co. N 1/2 Lot 5 and 6 and N 1/2 of Lot 4 Sect. 25 Tp. 14 R. 23, south and east.

**535. CALDWELL, Joseph**
(Also **Thomas Wilson CALDWELL** and **John Glenn CALDWELL**) Mar. 2, 1847, county unknown, S 1/2 SW 1/4 Sect. 25 Tp. 12 R. (?). Transferred Dec. 13, 1851 to **Joseph CALDWELL**. This receipt has a piece torn out. Patent delivered Aug. 10, 1855.

**536. CALDWELL, Joseph**
(Also **Thomas Wilson CALDWELL** and **John Glenn CALDWELL**) Mar. 2, 1847, 1 miles NE Ocala, Marion Co. NW 1/4 S(?) Sect. 9 Tp. 15 R. 22. Patent forwarded per order of CALDWELL, Aug. 10, 1855. CALDWELL's were from South Carolina.

**600. CALDWELL, Joseph**
Nov. 30, 1847, at Ocala, Marion Co. Lot No. 1 Sect. 17 Tp. 15 R. 22, south and east.

**CALDWELL, Joseph and T. W.** see **Stephen BRYAN #401**

**733. CALDWELL, Thomas Wilson**
April 17, 1850, near Ocala, Marion Co. SW 1/4 NW 1/4 Sect. 9 Tp. 15 R. 21, south and east.

**9327. CALHOUN, Sidney Ann A.**
(Widow of **Andrew CALHOUN**) May 15, 1891 2 1/4 miles SW Half Moon, Alachua Co. SE 1/4 Sect. 34 Tp. 10S R. 17E.

**593. CALL, Richard K.**
(DUP) Dec. 6, 1825, 1 mile NNW Tallahassee, Leon Co. W 1/2 NW 1/4 Sect. 23 Tp. 1 R. 1, north and west.

**718. Call, Richard K.**
(DUP) (Of Fla.) June 8, 1826, 2 miles E Helena, Leon Co. E 1/2 NW 1/4 Sect. 23 Tp.1 R. 1, north and west.

**766. CALL, Richard K.**
(Of Fla.) Sept. 1826, 5 miles ENE Centerville, Leon Co. W 1/2 SE 1/4 Sect. 15 Tp. 2 R. 2, north and east.

**1194. CALL, Richard K.**
Mar. 7, 1827, 6 miles W Lamont, Jefferson Co. W 1/2 SW 1/4 Sect. 23 Tp. 1 R. 4, south and east.

**1867. CALL, Richard K.**

(DUP) June 6, 1827, 4 miles S Waukenah, Jefferson Co. E 1/2 NW 1/4 Sect. 22 Tp. 1 R. 4, south and east.

**1868. CALL, Richard K.**
June 6, 1827, 4 miles S Waukenah, Jefferson Co. NE 1/4 Sect. 22 Tp. 1 R. 4, south and east.

**2064. CALL, Richard K.**
Sept. 18, 1827, 3 miles NW Alma, Jefferson Co. E 1/2 NE 1/4 Sect. 31 Tp. 3 R. 4, north and east. Transferred Oct. 6, 1827, to **Samuel GARRETT**.

**2342. CALL, Richard K.**
April 14, 1828, c. 3 miles SW Meridian, Leon Co. Lot No. 2 Fractional Sect. 35 Tp. 3 R. 1, north and west.

**2344. CALL, Richard K.**
April 14, 1828, c. 3 miles E Meridian, Leon Co. Lot No. 3 Fractional Sect. 35 Tp. 3 R. 1, north and west.

**2421. CALL, Richard K.**
May 23, 1828, 6 miles E Havana, Leon Co. E 1/2 SE 1/4 Sect. 34 Tp. 3 R. 1, north and west.

**2453. CALL, Richard K.**
Aug. 8, 1828, 3 miles E by S Sawdust, Gadsden Co. W 1/2 SE 1/4 Sect. 25 Tp. 2 R. 4, north and west.

**2519. CALL, Richard K.**
Oct. 9, 1828, 4 1/2 miles WNW Waukenah, Jefferson Co. W 1/2 SW 1/4 Sect. 31 Tp. 1 R. 4, north and east.

**2477. CALL, Richard K.**
Aug. 27, 1828, c. 7 miles E Havana, Leon Co. Lot No.4 Fractional Sect. 25 Tp. 3 R. 1, north and west.

**4685. CALL, Richard K.**
Dec. 8, 1834, 5 1/2 miles NW of Bradfordville, Leon Co. W 1/2 NE 1/4 Sect. 6 Tp. 2 R. 1, north and east.

**4686. CALL, Richard K.**
Dec. 12, 1834, 5 1/2 miles W of Bradfordville, Leon Co. W 1/2 SE 1/4 Sect. 3 Tp. 2 R. 1, north and west.

**4702. CALL, Richard K.**
Dec. 12, 1834, 3 1/2 miles SW of Tallahassee, Leon Co. SW 1/4 NE 1/4 Sect. 3 Tp. 1 R. 1, south and west.

**4991. CALL, Richard K.**
June 12, 1835, 3 1/2 miles S of St. Marks, Wakulla Co. Lot No. 5 Sect. 25 Tp. 4 R. 1, south and east.

**4992. CALL, Richard K.**
June 13, 1835, 4 miles S of St. Marks, Wakulla Co. Lot No. 1 Sect. 36 Tp. 4 R. 1, south and east.

**4993. CALL, Richard K.**
June 13, 1835, 3 1/2 miles S of St. Marks, Wakulla Co. Lot No. 7 Sect. 25 Tp. 4 R. 1, south and east.

**4994. CALL, Richard K.**
June 13, 1835, 3 1/2 miles S of St. Marks, Wakulla Co. Lot No. 6 Sect. 25 Tp. 4 R. 1, south and east.

**5026. CALL, Richard K.**
July 7, 1835, Apalachee Bay, 8 miles E of Bald Point, Franklin Co. Lot No. 1 Fractional Sect. 26 Tp. 4 R. 1, south and east.

**5060. CALL, Richard K.**
(With **John G. GAMBLE** and **Thomas PENNY**) July 9, 1835, 3 1/2 miles NNW of Port St. Joe, Gulf Co. Lots 1,2,3,4,5,6,7,8,9, 10, and 11 Sect. 22 Tp. 7 R. 11, south and west.

**5061. CALL, Richard K.**
(With **John G. GAMBLE** and **Thomas PENNY**) July 9, 1835, 3 1/2 miles N of Port St. Joe, Gulf Co. W 1/2 Sect. 23 Tp. 7 R. 11, south and west.

**5062. CALL, Richard K.**
(With **John G. GAMBLE** and **Thomas PENNY**) July 9, 1835, 1 mile NNE of Port St. Joe, Gulf Co. W 1/2 Sect. 23 Tp. 7 R. 11, south and west.

**5063. CALL, Richard K.**
(With **John G. GAMBLE** and **Thomas PENNY**) July 9, 1835, 1 1/4 miles NNE of Port St. Joe, Gulf Co. NE 1/4 Sect. 36 Tp. 7 R. 11, south and west.

**5064. CALL, Richard K.**
(With **John G. GAMBLE** and **Thomas PENNY**) July 9, 1835, 1 1/2 miles N of Port St. Joe, Gulf Co. NW 1/4 Sect. 25 Tp. 7 R. 11, south and west.

**5065. CALL, Richard K.**
(With **John G. GAMBLE** and **Thomas PENNY**) July 9, 1835, 2 1/2 miles N of Port St. Joe, Gulf Co. SE 1/4 Sect. 23 Tp.7 R. 11, south and west.

**5068. CALL, Richard K.**
(With **John G. GAMBLE** and **Thomas PENNY**) July 10, 1835, 1 1/4 miles N of Port St. Joe, Gulf Co. SW 1/4 Sect. 25 Tp. 7 R. 11, south and west.

**5071. CALL, Richard K.**
July 11, 1835, 3 1/2 miles S of St. Marks, Wakulla Co. Lots No. 1, 2, 3,

and 4 Sect. 23 Tp. 4 R. 1, south and east.

**5072. CALL, Richard K.**
July 11, 1835, 2 1/2 miles W by S of St. Marks, Wakulla Co. S 1/2 Sect. 24 Tp. 4 R. 1, south and east.

**5073. CALL, Richard K.**
July 11, 1835, 2 1/2 miles W by S of St. Marks, Wakulla Co. NW 1/4 Sect. 24 Tp. 4 R. 1, south and east.

**5074. CALL, Richard K.**
July 11, 1835, 2 1/2 miles W by S of St. Marks, Wakulla Co. W 1/2 NE 1/4 Sect. 24 Tp. 4 R. 1, south and east.

**5561. CALL, Richard K.**
Mar. 28, 1836, 3 1/2 miles SE of Concord, Gadsden Co. E 1/2 SW 1/4 Sect. 2 Tp. 2 R. 1, north and west; and W 1/2 SE 1/4 and E 1/2 NE 1/4 Sect. 34 Tp. 3 R. 1, north and west.

**6819. CALL, Richard K.**
Mar. 1, 1837, 2 miles SE St. Marks, Wakulla Co. Sect. 13 Tp. 4 R. 1, south and east.

**6822. CALL, Richard K.**
March 1, 1837, 1 1/2 miles WSW Marina, Hamilton Co. W 1/2 NE 1/4 Sect. 1 Tp. 1 R. 13, south and east.
See **John G. GAMBLE** and **Thomas PENNY**

**574. CALL, Rich. K.**
July 29, 1825, 5 miles WNW of Tallahassee, Leon Co. E 1/2 SE 1/4 Sect. 21 Tp. 1 R. 1, north and west.

**752. CALL, R. K.**
(Of Fla.) Sept. 5, 1826, 4 miles NW Wadesboro, Leon Co. E 1/2 SW 1/4 Sect. 15 Tp. 2 R. 2, north and east.

**753. CALL, R. K.**
(Of Fla.) Sept. 5, 1826, 4 miles NW Wadesboro, Leon Co. E 1/2 NE 1/4 Sect. 22 Tp. 2 R. 2, north and east.

**754. CALL, R. K.**
(Of Fla.) Sept. 6, 1826, 2 miles S Wadesboro, Leon Co. W 1/2 NW 1/4 Sect. 18 Tp. 1 R. 3, north and east. Transferred to **Robt. W. WILLIAMS**, no date given.

**755. CALL, R. K.**
(Of Fla.) Sept. 6, 1826, 2 miles S Wadesboro, Leon Co. E 1/2 NE 1/4 Sect. 13 Tp. 1 R. 2, north and east. Transferred to **Robt. W. WILLIAMS**, no date given.

**1878. CALL, R. K.**
June 7, 1827, 9 miles N Tallahassee, Leon Co. Lot No. 1 Fractional Sect. 11 Tp. 2 R. 1, north and west.

**1879. CALL, R. K.**
June 7, 1827, 9 miles N Tallahassee, Leon Co. NW 1/4 Sect. 10 Tp. 2 R. 1, north and west.

**1956. CALL, R. K.**
June 26, 1827, 5 1/2 miles SW Meridian, Leon Co. E 1/2 NE 1/4 Sect. 3 Tp. 2 R. 1, north and west.

**7980. CALLAWAY, Elizabeth**
June 1, 1839, 1 mile SE Campbellton, Jackson Co. SW 1/4 SW 1/4 Sect. 5 Tp. 6 R. 11, north and west.

**3823. CALLOWAY, Daniel**
Dec. 29, 1830, 1/2 mile SE Moseley Hall, Madison Co. E 1/2 NE 1/4 Sect. 26 Tp. 1 R. 8, south and east.

**3587. CALLOWAY, David**
Aug. 13, 1830, 3 miles E Moseley Hall, Madison Co. W 1/2 NW 1/4 Sect. 25 Tp. 1 R. 8, south and east.

**2164. CALLOWAY, Elisha**
Dec. 24, 1827, 3 miles W Ellis, Jackson Co. E 1/2 NE 1/4 Sect. 12 Tp. 6 R. 11, north and west.

**2529. CALLOWAY, Elijah H.**
Oct. 23, 1828, 6 miles ENE Campbellton, Houston Co. (Alabama) SW 1/4 Sect. 23 Tp. 7 R. 11, north and west.

**2530. CALLOWAY, Elijah H.**
Oct. 23, 1828, 3 miles W Ellis, Jackson Co. E 1/2 NW 1/4 Sect. 12 Tp. 6 R. 11, north and west.

**346. CALLOWAY, Elijah N.**
April 16, 1827, 2 miles SE Campbellton, Jackson Co. E 1/2 SW 1/4 Sect. 5 Tp. 6 R. 11, north and west.

**2613. CAMERON, Alex.**
Jan. 12, 1829, 3 miles WSW Midway, Gadsden Co. Lot No. 4 Sect. 12 Tp. 1 R. 3, north and west. Transferred to **Wm. MANNER** on Jan. 12, 1829.

**1763. CAMERON, JAMES**
(DUP) June 4, 1827, 3 miles W of Tallahassee, Leon Co. E 1/2 SW 1/4 Sect. 35 Tp. 1 R. 1, north and west.

**3. CAMP, Sextus**
Aug. 27, 1826, near Campbellton, Jackson Co. $200.62 1/2 for SE 1/4 of Sect. 18 Tp. 6 R. 11, north and west. 160.51/100 acres.

**19. CAMPBELL, Alex.**
Oct. 4, 1826, near Sawdust Post Ofice, Gadsden Co. $198.98 3/4 for NE 1/4 Sect. 26 Tp. 2 R. 4, north and west. 159.69 acres. Under Premption Law. **R. K. CALL**, Receiver. Transferred to **Jesse BYRD** on Oct. 4, 1826, by **Alex CAMPBELL**.

**1460. CAMPBELL, Alex.**
(DUP) May 22, 1827, 5 miles N Quincy, Gadsden Co. E 1/2 SW 1/4 Sect. 12 Tp. 3 R. 4, north and west.

**1461. CAMPBELL, Alex.**
(DUP) May 22, 1827, 5 1/2 miles N Quincy, Gadsden Co. W 1/2 SE 1/4 Sect. 12 Tp. 3 R. 4, north and west.

**146. CAMPBELL, Alex.**
(DUP) May 27, 1827, at Mt. Pleasant, Gadsden Co. Sect. 12 Tp. 3 R. 4, north and west.

**426. CAMPBELL, Christian**
Dec. 10, 1828, 1 mile N Eucheanna, Walton Co. Sect. 27 Tp. 2 R. 18, north and west.

**135. CAMPBELL, Daniel**
Dec. 25, 1826, at Mt. Pleasant Station, Gadsden Co. SE 1/4 Sect. 12 Tp. 3 R. 4, north and west.

**425. CAMPBELL, Daniel D.**
Dec. 10, 1828, 1 mile NE Eucheanna, Walton Co. W 1/2 SW 1/4 Sect. 26, Tp. 2 R. 18, north and west.

**8350. CAMPBELL, Daniel**
June 18, 1840, 6 1/2 miles N Redbay, Walton Co. W 1/2 SW 1/4 Sect. 4 Tp. 3 R. 17, north and west.

**2188. CAMPBELL, Duncan**
(Of Fla.) Dec. 31, 1827, 2 miles WSW Alma, Jefferson Co. E 1/2 NW 1/4 Sect. 4 Tp. 2 R. 4, north and west.

**471. CAMPBELL, John**
Jan. 15, 1830, 1 mile E Laurel Hill, Okaloosa Co. E 1/2 SW 1/4 Sect. 4 Tp. 5 R. 23, north and west.

**CAMPBELL, John W. see William M. LOFTIN, #554.**

**2818. CAMPBELL, James O. B.**
July 15, 1854, 1/2 mile N of Standard, Marion Co. S 1/2 NE 1/4 and N 1/2 SE 1/4 Sect. 17 Tp. 14 R. 20, south and east.

**3211. CAMPBELL, Neil**
Jan. 13, 1830, 5 miles NW Bradfordville, Leon Co. W 1/2 SE 1/4 Sect. 6 Tp. 1 R. 2, north and east.

**7383. CANADA, Caroline**
May 17, 1889, 1 3/4 miles SE Christman, Orange Co. S 1/2 SE 1/4 and E 1/2 SW 1/4 Sect. 20 Tp. 22S R. 32E.

**5295. CANNON, Henry R.**
Dec. 16, 1885, 3 miles N by W Wylly, Levy Co. W 1/2 NE 1/4 and E 1/2 NW 1/4 Sect. 4 Tp.13S R. 14E.

**6884. CANNON, Wm.**
March 11, 1837, 1/2 mile SW Lamont, Jefferson Co. W 1/2 SE 1/4 Sect. 27 Tp. 1 R. 5, south and east. Transferred to **Thomas RANDALL** in payment of $125.(no date). Witnesses: **Romeo LEWIS** and **Henry WASHINGTON**.

**2411. CARAWAY, Elijah**
Feb. 21, 1854, 2 1/2 miles E of Rixford, Suwannee Co. S 1/2 SE 1/4 Sect. 33 Tp. 1 R. 14, south and east. Patent delivered Oct. 11, 1869.

**1691. CARLETON, Isaac**
Feb. 3, 1853, 5 miles NNW of Dukes, Union Co. SE 1/4 SE 1/4 Sect. 12 Tp. 6 R. 18, south and east. Patent delivered June 3, 1856.

**1831. CARLETON, Isaac**
Apr. 18, 1853, 2 1/4 miles NW of Dukes, Union Co. SW 1/4 SW 1/4 Sect. 7 Tp. 6 R. 19, south and east. Patent delivered June 30, 1856.

**2551. CARLETON, Isaac**
Mar. 4, 1854, 5 1/2 miles E of Providence, Union Co. NE 1/4 NW 1/4 and SW 1/4 NE 1/4 Sect. 7 Tp. 6 R. 19, south and east.

**34. CARLTON, Alderman**
May 13, 1843, near Edgar, Putnam Co. Lot No. 3 Sect. 36 Tp. 10 R. 23, south and east

**8969. CARMICHAEL, John**
Aug. 14, 1846, 4 miles N by W Champaign, Madison Co. NW 1/4 SW 1/4 Sect. 35 Tp. 2 R. 8, north and east.

**8970. CARMICHAEL, John**
Aug. 14, 1846, 4 miles N by W Champaign, Madison Co. SW 1/4 SE 1/4 Sect. 34 Tp. 2 R. 8, north and east.

**8971. CARMICHAEL, John**
Aug. 14, 1846, 4 miles NNW Champaign, Madison Co. NE 1/4 SW 1/4 Sect. 3 Tp. 1 R. 8, north and east.

**2249. CARN, Jacob**
Feb. 9, 1828, 4 miles SW Miccosukee, Leon Co. E 1/2 SW 1/4 Sect. 24 Tp. 2 R. 2, north and east.

**1911. CARNEY, John**
June 14, 1827, 1 mile WSW Chaires, Leon Co. W 1/2 NW 1/4 Sect. 34 Tp. 1 R. 2, north and east.

**4398. CARNEY, John**
Aug. 24, 1833, 1 1/2 miles SSW of Chaires, Leon Co. NW 1/4 NW 1/4 Sect. 3 Tp. 1 R. 2, south and east.

**6460. CARNEY, John**
Jan. 9, 1837, just N Waukenah, Jefferson Co. E 1/2 NE 1/4 Sect. 3 Tp. 1 R. 4, south and east.

**6590. CARNEY, John**
Jan. 18, 1837, 1 mile NNE Waukenah, Jefferson Co. W 1/2 NW 1/4 Sect. 35 Tp. 1 R. 4, north and east.

**6620. CARNEY, John**
Jan. 20, 1837, 1/2 mile N Waukenah, Jefferson Co. E 1/2 NE 1/4 and E 1/2 SE 1/4 Sect. 34 Tp. 1 R. 4, north and east.

**6682. CARNEY, John**
Jan. 27, 1837, 1 mile SE Capps, Jefferson Co. NW 1/4 NW 1/4 Sect. 7 Tp. 1 R. 5, south and east.

**7549. CARNEY, John**
July 26, 1838, 2 miles SSW Nash, Jefferson Co. W 1/2 SE 1/4 Sect. 34 Tp. 1 R. 4, north and east.

**8390. CAROWAY, James**
Aug. 20, 1840, 2 miles Selman, Calhoun Co. NE 1/4 Sect. 25 Tp. 2 R. 8, north and west.

**4544. CARPENTER, William**
Feb. 10, 1834, 3/4 mile N by W of Selman, Calhoun Co. SE 1/4 NE 1/4 Sect. 21 Tp. 4 R. 8, north and west.

**2282. CARR, Henry**
March 7, 1828, 2 miles SE Lake Jackson Station, Leon Co. W 1//2 SW 1/4 Sect. 4 Tp. 1 R. 1, north and west.

**2480. CARR, Jacob**
Sept. 3, 1828, 3 miles NNE Wadesboro, Leon Co. W 1/2 SW 1/4 Sect. 24 Tp. 2 R. 2, north and east.

**3877. CARR, Jacob**
Feb. 11, 1831, 3 miles N by W Wadesboro, Leon Co. W 1/2 SE 1/4 Sect. 24 Tp. 2 R. 2, north and east.

**5988. CARR, Jacob**
Nov. 8, 1836, 4 miles E by S of Centerville, Leon Co. E 1/2 SE 1/4 Sect. 23 Tp. 2 R. 2, north and east.

**5509. CARR, William / William A.**
Mar. 3, 1836, 3 1/4 miles NNW of Bradfordville, Leon Co. NW 1/4 Sect. 9 Tp. 2 R. 1, north and east.

**1874. CARR, William / William A.**
June 7, 1827, 2 miles E Lake Jackson Station, Leon Co. E 1/2 NE 1/4 Sect. 4 Tp. 1 R. 1, north and west.

**1875. CARR, William / William A.**
June 7, 1827, 2 miles SE Lake Jackson Station, Leon Co. E 1/2 SW 1/4 Sect. 4 Tp. 1 R. 1, north and west.

**4324. CARR, William / William A.**
Mar. 15, 1833, 4 miles NW of Bradfordville, Leon Co. NW 1/4 SW 1/4 Sect. 7 Tp. 2 R. 1, north and east.

**8537. CARR, William / William A.**
April 6, 1842, 9 1/2 miles NW Bradfordville, Leon Co. Lot No. 7 Sect. 4 Tp. 2 R. 1, north and west.

**4502. CARR, William / William A.**
Jan. 3, 1834, 3 1/2 miles NNE of Bradfordville, Leon Co. SW 1/4 SW 1/4 Sect. 7 Tp. 2 R. 1, north and east.

See **Patrick KERR**

**3882. CARR, Wm. Alex'r A.**
Feb. 17, 1831, 10 miles N Tallahassee, Leon Co. Lot No. 2 Sect. 12 Tp. 2 R. 1, north and east.

**548. CARRAWAY, James**
Nov. 14, 1834, 3 miles SSW Ocheesee, Calhoun Co. E 1/2 SE 1/4 Sect. 14 Tp. 2 R. 8, north and west.

**5672. CARROL, Jesse**
Mar 13, 1836, at San Helena, Leon Co. NW 1/4 SE 1/4 Sect. 17, Tp. 1 R. 1, north and west.

**2688. CARSON, John**
Jan. 28, 1829, 1 mile NE Miccosukee, Leon Co. W 1/2 SE 1/4 Sect. 3 Tp. 2 R. 3, north and east.

**2689. CARSON, John**
Jan. 28, 1829, 5 1/2 miles NW Monticello, Jefferson Co. E 1/2 NW 1/4 Sect. 10 Tp. 2 R. 3, north and east.

**765. CARTER, Blake Anderson**
Dec. 3, 1850, c. 3 miles SE Kendrick, Marion Co. SE 1/4 NE 1/4 and NE 1/4 SE 1/4 Sect. 31 Tp. 14 R. 21, south and east. Patent delivered Feb.

14, 1858.

**815. CARTER, Blake Anderson**
Jan. 23, 1851, 1 mile S Kendrick, Marion Co. NW 1/4 NE 1/4 Sect. 35 Tp. 14 R. 21, south and east. Patent delivered Feb. 13, 1857.

**4126. CARTER, Aaron**
Jan. 24, 1832, 3 miles S by E of Sirmans, Madison Co. E 1/2 NW 1/4 Sect. 31 Tp. 1 R. 8, south and east.

**2721. CARTER, Blake A.**
May 2, 1854, 4 1/2 miles W of Ocala Junction, Marion Co. N 1/2 NE 1/4 Sect. 5 Tp. 15 R. 21, south and east. Patent delivered Feb. 13, 1857.

**2722. CARTER, Blake A.**
Mar. 2, 1854, 5 miles W of Ocala Junction, Marion Co. SE 1/4 NW 1/4 and NE 1/4 SW 1/4 Sect. 6 Tp. 15 R. 21, south and east. Patent delivered Feb. 13, 1857.

**2643. CARTER, Blake A.**
Mar. 20, 1854, 1/2 mile NNW of Zuber, Marion Co. SW 1/4 SW 1/4 Sect. 29 Tp. 14 R. 21, south and east. Patent delivered Feb. 16, 1857.

**2145. CARTER, Elizabeth**
Dec. 12, 1827, 2 miles W Mosely Hall, Madison Co. W 1/2 SW 1/4 Sect. 30 Tp. 1 R. 8, south and east.

**329. CARTER, Farish**
April 6, 1827, 2 miles NW Campbellton, Jackson Co. NE 1/4 Sect. 27 Tp. 7 R. 12, north and west.

**338. CARTER, Farish**
(Assignee of **Wm. BRITT**) April 12, 1827, 6 miles SE Campbellton, Jackson Co. SW 1/4 Sect. 17 Tp. 6 R. 11, north and west.

**409. CARTER, Farish**
(Assignee of **Miley PORTER**, heiress of **Ann HAMMOCK**) May 7, 1827, 8 miles ENE Graceville, Jackson Co. SE 1/4 Sect. 22 Tp. 7 R. 12, north and west.

**1856. CARTER, Farish**
June 5, 1827, 1/2 mile E Lake Jackson Station, Leon Co. W 1/2 NE 1/4 Sect. 5 Tp. 1 R. 1, north and west.

**1857. CARTER, Farish**
June 6, 1827, at Lake Jackson Station, Leon Co. E 1/2 NW 1/4 Sect. 5 Tp.1 R. 1, north and west.

**1858. CARTER, Farish**
June 6, 1827, 1 mile S by E Lake Jackson Station, Leon Co. E 1/2 NW 1/4 Sect. 8 Tp. 1 R. 1, north and west.

**8901. CARTER, Farish**
Feb. 16, 1846, 3 miles NNE Aycock, Jackson Co. E 1/2 SE 1/4 Sect. 24 Tp. 5 R. 12, north and west.

**2349. CARUTHERS, Elizabeth**
Aug. 16, 1862, see **William CARUTHERS**

**652. CARUTHERS, John**
(Of Fla.) Jan. 21, 1825, 2 miles SW Tallahassee, Leon Co. W 1/2 NE 1/4 Sect. 10 Tp. 1 R. 1, south and east.

**2485. CARUTHERS, Samuel**
Feb. 24, 1854, 2 1/4 miles NNW of Orange Home, Sumter Co. SW 1/4 SE 1/4 Sect. 8 and NW 1/4 NE 1/4 Sect. 17 and NE 1/4 NW 1/4 Sect. 17 Tp. 19 R. 23, south and east. Transferred to **Samuel A. CURRY** on Feb. 16, 1855.

**2349. CARUTHERS, William C.**
Nov. 3, 1853, 2 miles SW of Oxford, Sumter Co. S 1/2 SE 1/4 and N 1/2 SE 1/4 Sect. 30 Tp. 18 R. 23, south and east. Transferred to **Elizabeth CARUTHERS** Aug 16, 1862. Transferred to **Asa R. RANDALL** Jan 1, 1863. Transferred to **Stephen GAMBLE** Aug. 25, 1866.

**4822. CARVER, John B.**
Sept. 7, 1858, 1/2 mile S of 30 Mile Siding Station, Alachua Co. N 1/2 Lot No. 4 and S 1/2 Lot No. 5 Sect. 18 Tp. 8 R. 20, south and east. (Endorsed by **A. R. HAGAN**)

**1167. CARVER, Wilson**
Feb. 11, 1852, 2 miles N of Mason, Columbia Co. E 1/2 NW 1/4, W 1/2 NE 1/4 Sect. 15 Tp. 5 R. 17, south and east.

**6036. CASH, James J. D.**
Nov. 16, 1836, 2 1/2 miles N Quincy, Gadsden Co. SW 1/4 NE 1/4 Sect. 19 Tp. 3 R. 3, north and west.

**CASH, Leonard H.** see **NEALE, Benj. A.**

**8430. CASH, Winefred**
Dec. 15, 1840, 4 miles N Cary, Gadsden Co. NW 1/4 SE 1/4 Sect. 20 Tp. 3 R. 3, north and west.

**544. CASON, James**
Mar. 20, 1847, near Santa Fe, Alachua Co. NW 1/4 SE 1/4 Sect. 5 Tp. 7

R. 19, south and east.

**4831. CASON, John**
Jan. 27, 1835, 3 miles S by W of Miccosukee, Leon Co. W 1/2 NE 1/4 Sect. 33 Tp. 2 R. 3, north and west.

**4919. CASON, John**
April 1, 1835, 4 1/2 miles NNW of Lloyd, Jefferson Co. E 1/2 NE 1/4 Sect. 29 Tp. 2 R. 3, north and east.

**4920. CASON, John**
April 1, 1835, 5 miles N by W of Lloyd, Jefferson Co. W 1/2 NW 1/4 Sect. 28 Tp. 2 R. 3, north and east.

**5449. CASON, John**
Feb. 9, 1836, 3 1/4 miles SE of Centerville, Leon Co. E 1/2 SW 1/4 Sect. 28 Tp. 2 R. 3, north and east.

**5631. CASON, John**
April 28, 1836, 2 1/4 miles NNE of Wadesboro, Jefferson Co. W 1/2 SW 1/4 Sect. 33 Tp.2 R. 3, north and east.

**6161. CASON, John**
Dec. 7, 1836, 1 1/4 miles E Wadesboro, Jefferson Co. W 1/2 NW 1/4 Sect. 4 Tp. 1 R. 3, north and east.

**6216. CASON, John**
Dec. 15, 1836, 1 mile ENE Wadesboro, Jefferson Co. E 1/2 SE 1/4 Sect. 32 Tp. 2 R. 3, north and east.

**7505. CASON, John**
June 29, 1838, 2 1/2 miles NNE Wadesboro, Jefferson Co. SW 1/4 NE 1/4 Sect. 32 Tp. 2 R. 3, north and east.

**7943. CASON, John**
April 16, 1839, 1 1/4 miles NNE Wadesboro, Jefferson Co. E 1/2 NE 1/4 Sect. 5 Tp. 1 R. 3, north and east.

**1639. CASON, John R.**
Jan. 14, 1853, 1/2 mile N of Traxler, Alachua Co. NE 1/4 NE 1/4 Sect. 8 Tp. 7 R. 18, south and east.

**2819. CASON, John R.**
July 15, 1854, at Traxler, Alachua Co. SE 1/4 NE 1/4 Sect. 8 Tp. 7 R. 18, south and east. Patent delivered Aug. 22, 1857.

**5073. CASON, Ransom**
April 21, 1859, 1/2 mile SW of Worthington Springs, Alachua Co. SE 1/4 SE 1/4 Sect. 6 Tp. 7 R. 19, south and east.

**5699. CASON, Silas**
June 10, 1836, 3 1/2 miles E of Bond, Madison Co. SE 1/4 SE 1/4 Sect. 6 Tp. 2 R. 9, north and east.

**148. CASON, Simon**
Nov. 15, 1873, 4 miles E Lake Butler, Union Co. S 1/2 SE 1/4 Sect. 26 Tp. 5S R. 20E.

**5142. CATHCART, James H.**
Nov. 28, 1859, 1 1/2 miles NW of Cadillac, Alachua Co. NW 1/4 and NW 1/4 of NE 1/4 Sect. 2 Tp. 9 R. 17, south and east.

**4121. CATHCART, Robert**
Jan. 24, 1856, 1/2 mile SE of West Alachua, Alachua Co. SE 1/4 of NW 1/4 and NE 1/4 of SW 1/4 Sect. 21 Tp. 8 R. 18, south and east. Patent delivered Aug. 20, 1856.

**4259. CATHCART, Robert L.**
March 21, 1856, 1/2 mile NWN of Siding, Alachua Co. SE 1/4 of NE 1/4 and NE 1/4 of SW 1/4 Sect. 20 Tp. 8 R. 18, south and east. Patent delivered Aug. 20, 1858.

**CATHEY, James W. see WRIGHT, Arthur I. T. #2729**

**8341. CAUSEY, Vara D.**
June 16, 1840, 1 mile SW McClellan, Jefferson Co. SW 1/4 Sect. 21 Tp. 1 R. 5, north and east.

**5451. CAUSEY, Vard D.**
Feb. 10, 1836, 4 1/2 miles NE of Lamont, Jefferson Co. E 1/2 NE 1/4 Sect. 13 Tp. 1 R. 5, south and east.

**2073. CELLAN, John A.**
Aug. 19, 1853, 2 1/4 miles NE of Hague, Alachua Co. W 1/2 SE 1/4 Sect. 15 Tp. 8 R. 19, south and east. Patent delivered Mar. 17, 1856.

**2409. CELLAN, John A.**
Feb. 21, 1854, 2 1/2 miles NNE of Burnetts Lake Station, Alachua Co. S 1/2 NE 1/4 Sect. 15 Tp. 8 R. 19, south and east. Patent delivered Nov. 17, 1856.

**5550. CHADWICK, Daniel**
Mar. 19, 1836, 3 1/4 miles E of Stringer, Jefferson Co. SW 1/4 SE 1/4 Sect. 25 Tp. 3 R. 2, north and east.

**757. CHAIRES, Benja.**
(Of Fla.) Sept. 12, 1826, in Monticello, Jefferson Co. W 1/2 SE 1/4 Sect. 24 Tp.2 R. 4, north and east.

**758. CHAIRES, Benja.**
(Of Fla.) Sept. 12, 1826, at Monticello, Jefferson Co. W 1/2 NW 1/4 Sect.

25 Tp. 2 R. 4, north and east.

**1475. CHAIRES, Ben**
May 23, 1827, 4 1/2 miles W Greensboro, Gadsden Co. E 1/2 SE 1/4 Sect. 3 Tp. 2 R. 6, north and west.

**1476. CHAIRES, Ben**
(DUP) May 23, 1827, 4 1/2 miles W Greensboro, Gadsden Co. W 1/2 SE 1/4 Sect. 3 Tp. 2 R. 6, north and west.

**1477. CHAIRES, Ben**
May 23, 1827, 5 miles WNW Greensboro, Gadsden Co. W 1/2 NE 1/4 Sect. 3 Tp. 2 R. 6, north and west.

**1478. CHAIRES, Ben**
(DUP) May 23, 1827, 5 miles WNW Greensboro, Gadsden Co. E 1/2 NE 1/4 Sect. 3 Tp. 2 R. 6, north and west.

**1479. CHAIRES, Ben**
May 23, 1827, 5 miles W Greensboro, Gadsden Co. W 1/2 SW 1/4 Sect. 2 Tp. 2 R. 6, north and west.

**1569. CHAIRES, Benj.**
May 25, 1827, 2 1/2 miles SSW Greenwood, Jackson Co. W 1/2 NW 1/4 Sect. 34 Tp. 5 R. 10, north and west.

**1570. CHAIRES, Benj.**
(DUP) May 25, 1827, 1 1/2 miles S Marianna, Jackson Co. W 1/2 NE 1/4 Sewct. 15 Tp. 4 R. 10, north and west. Transferred to **Grove A. PARK**, with request to deliver the patent to him.

**1571. CHAIRES, Benj.**
May 25, 1827, 1 mile S Marianna, Jackson Co. W 1/2 SE 1/4 Sect. 10 Tp. 4 R. 10, north and west.

**1572. CHAIRES, Benj.**
May 25, 1827, 1 1/2 miles N Marianna, Jackson Co. W 1/2 NE 1/4 Sect. 33 Tp. 5 R. 10, north and west.

**1573. CHAIRES, Benj.**
May 25, 1827, 2 miles NW Marianna, Jackson Co. E 1/2 SE 1/4 Sect. 28 Tp. 5 R. 10, north and west.

**1575. CHAIRES, Benj.**
May 25, 1827, 3 miles NNW Marianna, Jackson Co. W 1/2 NW 1/4 Sect. 28 Tp. 5 R. 10, north and west.

**1576. CHAIRES, Benj.**
May 25, 1827, 3 miles NNW Marianna, Jackson Co. E 1/2 NW 1/4 Sect. 28 Tp. 5 R. 10, north and west.

**1577. CHAIRES, Benj.**
(DUP) May 25, 1827, 4 miles NW Marianna, Jackson Co. E 1/2 NW 1/4 Sect. 30 Tp. 5 R. 10, north and west.

**1578. CHAIRES, Benj.**
(DUP) May 25, 1827, 1 1/2 miles N Marianna, Jackson Co. E 1/2 NE 1/4 Sect. 33 Tp. 5 R. 10, north and west.

**1579. CHAIRES, Benj.**
May 25, 1827, 2 miles N Marianna, Jackson Co. W 1/2 SE 1/4 Sect. 28 Tp. 5 R. 10, north and west.

**1303. CHAIRES, Benjamin**
April 25, 1827, 3 miles SW Chaires, Leon Co. W 1/2 NE 1/4 Sect. 9 Tp 1 R. 2, south and east.

**1304. CHAIRES, Benjamin**
April 25, 1827, 5 miles E Lutterloh, Leon Co. W 1/2 SW 1/4 Sect. 31 Tp. 1 R. 2, north and east.

**1305. CHAIRES, Benjamin**
April 25, 1827, 3 1/2 miles SW Chaires, Leon Co. W 1/2 NE 1/4 Sect. 9 Tp. 1 R. 2, south and east.

**1743. CHAIRES, Benjamin**
June 4, 1827, 3 miles W by S Chaires, Leon Co. SW 1/4 Sect. 32 Tp. 1 R. 2, north and east.

**1744. CHAIRES, Benjamin**
June 4, 1827, 3 1/2 miles W by S Chaires, Leon Co. E 1/2 SE 1/4 Sect. 31 Tp. 1 R. 2, north and east.

**1745. CHAIRES, Benjmain**
June 4, 1827, 3 1/2 miles W Chaires, Leon Co. NE 1/4 Sect. 31 Tp.1 R. 2, north and east.

**1746. CHAIRES, Benjamin**
(DUP) June 4, 1827, 1 1/2 miles W Chaires, Leon Co. S 1/2 Sect. 28 Tp. 1 R. 2, north and east.

**1747. CHAIRES, Benjmain**
June 4, 1827, 1 1/2 miles W by S of Chaires, Leon Co. E 1/2 SE 1/4 Sect. 33 Tp. 1 R. 2, north and east.

**1748. CHAIRES, Benjamin**
(DUP) June 4, 1827, 1 3/4 miles W by S of Chaires, Leon Co. E 1/2 NW 1/4 Sect. 33 Tp. 1 R. 2, north and east.

**1749. CHAIRES, Benjamin**
(DUP) June 4, 1827, 3 3/4 miles W by S of Chaires, Leon Co. E 1/2 SW 1/4 Sect. 30 Tp. 1 R. 2, north and east.

**1750. CHAIRES, Benjamin**
(DUP) June 4, 1827, 2 1/2 miles NW of Chaires, Leon Co. W 1/2 NW 1/4 Sect. 22 Tp. 1 R. 2, north and east.

**1768. CHAIRES, Benjamin**
June 4, 1827, 3 miles NW of Chaires, Leon Co. E 1/2 NE 1/4 Sect. 21 Tp. 1 R. 2, north and east.

**1769. CHAIRES, Benjamin**
June 4, 1827, 2 1/2 miles NW of Chaires, Leon Co. E 1/2 NE 1/4 Sect. 21 Tp. 1 R. 2, north and east.

**1933. CHAIRES, Benjamin**
June 23, 1827, at Bradfordville, Leon Co. W 1/2 SW 1/4 Sect. 22 Tp. 1 R. 2, north and east.

**1934. CHAIRES, Benjamin**
June 23, 1827, 1/2 mile S Waukenah, Jefferson Co. W 1/2 NE 1/4 Sect. 10 Tp. 1 R. 4, south and east.

**1935. CHAIRES, Benjamin**
June 23, 1827, 9 miles ESE Tallahassee, Leon Co. W 1/2 NW 1/4 Sect. 20 Tp. 1 R. 2, south and east.

**1936. CHAIRES, Benjamin**
June 23, 1827, 8 miles E by N Talla$hassee, Leon Co. E 1/2 NW 1/4 Sect. 27 Tp. 1 R. 2, north and east.

**1937. CHAIRES, Benjamin**
June 23, 1827, 1/2 mile W Chaires, Leon Co. E 1/2 SW 1/4 Sect. 27 Tp. 1 R. 2, north and east.

**1798. CHAIRES, Benjamin**
(Benj.) June 5, 1827, N of Marianna, Jackson Co. E 1/2 NW 1/4 Sect. 3 Tp. 4 R. 10, north and west.

**1964. CHAIRES, Benjamin**
(Benj.) June 29, 1827, 5 miles SW El Destino, Leon Co. W 1/2 SW 1/4 Sect. 20 Tp. 1 R. 2, south and east.

**1965. CHAIRES, Benjamin**
June 29, 1827, 4 miles E Tallahassee, Leon Co. E 1/2 SW 1/4 Sect. 2 Tp. 1 R. 1, south and east.

**1966. CHAIRES, Benjamin**
(Ben) June 29, 1827, 5 miles SW El Destino, Leon Co. SE 1/4 Sect. 19 Tp. 1 R. 2, south and east.

**2066. CHAIRES, Benjamin**
Sept. 23, 1827, 1/2 mile SE Capitola, Leon Co. W 1/2 SE 1/4 Sect. 29 Tp. 1 R. 3, north and east.

**2067. CHAIRES, Benjamin**
Sept. 23, 1827, 1/2 mile E Capitola, Leon Co. W 1/2 NE 1/4 Sect. 29 Tp. 1 R. 3, north and east.

**2068. CHAIRES, Benjamin**
Sept. 23, 1827, 1/4 mile E Capitola, Leon Co. NW 1/4 Sect. 29 Tp. 1 R. 3, north and east.

**2069. CHAIRES, Benjamin**
Sept. 23, 1827, at Capitola, Leon Co. E 1/2 NE 1/4 Sect. 31 Tp. 1 R. 3, north and east.

**2070. CHAIRES, Benjamin**
Sept. 23, 1827, 1/2 mile SE Capitola, Leon Co. E. 1/2 SW 1/4 Sect. 29 Tp. 1 R. 3, north and east.

**2231. CHAIRES, Benjamin**
(Ben) Jan. 21, 1828, 1/4 mile W Chaires, Leon Co. W 1/2 SE 1/4 Sect. 27 Tp. 1 R. 2, north and east.

**2230. CHAIRES, Benjamin**
(Benj.) Jan. 22, 1828, 1/2 mile SW Chaires, Leon Co. W 1/2 NE 1/4 Sect. 34 Tp. 1 R. 2, north and east.

**2762. CHAIRES, Benjamin**
(Benj.) Feb. 25, 1829, 1 mile S Cody, Jefferson Co. E 1/2 NE 1/4 Sect. 31 Tp. 1 R. 3, south and east.

**2287. CHAIRES, Benjamin**
(Ben) March 10, 1828, in Marianna, Jackson Co. W 1/2 NW 1/4 Sect. 10 Tp. 4 R. 10, north and west.

**3160. CHAIRES, Benjamin**
Dec. 10, 1829, c. 2 miles SW Alma, Leon Co. (157 acres) Lot No. 5 Sect. 3 Tp. 2 R. 4, north and east.

**5263. CHAIRES, Benjamin**
Nov. 14, 1835, 1 1/4 miles N of Corey, Leon Co. NE 1/4 Sect. 17 Tp. 1 R. 2, south and east.

**6950. CHAIRES, Benjamin**
March 25, 1837, 3/4 miles SW Simsville, Jackson Co. W 1/2 NW 1/4 and E 1/2 SE 1/4 Sect. 13 Tp. 3 R. 10, north and west.

**6951. CHAIRES, Benjamin**
March 25, 1837, just W Simsville, Jackson Co. SE 1/4 Sect. 12 Tp. 3 R. 10, north and west.

**6952. CHAIRES, Benjamin**
Mar. 25, 1837, 3/4 mile SSE Rock Creek, Jackson Co. E 1/2 NE 1/4 and NW 1/4 NE 1/4 Sect. 30 Tp. 3 R. 9, north and west.

**6953. CHAIRES, Benjamin**
Mar. 25, 1837, 1/2 mile SW Rock Creek, Jackson Co. E 1/2 SE 1/4 Sect. 19 Tp. 3 R. 9, north and west.

**6954. CHAIRES, Benjamin**
Mar. 25, 1837, 1 mile SW Simsville,

Jackson Co. NW 1/4 SE 1/4 Sect. 13 Tp. 3 R. 10, north and west.

**1326. CHAIRES, Green N.**
May 7, 1827, 1 mile SW Capps, Jefferson Co. W 1/2 NW 1/4 Sect. 12 Tp. 1 R. 4, south and east.

**1327. CHAIRES, Green N.**
May 7, 1827, 3/4 mile S Waukenah, Jefferson Co. E 1/2 NW 1/4 Sect. 11 Tp. 1 R. 4, south and east.

**1355. CHAIRES, Green N.**
May 12, 1827, 1/2 mile SSE Waukenah, Jefferson Co. W 1/2 NW 1/4 Sect. 10 Tp. 1 R. 4, south and east.

**1356. CHAIRES, Green N.**
May 12, 1827, 1/2 mile SSE Waukenah, Jefferson Co. E 1/2 SW 1/4 Sect. 10 Tp. 1 R. 4, south and east.

**1357. CHAIRES, Green N.**
May 12, 1827, 3/4 mile S Waukenah, Jefferson Co. W 1/2 SE 1/3 Sect. 10 Tp. 1 R. 4, south and east.

**2159. CHAIRES, Green H.**
Dec. 24, 1827, 2 1/2 miles W by S Chaires, Leon Co. E 1/2 NE 1/4 Sect. 32 Tp. 1 R. 2, north and east.

**2250. CHAIRES, Green H.**
Feb. 11, 1828, 2 miles WNW Capitola, Leon Co. W 1/2 NE 1/4 Sect. 23 Tp. 1 R. 2, north and east.

**2251. CHAIRES, Green H.**
Feb. 11, 1828, 2 miles NW Chaires, Leon Co. E 1/2 NW 1/4 Sect.22 Tp. 1 R. 2, north and east.

**2288. CHAIRES, Green H.**
March 10, 1828, in Marianna, Jackson Co. E 1/2 NE 1/4 Sect. 3 Tp. 4 R. 10, north and west.

**2289. CHAIRES, Green H.**
March 10, 1828, 2 1/2 miles NE Round Lake, Jackson Co. E 1/2 SE 1/4 Sect. 7 Tp. 3 R. 11, north and west.

**3231. CHAIRES, Green H.**
Jan. 25, 1830, 2 miles NE Chaires, Leon Co. E 1/2 SW 1/4 Sect. 24 Tp. 1 R. 2, north and east. Transferred to **Wm. COPELAND**, Jan. 25, 1830. Witness: **Ben CHAIRES**. (This transfer was registered and filed in the Register's Office, Feb. 1, 1830. **G. W. WARD**, Reg.)

**4843. CHAIRES, Green H.**
Feb. 3, 1835, 3 miles W of Chaires, Leon Co. W 1/2 NW 1/4 Sect. 33 Tp. 1 R. 2, north and east.

**4865. CHAIRES, Green H.**
Feb. 14, 1835, 2 miles N by W of Chaires, Leon Co. W 1/2 SW 1/4 Sect. 15 Tp.1 R. 2, north and east.

**5293. CHAIRES, Green H.**
Dec. 1, 1835, 1 mile W of Chaires, Leon Co. E 1/2 NW 1/4 Sect. 34 Tp. 1 R. 2, north and east.

**5916. CHAIRES, Green H.**
Oct. 22, 1836, 3/4 mile N of Midway, Gadsden Co. NE 1/4 NW 1/4 Sect. 4 Tp.1 R. 2, south and east.

**6417. CHAIRES, Green H.**
Jan. 4, 1837, 3 miles W by S Chaires, Leon Co. NW 1/4 NE 1/4 Sect. 32 Tp. 1 R. 2, north and east.

**818. CHAIRES, Tom Peter**
(Of Fla.) Dec. 4, 1826, 4 miles SSW Waukenah, Jefferson Co. E 1/2 SE 1/4 Sect. 21 Tp. 1 R. 4, south and east.

**820. CHAIRES, Tom Peter**
(Of Fla.) Dec. 4, 1826, a mile ENE Wacissa, Jefferson Co. E 1/2 NE 1/4 Sect. 28 Tp. 1 R. 4, south and east.

**819. CHAIRES, Tom Peter**
(Of Fla.) Dec. 4, 1826, 3 miles S of Waukenah, Jefferson Co. W 1/2 SW 1/4 Sect. 22 Tp. 1 R. 4, south and east.

**3049. CHAIRES, Tom Peter**
Sept. 17, 1829, 3 miles WSW El Destino, Leon Co. N 1/2 SW 1/4 Sect. 15 Tp. 1 R. 2, south and east.

**3544. CHAIRES, Tom Peter**
June 26, 1830, 1/2 mile NE El Destino, Jefferson Co. E 1/2 SE 1/4 Sect. 6 Tp. 1 R. 3, south and east.

**3545. CHAIRES, Tom Peter**
June 26, 1830, just N El Destino, Jefferson Co. W 1/2 SW 1/4 Sect. 6 Tp. 1 R. 3, south and east.

**3996. CHAIRES, Tom Peter**
July 6, 1831, at Corey, Leon Co. W 1/2 NE 1/4 Sect. 22 Tp. 1 R. 2, south and east.

**3997. CHAIRES, Tom Peter**
July 6, 1831, at Corey, Leon Co. E 1/2 NE 1/4 Sect. 21 Tp. 6 R. 11, north and west.

**4269. CHAIRES, Tom Peter**
Jan. 7, 1833, 2 miles SW Chaires, Leon Co. W 1/2 NE 1/4 Sect. 10 Tp. 1 R. 2, south and east.

**4270. CHAIRES, Tom Peter**
Jan. 7, 1833, 1 3/4 miles E of Chaires, Leon Co. W 1/2 SE 1/4 Sect. 10 Tp. 1 R. 2, south and east.

**4034. CHAIRS, Benjamin**
July 19, 1831, 7 miles SW of Westlake, Hamilton Co. SE 1/4 Sect. 31 Tp. 1 R. 13, north and east.

**2843. CHAMBERS, John C.**
July 26, 1854, 1 1/2 miles N by E of Citra, Marion Co. NE 1/4 NE 1/4 Sect. 26 Tp. 12 R. 22, south and east. Transferred to **James HOBKIRK**, Feb. 20, 1856. Patent delivered Mar. 21, 1868.

**202. CHAMBLISS, Ephriam**
(DUP) Dec. 30, 1826, 2 miles W Campbellton, Jackson Co. E 1/2 NE 1/4 Sect. 3 Tp. 6 R. 12, north and west.

**949. CHANCE, Joseph**
Jan. 20, 1827, 1 mile NW Monticello, Jefferson Co. W 1/2 NW 1/4 Sect. 36 Tp. 2 R. 4, north and east.

**2446. CHANCE, Joseph**
July 28, 1828, 2 1/4 miles W Dills, Jefferson Co. W 1/2 NE 1/4 Sect. 3 Tp. 2 R. 5, north and east.

**1550. CHAPMAN, Daniel B.**
Dec. 9, 1852, 1/2 mile W of Spink, Sumter Co. NW 1/4 SW 1/4 Sect. 23 Tp. 19 R. 23, south and east. Patent delivered Mar. 15, 1875.

**2281. CHAPMAN, John**
Mar. 7, 1823, at Stringer, Leon Co. W 1/2 SW 1/4 Sect. 4 Tp. 1 R. 1, north and west.

**4181. CHAPMAN, John**
June 28, 1832, 5 1/4 miles E of Iamonia, Leon Co. NW 1/4 NW 1/4 Sect. 24 Tp. 3 R. 2, north and east.

**4301. CHAPMAN, John**
Feb. 7, 1833, 3 1/4 miles SW by S of Miccosukee, Leon Co. E 1/2 SE 1/4 Sect. 19 Tp. 3 R. 3, north and east.

**4302. CHAPMAN, John**
Feb. 8, 1833, 1 mile NW of Stringer, Leon Co. NW 1/4 SW 1/4 Sect. 20 Tp. 3 R. 3, north and east.

**4844. CHAPMAN, John**
Feb. 5, 1835, 3/4 mile N of Stringer, Jefferson Co. W 1/2 NW 1/4 Sect. 21 Tp. 3 R. 3, north and east.

**5187. CHAPMAN, John**
Oct. 5, 1835, 1 1/4 miles NNW of Stringer, Leon Co. E 1/2 NE 1/4 Sect. 20 Tp. 3 R. 3, north and east.

**5249. CHAPMAN, John**
Nov. 6, 1835, 1/4 mile SW of Lloyd, Jefferson Co. E 1/2 SW 1/4 Sect. 21 Tp. 3 R. 3, north and east.

**5846. CHAPMAN, John**
Sept. 14, 1836, 2 1/2 miles NW of Stringer, Jefferson Co. W 1/2 NW 1/4 Sect. 19 Tp. 3 R. 3, north and east.

**6064. CHAPMAN, John**
Nov. 21, 1836, 1 1/2 miles E Stringer, Leon Co. W 1/2 NE 1/4 Sect. 19 Tp. 3 R. 3, north and east.

**6524. CHAPMAN, John**
Jan. 12, 1837, 3 miles NW Copeland, Leon Co. E 1/2 NW 1/4 Sect. 19 Tp. 3 R. 3, north and east.

**6730. CHAPMAN, John**
Feb. 2, 1837, 3 miles WNW Copeland, Jefferson Co. E 1/2 SW 1/4 Sect. 24 Tp. 3 R. 2, north and east.

**6835. CHAPMAN, John**
March 4, 1837, 2 miles W by N Stringer, Leon Co. E 1/2 SW 1/4 Sect. 24 Tp. 3 R. 2, north and east.

**8129. CHAPMAN, John C.**
Nov. 8, 1839, 4 miles SE by S Parker, Holmes Co. N 1/2 Lot No. 5 Sect. 31 Tp. 6 R. 16, north and west.

**3149. CHAPMAN, Joshua**
Dec. 3, 1829, 4 miles E Iamonia, Leon Co. E 1/2 NE 1/4 Sect. 23 Tp. 3 R. 2, north and east.

**4719. CHAPMAN, Joshua**
Dec. 16, 1834, 3 1/2 miles E of Iamonia, Leon Co. E 1/2 SE 1/4 Sect. 15 Tp. 3 R. 2, north and east.

**3144. CHAPPELL, Benjamin**
Dec. 2, 1829, just S Jamieson, Gadsden Co. W 1/2 SE 1/4 Sect. 7 Tp. 3 R. 2, north and west.

**CHAPPELL, Benj.** see **BUTLER, Wm.** #3064

**668. CHARLES, Rebecca**
Oct. 26, 1848, c. 2 miles SE Dell, Suwannee Co. Lot No. 1 Sect. 21 Tp. 4 R. 11, south and east. Patent delivered March 5, 1860.

**669. CHARLES, Rebecca**
Nov. 14, 1848, c. 2 miles SE Dell, Suwannee Co. Lot No. 2 Fractional Sect. 21 Tp. 4 R. 11, south and east.

Patent delivered March 5, 1860.
**5019. CHARLES, Andrew J.**
Sept. 19, 1832, at Chancey, Lafayette Co. Lot No. 3 Sect. 6 Tp. 3 R. 11, south and east.
**7619. CHARLES, Andrew J.**
Aug. 31, 1838, 6 miles NNW Luraville, Suwannee Co. Lot No. 6 Sect. 5 Tp. 4 R. 11, south and east.
**5001. CHASE, William H.**
June 16, 1835, 1/2 mile NE of Pensacola, Escambia Co. Fractional Sect. 29 Tp. 2 R. 30, south and west.
**5008. CHASE, William H.**
June 16, 1835, 1/2 mile N of Pensacola, Escambia Co. Fractional Sect. 27 Tp. 2 R. 30, south and west.
**7869. CHASON, Jacob**
Feb. 14, 1839, 2 miles NE Gadsden, Gadsden Co. E 1/2 SE 1/4 Sect. 12 Tp. 1 R. 2, north and west.
**7917. CHASON, Jacob**
Mar. 11, 1839, 2 miles NNW Lake Jackson, Leon Co. S 1/2 Lot No. 7 Sect. 25 Tp. 2 R. 2, north and west.
**8556. CHASON, Jacob**
Sept. 19, 1842, 1 mile NNW San Helena, Leon Co. NE 1/4 NW 1/4 Sect. 18 Tp. 1 R. 1, north and west.
**8738. CHASON, Lucinda**
Dec. 10, 1844, 3/4 mile S Lake Jackson, Leon Co. NW 1/4 NE 1/4 Sect. 18 Tp. 1 R. 1, north and west.
**5171. CHASTEEN, Thomas**
Sept. 30, 1835, 1 mile W by N of Copeland, Leon Co. W 1/2 NW 1/4 Sect. 36 Tp. 3 R. 2, north and east.
**5172. CHASTEEN, Thomas**
Sept. 30, 1835, 1 1/2 miles W by N of Copeland, Leon Co. E 1/2 NE 1/4 Sect. 35 Tp. 3 R. 2, north and east.
**2596. CHATMAN, John**
Dec. 31, 1828, 1/2 mile E Stringer, Leon Co. E 1/2 SW 1/4 Sect. 27 Tp. 3 R. 3, north and east.
**5932. CHESHIRE, Barnabas**
Oct. 27, 1836, 1 mile S by E of Facil, Hamilton Co. SE 1/4 SE 1/4 Sect. 34 Tp. 1 R. 15, south and east.
**6320. CHESHIRE, Hander**
May 14, 1840, 4 miles NNE Westlake, Hamilton Co. SW 1/4 NW 1/4 Sect. 36 Tp. 2 R. 12, north and east.
**6276. CHESHIRE, William**
Dec. 22, 1836, 1 1/2 miles W Facil, Hamilton Co. NE 1/4 NE 1/4 Sect. 29 Tp. 1 R. 15, south and east.
**8727. CHESNUTT, William**
Nov. 28, 1844, 4 miles N by E Aucilla, Jefferson Co. E 1/2 NW 1/4 Sect. 1 Tp. 1 R. 4, north and east.
**5815. CHESTER, Abner**
Aug. 30, 1836, 1 mile SE by S of Concord, Gadsden Co. SW 1/4 SW 1/4 Sect. 20 Tp. 3 R. 1, north and west.
**5821. CHESTER, Abner**
Sept. 2, 1836, 2 miles SE Concord, Gadsden Co. W 1/2 NW 1/4 Sect. 29 Tp. 3 R. 1, north and west.
**7819. CHESTER, Abner**
Jan. 16, 1839, 3 miles N Lake Jackson, Leon Co. E 1/2 NE 1/4 Sect. 30 Tp. 3 R. 1, north and west.
**947. CHICK, Wm. M. F.**
Jan. 19, 1827, 6 miles S Quincy, Gadsden Co. E 1/2 W 1/2 Sect. 28 Tp. 2 R. 3, north and west. Transferred to **Henry GEE**, Mar. 2, 1827.
**3603. CHIFFER, Richard**
Sept. 6, 1830, 1/2 mile NW Lake Jackson Station, Leon Co. W 1/2 NW 1/4 Sect. 31 Tp. 2 R. 1, north and west. Paid in Script Certificate No. 167, issued to **Alex'r MACOMB**, survivor of Edgar and Macomb.
**7075. CHILDRESS, William**
Nov. 6, 1837, at Ross, Leon Co. NW 1/4 NW 1/4 Sect. 27 Tp. 1 R. 2, south and east.
**4500. CHISLER, Abner**
Jan. 1, 1833(1834?) 1/2 mile S of Concord, Gadsden Co. NE 1/4 SE 1/4 Sect. 19 Tp. 3 R. 1, north and west.
**41. CHRISTOFF, Lewis**
Nov. 7, 1826, c. 3 miles SW Greenwood, Jackson Co. W 1/2 NW 1/4 Sect. 8 Tp. 5 R. 10, north and west. Transferred Nov. 7, 1826, to **L. M. STONE** by David **THOMAS**, atty. in fact for **Lewis CHRISTOFF**. Transferred May 2, 1827, to **R. C. ALLEN & Co.** by L. M. STONE.
**1205. CHRISTOPHER, S.**
(DUP) Mar. 13, 1827, 4 miles SSE Miccosukee, Leon Co. NW 1/4 Sect. 26 Tp. 2 R. 3, north and east.
**1206. CHRISTOPHER, S.**
(DUP) Mar. 13, 1827, 3 mile S

Miccosukee, Leon Co. E 1/2 NE 1/4 Sect. 27 Tp. 2 R. 3, north and east.
**1207. CHRISTOPHER, S.**
(DUP) Mar. 13, 1827, 5 miles SSE Miccosukee, Leon Co. E 1/2 NE 1/4 Sect. 34 Tp. 2 R. 3, north and east.
**2355. CHRISTOPHER, Sam'l S.**
April 29, 1828, 3 1/2 miles E Wadesboro, Jefferson Co. W 1/2 NW 1/4 Sect. 2 Tp. 1 R. 3, north and east.
**2730. CHRISTOPHER, Sam'l S.**
Feb. 12, 1829, 3 1/2 miles E Wadesboro, Jefferson Co. E 1/2 SW 1/4 Sect. 2 Tp. 1 R. 3, north and east.
**2731. CHRISTOPHER, Sam'l S.**
Feb. 12, 1829, 2 1/2 miles E Wadesboro, Jefferson Co. W 1/2 SE 1/4 Sect. 2 Tp. 1 R. 3, north and east.
**5207. CHRISTOPHER, Samuel**
Oct. 13, 1835, 2 miles N of Lloyd, Jefferson Co. E 1/2 SW 1/4 Sect. 34 Tp. 2 R. 3, north and east.
**2525. CHRISTOPHER, Samuel S.**
Oct. 15, 1828, 3 miles E by N Wadesboro, Leon Co. W 1/2 SW 1/4 Sect. 34 Tp. 2 R. 3, north and east.
**5059. CHRISTOPHER, Samuel S.**
Dec. 9, 1835, 3 1/2 E by N of Wadesboro, Leon Co. W 1/2 NE 1/4 Sect. 2 Tp. 1 R. 3, north and east.
**5344. CHRISTOPHER, Samuel S.**
Dec. 11, 1835, at Lloyd, Jefferson Co. E 1/2 SW 1/4 Sect. 11 Tp. 1 R. 3, north and east.
**7018. CHURCH, Lucius**
June 15, 1837, 1/4 mile N Cherrylake, Madison Co. W 1/2 SW 1/4 Sect. 9 Tp. 2 R. 9, north and east.
**7019. CHURCH, Lucius**
June 15, 1837, 1/2 mile N Cherrylake, Madison Co. W 1/2 SW 1/4 Sect. 4 Tp. 2 R. 9, north and east.
**7292. CHURCH, Lucius**
Feb. 2, 1838, 1/4 mile N Cherrylake (town), Madison Co. NE 1/4 NW 1/4 Sect. 9 Tp. 2 R. 9, north and east.
**7293. CHURCH, Lucius**
Feb. 2, 1838, 1/4 mile W Cherrylake, Madison Co. E 1/2 SW 1/4 Sect. 8 Tp. 2 R. 9, north and east.
**7294. CHURCH, Lucius**
Feb. 2, 1838, 1/4 mile SW Cherrylake, Madison Co. E 1/2 NW 1/4 Sect. 17 Tp. 2 R. 9, north and east.
**7296. CHURCH, Lucius**
Feb. 2, 1838, at Cherrylake (town), Madison Co. W 1/2 SE 1/4 Sect. 8 Tp. 2 R. 9, north and east.
**8076. CHURCH, Lucius**
Sept. 19, 1839, 3/4 mile N Cherrylake (town), Madison Co. E 1/2 SW 1/4 Sect. 4 Tp. 2 R. 9, north and east.
**8077. CHURCH, Lucius**
Sept. 19, 1839, at Cherrylake, Madison Co. E 1/2 NE 1/4 and E 1/2 SE 1/4 Sect. 8 Tp. 2 R. 9, north and east.
**8079. CHURCH, Lucius**
Sept. 19, 1839, 1/4 mile W Cherrylake, Madison Co. NE 1/4 W 1/2 SE 1/4 Sect. 5 Tp. 2 R. 9, north and east.
**8079. CHURCH, Lucius**
Sept. 19, 1839, 1/4 mile S Cherrylake, Madison Co. W 1/2 SE 1/4 Sect. 17 Tp. 2 R. 9, north and east.
**159. CLARK, Jno. or John**
(Assignee **B. MAYO**) Dec. 28, 1826, 4 miles N Cottondale, Jackson Co. NE 1/4 Sect. 14 Tp. 5 R. 11, north and west.
**160. CLARK, Jno. or John**
(Assignee of **Wm. PADGETT**) Dec. 28, 1826, 3 miles NW Cottondale, Jackson Co. (Pre-emption) SE 1/4 Sect. 13 Tp. 5 R. 11, north and west.
**161. CLARK, Jno. or John**
(Assignee of **Peter THOMPSON**) Dec. 28, 1826, 4 miles N Cottondale, Jackson Co. NW 1/4 Sect. 12 Tp. 5 R. 11, north and west.
**162. CLARK, Jno. or John**
(Assignee of **Nathan SPEARS**) Dec. 28, 1826, 3 miles N Cottondale, Jackson Co. SE 1/4 Sect. 11 Tp. 5 R. 11, north and west.
**163. CLARK, Jno or John**
(Assignee of **Jno. SULLIVAN**) Dec. 28, 1826, 3 1/2 miles NW Cottondale, Jackson Co. NW 1/4 Sect. 13 Tp. 5 R. 11, north and west.
**365. CLARK, Jno. or John**
(Asssignee of **Mather NUGENT**) April 24, 1827, 5 miles ENE of Cottondale, Jackson Co. NE 1/4 Sect. 24 Tp. 5 R. 11, north and west.
**367. CLARK, Jno. or John**
(Assigneee of **Elijah PADGET**) May 1, 1827, 5 miles NE Cottondale, Jackson Co. W 1/2 NW 1/4 Sect. 14 Tp. 5

R. 11, north and west.

**368. CLARK, Jno. or John**
May 1, 1827, 6 miles NE of Cottondale, Jackson Co. NE 1/4 Sect.11 Tp. 5 R. 11, north and west.
See **Chas. WILLIAMSON**

**CLARK, John R. W.** see **William M. LOFTIN # 554**

**8654. CLARK, Thomas V.**
Mar. 15, 1844, 5 1/2 miles E Stringer, Jefferson Co. NE 1/4 Sect. 34 Tp. 3 R. 4, north and east.

**2082. CLARK, Thos.**
(Of Ga.) Oct. 27, 1827, 3 miles E Stringer, Jefferson Co. W 1/2 SE 1/4 Sect. 25 Tp. 3 R.3, north and east.

**4049. CLARK, William G.**
July 28, 1831, 2 miles SE of Waukeenah, Jefferson Co. E 1/2 NE 1/4 Sect. 13 Tp. 1 R. 4, south and east.

**4050. CLARK, William G.**
July 28, 1831, 2 miles S by E of Capps, Jefferson Co. E 1/2 NW 1/4 Sect. 18 Tp. 1 R. 5, south and east.

**5496. CLARK, William G.**
Feb. 27, 1836, 2 1/2 miles N by E of Braswells, Jefferson Co. W 1/2 SW 1/4 Sect. 3 Tp. 1 R. 4, south and east.

**2092. CLARK, William D.**
Aug. 22, 1853, 2 miles SE of Thomasville, Alachua Co. S 1/2 Lot No. 13 Sect. 31 Tp. 7 R. 20, south and east.

**2093. CLARK, William D.**
Aug. 22, 1853, 2 1/4 miles SE of Thomasville, Alachua Co. S 1/2 Lot No. 11 Sect. 31 Tp. 7 R. 20, south and east. Patent delivered Nov. 21, 1856.

**3601. CLARK, Wm. G.**
Sept. 4, 1830, at Waukenah, Jefferson Co. W 1/2 NE 1/4 Sect. 3 Tp. 1 R. 4, south and east. Purchased with Script issued to **Alex'r MACOMB**, survivor of Edgar and Macomb dated May 30, 1829.

**3602. CLARK, Wm. G.**
Sept. 4, 1830, at Waukenah, Jefferson Co. E 1/2 NW 1/4 Sect. 3 Tp. 1 R. 4, south and east. Purchased with Scrip No. 218, issued to **Alex'r MACOMB**, survivor of Edgar and Macomb, dated May 30, 1829.

**7467. CLARK, William G.**
May 12, 1838, 1/2 mile SSW Waukenah, Jefferson Co. E 1/2 NW 1/4 Sect. 9 Tp. 1 R. 4, south and east.

**CLARK, Wylie P.** see **William M. LOFTIN**

**3926. CLARKE, Thomas**
March 26, 1831, 3 miles E Stringer, Leon Co. W 1/2 NE 1/4 Sect. 25 Tp. 3 R. 3, north and east.

**6361. CLARKE, Thomas**
Dec. 31, 1836, 1/2 mile E Felkel, Leon Co. SW 1/4 Sect. 2 Tp. 2 R. 2, north and east.

**6362. CLARKE, Thomas**
Dec. 31, 1836, 3/4 mile SE Felkel, Leon Co. NW 1/4 NW 1/4 Sect.11 Tp. 2 R. 2, north and east.

**6363. CLARKE, Thomas**
Dec. 31, 1836, 1/2 mile S Felkel, Leon Co. E 1/2 NE 1/4 Sect. 10 Tp. 2 R. 2, north and east.

**6364. CLARKE, Thomas**
Dec. 31, 1836, at Felkel, Leon Co. SE 1/4 SE 1/4 Sect. 3 Tp. 2 R. 2, north and east.

**188. CLEMENTS, Ben or Benj.**
(Of Tennessee) May 19, 1825, 2 miles SE Tallahassee, Leon Co. W 1/2 NE 1/4 Sect. 11 Tp. 1 R. 1, south and east.

**189. CLEMENTS, Ben or Benj.**
(Of Tennessee) May 19, 1825, 2 miles SE Tallahassee, Leon Co. E 1/2 NE 1/4 Sect. 11 Tp. 1 R. 1, south and east.

**1797. CLEMENTS, Ben or Benj.**
June 5, 1827, 3 miles E Graceville, Jackson Co. W 1/2 NE 1/4 Sect. 30 Tp. 7 R. 12, north and west.

**1786. CLEMENTS, Ben or Benj.**
(DUP) June 5, 1827, 4 miles W by S Greenwood, Jackson Co. W 1/2 NW 1/4 Sect. 3 Tp. 5 R. 10, north and west.

**1790. CLEMENTS, Ben or Benj.**
June 5, 1827, 5 miles E Welchton, Jackson Co. W 1/2 NE 1/4 Sect. 28 Tp. 6 R. 11, north and west.

**1791. CLEMENTS, Ben or Benj.**
(DUP) June 5, 1827, 4 miles N by E of Campbellton, in Alabama. E 1/2 NE 1/4 Sect. 19 Tp. 7 R. 11, north and west.

**1792. CLEMENTS, Ben or Benj.**
June 5, 1827, 4 miles N Campbellton, in Alabama. E 1/2 NW 1/4 Sect. 20 Tp. 7 R. 11, north and west.

**1793. CLEMENTS, Ben or Benj.**

June 5, 1827, 4 miles N Campbellton, in Alabama. W 1/2 NW 1/4 Sect. 20 Tp. 7 R. 11, north and west.

**1794. CLEMENTS, Ben or Benj.**
June 5, 1827, 5 miles NNE Campbellton, in Alabama. E 1/2 NE 1/4 Sect. 20 Tp. 7 R. 11, north and west.

**1795. CLEMENTS, Ben or Benj.**
(DUP) June 5, 1827, 5 miles NE of Campbellton, in Alabama. W 1/2 NE 1/4 Sect. 20 Tp. 7 R. 11, north and west.

**1796. CLEMENTS, Ben or Benj.**
June 5, 1827, 4 miles ENE Graceville, Jackson Co. E 1/2 NE 1/4 Sect. 30 Tp. 7 R. 12, north and west.

**1825. CLEMENTS, Ben or Benj.**
June 5, 1827, 4 miles ENE of Graceville, Jackson Co. E 1/2 SE 1/4 Sect. 19 Tp. 7 R. 12, north and west.

**1826. CLEMENTS, Ben or Benj.**
June 5, 1827, 1 1/4 miles E Welchton, Jackson Co. E 1/2 NW 1/4 Sect. 31 Tp. 6 R. 11, north and west.(79.94 acres) Sold Jan. 23, 1827 to **W. S. MOORING** for $200.

**1827. CLEMENTS, Ben or Benj.**
June 5, 1827, 2 miles NE Graceville, Jackson Co. (and Alabama) W 1/2 SE 1/4 Sect. 19 Tp. 7 R. 12, north and west.

**1705. CLEMENTS, Jesse B.**
(DUP) May 30, 1827, 4 miles E Jacob, Jackson Co. E 1/2 NE 1/4 Sect. 21 Tp. 6 R. 11, north and west. Transferred June 4, 1827 to **Charles WILLIAMSON**.

**1706. CLEMENTS, Jesse B.**
(DUP) May 30, 1827, 4 miles E Jacob, Jackson Co. W 1/2 NE 1/4 Sect. 21 Tp. 6 R. 11, north and west. Transferred June 6, 1827, to **C. WILLIAMSON**.

**7281. CLEMENTS, John**
Jan. 30, 1838, 1/4 mile E Hamburg, Madison Co. SE 1/4 NE 1/4 Sect. 13 Tp. 2 R. 8, north and east.

**5750. CLEMENTS, John W.**
July 2, 1836, 3/4 mile W of Cherrylake (town), Madison Co. E 1/2 SE 1/4 Sect. 7 Tp. 2 R. 9, north and east.

**5751. CLEMENTS, John W.**
July 2, 1836, 2 miles SSE of Hamburg, Madison Co. NW 1/4 NE 1/4 and NE 1/4 NE 1/4 Sect. 13 Tp. 2 R. 8, north and east.

**6339. CLEMENTS, William**
Mar. 6, 1837, 5 miles E Iamonia, Leon Co. NW 1/4 SE 1/4 Sect. 24 Tp. 3 R. 2, north and east.

**9003. CLEMMONS, Chancy**
Jan. 26, 1891, 1 1/4 miles S by E Montbrook, Levy Co. SE 1/4 Sect. 32 TP. 13S R. 19E.

**5886. CLIFTON, Jack S.**
Oct. 6, 1836, 2 miles N by E of Bond, Madison Co. SW 1/4 NE 1/4 Sect. 2 Tp. 2 R. 8, north and east.

**7592. CLIFTON, Jack S.**
Aug. 15, 1838, 1/2 mile SE Hanson, Madison Co. W 1/2 SW 1/4 Sect. 35 Tp. 2 R. 10, north and east.

**2758. CLINE, George M.**
June 2, 1854, 3 miles N by E of Bass, Columbia Co. N 1/2 Lot No. 6 and N 1/2 Lot No. 7 Sect. 12 Tp. 4 R. 16, south and east.

**2007. CLOUD, Reuben**
July 20, 1827, 1 1/2 miles WSW Hermitage, Gadsden Co. E 1/2 NE 1/4 Sect.1 Tp. 3 R. 5, north and west. Endorsed to **Wiley LEWIS**, Dec. 31, 1832. Endorsed to **Jesse WATSON**, June 23, 1835.

**4253. CLOW, Dan C.**
Dec. 20, 1832. Illegible.

**295. CLYATT, Samuel M.**
Jan. 28, 1846, at Chiefland, Levy Co. E 1/2 NE 1/4 Sect. 12 Tp. 12 R. 14, south and east.

**698. CLYATT, Samuel M.**
Jan. 4, 1850, 2 miles SE Chiefland, Levy Co. E 1/2 SW 1/4 and SW 1/4 SE 1/4 Sect. 8 Tp. 12 R. 15, south and east. Patent delivered July 28, 1857.

**700. CLYATT, Samuel M.**
Jan. 4 1850, at Chiefland, Levy Co. SE 1/4 SW 1/4 Sect. 1 Tp. 12 R. 14, south and east. Patent delivered July 28, 1857.

**714. CLYATT, Samuel M.**
March 8, 1850, 1 mile SE Chiefland, Levy Co. NE 1/4 NE 1/4 Sect. 7 Tp. 12 R. 15, south and east.

**715. CLYATT, Samuel M.**
March 8, 1850, c. 2 miles SE Chiefland, Levy Co. E 1/2 SE 1/4 Sect. 18 and NW 1/4 NE 1/4 Sect. 19 Tp. 12

R. 15, south and east.

**1350. CLYATT, Samuel M.**
June 2, 1852, 1 1/4 miles W of Chiefland, Levy Co. NW 1/4 SW 1/4 Sect. 1 Tp. 12 R. 14, south and east. Patent delivered July 28, 1857.

**1351. CLYATT, Samuel M.**
June 2, 1852, 1 1/4 miles W of Chiefland, Levy Co. E 1/2 NE 1/4 and SE 1/4 NW 1/4 Sect. 3 Tp. 12 R. 14, south and east.

**2618. CLYATT, Samuel M.**
Mar. 15, 1854, 1 1/4 miles W by N of Chiefland, Levy Co. SE 1/4 SE 1/4 Sect. 34 Tp. 11 R. 14, south and east. Patent delivered Sept. 19, 1856.

**2619. CLYATT, Samuel M.**
Mar. 15, 1854, 1 1/4 miles E of Chiefland, Levy Co. SE 1/4 SE 1/4 Sect. 6 Tp. 12 R. 15, south and east. Patent delivered July 28, 1857.

**4932. CLYATT, William H.**
Jan. 5, 1859, 1 mile SSE of Columbia, Columbia Co. NW 1/4 and W 1/2 of NE 1/4 Sect. 14 Tp. 5 R. 10, south and east.

**COALTER, John see John H. BROCK**

**2326. COBB, Robert S.**
Mar. 21, 1828, 3 miles E by N MArianna, Jackson Co. W 1/2 SW 1/4 Sect. 31 Tp. 5 R. 9, north and west. Transferred May 3, 1828, to **Samuel STOWERY**.

**8906. COBERN, James**
Feb. 18, 1846, 2 miles N Dills, Jefferson Co. E 1/2 SW 1/4 Sect. 19 Tp. 3 R. 6, north and east.

**839. CODY, Burnett**
Jan. 10, 1827, 3 miles S Capps, Jefferson Co. W 1/2 NE 1/4 Sect. 24 Tp. 1 R. 4, south and east.

**3548. COE, Jesse**
July 2, 1830, 2 1/2 miles WNW Sawdust, Gadsden Co. W 1/2 NW 1/4 Sect. 19 Tp. 2 R. 4, north and west.

**3549. COE, Jesse**
July 2, 1830, c. 3 miles NW Sawdust, Gadsden Co. Lot No. 2 Sect. 18 Tp. 2 R. 4, north and west.

**4008. COE, Jesse**
July 16, 1831, 1/2 mile S of Sawdust, Gadsden Co. Lot No. 1 Sect. 28 Tp. 2 R. 4, north and west.

**4009. COE, Jesse**
July 16, 1831, 3 miles SE Sawdust, Gadsden Co. Lot No. 1 Sect. 34 Tp. 2 R. 4, north and west.

**4010. COE, Jesse**
July 16, 1831, 2 3/4 miles SW Sawdust, Gadsden Co. Lot No. 2 Sect. 34 Tp. 2 R. 4, north and west.

**4011. COE, Jesse**
July 16, 1831, 2 1/2 miles SW Sawdust, Gadsden Co. Lot No. 3 Sect. 34 Tp. 2 R. 4, north and west.

**6054. COE, Jesse**
Nov. 18, 1836, c. 1 mile W Watson, Liberty Co. Lot No. 3 Fractional Sect. 31 Tp. 2 R. 7, north and west.

**6720. COKER, Daniel**
Feb. 1, 1837, 2 miles W Myrick, Madison Co. NW 1/4 NE 1/4 Sect. 2 Tp. 1 R. 6, south and east.

**7254. COKER, Daniel**
Jan. 17, 1838, 5 miles W Myrick, Madison Co. NE 1/4 SE 1/4 Sect. 1 Tp. 1 R. 6, south and east.

**5000. COLE, Charles**
June 15, 1835, 3 miles NNE of Bradfordville, Leon Co. NE 1/4 NW 1/4 Sect. 11 Tp. 2 R. 1, north and east.

**601. COLE, James B.**
  **PRESCOTT, D.C.**
  **WILSON, Benj.**
Dec. 4, 1847, 8 1/2 miles E Highland, Clay Co. SW 1/4 SE 1/4 Sect. 28 Tp. 4 R. 24, south and east. Transferred to **George BRANNING** June 13, 1851. Patent delivered July 19, 1856.

**COLD, Joseph see Stephen BRYAN #320**

**572. COLE, Rich K.**
July 29, 1825, 5 miles WNW Tallahassee, Leon Co. SW 1/4 Sect. 21 Tp. 1 R. 1, north and west.

**6260. COLEMAN, Zacheus**
Dec. 21, 1836, 3 1/2 miles NW Alma, Leon Co. NE 1/4 SE 1/4 Sect. 20 Tp. 3 R. 4, north and east.

**8495. COLEMAN, Zachus**
Aug. 10, 1841, 5 miles SSE Fincher, Jefferson Co. SW 1/4 SW 1/4 Sect. 21 Tp. 3 R. 4, north and east.

**2642. COLLINS, Charles E. W.**
Mar. 18, 1854, 1 1/2 miles NNE Lake City Junction, Columbia Co. N 1/2 SE 1/4 and SE 1/4 NW 1/4 also NW 1/4 NE 1/4 Sect. 17 Tp. 6 R. 16, south and east. Patent delivered Feb. 14,

1857.

**2032. COLLINS, Charles H. B.**
Aug. 10, 1853,, 4 miles E of Fort White, Columbia Co. E 1/2 SE 1/4 Sect. 31 Tp. 6 R. 17, south and east. Patent delivered July 3, 1857.

**2652. COLLINS, Charles H. B.**
Mar. 21, 1854, 6 1/2 miles S by E of Fort White, Columbia Co. N 1/2 Lot No. 1 Sect. 6 Tp. 7 R. 17, south and east. Patent delivered July 3, 1857.

**2653. COLLINS, Charles H. B.**
Mar. 21, 1854, 3 1/2 miles ESE of Fort White, Columbia Co. SE 1/4 NE 1/4 Sect. 31 Tp. 6 R. 17, south and east. Patent delivered July 3, 1857.

**1202. COLLINS, David**
Feb. 23, 1852, 3 miles E of Meadows, Marion Co. NE 1/4 SW 1/4 and NW 1/4 SE 1/4 Sect. 13 Tp.22 R. 22, south and east.

**7005. COLLINS, Francis**
April 28, 1837, 1 1/4 miles NNE Olive, Escambia Co. SW 1/4 SE 1/4 Sect. 23 Tp. 1 R. 30, south and west.

**5990. COLLINS, Francisco**
Nov. 9, 1836, 1 1/2 miles E of Olive, Escambia Co. SE 1/4 SE 1/4 Sect. 23 Tp. 1 R. 30, south and west.

**5053. COLLINS, Henry M.**
July 14, 1859, 6 miles SSE of Fort White, Columbia Co. SW 1/4 NW 1/4 and NW 1/4 SW 1/4 Sect. 5 Tp.(?) R. 17, south and east.

**5123. COLLINS, John F.**
Aug. 5, 1835, 3 miles SE of Jumper, Gadsden Co. SW 1/4 NW 1/4 Sect. 34 Tp. 2 R. 5, north and west.

**5714. COLLINS, Thomas G.**
June 22, 1836, 1 1/4 miles WSW of Centerville, Leon Co. SE 1/4 SW 1/4 Sect. 23 Tp. 2 R. 1, north and east.

**6535. COLLINS, Thomas G.**
Jan. 13, 1837, 6 1/4 miles W Bradfordville, Leon Co. SW 1/4 SE 1/4 Sect. 23 Tp. 2 R. 1, north and east.

**7694. COLLINS, Thomas G.**
Nov. 1, 1838, at Bayhead, Bay Co. SW 1/4 SW 1/4 Sect. 17 Tp. 2 R. 13, south and west.

**7695. COLLINS, Thomas G.**
Nov. 1, 1838, 1/2 mile NNW Bayhead, Bay Co. Lot No. 1 Fractional Sect. 18 Tp. 2 R. 13, south and west.

**7865. COLLINS, Thomas**
Feb. 13, 1838, 1/2 mile SSW.Cherrylake, Madison Co. W 1/2 NW 1/4 Sect. 8 Tp. 2 R. 9, north and east.

**3854. COLLINS, William**
Jan. 20, 1831, 1 1/2 miles SE Greenville, Madison Co. E 1/2 NW 1/4 Sect. 6 Tp. 2 R. 1, north and east.

**3935. COLLINS, William**
April 2, 1831, 3 miles N Bradfordville, Leon Co. E 1/2 SE 1/4 Sect. 1 Tp. 2 R. 1, north and west.

**4142. COLLINS, William**
Feb. 18, 1832, at Blackcreek, Leon Co. W 1/2 NE 1/4 Sect. 12 Tp. 1 R. 2, north and east.

**1921. COLLINS, William C.**
July 4, 1853, 5 miles E of Fort White, Columbia Co. SE 1/4 SE 1/4 Sect. 32 Tp. 6 R. 17, south and east. Patent delivered Oct. 3, 1859.

**2687. COLLINS, William C.**
April 15, 1854, 8 miles E of Fort White, Columbia Co. SW 1/4 SW 1/4 Sect. 33 Tp. 6 R. 17, south and east. Patent delivered Oct. 3, 1857.

**7610. COLMON, Zachua**
Aug. 22, 1838, 2 miles SE Fincher, Jefferson Co. SE 1/4 SE 1/4 Sect. 20 Tp. 3 R. 4, south and east.

**304. COLSON, Elijah**
Feb. 7, 1846, c. 4 miles W Thomasville, Alachua Co. E 1/2 NW 1/4 Sect. 20 Tp. 7 R. 19, south and east. Patent delivered Aug. 1, 1847.

**684. CONE, William McCORMICK, Abner H.**
May 10, 1849, 1 mile E Ladonia, Citrus Co. NE 1/4 NW 1/4 Sect. 23 Tp. 17 R. 19, south and east. Transferred to **Abner H. McCORMICK** July 13, 1851. Witnesses: **CONE, Wm.** and **McCORMICK, Paul.** Patent delivered May 12, 1856.

**4484. COLSON, George**
Jan. 10, 1857, 1/4 mile NW of Judson, Levy Co. SE 1/4 of SW 1/4 Sect. 26 and NE 1/4 of NW 1/4 Sect. 35 Tp. 10 R. 15, south and east. Transferred to **Chas. F. HIESS,** Aug. 26, 1857. Patent delivered Jan. 2, 1872.

**4156. COLSON, James D.**
Feb. 13, 1856, 2 miles NE of Traxler, Alachua Co. SW 1/4 SE 1/4 Sect. 9

Tp. 7 R. 19, south and east.

**291. COLSON, John**
Jan. 1, 1827, 4 miles NW of Quincy, Gadsden Co. E 1/2 NW 1/4 Sect. 33 Tp. 3 R. 4, north and west.

**306. COLSON, John**
Jan. 1, 1827, 5 miles W of Quincy, Gadsden Co. W 1/2 SW 1/4 Sect. 35 Tp. 3 R. 4, north and west.

**1438. COLSON, John**
May 22, 1827, 2 1/2 miles NW Quincy, Gadsden Co. E 1/2 SW 1/4 Sect. 35 Tp. 3 R. 4, north and west.

**1439. COLSON, John**
May 22, 1827, 3 miles NW Quincy, Gadsden Co. E 1/2 SE 1/4 Sect. 34 Tp. 3 R. 4, north and west.

**1861. COLSON, John**
June 6, 1827, 2 miles E Mear's Spur, Gadsden Co. E 1/2 SE 1/4 Sect. 8 Tp. 3 R. 5, north and west.

**1862. COLSON, John**
June 6, 1827, 4 miles W by N Mt. Pleasant, Gadsden Co. W 1/2 SW 1/4 Sect. 9 Tp. 3 R. 5, north and west.

**1917. COLSON, John**
June 16, 1827, 5 1/2 miles NW Greensboro, Gadsden Co. E 1/2 NW 1/4 Sect. 35 Tp. 3 R. 6, north and west.

**1918. COLSON, John**
June 16, 1827, 3 1/2 miles NW Greensboro, Gadsden Co. SW 1/4 Sect. 36 Tp. 3 R. 6, north and west.

**9519. COLSON, Ruben**
Aug. 25, 1891, 1 1/2 miles SE Perry, Taylor Co. N 1/2 NW 1/4 and NW 1/4 NE 1/4 and SE 1/4 NW 1/4 Sect. 31 Tp. 4S R. 8E.

**1151. COMBS, John**
Feb. 4, 1852, 3 3/4 miles SW of Mason, Columbia Co. E 1/2 SE 1/4 Sect. 1 Tp. 6 R. 17, south and east.

**8361. COMERFORD, John**
June 20, 1840, 2 miles SE Greenwood, Jackson Co. SW 1/4 NW 1/4 and NW 1/4 SW 1/4 Sect. 3 Tp. 2 R. 9, north and west.

**7674. COMERFORD, Philip**
Oct. 16, 1838, 3 1/2 miles NNE Crigler, Jackson Co. SE 1/4 NW 1/4 Sect. 10 Tp. 4 R. 9, north and west.

**7747. COMERFORD, Philip**
Dec. 3, 1838, 5 1/2 miles NNE Graceville, Jackson Co. (State line) E 1/2 NW 1/4 Sect. 19 Tp. 7 R. 12, north and west.

**5435. COMMYNS, Florence F.**
Feb. 3, 1836, at Gull Point, Escambia Co. Lot No. 3 Sect. 38 Tp. 1 R. 30, south and west.

**4430. COMPTON, Richard J.**
Oct. 9, 1833, 2 miles S by W of Fentress, Santa Rosa Co. SE 1/4 SE 1/4 Sect. 24 Tp. 3 R. 27, north and west.

**7698. CONDREY, Thomas H.**
Nov. 7, 1838, at Florence, Gadsden Co. SE 1/4 SE 1/4 Sect. 2 Tp. 2 R. 3, north and west.

**6472. CONE, Arnold**
Jan. 9, 1837, 4 miles E by N Alma, Jefferson Co. E 1/2 SW 1/4 Sect. 29 Tp. 3 R. 5, north and east.

**6473. CONE, Arnold**
Jan. 9, 1837, 4 miles E Alma, Jefferson Co. NW 1/4 NE 1/4 Sect. 32 Tp. 3 R. 5, north and east.

**3147. CONE, Emily**
April 26, 1882, 2 miles N Brooker, Bradford Co. N 1/2 Lots 10 and 11 Sect. 6 Tp. 7S R. 20E.

**4137. CONE, William**
Feb. 8, 1832, 7 miles E by S of Stringer, NE shore of Lake Miccasukee, Jefferson Co. Lot No. 3 Sect. 36 Tp. 3 R. 4, north and east.

**4437. CONER, Sam**
Oct. 22, 1833, 3 1/2 miles NNE of Centerville, Leon Co. NW 1/4 NE 1/4 Sect. 15 Tp. 2 R. 2, north and east.

**4438. CONER, Sam**
Oct. 22, 1833, 3 1/4 miles NNE of Centerville, Leon Co. NE 1/4 NE 1/4 Sect. 15 Tp. 2 R. 2, north and east.

**518. CONGERS, Isaac**
May 9, 1831, 3 miles NNE Dills, Jefferson Co. E 1/2 NW 1/4 Sect. 29 Tp. 3 R. 6, north and east.

**5420. CONNELL, James**
Jan. 21, 1836, 3 1/2 miles SSW of Greensboro, Gadsden Co. E 1/2 SW 1/4 Sect. 18 Tp. 2 R. 5, north and east.

**5800. CONNELL, James**
Aug. 17, 1836, 2 1/2 miles N by E of Monticello, Jefferson Co. W 1/2 SW 1/4 Sect. 17 Tp. 2 R. 5, north and east.

**6163. CONNELL, James**

Dec. 8, 1836, 2 miles N by W Dills, Jefferson Co. NW 1/4 NW 1/4 Sect. 35 Tp. 3 R. 5, north and east.

**6164. CONNELL, James**
Dec. 8, 1836, 3 miles NW Dills, Jefferson Co. SE 1/4 SW 1/4 Sect. 27 Tp. 3 R. 5, north and east.

**6925. CONNELL, James**
March 18, 1837, 2 miles WNW Dills, Jefferson Co. NW 1/4 SW 1/4 Sect. 35 Tp. 3 R. 5, north and east.

**6926. CONNELL, James**
March 18, 1837, 2 miles W Sills (Dills), Jefferson Co. NW 1/4 NW 1/4 Sect. 2 Tp. 2 R. 5, north and east. Note on back states: "**John CONNELL** for **John H. HAGIX**".

**7677. CONNELL, Thomas**
Oct. 19, 1838, 2 miles SE by E Concord, Gadsden Co. NE 1/4 NE 1/4 Sect. 20 Tp. 3 R. 1, north and west.

**5115. CONNELL, William**
July 27, 1835, 1/4 mile NE of Monticello, Jefferson Co. W 1/2 SW 1/4 Sect. 20 Tp. 2 R. 5, north and east.

**2856. CONNELL, William**
July 2, 1829, 1/4 mile NE Monticello, Jefferson Co. W 1/2 NW 1/4 Sect. 20 Tp. 2 R. 5, north and east.

**2857. CONNELL, William**
July 2, 1829, 1/2 mile NE Monticello, Jefferson Co. E 1/2 NE 1/4 Sect. 19 Tp. 2 R. 5, north and east.

**2768. CONNELL, William**
March 4, 1829, 3 miles NNE Monticello, Jefferson Co. W 1/2 SE 1/4 Sect. 9 Tp. 2 R. 5, north and east.

**5512. CONNER, Lewis**
Mar. 5, 1836, 5 3/4 miles NNW of Florence, Gadsden Co. SE 1/4 NE 1/4 Sect. 15 Tp. 2 R. 2, north and east.

**6323. CONNER, Lewis**
Dec. 27, 1836, 4 miles W Copeland, Leon Co. W 1/2 SW 1/4 Sect. 35 Tp. 3 R. 2, north and east.

**6324. CONNER, Lewis**
Dec. 27, 1836, 4 1/2 miles W Copeland, Leon Co. E 1/2 SE 1/4 Sect. 34 Tp. 3 R. 2, north and east.

**6325. CONNER, Lewis**
Dec. 25, 1836, 4 1/4 miles W Copeland, Leon Co. E 1/2 SW 1/4 Sect. 35 Tp.3 R. 2, north and east.

**4463. CONNER, William**
Dec. 2, 1833, 1/2 mile W by S of Norfleet, Leon Co. NE 1/4 SW 1/4 Sect. 31 Tp. 2 R. 1, north and west.

**7867. CONYERS, Daniel**
Feb. 13, 1839, 1/2 mile NW Cherrylake, Madison Co. SE 1/4 Sect. 29 Tp. 3 R. 6, north and east.

**8309. CONYERS, Isaac**
April 29, 1840, 2 miles N Dills, Jefferson Co. W 1/2 NW 1/4 Sect. 29 Tp. 3 R. 6, north and east.

**1018. COOK, Ambrose**
Jan. 29, 1827, 12 miles N Tallahassee, Leon Co. Lot No. 2 Fractional Sect. 36 Tp. 3 R. 1, north and west. Transferred to **Benjamin SINGLETARY**, Feb. 19, 1827. Teste: **Nat BRYAN**.

**3063. COOK, Henry**
Sept. 25, 1829, 1/2 mile S Centerville, Leon Co. W 1/2 NE 1/4 Sect. 25 Tp. 2 R. 1, north and east. Transferred to **Edmond P. WESTEN (WESTER?)**, May 5, 1830. Transferred to **Sion PARIASH (PEVIASH?)**, Dec. 31, 1830.

**3065. COOK, Henry**
Sept. 27, 1829, 3/4 mile S by W Centerville, Leon Co. E 1/2 NE 1/4 Sect. 25 Tp. 2 R. 1, north and east. Transferred to **Edmond P. WESTEN** May 5, 1830. Transferred to **Sion FIRASH**, Dec. 31, 1830.

**COOK, John see Samuel THEUS**

**5394. COOK, John**
Jan. 9, 1836, 5 1/2 miles SSE of Centerville, Leon Co. NW 1/4 SW 1/4 Sect. 25 Tp. 2 R. 1, north and east.

**2592. COOK, Levi**
Mar. 9, 1854, 3 1/4 miles W of Jefferson, Columbia Co. SW 1/4 SW 1/4 Sect. 15 Tp. 4 R. 17, south and east.

**40. COOK, Simon**
Nov. 6, 1826, c. 5 miles NE Marianna, Jackson Co. NW 1/4 Sect. 18 Tp. 5 R. 10, north and west. Transferred to **Richard C. ALLEN & Co.** Nov. 7, 1826, by **L. M. STONE**, Atty. in fact for **Simon COOK**.

**2729. COOKSEY, Wm. E.**
Feb. 12, 1829, 1 mile S San Helena, Leon Co. E 1/2 NW 1/4 Sect. 29 Tp. 1 R. 1, north and west.

**3033. COOKSEY, Wm. E.**

Sept. 9, 1829, 1 mile S San Helena, Leon Co. W 1/2 NW 1/4 Sect. 29 Tp. 1 R. 1, north and west.

**67. COOLEY, William**
Dec. 3, 1844, at Homosassa, Citrus Co. W 1/2 SE 1/4 Sect. 32 Tp. 19 R. 17, south and east.

**68. COOLEY, William**
Dec. 3, 1844, at Homosassa Springs, Citrus Co. NE 1/4 NW 1/4 Sect. 28 Tp. 19 R. 17, south and east. Patent delivered April 14, 1845.

**356. COOLEY, William**
March 26, 1846, just NE Homosassa Springs, Citrus Co. NW 1/4 NW 1/4 Sect. 27 Tp. 19 R. 17, south and east.

**384. COOLEY, William**
May 4, 1846, at Homosassa Springs, Citrus Co. NE 1/4 NW 1/4 Sect. 27 Tp. 19 R. 17, south and east.

**400. COOLEY, William**
May 7, 1846, 1 mile N Hernando, Citrus Co. Lot No. 3 Fractional Sect. 23 Tp. 18 R. 19, south and east.

**138. COOLEY, William**
Mar. 19, 1845, 4 1/2 miles E Homasassa, Citrus Co. W 1/2 SE 1/4 Sect. 29 Tp. 19 R. 17, south and east.

**138. COOLEY, William**
Mar. 19, 1845, 4 1/2 miles E Homasassa, Citrus Co. Lot No. 6 Sect. 29 Tp 19 R. 17, south and east.

**140. COOLEY, William**
Mar. 19, 1845, 4 1/2 miles E by N Homasassa, Citrus Co. E 1/2 SE 1/4 Sect. 29 Tp. 19 R. 17, south and east.

**6503. COOPER, Ezekial**
Jan. 10, 1837, 2 miles S Chattahoochee, Gadsden Co. SW 1/4 SW 1/4 Sect. 10 Tp. 3 R. 6, north and west.

**8333. COOPER, James R.**
June 14, 1890, 1 mile W Kenney, Pasco Co. E 1/2 NE 1/4 Sect. 28 Tp. 26S R. 20E.

**775. COOPER, Thomas White**
Dec. 14, 1850, c. 1 1/2 miles W Orange Lake, Marion Co. NW 1/4 NW 1/4 Sect. 26 Tp. 12 R. 20, south and east.

**775. COOPER, Thomas White**
Dec. 14, 1850, c. 1 1/2 miles W Orange Lake, Marion Co. NW 1/4 NW 1/4 Sect. 26 Tp. 12 R. 20, south and east.

**7947. COOPER, William B.**
April 29, 1839, 4 miles SSW Avoca, Hamilton Co. E 1/2 NE 1/4 and W 1/2 SE 1/4 Sect. 33 Tp. 2 R. 13, north and east.

**8086. COOPER, William B.**
Sept. 21, 1839, 4 miles W Jasper, Hamilton Co. E 1/2 NW 1/4 and W 1/2 NE 1/4 Sect. 4 Tp. 1 R. 13, north and east.

**8087. COOPER, William B.**
Sept. 21, 1839, 4 miles S by W Avoca, Hamilton Co. E 1/2 SW 1/4 Sect. 33 Tp. 2 R. 13, north and east.

**3574. COPELAND, Ann**
July 19, 1830, 6 1/2 miles WSW Madison, Madison Co. W 1/2 NW 1/4 Sect. 11 Tp. 1 R. 8, south and east.

**3575. COPELAND, Ann**
July 19, 1830, 1 mile NE Moseley Hall, Madison Co. W 1/2 SE 1/4 Sect. 23 Tp. 1 R. 8, south and east.

**3515. COPELAND, Eliza**
May 19, 1830, 3 miles ENE Moseley Hall, Madison Co. E 1/2 SE 1/4 Sect. 14 Tp. 1 R. 8, south and east.

**3516. COPELAND, Eliza**
May 19, 1830, 3 1/4 miles ENE Moseley Hall, Madison Co. W 1/2 SW 1/4 Sect. 13 Tp. 1 R. 8, south and east.

**3517. COPELAND, ELiza**
May 19, 1830, 3 miles NNE Moseley Hall, Madison Co. E 1/2 NE 1/4 Sect. 14 Tp. 1 R. 8, south and east.

**3518. COPELAND, Henry**
May 19, 1830, 6 miles SW Madison, Madison Co. E 1/2 NE 1/4 Sect. 12 Tp. 1 R. 8, south and east.

**3572. COPELAND, Henry**
July 19, 1830, 5 1/2 miles WSW Madison, Madison Co. SW 1/4 Sect. 1 Tp. 1 R. 8, south and east.

**3573. COPELAND, Henry**
July 19, 1830, 6 miles SW Madison, Madison Co. W 1/2 NE 1/4 Sect. 12 Tp. 1 R. 8, south and east.

**3521. COPELAND, Jane**
May 19, 1830, 3 miles SW Madison, Madison Co. NE 1/4 Sect. 6 Tp. 1 R. 9, south and east.

**3522. COPELAND, Jane**
May 19, 1830, 3 1/2 miles SW Madison, Madison Co. W 1/2 SE 1/4 Sect.

6 Tp. 1 R. 9, south and east.
**2043. COPELAND, Robert**
Aug. 23, 1827, Copeland, Leon Co. E 1/2 SW 1/4 Sect. 33 Tp. 3 R. 3, north and east.
**2044. COPELAND, Robert**
Aug. 23, 1827, 4 miles WNW Copeland, Leon Co. E 1/2 SE 1/4 Sect. 26 Tp. 3 R. 2, north and east.
**2045. COPELAND, Robert**
Aug. 23, 1827, 4 miles E by S Iamonia, Leon Co. E 1/2 NW 1/4 Sect.23 Tp. 3 R. 2, north and east.
**2104. COPELAND, Robert**
Nov. 15, 1827, Jefferson Co. W 1/2 NE 1/4 Sect. 20 Tp. 3 R. 4, north and east.
**2332. COPELAND, Robert**
April 8, 1828, 2 miles SE Iamonia, Leon Co. NE 1/4 Sect. 28 Tp. 3 R. 2, north and east.
**2333. COPELAND, Robert**
April 8, 1828, 4 miles WNW Copeland, Leon Co. W 1/2 NE 1/4 Sect. 26 Tp. 3 R. 2, north and east.
**2334. COPELAND, Robert**
April 8, 1828, 5 miles WNW Copeland, Leon Co. E 1/2 NW 1/4 Sect. 26 Tp. 3 R. 2, north and east.
**3714. COPELAND, Robert**
Oct. 26, 1830, 2 miles E Bailey, Madison Co. SW 1/4 Secr. 21 Tp. 2 R. 7, north and east.
**4800. COPELAND, William**
Jan. 21, 1835, 1 mile N of Chaires, Leon Co. NW 1/4 NW 1/4 Sect. 25 Tp. 1 R. 2, north and east.
**1894. COPELAND, William**
June 9, 1837, 1 mile NW Capitola, Leon Co. NW 1/4 Sect. 24 Tp. 1 R. 2, north and east.
**4839. COPELAND, William**
Feb. 3, 1835, 5 miles W of Lloyd, Jefferson Co. W 1/2 SW 1/4 Sect. 19 Tp. 1 R. 3, north and east.
**4840. COPELAND, William**
Feb. 3, 1835, 2 miles NNE Chaires, Leon Co. W 1/2 NE 1/4 Sect. 25 Tp. 1 R. 2, north and east.
**4841. COPELAND, William**
Feb. 3, 1835, 1 1/2 miles NNE Chaires, Leon Co. NE 1/4 NE 1/4 Sect. 25 Tp. 1 R. 2, north and east.
**3576. COPELAND, Robert**
July 19, 1830, just N of Moseley Hall, Madison Co. SE 1/4 Sect.22 Tp. 1 R. 8, south and east.
**2210. COPELAND, Wm.**
(Of Fla.) Jan. 5, 1828, 5 miles SW Miccosukee, Leon Co. W 1/2 SW 1/4 Sect. 24 Tp. 1 R. 2, north and east.
**2229. COPELAND, Wm.**
(Of Fla.) Jan. 21, 1828, 1 mile WNW Capitola, Leon Co. E 1/2 SE 1/4 Sect. 23 Tp. 1 R. 2, north and east.
**COPELAND, Wm. see Green H. CHAIRES**
**5783. CORBETT, William L.**
July 27, 1836, 4 miles NNW of Haywood, Jackson Co. Lot No. 7 Fractional Sect. 19 Tp. 6 R. 7, north and west.
**375. CORLEY, Jeremiah**
May 3, 1827, 3 miles W Malone, Jackson Co. E 1/2 NE 1/4 Sect. 34 Tp. 6 R. 10, north and west.
**4. CORNISH, Wm.**
Aug. 27, 1826, c. 2 miles SW Graceville, Jackson Co. SE 1/4 Sect. 13 Tp. 6 R. 12, north and west. Received $200. 22 1/2.
**3204. CORNWELL, Geo. D.**
Jan. 6, 1830, 5 miles SSE Quincy, Gadsden Co. Lot No. 1 Fractional Sect. 33 Tp. 2 R. 3, north and west.
**6770. COTTRELL, Joseph B.**
June 12, 1888, 2 miles SW Valaha, Lake Co. SW 1/4 NW 1/4 and NW 1/4 SW 1/4 Sect. 27 and SE 1/4 NE 1/4 and NE 1/4 SE 1/4 Sect. 28 Tp. 20S R. 25E.
**1090. COUDRY, George M.**
Jan. 10, 1852, 3/4 mile E of Coleman, Sumter Co. SW 1/4 SW 1/4 Sect. 21 Tp. 1 R. 23, south and east. Patent delivered Oct. 13, 1856.
**3766. COURTNEY, Philip W.**
Nov. 29, 1830, 3 miles WSW Bradfordville, Leon Co. W 1/2 NW 1/4 Sect. 23 Tp. 2 R. 1, north and east.
**3767. COURTNEY, Philip W.**
Nov. 29, 1830, 2 1/2 miles WSW Bradfordville, Leon Co. W 1/2 NE 1/4 Sect. 28 Tp. 2 R. 1, north and east.
**4312. COVINGTON, Tristram**
Feb. 18, 1833, 3 miles NE of Centerville, Leon Co. SE 1/4 SW 1/4 Sect. 8 Tp. 2 R. 2, north and east.

**3230. COWARD, Zechariah**
Jan. 25, 1830, 1 mile S Marianna, Gadsden Co. W 1/2 NW 1/4 Sect. 15 Tp. 4 R. 10, south and west.

**7387. COX, Samuel H.**
Mar. 6, 1838, 1 3/4 miles SSW Avoca, Hamilton Co. NE 1/4 SE 1/4 Sect. 23 Tp. 2 R. 13, north and east.

**8954. COX, Starkey A.**
July 3, 1846, 8 miles N Gadsden, Gadsden Co. E 1/2 SW 1/4 Sect. 20 Tp. 3 R. 3, north and west.

**8955. COX, Starkey A.**
July 3, 1846, 5 1/2 miles NNE Lamont, Jefferson Co. SW 1/4 NW 1/4 Sect. 20 Tp. 3 R. 3, north and west.

**51. COX, William**
Nov. 8, 1826, near Littman, Gadsden Co. SE 1/4 Sect. 8 Tp. 2 R. 3, north and west. Transferred Nov. 8, 1826, to **Hezekiah WILDER** by Wm. Cox.

**5415. COX, William**
Jan. 19, 1836, 1 3/4 miles S of Quincy, Gadsden Co. NW 1/4 SE 1/4 Sect. 13 Tp. 2 R. 4, north and east.

**16. COY, Amaziah**
Jan. 13, 1843, 2 miles SE Oypas, Clay Co. NE 1/4 NE 1/4 Sect. 36 Tp. 5 R. 23, south and east.

**3625. CRAICY, Henry**
Oct. 6, 1830, c. 4 miles E Meridian, Leon Co. Lot No. 3 Sect. 23 Tp. 3 R. 1, north and east. Pd. in script issued to **Alex'r MACOMB**, survivor of Edgar and Macomb, dated May 30, 1829.

**2803. CRANE, Alex. P. W.**
April 13, 1829, c. 1 mile E St. Marks, Wakulla Co. Lot No. 3 Sect. 1 Tp. 4 R. 1, south and east.

**CRANE, Ambrose** see **Thomas J. GREEN #4441**

**4387. CRAVEY, Henry**
Aug. 16, 1838, 2 miles SSW of Iamonia, Leon Co. SW 1/4 NE 1/4 Sect. 14 Tp. 3 R. 1, north and east.

**4386. CRAVEY, Henry**
Aug. 16, 1833, 2 1/4 miles SSW of Iamonia, Leon Co. SW 1/4 NW 1/4 Sect. 14 Tp. 3 R. 1, north and east.

**2740. CRAWFORD, Adam**
Feb. 16, 1829, 2 miles SSW Campbellton, Jackson Co. E 1/2 SW 1/4 Sect. 11 Tp. 6 R. 12, north and west.

**4383. CREME, Ambrose Byron**
Aug. 5, 1833, 3 miles S of St. Marks, Wakulla Co. Lot No. 1 Sect. 23 Tp. 4 R. 1, south and east.

**CRESWELL, Pickens** see **Andrew McFALL**

**2163. CREWS, Elias**
Sept. 12, 1853, 2 miles NE of Taylor, Baker Co. Lot No. 4 Sect. 31 Tp. 2 R. 21, north and east. Patent delivered June 25, 1872.

**4175. CREWS, James B.**
Feb., 18, 1856, 5 1/4 miles E of Lake City Junction, Columbia Co. SE 1/4 of SW 1/4 Sect. 19 Tp. 6 R. 17, south and east.

**997. CREWS, John**
Nov. 6, 1851, near Baxter, Baker Co. Lot No. 1 Fractional Sect. 5 Tp. 1 R. 21, north and east. Patent delivered Oct. 26, 1857.

**1174. CREWS, John**
Feb. 12, 1852, 3 miles NNE Taylor, Baker Co. SE 1/4 NE 1/4 Sect. 6 Tp. 1 R. 21, north and east. Patent delivered April 26, 1857.

**2179. CREWS, John**
Sept. 15, 1853, 3/4 mile NNE of Taylor, Baker Co. Lot No. 2 Sect. 5 Tp. 1 R. 21, south and east. Patent delivered Oct. 26, 1859.

**4263. CREWS, Joseph M.**
Mar. 24, 1856, 5 1/2 miles W by N Worthington Springs, Bradford Co. SE 1/4 SE 1/4 of Sect. 9 and NE 1/4 NE 1/4 Sect. 30 Tp. 6 R. 18, south and east.

**2509. CREWS, Samuel**
Feb. 27, 1854, 4 3/4 miles NW of Claymo, Bradford Co. Lot No. 7 Sect. 31 Tp. 6 R. 20, south and east. Patent delivered Feb. 6, 1857.

**2510. CREWS, Samuel**
Feb. 27, 1854, 5 3/4 miles NNW of Claymo, Bradford, Co. NE 1/4 SE 1/4 Sect. 36 Tp. 6 R. 19, south and east. Patent delivered Feb. 7, 1857.

**1021. CRISMAN, Robert**
Nov. 29, 1851, 1 1/4 miles S Valrico, Hillsborough Co. NW 1/4 Sect. 36 Tp. 29 R. 20, south and east.

**481. CROM, Harmon**
Nov. 18, 1846, 1 1/2 miles SW Summerfield, Marion Co. SW 1/4 NW 1/4 Sect. 24 Tp. 17 R. 22, south and

east.

**1240. CROMARTIE, A.**
April 3, 1827, 5 miles N Centerville, Leon Co. Lot No. 2 Sect. 25 Tp. 3 R. 1, north and east.'

**627. CROMARTIE, Alex.**
(Of N. Car.)Dec. 7, 1825, 4 miles NNE of Bradfordville, Leon Co. Lot No.1 Sect. 32 Tp. 3 R. 1, north and east.

**628. CROMARTIE, Alex.**
(Of N. C.) Dec. 8, 1825, 1 mile E of Meridian, Leon Co. Lot No. 2 Sect. 20 Tp. 3 R. 1 north and east.

**629. CROMARTIE, Alex.**
(Of N. C.) Dec. 8, 1825, 1 mile E Meridian, Leon Co. Lot 3 Sect. 20 Tp. 3 R. 1, north and east.

**691. CROMARTIE, Alex.**
(Of N. C.) March 30, 1826, 2 miles E Meridian, Leon Co. W 1/2 SW 1/4 Sect. 15 Tp. 3 R. 1, north and east.

**692. CROMARTIE, Alex.**
(Of N. C.) March 30, 1826, 3 miles NE Lake Jackson Station, Leon Co. Lot No. 2 in Fractional Sect. 21 Tp. 3 R. 1, north and east.

**693. CROMARTIE, Alex.**
(Of N. C.) March 30, 1826, 6 miles NNW of Bradfordville, Leon Co. Lot No. 6 Sect. 32 Tp. 3 R. 1, north and east.

**694. CROMARTIE, Alex.**
(Of N. C.) March 30, 1826, 1/2 mile NE Meridian, Leon Co. W 1/2 SW 1/4 Sect. 17 Tp. 3 R. 1, north and east.

**695. CROMARTIE, Alex.**
(Of N. C.) March 30, 1826, 4 miles WNW Centerville, Leon Co. Lot No. 2 Sect. 26 Tp. 3 R. 1, north and east.

**4989. CROMARTIE, Alexander**
June 5, 1835, 1/2 mile SW of Meridian, Leon Co. NW 1/4 SE 1/4 Sect. 18 Tp. 3 R. 1, north and east.

**1988. CROMARTIE, James**
July 7, 1827, 1 mile NW Meridian, Leon Co. E 1/2 NW 1/4 Sect. 13 Tp. 3 R. 1, north and west.

**1989. CROMARTIE, James**
July 7, 1827, 1 mile NW Meridian, Leon Co. W 1/2 NE 1/4 Sect. 13 Tp. 3 R. 1, north and west.

**1990. CROMARTIE, James**
July 7, 1827, 3/4 mile W Meridian, Leon Co. SW 1/4 Sect. 13 Tp. 3 R. 1, north and west.

**5294. CROMARTIE, James**
Dec. 1, 1835, 2 1/2 miles SSW of St. Marks, Wakulla Co. SE 1/4 SE 1/4 Sect. 14 Tp. 3 R. 1, south and west.

**2478. CROMARTIE, James**
Aug. 29, 1828, 3/4 mile NW Meridian, Leon Co. SE 1/4 Sect. 13 Tp. 3 R. 1, north and west.

**4824. CROMARTIE, John**
Jan. 26, 1835, 3 miles W by S of Felkel, Gadsden Co. NE 1/4 SE 1/4 Sect. 1 Tp.2 R. 1, north and east.

**5752. CROMARTIE, John**
July 4, 1836, 1 mile SE of Florence, Gadsden Co. S 1/2 SW 1/4 Sect. 6 Tp. 2 R. 2, north and east.

**5753. CROMARTIE, John**
July 4, 1836, 3 1/2 miles NNE of Bradfordville, Leon Co. SW 1/4 SE 1/4 Sect. 1 Tp. 2 R. 1, north and east.

**6358. CROMARTIE, John**
Dec. 31, 1836, 3 miles NNW Bradfordville, Leon Co. NE 1/4 SW 1/4 and SE 1/4 SE 1/4 Sect. 1 Tp. 2 R. 1, north and east.

**6359. CROMARTIE, John**
Dec. 31, 1836, 2 miles N by E Centerville, Leon Co. NW 1/4 NW 1/4 and NE 1/4 NW 1/4 Sect. 7 Tp. 2 R. 2, north and east.

**6360. CROMARTIE, John**
Dec. 31, 1836, 2 miles N Centerville, Leon Co. E 1/2 NE 1/4 Sect. 12 Tp. 2 R. 1, north and east.

**4121. CROOM, Hardy B.**
Jan. 12, 1832, 3 3/4 miles SW of Sawdust, Gadsden Co. E 1/2 SW 1/4 Sect. 25 Tp. 2 R. 4, north and west.

**1751. CROOM, Joshua**
June 4, 1827, 2 1/2 miles E by N Stringer, Leon Co. E 1/2 SW 1/4 Sect. 24 Tp. 3 R. 3, north and east.

**1752. CROOM, Joshua**
June 4, 1827, at Miccosukee, Leon Co. SW 1/4 Sect. 9 Tp. 2 R. 3, north and east.

**1753. CROOM, Joshua**
June 4, 1827, 1/2 mile SW of Miccosukee, Leon Co. E 1/2 SE 1/4 Sect. 8 Tp. 2 R. 3, north and east.

**8502. CROOM, William W.**
Sept. 25, 1841, 4 miles NNE Mt.

Pleasant, Gadsden Co. NW 1/4 NE 1/4 Sect. 4 Tp. 3 R. 4, north and west. Transferred to **N. J. ZEIGLER**, May 23, 1856. Certified by **L. C. LASTER** Clerk of the County of Gadsden.

**8644. CROSBY, Joseph**
Feb. 21, 1844, 1 3/4 miles N Dills, Jefferson Co. W 1/2 SW 1/4 Sect. 30 Tp. 3 R. 6, north and east.

**1635. CROSBY, William**
Jan. 13, 1853, 3 miles S of Saxton, Bradford Co. SW 1/4 NE 1/4 Sect. 22 Tp. 6 R. 21, south and east. Patent delivered Feb. 2, 1857.

**2054. CROSBY, William**
Aug. 15, 1853, 1 mile SW Starke, Bradford Co. Lot No. 1 Sect. 25 Tp. 6 R. 21 and W 1/2 Lot 1, 2 and 3 Sect. 30 Tp. 6 R. 22, south and east.

**2788. CROW, Eliza**
July 4, 1854, 1/2 mile S by W of Fruitland Park, Lake Co. SE 1/4 NW 1/4 Sect. 28 Tp. 19 R. 24, south and east. Transferred to **James C. FUSSELL**, Nov. 28, 1855. Patent delivered (no date).

**3501. CROWELL, Richard H.**
May 3, 1830, 1 1/2 miles NNW of Bradfordville, Leon Co. W 1/2 SW 1/4 Sect.10 Tp. 2 R. 1, north and east. A certified copy made from the record in the Receiver's Office. Made March 14, 1838, by **M. Q. ALLEN**, Receiver.

**CROWELL, R. H.** see **Thomas BRADFORD #4649**.

**8421. CRUM, Harmon**
Nov. 19, 1840, 3 miles NNW Calhoun, Madison Co. E 1/2 NE 1/4 Sect. 4 Tp. 1 R. 9, south and east.

**2451. CULVER, Sam'l**
(And child **B. GUESS**) Aug. 5, 1828, 2 miles NNE Newport, Wakulla Co. Lot No. 5 Sect. 18 Tp. 3 R. 2, south and east.

**1316. CUMBO, Willbend**
(Alias **William BARKER**) Sept. 29, 1854, 3 miles SE of High Springs, Alachua Co. 26 acres and 62/100. Lot 3 SW 1/4 Sect. 6 Tp. 8 R. 18, south and east.

**550. CUMERFORD, Philip**
Nov. 15, 1834, 3 miles W Leonards Siding, Calhoun Co. NW 1/4 SE 1/4 Sect. 7 Tp. 1 R. 9, north and west.

**5761. CUNYUS, Joel**
July 8, 1836, 1 3/4 miles SSE of Lloyd, Jefferson Co. NE 1/4 SW 1/4 Sect. 25 Tp. 1 R. 3, north and east.

**69. CURRY, John**
Dec. 6, 1844, 6 1/2 miles W Irvine, Marion Co. SE 1/4 SW 1/4 Sect. 25 and NE 1/4 NW 1/4 Sect. 36 Tp. 12, south and west. No Range given.

**CURRY, Samuel A.** see **Samuel CARUTHERS #2485**

**1882. CURRY, William**
June 6, 1853, 2 1/2 miles E of Fairfield, Alachua Co. W 1/2 NE 1/4 NE 1/4 Sect. 15 Tp. 13 R. 20, south and east. Patent delivered (no date).

**2571. CURRY, William**
(Sr.) Mar. 6, 1854, 2 1/2 miles SW of Fairfield, Marion Co. SE 1/4 NE 1/4 Sect. 15 Tp. 13 R. 20, south and east. Patent delivered (no date).

**2572. CURRY, William**
(Sr.) Mar. 6, 1854, 3 1/2 miles NW of Fairfield, Marion Co. W 1/4 SE 1/4 Sect. 9 Tp. 13 R. 20, south and east.

**4247. CURRY, William**
(Sr.) Mar. 15, 1856, 1 mile SW of Fairfield, Marion Co. N 1/2 of SE 1/4 and NE 1/4 of SW 1/4 and SE 1/4 of NW 1/4 Sect. 15 Tp.. 13 R. 20, south and east. Patent delivered.

**3123. CUTHBERT, John A.**
Nov. 14, 1829, 4 miles WNW Waukenah, Jefferson Co. E 1/2 SW 1/4 Sect. 30 Tp. 1 R. 4, north and east.

**2294. CUTHBERT & MURRAY**
March 11, 1828, 3/4 mile SW Braswell, Jefferson Co. W 1/2 SE 1/4 Sect. 17 Tp.1 R. 4, north and east.

**2295. CUTHBERT & MURRAY**
March 11, 1828, 1 mile SW Braswell, Jefferson Co. W 1/2 NE 1/4 Sect. 20 Tp. 1 R. 4, north and east.

**2296. CUTHBERT & MURRAY**
March 11, 1828, 1 1/4 miles WSW Braswell, Jefferson Co. E 1/2 NW 1/4 Sect. 20 Tp. 1 R. 4, north and east.

**2297. CUTHBERT & MURRAY**
March 11, 1828, 2 miles SW Braswell, Jefferson Co. W 1/2 SE 1/4 Sect. 20 Tp. 1 R. 4, north and east.

**2298. CUTHBERT & MURRAY**
March 11, 1828, 2 miles SW Braswell, Jefferson Co. E 1/2 SW 1/4 Sect. 20

Tp. 1 R. 4, north and east.
**2299. CUTHBERT & MURRAY**
March 11, 1828, 2 1/2 miles SW Braswell, Jefferson Co. E 1/2 NW 1/4 Sect. 29 Tp.1 R. 4, north and east.
**2300. CUTHBERT & MURRAY**
March 11, 1828, 3 miles SW Braswell, Jefferson Co. W 1/2 SE 1/4 Sect. 30 Tp.1 R. 4, north and east.
**2382. CUTHBERT & MURRAY**
May 23, 1828, 3 miles SW Monticello, Jefferson Co. NE 1/4 Sect. 21 Tp. 1 R. 4, north and east.
**2706. CUTHBERT & MURRAY**
Feb. 3, 1829, 3 miles NW Waukenah, Jefferson Co. W 1/2 SE 1/4 Sect. 29 Tp. 1 R. 4, north and east.

## * D *

**2189. DABNEY, James W.**
Dec. 31, 1827, 3 miles W Tallahassee, Leon Co. W 1/2 SE 1/4 Sect. 32 Tp. 1 R. 1, north and west.

**8583. DABNEY, James W.**
March 20, 1843, 2 1/2 miles W by W Tallahassee, Leon Co. NW 1/4 NE 1/4 Sect. 33 Tp. 1 R. 1, north and west.

**8792. DABNEY, James H.**
July 8, 1845, 4 miles NNW Tallahassee, Leon Co. E 1/2 NW 1/4 Sect. 33 Tp. 1 R. 1, north and west.

**3397. DABNEY, Jas. W.**
Feb. 16, 1830, c. 1 mile SE Old Town, Dixie Co. Lot No. 2 Fractional Sect. 24 Tp. 10 R. 13, south and east.

**2180. DABNEY, J. W.**
Dec. 28, 1827, 3 miles W Tallahassee, Leon Co. E 1/2 SE 1/4 Sect. 32 Tp. 1 R. 1, north and west.

**DABNEY, James W.** see **Alex WATSON**

**2376. DAMPIER, John G.**
Feb. 20, 1854, 5 miles W of Orange Springs, Marion Co. Lot No. 6 Sect. 20 Tp. 11 R. 23, south and east.

**345. DANIEL, Appellas**
April 16, 1827, 8 miles NNE Cottondale, Jackson Co. SW 1/4 Sect. 19 Tp. 6 R. 11, north and west.

**1471. DANIEL, James**
Oct. 13, 1852, 3 miles NE of McKinley, Columbia Co. SW 1/4 SW 1/4 Sect. 8 Tp. 3 R. 16, south and east. Patent delivered July 7, 1857.

**2841. DANIEL, Jessee**
June 4, 1829, 3 miles SW Quincy, Gadsden Co. E 1/2 SW 1/4 Sect. 14 Tp. 2 R. 4, north and east.

**937. DANIEL, John**
(Jr.) Jan. 19, 1827, 5 miles S Quincy, Gadsden Co. W 1/2 NE 1/4 Sect. 30 Tp. 2 R. 3, north and west.

**1442. DANIEL, John**
(DUP) May 22, 1827, 2 1/2 miles SSW Quincy, Gadsden Co. W 1/2 SE 1/4 Sect. 14 Tp. 2 R. 4, north and west.

**1443. DANIEl, John**
(DUP) May 22, 1827, 2 1/2 miles SSW Quincy, Gadsden Co. E 1/2 SE 1/4 Sect. 14 Tp. 2 R. 4, north and west.

**249. DANIEL, Jonas**
Dec. 30, 1826, 3 miles SE of Campbellton, Jackson Co. SE 1/4 Sect. 3 Tp. 6 R. 11, north and west.

**6756. DANIEL, Josiah**
Feb. 6, 1837, 5 miles E Campbellton, Jackson Co. SW 1/4 SE 1/4 Sect. 34 Tp. 7 R. 11, north and west.

**7484. DANIEL, Josiah**
April 3, 1838, 1 mile SE by S Campbellton, Jackson Co. NE 1/4 NE 1/4 Sect. 7 Tp. 6 R. 11, north and west.

**7979. DANIEL, Josiah**
June 1, 1839, 3/4 mile SSE Campbellton, Jackson Co. E 1/2 NW 1/4 and SW 1/4 NE 1/4 Sect. 7 Tp. 6 R. 11,north and west.

**173. DANIEL, Stephen**
Dec. 29, 1826, 4 miles E of Graceville, Jackson Co. SW 1/4 Sect. 26 Tp. 7 R. 12, north and west.

**1942. DARBY, Jacob**
June 25, 1827, 5 miles SW Quincy, Gadsden Co. W 1/2 SE 1/4 Sect. 22 Tp. 2 R. 3, north and west.

**8319. DARRACATT, John A.**
May 13, 1840, 5 1/2 miles SSE Bennett, Madison Co. W 1/2 NE 1/4 Sect. 35 Tp. 2 R. 8, north and east.

**8454. DASHA, Joshua**
Jan. 19, 1841, 1/4 mile W Octahatchee, Hamilton Co. W 1/2 NE 1/4 Sect. 15 Tp. 2 R. 11, north and east.

**8455. DASHA, Joshua**
Jan. 19, 1841, 1 mile SW Octahatchee, Hamilton Co. NW 1/4 SE 1/4 Sect. 15 Tp. 2 R. 11, north and east.

**8456. DASHA, Joshua**
Jan. 19, 1841, 1/4 mile W Octahatchee, Hamilton Co. NE 1/4 NE 1/4 Sect. 15 Tp. 2 R. 11, north and east.

**73. DAUGHERTY, Nancy**
Nov. 24, 1826, c. 3 miles SW Jamieson, Gadsden Co. SW 1/4 Sect. 10 Tp. 3 R. 3, north and west. Transferred to **Wm. McELOY** on Nov. 24, 1826.

**7390. DAUGHERTY, William**
March 6, 1838, 1 1/4 miles NNE Avoca, Hamilton Co. NE 1/4 NW 1/4 Sect. 13 Tp. 2 R. 13, north and east.

**2277. DAVIDSON, Ann**
(Of Va.) Feb 28, 1828, 3 miles WSW

Wadesboro, Leon Co. E 1/2 SW 1/4 Sect. 3 Tp. 1 R. 2, north and east.

**2278. DAVIDSON, Ann**
(Of Va.) Feb. 28, 1828, 3 miles W by S Wadesboro, Leon Co. W 1/2 NW 1/4 Sect. 3 Tp. 1 R. 2, north and east.

**2792. DAVIDSON, David**
March 26, 1829, 3 miles W Wadesboro, Leon Co. E 1/2 NE 1/4 Sect. 4 Tp. 1 R. 2, north and east.

**3587. DAVIDSON, David**
Aug. 6, 1830, 3 1/2 miles W Wadesboro, Leon Co. W 1/2 NE 1/4 Sect. 4 Tp. 1 R. 2, north and east. Transferred, by deed, to **Robt. K. WEST** of Tallahassee on April 18, 1833.

**214. DAVIDSON, John**
Dec. 30, 1826, 5 miles NE Cottondale, Jackson Co. NE 1/4 Sect. 9 Tp. 5 R. 11, north and west.

**1818. DAVIDSON, Jno.**
(DUP) June 5, 1827, 1/2 mile SE Aberdeen, Jackson Co. E 1/2 SW 1/4 Sect. 3 Tp. 4 R. 11, north and west.

**3853. DAVIS, David**
Jan. 19, 1831, 4 miles S by W Graceville, Jackson Co. W 1/2 SE 1/4 Sect. 17 Tp. 6 R. 13, north and west.

**2769. DAVIS, Dennis**
March 5, 1829, 6 miles NE Wadesboro, Leon Co. Lot No. 4 Sect. 14 Tp. 2 R. 3, north and east.

**2771. DAVIS, Dennis**
March 5, 1829, 2 miles SE Miccosukee, Leon Co. W 1/2 SE 1/4 Sect. 15 Tp. 2 R. 3, north and west.

**3001. DAVIS, Dennis**
Aug. 29, 1829, 3 miles E by N Copeland, Leon Co. W 1/2 NE 1/4 Sect. 36 Tp. 3 R. 3, north and east.

**3002. DAVIS, Dennis**
Aug. 29, 1829, 2 3/4 miles E by N Copeland, Leon Co. E 1/2 NE 1/4 Sect. 36 Tp. 3 R. 3, north and east.

**6217. DAVIS, Dennis**
Dec. 15, 1836, 1 1/2 miles SSE Wadesboro, Leon Co. W 1/2 SW 1/4 Sect. 4 Tp. 1 R. 3, north and east.

**6218. DAVIS, Dennis**
Dec. 15, 1836, 1 mile SE Wadesboro, Leon Co. NE 1/4 Sect. 8 Tp. 1 R. 3, north and east.

**5912. Davis, Edmund**
Oct. 20, 1836, 1/2 mile SE of Mt. Pleasant, Gadsden Co. E 1/2 NW 1/4 Sect. 19 Tp. 3 R. 4, north and west.

**5915. DAVIS, Edmund**
Oct. 20, 1836, at Mt. Pleasant, Gadsden Co. SW 1/4 NW 1/4 Sect. 19 Tp. 3 R. 4, north and west.

**8187. DAVIS, Edmund**
Dec. 27, 1839, 1 1/4 miles SSE Fincher, Jefferson Co. E 1/2 NW 1/4 and SW 1/4 NW 1/4 Sect. 19 Tp. 3 R. 4, north and east.

**8140. DAVIS, James A.**
Nov. 14, 1839, at Blountstown, Calhoun Co. Lot No. 15 Sect. 28 Tp. 1 R. 8, north and west.

**104. DAVIS, John**
Dec. 19, 1826, at Marina, Jackson Co. W 1/2 NE 1/4 Sect. 3 Tp. 4 R. 10, north and west.

**3027. DAVIS, Samuel**
Sept. 8, 1829, 3 1/2 miles NW Rockhill, Walton Co. W 1/2 NE 1/4 Sect. 32 Tp. 2 R. 19, north and west.

**2085. DAVIS, Sam'l**
Oct. 29, 1827, at Florence, Gadsden Co. E 1/2 NW 1/4 Sect. 36 Tp. 3 R. 3, north and west.

**2520. DAVIS, Sam'l**
Oct. 10, 1828, 2 1/2 miles E Stringer, Jefferson Co. E 1/2 SW 1/4 Sect. 25 Tp. 3 R. 3, north and east.

**2802. DAVIS, Sam'l**
April 7, 1829, 8 miles SSW DeFuniak Springs, Walton Co. W 1/2 SE 1/4 Sect. 29 Tp. 2 R. 19, north and west.

**5196. DAWKINS, Ephram**
Oct. 9, 1835, 2 1/4 miles S by E of Iamonia, Leon Co. SW 1/4 NW 1/4 Sect. 31 Tp. 3 R. 2, north and east.

**6322. DAWKINS, Francis A.**
Dec. 27, 1836, 3 miles NNW Alma, Jefferson Co. NW 1/4 Sect. 22 Tp. 3 R. 4, north and east.

**4940. DAWKINS, Francis A.**
April 24, 1835, 9 miles E of Monticello, Jefferson Co. SE 1/4 SW 1/4 Sect. 29 Tp. 2 R. 3, north and east.

**6353. DAWKINS, Francis A.**
Dec. 30, 1836, 2 miles NNW Alma, Jefferson Co. NE 1/4 Sect. 22 Tp. 3 R. 4, north and east.

**6354. DAWKINS, Francis A.**
Dec. 30, 1836, 2 1/2 miles NNW Alma, Jefferson Co. E 1/2 SW 1/4

and W 1/2 SE 1/4 Sect. 22 Tp. 3 R. 4, north and east.

**2709. DAWKINS, Guilford B.**
Feb. 5, 1829, 1 1/2 miles SE Capitola, Jefferson Co. W 1/2 SE 1/4 Sect. 29 Tp. 2 R. 3, north and east.

**5369. DAWKINS, John**
Dec. 28, 1835, 5 miles NW of Lloyd, Jefferson Co. NW 1/4 NE 1/4 Sect. 32 Tp.2 R.3, north and east.

**5370. DAWKINS, John**
Dec. 28, 1835, 5 miles NW of Lloyd, Jefferson Co. NE 1/4 NW 1/4 Sect. 32 Tp. 2 R. 3, north and east.

**7823. DAWKINS, John**
Jan. 17, 1839, 2 miles SE Fincher, Leon Co. E 1/2 SE 1/4 Sect. 21 Tp. 3 R. 4, north and east.

**5671. DAWKINS, William**
May 12, 1836, 3 miles NNE Wadesboro, Jefferson Co. NE 1/4 SE 1/4 and NE 1/4 SW 1/4 Sect. 29 Tp. 2 R. 3, north and east.

**3994. DAWSEY, James**
July 1, 1831, 2 1/2 miles SW Chattahoochee, Gadsden Co. W 1/2 SE 1/4 Sect. 10 Tp. 3 R. 6, north and west.

**6506. DAWSEY, James**
Jan. 10, 1837, 2 1/2 miles SSE Chattahoochee, Gadsden Co. SE 1/4 NE 1/4 Sect. 10 Tp. 3 R. 6, north and west.

**1520. DAWSEY. Thomas**
May 23, 1827, 1 1/2 miles S Hermitage, Gadsden Co. E 1/2 NW 1/4 Sect. 3 Tp. 3 R. 5, north and west.

**1521. DAWSEY, Thomas**
(DUP) May 23, 1827, 1 1/2 miles SE Hermitage, Gadsden Co. W 1/2 SE 1/4 Sect. 3 Tp. 3 R. 5, north and west.

**4003. DAWSKY, Thomas A.**
July 13 (year missing), 1 1/4 miles N of Ashville, Madison Co. E 1/2 SE 1/4 Sect. 10 Tp. 3 R. 6, north and west.

**198. DAWSON, David**
Dec. 29, 1826, 5 miles ENE Welchton, Jackson Co. SE 1/4 Sect. 20 Tp. 6 R. 11, north and west.

**4884. DAY, Samuel T.**
Oct. 19, 1858, 3 miles SW of Providence, Columbia Co. S 1/2 NE 1/4 and SE 1/4 SE 1/4 Sect. 2 Tp. 6 R. 17, south and east.

**7883. DAY, William**
Feb. 22, 1839, 3 1/2 miles SW Jasper, Hamilton Co. W 1/2 NW 1/4 Sect. 14 Tp. 1 R. 13, north and east.

**7187. DEACON, Nathaniel**
Jan. 4, 1838, 3 miles W Marion, Hamilton Co. E 1/2 NE 1/4 and SE 1/4 SE 1/4 Sect. 35 Tp. 1 R. 13, north and east.

**158. DEAN, Jane**
(DUP) Dec. 28, 1826, at Havana, Gadsden Co. NW 1/4 Sect. 28 Tp. 3 R. 2, north and west. Transferred to **Savage STRICKLIN**, Jan. 10, 1827.

**33. DEAN, Norval**
Nov. 4, 1826, near Havana, Gadsden Co. NE 1/4 Sect. 29 Tp. 3 R. 2, north and west.

**4007. DEAN, Thaddeus**
Dec. 17, 1855, 2 miles SW of Peacock's, Levy Co. S 1/2 and NW 1/4 of SE 1/4 Sect. 14 Tp. 13 R. 18, south and east.

**2403. DEAS, John S.**
Feb. 21, 1854, at Wilmarth, Suwannee Co. NE 1/4 NW 1/4 Sect.22 Tp. 4 R. 11, south and east. Patent delivered Feb. 14, 1872.

**2401. DEAS, Lewis M.**
Feb. 20, 1854, 2 1/4 miles W of Luraville, Suwannee Co. SE 1/4 NE 1/4 Sect. 15 Tp. 4 R. 11, south and east. Patent delivered Oct. 13, 1859.

**2545. DEAS, Lewis M.**
Mar. 4, 1854, 2 3/4 miles E of Luraville, Suwannee Co. SW 1/4 NE 1/4 Sect. 15 Tp. 4 R. 11, south and east. Patent delivered Feb. 14, 1872.

**5151. DEAS, Mathew M.**
Sept. 23, 1835, 3 miles S by W of Hanson, Madison Co. E 1/2 SE 1/4 Sect. 4 Tp. 2 R. 9, north and east.

**5698. DEAS, Mathew M.**
June 10, 1836, 1 1/2 miles NE of Cherrylake (town), Madison Co. E 1/2 NE 1/4 Sect. 4 Tp. 2 R. 9, north and east.

**2319. DEAS, Moses**
Oct. 31, 1853, 7 miles SW of Guilford, Union Co. NW 1/4 SE 1/4 and SE 1/4 SE 1/4 Sect. 28 Tp. 5 R. 18, south and east.

**2519. DEAS, Moses**
Feb. 28, 1854, 4 1/2 miles W of Providence, Union Co. NW 1/4 NW

1/4 Sect. 2 Tp. 6 R. 18, south and east. Patent delivered Aug. 29, 1857.

**7527. DeBUSH, Andrew W.**
Aug. 13, 1889, 1 1/2 miles Rutland, Hernando Co. SW 1/4 NE 1/4 and SE 1/4 NW 1/4 Sect. 36 Tp. 18S R. 20E.

**8. DEEN, Micajah**
Jan. 3, 1843, at Rixford, Suwannee Co. E 1/2 NW 1/4 Sect. 36 Tp. 1 R. 13, south(?) and east.

**9. DEEN, Micajah**
Jan. 3, 1843, near Brandford, Suwanee Co. Lot No. 7 Fractional Sect. 17 Tp. 6 R. 14, south and east.

**1708. DEES, James**
Feb. 12, 1853, 6 miles SW of Guilford, Union Co. SW 1/4 NW 1/4 Sect.22 Tp. 5 R. 18, south and east.

**8651. DEES, Leonard**
Mar. 8, 1844, 2 3/4 miles E Chason, Calhoun Co. W 1/2 NW 1/4 Sect. 36 Tp. 2 R. 11, north and east.

**3796. DEES, Matthew M.**
Dec. 13, 1830, 1 1/2 miles ESE Cherry Lake Post Office, Madison Co. W 1/2 NE 1/4 Sect. 15 Tp. 2 R. 9, north and east.

**3915. DEES, Matthew M.**
March 15, 1831, 1 1/2 miles ESE Cherry Lake, Madison Co. E 1/2 NW 1/4 Sect. 15 Tp. 2 R. 9, north and east.

**5020. DEES, Matthew M.**
Sept. 29 (year missing) 1/2 mile E of Copeland, Jefferson Co. SE 1/4 SW 1/4 Sect. 33 Tp. 3 R. 9, north and east.

**8868. DEES, William**
Dec. 31, 1845, 1/2 miles SW Jennings, Hamilton Co. E 1/2 NW 1/4 Sect. 11 Tp. 2 R. 12, north and east.

**8874. DEES, William**
Jan. 17, 1846, 1/2 mile SE Jennings, Hamilton Co. NE 1/4 NE 1/4 Sect. 10 Tp. 2 R. 12, north and east.

**8875. DEES, William**
Jan. 17, 1846, 1/2 mile SW Jennings, Hamilton Co. NW 1/4 NW 1/4 Sect. 11 Tp. 2 R. 12, north and east.

**1505. DEKLE, Thomas E.**
Nov. 10, 1852, 2 1/4 miles NW of Dukes, Union Co. E 1/2 SW 1/4 Sect. 18 Tp. 1 R. 19, south and east. Patent delivered Sept. 14, 1857.

**1508. DEKLE, Thomas E.**
Nov. 13, 1852, 1 1/4 miles NW of Dukes, Union Co. NE 1/4 NW 1/4 Sect. 19 Tp. 6 R. 19, south and east. Patent delivered Sept. 14, 1857.

**2535. DeLEGAL, Thomas P.**
Mar. 3, 1854, 4 miles SSW of Rixford, Suwannee Co. NW 1/4 SE 1/4 Sect. 2 and SE 1/4 NE 1/4 Sect. 10 Tp. 2 R. 14, south and east. Patent delivered Nov. 10, 1869.

**2620. DeLEGAL, Thomas P.**
Mar. 15, 1854, 6 miles ESE of Rixford, Suwannee Co. N 1/2 SW 1/4 and NE 1/4 SE 1/4 Sect. 2 Tp. 2 R. 14, south and east. Patent delivered Oct. 11, 1869.

**365. DELL, Bennett Maxey(Maxy)**
April 20, 1846, 1 1/2 miles NW Alachua, Alachua Co. SE 1/4 Sect. 2 Tp. 8 R. 18, south and east.

**431. DELL, Bennett Maxey(Maxy)**
June 13, 1846, 2 miles N by E Alachua, Alachua Co. W 1/2 NW 1/4 Sect. 1 and E 1/2 NE 1/4 Sect. 2 Tp. 8 R. 18, south and east. Patent delivered Nov. 7, 1856.

**453. DELL, Bennett Maxey (Maxy)**
Aug. 10, 1846, at Orange Springs, Marion Co. NE 1/4 SE 1/4 Sect. 25 Tp. 11 R. 23, south and east. Patent delivered Dec. 2, 1854.

**1065. DELL, Bennett M.**
Dec. 30, 1851, 1 mile SW of Haynesworth, Alachua Co. Lot No. 5 NE 1/4 Sect. 1 Tp. 8 R. 18, south and east. Patent delivered Nov. 7, 1856.

**1066. DELL, Bennett M.**
Dec. 30, 1851, 1 1/4 miles SW of Haynesworth, Alachua Co. NE 1/4 SE 1/4 Sect. 36 Tp. 7 R. 18, south and east. Patent delivered Nov. 7, 1856.

**2473. DELL, Bennett M.**
Feb. 23, 1854, 2 miles N of Haynesworth, Alachua Co. SW 1/4 NW 1/4 Sect. 29 Tp. 7 R. 19, south and east. Patent delivered Nov. 7, 1856.

**143. DELL, James**
Mar. 9, 1844, 3 1/4 miles WNW Haynesworth, Alachua Co. W 1/2 SW 1/4 Sect. 34 Tp. 7 R. 18, south and east.

**328. DELL, James**
Feb. 27, 1846, 3 1/2 miles W Haynesworth, Alachua Co. E 1/2 NW 1/4

Sect. 34 Tp. 7 R. 18, south and east.

**329. DELL, James**
Feb. 27, 1846, 4 1/2 miles W Haynesworth, Alachua Co. W 1/2 NE 1/4 Sect. 33 Tp. 7 R. 18, south and east.

**920. DELL, James G.**
(For Alachua Steam Mill Co.) Aug. 7, 1851, c. 1 mile SW of Haynesworth, Alachua Co. N 1/2 Lot No. 4 Sect. 6 Tp. 8 R. 19, south and west. Patent delivered June 23, 1858.

**209. DELL, Philip**
Nov. 14, 1845, 4 1/2 miles SW Santa Fe, Alachua Co. SE 1/4 SW 1/4 Sect. 23 Tp. 7 R.18, south and east.

**1720. DELL, Simeon**
Feb. 19, 1853, 2 1/2 miles N of High Springs, Alachua Co. NW 1/4 SW 1/4 Sect. 26 Tp. 7 R. 17, south and east. Patent delivered June 23, 1858.

**2162. DELL, Simeon**
Sept. 8, 1853, 1 1/4 miles SW of Traxler, Alachua Co. Lot No. 1 Sect. 18 and Lot No. 1 Sect. 19 Tp. 7 R. 18, south and east. Patent delivered June 23, 1858.

**2174. DELL, Simeon**
Sept. 14, 1853, at Traxler, Alachua Co. Lot No. 2 and S 1/2 Lot No. 1 Sect. 8 and Lots No. 1 and 2 Sect. 17 Tp. 7 R. 18, south and east. Patent delivered June 23, 1858.

**2202. DELL, Simeon**
Sept. 24, 1853, 3 3/4 miles NNE of High Springs, Alachua Co. Lot No. 2 Sect. 23 Tp. 7 R. 18, south and east. Patent delivered June 23, 1858.

**1149. DELL, William**
Feb. 3, 1852, 2 miles NW of Haynesworth, Alachua Co. SE 1/4 SE 1/4 Sect. 26 Tp. 7 R. 18, south and east. Patent delivered July 4, 1859.

**8766. DENCY, Henry**
Mar. 29, 1845, 1 mile E by N Maysland, Madison Co. W 1/2 SW 1/4 Sect. 36 Tp. 3 R. 7, north and east.

**2557. DENISON, Coatts R.**
Dec. 1, 1828, 1 1/2 miles W of Dills, Jefferson Co. E 1/2 NW 1/4 Sect. 2 Tp. 2 R. 5, north and east.

**1609. DENISON, Coatts R.**
Jan. 6, 1853, 1 mile W of New River, Bradford Co. SW 1/4 NW 1/4 and NW 1/4 SW 1/4 Sect. 28 Tp. 6 R. 20, south and east. Patent delivered Feb. 2, 1857.

**8427. DENNIS, George E.**
Dec. 12, 1840, 2 miles S Cherrylake, Madison Co. SE 1/4 SE 1/4 Sect. 20 Tp. 2 R. 9, north and east.

**8428 DENNIS, George E.**
Dec. 12, 1840, 2 1/2 miles S by W Cherrylake, Madison Co. W 1/2 SW 1/4 Sect. 21 Tp. 2 R. 9, north and east.

**216. DEVINE, John**
(DUP) Dec. 30, 1826, 3 miles SW Ellis Post Office, Jackson Co. NE 1/4 Sect. 19 Tp. 6 R. 11, north and west.

**240. DEW, Philip**
Jan. 1, 1846, 3 1/2 miles NW Haynesworth, Alachua Co. SW 1/4 SW 1/4 Sect. 23 Tp. 7 R. 18, south and east.

**995. DEXTER, Thomas D.**
Nov. 5, 1851, 5 1/2 miles E Live Oak, Suwannee Co. SW 1/4 NE 1/4 Sect. 14 Tp. 2 R. 14, south and east.

**4234. DEXTER, Thomas D.**
Mar. 7, 1856, 1 1/2 miles NNE Houston, Suwannee Co. SE 1/4 SE 1/4 Sect. 23 Tp. 2 R. 14, south and east.

**4235. DEXTER, Thomas D.**
Mar. 7, 1856, 1 1/4 miles NNE of Houston, Suwannee Co. SE 1/4 NE 1/4 Sect. 23 Tp. 2 R. 14, south and east. Patent delivered Nov. 5, 1856.

**4236. DEXTER, Thomas D.**
Mar. 7, 1856, 2 miles W of Houston, Suwannee Co. NE 1/4 NW 1/4 Sect. 22 Tp. 2 R. 14, south and east.

**4238. DEXTER, Thomas G.**
Mar. 7, 1856, 3 miles NNE Houston, Suwannee Co. N 1/2 NE 1/4 Sect. 26 Tp. 2 R. 14, south and east.

**1297. DICKERSON, John**
April 24, 1827, 2 miles SW Iamonia, Leon Co. Lot No. 1 Fractional Sect. 24 Tp. 3 R. 1, north and east.

**5840. DICKERSON, William**
Sept. 9, 1836, at Iamonia, Leon Co. NW 1/4 SW 1/4 Sect. 18 Tp. 3 R. 2, north and east.

**7404. DICKENSON, John P.**
Mar. 13, 1838, 2 1/2 miles N by E Monticello, Jefferson Co. SE 1/4 Sect. 8 Tp. 2 R. 5, north and east.

**7536. DICKENSON, John P.**
July 14, 1838, 4 1/2 miles SSW Dills,

Jefferson Co. W 1/2 SW 1/4 Sect. 9 Tp. 2 R. 5, north and east.

**4848. DICKINSON, John**
Feb. 9, 1835, 6 1/2 miles W of Bradfordville, Leon Co. Lot No. 5 Sect. 20 Tp. 2 R. 1, north and west.

**4849. DICKINSON, John**
Feb. 9, 1835, 1 1/2 miles N of Lake Jackson (town), Leon Co. SE 1/4 NE 1/4 Sect. 30 Tp. 2 R. 1, north and west.

**8759. DICKINSON, Samuel H.**
Mar. 22, 1845, 3 3/4 miles W by S St. Marks, Leon Co. SW 1/4 SW 1/4 Sect. 22 Tp. 1 R. 1, south and west.

**4490. DICKINSON, William**
Dec. 24, 1833, at Iamonia, Leon Co. NW 1/4 NW 1/4 Sect. 18 Tp. 3 R. 2, north and east.

**8707. DICKSON, Marmaduke N.**
(See **John P. MADDUX**) Oct. 4, 1844, 1 1/4 miles SE Greenwood, Jackson Co. W 1/2 SE 1/4 Sect. 5 Tp. 5 R. 9, north and west.

**3141. DICKSON, William**
Dec. 1, 1829, 5 miles SSW Chattahoochee, Gadsden Co. E 1/2 SW 1/4 Sect. 19 Tp. 3 R. 6, north and west.

**3142. DICKSON, William**
Dec. 1, 1829, 5 1/2 miles SSW Chattahoochee, Gadsden Co. NW 1/4 Sect. 30 Tp. 3 R. 6, north and west.

**3190. DICKSON, Wm. S.**
Dec. 30, 1829, 5 miles SSW Chattahoochee, Gadsden Co. W 1/2 SE 1/4 Sect. 19 Tp. 3 R. 6, north and west.

**4326. DILLARD, Sampson**
Mar. 18, 1833, 9 1/2 miles E of Stringer, Leon Co. SE 1/4 Sect. 25 Tp. 3 R. 4, north and east.

**4332. DILLARD, Sampson**
Mar. 20, 1833, 10 miles SE of Stringer, Leon Co. SW 1/4 SE 1/4 Sect. 36 Tp. 3 R. 4, north and east.

**4595. DINN, Shadrach**
July 8, 1834, 2 1/4 miles N of Lloyd, Jefferson Co. NE 1/4 NW 1/4 Sect. 4 Tp. 1 R. 3, north and east.

**810. DITTS, Daniel**
(Of Fla.) Nov. 28, 1826, 4 miles W Tallahassee, Leon Co. E 1/2 NE 1/4 Sect. 32 Tp. 1 R. 1, north and west.

**4090. DIXON, Shadrach**
Sept. 26, 1831, 1/4 mile NE of Wadesboro, Leon Co. E 1/2 SW 1/4 Sect. 33 Tp. 2 R. 3, north and east.

**4091. DIXON, Shadrach**
Sept. 26, 1831, 4 1/4 miles NE of Wadesboro, Leon Co. W 1/2 SE 1/4 Sect. 33 Tp. 2 R. 3, north and east.

**185. DOBRON, Isaiah**
Dec. 29, 1826, 3 miles S Havana, Gadsden Co. SE 1/4 Sect. 15 Tp. 2 R. 2, north and west. Transferred "this day (no date), to **Seaborn RAWLS**.

**8728. DOLON, Martin**
Dec. 2, 1844, 1/4 mile SSE Hardaway, Gadsden Co. W 1/2 NE 1/4 Sect. 29 Tp. 3 R.5, north and west. Transferred to **J. SMALLWOOD**, Jan. 13, 1849.

**327. DOMSEY, John**
(DUP) April 3, 1827, 5 miles W of Quincy, Gadsden Co. W 1/2 NE 1/4 Sect. 12 Tp.2 R. 4, north and west.

**9398. DONALD, Louis**
June 24, 1891, 3 miles N by E Gretna, Gadsden Co. SW 1/4 NE 1/4 Sect. 10 Tp. 3N R. 4W.

**105. DONALD, Wm.**
Dec. 19, 1826, 3 miles W of Campbellton, Jackson Co. NW 1/4 Sect. 3 Tp. 6 R. 12, north and west.

**272. DONALD, Wm.**
Jan. 1, 1827, 7 miles SE of Graceville, Jackson Co. E 1/2 SE 1/4 Sect. 4 Tp. 6 R. 12, north and west.

**380. DONALD, Wm.**
(Assignee of **Chas. McKAY**) May 3, 1827, 5 miles ESE Graceville, Jackson Co. W 1/2 SE 1/4 Sect. 4 Tp. 6 R. 12, north and west.

**2270. DONALD, Wm.**
(Of Fla.) Feb. 21, 1828, 3 miles WSW Campbellton, Jackson Co. W 1/2 SE 1/4 Sect. 3 Tp. 6 R. 12, north and west.

**2587. DONALD, Wm.**
Dec. 27, 1828, 2 1/2 miles SSW Campbellton, Jackson Co. NE 1/4 Sect. 10 Tp. 6 R. 12, north and west.

**1796. DOUBERLY, William**
Mar. 30, 1853, 2 miles WNW of Jefferson, Columbia Co. NE 1/4 NE 1/4 and SW 1/4 NE 1/4 Sect. 14 Tp. 4 R. 17, south and east.

**1797. DOUBERLY, William**
Mar. 30, 1853, 2 miles W of Jefferson,

Co. NE 1/4 NW 1/4 Sect. 14 Tp. 4 R. 17, south and east.

**DOUGHTON, Lonnie** see **Lucius D. ROGERS, #233**

**1141. DOUGLAS, Charles F.**
Jan. 30, 1852, 2 1/2 miles NE Lulu, Columbia Co. NE 1/4 NE 1/4 Sect. 25 Tp. 4 R. 18, south and east.

**108. DOUGLASS, Alex.**
Dec. 20, 1826, c. 3 miles NW of Lake Jackson Station, Gadsden Co. W 1/2 NW 1/4 Sect. 30 Tp. 2 R. 2, north and west.

**1030. DOUGLASS, Alex.**
Jan. 30, 1827, 7 miles SE Quincy, Gadsden Co. E 1/2 SE 1/4 Sect. 24 Tp. 2 R. 3, north and west.

**8205. DOUGLASS, Allen D.**
Jan. 7, 1840, 3 miles NNE Marion, Hamilton Co. SW 1/4 NE 1/4 Sect. 21 Tp. 1 R. 14, north and east.

**107. DOUGLASS, Daniel B.**
Dec. 20, 1826, 4 miles SE Sawdust Post Office, Gadsden Co. NE 1/4 Sect. 25 Tp. 2 R. 3, north and west.

**2706. DOUGLASS, John**
May 15, 1854, 4 miles NE Lulu, Columbia Co. Lot No. 4 Sect. 19, Lot No. 1 Sect. 30 Tp. 4 R. 19, south and east; and SE 1/4 SE 1/4 Sect. 24 Tp. 4 R. 18, south and east.

**4539. DOWLING, William H.**
Feb. 3, 1834, 1 mile W of Iamonia, Leon Co. NE 1/4 SE 1/4 Sect. 17 Tp. 3 R. 2, north and east.

**3449. DOWLING, Zacchus(Zaccaheus)**
Mar. 13, 1830, 4 1/2 miles W Wadesboro, Leon Co. E 1/2 SW 1/4 Sect. 5 Tp. 1 R. 2, north and east. "Received for the within Treasury Scrip No. 57, dated May 30, 1829, in favor of **Alex'r MACOMB**, survivor of Edgar and Macomb."

**3450. DOWLING, Zacchus (Zaccaheus)**
March 12, 1830, 3 miles SSE of Centerville, Leon Co. W 1/2 NW 1/4 Sect. 5 Tp. 1 R. 2, north and east. "Received for the within Treasury Scrip No. 56, dated May 30, 1829, in favor of **Alex'r MACOMB**, survivor of Edgar and Macomb."

**2941. DOWLING, Zucchus**
July 17, 1829, 5 miles W Wadesboro, Leon Co. SE 1/4 Sect. 5 Tp. 1 R. 2, north and east.

**1593. DRAKE, Wm. B.**
May 25, 1827, 1 mile ENE Marianna, Jackson Co. E 1/2 NW 1/4 Sect. 2 Tp. 4 R. 10, north and west. Transferred to **Charles WILLIAMSON**, on May 28, 1827. Register: **G. W. WARD**.

**1620. DRAKE, Wm. B.**
May 26, 1827, 2 miles S Welchton, Jackson Co. E 1/2 SW 1/4 Sect. 1 Tp. 3 R. 12, north and west. Transferred May 28, 1827, to **Chas. WILLIAMSON**.

**1621. DRAKE, Wm. B.**
May 26, 1827, 2 miles S Welchton, Jackson Co. W 1/2 SW 1/4 Sect. 1 Tp. 3 R. 12, north and west. Transferred to **Chas. WILLIAMSON**, on May 28, 1827.

**1632. DRAKE, Wm. B.**
May 28, 1827, 3 1/2 miles WNW Monticello, Jefferson Co. Lot No. 4 Fractional Sect. 21 Tp. 2 R. 4, north and east. Transferred May 29, 1827, to **John G. GAMBLE**.

**1707. DRAKE, Wm. B.**
May 30, 1827, 5 miles E by N Jacob, Jackson Co. E 1/2 NE 1/4 Sect. 10 Tp. 6 R. 11, north and west. Transferred to **John G. GAMBLE**, June 6, 1827.

**1708. DRAKE, Wm. B.**
(DUP) May 30, 1827, 5 miles ESE Campbellton, Jackson Co. E 1/2 SW 1/4 Sect. 10 Tp. 6 R. 11, north and west. Transferred June 6, 1827, to **John G. GAMBLE**.

**1709. DRAKE, Wm. B.**
May 30, 1827, 5 miles ESE Campbellton, Jackson Co. W 1/2 SE 1/4 Sect. 10 Tp. 6 R. 11, north and west. Transferred June 6, 1827, to **John G. GAMBLE**.

**2985. DREW, Farnell**
Aug. 24, 1829, c. 5 miles W Alma, Jefferson Co. E 1/2 SE 1/4 Sect. 34 Tp. 3 R. 5, north and east.

**DREW, Rachel** see **James RAMSEY**

**532. DREW, William**
May 30, 1831, 4 miles ENE Dills, Jefferson Co. E 1/2 SE 1/4 Sect. 27 Tp. 3 R. 6, north and east.

**4111. DREW, William**
Dec. 2, 1831, 6 miles W by S Dennett,

Madison Co. E 1/2 SE 1/4 Sect. 20 Tp. 2 R. 6, north and east.

**2009. DRIGGERS, Jonas**
Aug. 5, 1853, 6 miles E of Haynesworth, Alachua Co. NW 1/4 SE 1/4 Sect. 36 Tp. 7 R. 19, south and east. Patent delivered Feb. 12, 1857.

**1814. DRIGGERS, William H.**
Mar. 5, 1853, 1 1/2 miles N Thomasville, Alachua Co. SW 1/4 NW 1/4 Sect. 13 Tp. 7 R. 19, south and east. Patent delivered Nov. 10, 1856.

**6243. DRUE, Farnel**
Dec. 19, 1836, 2 miles W Dills, Jefferson Co. SW 1/4 SW 1/4 Sect. 35 Tp. 3 R. 5, north and east.

**7286. DRUE, Farnel**
Jan. 31, 1838, 1 3/4 miles W Hamburg, Madison Co. NW 1/4 SW 1/4 Sect. 17 Tp. 2 R. 8, north and east.

**2605. DUBERLY, William**
Mar. 13, 1854, 6 1/2 miles SSW of Mt. Carrie Station, Columbia Co. SW 1/4 NW 1/4 Sect. 13 Tp. 4 R. 17, south and east. Patent delivered Nov. 26, 1863.

**120. DUBOSE, Wade H.**
Dec. 23, 1826, 5 miles NW Cottondale, Jackson Co. NW 1/4 Sect. 8 Tp. 5 R. 11, north and west. Transferred to **Wm. J. WATSON**, Jan. 16, 1828. Teste: **Samuel DUBOSE**.

**7497. DUERR, Chuslean F. and BRADEN, Hector W.**
June 20, 1838, 2 3/4 miles SSW Jasper, Hamilton Co. W 1/2 SW 1/4 Sect. 18 Tp. 1 R. 14, north and east.

**1748. DUKES, Jonathan**
Mar. 3, 1853, at Worthington Springs, Alachua Co. NW 1/4 NE 1/4 Sect. 33 Tp. 6 R. 19, south and east. Patent delivered Jan. 9, 1857.

**2540. DUKES, Jonathan**
Mar. 3, 1854, 1 1/4 miles S of Dukes, Union Co. W 1/2 SE 1/4 Sect. 28 Tp. 6 R. 19, south and east. Patent delivered Jan. 9, 1857.

**4726. DUKES, Jonathan**
Feb. 26, 1858, 1 mile S of Dukes, Union Co. SE 1/4 SE 1/4 Sect. 28 Tp. 6 R. 19, south and east. Patent delivered Sept. 8, 1863.

**7699. DULANEY, Benjamin**
Nov. 7, 1838, 2 miles E by N Brick, Okaloosa Co. E 1/2 NE 1/4 Sect. 4 Tp. 5 R. 23, north and west.

**217. DUNCAN, Dread**
Dec. 30, 1826, 6 miles SW Campbellton, Jackson Co. SW 1/4 Sect. 20 Tp. 6 R. 11, north and west.

**8842. DUNCAN, Jane**
Nov. 18, 1845, 3 3/4 miles NW Marion, Hamilton Co. SW 1/4 NW 1/4 Sect. 27 Tp. 1 R. 13, north and east.

**8838. DUNCAN, Thomas**
Nov. 15, 1845, 2 1/2 miles W by N Mt. Pleasant, Gadsden Co. NE 1/4 SW 1/4 Sect. 15 Tp. 3 R. 5, north and west.

**688. DUNLAP, Thos.**
Mar. 4, 1826, 4 miles NW Tallahassee, Leon Co. E 1/2 NW 1/4 Sect. 22 Tp. 1 R. 1, north and west.

**6135. DUNN, Daniel B.**
Sept. 8, 1887, 1 1/4 miles NW Rosewood, Levy Co. E 1/2 SW 1/4 Sect. 30 Tp. 14S R. (?)E.

**4553. DURHAM, William T.**
Feb. 24, 1834, 5 miles WSW of Dellwood, Jackson Co. NE 1/4 SW 1/4 Sect. 20 Tp. 5 R. 9, north and west. Transferred to **Elijah BRYAN**, Nov. 27, 1835. Sworn before **Thomas M. BUSH**, Clerk of Jackson Co.

**1440. DUPONT, Archie**
June 11, 1878, 1 1/2 miles N by E Midway, Gadsden Co. SW 1/4 SE 1/4 Sect. 32 Tp. 2N R.W.

**7864. DUPREE, Simon D.**
Jan. 23, 1890, 1 1/4 miles SW McKinley, Columbia Co. S 1/2 NE 1/4 and N 1/2 SE 1/4 Sect. 26 Tp. 3S R. 15E.

**1967. DUVAL, Jno. P.**
June 29, 1827, at Maxwell's Spur, Leon Co. N 1/2 Sect. 13 Tp. 1 R. 1, south and west. (319.37 acres)

**1968. DUVAL, Jno. P.**
June 29, 1827, 2 miles S Tallahassee, Leon Co. SW 1/4 Sect. 12, Tp.1 R. 1, south and west.

**1969. DUVAL, Jno. P.**
June 29, 1827, 3 1/2 miles SW Tallahassee, Leon Co. E 1/2 NE 1/4 Sect. 14 Tp. 1 R. 1, south and west.

**1981. DUVAL, Jno. P.**
July 2, 1827, 3 1/2 miles SE Tallahassee, Leon Co. SW 1/4 Sect. 15 Tp. 1

R. 1, south and east.

**806. DUVAL, John P. Formey**
Jan. 15, 1851, 2 1/2 miles SW Spring Park, Marion Co. NW 1/4 SW 1/4 Sect. 33 Tp. 14 R. 20, south and east. Patent delivered Dec. 4, 1856.

**5438. DUVAL, William P.**
Feb. 4, 1836, 1/4 mile S of Indian Pass, Gulf Co. Lot No. 4 Sect. 20 Tp. 9 R. 11, south and west.

**5439. DUVAL, William P.**
Feb. 4, 1836, 1/4 mile S of Indian Pass, Gulf Co. Lot No. 1 Sect. 22 Tp. 9 R. 11, north and west.

**301. DUVAL, Wm. P.**
Jan. 1, 1827, 5 miles E of Tallahassee, Leon Co. NW 1/4 Sect. 6 Tp. 1 R. 1, south and east. Under a Mandamus from the Judge of the Superior Court of Middle Florida.

**1976. DUVAL, Wm. P.**
(DUP) July 2, 1827, 6 miles ESE Tallahassee, Leon Co. E 1/2 SE 1/4 Sect. 14 Tp. 1 R. 1, south and east.

**1977. DUVAL, Wm. P.**
(DUP) July 2, 1827, 6 miles SW Tallahassee, Leon Co. E 1/2 SW 1/4 Sect. 14 Tp. 1 R. 1, south and east.

**2838. DYER, Aaron**
May 26, 1829, 2 miles N by W Fanlew, Leon Co. E 1/2 NE 1/4 Sect. 29 Tp. 2 R. 2, south and east.

**2575. DYER, Aaron**
(And **Josiah DYER**) Dec. 22, 1826, 1 1/2 miles S Felkel, Leon Co. E 1/2 NW 1/4 Sect. 22 Tp. 2 R. 2, north and east.

**DYER, Josiah** see **Aaron DYER, # 2575.**

**5938. DYKES, Henry**
Oct. 29, 1836, 2 3/4 miles NNE Hinson, Gadsden Co. NW 1/4 NW 1/4 Sect. 23 Tp. 3 R. 2, north and west.

**3051. DYKES, Jacob H.**
Sept. 18, 1829, 3 miles E by S Iamonia, Leon Co. E 1/2 SW 1/4 Sect. 17 Tp. 3 R. 2, north and west.

**6160. DYKES, Jacob H.**
Dec. 7, 1836, 1 1/4 miles N Havana, Gadsden Co. SE 1/4 SE 1/4 Sect. 22 Tp. 3 R. 2, north and west.

## * E *

**8736. EAGERTON, Henry L.**
Dec. 5, 1844, 2 1/2 miles S by W Hardaway, Walton Co. SW 1/4 SW 1/4 Sect. 32 Tp. 3 R. 5, north and west.

**8739. EAGERTON, Henry L.**
Dec. 12, 1844, 2 1/4 miles S Hardaway, Walton Co. SE 1/4 SE 1/4 Sect. 31 Tp. 3 R. 5, north and west.

**4273. EATON, Joseph**
Jan. 14, 1833, 3 1/2 miles E by S of Capitola, Jefferson Co. NW 1/4 NW 1/4 Sect. 25 Tp. 1 R. 3, north and east.

**4274. EATON, Joseph**
Jan. 14, 1833, 3 miles E by S of Capitola, Jefferson Co. SW 1/4 SW 1/4 Sect. 24 Tp. 1 R. 3, north and east.

**5987. EATON, Joseph**
Nov. 8, 1836, 1 1/2 miles SE by E of Lloyd, Jefferson Co. NE 1/4 NE 1/4 Sect. 20 Tp. 1 R. 3, north and east.

**6264. EATON, Joseph**
Dec. 21, 1836, 2 miles E Lloyd, Jefferson Co. NW 1/4 SW 1/4 Sect. 24 Tp. 1 R. 3, north and east.

**6270. EBBS, William P.**
Oct. 24, 1887, 5 miles W Hernando, Citrus Co. NE 1/4 Sect. 26 Tp. 18S R. 24E.

**4547. ECCLES, John**
Mar. 25, 1857, 3 miles SSW of Hildreth, Suwannee Co. SW 1/4 of SE 1/4 Sect. 14 Tp. 6 R. 14, south and east. Patent delivered June 11, 1870.

**4933. ECCLES, John**
Jan. 5 1859, 1 mile E of McAlpin, Suwannee Co. N 1/2 NW 1/4 Sect. 8 Tp. 4 R. 14, south and east.

**4552. ECCLES, Mary J.**
Mar. 31, 1857, 2 1/2 miles E of Branford, Suwannee Co. SE 1/4 SE 1/4 Sect. 15 Tp. 6 R. 14, south and east. Patent delivered June 11, 1857.

**2172. EDENFIELD, Jno.**
(Of Fla.) Dec. 25, 1827, 3 miles NNW Sawdust, Gadsden Co. W 1/2 SE 1/4 Sect. 8 Tp. 2 R. 4, north and west.

**8772. EDENFIELD, Sarah Ann Martha**
April 16, 1845, 1 1/2 miles N by W Watson, Liberty Co.. NE 1/4 NE 1/4 Fractional Lot No. 1 Sect. 20 Tp. 2 R. 7, north and west.

**4256. EDES, Peter**
Dec. 28, 1832, 1 1/4 miles NNE of Chattahoochee, Gadsden Co. W 1/2 SE 1/4 Sect. 33 Tp. 4 R. 6, north and west.

**4257. EDES, Peter**
Dec. 28, 1832, 1 mile NNE of Chattahoochee, Gadsden Co. SW 1/4 Sect. 33 Tp. 4 R. 6, north and west.

**4258. EDES, Peter**
Dec. 28, 1832, 1/2 mile SSE of Chattahoochee, Gadsden Co. NW 1/4 Sect. 4 Tp. 3 R. 6, north and west.

**333. EDINFIELD, John**
April 6, 1827, 3 miles W Sawdust, Gadsden Co. SW 1/4 Sect. 23 Tp. 2 R. 4, north and west.

**4560. EDWARDS, Abram B. M.**
Mar. 24, 1834, 5 1/4 miles W by N of Dellwood, Jackson Co. SW 1/4 NE 1/4 Sect. 20 Tp. 5 R. 9, north and west.

**4561. EDWARDS, Abram B. M.**
Mar. 24, 1834, 5 3/4 miles W by N of Dellwood, Jackson Co. SE 1/4 NW 1/4 Sect. 20 Tp. 5 R. 9, north and west.

**8360. EDWARDS, Brittain**
June 20, 1840, 1 mile SSW Lovett, Madison Co. W 1/2 SE 1/4 Sect. 28 Tp. 3 R. 7, north and east.

**22. EDWARDS, Cullin**
Oct. 23, 1826, near and 3 miles NW Quincy, Gadsden Co. $199.60 1/4 for NE 1/4 Sect. 2 Tp. 2 R. 4, north and west.

**334. EDWARDS, Cullin**
April 6, 1827, 5 miles W Quincy, Gadsden Co. E 1/2 NW 1/4 Sect. 2 Tp. 2 R. 4, north and west.

**6140. EDWARDS, Cullin**
Dec. 5, 1836, 2 1/2 miles SSE Greensboro, Gadsden Co. SE 1/4 SW 1/4 and SW 1/4 NE 1/4 Sect. 22 Tp. 2 R. 5, north and west.

**475. EDWARDS, Elias**
Aug. 31, 1830, 3 miles SW Ashville, Jefferson Co. NE 1/4 Sect. 12 Tp. 2 R. 6, north and east.

**3930. EDWARDS, Elias**
March 30, 1831, 2 miles SW Ashville, Jefferson Co. E 1/2 NW 1/4 Sect. 12 Tp. 2 R. 6, north and east.

**5089. EDWARDS, Elias**
July 22, 1835, 5 3/4 miles SSE of Dills, Jefferson Co. NW 1/4 SW 1/4 Sect. 12 Tp. 2 R. 6, north and east.

**5088. EDWARDS, Elias**
July 22, 1835, 5 miles SSE of Dills, Jefferson Co. NE 1/4 NE 1/4 Sect. 11 Tp. 2 R. 6, north and east.

**8541. EDWARDS, Elias**
May 12, 1842, 1/4 mile NW Ashville, Jefferson Co. E 1/2 SE 1/4 Sect. 31 Tp. 3 R. 7, north and east.

**8420. EDWARDS, Harriet R.**
Nov. 17, 1840, 2 1/2 miles SW by W Waukenah, Jefferson Co. E 1/2 NE 1/4 Sect. 8 Tp. 1 R. 4, south and east.

**2517. EDWARDS, Henry**
Oct. 9, 1828, 5 miles E Wadesboro, Leon Co. E 1/2 SE 1/4 Sect. 35 Tp. 2 R. 3, north and east.

**6147. EDWARDS, Henry R.**
Dec. 5, 1836, 8 miles E Ocklockonee Post Office, Leon Co. E 1/2 SE 1/4 Sect. 28 Tp. 1 R. 3, north and east.

**5133. EDWARDS, James**
Aug. 17, 1835, 2 1/2 miles N by W of Lloyd, Jefferson Co. E 1/2 SE 1/4 Sect. 4 Tp. 1 R. 3, north and east.

**2815. EDWARDS, Jas.**
May 6, 1829, 1 mile SE Capitola, Jefferson Co. W 1/2 NE 1/4 Sect. 31 Tp. 1 R. 3, north and east.

**292. EDWARDS, Jno.**
Jan. 1, 1827, 2 miles W of Quincy, Gadsden Co. E 1/2 NW 1/4 Sect. 8 Tp. 2 R. 4, north and west.

**293. EDWARDS, Jno.**
Jan. 1, 1827, 5 miles NW Quincy, Gadsden Co. W 1/2 NW 1/4 Sect. 35 Tp. 3 R. 4, north and west.

**587. EDWARDS, John**
Aug. 10, 1825, 5 miles ENE Wadesboro, Leon Co. E 1/2 SW 1/4 Sect. 26 Tp. 2 R. 3, north and east.

**654. EDWARDS, John**
(Of Fla.) Jan. 24, 1826, 4 miles E Wadesboro, Leon Co. W 1/2 NW 1/4 Sect. 35 Tp. 2 R. 3, north and east.

**655. EDWARDS, John**
(Of Fla.) Jan. 24, 1826, 4 miles E Wadesboro, Leon Co. E 1/2 SW 1/4 Sect. 35 Tp. 2 R. 3, north and east.

**656. EDWARDS, John**
Jan. 24, 1826, 4 miles E Wadesboro, Leon Co. E 1/2 NW 1/4 Sect. 2 Tp. 1 R. 3, north and east.

**2477. EDWARDS, John**
Feb. 24, 1854, 3 1/4 miles SSW of O'Brien, Suwannee Co. NW 1/4 SE 1/4 Sect. 31 Tp. 5 R. 14, south and east.

**2754. EDWARDS, John**
Feb. 23, 1829, 5 miles W Quincy, Gadsden Co. W 1/2 NE 1/4 Sect. 8 Tp. 2 R. 4, north and west.

**2492. EDWARDS, Jno. D.**
Sept. 13, 1828, 1 1/2 miles NW Capitola, Leon Co. W 1/2 SE 1/4 Sect. 17 Tp. 1 R. 3, north and east.

**4501. EDWARDS, John D.**
Jan. 2, 1834, 3 miles NNE of Lloyds, Jefferson Co. SW 1/4 SE 1/4 Sect. 4 Tp. 1 R. 3, north and east.

**6146. EDWARDS, John D.**
Dec. 5, 1836, 3 miles S Bradwell's Station, Leon Co. NW 1/4 SE 1/4 Sect. 28 Tp. 1 R. 3, north and east.

**7480. EDWARDS, John D.**
May 30, 1838, 2 miles SE by S Lloyds, Jefferson Co. W 1/2 NE 1/4 Sect. 26 Tp. 1 R. 3, north and east.

**7767. EDWARDS, John D.**
Dec. 18, 1838, 4 miles SSW Gadsden, Gadsden Co. W 1/2 SW 1/4 Sect. 27 Tp. 1 R. 3, north and east.

**5490. EDWARDS, John I.**
Feb. 25, 5 1/4 miles W of Dellwood, Jackson Co. SE 1/4 Sect. 20 Tp. 5 R. 9, north and west.

**5491. EDWARDS, John I.**
Feb. 25, 1836, 3 miles S by W of Haywood, Jackson Co. E 1/2 SW 1/4 Sect. 20 Tp. 5 R. 9, north and west.

**3097. EDWARDS, John J.**
Oct. 28, 1829, 4 miles S Greenwood, Jackson Co. W 1/2 SW 1/4 Sect. 18 Tp. 5 R. 9, north and west.

**5560. EDWARDS, John J.**
Mar. 28, 1836, 4 3/4 miles W of Dellwood, Jackson Co. SW 1/4 NW 1/4 Sect. 21 Tp. 5 R. 9, north and west.

**8043. EDWARDS, John J.**
Aug. 17, 1839, 1 mile NW Bond, Jackson Co. NE 1/4 SW 1/4 Sect. 5 Tp. 2 R. 7, north and east.

**8435. EDWARDS, John J.**
Dec. 23, 1840, 3/4 mile S by W

Ashville, Jefferson Co. SW 1/4 Sect. 32 Tp. 3 R. 7, north and east.

**2515. EDWARDS, Mary**
Oct. 9, 1828, 3 miles ENE Wadesboro, Leon Co. W 1/2 NE 1/4 Sect. 34 Tp. 2 R. 3, north and east.

**2516. EDWARDS, Mary**
Oct. 9, 1828, 3 miles ENE Wadesboro, Leon Co. E 1/2 SW 1/4 Sect. 27 Tp. 2 R. 3, north and east.

**50. EDWARDS, Samuel**
Nov. 8, 1826, near Florence Post Office, Gadsden Co. SE 1/4 Sect. 7 Tp. 2 R. 3, north and west. Transferred Nov. 8, 1826, to **Hezekiah WILDER** by **Samuel EDWARDS**.

**1453. EDWARDS, Samuel**
(DUP) May 10, 1827, 2 1/2 miles W Quincy, Gadsden Co. W 1/2 NE 1/4 Sect. 10 Tp. 2 R. 4, north and west.

**1454. EDWARDS, Samuel**
(DUP) May 22, 1827, 2 miles W Quincy, Gadsden Co. E 1/2 NE 1/4 Sect. 10 Tp. 2 R. 4, north and west.

**4047. EDWARDS, Samuel**
July 26, 1831, 3/4 mile NNE of Sawdust, Gadsden Co. W 1/2 SE 1/4 Sect. 10 Tp. 2 R. 4, north and west.

**8950. EDWARDS, Sherrod**
June 9, 1846, 6 miles SSW Westlake, Hamilton Co. Lots No. 1 and 2 NE 1/4 Fractional Sect. 23 Tp. 1 R. 11, south and east.

**6210. EDWARDS, Thomas**
Dec. 15, 1836, 3 miles W Hermitage, Gadsden Co. W 1/2 NW 1/4 Sect. 26 Tp. 4 R. 6, north and west.

**7798. EDWARDS, Thomas W.**
Jan. 5, 1839, 1 1/2 miles SE Greenwood, Jackson Co. E 1/2 SE 1/4 Sect. 8 Tp. 5 R. 9, north and west.

**8681. EDWARDS, Thomas W.**
Aug. 3, 1844, Location not given. W 1/2 NW 1/4 and W 1/2 SW 1/4 Sect. 9 Tp. 5 R. 9.

**6139. EDWARDS, William**
Dec. 5, 1836, 5 miles W Quincy, Gadsden Co. SE 1/4 NE 1/4 Sect. 7 Tp. 2 R. 4, north and west.

**195. EDWARDS, Wm.**
(DUP) Dec. 29, 1825, at Quincy, Gadsden Co. NW 1/4 Sect. 1 Tp. 2 R. 4, north and west.

**4503. EDUDORS, Stephen**
Jan. 4, 1834, 2 miles S of Iamonia, Leon Co. N 1/2 Lot No. 2 Sect. 25 Tp. 3 R. 1, north and west.

**2918. EICHELBERGER, Adam L.**
Sept. 22, 1854, 5 1/2 miles W by N of Bellview, Marion Co. N 1/2 NE 1/4 Sect. 6 Tp. 17 R. 22, south and east. Patent delivered June 24, 1863.

**2919. EICHELBERGER, John B.**
Sept. 22, 1854, 4 1/2 miles W by N of Belleview, Marion Co. NE 1/4 SE 1/4 Sect. 28 Tp. 16 R. 22, south and east

**7482. ELKINS, John B.**
May 31, 1838, 3 1/2 miles N by E Champaign, Madison Co. NE 1/4 SE 1/4 Sect. 1 Tp. 1 R. 8, north and east.

**7483. ELKINS, John B.**
May 31, 1838, 3 miles W by S Chipola, Calhoun Co. SW 1/4 SW 1/4 Sect. 6 Tp. 1 R. 9, north and east.

**5358. ELLIOTT, James M.**
Sept. 22, 1836, 3 miles N of Quincy, Gadsden Co. SE 1/4 NE 1/4 Sect. 19 Tp. 3 R. 3, north and west.

**6009. ELLIOTT, James M.**
Nov. 14, 1836, 3 miles N by E Quincy, Gadsden Co. W 1/2 SW 1/4 Sect. 20 Tp. 3 R. 3, north and west.

**6010. ELLIOTT, James M.**
Nov. 14, 1836, 3 1/4 miles N by E Quincy, Gadsden Co. NE 1/4 SE 1/4 Sect. 19 Tp. 3 R. 3, north and west.

**2172. ELLIS, Giles U.**
Sept. 14, 1853, 2 miles SE of Providence, Union Co. W 1/2 SE 1/4 Sect. 33 and NW 1/4 NW 1/4 Sect. 34 Tp. 6 R. 17, south and east. Patent delivered June 2, 1858.

**4557. ELLIS, Giles U.**
June 1, 1857, 6 miles SE of Fort White, Columbia Co. N 1/2 NW 1/4 Sect. 3 and N 1/2 NE 1/4 Sect. 4 Tp. 7 R. 17, south and east. Patent delivered Feb. 6, 1870.

**4673. ELLIS, Giles U.**
Nov. 2, 1857, 6 1/2 miles SE of Fort White, Columbia Co. S 1/2 of NE 1/4 Sect. 4 Tp. 7 R. 17, south and east. Patent delivered Mar. 6, 1870.

**4776. ELLIS, Giles U.**
Sept. 2, 1858, 6 miles SSW of Fort White, Columbia Co. NE 1/4 SE 1/4 Sect. 4 Tp. 7 R. 17, south and east.

**4746. ELLIS, Giles U.**

April 21, 1858, 6 miles E of Fort White, Columbia Co. W 1/2 NE 1/4 and NW 1/4 SE 1/4 Sect. 34 Tp.6 R. 17, south and east. Patent delivered Feb. 6, 1870.

**2822. ELLIS, James M.**
July 19, 1854, 2 1/2 miles N by W of Haynesworth, Alachua Co. SE 1/4 NE 1/4 Sect. 30 Tp. 7 R. 19, south and east.

**4576. ELLIS, John**
May 15, 1834, 1 1/4 miles SSW of Fentress, Santa Rosa Co. NW 1/4 SW 1/4 Sect. 24 Tp. 3 R. 27, north and west.

**2217. ELLIS, Moses**
Jan. 10, 1828, 2 1/2 miles SE Capitola, Jefferson Co. S 1/2 NE 1/4 Sect. 25 Tp. 1 R. 3, north and east.

**4109. ELLIS, Moses**
Nov. 24, 1831, 5 1/2 miles E by S of Capitola, Jefferson Co. E 1/2 SW 1/4 Sect. 25 Tp. 1 R. 3, north and east.

**4884. ELLIS, Moses**
Mar. 10, 1835, 2 miles SSE of Lloyd, Jefferson Co. SW 1/4 NW 1/4 Sect. 25 Tp. 1 R. 3, north and east.

**5986. ELLIS, Moses**
Nov. 8, 1836, 1 1/2 miles SE by E of Lloyd, Jefferson Co. SE 1/4 NE 1/4 Sect. 20 Tp. 1 R. 3, north and east.

**657. ELLIS, Thomas C.**
Aug. 4, 1848, 2 miles S Oldsmar, Hillsborough Co. Lots No. 1 and 3 Sect. 36 Tp. 28 R. 16, south and east.

**1238. ELLIS, William**
March 31, 1827, 3 miles W Gadsden, Gadsden Co. Lot No. 1 Sect. 18 Tp. 1 R. 2, north and west.

**1115. ELLIS, Wm. H.**
(DUP) Feb. 12, 1827, at San Helena, Leon Co. Lot No. 3 Sect. 17 Tp. 1 R. 2, north and west.

**4401. EMANUEL, David**
Aug. 27, 1833, 2 miles S of Iamonia, Leon Co. SE 1/4 SW 1/4 Sect. 19 Tp. 3 R. 2, north and east.

**4402. EMANUAL, David**
Aug. 27, 1833, 2 1/4 miles S of Iamonia, Leon Co. W 1/2 NW 1/4 Sect. 19 Tp. 3 R. 2, north and east.

**7164. ENGLISH, Charles G.**
Dec. 25, 1837, 2 miles NNW Dills, Jefferson Co. E 1/2 SW 1/4 Sect. 35 Tp. 3 R. 5, north and east. Transferred to **Mrs. Nancy HOGAN** on Jan. 4, 1838.

**3109. ENGLISH, Cornelius**
Nov. 8, 1829, 3 1/2 miles S by W Corey, Leon Co. W 1/2 NE 1/4 Sect. 18 Tp. 2 R. 2, south and east.

**495. ENTERKIN, James**
Oct. 25, 1830, 3 miles E Dills, Jefferson Co. E 1/2 SW 1/4 Sect. 33 Tp. 3 R. 6, north and east.

**2717. EPPS (EPPES), Francis**
Feb. 10, 1829, 3 miles E Centerville, Leon Co. W 1/2 NE 1/4 Sect. 22 Tp. 2 R. 2, north and east.

**2718. EPPS (EPPES), Francis**
Feb. 10, 1829, 3 miles E Centerville, Leon Co. E 1/2 NW 1/4 Sect. 22 Tp. 2 R. 2, north and east.

**2719. EPPS (EPPES), Francis**
Feb. 10, 1829, 3 1/2 miles E Centerville, Leon Co. E 1/2 SE 1/4 Sect. 22 Tp. 2 R. 2, north and east.

**2720. EPPS (EPPES), Francis**
Feb. 10, 1829, 4 miles E by N Centerville, Leon Co. E 1/2 SE 1/4 Sect. 15 Tp. 2 R. 2, north and east.

**2732. EPPS (EPPES), Francis**
Feb. 12, 1829, 6 miles WSW Miccosukee, Leon Co. E 1/2 NW 1/4 Sect. 15 Tp. 2 R. 2, north and east.

**2791. EPPS (EPPES). Francis**
Aug. 1, 1829, 2 miles WNW Wadesboro, Leon Co. SE 1/4 Sect. 27 Tp. 2 R. 2, north and east.

**4522. EPPS (EPPES), Francis**
Jan. 18, 1834, 5 miles E of Centerville, Leon Co. SW 1/4 SW 1/4 Sect. 14 Tp. 2 R. 2, north and east.

**4523. EPPS (EPPES), Francis**
Jan. 18, 1834, 4 3/4 miles E of Centerville, Leon Co. NW 1/4 SW 1/4 Sect.23 Tp. 2 R. 2, north and east.

**4666. EPPS (EPPES), Francis**
Nov. 22, 1834, 3 miles SSE of Bradfordville, Liberty Co. W 1/2 NW 1/4 Sect. 26 Tp. 2 R. 2, north and east.

**4667. EPPS (EPPES), Francis**
Nov. 22, 1834, 3 1/4 miles E of Centerville, Leon Co. SW 1/4 SW 1/4 Sect. 23 Tp. 2 R. 2, north and east.

**4769. EPPS (EPPES), Francis**
Jan. 12, 1835, 3 1/2 miles SSE of Centerville, Leon Co. E 1/2 NE 1/4

Sect. 27 Tp. 2 R, 2, north and east.
**ERNEST, James** see **Wilson GAINES**
**3036. ESLICK, James**
Sept. 12, 1829, 2 1/4 miles E Tallahassee, Leon Co. E 1/2 NE 1/4 Sect. 4 Tp. 1 R. 1, south and west.
**7511. ESTASTERS, Giles**
July 7, 1838, 2 1/2 miles S by E Dills, Jefferson Co. SE 1/4 SW 1/4 Sect. 13 Tp.2 R. 5, north and east.
**5429. ESTERS, Giles**
Feb.1, 1836, 4 1/2 miles SW by S of Dills, Jefferson Co. W 1/2 SW 1/4 Sect. 21 Tp. 2 R. 6, north and east.
**3459. EUBANKS, Major**
March 18, 1830, 3 1/2 miles S by W Monticello, Jefferson Co. W 1/2 NE 1/4 Sect. 12 Tp. 1 R. 4, north and east. Received for the within Treasury Scrip No. 58, dated May 30, 1829, in favor of **Alex'r MACOMB**, survivor of Edgar and Macomb.
**1869. EUBANK, Stephen**
June 6, 1827, 2 1/2 miles W Dills, Jefferson Co. E 1/2 SW 1/4 Sect. 34 Tp. 3 R. 5, north and east.
**1870. EUBANK, Stephen**
June 6, 1827, 3 miles WNW Dills, Jefferson Co. W 1/2 NE 1/4 Sect. 34 Tp. 3 R. 5, north and east.
**1871. EUBANK, Stephen**
June 6, 1827, 2 miles W Dills, Jefferson Co. W 1/2 SE 1/4 Sect. 34 Tp. 3 R. 5, north and east.
**452. EVANS, David**
Jan. 1, 1829, 7 miles SW DeFuniak Sprgs, Walton Co. E 1/2 NW 1/4 Sect. 18 Tp. 2 R. 19, north and west.
**4303. EVANS, Hezekiar**
(Georgia) Feb. 9, 1833, 3 miles SW Dill, Jefferson Co. W 1/2 SW 1/4 Sect. 11 Tp. 2 R. 5, north and east.
**4304. EVANS, Hezekiar**
Feb. 9, 1833, information inadequate for location-presumably as above.
**3202. EVANS, James**
Jan. 4, 1830, 6 miles SW DeFuniak Springs, Walton Co. W 1/2 SE 1/4 Sect. 18 Tp. 2 R. 19, north and west.
**2121. EVANS, Jonah**
Dec. 4, 1827, 2 miles N Braswell, Jefferson Co. E 1/2 NW 1/4 Sect. 9 Tp. 1 R. 4, north and east.
**2011. EVANS, Josiah**
Aug. 2, 1827, 2 miles N Wadesboro, Leon Co. NE 1/4 Sect. 25 Tp. 2 R. 2, north and east.
**5253. EVANS, Sharples**
Nov. 6, 1835, 1 1/2 miles SW of Econfina, Bay Co. SW 1/4 NW 1/4 Sect. 21 Tp. 1 R. 13, south and west.
**5252. EVANS, William**
Nov. 6, 1835, 1 3/4 miles NNE of Econfina, Bay Co. SE 1/4 SW 1/4 Sect. 10 Tp. 1 R. 13, south and west.
**2378. EVERETT, Joseph A.**
Feb. 20, 1854, 3/4 mile NNW of Crosby, Marion Co. SW 1/4 SW 1/4 Sect. 30 Tp. 16 R. 18, south and east. Patent delivered July 27, 1857.
**2586. EVERETT, Josiah**
Dec. 26, 1828, 3 miles N by W Monticello, Jefferson Co. Lot No. 2 Sect. 11 Tp. 2 R. 4, north and east. Transferred to **Marshall HART**, Jan. 9, 1829.
**3028. EVERETT, Myles**
Sept. 8, 1829, 3 miles E verett, Washington Co. W 1/2 NW 1/4 Sect. 11 Tp. 3 R. 13, north and west.
**3029. EVERETT, Myles**
Sept. 8, 1829, 2 1/2 miles ESE Everett, Washington Co. W 1/2 SE 1/4 Sect. 15 Tp. 3 R. 13, north and west.
**3030. EVERETT, Myles**
Sept. 8, 1829, 4 miles E Everett, Washington Co. E 1/2 NW 1/4 Sect. 11 Tp. 3 R. 13, north and west.
**3031. EVERETT, Myles**
Sept. 8, 1829, 3 1/2 miles E by N Everett, Washington Co. W 1/2 NE 1/4 Sect. 12 Tp. 3 R. 13, north and west.
**4211. EVERETT, Myles**
Sept. 3, 1832, 2 1/4 miles E of Everett, Washington Co. SW 1/4 SE 1/4 Sect. 10 Tp. 3 R. 13, north and west.
**8024. EVERETT, Myles**
Aug. 1, 1839, 2 1/2 miles E Everett, Washington Co. W 1/2 SW 1/4 Sect. 11 Tp. 3 R. 13, north and west.
**8025. EVERETT, Myles**
Aug. 1, 1839, 4 miles SE Everett, Washington Co. NE 1/4 NE 1/4 Sect. 22 Tp.3 R. 13, north and west.
**8026. EVERETT, Myles**
Aug. 1, 1839, 2 3/4 miles E Everett, Washington Co. E 1/2 NW 1/4 Sect.

15 Tp. 3 R. 13, north and west.

**8028. EVERETT, Myles**
Aug. 12, 1839, 2 1/2 miles E Everett, Washington Co. E 1/2 SE 1/4 NW 1/4 SE 1/4 Sect. 10 Tp. 3 R. 13, north and west. See **John BROWN**

**6270. EWING, David B.**
Dec. 22, 1836, 1 mile N Fowler, Madison Co. SW 1/4 SE 1/4 Sect. 6 Tp. 1 R. 7, north and east.

**6271. EWING, David B.**
Dec. 22, 1836, 1/2 mile N Fowler, Madison Co. NW 1/4 NE 1/4 Sect. 7 Tp.1 R. 7, north and east.

**7358. EWING, David B.**
Feb. 27, 1838, 2 miles SSE Hamburg, Madison Co. W 1/2 NW 1/4 Sect. 24 Tp. 2 R. 8, north and east.

**7578. EWING, David B.**
Aug. 9, 1838, 2 miles SSE Hamburg, Madison Co. E 1/2 SW 1/4 Sect. 24 Tp. 2 R. 8, north and east.

## * F *

**619. FAGAN, Stephen**
Feb. 21, 1848, 1 mile NE Alachua, Alachua Co. NW 1/4 NW 1/4 Sect. 12 Tp. 8 R. 18, south and east.

**876. FAIN, Mathew**
Jan. 16, 1827, 2 miles S Quincy, Gadsden Co. W 1/2 SE 1/4 Sect. 18 Tp. 3 R. 2, north and west. Transferred to **Wm. SLADE** of Georgia, Jan. 15, 1827. Teste: **G. W. WARD**,Regr.

**8979. FAIN, Mathew**
Oct. 15, 1846, 2 1/2 miles E Greenville, Madison Co. E 1/2 NW 1/4 Sect. 19 Tp. 1 R. 7, north and west.

**3016. FAIR, Mathew**
Sept. 7, 1829, 1/2 mile N Hinson, Gasdsden Co. E 1/2 NW 1/4 Sect. 21 Tp. 3 R. 2, north and west.

**17. FAIR, Mathew**
Sept. 20, 1826, at Bradfordville, Leon Co. NE 1/4 Sect. 20 Tp. 3 R. 2, north and east. 159.94 acres. "Received $199.92 1/2", **R. K. CALL**, receiver.

**6618. FAIRCLOTH, Allen**
Jan. 20, 1837, 3 miles SSE El Destino, Jefferson Co. SE 1/4 SW 1/4 Sect. 20 Tp. 1 R. 3, south and east.

**3972. FAIRCLOTH, Allen C.**
May 21, 1831, 2 miles W Cody, Leon Co. W 1/2 NW 1/4 Sect. 26 Tp. 1 R. 2, south and east.

**3066. FARMER, David J.**
Sept. 27, 1829, 2 miles E Copeland, Leon Co. E 1/2 NE 1/4 Sect. 35 Tp. 3 R. 3, north and east.

**3034. FARMER, David Y.**
Sept. 10, 1829, 2 1/2 miles E Copeland, Leon Co. W 1/2 NE 1/4 Sect. 35 Tp. 3 R. 3, north and east.

**3082. FARMER, David Y.**
Oct. 9, 1829, 1 mile WSW Alma, Jefferson Co. E 1/2 SW 1/4 Sect. 35 Tp. 3 R. 3, north and east.

**2311. FARMER, John**
March 17, 1828, 1 mile NE Miccosukee, Leon Co. E 1/2 SW 1/4 Sect. 3 Tp. 2 R. 3, north and east.

**FARN, Titus** see **Ira SANBURN**

**486. FARNELL, Benj.**
Oct. 8, 1830, at Dills, Jefferson Co. E 1/2 SE 1/4 Sect. 6 Tp. 2 R. 6, north and east.

**2430. FARR, Titus**
June 23, 1828, 1 mile S Centerville, Leon Co. E 1/2 SW 1/4 Sect. 25 Tp. 2 R. 1, north and east.

**1881. FAUST. Daniel**
(DUP) June 8, 1827, 2 miles W Tallahassee, Leon Co. E 1/2 SW 1/4 Sect. 34 Tp. 1 R. 1, north and west.

**3613. FAUST, Daniel**
Sept. 14, 1830, 4 miles W Black Creek, Leon Co. W 1/2 SE 1/4 Sect. 8 Tp. 1 R. 2, north and east.

**4040. FAUST, Daniel**
July 19, 1831, 4 miles NNW of Chaires, Leon Co. E 1/2 NW 1/4 Sect. 9 Tp. 1 R. 2, north and east.

**4481. FELKEL, Daniel**
Dec. 14, 1833, 1/2 mile SE of Centerville, Leon Co. NW 1/4 SW 1/4 Sect. 30 Tp. 2 R. 2, north and east.

**4335. FELKEL, David**
Mar. 25, 1833, 1 1/4 miles S by E of Centerville, Leon Co. NE 1/4 SW 1/4 Sect. 30 Tp. 2 R. 2, north and east.

**5181. FELKEL, David**
Oct. 2, 1835, 1 mile S of Centerville, Leon Co. NE 1/4 SE 1/4 Sect. 25 Tp. 2 R. 1, north and east.

**4477. FELKEL, Jacob S.**
Dec. 14, 1833, 2 1/2 miles SSE of Centerville, Leon Co. W 1/2 NW 1/4 Sect. 29 Tp. 2 R. 2, north and east.

**4478. FELKEL, Jacob S.**
Dec. 14, 1833, 1 1/4 miles S by E of Centerville, Leon Co. NE 1/4 NE 1/4 Sect. 30 Tp. 2 R. 2, north and east.

**4480. FELKEL, Jacob S.**
Dec. 14, 1833, 1/4 mile SE of Centerville, Leon Co. NE 1/4 SW 1/4 Sect. 19 Tp. 2 R. 2, north and east.

**5174. FELKEL, Jacob S.**
Sept. 30, 1835, 1/4 mile S of Centerville, Leon Co. E 1/2 NE 1/4 Sect. 25 Tp. 2 R. 1, north and east.

**5175. FELKEL, Jacob S.**
Sept. 30, 1835, 3/4 mile SSE of Centerville, Leon Co. NW 1/4 NE 1/4 Sect. 30 Tp. 2 R. 2, north and east.

**5200. FELKEL, Jacob L.**
Oct. 12, 1835, 2 1/2 miles SE by S of

Centerville, Leon Co. SE 1/4 NE 1/4 Sect. 30 Tp. 2 R. 2, north and east.

**4483. FELKEL, John**
Dec. 19, 1833, 1/4 mile E of Centerville, Leon Co. NW 1/4 SW 1/4 Sect. 19 Tp. 2 R. 2, north and east.

**4108. FERGERSON, Malcom**
Nov. 21, 1831, 1 mile NE of El Destino, Jefferson Co. E 1/2 SE 1/4 Sect. 1 Tp. 1 R. 2, south and east.

**5769. FERGUS, Alexander**
July 14, 1836, 3/4 mile N by E of Macom, Washington Co. SW 1/4 SW 1/4 Sect. 11 Tp. 2 R. 14, north and west.

**7216. FERGUSON, Alexander**
Jan. 11, 1836, 3/4 mile NNE of Macom, Washington Co. NW 1/4 SW 1/4 Sect. 11 Tp. 2 R. 14, north and west.

**964. FERGUSON, David**
(DUP) Jan. 20, 1827, 3 miles SE Quincy, Gadsden Co. W 1/2 NE 1/4 Sect. 15 Tp. 2 R. 3, north and west.

**963. FERGUSON, David**
(DUP) Jan. 20, 1827, 3 miles SE Quincy, Gadsden Co. W 1/2 Sect. 15 Tp. 2 R. 3, north and west.

**965. FERGUSON, David**
(DUP) Jan. 20, 1827, 3 miles SE Quincy, Gadsden Co. W 1/2 SE 1/4 Sect. 15 Tp. 2 R. 3, north and west.

**2052. FERGUSON, Jas.**
Sept. 7, 1827, 5 miles W Quincy, Gadsden Co. W 1/2 NW 1/4 Sect. 8 Tp. 2 R. 4, north and west.

**4823. FERGUSON, John**
Jan. 26, 1835, 1/2 mile N of Macom, Washington Co. SE 1/4 SE 1/4 Sect. 10 Tp. 2 R. 14, north and west.

**7215. FERGUSON, John**
Jan. 11, 1838, 1/4 mile N by E Macom, Washington Co. SE 1/4 SW 1/4 Sect.11 Tp. 2 R. 14, north and west.

**387. FERGUSON, Niel**
May 4, 1846, at Crystal River, Citrus Co. SE 1/4 NE 1/4 Sect. 21 Tp. 18 R. 17, south and east.

**399. FERGUSON, Niel**
May 6, 1846, 1 1/2 miles W Crystal River, Citrus Co. SE 1/4 NW 1/4 Sect. 21 Tp. 18 R. 17, south and east.

**7097. FERNANDIZ, Stephen D.**
Nov. 17, 1837, 2 miles W Waukenah, Jefferson Co. SE 1/4 NW 1/4 Sect. 5 Tp. 1 R. 4, south and east.

**5839. FERRELL, Luday C.**
Sept. 9, 1836, at Iamonia, Leon Co. SW 1/4 NW 1/4 Sect. 18 Tp. 3 R. 2, north and east.

**5637. FERRELL, Ludy**
April 30, 1836, 1 1/4 miles NNW of Iamonia, Jefferson Co. N 1/2 Lot No.? Sect. 13 Tp. 3 R. 1, north and east.

**4152. FERRELL, William**
Mar. 19, 1832, 1 1/4 miles E of Concord, Gadsden Co. W 1/2 NW 1/4 Sect. 15 Tp. 3 R. 1, north and east.

**4376. FERRELL, William**
July 13, 1833, 7 miles SSE of Concord, Gadsden Co. NW 1/4 SE 1/4 Sect. 1 Tp. 2 R. 1, north and east.

**2023. FETNER, John Z.**
Aug. 8, 1853, 2 1/2 miles E of Proctor, Marion Co. NE 1/4 SE 1/4 Sect. 28 Tp. 12 R. 22, south and east. Transferred to **Brent MITCHELL** on Jan. 28, 1854. Patent delivered Nov. 7, 1856.

**71. FIELDS, Jos. W.**
(Of Ala.) May 18, 1825, 3 miles N Lake Jackson Post Office, Leon Co. W 1/2 NW 1/4 Sect. 24 Tp. 2 R. 1, north and west.

**72. FIELDS, Jos. W.**
(Of Ala.) May 18, 1825, 3 miles N Lake Jackson Post Office, Leon Co. E 1/2 NW 1/4 Sect. 24 Tp. 2 R.1, north and west.

**73. FIELDS, Jos. W.**
(Of Ala.) May 18, 1825, c. 3 miles NW of Lake Jackson Post Office, Gadsden Co. Lot No. 2, 48 acres, in Fractional Sect. 23 Tp. 2 R. 1, north and west.

**74. FIELDS, Jos. W.**
(Of Ala.) May 18, 1825, C. 3 miles NE of Lake Jackson Post Office, Leon Co. Lot No. 1, of 112 acres, of Fractional Sect. 23 Tp. 2 R. 1, north and west.

**75. FIELDS. Jos. W.**
(Of Ala.) May 18, 1825, c. 4 miles N of Lake Jackson, Leon or Gadsden Co.

Sect. 13 Tp. 2 R. 1, north and west. Lot 2 in Fractional Sect. 13 Tp. 2 R. 1, north and west. 109 acres. See **Thomas P. RANDOLPH**

**8486. FINLEY, James**
April 29, 1841, 2 1/2 miles W by N Simsville, Jackson Co. NW 1/4 NW 1/4 Sect. 10 Tp. 3 R. 10, north and west. Transferred to **John MILTON**, Feb. 2, 1852.

**8487. FINLEY, James**
April 29, 1841, 3 1/2 miles W Simsville, Jackson Co. NW 1/4 NE 1/4 Sect. 9 Tp. 3 R. 10, north and west. Transferred to **John MILTON**, Feb. 2, 1852.
See **John BUSH, #7997**

**3489. FIREASH, Sion**
Jan. 14, 1831, 1 mile S Centerville, Leon Co. W 1/2 SE 1/4 Sect. 25 Tp. 2 R. 1, north and east.
See **Henry COOK, #3065**

**6372. FISHER, Alexander J.**
Dec. 31, 1836, 2 miles WSW Chaires, Leon Co. NE 1/4 NE 1/4 Sect. 4 Tp. 1 R. 2, south and east.

**6829. FISHER, Alfred A.**
Mar. 2, 1837, 1/2 mile NW Eridu, Madison Co. E 1/2 SW 1/4 and W 1/2 SE 1/4 Sect. 12 Tp.2 R. 5, south and east.

**6830. FISHER, Alfred A.**
Mar. 2, 1837, just SW Eridu, Madison Co. W 1/2 NE 1/4 and E 1/2 NW 1/4 Sect. 13 Tp. 2 R. 5, south and east.

**6831. FISHER, Alfred A.**
Mar. 2, 1837, just W Eridu, Madison Co. W 1/2 NW 1/4 Sect. 13 Tp. 2 R. 5, south and east.

**6832. FISHER, Alfred A.**
Mar. 2, 1837, 1/2 mile W Eridu, Madison Co. W 1/2 SW 1/4 Sect. 12 Tp. 2 R. 5, south and east.

**2852. FISHER, Daniel B.**
July 29, 1854, 6 miles N by E of Houston, Suwannee Co. SE 1/4 SE 1/4 Sect. 2 Tp. 2 R. 14, south and east. Patent delivered (no date).

**5378. FISHER, Robert**
Dec. 31, 1835, 2 1/4 miles N by W of Wadesboro, Leon Co.(on the state line). W 1/2 NE 1/4 Sect. 26 Tp. 2 R. 2, north and east.

**5379. FISHER, Robert**
Dec. 31, 1835, 2 1/4 miles N by W of Wadesboro, Leon Co. (on the state line), W 1/2 SE 1/4 Sect. 23 Tp. 2 R. 2, north and east.

**5589. FISHER, Robert**
April 9, 1836, 2 3/4 miles S by E Wadesboro, Leon Co. SE 1/4 NW 1/4 Sect. 26 Tp. 2 R. 2, north and east.

**5590. FISHER, Robert**
April 9, 1836, 3 1/4 miles SE Wadesboro, Leon Co. W 1/2 SE 1/4 Sect. 27 Tp. 2 R. 2, north and east.

**5625. FISHER, Robert**
April 27, 1836, 5 miles E by S of Centerville, Leon Co. NE 1/4 NW 1/4 Sect. 26 Tp. 2 R. 2, north and east.

**5626. FISHER, Robert**
April 27, 1836, 4 3/4 miles E by S of Centerville, Leon Co. SW 1/4 NE 1/4 Sect. 27 Tp. 2 R. 2, north and east.

**5592. FISHER, Robert**
April 12, 1836, 4 miles SE by E of Centerville, Leon Co. E 1/2 NW 1/4 Sect. 27 Tp. 2 R. 2, north and east.

**5632. FISHER, Robert**
April 29, 1836, 3 miles W of Copeland, Leon Co. SE 1/4 NW 1/4 and SW 1/4 NE 1/4 Sect. 34 Tp. 3 R. 2, north and east.

**5633. FISHER, Robert**
April 29, 1836, 3 miles W of Copeland, Leon Co. SW 1/4 and W 1/2 SE 1/4 Sect. 34 Tp. 3 R. 2, north and east.

**5634. FISHER, Robert**
April 29, 1836, 1836, 3 1/4 miles W of Copeland, Leon Co. E 1/2 SE 1/4 Sect. 33 Tp. 3 R. 2, north and east.

**2765. FISHER, Wm.**
Feb. 27, 1829, 3 1/2 miles N Lake Jackson, Leon Co. Lot No. 1 of Sect. 18 Tp. 2 R. 1, north and west.

**2143. FITCH, Eli**
Sept. 5, 1853, at Santa Fe, Alachua Co. SE 1/4 NE 1/4 Sect. 20 Tp. 7 R. 19, south and east. Patent delivered Oct. 5, 1857.

**3939. FITZGERALD, Freeman**
April 8, 1831, 3 miles NW Midway, Gadsden Co. W 1/2 NW 1/4 Sect. 36 Tp. 2 R. 3, north and west.

**5406. FITZGERALD, Freeman**
Jan. 15, 1836, 2 1/4 miles S of Florence, Gadsden Co. SW 1/4 Sect.

24 Tp. 2 R. 3, north and west.

**5407. FITZGERALD, Freeman**
Jan. 15, 1836, 2 1/2 miles SE by S of Florence, Gadsden Co. W 1/2 SE 1/4 Sect. 24 Tp. 2 R. 3, north and west.

**6266. FITZGERALD, Freeman**
Dec. 22, 1836, 2 miles N Midway, Gadsden Co. SW 1/4 Sect. 28 Tp. 2 R. 2, north and west.

**6268. FITZGERALD, Freeman**
Dec. 22, 1836, 1 1/2 miles NNE Midway, Gadsden Co. W 1/2 NE 1/4 Sect. 33 Tp. 2 R. 2, north and west.

**4077. FLAKE, William**
Sept. 5, 1831, 2 1/4 miles SE of Jamieson, Gadsden Co. E 1/4 NW 1/4 Sect. 18 Tp. 3 R. 21, north and west.

**9294. FLEMMIING, Jordan**
May 13, 1891, 2 miles S Ogden, Columbia Co. NE 1/4 SW 1/4 Sect. 32 Tp.3S R. 16E.

**8439. FLETCHER, Charles J.**
Dec. 29, 1840, 4 miles SW Madison, Madison Co. SW 1/4 SE 1/4 Sect. 5 Tp. 1 R. 9, south and east.

**4462. FLETCHER, Griffin K.**
Nov. 29, 1833, 3 1/2 miles E of Lake Jackson, Leon Co. SE 1/4 NE 1/4 Sect. 28 Tp. 3 R. 2, north and west.

**5273. FLETCHER, Griffin M.**
Nov. 20, 1835, 1/4 mile NE of Hinson, Gadsden Co. NE 1/4 NE 1/4 Sect. 28 Tp. 3 R. 2, north and west.

**2983. FLETCHER, James**
Aug. 22, 1829, at Ocklokonee, Leon Co. W 1/2 SE 1/4 Sect. 25 Tp. 1 R. 2, north and west.

**63. FLETCHER, John**
Nov. 15, 1826, 3 miles N Midway, Gadsden Co. SE 1/4 Sect. 20 Tp. 2 R. 2, north and west. Transferred Nov. 15, 1826, to **Augustus H. LANIER**.

**6336. FLETCHER, John**
Dec. 28, 1836, in Havana, Gadsden Co. SW 1/4 SW 1/4 Sect. 34 Tp. 3 R. 2, south and west.

**24. FLETCHER, Mary**
Oct. 24, 1826, c. 2 miles SW Greenwood, Jackson Co. NW 1/4 Sect. 7 Tp. 5 R. 10, north and west. Transferred to **R.C. ALLEN & CO.**, Nov. 7, 1826, signed by **David THOMAS** as atty. in fact for **M. FLETCHER**.

**8347. FLETCHER, Mary**
June 18, 1840, 2 miles E by N Blountstown, Calhoun Co. SE 1/4 Sect. 26 Tp. 1 R. 8, north and west.

**881. FLETCHER, Zabud**
Jan. 16, 1827, at Havana, Gadsden Co. W 1/2 NE 1/4 Sect. 33 Tp. 3 R. 2, north and west.

**2248. FLETCHER, Zabud**
Feb. 9, 1828, at Hinson, Gadsden Co. W 1/2 NE 1/4 Sect. 28 Tp. 3 R. 2, north and west.

**4538. FLETCHER, Zalud**
Jan. 30, 1834, 1/4 mile N of Havana, Gadsden Co. SE 1/4 NE 1/4 Sect. 33 Tp. 3 R. 2, north and west.

**FLOURNEY, Robert** (heirs of) see **James PATTERSON**

**8767. FLOWERS, John**
Mar. 29, 1845, 1 mile E by N Maysland, Madison Co. W 1/2 NW 1/4 Sect. 36 Tp. 3 R. 7, north and east.

**573. FLOWERS, Joseph**
June 7, 1836, 1 mile E Lovett, Madison Co. NE 1/4 Sect. 35 Tp. 3 R. 7, north and east. Received from **W. J. BAILEY**, Oct. 18, 1847.

**8899. FLOWERS, Joseph**
Feb. 12, 1846, 1 mile SW Bailey, Madison Co. NW 1/4 NW 1/4 Sect. 29 Tp. 2 R. 8, north and east.

**8900. FLOWERS, Joseph**
Feb. 12, 1846, 3 miles E Dennett, Madison Co. NE 1/4 NE 1/4 Sect. 31 Tp. 2 R. 8, north and east.

**858. FLOYD, Arthur**
April 1, 1851, 2 1/2 miles NE Alachua, Alachua Co. N 1/2 Lot No. 3 Sect. 1 Tp. 8 R. 18, south and east. Patent delivered June 5, 1856.

**1111. FLOYD, Arthur**
Jan. 15, 1852, 1 mile NE by E High Springs, Alachua Co. SE 1/4 SW 1/4 Sect. 1 Tp. 8 R. 18, south and east. Patent delivered Aug. 19, 1856.

**7913. FLOYD, Lewis B.**
Mar. 5, 1839, at Ellis, Jackson Co. SW 1/4 NE 1/4 Sect. 4 Tp. 6 R. 10, north and west.

**5102. FLOYD, Robert I.**
July 23, 1835, on St. Josephs

Bay, 6 1/2 miles NNW of Port St. Joe, Gulf Co. Lot No. 4 Fractional Sect. 5 Tp. 7 R. 11, south and west.

**5458. FOLSOM, Chesley**
Feb. 11, 1836, 2 1/2 miles NNE of Simsville, Jackson Co. SE 1/4 SE 1/4 and SE 1/4 SW 1/4 Sect. 4 Tp. 3 R. 9, north and west.

**694. FOLSOM, Elijah**
Dec. 13, 1849, 4 miles SW Columbia, Columbia Co. SE 1/4 SW 1/4 Sect. 15 Tp. 6 R. 20, south and east. Transferred to **Cain STRICKLAND**, Jan. 28, 1850. **A. M. ANDREWS**, Justice of Peace.

**8433. FOLSOM, Malinda**
Dec. 22, 1840, 3 1/2 miles NNE Dills, Jefferson Co. W 1/2 SW 1/4 Sect. 28 Tp. 3 R. 5, north and east.

**4924. FOLSOM, Needham B.**
April 6, 1835, 1/2 mile S of Copeland, Jefferson Co. E 1/2 NE 1/4 Sect. 5 Tp. 2 R. 4, north and east.

**5641. FOLSOM, Needham B.**
May 2, 1836, 3 3/4 miles NNE of Wadesboro, Jefferson Co. W 1/2 NW 1/4 Sect. 29 Tp. 2 R. 3, north and east.

**5642. FOLSOM, Needham B.**
May 2, 1836, 6 miles SE by S of Stringer, Jefferson Co. W 1/2 NW 1/4 Sect. 4 Tp. 2 R. 4, north and east.

**6252. FOLSOM, Needham B.**
Dec. 20, 1836, 4 miles SW Alma, Leon Co. W 1/2 SW 1/4 Sect. 4 Tp. 2 R. 4, north and east.

**4456. FOLSOM, Sidney S.**
Dec. 12, 1833, 4 3/4 miles E by S of Oakdale, Jackson Co. SW 1/4 SE 1/4 Sect. 4 Tp. 3 R. 9, north and west.

**4230. FOLSOM, Thomas**
Oct. 15, 1832, 1 3/4 miles W of Simsville, Jackson Co. NE 1/4 NE 1/4 Sect. 9 Tp. 3 R. 9, north and west.

**4440. FOLSOM, Thomas**
Oct. 23, 1833, 1 1/2 miles E of Simsville, Jackson Co. NW 1/4 NE 1/4 Sect. 9 Tp. 2 R. 3, north and east.

**3537. FOLSON, Ebenezer**
June 6, 1830, 1 1/2 miles SSE Mickasukee, Leon Co. E 1/2 SW 1/4 Sect. 15 Tp. 2 R. 3, north and east.

**7331. FOLSON, Ebenezer**
Feb. 15, 1838, 1 1/4 miles N Monticello, Jefferson Co. SE 1/4 NW 1/4 and SW 1/4 NE 1/4 Sect. 18 Tp. 2 R. 5, north and east.

**4877. FONTS, Martin**
Oct. 9, 1858, 1/2 mile SE of Lake Butler Station, Union Co. N 1/2 of Lots No. ?, 5 and 6 Sect. 6 Tp. 6 R. 20, south and east.

**1. FORBES, Robert**
Aug. 24, 1826, near Sawdust, Gadsden Co. SE 1/4 Sect. 2 Tp. 2 R. 4, north and west. Contains 159.88/100 acres. Rec'd of **Robert FORBES** $196.60 in full. Signed **R. K. CALL**, Receiver

**283. FORBES, Robert**
Jan. 1, 1827, 5 miles W of Quincy, Gadsden Co. E 1/2 NE 1/4 Sect. 12 Tp. 2 R. 4, north and west.

**2000. FORBES, Robert**
July 17, 1827, 1 mile W Quincy, Gadsden Co. W 1/2 NW 1/4 Sect. 12 Tp. 1 R. 4, north and west.

**3042. FORBES, Robert**
Sept. 15, 1829, 1/2 mile SW Quincy, Gadsden Co. E 1/2 NW 1/4 Sect. 29 Tp. 2 R. 3, north and east.

**3916. FORBES, Robert**
Mar. 16, 1831, 1 mile SW Quincy, Gadsden Co. SW 1/4 Sect. 12 Tp. 2 R. 4, north and west.

**3293. FORBES, Wesley**
Feb. 12, 1830, 5 miles ENE Wadesboro, Jefferson Co. E 1/2 NW 1/4 Sect. 29 Tp. 2 R. 3, north and east.

**3294. FORBES, Wesley**
Feb. 12, 1830, 3 miles NE Wadesboro, Leon Co. W 1/2 NW 1/4 Sect. 29 Tp. 2 R. 3, north and east.

**3488. FORBES, Wesley**
April 21, 1830, 2 1/2 miles N by E Wadesboro, Leon Co. E 1/2 NW 1/4 Sect. 20 Tp. 2 R. 3, north and east.

**5593. FORBES, William**
April 13, 1836, 2 1/2 miles W of Quincy, Gadsden Co. W 1/2 NW 1/4 Sect. 14 Tp. 2 R. 4, north and west.

**5594. FORBES, William**
April 13, 1836, 1 3/4 miles W of Quincy, Gadsden Co. W 1/2 SW 1/4 Sect.11 Tp. 2 R. 4, north and west.

**4094. FORBES, Wm.**
Oct. 5, 1831, 1 mile SE Quincy, Gadsden Co. E 1/2 SE 1/4 Sect. 17 Tp. 2 R. 3, north and west.

**946. FORCUE, Benjamin**
Jan. 19, 1827, 7 miles SW Havana, Gadsden Co. E 1/2 SW 1/4 Sect. 19 Tp. 2 R. 2, north and west.

**7888. FORD, David**
Jan. 28, 1890, 1 1/2 miles SE Loughman, Polk Co. NE 1/4 NE 1/4 Sect. 19 and E 1/2 SE 1/4 Sect. 18 and NW 1/4 SE 1/4 Sect. 18 Tp. 26 R. 28, south and east.

**3253. FOREHAND, James**
Feb. 5, 1830, at Lake Jackson Post Office, Leon Co. E 1/2 SW 1/4 Sect. 6 Tp. 1 R. 1, north and west.

**7894. FOREHAND, James**
Feb. 26, 1839, 1 mile SSW Lake Jackson, Leon Co. SW 1/4 SW 1/4 Sect. 7 Tp.1 R. 1, north and west.

**8553. FOREHAND, James**
Aug. 27, 1842, 1 1/4 miles SE Lake Jackson, Leon Co. NE 1/4 NW 1/4 Sect. 7 Tp. 1 R. 1, north and west.

**5292. FOREHAND, William**
Nov. 28, 1835, 1 mile SW of Lake Jackson (town), Leon Co. SW 1/4 SW 1/4 Sect. 6 Tp. 1 R. 1, north and west.

**3619. FORGE, Wm.**
Sept. 23, 1830, 3 miles SSW Quincy, Gadsden Co. W 1/2 NW 1/4 Sect. 24 Tp. 2 R. 4, north and west.

**8975. FORREST, Caswell**
Aug. 31, 4 3/4 miles SE Juniper, Gadsden Co. NW 1/4 SE 1/4 Sect. 33 Tp. 2 R. 5, north and west.

**225. FORTUNE, Adam**
(DUP) (Assignee of **Ben H. SWEARINGER**) 1 mile N Marianna, Jackson Co. SW 1/4 Sect. 34 Tp. 5 R. 10, north and west. Transferred to **Wm. J. WATSON**, Sept. 21, 1828.

**2010. FORTUNE, Adam**
Aug. 1, 1827, 1 mile NE Marianna, Jackson Co. W 1/2 SE 1/4 Sect. 34 Tp. 3 R. 10, north and west. Indorsed to **Wm. J. McARON**, Sept. 21, 1827.

**2092. FORTUNE, Adam**
Nov. 8, 1827, in Marianna, Jackson Co. W 1/2 NW 1/4 Sect. 3 Tp. 4 R. 10, north and west.

**2114. FORTUNE, Adam**
(Of Fla.) Nov. 24, 1827, 4 miles NNE Marianna, Jackson Co. E 1/2 SE 1/4 Sect. 33 Tp. 5 R. 10, north and west.

**2614. FORTUNE, Adam**
Jan. 23, 1829, 3 miles NNE Marianna, Jackson Co. E 1/2 SE 1/4 Sect. 23 Tp. 5 R. 10, north and west.

**2659. FORTUNE, Adam**
Jan. 23, 1829, 4 miles NNE Marianna, Jackson Co. W 1/2 SE 1/4 Sect. 23 Tp. 5 R. 10, north and west.

**2755. FORTUNE, Adam**
Feb. 23, 1829, 3 1/2 miles NNE Marianna, Jackson Co. W 1/2 NW 1/4 Sect. 24 Tp. 5 R. 10, north and west.

**2794. FORTUNE, Adam**
March 31, 1829, 3 1/2 miles NNE Marianna, Jackson Co. E 1/2 NW 1/4 Sect. 24 Tp. 5 R. 10, north and west.

**2795. FORTUNE, Adam**
March 31, 1829, 3 1/2 miles NNE Marianna, Jackson Co. E 1/2 SW 1/4 Sect. 24 Tp. 5 R. 10, north and west.

**2814. FORTUNE, Adam**
May 4, 1829, 4 miles NE Marianna, Jackson Co. W 1/2 SW 1/4 Sect. 24 Tp. 5 R. 10, north and west.

**4381. FORTUNE, Adam**
July 25, 1833, 6 miles NE of Fairgrounds, Jackson Co. NW 1/4 NE 1/4 Sect. 24 Tp. 5 R. 10, north and west.

**4584. FORTUNE, Adam**
June 12, 1834, 3 miles NNE of Marianna, Jackson Co. E 1/2 NE 1/4 Sect. 25 Tp. 5 R. 10, north and west.

**4585. FORTUNE, Adam**
June 12, 1834, 3 1/4 miles NNE of Marianna, Jackson Co. SW 1/4 NE 1/4 Sect. 25 Tp. 5 R. 10, north and west.

**4586. FORTUNE, Adam**
June 12, 1834, 2 1/2 miles NNE of Marianna, Jackson Co. NE 1/4 SE 1/4 Sect. 25 Tp. 5 R. 10, north and west.

**2. FOSCUE, Benjamin, Benj., or Ben**
Aug. 27, 1826, near Campbellton, Jackson Co. SW 1/4 Sect. 18 Tp. 6 R. 11, north and west. 160.51 acres. Received of **Benjamin FOSCUE**, $200.62 1/2. **R. K. CALL**, Receiver.

**942. FOSCUE, Benjamin, Benj. or Ben**
Jan. 19, 1827, 5 miles SW Havana, Gadsden Co. NE 1/4 Sect. 19 Tp. 2 R. 2, north and west.

**943. FOSCUE, Benjamin, Benj. or Ben**
Jan. 19, 1827, 5 miles SW Havana, Gadsden Co. E 1/2 NW 1/4 Sect. 19 Tp. 2 R. 2, north and west.

**2783. FOSCUE, Benjamin, Benj. or Ben**
March 16, 1829, 4 miles E Jacob, Jackson Co. E 1/2 NW 1/4 Sect. 14 Tp. 6 R. 11, north and west.

**2784. FOSCUE, Benjamin**
March 16, 1829, 4 1/2 miles E Jacob, Jackson Co. W 1/2 NE 1/4 Sect. 14 Tp. 6 R. 11, north and west.

**2785. FOSCUE, Benjamin**
March 16, 1829, 3 miles ENE Jacob, Jackson Co. SE 1/4 Sect. 8 Tp. 6 R. 11, north and west.

**2786. FOSCUE, Benjamin**
March 16, 1829, 6 miles E by N Jacob, Jackson Co. SW 1/4 Sect. 8 Tp. 6 R. 11, north and west.

**2788. FOSCUE, Benjamin**
March 16, 1829, 2 miles S Welchton, Jackson Co. NE 1/4 Sect. 12 Tp. 5 R. 12, north and west.

**2957. FOSCUE, Benjamin**
July 24, 1829, 1 1/2 miles S Welchton, Jackson Co. E 1/2 SE 1/4 Sect. 1 Tp. 5 R. 12, north and west.

**2165. FOSCUE, Benjamin**
Dec. 24, 1827, 3 miles W Millspring, Jackson Co. NW 1/4 Sect. 13 Tp. 3 R. 8, north and west.

**2166. FOSCUE, Benjamin**
Dec. 24, 1827, 3 miles SW Campbellton, Jackson Co. NW 1/4 Sect. 10 Tp. 6 R. 12, north and west.

**1718. FOSTER, Arthur**
May 31, 1827, 1 mile S Jacob, Jackson Co. W 1/2 SW 1/4 Sect. 24 Tp. 6 R. 12, north and west.

**1719. FOSTER, Arthur**
May 31, 1827, 1 mile S by E Jacob, Jackson Co. E 1/2 SW 1/4 Sect. 24 Tp. 6 R. 12, north and west.

**174. FOSTER, Wm.**
Dec. 29, 1826, 3 mile NW Glass Post Office, Jackson Co. NE 1/4 Sect. 25 Tp. 6 R. 12, north and west.

**5280. FOSTER, James**
Feb. 5, 1861, 3 1/2 miles E of Houston, Suwannee Co. SW 1/4 NE 1/4 Sect. 36 Tp. 2 R. 14, south and east.

**8186. FOWLER, William R. or Wm. R.**
Dec. 24, 1839, 2 1/2 miles SE by S Jennings, Hamilton Co. SW 1/4 NW 1/4 Sect. 18 Tp. 2 R. 13, north and east.

**6874. FOWLER, William R. or Wm. R.**
Mar. 9, 1837, c. 1 mile SE Jennings, Hamilton Co. Lot No. 6 Fractional Sect. 12 Tp. 2 R. 12, north and east.

**4260. FORSYTH, Joseph**
(And **Andrew P. SIMPSON**) Dec. 29, 1832, 3 1/4 miles NE of Indian Ford, Santa Rosa Co. W 1/2 NW 1/4 Sect. 30 Tp. 3 R. 26, north and west.

**7721. FORSYTH, Joseph**
Nov. 23, 1838, 1 3/4 miles NNW Galt City, Santa Rosa Co. W 1/2 NE 1/4 and W 1/2 NW 1/4 Sect. 15 Tp. 1 R. 28, north and west.

**7848. FORSYTH, Joseph**
Feb. 4, 1839, at Milton, Santa Rosa Co. Lot No. 4 Fractional Sect. 10 Tp. 1 R. 28, north and west.

**7884. FORSYTH, Joseph**
Feb. 23, 1839, 1 1/2 miles SE Indian Ford, Santa Rosa Co. W 1/2 SW 1/4 Sect. 1 Tp. 2 R. 27, north and west.

**7885. FORSYTH, Joseph**
Feb. 23, 1839, 1 mile SE Indian Ford, Santa Rosa Co. SE 1/4 Sect. 2 Tp. 2 R. 27, north and west.

**7886. FORSYTH, Joseph**
Feb. 23, 1839, 3 miles NNE Coldwater, Santa Rosa Co. NW 1/4 SW 1/4 NE 1/4 Sect.11 Tp. 2 R. 27, north and west.

**7887. FORSYTH, Joseph**
Feb. 23, 1839, 1 1/4 miles NNE Coldwater, Santa Rosa Co. E 1/2 NE 1/4 Sect. 10 Tp. 2 R. 27, north and west.

**7888. FORSYTH, Joseph**
Feb. 23, 1839, 2 1/2 miles SSE Coldwater, Santa Rosa Co. E 1/2 SE 1/4 Sect. 17 Tp. 2 R. 27, north and west.

**7889. FORSYTH, Joseph**
Feb. 23, 1839, 3/4 mile NW Coldwater, Santa Rosa Co. E 1/2 SE 1/4 Sect. 5 Tp. 2 R. 27, north and west.

**7890. FORSYTH, Joseph**
Feb. 23, 1839, 1/4 mile W Coldwater, Santa Rosa Co. E 1/2 NE 1/4 and E 1/2 SE 1/4 Sect. 8 Tp. 2 R. 27, north and west.

**7891. FORSYTH, Joseph**
Feb. 23, 1839, 3 1/2 miles E Indian

Ford, Santa Rosa Co. E 1/2 SE 1/4 Sect. 32 Tp. 3 R. 26, north and west.

**7892. FORSYTH, Joseph**
Feb. 23, 1839, 4 1/2 miles E by N Indian Ford, Santa Rosa Co. SE 1/4 Sect. 33 Tp. 3 R. 26, north and west.

**8236. FORSYTH, Joseph W.**
Feb. 27, 1840, 1 mile NE Indian Ford, Santa Rosa Co. SE 1/4 SW 1/4 Sect. 36 Tp. 3 R. 27, north and west.

**8582. FOX, Edmund B.**
Nov. 21, 1843, 1 mile NW Aucilla, Jefferson Co. E 1/4 SW 1/4 Sect. 9 Tp. 1 R. 6, north and east. The above is a provisional receipt issued to owner by **H. R. W. ANDREWS** to replace the lost original.

**8145. FRENCH, James**
Nov. 18, 1839, 6 miles SSE Barker, Holmes Co. NW 1/4 NW 1/4 Sect. 32 Tp. 6 R. 16, north and west.

**3252. FREEMAN, Ezekila K.**
Feb. 5, 1830, 3 1/2 miles W Tallahassee, Leon Co. E 1/2 SE 1/4 Sect. 31 Tp. 1 R. 1, north and west.

**2854. FREEMAN, Job**
June 26, 1829, 3 miles NW Wacissa, Jefferson Co. E 1/2 SW 1/4 Sect. 25 Tp. 1 R. 3, south and east.

**3909. FREEMAN, Job**
March 7, 1831, 3 miles NW Wacissa, Jefferson Co. W 1/2 SE 1/4 Sect. 25 Tp. 1 R. 3, south and east. See **Patrick KERR**

**3921. FREEMAN, John**
Mar. 28, 1831, 2 miles NW Wacissa, Jefferson Co. E 1/2 NE 1/4 Sect. 36 Tp. 1 R. 3, south and east.

**5126. FREEMAN, John**
Aug. 5, 1835, 1 1/4 miles E by N of Cay, Jefferson Co. SE 1/4 NE 1/4 Sect. 36 Tp. 1 R. 3, south and east.

**7785. FREEMAN, John**
Dec. 31, 1838, 2 1/2 miles NNE Cay, Jefferson Co. NW 1/4 NE 1/4 Sect. 36 Tp. 1 R. 3, south and east.

**8895. FREEMAN, William**
Feb. 2, 1846, 1/2 mile W by E Macon, Washington Co. NW 1/4 NW 1/4 Sect. 14 Tp. 2 R. 14, north and west.

**1935. FREEZE, Martin H.**
July 8, 1853, 1/4 mile S of Watertown, Columbia Co. SW 1/4 SE 1/4 Sect. 34 Tp. 3 R. 17, south and east. Patent delivered Oct. 28, 1856.

**4753. FRENCH, Tilman J.**
Dec. 31, 1834, 1 mile E of Jamieson, Gadsden Co. NW 1/4 SE 1/4 Sect. 8 Tp. 3 R. 2, north and west.

**4172. FRIER, Alexander A.**
Feb. 18, 1856, 1/2 mile N Santa Fe, Alachua Co. S 1/2 SE 1/4 Sect. 48 NE 1/4 NE 1/4 Sect. 17 Tp. 7 R. 19, south and east.

**2464. FRIER, David A.**
Feb. 23, 1854, 3 1/2 miles NNW of Blitchton, Marion Co. N 1/2 NE 1/4, N 1/2 NW 1/4 and SW 1/4 NW 1/4 Sect.2 Tp. 14 R. 19, south and east. Transferred to **Ephriam BLITCH**, Dec. 12, 1854, before **John M. McINTOSH**, Judge of Probate, N. C., Marion Co.

**238. FROOMAN, Jno.**
Dec. 30, 1826, 2 miles S Havana, Gadsden, Co. NW 1/4 Sect. 8 Tp. 2 R. 2, north and west.

**2029. FRY, James W.**
Sept. 1, 1880, 3/8 mile NW Live Oak, Suwannee Co. SE 1/4 NW 1/4 Sect. 22 Tp. 2S R. 13E.

**1055. FUSELL, James C.**
Dec. 23, 1851, on NW shore of Lake Griffin, Lake Co. N 1/2 Lot No. 3 and S 1/2 Lot No. 5 Sect. 23 Tp. 19 R. 24, south and east.

**1056. FUSELL, James C.**
Dec. 23, 1851, on NW shore of Lake Griffin, Lake Co. SE 1/4 of NW 1/4 Sect. 26 Tp. 19. R. 24, south and east. See **Eliza CROW, #2788**

**3431. FULLER, Zaccheus**
March 2, 1830, 4 miles SW Meridian, Leon Co. W 1/2 NW 1/4 Sect. 2 Tp. 2 R. 1, north and west.

**3432. FULLER, Zaccheus**
Mar. 2, 1830, 3 miles N Bradfordville, Leon Co. NE 1/4 Sect. 3 Tp. 2 R. 1, north and east.

**5571. FULLER, Zachrus**
April 2, 1836, 3 1/2 miles SSW of Boyd, Taylor Co. SW 1/4 Sect. 35 Tp. 3 R. 7, north and east.

**5571. FULLER, Zachrus**
April 2, 1836, 3 1/4 miles SSW of Boyd, Taylor Co. SE 1/4 NE 1/4 Sect.

34 Tp. 3 R. 7, north and east.
**992. FUPELL, James C.**
Nov. 5, 1851, at Leesburg, Lake Co.
Lots No. 6 & 7 Sect. 23 Tp. 19 R. 24, south and east.

## * G *

**2292. GADSDEN, James**
March 11, 1828, 3 miles ENE El Destino, Jefferson Co. W 1/2 SW 1/4 Sect. 3 Tp. 1 R. 3, south and east.

**2835. GADSDEN, James**
May 26, 1829, 3 miles E El Destino, Jefferson Co. W 1/2 SE 1/4 Sect. 10 Tp. 1 R. 3, south and east.

**2836. GADSDEN, James**
May 26, 1829, 2 3/4 miles E El Destino, Jefferson Co. E 12 SW 1/4 Sect. 3 Tp. 1 R. 3, south and east.

**2837. GADSDEN, James**
May 26, 1829, 3 1/2 miles E El Destino, Jefferson Co. W 1/2 NW 1/4 Sect. 11 Tp. 1 R. 3, south and east.

**2849. GADSDEN, James**
June 12, 1829, 2 1/2 miles NW Wacissa, Jefferson Co. E 1/2 NW 1/4 Sect. 25 Tp. 1 R. 3, south and east.

**3434. GADSDEN, James**
March 4, 1830. 2 1/2 miles N Mandalay, Jefferson Co. E 1/2 NE 1/4 Sect. 6 Tp. 4 R. 4, south and east.

**3435. GADSDEN, James**
March 4, 1830, 2 miles NNE Mandalay, Jefferson Co. E 1/2 SW 1/4 Sect. 32 Tp. 3 R. 4, south and east.

**3485. GADSDEN, James**
Apr. 21, 1830, 4 miles ESE El Destino, Jefferson Co. NE 1/4 Sect. 23 Tp. 1 R. 3, south and east. Delivered the patent for the within Certificate to **Achille MURAT**, (signed) **James D. GADSDEN**, June 15, 1835.

**4217. GADSDEN, James**
Sept. 10, 1832, 2 1/4 miles E of El Destino, Jefferson Co. SW 1/4 SE 1/4 Sect. 3 Tp. 1 R. 3, south and east.

**4218. GADSDEN, James**
Sept. 10, 1832, 2 miles E of El Destino, Jefferson Co. NE 1/4 SE 1/4 Sect. 10 Tp. 1 R. 3, south and east.

**4821. GADSDEN, James**
Jan. 24, 1835, 3 1/2 miles S of El Destino, Leon Co. E 1/2 NW 1/4 Sect. 15 Tp. 1 R. 3, south and east.
See **Wm. B. MITTALL** and **Horatio N. GRAY**

**1773. GADSDEN, Jas.**
(DUP) June 4, 1827, 2 miles E of Lloyd, Jefferson Co. E 1/2 NE 1/4 Sect. 24 Tp. 1 R. 3, south and east. "Deliver the patent of the within to **Mr. Claude D. JACMIENT** signed James GADSDEN, June 14, 1834."

**1774. GADSDEN, Jas.**
(DUP) June 4, 1827, 1 1/2 miles E of Lloyd, Jefferson Co. NW 1/4 Sect. 24 Tp. 1 R. 3, south and east. "Deliver the patent of the within certificate to **Achille MURAT**" signed **James GADSDEN**, June 15, 1835.

**3483. GADSDEN, John**
April 21, 1830, 4 1/2 miles W by S El Destino, Jefferson Co. W 1/2 NW 1/4 Sect. 13 Tp. 1 R. 3, south and east.

**3484. GADSDEN, John**
April 21, 1830, 2 1/2 miles S by E El Destino, Jefferson Co. E 1/2 SE 1/4 Sect. 14 Tp. 1 R. 3, south and east. Delivered the patent for the within to **A. L. KEKING(?)**. Signed **Ida GADSDEN** per **Jas. GADSDEN**.

**4358. GADSDEN, Octavius**
May 3, 1833, 4 miles E by NE of El Destino, Jefferson Co. SW 1/4 SW 1/4 Sect. 2 Tp. 1 R. 2, south and east.

**4359. GADSDDEN, Octavius**
May 3, 1833, 4 miles E of El Destino, Jefferson Co. E 1/2 NW 1/4 Sect. 11 Tp.1 R. 3, south and east.

**4777. GADSDEN, Octavus**
Jan. 15, 1835, 3 1/2 miles E of El Destino, Jefferson Co. W 1/2 SE 1/4 Sect. 11 Tp. 1 R. 3, south and east.

**4778. GADSDEN, Octavus**
Jan. 15, 1835, 3 3/4 miles E of El Destino, Jefferson Co. E 1/2 SW 1/4 Sect. 11 Tp. 1 R. 3, south and east.

**4779. GADSDEN, Octavus**
Jan. 15, 1835, 3 1/2 miles E of El Destino, Jefferson Co. W 1/2 SW 1/4 Sect. 11 Tp. 1 R. 3, south and east.

**5795. GADSDEN, Octavus**
Aug. 15, 1836, 4 miles NNE of El Destino, Jefferson Co. SE 1/4 SW 1/4 Sect. 2 Tp. 1 R. 3, south and east.

**GADSDEN, O. H.** see **Willis LAING, #4658**

**695. GAINES, Mary Ann Jane**
Dec. 15, 1849, 2 1/2 miles S Ocala, Marion Co. Lot No. 4 Sect. 36 Tp. 15 R. 21, south and east.

**716. GAINES, Mary Ann Jane**

Mar. 8, 1850, at Agnew, Marion Co. SW 1/4 SE 1/4 Sect. 10 Tp. 15 R. 21, south and east.
**741. GAINES, Mary Ann Jane**
June 6, 1850, at Agnew, Marion Co. NE 1/4 NW 1/4 Sect. 15 Tp. 15 R. 21, south and east.
**2140. GAINES, Mary Ann Jane**
Sept. 5, 1853, 2 miles W of Ocala, Marion Co. SE 1/4 NE 1/4 Sect. 22 and SW 1/4 SW 1/4 Sect. 23 Tp. 15 R. 21, south and east.
**2141. GAINES, Mary Ann Jane**
Sept. 5, 1853, 1 1/2 miles W of Ocala, Marion Co. SW 1/4 SE 1/4 Sect. 14 and NW 1/4 NE 1/4 Sect. 23 Tp. 15 R. 21, south and east.
**2142. GAINES, Mary Ann Jane**
Sept. 5, 1853, 2 1/2 miles W of Ocala, Marion Co. SW 1/4 SE 1/4 Sect. 22 Tp. 15 R. 21, south and east.
**4162. GAINES, Wilson**
(And **James ERNEST**) April 14, 1832, 4 1/2 miles NW of Indian Ford, Santa Rosa Co. W 1/2 NE 1/4 Sect. 30 Tp. 3 R. 27, north and west.
**4330. GAMBLE, James B.**
Mar. 19, 1833, 1/2 mile SE of Cody, Jefferson Co. SW 1/4 SW 1/4 Sect. 29 Tp. 1 R. 3, south and east.
**4331. GAMBLE, James B.**
Mar. 19, 1833, at Cody, Jefferson Co. SE 1/4 SE 1/4 Sect. 30 Tp. 1 R. 3, south and east.
**2623. GAMBLE, John G./ Jno. G.**
Jan. 14, 1829, 6 1/2 miles SSW Waukenah, Jefferson Co. E 1/2 NE 1/4 Sect. 31 Tp. 1 R. 4, south and east.
**1246. GAMBLE, John G./Jno. G.**
April 9, 1827, 5 miles SSW Waukenah, Jefferson Co. NW 1/4 Sect. 28 Tp. 1 R. 4, south and east.
**1247. GAMBLE, John G./or Jno. G.**
(DUP) April 9, 1827, 3 miles SSW Waukenah, Jefferson Co. W 1/2 SE 1/4 Sect. 21 Tp. 1 R. 4, south and east.
**1248. GAMBLE, John G./Jno. G.**
(DUP) April 9, 1827, 3 miles SSW Waukenah, Jefferson Co. SW 1/4 Sect. 21 Tp. 1 R. 4, south and east.
**1249. GAMBLE, John G./Jno. G.**
(DUP) April 9, 1827, 3 miles SSW Waukenah, Jefferson Co. NE 1/4 Sect. 21 Tp. 1 R. 4, south and east.
**1250. GAMBLE, John G./Jno. G.**
(DUP) April 9, 1827, 3 miles SSW Waukenah, Jefferson Co. E 1/2 NW 1/4 Sect. 21 Tp. 1 R. 4, south and east.
**1251. GAMBLE, John G./Jno. G.**
(DUP) April 9, 1827, 4 miles SW Waukenah, Jefferson Co. W 1/2 NE 1/4 Sect. 20 Tp. 1 R. 4, south and east.
**1252. GAMBEL, John G./Jno. G.**
(DUP) April 9, 1827, 5 miles SSW Waukenah, Jefferson Co. W 1/2 NE 1/4 Sect. 28 Tp. 1 R. 4, south and east.
**1252. GAMBLE, John G./Jno. G.**
(DUP) April 9, 1827, 3 miles WSW Waukenah, Jefferson Co. E 1/2 SW 1/4 Sect. 8 Tp. 1 R. 4, south and east.
**1254. GAMBLE, John G./Jno. G.**
(DUP) April 9, 1827, 3 miles WSW Waukenah, Jefferson Co. W 1/2 SE 1/4 Sect. 8 Tp. 1 R. 4, south and east.
**1270. GAMBLE, John G./Jno. G.**
April 12, 1827, 5 1/2 miles SSW Waukenah, Jefferson Co. SE 1/4 Sect. 20 Tp. 1 R. 4, south and east.
**1299. GAMBLE, John G./Jno. G.**
April 24, 1827, 7 miles SSE Waukenah, Jefferson Co. NW 1/4 Sect. 36 Tp. 1 R. 4, north and east. Transferred Aug. 25, 1827, to **Robert GAMBLE**.
**1300. GAMBLE, John G./Jno. G.**
April 24, 1827, 7 miles SSE Waukenah, Jefferson Co. SW 1/4 Sect. 36 Tp. 1 R. 4, north and east. Transferred to **Robert GAMBLE** on Aug. 25, 1827.
**1301. GAMBLE, John G./Jno. G.**
April 24, 1827, 7 miles SSE Waukenah, Jefferson Co. W 1/2 SE 1/4 Sect. 26 Tp. 1 R. 4, north and east. Transferred Aug. 25, 1827, to **Robert GAMBLE**.
**1302. GAMBLE, John G./Jno. G.**
April 24, 1827, 6 miles SSE Waukenah, Jefferson Co. E 1/2 SW 1/4 Sect. 24 Tp. 1 R. 4, south and east. **1317. GAMBLE, John G./Jno. G.**
May 1, 1827, 5 1/2 miles SW Waukenah, Jefferson Co. W 1/2 SW 1/4 Sect. 29 Tp. 1 R. 4, south and east.
**1318. GAMBLE, John G./Jno. G.**
May 1, 1827, 6 miles SW Waukenah, Jefferson Co. E 1/2 SE 1/4 Sect. 30 Tp. 1 R. 4, south and east.
**1329. GAMBLE, John G.**
(DUP) May 7, 1827, 5 1/2 miles S

Capps, Jefferson Co. E 1/2 SE 1/4 Sect. 36 Tp. 1 R. 4, north and east. Transferred to **Robert GAMBLE**, on Aug. 25, 1827.

**1350. GAMBLE, John G.**
(Of Virginia) May 11, 1827, 2 miles NE Wacissa, Jefferson Co. W 1/2 SE 1/4 Sect. 29 Tp. 1 R. 4, south and east.

**1351. GAMBLE, John G.**
(Of Virginia) May 11, 1827, 3 miles NE Wacissa, Jefferson Co. W 1/2 NW 1/4 Sect. 29 Tp. 1 R. 4, south and east.

**1352. GAMBLE, John G.**
(Of Virginia) May 11, 1827, 2 1/2 miles NE Wacissa, Jefferson Co. SW 1/4 Sect. 20 Tp. 1 R. 4, south and east.

**1353. GAMBLE, John G.**
May 11, 1827, 5 miles NW Waukenah, Jefferson Co. W 1/2 SW 1/4 Sect. 25 Tp. 1 R. 4, south and east. Transferred August. 25, 1827 to **Robert GAMBLE**.

**1364. GAMBLE, John G.**
May 14, 1827, at Nash, Jefferson Co. W 1/2 SE 1/4 Sect. 25 Tp. 1 R. 4, north and east. Transferred at Richmond to **Robert GAMBLE**, Aug. 25, 1827.

**1376. GAMBLE, John G.**
May 15, 1827, 2 miles NW Chaires, Leon Co. E 1/2 NW 1/4 Sect. 21 Tp. 1 R. 2, north and east.

**1377. GAMBLE, John G.**
May 15, 1827, 2 miles NW Chaires, Leon Co. W 1/2 NE 1/4 Sect. 21 Tp. 1 R. 2, north and east.

**1428. GAMBLE, John G.**
(Of Virginia) May 21, 1827, 4 1/2 miles WNW Monticello, Jefferson Co. NE 1/4 Sect. 21 Tp. 2 R. 4, north and east. Transferred to **Chas. WILLIAMSON**, May 30, 1827, (signed **G. W. WARD**, Register).

**1631. GAMBLE, John G.**
(DUP) May 28, 1827, 4 miles WNW Monticello, Jefferson Co. Lot No. 3 Fractional Sect. 21 Tp. 2 R. 4, north and east. Transferred May 30, 1827, to **Chas. WILLIAMSON. G. W. WARD**, Register.

**1633. GAMBLE, John G.**
May 23, 1827, 3 1/2 miles WNW Monticello, Jefferson Co. Lot No. 5 Fractional Sect. 21 Tp. 3 R. 4, north and east. Transferred to **Chas. WILLIAMSON**, May 30, 1827.

**1634. GAMBLE, John G.**
May 28, 1827, 3 1/2 miles WNW Monticello, Jefferson Co. Lot No. 1 Fractional Sect. 22 Tp. 2 R. 4, north and east. Transferred May 30, 1827, to **Chas. WILLIAMSON**.

**1787. GAMBLE, John G.**
June 5, 1827, 5 miles SW Campbellton, Jackson Co. W 1/2 SW 1/4 Sect. 10 Tp. 6 R. 11, north and west.

**1788. GAMBLE, John G.**
June 5, 1827, 7 miles E by S Campbellton, Jackson Co. E 1/2 NW 1/4 Sect. 15 Tp. 6 R. 11, north and west.

**1789. GAMBLE, John G.**
June 5, 1827, 3 miles W Jacob, Jackson Co. W 1/2 NW 1/4 Sect. 15 Tp. 6 R. 11, north and west.

**1800. GAMBLE, John G.**
June 5, 1827, 3 miles WSW Waukenah, Jefferson Co. W 1/2 SW 1/4 Sect. 8 Tp. 1 R. 4, south and east.

**1906. GAMBLE, John G.**
June 12, 1827, 4 miles NNE Waukenah, Jefferson Co. E 1/2 NE 1/4 Sect. 24 Tp. 1 R. 5, north and east.

**1907. GAMBLE, John G.**
June 12, 1827, 1 mile S Drifton, Jefferson Co. W 1/2 NW 1/4 Sect. 19 Tp. 1 R. 5, north and east.

**1908. GAMBLE, John G.**
June 12, 1827, 1/2 mile S Drifton, Jefferson Co. W 1/2 SW 1/4 Sect. 18 Tp. 1 R. 5, north and east.

**1928. GAMBLE, John G.**
June 18, 1827, 2 miles S Waukenah, Jefferson Co. W 1/2 SW 1/4 Sect. 15 Tp. 1 R. 4, south and east.

**1929. GAMBLE, John G.**
June 18, 1827, 4 miles SW by W Waukenah, Jefferson Co. NW 1/4 Sect. 18 Tp. 1 R. 4, south and east.

**1943. GAMBLE, John G.**
June 25, 1827, 3 miles WNW Waukenah, Jefferson Co. NE 1/4 Sect. 31 Tp. 1 R. 4, north and east.

**1944. GAMBLE, John G.**
June 25, 1827, 3 miles WNW Waukenah, Jefferson Co. W 1/2 NW 1/4 Tp. 1 R. 4, north and east.

**1945. GAMBLE, John G.**

June 25, 1827, 3 miles NE Waukenah, Jefferson Co. E 1/2 NW 1/4 Sect. 24 Tp. 1 R. 4, north and east.

**1946. GAMBLE, John G.**
June 25, 1827, 4 miles NE Waukenah, Jefferson Co. W 1/2 NE 1/4 Sect. 24 Tp. 1 R. 4, north and east.

**1947. GAMBLE, John G.**
(DUP) June 25, 1827, 1 1/2 miles SW Drifton, Jefferson Co. E 1/2 SW 1/4 Sect. 13 Tp. 1 R. 4, north and east.

**1948. GAMBLE, John G.**
June 25, 1827, 1 3/4 miles SW Drifton, Jefferson Co. W 1/2 SW 1/4 Sect. 13 Tp. 1 R. 4, north and east.

**1960. GAMBLE, John G.**
June 27, 1827, 1 mile SW Drifton, Jefferson Co. E 1/2 SE 1/4 Sect. 13 Tp. 1 R. 4, north and east.

**1982. GAMBLE, John G.**
#1983 Receipts were lost but patents for these were delivered #1984 to **John G. GAMBLE**, and receipted for by him. No descriptions are on this subject.

**2323. GAMBLE, John G.**
March 29, 1828, 3 miles S Waukenah, Jefferson Co. W 1/2 NW 1/4 Sect. 22 Tp. 1 R. 4, south and east.

**2678. GAMBLE, John G.**
Jan. 27, 1829, 3 miles SW Waukenah, Jefferson Co. E 1/2 NW 1/4 Sect. 20 Tp. 1 R. 4, south and east.

**3090. GAMBLE, John G.**
Oct. 26, 1829, 5 miles SW Waukenah, Jefferson Co. SE 1/4 Sect. 19 Tp. 1 R. 4, south and east.

**3200. GAMBLE, John G.**
Jan. 1, 1830, 1/2 mile W Waukenah, Jefferson Co. E 1/2 NE 1/4 Sect. 19 Tp. 1 R. 4, south and east.

**3389. GAMBLE, John G.**
Feb. 16, 1830, 2 miles S Mandelay, Taylor Co. W 1/2 SW 1/4 Sect. 30 Tp. 4 R. 4, south and east.

**3390. GAMBLE, John G.**
Feb. 16, 1830, 1 mile S by W Mandalay, Taylor Co. W 1/2 NW 1/4 Sect. 30 Tp. 4 R. 4, south and east.

**3391. GAMBLE, John G.**
Feb. 16, 1830, at Mandalay, Taylor Co. N 1/2 Sect. 19 Tp. 4 R. 4, south and east. 218.24 acres.

**3392. GAMBLE, John G.**
Feb. 16, 1830, 1/2 mile SW Mandalay, Taylor Co. SW 1/4 Sect. 19 Tp. 4 R. 4, south and east. 159.12 acres.

**3393. GAMBLE, John G.**
Feb. 16, 1830, 1/4 mile S Mandalay, Taylor Co. W 1/2 SE 1/4 Sect. 19 Tp. 4 R. 4, south and east. 79.50 acres.

**3394. GAMBLE, John G.**
Feb. 16, 1830, 1/2 mile SE Mandalay, Taylor Co. E 1/2 SE 1/4 Sect. 19 Tp. 4 R. 4, south and east.

**3950. GAMBLE, John G.**
April 13, 1831, 4 miles SW Waukenah, Jefferson Co. W 1/2 NW 1/4 Sect. 20 Tp. 1 R. 4, south and east.

**4134. GAMBLE, John G.**
Feb. 6, 1832, 3 1/4 miles S by E of Mandalay, Jefferson Co. W 1/2 NW 1/4 Sect. 32 Tp. 1 R. 4, south and east.

**4367. GAMBLE, John G.**
June 8, 1833, 1 1/2 miles W by N of Braswell, Jefferson Co. W 1/2 SE 1/4 Sect. 18 Tp. 1 R. 4, south and east.

**4368. GAMBLE, John G.**
June 8, 1833, 2 miles NNE Lloyd, Jefferson Co. E 1/2 NE 1/4 Sect. 13 Tp. 1 R. 3, south and east.

**4895. GAMBLE, John G.**
(And **Robert GAMBLE**), Trustees of **Agnes S. B. CABELL**, Mar. 19, 1835, 1/2 mile SW of Nash, Jefferson Co. SE 1/4 Sect. 26 Tp. 1 R. 4, north and east.

**4896. GAMBLE, John G.**
(And **Robert GAMBLE**), Trustees of **Agnes S. B. CABELL**, Mar. 19, 1835, 3/4 mile SW of Nash, Jefferson Co. W 1/2 NE 1/4 Sect. 35 Tp. 1 R. 4, north and east.

**4897. GAMBLE, John G.**
(And **Robert GAMBLE**), Trustees of **Agnes S. B. CABELL**, Mar. 19, 1835, 3/4 mile SW of Nash, Jefferson Co. E 1/2 NW 1/4 Sect. 35 Tp. 1 R. 4, north and east.

**4898. GAMBLE, John G.**
Mar. 19, 1835, 2 miles SE of Nash, Jefferson Co. W 1/2 NW 1/4 Sect. 31 Tp. 1 R. 5, north and east.

**4983. GAMBLE, John G.**
May 26, 1835, 2 miles W by N of Braswells, Jefferson Co. SE 1/4 SW 1/4 Sect. 18 Tp. 1 R. 4, south and east.

**4984. GAMBLE, John G.**

May 26, 1835, 1 3/4 miles W by N of Braswells, Jefferson Co. W 1/2 SW 1/4 Sect. 18 Tp. 1 R. 4, south and east.

**5018. GAMBLE, John G.**
June 30, 1835, 3 1/2 miles NNW of Waukenah, Jefferson Co. W 1/2 SW 1/4 Sect. 31 Tp. 1 R. 4, south and east.

**5037. GAMBLE, John G.**
(With **Richard K. CALL** and **Thomas PENNY**) July 8, 1835, 6 miles E of Steinhatchee Springs, Lafayette Co. Lots 1, 2, 3, 4, 6, 7, 8, 9, 10, and 15 Fractional Sect. 26 Tp. 7 R. 11, south and west.

**5038. GAMBLE, John G.**
(With **Richard K. CALL** and **Thomas PENNY**) July 8, 1835, 7 miles SSW of Howell, Lafayette Co. Fractional Sect. 2 Tp. 8 R. 12, south and west.

**5039. GAMBLE, John G.**
(With **Richard K. CALL** and **Thomas PENNY**) July 8, 1835, 4 1/2 miles W of Linnie, Lafayette Co. Fractional Sect. 11 Tp. 8 R. 12, south and west.

**5040. GAMBLE, John G.**
(With **Richard K. CALL** and **Thomas PENNY**) July 8, 1835, 1/4 mile of Port St. Joe, Gulf Co. W 1/2 Sect. 36 Tp. 7 R. 11, south and west.

**5041. GAMBLE, John G.**
(With **Richard K. CALL** and **Thomas PENNY**) July 8, 1835, at Port St. Joe, Gulf Co. W 1/2 Fractional Sect. 1 Tp. 8 R. 11, south and west.

**5042. GAMBLE, John G.**
(With **Richard K. CALL** and **Thomas PENNY**) July 8, 1835, 1/2 mile of Port St. Joe, Gulf Co. Fractional Sect. 35 Tp. 7 R. 11, south and west.

**5043. GAMBLE, John G.**
(With **Richard K. CALL** and **Thomas PENNY**) July 8, 1835, 7 miles E of Port St. Joe, Gulf Co. E 1/2 Sect. 1 Tp. 8 R. 11, south and west.

**5044. GAMBLE, John G.**
(With **Richard K. CALL** and **Thomas PENNY**) July 8, 1835, St. Joseph's Bay, 2 miles SW of Port St. Joe, Gulf Co. Fractional Sect. 14 Tp. 8 R. 12, south and west.

**5045. GAMBLE, John G.**
(With **Richard K. CALL** and **Thomas PENNY**) July 8, 1835, 1/4 mile N of Port St. Joe, Gulf Co. Fractional Sect. 2 Tp. 8 R. 10, south and west.

**5046. GAMBLE, John G.**
(With **Richard K. CALL** and **Thomas PENNY**) July 8, 1835, 8 miles N of Port St. Joe, Gulf Co. Lots 5, 10, 12, and 13 Sect. 9 Tp. 7 R. 11, south and west.

**5047. GAMBLE, John G.**
(With **Richard K. CALL** and **Thomas PENNY**) July 8, 1835, 2 1/2 miles N by W of Port St. Joe, Gulf Co. Lots 14, 15, and 16 Sect. 22 Tp. 7 R. 11, south and west.

**5048. GAMBLE, John G.**
(With **Richard K. CALL** and **Thomas PENNY**) July 8, 1835, 5 miles N by W of Port St. Joe, Gulf Co. Lots No. 1 and 2 Sect. 21 Tp. 7 R. 11, south and west.

**5049. GAMBLE, John G.**
(With **Richard K. CALL** and **Thomas PENNY**) July 8, 1835, St. Joseph's Bay, 6 miles S by W of Port St. Joe, Gulf Co. Lots 1, 3, and 4 Sect. 25 Tp. 8 R. 12, south and west.

**5050. GAMBLE, John G.**
(With **Richard K. CALL** and **Thomas PENNY**) July 8, 1835, St. Joseph's Bay, 3 miles S by W of Port St. Joe, Gulf Co. Fractional Sect. 26 Tp. 8 R. 11, south and west.

**5051. GAMBLE, John G.**
(With **Richard K. CALL** and **Thomas PENNY**) July 8, 1835, St. Joseph's Bay, 5 miles SSW of Port St. Joe, Gulf Co. Fractional Sect. 23 Tp. 8 R. 12, south and west.

**5052. GAMBLE, John G.**
(With **Richard K. CALL** and **Thomas PENNY**) July 8, 1835, 2 1/2 miles N by W of Port St. Joe, Gulf Co. Lots No. 1 and 3 Fractional Sect. 27 Tp. 7 R. 11, south and west.

**5053. GAMBLE, John G.**
(With **Richard K. CALL** and **Thomas PENNY**) July 8, 1835, 2 3/4 miles N by W of Port St. Joe, Gulf Co. Lots No. 12 and 13 Fractional Sect. 22 Tp. 7 R. 11, south and west.

**5054. GAMBLE, John G.**
(With **Richard K. CALL** and **Thomas PENNY**) July 8, 1835, 2 miles SSW of Niles, Gulf Co. Fractional Sect. 23 Tp. 8 R. 11, south and west.

**5055. GAMBLE, John G.**
(With **Richard K. CALL** and **Thomas PENNY**) July 8, 1835, St. Joseph's Bay, 4 1/2 miles W of Higgins, Gulf Co. Fractional Sect. 35 Tp. 8 R. 11, south and west.

**5056. GAMBLE, John G.**
(With **Richard K. CALL** and **Thomas PENNY**) July 8, 1835, St. Joseph's Bay, 6 miles SW of Niles, Gulf Co. Fractional Sect. 24 Tp. 8 R. 12, south and west.

**5057. GAMBLE, John G.**
(With **Richard K. CALL** and **Thomas PENNY**) July 8, 1835, 8 miles NNW of Port St. Joe, Gulf Co. Fractional Sect. 8 Tp. 7, R. 11, south and west.

**5058. GAMBLE, John G.**
(With **Richard K. CALL** and **Thomas PENNY**) July 8, 1835, St. Joseph's Bay, 12 miles W by S of Niles, Gulf Co. Fractional Sect. 13 Tp. 8 R. 12, south and west.

**7408. GAMBLE, John G.**
Mar. 15, 1838, 4 1/2 miles E by S El Destino, Jefferson Co. E 1/2 SE 1/4 Sect. 13 Tp. 1 R. 3, south and east.

**7409. GAMBLE, John G.**
Mar. 15, 1838, 4 1/2 miles NNE Cay, Jefferson Co. N 1/2 NW 1/4 Sect. 19 Tp. 1 R. 4, south and east.
See **Elizabeth VICKERS**, **Robert GAMBLE** and **Adam GRANTHAM**

**922. GAMBLE, Robert**
Jan. 18, 1827, 1 mile E Waukenah, Jefferson Co. E 1/2 SW 1/4 Sect. 1 Tp. 1 R. 4, south and east.

**923. GAMBLE, Robert**
Jan. 18, 1827, 2 miles SE Waukenah, Jefferson Co. W 1/2 SW 1/4 Sect. 12 Tp. 1 R. 4, south and east.

**924. GAMBLE, Robert**
Jan. 18, 1827, 2 miles SE Waukenah, Jefferson Co. E 1/2 SE 1/4 Sect. 12 Tp. 1 R. 4, south and east.

**925. GAMBLE, Robert**
Jan. 18, 1827, 1 mile SE Waukenah, Jefferson Co. SW 1/4 Sect. 11 Tp. 1 R. 4, south and east.

**926. GAMBLE, Robert**
Jan. 18, 1827, at Capps, Jefferson Co. NW 1/4 Sect. 1 Tp. 1 R. 4, south and east.

**927. GAMBLE, Robert**
Jan. 18, 1827, 1 mile E Waukenah, Jefferson Co. E 1/2 NE 1/4 Sect. 21 Tp. 1 R. 4, south and east.

**928. GAMBLE, Robert**
Jan. 18, 1827, 1 mile SE Waukenah, Jefferson Co. E 1/2 SW 1/4 Sect. 2 Tp. 1 R. 4, south and east.

**929. GAMBLE, Robert**
Jan. 18, 1 mile SE Waukenah, Jefferson Co. W 1/2 SE 1/4 Sect. 2 Tp. 1 R. 4, south and east.

**1025. GAMBLE, Robert**
Jan. 30, 1827, 6 miles E Bloxham, Jefferson Co. E 1/2 NE 1/4 Sect. 1 Tp. 1 R. 4, south and east.

**1039. GAMBLE, Robert**
Jan. 31, 1827, 1 mile SE Waukenah, Jefferson Co. E 1/2 SE 1/4 Sect. 11 Tp. 1 R. 4, south and east.

**1040. GAMBLE, Robert**
Jan. 31, 1827, 2 1/2 miles ESE Waukenah, Jefferson Co. E 1/2 NW 1/4 Sect. 12 Tp. 1 R. 4, south and east.

**1079. GAMBLE, Robert**
Feb. 5, 1827, 2 1/2 miles SE Waukenah, Jefferson Co. W 1/2 SE 1/4 Sect. 12 Tp. 1 R. 4, south and east.

**1080. GAMBLE, Robert**
Feb. 5, 1827, 3 miles W Waukenah, Jefferson Co. W 1/2 SW 1/4 Sect. 6 Tp. 1 R. 4, south and east.

**1081. GAMBLE, Robert**
Feb. 5, 1827, 1/2 mile SE Waukenah, Jefferson Co. W 1/2 SW 1/4 Tp. 1 R. 4, south and east.

**1082. GAMBLE, Robert**
Feb. 5, 1827, at Waukenah, Jefferson Co. E 1/2 SE 1/4 Sect. 3 Tp. 1 R. 4, south and east.

**1131. GAMBLE, Robert**
Feb. 17, 1827, 5 miles W Lamont, Jefferson Co. SE 1/4 Sect. 23 Tp. 1 R. 4, south and east.

**1148. GAMBLE, Robert**
(DUP) Feb. 19, 1827, 5 miles W by S of Lamont, Jefferson Co. E 1/2 NE 1/4 Sect. 36 Tp. 1 R.4, south and east.

**1177. GAMBLE, Robert**
(DUP) Feb. 27, 1827, 2 1/2 miles SW Waukenah, Jefferson Co. E 1/2 NE 1/4 Sect. 17 Tp. 1 R. 4, south and east. Transferred Aug. 25, 1827, to **John G. GAMBLE**.

**1178. GAMBLE, Robert**

(DUP) Feb. 27, 1827, 3 miles SW Waukenah, Jefferson Co. W 1/2 SW 1/4 Sect. 17 Tp. 1 R. 4, south and east. Transferred Aug. 25, 1827, to **John G. GAMBLE**.

**1179. GAMBLE, Robert**
(DUP) Feb. 27, 1827, 4 miles W Lamont, Jefferson Co. E 1/2 SE 1/4 Sect. 25 Tp. 1 R. 4, south and east.

**1180. GAMBLE, Robert**
(DUP) Feb. 27, 1827, 5 miles W Lamont, Jefferson Co. W 1/2 NE 1/4 Sect. 26 Tp. 1 R. 4, south and east.

**1181. GAMBLE, Robert**
(DUP) Feb. 27, 1827, 7 miles W Lamont, Jefferson Co. W 1/2 NW 1/4 Sect. 21 Tp. 1 R. 4, south and east. Transferred to **John G. GAMBLE** on Aug. 25, 1827.

**1182. GAMBLE, Robert**
(DUP) Feb. 27, 1827, 8 miles W Lamont, Jefferson Co. E 1/2 NE 1/4 Sect. 20 Tp. 1 R. 4, south and east. Transferred to **John G. GAMBLE** on Aug. 5, 1827.

**1192. GAMBLE, Robert**
Mar. 6, 1827, 5 1/2 miles W Lamont, Jefferson Co. E 1/2 NW 1/4 Sect. 26 Tp. 1 R. 4, south and east.

**1193. GAMBLE, Robert**
(DUP) Mar. 6, 1827, 5 miles W by S Lamont, Jefferson Co. W 1/2 NE 1/4 Sect. 36 Tp. 1 R. 4, south and east.

**1227. GAMBLE, Robert**
Mar. 27, 1827, 5 miles S Waukenah, Jefferson Co. NE 1/4 Sect. 34 Tp. 1 R. 4, south and east.

**1228. GAMBLE, Robert**
Mar. 27, 1827, 5 miles S Waukenah, Jefferson Co. SW 1/4 Sect. 27 Tp. 1 R. 4, south and east.

**1255. GAMBLE, Robert**
April 9, 1827, 5 miles S Waukenah, Jefferson Co. NW 1/4 Sect. 34 Tp. 1 R. 4, south and east.

**1256. GAMBLE, Robert**
April 9, 1827, 5 miles S Waukenah, Jefferson Co. W 1/2 SW 1/4 Sect. 26 Tp. 1 R. 4, south and east.

**1257. GAMBLE, Robert**
April 9, 1827, 5 miles S Waukenah, Jefferson Co. W 1/2 NW 1/4 Sect. 35 Tp. 1 R. 4, south and east.

**1271. GAMBLE, Robert**
April 12, 1827, 5 miles WSW Waukenah, Jefferson Co. E 1/2 SW 1/4 Sect. 22 Tp. 1 R. 4, south and east.

**1272. GAMBLE, Robert**
(DUP) April 12, 1827, 5 miles S Waukenah, Jefferson Co. E 1/2 NW 1/4 Sect. 27 Tp. 1 R. 4, south and east.

**1310. GAMBLE, Robert**
April 30, 1827, 3 miles S Waukenah, Jefferson Co. NW 1/4 Sect. 23 Tp. 1 R. 4, south and east.

**1311. GAMBLE, Robert**
April 30, 1827, 3 miles S Waukenah, Jefferson Co. W 1/2 NE 1/4 Sect. 23 Tp. 1 R. 4, south and east.

**1312. GAMBLE, Robert**
Aprill 30, 1827, 3 miles S Waukenah, Jefferson Co. E 1/2 SW 1/4 Sect. 23 Tp. 1 R. 4, south and east.

**1314. GAMBLE, Robert**
April 30, 1827, 2 miles S Waukenah, Jefferson Co. E 1/2 NE 1/4 Sect. 15 Tp. 1 R. 4, south and east.

**1316. GAMBLE, Robert**
April 30, 1827, 5 1/2 miles S Waukenah, Jefferson Co. W 1/2 SE 1/4 Sect. 34 TP. 1 R. 4, south and east. **1331. GAMBLE, Robert**
(DUP) May 7, 1827, 4 miles SE Waukenah, Jefferson Co. E 1/2 SW 1/4 Sect. 24 Tp. 1 R. 4, south and east.

**1332. GAMBLE, Robert**
(DUP) May 7, 1827, 4 miles SE Waukenah, Jefferson Co. W 1/2 SE 1/4 Sect. 24 Tp. 1 R. 4, south and east.

**1360. GAMBLE, Robert**
May 14, 1827, 3 miles SE Waukenah, Jefferson Co. W 1/2 SE 1/4 Sect. 13 Tp. 1 R. 4, south and east.

**1361. GAMBLE, Robert**
May 14, 1827, 3 miles SSE Waukenah, Jefferson Co. E 1/2 NE 1/4 Sect. 23 Tp. 1 R. 4, south and east.

**1362. GAMBLE, Robert**
May 14, 1827, 3 1/2 miles S Waukenah, Jefferson Co. W 1/2 NW 1/4 Sect. 27 Tp. 1 R. 4, south and east.

**1363. GAMBLE, Robert**
May 14, 1827, 2 1/2 miles SSE Waukenah, Jefferson Co. SE 1/4 Sect. 14 Tp. 1 R. 4, south and east.

**1372. GAMBLE, Robert**
May 15, 1827, 1 mile NE Waukenah, Jefferson Co. W 1/2 NE 1/4 Sect. 2

Tp. 1 R. 4, south and east.

**1373. GAMBLE, Robert**
May 15, 1827, 2 miles SSE Waukenah, Jefferson Co. W 1/2 NW 1/4 Sect. 14 Tp. 1 R. 4, south and east.

**1738. GAMBLE, Robert**
June 2, 1827, 4 1/2 miles E Wacissa, Jefferson Co. E 1/2 NW 1/4 Sect. 1 Tp. 2 R. 4, south and east.

**1739. GAMBLE, Robert**
June 2, 1827, 4 1/2 miles E Wacissa, Jefferson Co. W 1/2 NW 1/4 Sect. 1 Tp. 2 R. 4, south and east.

**1740. GAMBLE, Robert**
June 2, 1827, 4 miles E Wacissa, Jefferson Co. E 1/2 NE 1/4 Sect. 2 Tp. 2 R. 4, south and east.

**1741. GAMBLE, Robert**
June 2, 1827, 3 1/2 miles E Wacissa, Jefferson Co. W 1/2 NE 1/4 Sect. 2 Tp. 2 R. 4, south and east.

**1742. GAMBLE, Robert**
June 2, 1827, 3 1/2 miles E Wacissa, Jefferson Co. E 1/2 NW 1/4 Sect. 2 Tp. 2 R. 4, south and east.

**2193. GAMBLE, Robert**
(Of Fla.) Dec. 31, 1827, 5 miles S Capps, Jefferson Co. E 1/2 NW 1/4 Sect. 36 Tp. 1 R. 4, south and east.

**2194. GAMBLE, Robert**
Dec. 31, 1827, 5 miles S Capps, Jefferson Co. E 1/2 SW 1/4 Sect. 36 Tp. 1 R. 4, south and east.

**2263. GAMBLE, Robert**
Feb. 18, 1828, 2 miles NW Waukenah, Jefferson Co. W 1/2 NW 1/4 Sect. 33 Tp. 1 R. 4, north and east. Transferred Mar. 10, 1828, to **D. M. QUAILES**; dated at Jefferson Co., Fla.

**2264. GAMBLE, Robert**
Feb. 18, 1828, 2 1/2 miles WNW Waukenah, Jefferson Co. E 1/2 NE 1/4 Sect. 32 Tp. 1 R. 4, north and east. Transferred Mar. 10, 1828, to **D. M. QUAILES**.

**2265. GAMBLE, Robert**
Feb. 18, 1828, 2 1/2 miles NW Waukenah, Jefferson Co. W 1/2 SW 1/4 Sect. 28 Tp. 1 R. 4, north and east. Transferred Feb. 18, 1828 to **D. M. QUAILES**.

**2266. GAMBLE, Robert**
Feb. 18, 1828, 3 miles NW Waukenah, Jefferson Co. E 1/2 SE 1/4 Sect. 29 Tp. 1 R. 4, north and east. Transferred Mar. 10, 1828, to **D. M. QUAILES**.

**2317. GAMBLE, Robert**
Mar. 20, 1828, 5 miles S by E Waukenah, Jefferson Co. W 1/2 NW 1/4 Sect. 26 Tp. 1 R. 4, south and east.

**2318. GAMBLE, Robert**
Mar. 20, 1828, 3 miles SE Waukenah, Jefferson Co. E 1/2 SW 1/4 Sect. 12 Tp. 1 R. 4, south and east.

**5510. GAMBLE, Robert**
Mar. 3, 1836, 1/4 mile E of Wetumka, Gadsden Co. W 1/2 SW 1/4 Sect. 35 Tp. 1 R. 4, south and east.

**5511. GAMBLE, Robert**
Mar. 3, 1836, at Wetumka, Gadsden Co. E 1/2 SE 1/4 Sect. 34 Tp. 1 R. 4, south and east.

**5924. GAMBLE, Robert**
Oct. 25, 1836, 3 3/4 miles E of Leonton, Jefferson Co. W 1/2 SE 1/4 Sect. 1 Tp. 2 R. 4, south and east.

**5925. GAMBLE, Robert**
Oct. 25, 1836, 4 miles E of Leonton, Jefferson Co. W 1/2 SW 1/4 Sect. 6 Tp. 2 R. 5, south and east.

**6492. GAMBLE, Robert**
Jan. 9, 1837, 4 1/2 miles W Lamont, Jefferson Co. W 1/2 SW 1/4 Sect. 24 Tp. 1 R. 4, south and east.

**6493. GAMBLE, Robert**
Jan. 9, 1837, 5 miles W Lamont, Jefferson Co. W 1/2 NW 1/4 Sect. 25 Tp. 1 R. 4, south and east.

**6494. GAMBLE, Robert**
Jan. 9, 1837, 4 1/2 miles W Lamont, Jefferson Co. E 1/2 NE 1/4 Sect. 25 Tp. 1 R. 4, south and east.

**7003. GAMBLE, Robert**
April 27, 1837, 2 3/4 miles S Capps, Jefferson Co. E 1/2 SE 1/4 Sect. 24 Tp. 1 R. 4, south and east.

**7004. GAMBLE, Robert**
April 27, 1837, 4 miles W by W Leonton, Jefferson Co. NE 1/4 SW 1/4 Sect. 1 Tp. 2 R. 4, south and east.

**7445. GAMBLE, Robert**
April 11, 1838, 1 1/2 miles W Lamont, Jefferson Co. Lot No. 6 Sect. 29 Tp. 1 R. 5, south and east.

**7446. GAMBLE, Robert**
April 11, 1838, 1 3/4 miles W Lamont, Jefferson Co. Lot No. 3 Sect. 29 Tp. 1 R. 5, south and east.

**7447. GAMBLE, Robert**
April 11, 1838, 1 3/4 miles W Lamont, Jefferson Co. Lot No. 5 Sect. 29 Tp. 1 R. 5, south and east.

**7448. GAMBLE, Robert**
April 11, 1838, 1 3/4 miles W Lamont, Jefferson Co. Lot No. 4 Tp. 1 R. 5, south and east.
See **John G. GAMBLE** and **R. C. ALLEN**

**408. GAMBLE, Robert, Jr.**
May 11, 1846, at Manavista, Manatee Co. NW 1/4 Sect. 17 Tp. 34 R. 18, south and east.

**GAMBLE, Stephen** see **William C. CARRUTHERS, #2349**

**2378. GANTT, Daniel**
May 16, 1828, c. 2 miles S Meridian, Leon Co. Island No. 41 Tp. 3 R. 1, north and west.

**2513. GANTT, Daniel**
Oct. 7, 1828, c. 6 miles ESE Havana, Leon Co. Lot No. 6 Sect. 4 Tp. 2 R. 1, north and west.

**2376. GANTT, Lucy**
May 16, 1828, c. 5 miles NNE Lake Jackson, Leon Co. Lot No. 2 Sect. 9 Tp. 2 R. 1, north and west.

**2377. GANTT, Lucy**
May 16, 1828, c. 5 miles NNE Lake Jackson, Leon Co. Lot No. 3 Sect. 9 Tp. 2 R. 1, north and west.

**3750. GARETT, William**
Nov. 21, 1830, 3 miles Alma, Leon Co. E 1/2 NE 1/4 Sect.32 Tp. 3 R. 4, north and east.

**1653. GARNER, James**
Jan. 24, 1853, 4 miles SW of Louise, Alachua Co. NE 1/4 SE 1/4 Sect. 4 Tp. 8 R. 20, south and east.

**2259. GARNER, James**
Oct. 19, 1853, 1 1/2 miles S of Atlas, Alachua Co. NW 1/4 SW 1/4 Sect. 3 Tp. 6 R. 20, south and east.

**5054. GARRETT, Milla**
July 15, 1859, 2 1/2 miles SSE of Kokoma, Alachua Co. N 1/2 NE 1/4 and NW 1/4 and N 1/2 SW 1/4 Sect. 34 Tp. 9 R. 17, south and east.

**2725. GARRETT, Sam'l**
Feb. 11, 1829, 2 1/2 miles WNW Alma, Leon Co. W 1/2 SE 1/4 Sect. 28 Tp.3 R. 4, north and east.

**3777. GARRETT, Samuel**
Dec. 6, 1830, 3 miles E Copeland, Leon Co. E 1/2 SE 1/4 Sect. 31 Tp. 3 R. 4, north and east.

**4037. GARRETT, Samuel**
July 19, 1831, 7 miles NW of Monticello, Gadsden Co. W 1/2 NE 1/4 Sect. 33 Tp. 3 R. 4, north and east. See **Richard K. CALL**

**2653. GARRETT, Wm.**
Jan. 20, 1829, 2 1/2 miles W Alma, Leon Co. W 1/2 NW 1/4 Sect. 32 Tp. 3 R. 4, north and east. See **Daniel McRAENG**

**703. GASKINS, Thomas**
Jan. 12, 1850, 3 1/2 miles SW Guilford, Union Co. W 1/2 NW 1/4 and NE 1/4 NW 1/4 and NW 1/4 NE 1/4 Sect. 27 Tp. 5 R. 18, south and east. Patent delivered Feb. 12, 1853.

**1217. GASKINS, Thomas**
Feb. 27, 1852, 5 miles SW of Guilford, Union Co. NE 1/4 NE 1/4 Sect. 27 Tp. 5 R. 18, south and east. Patent delivered Feb. 27, 1856.

**4487. GAUSE, Benjamin W.**
Dec. 23, 1832, 5 miles E by S of Centerville, Jefferson Co. SW 1/4 SW 1/4 Sect. 26 Tp. 2 R. 2, north and east.

**5489. GAUSE, Benjamin W.**
Feb. 24, 1836, 2 1/4 miles NNW of Wadesboro, Leon Co. E 1/2 NW 1/4 Sect. 35 Tp. 2 R. 2, north and east.

**2494. GAUTIER, Peter W.**
(Sen'r of Fla) Sept. 15, 1828, 5 miles E by N Cottondale, Jackson Co. E 1/2 SW 1/4 Sect. 19 Tp. 5 R. 10, north and west.

**2495. GAUTIER, Peter W.**
(Sen'r of Fla.) Sept. 15, 1828, 5 miles E Cottondale, Jackson Co. W 1/2 NW 1/4 Sect. 30 Tp. 5 R. 10, north and west.

**6672. GAUTIER, Peter W.**
(Jr.) Jan. 25, 1837, just NW Marianna, Jackson Co. E 1/2 NE 1/4 Sect. 31 Tp. 5 R. 10, north and west.

**6736. GAUTIER, Peter W.**
(Jr.) Feb. 3, 1837, 1/2 miles W Fair Grounds, Jackson Co. E 1/2 SE 1/4 Sect. 19 Tp. 5 R. 10, north and west.
See **William M. LOFTIN, #554**

**2602. GAVIN, Charles**
Mar. 11, 1854, 4 miles E of High Springs, Alachua Co. S 1/2 Lot No. 1

and S 1/2 Lot No. 2 Sect. 5 and S 1/2 Lot No. 4 Tp. 8 R. 18, south and east. Patent delivered Sept. 8, 1857.

**2727. GAVIN, Charles**
May 2, 1854, 3 1/2 miles E of High Springs, Alachua Co. NW 1/4 SW 1/4 Sect. 32 Tp. 7 R. 18, south and east. Patent delivered Sept. 8, 1857.

**4338. GAVIN, Charles**
April 19, 1856, 1 1/2 miles NE of Mile Siding Station, Alachua Co. E 1/2 SE 1/4 Sect.5 Tp. 8 R. 18, south and east. Patent delivered Sept. 8, 1857.

**2581. GAVIN, William**
Mar. 6, 1854, 3 3/4 miles WNW of Haynesworth, Columbia Co. Lot No. 2 and S 1/2 Lot No. 4 Sect. 32 and Lot No. 1 Sect. 33 Tp. 7 R. 18, south and east. Patent delivered Sept. 8, 1857.

**2601. GAVIN, William**
Mar. 11, 1854, 4 1/2 miles E of High Springs, Alachua Co. SE 1/4 SE 1/4 Sect. 31 Tp. 7 and NE 1/4 NE 1/4 Sect. 6 and N 1/2 NW 1/4 Sect. 5 Tp. 8 R. 18, south and east. Patent delivered Sept. 8, 1857.

**4123. GAYLAND, Nathan R.**
Jan. 26, 1856, 6 1/2 miles E of Pine Mount, Suwannee Co. Lot No. 7 and N 1/2 of Lots No. 5 and 6 Sect. 6 Tp. 4 R. 15, south and east.

**GAY, Thomas** see **Cornelius GRANTHAM**

**6447. GAYLER, Elijah**
Jan. 6, 1837, 5 miles E by S Bluff Springs, Santa Rosa Co. NE 1/4 SE 1/4 Sect. 23 Tp. 5 R. 30, north and west. Patent receipted for Dec., 1846.

**5228. GAYLORD, Nathan R.**
5 1/2 miles E of Pinemount, Suwannee Co. SW 1/4 SW 1/4 Sect. 6 Tp. 4 R. 15, south and east. Mar. 19, 1860.

**1049. GEE, Henry**
Feb. 1, 1827, 3 1/2 miles SE Quincy, Gadsden Co. E 1/2 SW 1/4 Sect. 21 Tp. 2 R. 3, north and west.

**1444. GEE, Henry**
(DUP) May 23, 1827, 1 1/2 miles SE Sawdust, Gadsden Co. Lot No. 1 Sect. 33 Tp. 2 R. 4, north and west.

**1445. GEE, Henry**
(DUP) May 22, 1827, 3 miles WSW Sawdust, Gadsden Co. Lot No. 1 Sect. 31 Tp. 2 R. 4, north and west.

**1785. GEE, Henry**
(DUP) June 5, 1827, at Mear's Spur, Gadsden Co. W 1/4 SW 1/4 Sect. 7 Tp. 3 R. 5, north and west.

**1831. GEE, Henry**
June 5, 1827, at Mear's Spur, Gadsden Co. W 1/2 NW 1/4 Sect. 18 Tp. 3 R. 5, north and west.

**2033. GEE, Henry**
Aug. 14, 1827, 4 miles SE Quincy, Gadsden Co. W 1/2 SE 1/4 Sect. 21 Tp. 2 R. 3, north and west.

**2161. GEE, Henry**
Dec. 24, 1827, at Steaphead(?), Gadsden Co. E 1/2 SE 1/4 Sect. 18 Tp. 2 R. 6, north and west.

**2162. GEE, Henry**
Dec. 24, 1827, 1 mile NW Steaphead(?), Gadsden Co. W 1/2 NW 1/4 Sect. 18 Tp. 2 R. 6, north and west.

**2163. GEE, Henry**
Dec. 24, 1827, 1 mile NW Steaphead(?), Gadsden Co. W 1/2 NE 1/4 Sect. 18 Tp. 2 R. 6, north and west.

**2183. GEE, Henry**
(Of Fla.) Dec. 28, 1827, 1 mile ESE Mear's Spur, Gadsden Co. W 1/2 NW 1/4 Sect. 7 Tp. 3 R. 5, north and west.

**2441. GEE, Henry**
July 12, 1828, 3 miles SSW Quincy, Gadsden Co. W 1/2 NE 1/4 Sect. 20 Tp. 2 R. 3, north and west.

**2463. GEE, Henry**
Aug. 19, 1828, 4 miles SSW Chattahoochee, Gadsden Co. W 1/2 SW 1/4 Sect. 19 Tp. 3 R. 6, north and west.

**2658. GEE, Henry**
Jan. 23, 1829, 3 miles NNW Rock Bluff, Gadsden Co. E 1/2 NW 1/4 Sect. 18 Tp. 2 R. 6, north and west.

**4023. GEE, Henry**
July 16, 1831, 1/2 mile W of Chattahoochee, Gadsden Co. Lot No. 3 Sect. 5 Tp. 3 R. 6, north and west.

**4024. GEE, Henry**
July 16, 1831, 2 miles SW of Chattahoochee, Gadsden Co. Lot No. 1 Sect. 7 Tp. 3 R. 6, north and west.

**4025. GEE, Henry**
July 16, 1831, 1 3/4 mile W of Chattahoochee, Gadsden Co. Lot No. 2 Sect. 7 Tp. 3 R. 6, north and west.

**4026. GEE, Henry**
July 16, 1831, 1 3/4 mile W of

Chattahoochee, Gadsden Co. Lot No. 5 Sect. 7 Tp. 3 R. 6, north and west.

**4035. GEE, Henry**
July 19, 1831, 1 3/4 miles NNE of Chattahoochee, Gadsden Co. Lot No. 2 Sect. 3 Tp. 3 R. 6, north and west.

**GEE, Homer see Boney PLAYER**

**8741. GEIGER, Abraham**
Dec. 14, 1844, 1/4 mile SW Avoca, Hamilton Co. NE 1/4 NE 1/4 Sect. 21 Tp. 2 R. 13, north and east.

**2713. GEIGER, Abraham**
May 1, 1854, at Emathla, Marion Co. Lot No. 1 Sect. 25 Tp. 14 R. 20, south and east. Patent delivered Dec. 4, 1856.

**2625. GEIGER, Felix**
Mar. 16, 1854, 3 miles S by W of Oypas, Clay Co. SW 1/4 SW 1/4 Sect. 30 Tp. 5 R. 24, south and east.

**358. GEIGER, James**
April 13, 1846, c. 2 1/2 miles SW Ft. McCoy, Marion Co. Lots No. 5 & 6 Fractional Sect. 7 Tp. 13 R. 23, south and east. Transferred to **James M. WALLENS**, Dec. 26, 1854.

**557. GEIGER, John Martin**
May 4, 1847, near Reynolds, Bradford Co. SE 1/4 NW 1/4 Sect.6 Tp. 7 R. 22, south and east.

**851. GIBSON, Allen**
March 26, 1851, 3 1/2 miles SW Santos, Marion Co. SE 1/4 SE 1/4 Sect. 19 Tp. 16 R. 22, south and east. Patent delivered July 15, 1858.

**GIBSON, Allen see David A. McDAVID, #121**

**5114. GIBSON, Elisha**
Oct. 18, 1859, 4 1/2 miles W of Newton, Levy Co. W 1/2 NE 1/4 Sect. 34 Tp. 11 R. 15, south and east. Patent delivered to **Emanuel STUDSTILL**, Feb. 24, 1875.

**663. GIBSON, Edward R.**
(Of Fla.) Feb. 7, 1826, at Monticello, Jefferson Co. W 1/2 SW 1/4 Sect. 30 Tp. 2 R. 5, north and east.

**1203. GIDDINGS, George W.**
Feb. 23, 1852, 2 miles S of St. Catherine, Sumter Co. SE 1/4 SW 1/4 Sect. 17 Tp. 22 R. 23, south and east.

**1060. GIEGER, Abraham**
Dec. 25, 1851, at Fessenden Academy, Marion Co. N 1/2 NW 1/4 Sect. 31 Tp. 14 R. 21, south and east. Patent delivered Dec. 4, 1886.

**4265. GIEGER, Felix**
Mar. 24, 1856, 1 3/4 miles W of Oypas, Clay Co. NW 1/4 SE 1/4 and NE 1/4 SW 1/4 Sect. 30 Tp. 5 R. 24, south and east.

**1148. GIEGER, John Martin**
Feb. 2, 1852, NW shore of Lake Grandin, Putnam Co. Lots 2 and 14, Sect. 9 Tp. 9 R. 24, south and east. Patent delivered Mar. 9, 1856.

**1913. GIEGER, John Martin**
June 30, 1853, 6 miles NE of Claymo, Bradford Co. SW 1/4 SE 1/4 Sect. 31 Tp. 6 R. 21, south and east.

**439. GIEGER, Joshua Daine**
June 29, 1846, 3 1/2 miles W Blitchton, Marion Co. NE 1/4 SW 1/4 Sect. 2 Tp. 14 R. 19, south and east. Patent received May 1, 1856.

**8318. GIFF, William C.**
May 13, 1840, 1 mile SSW Bond, Madison Co. SW 1/4 Sect. 31 Tp. 3 R. 8, north and west.

**1400. GILCHRIST, Malcolm**
(Of Ala.) May 21, 1827, 4 miles NE Quincy, Gadsden Co. E 1/2 SE 1/4 Sect. 31 Tp. 3 R. 3, north and west.

**1401. GILCHRIST, Malcolm**
(Of Ala.) May 21, 1827, 1 mile N Quincy, Gadsden Co. W 1/2 SE 1/4 Sect. 31 Tp. 3 R. 3, north and west.

**1402. GILCHRIST, Malcolm**
(Of Ala.) May 21, 1827, 1 mile N Quincy, Gadsden Co. E 1/2 SW 1/4 Sect. 31 Tp. 3 R. 3, north and west.

**1403. GILCHRIST, Malcolm**
(Of Ala.) May 21, 1827, 1 mile N Quincy, Gadsden Co. W 1/2 NW 1/4 Sect. 31 Tp. 3 R. 3, north and west.

**1404. GILCHRIST, Malcolm**
(Of Ala.) May 21, 1827, 3 miles NE Quincy, Gadsden Co. W 1/2 NE 1/4 Sect. 21 Tp. 3 R. 3, north and west.

**1406. GILCHRIST, Malcolm**
(Of Ala.) May 21, 1827, 6 miles NE Quincy, Gadsden Co. W 1/2 NE 1/4 Sect. 14 Tp. 3 R. 3, north and west.

**1407. GILCHRIST, Malcolm**
(Of Ala.) May 21, 1827, 7 miles W Quincy, Gadsden Co. W 1/4 NW 1/4 Sect. 6 Tp. 3 R. 3, north and west.

**1432. GILCHRIST, Malcolm**

May 22, 1827, 6 miles N Quincy, Gadsden Co. E 1/2 SE 1/4 Sect. 1 Tp. 3 R. 4, north and west.

**1433. GILCHRIST, Malcolm**
May 22, 1827, 2 miles W Quincy, Gadsden Co. W 1/2 NW 1/4 Sect. 11 Tp. 3 R. 4, north and west.

**1434. GILCHRIST, Malcolm**
May 22, 1827, 5 miles W Quincy, Gadsden Co. W 1/2 SW 1/4 Sect. 8 Tp. 2 R. 4, north and west. Transferred to **Wm. EDWARDS**, June 5, 1827. G. W. WARD, Reg.

**1435. GILCHRIST, Malcolm**
May 22, 1827, 4 1/2 miles W Quincy, Gadsden Co. E 1/2 SW 1/4 Sect. 8 Tp. 2 R. 4, north and west. Transferred to **Wm. EDWARDS**, June 5, 1827.

**1473. GILCHRIST, Malcolm**
May 23, 1827, 1/2 mile NE Mear's Spur, Gadsden Co. E 1/2 SE 1/4 Sect. 12 Tp. 3 R. 6, north and west. Transferred to **Henry GEE**, June 6, 1827. G. W. WARD, Reg.

**1474. GILCHRIST, Malcolm**
May 23, 1827, 2 miles NW Mear's Spur, Gadsden Co. E 1/2 SE 1/4 Sect. 2 Tp. 3 R. 6, north and west.

**1717. GILCHRIST, Malcolm**
May 31, 1827, 1 mile SSW Jacob, Jackson Co. W 1/2 SE 1/4 Sect. 23 Tp. 6 R. 12, north and west. Transferred June 4, 1827, to **Benj. CLEMENTS**. G. W. WARD, Reg.

**1728. GILCHRIST, Malcolm**
June 1, 1827, 2 miles SSW Moody, Wakulla Co. W 1/2 NW 1/4 Sect. 30 Tp. R. 1, south and east. Transferred to **R. C. ALLEN**, June 5, 1827. G. W. WARD, Reg.

**1757. GILCHRIST, Malcolm**
(DUP) June 4, 1827, 2 mile WNW of Monticello, Jefferson Co. Lot No. 5 Sect. 23 Tp. 2 R. 4, north and east.

**1758. GILCHRIST, Malcolm**
(DUP) June 4, 1827, 1 3/4 miles W of Monticello, Jefferson Co. E 1/2 NW 1/4 Sect. 26 Tp. 2 R. 4, north and east.

**1759. GILCHRIST, Malcolm**
(DUP) June 4, 1827, 1 1/2 miles W of Monticello, Jefferson Co. Lot No. 4 Fractional Sect. 23 Tp. 2 R. 4, north and east.

**1429. GILCHRIST, Malcolm**

May 22, 1827, 2 1/2 miles NNE Quincy, Gadsden Co. E 1/2 NW 1/4 Sect. 25 Tp. 3 R. 4, north and west.

**1430. GILCHRIST, Malcolm**
May 22, 1827, 3 1/2 miles N by E of Quincy, Gadsden Co. E 1/2 SW 1/4 Sect. 24 Tp. 3 R. 4, north and west.

**1544. GILCHRIST, Malcolm**
May 24, 1827, 1 1/2 miles NE Simsville, Jackson Co. W 1/2 NE 1/4 Sect. 8 Tp. 2 R. 9, north and west. Transferred to **Charles WILLIAMSON**, June 4, 1827. G. W. WARD, Reg.

**1545. GILCHRIST, Malcolm**
May 24, 1827, just north of Rock Creek, Jackson Co. W 1/2 SW 1/4 Sect. 17 Tp. 3 R. 9, north and west.

**1546. GILCHRIST, Malcolm**
(DUP) May 24, 1827, 1 mile NE Simsville, Jackson Co. E 1/2 NW 1/4 Sect. 8 Tp. 3 R. 9, north and west. Transferred to **Charles WILLIAMSON**, June 4, 1827. G. W. WARD, Reg.

**1597. GILCHRIST, Malcolm**
May 25, 1827, 1/2 miles SW Oakdale, Jackson Co. W 1/2 NE 1/4 Sect. 35 Tp. 4 R. 10, north and west. Transferred June 4, 1827, to **Charles WILLIAMSON**. G. W. WARD, Reg.

**1599. GILCHRIST, Malcolm**
(DUP) May 25, 1827, at Oakdale, Jackson Co. E 1/2 NE 1/4 Sect. 35 Tp. 4 R. 10, north and west. Transferred June 4, 1827 to **Charles WILLIAMSON**.

**1652. GILCHRIST, Malcolm**
(DUP) May 29, 1827, 12 1/2 miles NNW Haywoood, in Alabama. W 1/2 NE 1/4 Sect. 15 Tp. 7 R. 8, north and west. Transferred June 4, 1827, to **Charles WILLIAMSON**.

**1658. GILCHRIST, Malcolm**
May 29, 1827, 10 1/2 miles NNW Haywood, Jackson Co. E 1/2 SE 1/4 Sect. 27 Tp. 7 R. 8, north and west. Transferred June 4, 1827, to **Charles WILLIAMSON**.

**1659. GILCHRIST, Malcolm**
(DUP) May 29, 1827, 9 miles NNW Haywood, Jackson Co. Lot No. 4 Sect. 36 Tp. 7 R. 8, north and west. Transferred to **Charles WILLIAMSON**, June 4, 1827.

**1661. GILCHRIST, Malcolm**
(DUP) May 29, 1827, 9 miles NNW Haywood, Jackson Co. Lot No. 1 Sect. 35 Tp. 7 R. 8, north and west. Transferred to **Charles WILLIAMSON** on June 4, 1827.

**1693. GILCHRIST, Malcolm**
(DUP) May 30, 1827, 4 miles ESE Campbellton, Jackson Co. W 1/2 NW 1/4 Sect. 10 Tp. 6 R. 11, north and west. Transferred June 4, 1827, to **Charles WILLIAMSON.**

**1694. GILCHRIST, Malcolm**
(DUP) May 30, 1827, 5 miles E Welchton, Jackson Co. W 1/2 NW 1/4 Sect. 35 Tp. 6 R. 11, north and west. Transferred to **Charles WILLIAMSON** on June 4, 1827.

**1695. GILCHRIST, Malcolm**
May 30, 1827, 6 miles E Welchton, Jackson Co. W 1/2 SW 1/4 Sect. 36 Tp. 6 R. 11, north and west. Transferred June 4, 1827, to **Charles WILLIAMSON.**

**1697. GILCHRIST, Malcolm**
(DUP) May 30, 1827, 6 1/2 miles E Welchton, Jackson Co. E 1/2 SW 1/4 Sect. 36 Tp. 6 R. 11, north and west. Transferred June 4, 1827, to **Charles WILLIAMSON.**

**1730. GILCHRIST, Malcolm**
June 1, 1827, 2 miles WNW Vereen, Wakulla Co. E 1/2 SW 1/4 Sect. 30 Tp. 2 R. 1, south and east. Transferred June 5, 1827, to **R. C. ALLEN & Co.**

**1806. GILCHRIST, Malcolm**
June 5, 1827, 4 miles NE Quincy, Gadsden Co. E 1/2 NW 1/4 Sect. 21 Tp. 3 R. 3, north and east.

**1898. GILCHRIST, Malcolm**
June 11, 1827, 1 1/2 miles S Oakdale, Jackson Co. NW 1/4 Sect. 1 Tp. 3 R. 10, north and west.

**1899. GILCHRIST, Malcolm**
June 11, 1827, 2 1/2 miles NW Simsville, Jackson Co. W 1/2 SW 1/4 Sect. 1 Tp. 3 R. 10, north and west.

**45. GILLET, Anderson**
Nov. 14, 1843, 1 mile N McKinley, Columbia Co. SE 1/4 SE 1/4 Sect. 9 Tp. 3 R. 16, south and east.

**2007. GILLET, George**
Aug. 4, 1853, 5 miles SE by S of Hawthorne, Alachua Co. Lot No. 1 Sect. 7 and NW 1/4 NW 1/4 Sect. 8 Tp. 10 R. 22, south and east. Patent delivered Oct. 2, 1857.

**5137. GILLET, Joshua J.**
Nov. 17, 1859, 1 mile E of Judson, Levy Co. SE 1/4 SE 1/4 Sect. 36 Tp. 10 R. 15, south and east.

**8116. GILLET, Marcus**
Oct. 16, 1839, at Florence, Gadsden Co. W 1/2 NW 1/4 Sect. 1 Tp. 2 R. 3, north and west.

**8121. GILLET, Marcus**
Oct. 19, 1829, 1/4 mile N Florence, Gadsden Co. W 1/2 SW 1/4 Sect. 36 Tp. 3 R. 3, north and west.

**2004. GILLETT, David**
Aug. 4, 1853, 4 miles SE of Hawthorne, Alachua Co. E 1/2 NW 1/4 Sect. 17 Tp. 10 R. 22, south and east. Patent delivered Oct. 2, 1858.

**2816. GILLETT, David**
July 14, 1854, 1 1/4 miles SW of Campville, Alachua Co. NW 1/4 SW 1/4 Sect. 5 Tp. 11 R. 22, south and east.

**2817. GILLETT, David**
July 14, 1854, 1 3/4 miles W by S of Campville, Alachua Co. Lot No. 2 Sect. 6 Tp. 10 R. 22, south and east.

**2988. GILLETT, David**
Oct. 16, 1854, 1 1/2 miles N by E of Campville, Alachua Co. E 1/2 SW 1/4 and SW 1/4 SW 1/4 Sect. 20 Tp. 10 R. 22, south and east.

**8238. GILLIS, Angus**
Feb. 28, 1840, 3 1/2 miles SW Ponce De Leon, Holmes Co. E 1/2 NW 1/4 Sect. 6 Tp. 4 R. 17, north and west.

**GILMER, Chas. L.** see **Wm. B. L. GILMER, #6635**

**6526. GILMER, Nicholas M.**
Jan. 12, 1837, 4 miles W Greensboro, Gadsden Co. SW 1/4 SW 1/4 Sect. 11 Tp. 2 R. 6, north and west.

**6527. GILMER, Nicholas M**
Jan. 12, 1837, 4 1/2 miles W Greensboro, Gadsden Co. NW 1/4 SW 1/4 Sect. 3 Tp. 2 R. 6, north and west.

**6635. GILMER, Wm. B. L.**
(And **Chas. L. Gilmer** and **Benj. S. BIBB**) Of Alabama. Jan. 23, 1837, 1 mile S Welchton, Jackson Co. NW 1/4 W 1/2 SE 1/4 Sect. 1 Tp. 5 R. 12, north and west.

**6636. GILMER, Wm. B. L.**
(And **Chas. L. GILMER** and **Benj. S. BIBB**) Of Alabama. Jan. 23, 1837, 3 miles NW by N Cottondale, Jackson Co. SW 1/4 Sect. 13 Tp. 5 R. 12, north and west.

**6637. GILMER, Wm. B. L.**
(And **Chas. L. GILMER** and **Benj. S. BIBB**) Of Alabama. Jan. 24, 1837, 6 miles NW by N Cottondale, Jackson Co. NE 1/4 Sect. 1 Tp. 5 R. 12, north and west.

**6688. GILMER, Wm. B. L.**
(And **Chas. L. GILMER** and **Benj. S. BIBB**) Of Alabama. Jan. 28, 1837, 5 miles NNW Cottondale, Jackson Co. E 1/2 SE 1/4 Sect. 11 Tp. 5 R. 12, north and west.

**6689. GILMER, Wm. B. L.**
(And **Chas. L. GILMER** and **Benj. S. BIBB**) Of Alabama. Jan. 28, 1837, 5 miles NNW Cottondale, Jackson Co. E 1/2 NW 1/4 Sect. 12 Tp. 5 R. 12, north and west.

**6705. GILMER, Wm. B. L.**
(And **Chas. L. GILMER** and **Benajah S. BIBB**) Jan. 31, 1837, 3 miles NW Cottondale, Jackson Co. W 1/2 NW 1/4 Sect. 24 Tp. 5 R. 12, north and west.

**6706. GILMER, Wm. B. L.**
(And **Chas. L. GILMER** and **Benajah S. BIBB**) Jan. 31, 1837, 4 1/2 Miles NNW Cottondale, Jackson Co. SW 1/4 Sect. 12 Tp. 5 R. 12, north and west.

**6707. GILMER, Wm. B. L.**
(And **Chas. L. GILMER** and **Benajah S. BIBB**) Jan. 31, 1837, 4 1/2 miles NNW Cottondale, Jackson Co. NE 1/4 NW 1/4 SE 1/4 SW 1/4 Sect. 11 Tp. 5 R. 12, north and west.

**GILSTRAP, John** see **MILLS & PERRY, #460**

**6757. GILSTRAP, Leon**
Feb. 6, 1837, 3 miles SW Campbellton, Jackson Co. NW 1/4 SW 1/4 Sect. 4 Tp. 6 R. 12, north and west.

**8592. GIRTMAN, David**
July 4, 1843, 4 miles NNE Prosperity, Holmes Co. Lot No. 4 Tp. 5 R. 16, north and west.

**8593. GIRTMAN, David**
July 25, 1843, 3 3/4 miles NNE Prosperity, Holmes Co. SW 1/4 SW 1/4 Sect. 8 Tp. 5 R. 16, north and west.

**8652. GIRTMAN, David**
March 9, 1844, 4 1/2 miles NNE Prosperity, Holmes Co. Lot No. 3 Sect. 7 Tp. 6 R. 16, north and west.

**7840. GLENN, HARDY**
Jan. 28, 1839, 1 1/4 miles SSE Greensboro, Gadsden Co. NE 1/4 SW 1/4 Sect. 15 Tp. 2 R. 5, north and west.

**2229. GODBOKE, James D.**
Oct. 4, 1853, 7 miles NNE of Houston, Suwannee Co. SW 1/4 SE 1/4 Sect. 35 Tp. 2 R. 15, south and east. Patent delivered Oct. 24, 1858.

**2676. GODBOLD, Nehemiah**
Jan. 27, 1829, 7 miles SSW DeFuniak Springs, Walton Co. E 1/2 SE 1/4 Sect. 29 Tp. 2 R. 19, north and west.

**8872. GODDARD, David C.**
Jan. 10, 1846, 5 1/2 miles E Macon, Washington Co. NW 1/4 W 1/2 and SW 1/4 Sect. 15 Tp. 2 R. 13, north and west.

**194. GODFREY, William**
Nov. 3, 1845, 3 1/2 miles N Lake City, Columbia Co. SE 1/4 NW 1/4 Sect. 1 Tp. 3 R. 16, south and east. Transferred Oct. 2, 1847, to **Abraham RIVERS. S. SCARBOROUGH**, Atteste.

**1613. GODWIN, Jacob**
Jan. 6, 1853, 5 miles NNW of Claymo, Bradford Co. Lot No. 2 Sect. 29 Tp. 6 R.. 20, south and east. Patent delivered Oct. 15, 1857.

**1705. GODWIN, Jacob**
Feb. 12, 1853, 5 miles NW of Claymo, Bradford Co. S 1/2 Lot 4 Sect. 31 Tp. 6 R. 20, south and east. Patent delivered Oct. 15, 1854.

**2352. GODWIN, Jacob**
Nov. 5, 1853, 4 1/2 miles NE of Claymo, Bradford Co. N 1/2 Lots No. 10 and 11 Sect. 31 Tp. 6 R. 20, south and east.

**2370. GODWIN, Jefferson**
Feb. 20, 1854, 2 1/4 miles SW Atlas, Alachua Co. NW 1/4 SW 1/4 Sect. 32 Tp. 7 R. 20, south and east. Patent delivered Nov. 10, 1856.

**2472. GODWIN, Solomon**
Feb. 23, 1854, 1 1/2 miles SW Crosby, Levy Co. SW 1/4 SW 1/4 Sect. 25

and NW 1/4 NW 1/4 Sect. 36 Tp. 16 R. 17, south and east. Patent delivered Nov. 10, 1856.

**5122. GOFF, James**
Aug. 4, 1835, 2 miles SE of Bond, Madison Co. SE 1/4 NW 1/4 Sect. 10 Tp. 2 R. 8, north and east.

**5412. GOFF, James A.**
Jan. 18, 1836, 1 3/4 miles NNE of Monticello, Jefferson Co. SW 1/4 NW 1/4 Sect. 17 Tp. 2 R. 5, north and east.

**6373. GOFF, James A.**
Jan. 2, 1837, 2 miles N by E Monticello, Jefferson Co. NW 1/4 NW 1/4 Sect. 17 Tp. 2 R. 5, north and east.

**6496. GOFF, James A.**
Jan. 10, 1837, 1 1/2 miles NNE Monticello, Jefferson Co. E 1/2 SE 1/4 and W 1/2 NE 1/4 Sect. 17 Tp. 2 R. 5, north and east.

**6085. GOFF, James A.**
Nov. 25, 1836, 2 miles NE Monticello, Jefferson Co. SE 1/4 NW 1/4 Sect. 17 Tp. 2 R. 5, north and east.

**310. GOFF, Thomas**
Jan. 1, 1827, 8 miles NW of Marianna, Jackson Co. NE 1/4 Sect. 10 Tp. 5 R. 11, north and west. Transferred to **A. PRINGEL** on Jan. 22, 1827. **R. LEWIS**, atty.

**1605. GOFF, Thomas**
May 25, 1827, at Kynesville, Jackson Co. W 1/2 SE 1/4 Sect. 9 Tp. 4 R. 11, north and west. Transferred to **CHARLES WILLIAMSON** on June 6, 1827.

**1606. GOFF, Thomas**
May 25, 1827, at Kynesville, Jackson Co. W 1/2 SW 1/4 Sect. 9 Tp. 4 R. 11, north and west.

**2602. GOFF, Thomas**
Jan. 8, 1829, at Kynesville, Jackson Co. E 1/2 SE 1/4 Sect. 9 Tp. 4 R. 11, north and west.

**GOINS, Daniel see Alexander McLEOD, #150 & 330**

**8403. GOIRTO, John G.**
Sept. 9, 1840, 2 miles N by W Calhoun, Madison Co. NE 1/4 NE 1/4 Sect. 10 Tp. 1 R. 9, north and east.

**3210. GOLDING, Samuel**
Jan. 8, 1830, 1 mile SW Copeland, Leon Co. W 1/4 NE 1/4 Sect. 5 Tp. 2 R. 5, north and east.

**3254. GOLDING, Samuel**
Deb. 6, 1830, 1 mile SW Copeland, Leon Co. E 1/2 NW 1/4 Sect. 5 Tp. 2 R. 3, north and east.

**4145. GOLDING, Samuel**
Mar. 2, 1832, 1 mile E of Stringer, Leon Co. E 1/2 NW 1/4 Sect. 27 Tp. 3 R. 3, north and east.

**4970. GOLDSBOROUGH, L. M.**
May 20, 1835, NE shore of Lake Miccosukee, 6 1/2 miles SE of Stringer, Leon Co. SE 1/4 Sect. 9 Tp. 1 R. 4, north and east.

**4971. GOLDSBOROUGH, L. M.**
May 20, 1835, NE shore of Lake Miccosukee, 6 1/2 miles SE of Stringer, Leon Co. E 1/2 SW 1/4 Sect. 9 Tp. 1 R. 4, north and east.

**4972. GOLDSBOROUGH, L. M.**
May 20, 1835, NE shore of Lake Miccosukee, 6 1/2 miles SE of Stringer, Leon Co. E 1/2 NE 1/4 Sect. 9 Tp. 1 R. 4, north and east.

**GOLDSBOROUGH, Louis M. see Isham G. SEARCY, #5029/#5036**

**4867. GONZALEZ, Joseph**
Feb. 15, 1835, from description apparently in Pensacola Bay, about 2 miles W of Pensacola. Lot No. 3 Sect. 33 Tp. 2 R. 30, south and west.

**218. GOODHEAD, Jacob Sarllin**
Nov. 24, 1845, 1 mile NE Suwannee Valley, Columbia Co. SE 1/4 NE 1/4 Sect. 13 Tp. 2 R. 16, south and east.

**6345. GOODMAN, David B.**
Dec. 29, 1836, 3 miles N by W Aucilla, Jefferson Co. NE 1/4 NE 1/4 Sect. 32 Tp. 2 R. 6, north and east.

**8526. GOODMAN, Robert**
Feb. 5, 1842, 1 mile N Dills, Jefferson Co. W 1/2 SW 1/4 Sect. 28 Tp. 3 R. 6, north and east.

**6426. GOODMAN, William W.**
Jan. 4, 1837, at Greenville, Madison Co. NE 1/4 NW 1/4 Sect. 22 Tp. 1 R. 7, north and east.

**4450. GOODSON, Alexander**
Nov. 4, 1856, 2 miles SE of Orange Heights, Alachua Co. Lot No. 7 Sect. 14 Tp. 9 R. 22, south and east.

**GOODWIN, Thomas see John P. MADDUX**

**424. GORDON, Alexander**
Dec. 10, 1828, 3 miles ENE Euchean-

na, Walton Co. SE 1/4 Sect. 25 Tp. 2 R. 18, north and west.

**423. GORDON, Ephriam**
Dec. 10, 1828, 3 miles NE Eucheanna, Walton Co. NE 1/4 Sect. 25 Tp. 2 R. 18, north and west.

**4392. GORLAND, Thomas**
Aug. 21, 1833, 3 1/2 miles S by W of Iamonia, Leon Co. Lot No. 1 Sect. 13 Tp. 3 R. 1, north and east.

**4393. GORLAND, Thomas**
Aug. 21, 1833, 3 1/2 miles S by W of Iamonia, Leon Co. Lot No. 9 Sect. 13 Tp. 3 R. 1, north and east.

**3111. GORMAN, John**
Nov. 8, 1829, 3/4 mile E Waukenah, Jefferson Co. E 1/2 NW 1/4 Sect. 2 Tp. 1 R. 4, south and east.

**3454. GORMAN, Richard**
March 15, 1830, 1/2 mile SW Capps, Jefferson Co. N 1/2 SW 1/4 Sect. 6 Tp. 1 R. 5, south and east. Transferred to **Benj. D. SIMS** (no date), and the transfer signed by **Edward T. SHEPHERD**.

**6628. GORMAN, Richard**
Jan. 21, 1837, 2 miles WNW Waukenah, Jefferson Co. NW 1/4 SE 1/4 Sect. 32 Tp. 1 R. 4, north and east.

**2853. GORMAN, William**
June 19, 1829, 1 mile NW Waukenah, Jefferson Co. E 1/2 SW 1/4 Sect. 35 Tp. 1 R. 4, north and east.

**3452. GORMAN, William**
March 15, 1830, 1 1/2 miles NE Capps, Jefferson Co. E 1/2 SW 1/4 Sect. 31 Tp. 1 R. 5, north and east. (Pencilled below the name of **R. K. CALL**, Receiver, is the name of **Simpson FOUCHE**).

**3453. GORMAN, William**
Mar. 15, 1830, 1/2 mile SE Capps, Jefferson Co. NW 1/4 Sect. 6 Tp. 1 R. 5, south and east. (Pencilled **Simpson FOUCHE** under **CALL**'s signature.)

**3896. GORMAN, William**
Feb. 25, 1831, 3 miles E Capps, Jefferson Co. SW 1/4 Sect. 4 Tp. 1 R. 5, south and east. Transferred to **Benj. D. SIMS**, no date. Signed **Edward T. SHEPHERD**.

**3897. GORMAN, William**
Feb. 25, 1831, 3 miles ESE Capps, Jefferson Co. W 1/2 NW 1/4 Sect. 9 Tp. 1 R. 5, south and east. Transferred to **Benj. D. SIMS**, no date. Signed **Edward T. SHEPHERD**.

**4906. GORMAN, William**
Mar. 21, 1835, 2 1/2 miles SW of Nash, Jefferson Co. NW 1/4 SW 1/4 Sect. 33 Tp. 1 R. 4, north and east.

**4907. GORMAN, William**
Mar. 21, 1835, 3 1/4 miles SE of Nash, Jefferson Co. SE 1/4 SW 1/4 Sect. 33 Tp. 1 R. 4, north and east.

**6461. GORMAN, William**
Jan. 9, 1837, 1 1/2 miles S Waukenah, Jefferson Co. E 1/2 SE 1/4 Sect. 10 Tp. 1 R. 4, south and east.

**6462. GORMAN, William**
Jan. 9, 1837, 2 miles NW Waukenah, Jefferson Co. NE 1/4 SW 1/4 and SW 1/4 SW 1/4 Sect. 33 Tp. 1 R. 4, north and east.

**7771. GORMAN, William**
Dec. 20, 1838, 2 3/4 miles SSW Waukenah, Gadsden Co. W 1/2 NE 1/4 and NE 1/4 NW 1/4 Sect. 8 Tp. 1 R. 4, south and east. See **Norman McLEOD**.

**66. GORREE, John**
Dec. 2, 1844, 1 1/2 miles S Gulf Hammock, Levy Co. E 1/2 NE 1/4 Sect. 31 Tp. 14 R. 16, south and east. Patent delivered Aug. 21, 1845.

**4832. GOUSE, Benjamin W.**
Jan. 28, 1830, 4 3/4 miles SSW of Centerville, Leon Co. SE 1/4 SW 1/4 Sect. 26 Tp. 2 R. 2, north and east.

**801. GRAFFORD, Ellis**
(Of Fla.) Nov. 15, 1826, 2 miles W Capitola, Leon Co. E 1/2 SE 1/4 Sect. 23 Tp. 1 R. 2, south and east.

**1440. GRAHAM, A.**
May 22, 1827, 3 1/2 miles WNW Quincy, Gadsden Co. E 1/2 SE 1/4 Sect. 33 Tp. 3 R. 4, north and west.

**1441. GRAHAM, A.**
May 22, 1827, 3 1/2 miles WNW Quincy, Gadsden Co. W 1/2 SE 1/4 Sect. 33 Tp. 3 R. 4, north and west.

**5817. GRAHAM, Archibald**
Aug. 31, 1836, 4 miles SE of Iamonia, Leon Co. NE 1/4 NW 1/4 Sect. 24 Tp. 3 R. 2, north and east.

**6807. GRAHAM, Archibald**
Mar. 1, 1837, 3 miles W by N Stringer, Leon Co. S 1/2 NW 1/4 Sect. 24

Tp. 3 R. 2, north and east.

**2722. GRAHAM, Daniel J.**
Feb. 10, 1829, 4 miles SW Monticello, Jefferson Co. E 1/2 NE 1/4 Sect. 4 Tp. 1 R. 4, north and east.

**2745. GRAHAM, Daniel S.**
Feb. 18, 1829, 5 miles SW Monticello, Jefferson Co. E 1/2 SE 1/4 Sect. 4 Tp. 1 R. 4, north and east.

**2746. GRAHAM, Daniel S.**
Feb. 18, 1829, 5 miles WSW Monticello, Jefferson Co. SE 1/4 Sect. 33 Tp. 2 R. 4, north and east.

**2747. GRAHAM, Daniel S.**
Feb. 18, 1829, 5 miles SW Monticello, Jefferson Co. W 1/2 SW 1/4 Sect. 3 Tp. 1 R. 4, north and east.

**2793. GRAHAM, Daniel S.**
March 30, 1829, 3 miles W by S Monticello, Jefferson Co. E 1/2 NE 1/4 Sect. 33 Tp. 2 R. 4, north and east.

**4589. GRAHAM, Thomas B.**
July 4, 1834, 2 miles S of Sawdust, Gadsden Co. NE 1/4 SW 1/4 Sect. 33 Tp. 3 R. 4, north and west.

**6059. GRAHAM, Thomas B.**
Nov. 19, 1836, 3 miles S Mt. Pleasant, Gadsden Co. W 1/2 NE 1/4 and SE 1/4 NW 1/4 Sect. 33 Tp. 3 R. 4, north and west.

**2539. GRAINGER, Alexander**
July 15, 1881, 1/2 mile SE Hunter, Putnam Co. N 1/2 of NW 1/4 and NW 1/4 NE 1/4 Sect. 20 Tp. 10S R. 26E.

**6744. GRAINGER, Farney**
Feb. 6, 1837, 3 miles W Waukenah, Jefferson Co. SW 1/4 SW 1/4 Sect. 5 Tp. 1 R. 4, south and east.

**6800. GRAINGER, Samuel**
Mar. 1, 1837, 3 miles NE Lamont, Jefferson Co. NW 1/4 NE 1/4 Sect. 12 Tp. 1 R. 5, south and east.

**6801. GRAINGER, Samuel**
Mar. 1, 1837, 3 1/2 miles NNE Lamont, Jefferson Co. SW 1/4 SE 1/4 Sect. 1 Tp. 1 R. 5, south and east.

**4526. GRAMLING, Adam**
Jan. 20, 1834, 1 1/4 miles S by E of Centerville, Leon Co. NE 1/4 NW 1/4 Sect. 31 Tp. 2 R. 2, north and east.

**5240. GRAMLING, Adam**
Oct. 29, 1835, 5 1/4 miles E by S of Centerville, Leon Co. W 1/2 NE 1/4 Sect. 24 Tp. 2 R. 1, north and east.

**5254. GRAMLING, Adam**
Nov. 7, 1835, at Centerville, Leon Co. NW 1/4 SE 1/4 Sect. 24 Tp. 2 R. 1, north and east.

**6273. GRAMLING, Adam**
Dec. 22, 1836, at Centerville, Leon Co. E 1/2 NW 1/4 Sect. 24 Tp. 2 R. 1, north and east.

**6321. GRAMLING, Adam**
Dec. 27, 1836, 2 miles E Bradfordville, Leon Co. NE 1/4 SW 1/4 Sect. 24 Tp. 2 R. 1, north and east.

**5304. GRAMLING, Christian**
Dec. 4, 1835, 3/4 mile SE of Felkel, Leon Co. NE 1/4 SE 1/4 Sect. 2 Tp. 2 R. 2, north and east.

**5305. GRAMLING, Christian**
Dec. 4, 1835, 3/4 mile SE Felkel, Leon Co. NW 1/4 SE 1/4 Sect. 2 Tp. 2 R. 2, north and east.

**6566. GRAMLING, Christian**
Jan. 16, 1837, at Centerville, Leon Co. E 1/2 NE 1/4 Sect. 24 Tp. 2 R. 1, north and east.

**5568. GRAMLING, John**
Mar. 31, 1836, 1/4 mile SW of Centerville, Leon Co. W 1/2 SW 1/4 Sect. 24 Tp. 2 R. 1, north and east.

**6456. GRAMLING, John**
Jan. 7, 1837, just W Centerville, Leon Co. SW 1/4 NW 1/4 Sect. 24 Tp. 2 R. 1, north and east.

**7687. GRANTHAM, Abraham**
Oct. 25, 1838, 1 mile W by S Waukenah, Jefferson Co. SE 1/4 SW 1/4 Sect. 4 Tp. 1 R. 4, south and east.

**4847. GRANGER, Taney**
Feb. 7, 1835, 2 miles W of Waukenah, Jefferson Co. NW 1/4 SW 1/4 Sect. 5 Tp. 1 R. 4, south and east.

**242. GRANTHAM, Cornelius**
Dec. 30, 1826, 5 miles NE Crigler Station, Jackson Co. W 1/2 SE 1/4 Sect. 5 Tp. 4 R. 9, north and west. Transferred to **David THOMAS**, Dec. 30, 1826, through attorney **Stephen RICHARDS**. Transferred from **David THOMAS** to **Miles SIMS**, Jan. 2, 1827, and from **Miles SIMS** to **Thomas GAY**.

**4912. GRANTHAM, Edward**
Mar. 25, 1835, 2 1/2 miles NE of Cay, Jefferson Co. NE 1/4 SW 1/4 Sect. 18

Tp. 1 R. 4, south and east.
**3894. GRANTHAM, James**
Feb. 24, 1831, 4 miles WSW Waukenah, Jefferson Co. E 1/2 SE 1/4 Sect. 7 Tp. 1 R. 4, south and east.
**2869. GRANTHAM, Seaton**
(Of Ga.) July 6, 1829, c. 2 miles S Ocheesee, Calhoun Co. Lot No. 5 Sect. 18 Tp. 2 R. 7, north and west.
**2870. GRANTHAM, Seaton**
(Of Ga.) July 6, 1829, c. 2 miles S Ocheesee, Calhoun Co. Lot No. 6 Sect. 18 Tp. 2 R. 7, north and west.
**2871. GRANTHAM, Seaton**
July 6, 1829, 3 miles S Ocheesee, Calhoun Co. Lot No.(?) Sect. 19 Tp. 2 R. 7, north and west.
**GRANTHAM (GRANTLAND), Seaton**
see **David C. STONE, Henry D. STONE, David THOMAS** and **Wm. WYATT**
**3937. GRANTHAME, Abram**
Apr. 5, 1831, 5 miles SE Waukenah, Jefferson Co. E 1/2 SE 1/4 Sect. 18 Tp.1 R. 4, south and east. Assigned (without date) to **John G. GAMBLE**.
**3990. GRANTHAN, Edward**
June 23, 1831, 5 miles E by S El Destino, Jefferson Co. W 1/2 NE 1/4 Sect. 13 Tp. 1 R. 3, south and east.
**2900. GRANTLAND, Seaton**
(Of Ga.) July 7, 1829, 4 miles SSW Chattahoochee, Gadsden Co. Lot No. 1 Sect. 24 Tp. 3 R. 7, north and west.
**2901. GRANTLAND, Seaton**
July 7, 1829, 4 miles SSW Chattahoochee, Gadsden Co. Lot No. 2 Sect. 24 Tp. 3 R. 7, north and west.
**2902. GRANTLAND, Seaton**
(Of Ga.) July 7, 1829, 3 miles E Millspring, Jackson Co. Lot No. 2 Sect. 13 Tp. 3 R. 7, north and west.
**2903. GRANTLAND, Seaton**
(Of Ga.) July 7, 1829, 3 miles E Millspring, Jackson Co. Lot No. 1 Sect. 13 Tp. 3 R. 7, north and west.
**2988. GRANTLAND, SEATON**
(Of Ga.) Aug. 25, 1829, 3 miles SSE Millspring, Jackson Co. Lot No. 2 Sect. 34 Tp. 3 R. 7, north and west.
**2989. GRANTLAND, Seaton**
Aug. 25, 1829, 2 miles NE Millspring, Jackson Co. E 1/2 SE 1/4 Sect. 10 Tp. 3 R. 7, north and west.
**2990. GRANTLAND, Seaton**
Aug. 25, 1829, 2 1/2 miles W Roy, Liberty Co. Lot No. 1 Sect. 4 Tp. 2 R. 7, north and west.
**2991. GRANTLAND, Seaton**
Aug. 25, 1829, 2 miles N by E Rock Bluff, Liberty Co. SE 1/4 Sect. 13 Tp. 2 R. 7, north and west.
**2992. GRANTLAND, Seaton**
Aug. 25, 1829, 2 1/2 miles NNE Rock Bluff, Liberty Co. E 1/2 NE 1/4 Sect. 13 Tp. 2 R. 7, north and west.
**2993. GRANTLAND, Seaton**
Aug. 25, 1829, 3 1/2 miles NW Rock Bluff, Liberty Co. Lot No. 2 Sect. 19 Tp. 2 R. 7, north and west.
**2994. GRANTLAND, Seaton**
(Of Ga.) Aug. 25, 1829, (location not given) Calhoun Co. Lot No. 4 Sect. 19 Tp. 2 R. 7, north and west.
**2995. GRANTLAND, Seaton**
(Of Ga.) Aug. 25, 1829, c. 4 miles SW Roy, Liberty Co. Lot No. 4 Sect. 20 Tp. 2 R. 7, north and west.
**2996. GRANTLAND, Seaton**
(Of Ga.) Aug. 25, 1829, c. 4 miles ESE Millspring, Jackson Co. Lot No. 4 Sect. 24 Tp. 3 R. 7, north and west.
**3552. GRANTLAND, Seaton**
(Of Ga.) July 6, 1830, 4 miles SE Mandalay, Taylor Co. NW 1/4 Sect. 33 Tp. 4 R. 4, south and east.
**3553. GRANTLAND, Seaton**
(Of Ga.) July 6, 1830, 4 miles SE Mandalay, Taylor Co. NE 1/4 Sect. 33 Tp. 4 R. 4, south and east.
**3554. GRANTLAND, Seaton**
July 6, 1830, 2 3/4 miles S by E Mandalay, Taylor Co. N 1/2 Sect. 32 Tp. 4 R. 4, south and east. 325.18 acres
**3555. GRANTLAND, Seaton**
July 6, 1830, 2 miles ESE Mandalay, Taylor Co. E 1/2 SE 1/4 Sect. 20 Tp. 4 R. 4, south and east.
**3556. GRANTLAND, Seaton**
July 6, 1830, 1/2 mile SE Mandalay, Taylor Co. N 1/2 Sect. 20 Tp. 4 R. 4, south and east. 321 acres.
**3557. GRANTLAND, Seaton**
July 6, 1830, 1/2 mile SE Buck Horn, Taylor Co. NW 1/4 Sect. 21 Tp. 4 R. 4, south and east.
**3558. GRANTLAND, Seaton**
July 6, 1830, 2 1/2 miles SE Mandalay, Taylor Co. SW 1/4 Sect. 28 Tp. 4

R. 4, south and east.

**3559. GRANTLAND, Seaton**
July 6, 1830, 2 miles S Buck Horn, Taylor Co. SE 1/4 Sect. 28 Tp. 4 R. 4, south and east.

**3560. GRANTLAND, Seaton**
July 6, 1830, 1 mile S Buck Horn, Taylor Co. NW 1/4 Sect. 28 Tp. 4 R. 4, south and east.

**3561. GRANTLAND, Seaton**
July 6, 1830, 2 miles SE Mandalay, Taylor Co. S 1/2 Sect. 29 Tp. 4 R. 4, south and east.

**3562. GRANTLAND, Seaton**
July 6, 1830, just S Buck Horn, Taylor Co. W 1/2 SE 1/4 Sect. 21 Tp. 4 R. 4, south and east.

**3563. GRANTLAND, Seaton**
July 6, 1830, 2 miles SE Mandalay, Taylor Co. E 1/2 SE 1/4 Sect. 29 Tp. 4 R. 4, south and east.

**2953. GRANTLAND, Setan**
(Of Ga.) July 21, 1829, 2 miles S Ocheesee, Calhoun Co. Lot No. 5 Sect. 19 Tp. 2 R. 7, north and west.

**2963. GRANTLAND, Seton**
(Of Ga.) July 17, 1829, 2 1/2 miles W Roy, Liberty Co. Lot No. 3 Sect. 4 Tp. 2 R. 7, north and west.

**3624. GRANY, Henry**
Oct. 6, 1830, 2 miles W Iamonia, Leon Co. SW 1/4 Sect. 14 Tp. 14 R. 1, north and east. Pd. in Scrip issued to **Alex'r MACOMB**. Certs. No. 153 and 154, May 30, 1829, endorsed by **MACOMB**.

**8396. GRAVES, John**
Aug. 21, 1840, 1 mile W Bristol, Liberty Co. Lots No. 1 and 2 Sect. 36 Tp. 1 R. 8, north and west.

**3004. GRAY, Edmund**
Aug. 31, 1829, 4 miles E Monticello, Jefferson Co. E 1/2 NW 1/4 Set. 25 Tp. 2 R. 5, north and east.

**4541. GRAY, Edmund**
Feb. 5, 1834, 4 1/2 miles NNE of Monticello, Jefferson Co. NW 1/4 SW 1/4 Sect. 24 Tp. 2 R. 5, north and east.

**6142. GRAY, John**
Dec. 19, 1836, 3 miles SSE Dills, Jefferson Co. NW 1/4 SW 1/4 and NE 1/4 SW 1/4 Sect. 17 Tp. 2 R. 6, north and east.

**2748. GRAY, Horatio N.**
Feb. 18, 1829, 5 miles ESE El Destino, Jefferson Co. W 1/2 NE 1/4 Sect. 14 Tp. 1 R. 3, south and east. Transferred to **Jas. GADSDEN** (no date given). Transferred by **Jas. GADSDEN** to **A. F. HOLMES** (no date given).

**2749. GRAY, Horatio N.**
Feb. 18, 1829, 4 3/4 miles ESE El Destino, Jefferson Co. E 1/2 SW 1/4 Sect. 14 Tp. 1 R. 3, south and east. Transferred to **Jas. GADSDEN** (no date given). Transferred by **Jas. GADSDEN** to **A. F. HOLMES** (no date given).

**2789. GRAY, Horatio N.**
Mar. 18, 1829, 5 miles SE Tallahassee, Leon Co. NW 1/4 Sect. 22 Tp. 1 R. 1, south and east.

**7414. GRAY, Susannah**
Mar. 19, 1838, 1 mile E by S Concord, Gadsden Co. NW 1/4 SW 1/4 Sect. 17 Tp. 3 R. 1, north and west.

**1863. GRAY, Thomas**
June 6, 1827, 3 miles S Quincy, Gadsden Co. W 1/2 NW 1/4 Sect. 30 Tp. 2 R. 3, north and west.

**121. GRAY, Thomas**
Dec. 23, 1826, 2 miles SE Sawdust Station, Gadsden Co. NW 1/4 Sect. 33 Tp. 2 R. 4, north and west. Transferred to **Wm. J. HAMANS**, June 17, 1829.

**985. GRAY, Thomas**
(DUP) Jan. 22, 1827, 1 mile SE Quincy, Gadsden Co. W 1/2 NW 1/4 Sect. 8 Tp. 2 R. 3, north and west.

**7504. GRAY, Zachariah**
June 28, 1838, 2 miles S by W Dills, Jefferson Co. NW 1/4 NW 1/4 Sect. 13 Tp. 2 R. 5, north and east.

**2897. GREEN, Caroline L.**
Sept. 2, 1854, 3 1/2 miles S by W of Bay Lake, Marion Co. Lot No. 7 Sect. 19 Tp. 12 R. 23, south and east.

**195. GREEN, Glover Foreman**
Nov. 3, 1845, 2 1/2 miles E Chiefland, Levy Co. NW 1/4 SE 1/4 and SE 1/4 NW 1/4 Sect. 4 Tp. 12 R. 15, south and east.

**417. GREEN, Glover Foreman**
May 19, 1846, 3/4 mile S Newton, Levy Co. E 1/2 SW 1/4 Sect. 4 Tp. 12 R. 15, south and east.

**7925. GREEN, John P.**
March 20, 1839, 2 miles SE St. Marks, Wakulla Co. W 1/2 SE 1/4 Sect. 12 Tp. 4 R. 1, south and east.

**8813. GREEN, Lewis**
Sept. 15, 1845, 1 mile NNE Ellaville, Madison Co. Lot No. 5 Fractional Sect. 13 Tp. 1 R. 11, south and east.

**3474. GREEN, Nat'l T.**
April 8, 1830, at St. Marks, Wakulla Co. Lot No. 4 Fractional Sect. 11 Tp. 4 R. 1, south and east. Asssigned 1/2 of the within to **Thos. Jef. GREEN** to be held in joint interest with **Nath'l T. GREEN**, May 8, 1830. Patent delivered to **Minor WALKER**, Dec. 5, 1848.

**GREEN, Nathaniel see Thomas J. GREEN, #3536.**

**3536. GREEN, Thomas J.**
June 3, 1830, 4 miles S St. Marks, Wakulla Co. Lot No. 2 Sect. 23 Tp. 4 R. 1, south and east. An undivided half (53.25 acres) was transferred Aug. 1, 1830 to **Nath'l. T. GREEN**. Delivered to **Marion WALKER**, Dec. 5, 1848.

**4441. GREEN, Thomas J.**
Oct. 23, 1833, 1 1/4 miles S of St. Marks, Wakulla Co. Lot No. 4 Tp. 4 R. 1, south and east. Transferred to **Ambrose CRANE**, Oct. 23, 1833.

**4004. GREEN, Thomas W.**
Dec. 17(?), 1855, 1 1/2 miles S of Thomasville, Alachua Co. SE 1/4 NW 1/4 Sect. 35 Tp. 7 R. 19, south and east. Patent delivered July 4, 1859.

**178. GREGORY, Jason**
Dec. 29, 1826, 2 miles N Sawdust Post Office, Gadsden Co. W 1/2 NW 1/4 Sect. 15 Tp. 2 R. 4, north and west.

**384. GREGORY, Jason**
May 4, 1827, 3 miles SW Quincy, Gadsden Co. E 1/2 NW 1/4 Sect. 15 Tp. 2 R. 4, north and west.

**2199. GREGORY, Jason**
(Of Fla.) Dec. 31, 1827, 3 miles SW Quincy, Gadsden Co. E 1/2 NE 1/4 Sect. 22 Tp. 2 R. 4, north and west.

**2200. GREGORY, Jason**
(Of Fla.) Dec. 31, 1827, 2 miles ENE Sawdust, Gadsden Co. W 1/2 NW 1/4 Sect. 23 Tp. 2 R. 4, north and west.

**5226. GREGORY, Jason**
Oct. 22, 1835, 3 miles W of Quincy, Gadsden Co. SW 1/4 Sect. 10 Tp. 2 R. 4, north and west.

**5227. GREGORY, Jason**
Oct. 22, 1835, 4 miles W of Quincy, Gadsden Co. NW 1/4 SE 1/4 Sect. 15 Tp. 2 R. 4, north and west.

**5228. GREGORY, Jason**
Oct. 22, 1835, 4 miles W of Quincy, Gadsden Co. E 1/2 SW 1/4 Sect. 15 Tp. 2 R. 4, north and west.

**5229. GREGORY, Jason**
Oct. 22, 1835, 4 1/4 miles W of Quincy, Gadsden Co. E 1/2 SE 1/4 Sect. 15 Tp. 2 R. 4, north and west.

**5231. GREGORY, Jason**
Oct. 23, 1835, 4 1/4 miles N by W of Quincy, Gadsden Co. W 1/2 NE 1/4 Sect. 15 Tp. 2 R. 4, north and west.

**64. GREGORY, Jesse**
Nov. 16, 1826, at Sawdust Post Office, Gadsden Co. SE 1/4 Sect. 22 Tp. 2 R. 4, north and west.

**1469. GREGORY, Jesse**
(DUP) May 22, 1827, 1 mile E Sawdust, Gadsden Co. E 1/2 SW 1/4 Sect. 22 Tp. 2 R. 4, north and west.

**1872. GREGORY, Jesse**
(DUP) June 6, 1827, 1/2 mile E Sawdust, Gadsden Co. W 1/2 SW 1/4 Sect. 22 Tp. 2 R. 4, north and west.

**2713. GREGORY, Jesse**
Feb. 6, 1829, 1 mile NE Sawdust, Gadsden Co. W 1/2 NW 1/4 Sect. 22 Tp. 2 R. 4, north and west.

**5013. GREGORY, Jesse**
June 24, 1835, 1 mile SE Sawdust, Gadsden Co. E 1/2 NW 1/4 Sect. 22 Tp. 2 R. 4, north and west.

**5014. GREGORY, Jesse**
June 24, 1835, 2 miles NE of Sawdust, Gadsden Co. SW 1/4 SE 1/4 Sect. 15 Tp. 2 R. 4, north and west. See **Henry W. PEEBLES**

**1824. GREGORY, John**
(DUP) June 6, 1827, 4 1/2 miles W by S Quincy, Gadsden Co. SE 1/4 Sect. 9 Tp. 2 R. 4, north and west.

**190. GREGORY, Lewis**
(DUP) Dec. 29, 1826, 1 mile NE Sawdust Post Office, Gadsden Co. Sect. 21 Tp. 2 R. 4, north and west.

**191. GREGORY, Lewis**
(DUP) Dec. 29, 1826, 1 mile NE Sawdust, Gadsden Co. W 1/2 NE 1/4

Sect. 21 Tp. 2 R. 4, north and west.
**1779. GREGORY, Lewis**
June 5, 1827, near Sawdust(northward), Gadsden Co. Lot No. 5 Sect. 21 Tp. 2 R. 4, north and west.

**1780. GREGORY, Lewis**
June 5, 1827, near Sawdust (northward), Gadsden Co. Lot No. 7 Sect. 21 Tp. 2 R. 4, north and west.

**1781. GREGORY, Lewis**
June 5, 1827, near Sawdust (northward), Gadsden Co. Lot No. 6 Sect. 21 Tp. 2 R. 4, north and west.

**4954. GREGORY, Lewis**
April 30, 1835, 1 mile NW of Sawdust, Gadsden Co. NE 1/4 SE 1/4 Sect. 8 Tp. 2 R. 4, north and west.

**7856. GREGORY, Lewis**
Feb., 6, 1839, 6 miles SSE Stringer, Leon Co. E 1/2 NE 1/4 Sect. 8 Tp. 2 R. 4, north and west.

**7868. GREGORY, Lewis**
Feb. 13, 1839, 3 miles W by N Quincy, Gadsden Co. NW 1/4 W 1/2 NE 1/4 Sect. 9 Tp. 2 R. 4, north and west.

**4975. GREGORY, Walter**
May 22, 1835, 1/2 mile N by W of Pensacola, Escambia Co. Lot No. 3 Sect. 20 Tp. 2 R. 30, south and west.

**4976. GREGORY, Walter**
May 22, 1835, 2 miles N of Pensacola, Escambia Co. Lot No. 1 Sect. 2 Tp. 2 R. 30, south and west.

**4977. GREGORY, Walter**
May 22, 1835, 2 1/2 miles NNW of Pensacola, Escambia Co. Lot No. 2 Sect. 6 Tp. 2 R. 29, south and west.

**4978. GREGORY, Walter**
May 22, 1835, 1/2 mile N by W of West Pensacola, Escambia Co. Lot No. 1 Sect. 20 Tp. 2 R. 30, south and west.

**4979. GREGORY, Walter**
May 22, 1835, 1/2 mile N by W of West Pensacola, Escambia Co. Lot No. 2 Sect. 20 Tp. 2 R. 30, south and west.

**4980. GREGORY, Walter**
May 22, 1835, 2 miles N of Pensacola, Escambia Co. Lot No. 2 Sect. 2 Tp. 2 R. 30, south and west.

**8109. GREGORY, Willoughby S.**
Oct. 5, 1839, 2 miles E Quincy, Gadsden Co. E 1/2 SE 1/4 Sect. 10 Tp. 2 R. 4, north and west.

**8110. GREGORY, Willoughby S.**
Sept. 5, 1839, 2 1/4 miles SW Qiuncy, Gadsden Co. W 1/2 SW 1/4 Sect. 14 Tp. 2 R. 4, north and west.

**8111. GREGORY, Willoughby S.**
Oct. 5, 1839, 2 miles SW Quincy, Gadsden Co. NE 1/4 NW 1/4 Sect. 14 Tp. 2 R. 4, north and west.

**8256. GREGORY, Willoughby S.**
Mar. 16, 1840, 2 3/4 miles N by W Monticello, Jefferson Co. NW 1/4 SE 1/4 Sect. 14 Tp. 2 R. 4, north and west.

**8356. GRIFFIN, James**
June 18, 1840, 3 1/4 miles E Selman, Calhoun Co. W 1/2 Sect. 25 Tp. 2 R. 8, north and west.

**2600. GRIFFIN, John**
Jan. 6, 1829, 2 miles N Havana, Gadsden Co. W 1/2 SW 1/4 Sect. 15 Tp. 3 R. 2, north and west.

**503. GRIFFIN, John**
Dec. 18, 1831, 2 miles E Monticello, Jefferson Co. W 1/2 NE 1/4 Sect. 33 Tp. 2 R. 5, north and east.

**8348. GRIFFIN, Lenn**
June 18, 1840, 3 miles E Selman, Calhoun Co. SE 1/4 Sect. 25 Tp. 2 R. 8, north and west.

**8635. GRIFFIN, Lenn**
Feb. 7, 1844, 1/4 mile E by N Watson, Liberty Co. SE 1/4 SE 1/4 Sect. 29 Tp. 2 R. 7, north and west.

**8712. GRIFFIN, Lenn**
Oct. 8, 1844, 1/4 mile NNE Watson, Liberty Co. NE 1/4 SE 1/4 Sect. 29 Tp. 2 R. 7, north and west.

**8713. GRIFFIN, Lenn**
Oct. 8, 1844, 1/4 mile NE Watson, Liberty Co. SW 1/4 SE 1/4 Sect. 29 Tp. 2 R. 7, north and west.

**379. GRIFFIN, Lucy**
May 3, 1827, 4 miles W Greenwood, Jackson Co. SE 1/4 Sect. 33 Tp. 6 R. 10, north and west. Transferred from **Lucy GRIFFIN** to **John LOTT**, Jan. 3, 1828

**4800. GRIFFIN, Thomas C.**
Sept. 6, 1858, 1 3/4 miles SE Cooper, Columbia Co. N 1/2 Sect. 6 Tp. 5 R. 16, south and east.

**3956. GRIMES, John**
Apr. 21, 1831, 1/2 mile WW Ocklok-

onee, Leon Co. E 1/2 SE 1/4 Sect. 26 Tp. 1 R. 2, north and west.

**5067. GRIMES, John**
Aug. 6, 1859, 1/2 mile NNE of Fleetnor, Alachua Co. W 1/2 Sect. 32 Tp. 9 R. 17, south and east.

**3481. GRINER, James**
Apr. 20, 1830, c. 1 mile SW Iamonia, Leon Co. Lot No. 5 Fractional Sect. 24 Tp. 3 R. 7, north and east.

**4049. GRIPIT, Percy**
Dec. 31, 1855, 2 1/2 miles SE Komoko,, Alachua Co. S 1/2 of SE 1/4 and S 1/2 of SW 1/4 Sect. 31 Tp. 9 R. 18, south and east.

**7378. GRUBBS, Robert B.**
Mar. 2, 1838, 2 1/2 miles NNE McClellan, Jefferson Co. SE 1/4 SW 1/4 Sect. 2 Tp. 1 R. 5, north and east.

**7379. GRUBBS, Robert B.**
Mar. 2, 1838, 2 miles NNE McClellan, Jefferson Co. NE 1/4 NW 1/4 Sect. 11 Tp. 1 R. 5, north and east.

**2436. GRUBER, Albert A.**
July 10, 1828, 6 miles N Tallahassee, Leon Co. E 1/2 SE 1/4 Sect. 25 Tp. 1 R. 2, north and west.

**8162. GUNN, William S.**
Dec. 3, 1839, 1 1/4 miles W Quincy, Madison Co. E 1/2 SW 1/4 and W 1/2 SE 1/4 Sect. 25 Tp. 1 R. 2, north and west.

**8220. GUNTER, Thomas**
Jan. 13, 1840, 1/4 mile SE Mount Pleasant, Gadsden Co. NW 1/4 NW 1/4 Sect. 19 Tp. 3 R. 4, north and east.

**1948. GUTHREY, Abraham**
July 18, 1853, 1 1/4 miles SSW of Campville, Alachua Co. SE 1/4 SW 1/4 Sect. 8 Tp. 10 R. 22, south and east. Patent delivered Oct. 2, 1858.

**1938. GUTHREY, Samuel**
July 13, 1853, 2 miles SSW Campville, Alachua Co. SW 1/4 NW 1/4 Sect. 8 Tp. 10 R. 22, south and east.

## * H *

**2982. HADLEY, Limon D.**
Aug. 12, 1829, 3 miles S by W Monticello, Jefferson Co. W 1/2 SW 1/4 Sect. 1 Tp. 1 R. 4, north and east.

**3519. HADLEY, Samuel**
May 19, 1830, 2 1/2 miles E by S Moseley Hall, Madison Co. E 1/2 SE 1/4 Sect. 25 Tp. 1 R. 8, south and east.

**3577. HADLEY, Samuel**
July 19, 1820, 2 1/2 miles ENE Moseley Hall, Madison Co. E 1/2 SW 1/4 Sect. 24 Tp. 1 R. 8, south and east.

**3578. HADLEY, Samuel**
July 19, 1830, 2 1/2 miles E Moseley Hall, Madison Co. W 1/2 SE 1/4 Sect. 24 Tp. 1 R. 8, south and east.

**3918. HADLEY, Samuel**
March 20, 1831, 3 miles E Moseley Hall, Madison Co. W 1/2 SE 1/4 Sect. 24 Tp. 1 R. 8, south and east.

**4087. HADLEY, Samuel**
Sept. 22, 1831, 8 miles W of Madison, Madison Co. E 1/2 NW 1/4 Sect. 24 Tp. 1 R. 8, north and east.

**4088. HADLEY, Samuel**
Sept. 22, 1831, 4 1/2 miles S by W of Madison, Madison Co. W 1/2 NE 1/4 Sect. 35 Tp. 1 R. 8, north and east.

**4089. HADLEY, Samuel**
Sept. 22, 1831, at Perkins, Leon Co. E 1/2 NW 1/4 Sect. 35 Tp. 1 R. 8, north and east.

**2667. HADLEY, Simon D.**
Jan. 26, 1829, 3 miles S Monticello, Jefferson Co. W 1/2 NW 1/4 Sect. 12 Tp. 1 R. 4, north and east.

**3076. HADLEY, Simon D.**
Oct. 1, 1829, 3 miles SSW Monticello, Jefferson Co. E 1/2 SW 1/4 Sect. 1 Tp. 1 R. 4, north and east.

**2752. HADLEY, Thomas**
Feb. 21, 1829, 3 miles SSW Monticello, Jefferson Co. E 1/2 NW 1/4 Sect. 12 Tp. 1 R. 4, north and east.

**6576. HAEKINS, Whitehurst J.**
Jan. 17, 1837, 3 miles S Chattahoochee, Gadsden Co. SE 1/4 NW 1/4 Sect. 23 Tp. 3 R. 3, north and west.

**4812. HAGEN, Andrew B.**
Sept. 6, 1858, 3 1/2 miles SW of Cooper, Columbia Co. E 1/2 Sect. 12 Tp. 5 R. 15, south and east.

**2108. HAGEN, Benj.**
Nov. 19, 1827, 1/4 mile W Black Creek, Leon Co. SW 1/4 Sect. 11 Tp. 1 R. 2, north and east.

**5375. HAGAN, Nancy**
Dec. 30, 1835, 1/4 mile E of Wadesboro, Jefferson Co. (on the county line) W 1/2 NE 1/4 Sect. 6 Tp. 1 R. 3, north and east.

**5675. HAGAN, Nancy**
May 18, 1836, 1/4 mile N of Wadesboro, Leon Co. SE 1/4 NW 1/4 Sect. 6 Tp. 1 R. 3, north and east.

**5376. HAGAN, Nancy**
Dec. 30, 1835, 1/4 mile E of Wadesboro, Leon Co. (on the county line) NE 1/4 NW 1/4 Sect. 6 Tp. 1 R. 3, north and east.

**6156. HAGAN, Nancy**
Dec. 5, 1836, just SE Wadesboro, Leon Co. NW 1/4 SE 1/4 Sect. 6 Tp. 1 R. 3, north and east.

**3101. HAGAN, Jesse**
Oct. 30, 1829, 5 miles E Copeland, Leon Co. E 1/2 SW 1/4 Sect. 31 Tp. 3 R. 4, north and east.

**2070. HAGAN, Jesse**
Aug. 19, 1853, at Melrose, Alachua Co. SE 1/4 SE 1/4 Sect. 24 Tp. 9 R. 22, south and east. Patent delivered April 28, 1858.

**2974. HAGAN, William**
Oct. 13, 1854, 5 miles SW Lulu, Columbia Co. E 1/2 SW 1/4 Sect. 6 Tp. 5 R. 18, south and east. Also S 1/2 NW 1/4 Sect. 1, SE 1/4 SW 1/4 Sect. 2, and NW 1/4 NE 1/4 Sect. 12 Tp. 5 R. 17, south and east.

**8144. HAGOOD, Richard R.**
Nov. 15, 1839, 2 miles SSW Miccosukee, Jefferson Co. NW 1/4 NW 1/4 Sect. 19 Tp. 2 R. 3, north and west.

**942. HAGUE, John R.**
Sept. 4, 1851, c. 2 miles SE Hague, Alachua Co. Lot No. 7 Sect. 33 Tp. 8 R. 19, south and east.

**59. HAGUE, Sarah**
July 31, 1844, 2 1/2 miles SE Hague, Alachua Co. SW 1/4 NW 1/4 Sect. 34 Tp. 8 R. 19, south and east.

**8509. HAIR, John**
Dec. 2, 1841, 2 miles E Greensboro, Gadsden Co. SW 1/4 SW 1/4 Sect. 11

Tp. 2 R. 5, north and west.

**5092. HAIRE, Charles**
July 23, 1835, 6 1/2 miles NNW of Port St. Joe, Gulf Co. Lots No. 5, 9, and 10 Fractional Sect. 5 Tp. 7, R. 11, south and west.

**5093. HAIRE, Charles**
July 23, 1835, on isthmus dividing St. Joseph's Bay from the Bay of San Blas, 4 miles SSW of Indian Pass, Gulf Co. Lots No. 3 and 4 Fractional Sect. 23 Tp. 9 R. 11, south and west.

**5094. HAIRE, Charles**
July 23, 1835, 3 miles S of Farmdale, Bay Co. Lot No. 1 Sect. 17 Tp. 6 R. 12, south and west.

**5095. HAIRE, Charles**
July 23, 1835, 6 miles NNW of Port St. Joe, Gulf Co. Lot No. 4 Fractional Sect. 9 Tp. 7 R. 11, south and west.

**5096. HAIRE, Charles**
July 23, 1835, 2 1/2 miles S of Farmdale, Gulf Co. SW 1/4 SW 1/4 Sect. 9 Tp. 6 R. 12, south and west.

**5097. HAIRE, Charles**
July 23, 1835, 1 3/4 miles SSW of Overstreet, Gulf Co. SE 1/4 SE 1/4 Sect. 8 Tp. 6 R. 12, south and west.

**5098. HAIRE, Charles**
July 23, 1835, 8 miles S by W of Overstreet, Gulf Co. Fractional Sect. 6 Tp. 7 R. 11, south and west.

**5570. HAIRE, Charles**
Mar. 31, 1836, apparently in San Blas Bay, E of Cape San Blas, Gulf Co.

**6084. HAIRE, Charles**
Nov. 23, 1836, c. 2 miles NE San Blas Light, Gulf Co. Lot No. 4 Fractional Sect. 21 Tp. 9 R. 11, south and west.

**6127. HAIRE, Charles**
Dec. 2, 1836, c. 1 1/2 miles N San Blas Light, Gulf Co. Lot No. 10 Fractional Sect. 20 Tp. 9 R. 11, south and west. 50.85 acres.

**6933. HAIRE, Charles**
(And **Henry PENNY**) March 23, 1837, at San Blas, Gulf Co. Lots No. 3 and 4 Fractional Sect. 31 Tp. 4 R. 13, south and east.

**6944. HAIRE, Charles**
March 25, 1837, 1 1/2 miles ENE Cook, Bay Co. E 1/2 SE 1/4 Sect. 14 Tp. 4 R. 13, south and west.

**6946. HAIRE, Charles**
March 25, 1837, 1 mile NE Overstreet, Gulf Co. E 1/2 NE 1/4 Sect. 34 Tp. 5 R. 11, south and west.

**6947. HAIRE, Charles**
March 25, 1837, 1 mile NE Overstreet, Gulf Co. W 1/2 NW 1/4 Sect. 35 Tp. 5 R. 11, south and west.

**6948. HAIRE, Charles**
March 25, 1837, 2 miles ENE Cook, Bay Co. W 1/2 SW 1/4 Sect. 13 Tp. 4 R. 13, south and west.

**6959. HAIRE, Charles**
March 28, 1837, 1 mile ENE Parker, Bay Co. W 1/2 SE 1/4 Sect. 17 Tp. 4 R. 13, south and west.

**2517. HAISTEEN, Frederick S.**
Feb. 28, 1854, 1/2 mile SW of Mason, Columbia Co. S 1/2 SW 1/4 Sect. 27 and SE 1/4 SE 1/4 Sect. 28 Tp. 5 R. 17, south and east. Patent delivered Oct. 27, 1856.

**2518. HAISTEEN, Frederick S.**
Feb. 28, 1854, 1/2 mile S by W of Mason, Columbia Co. E 1/2 NE 1/4 Sect. 33 and NW 1/4 NW 1/4 Sect. 34 Tp. 5 R. 17, south and east.

**5824. HALE, Benjamin**
Sept. 5, 1836, 2 1/4 miles SSW of Tallahassee, Leon Co. SW 1/4 SE 1/4 Sect. 9 Tp. 1 R. 1, south and west.

**5825. HALE, Benjamin**
Sept 5, 1836, 2 3/4 miles SW of Tallahassee, Leon Co. SW 1/4 SW 1/4 Sect. 10 Tp. 1 R. 1, south and west.

**5822. HALE, James**
Sept. 5, 1836, 2 1/4 miles W of St. Marks Junction, Leon Co. NW 1/4 NE 1/4 Sect. 15 Tp. 1 R. 1, south and west.

**8391. HALE, Jesse**
Aug. 20, 1840, 2 1/2 miles NNE Blountstown, Calhoun Co. NE 1/4 Sect. 22 Tp. 1 R. 8, north and west.

**2315. HALE, Jno. W.**
March 20, 1828, 1/2 mile N Florence, Gadsden Co. E 1/2 NE 1/4 Sect. 35 Tp. 3 R. 3, north and west.

**2943. HALE, John W.**
July 20, 1829, 3 miles W Ocklockonee, Leon Co. W 1/2 SE 1/4 Sect. 27 Tp. 1 R. 2, north and west.

**2314. HALE, Joseph**
March 18, 1828, 5 1/2 miles WSW

Bradfordville, Leon Co. NW 1/4 Sect. 26 Tp. 1 R. 2, north and west.

**2619. HALE, Joseph**
Jan. 29, 1829, at Lawrence Switch, Leon Co. E 1/2 SW 1/4 Sect. 26 Tp. 1 R. 2, north and west.

**5428. HALE, Joseph**
Feb. 1, 1836, 3/4 miles E of Chaires, Leon Co. NW 1/4 SE 1/4 Sect. 26 Tp. 1 R. 2, north and west.

**5487. HALE, Joseph**
Feb. 22, 1836, 1/4 mile E of Lawrence, Leon Co. S 1/2 Lot No. 5 Fractional Sect. 23 Tp. 1 R. 2, north and west.

**6060. HALE, Joseph**
Nov. 19, 1836, 2 miles W Ocklockonee Post Office, Leon Co. W 1/2 SW 1/4 Sect. 27 Tp. 1 R. 2, north and west.

**7757. HALE, Joseph**
Dec. 11, 1838, at Ocklockonee, Leon Co. SW 1/4 NW 1/4 Sect. 25 Tp. 1 R. 2, north and west.

**8201. HALE, Joseph**
Jan. 3, 1840, 1/2 mile NNW Nash, Jefferson Co. SW 1/4 SW 1/4 Sect. 24 Tp. 1 R. 4, north and east.

**7804. HALE, Joseph H. F.**
Jan. 9, 1839, at Nash, Jefferson Co. NW 1/4 SW 1/4 Sect. 24 Tp. 1 R. 4, north and east.

**1063. HALE, Peter**
Dec. 30, 1851, 3 miles NW of Santos, Marion Co. NW 1/4 SE 1/4 Sect. 5 Tp. 16 R. 22, south and east. Patent delivered May 12, 1856.

**2088. HALE, Wm.**
Nov. 7, 1827, 6 miles N Tallahassee, Leon Co. E 1/2 SW 1/4 Sect. 30 Tp. 2 R. 1, north and east.

**2089. HALE, Wm.**
Nov. 7, 1827, 6 miles NNE Tallahassee, Leon Co. E 1/2 SE 1/4 Sect. 32 Tp. 2 R. 1, north and east.

**2014. HALEY, Holiday**
Aug. 4, 1827, 2 1/2 miles SW Jacob, Jackson Co. W 1/2 NW 1/4 Sect. 26 Tp. 6 R. 12, north and west.

**3617. HALL, Benjamin**
Sept. 21, 1830, 3 miles WSW Tallahassee, Leon Co. W 1/2 NE 1/4 Sect. 9 Tp. 1 R. 1, south and west.

**3156. HALL, Harvey M.**
Dec. 9, 1829, 3/4 mile E Ockloklonee, Leon Co. W 1/2 NE 1/4 Sect. 30 Tp. 1 R. 1, north and west.

**3157. HALL, Harvey M.**
Dec. 9, 1829, 1 mile NE Ocklokonee, Leon Co. W 1/2 SE 1/4 Sect. 19 Tp. 1 R. 1, north and west.

**HALL, John C. see Kenneth BIMBY**

**8886. HALL, John**
Jan. 26, 1846, 4 3/4 miles SW Jasper, Hamilton Co. SW 1/4 SE 1/4 Sect. 15 Tp. 1 R. 13, north and east.

**7100. HALL, John C.**
Nov. 18, 1837, 2 1/2 miles N by W Lake Jackson (town), Leon Co. NE 1/4 SW 1/4 Sect. 26 Tp. 2 R. 2, north and west.

**7064. HALL, John Choice**
Oct. 25, 1837, 2 miles NNW Lake Jackson (town), Leon Co. W 1/2 SE 1/4 SE 1/4 NW 1/4 Sect. 26 Tp. 2 R. 2, north and west.

**7996. HALL, Nehemiah**
June 22, 1839, 4 1/2 miles SW Jasper, Hamilton Co. W 1/2 SW 1/4 Sect. 14 Tp. 1 R. 13, north and east.

**311. HALL, Sarah**
Jan. 1, 1827, 11 miles NW of Marianna, Jackson Co. SW 1/4 Sect. 2 Tp. 5 R. 11, north and west.

**4150. HALL, Thomas L.**
Mar. 8, 1832, 1 1/4 miles E of Hardaway, Gadsden Co. E 1/2 SW 1/4 Sect. 15 Tp. 3 R. 1, north and east.

**4391. HALL, Thomas L.**
Aug. 21, 1833, 4 miles SW of Iamonia, Leon Co. SW 1/4 NE 1/4 Sect. 15 Tp. 3 R. 1, north and east.

**5628. HALL, Thomas Sant**
April 28, 1836, 3 1/2 miles NW of Iamonia, Leon Co. NW 1/4 NE 1/4 Sect. 14 Tp. 3 R. 1, north and east.

**437. HALL, William**
Dec. 22, 1828, 2 miles E Norum, Washington Co. NE 1/4 Sect. 9 Tp. 2 R. 15, north and west.

**3470. HALL, William**
April 3, 1830, in Lake Hall, Leon Co. W 1/2 SE 1/4 Sect. 32 Tp. 2 R. 1, north and east. Pd. for with Treasury Scrip No. 68, issued in favour of Edgar and Macomb.

**6332. HALL, Wm.**
Dec. 28, 1836, 3 miles W Millspring, Jackson Co. NE 1/4 NE 1/4 and Nw 1/4 NE 1/4 Sect. 14 Tp. 3 R. 8, north

and west.

**1779. HALL, William E.**
July 25, 1853, 3 1/2 miles SE of Silver Springs, Marion Co. S 1/2 NW 1/4 Sect. 11 Tp. 15 R. 22, south and east. Patent delivered Sept. 24, 1857.

**1978. HALL, William E.**
July 25, 1853, 3 miles SE of Campville, Alachua Co. NE 1/4, NE 1/4 of NW 1/4 Sect. 10 Tp. 15 R. 22, south and east. Patent delivered (no date).

**1980. HALL, William E.**
July 25, 1853, 4 miles NE of Ocala, Marion Co. S 1/2 SW 1/4 and SE 1/4 SE 1/4 Sect. 3 Tp. 15 R. 22, south and east. Patent delivered Sept. 24, 1857.

**2425. HALL, William E.**
Feb. 21, 1854, at Blitchton, Marion Co. N 1/2 Sect. 12 Tp. 14 R. 20, south and east. Patent delivered Sept. 24, 1857.

**2426. HALL, William E.**
Feb. 21, 1854, 1 1/2 miles E of Melton, Alachua Co. SW 1/4 SW 1/4 Sect. 31 Tp. 13 R. 21, south and east. Patent delivered Sept. 24, 1857.

**2430. HALL, William E.**
Feb. 21, 1854, 2 3/4 miles NE of Martin, Marion Co. SW 1/4 SW 1/4 and NE 1/4 SE 1/4 Sect. 7 Tp. 14 R. 21, south and east.

**2749. HALL, William E.**
May 24, 1854, 3 1/2 miles NNE of Ocala, Marion Co. SW 1/4 SW 1/4 Sect. 11 Tp. 15 R. 22, south and east. Patent delivered Sept. 24, 1857.

**2750. HALL, William E.**
May 24, 1854, 1 mile N of Zuber, Marion Co. NW 1/4 SE 1/4 Sect. 7 Tp. 14 R. 21, south and east. Patent delivered Sept. 24, 1857.

**1981. HALL, William E.**
July 25, 1855, 3 1/2 miles SSE of Ocala, Marion Co. NW 1/4 SW 1/4 Sect. 23 Tp. 14 R. 22, south and east. Patent delivered Sept. 24, 1857.

**8748. HALLMAN, John A.**
Dec. 28, 1844, 1 3/4 miles NNW Dills, Jefferson Co. NE 1/4 NW 1/4 Sect. 35 Tp. 3 R. 5, north and east.

**7682. HALTON, Jesse**
Oct. 24, 1838, 1 1/2 miles SE by S McClellan, Jefferson Co. SW 1/4 SE 1/4 Sect. 22 Tp. 1 R. 5, south and east.

**8914. HAMILTON, David**
Feb. 25, 1846, 2 1/4 miles N Dills, Jefferson Co. E 1/2 NW 1/4 Sect. 30 Tp. 3 R. 6, north and east.

**5131. HAMILTON, Isaac**
Aug. 13, 1835, 1 mile W of Copeland, Leon Co. SE 1/4 Sect. 36 Tp. 3 R. 2, north and east.

**7101. HAMILTON, Isaac**
Nov. 18, 1837, 5 miles NNE of Felkel, Leon Co. E 1/2 SW 1/4 Sect. 35 Tp. 3 R. 2, north and east.

**7109. HAMILTON, Isaac**
Nov. 22, 1837, 3 1/4 miles NNE Felkel, Leon Co. W 1/2 NE 1/4 Sect. 25 Tp. 3 R. 2, north and east.

**7366. HAMILTON, Isaac**
Mar. 1, 1838, 5 miles SSE Iamonia, Leon Co. SW 1/4 SE 1/4 Sect. 24 Tp.3 R. 2, north and east.

**443. HAMILTON, James**
Dec. 24, 1828, 5 miles ESE Norum, Washington Co. E 1/2 NW 1/4 Sect. 14 Tp. 2 R. 15, north and west.

**93. HAMILTON, James**
Dec. 13, 1826, at Norum, Washington Co. E 1/2 SW 1/4 Sect. 11 p. 2 R. 15, north and west.

**3622. HAMILTON, John**
Oct. 1, 1830, 2 1/2 miles SE Fincher, Leon Co. E 1/2 NW 1/4 Sect. 20 Tp.3 R. 4, north and east.

**3929. HAMILTON, John**
March 29, 1831, 2 miles W Alma, Leon Co. E 1/2 NE 1/4 Sect. 33 Tp. 3 R. 4, north and east.

**1950. HAMLIN, George**
June 25, 1827, c. 4 miles NE Newport, Wakulla Co. Lot No. 7 Sect. 18 Tp. 3 R. 2, south and east.

**1951. HAMLIN, George**
June 25, 1827, c. 2 miles NE Newport, Wakulla Co. Lot No. 3 Sect. 19 Tp. 3 R. 2, south and east.

**1952. HAMLIN, George**
June 25, 1827, 3 miles NNE Newport, Wakulla Co. E 1/2 SW 1/4 Sect. 8 Tp. 3 R. 2, south and east.

**1955. HAMLIN, George**
June 26, 1827, 4 miles ESE Wakulla, Wakulla Co. Lot No. 6 Sect. 18 Tp. 3 R. 2, south and east.

**1985. HAMLIN, George**
(DUP) July 6, 1827, 4 miles E by S

Wakulla, Wakulla Co. Lot No. 8 Sect. 18 Tp. 3 R. 2, south and east.

**2065. HAMLIN, George**
Sept. 18, 1827, c. 1 mile NE Newport, Wakulla Co. Lot No. 2 Sect. 19 Tp. 3 R. 2, south and east.

**2071. HAMLIN, George**
Oct. 3, 1827, c. 2 miles NNE Newport, Wakulla Co. Lot No. 4 Sect. 19 Tp. 3 R. 2, south and east.

**2351. HAMLIN. J. G. and N.**
April 24, 1828, c. 5 miles W Wakulla, Wakulla Co. Lot No. 1 Sect. 8 Tp. 3 R. 2, south and east.

**2362. HAMLIN, J. C. and N.**
May 3, 1828, at Newport, Wakulla Co. Lot No. 1 Sect. 25 Tp. 1 R. 1, south and east. **2493. HAMLIN, J. G. and N.**
Sept 15, 1828, 2 1/2 miles N by E of Fanlew, Jefferson Co. W 1/2 SW 1/4 Sect. 17 Tp. 3 R. 2, south and east.

**HAMLIN, N. see J. G. HAMLIN**

**2516. HAMMOND, Benjamin F.**
Feb. 27, 1854, 4 miles ENE of Elmwood, Marion Co. NW 1/4 SE 1/4 Sect. 34 Tp. 12 R. 19, south and east. Patent delivered Nov. 28, 1856.

**1171. HANCOCK, Durham**
Feb. 12, 1852, 1 3/4 miles SW Lulu, Columbia Co. NW 1/4 NW 1/4 Sect. 9 Tp. 5 R. 18, south and east. Patent delivered April 11, 1856.

**1778. HANCOCK, Shadrach**
Mar. 19, 1853, 6 miles E of Fort White, Columbia Co. SE 1/4 SE 1/4 Sect. 34 Tp. 6 R. 17, south and east.

**2614. HANCOCK, Shadrach**
Mar. 15, 1854, 3/4 mile N by E of Mason, Columbia Co. NE 1/4 NW 1/4 and NW 1/4 NE 1/4 Sect. 22 Tp. 5 R. 17, south and east.

**2460. HANCOCK, Shadrack**
Feb. 23, 1854, 1 1/4 miles N of Mason, Columbia Co. SE 1/4 SW 1/4 and SW 1/4 SE 1/4 Sect. 15 Tp. 5 R. 17, south and east.

**2461. HANCOCK, Shadrack**
Feb. 23, 1854, 8 miles SE of Fort White, Columbia Co. W 1/2 NE 1/4 and SE 1/4 NE 1/4 Sect. 3 Tp. 7 Tp. 17, south and east.

**2903. HANCOCK, Shadrack**
Sept. 7, 1854, 3/4 mile N of Mason, Columbia Co. N 1/2 SW 1/4 Sect. 17 Tp. 3 R. 17, south and east.

**4213. HANCOCK, Simon**
Feb. 29, 1856, at McKinley, Columbia Co. N 1/2 SW 1/4 Sect. 17 Tp. 3 R. 17, south and east.

**2615. HANCOCK, William H.**
Mar. 15, 1854, 2 1/2 miles NNE Mason, Columbia Co. W 1/2 NW 1/4 Sect. 14 Tp. 5 R. 17, south and east. Patent delivered Sept. 19, 1856.

**5347. HAND, Abraham**
Dec. 12, 1835, 6 miles S by E of Havana, Gadsden Co. NE 1/4 NW 1/4 Sect. 22 Tp. 5 R. 2, north and west.

**8114. HAND, Abraham**
Oct. 14, 1839, 1 mile SW Concord, Gadsden Co. E 1/2 SW 1/4 Sect. 24 Tp. 3 R. 2, north and west. **7712. HAND, Nathaniel R.**
Nov. 20, 1838, 1 mile SSW Concord, Gadsden Co. SE 1/4 SW 1/4 Sect. 13 Tp. 3 R. 2, north and west.

**6505. HANDLE, Margaret**
Jan. 10, 1837, 4 1/2 miles SSW Tallahassee, Leon Co. SE 1/4 SE 1/4 Sect. 22 Tp. 1 R. 1, south and west. (On back "Margaret **HANDLEY**").

**6964. HANDLEY, Margaret**
Mar. 30, 1837, 4 miles SSW Tallahassee, Leon Co. SW 1/4 SW 1/4 Sect. 23 Tp. 1 R. 1, south and west.

**5255. HANKINS, David**
(No date) 1 1/4 miles NW of Pinetta, Madison Co. E 1/2 SW 1/4 Sect. 1 Tp. 2 R. 9, north and east.

**3842. HANKINS, Dennis**
Jan. 10, 1831, 1 mile NW Waco, Madison Co. E 1/2 SW 1/4 Sect. 18 Tp. 1 R. 9, south and west.

**4571. HANKINS, Dennis**
April 16, 1834, 1 mile SE by E of Clarksville, Jackson Co. SE 1/4 NE 1/4 Sect. 5 Tp. 1 R. 9, south and east.

**4572. HANKINS, Dennis**
April 16, 1834, 3/4 mile SE by E of Clarksville, Jackson Co. NW 1/4 NE 1/4 Sect. 5 Tp. 1 R. 9, south and east.

**4893. HANKINS, Dennis**
Mar. 19, 1835, 4 miles W by S of Madison, Madison Co. W 1/2 SE 1/4 Sect. 30 Tp. 1 R. 9, north and east.

**4894. HANKINS, Dennis**

Mar. 19, 1835, 3 miles SW of Madison, Madison Co. W 1/2 NW 1/4 Sect. 5 Tp. 1 R. 9, south and east.

**6070. HANKINS, Dennis**
Nov. 22, 1836, 2 1/4 miles E Cherrylake Post Office, Madison Co. E 1/2 SW 1/4 Sect. 11 Tp. 2 R. 9, north and east.

**6071. HANKINS, Dennis**
Nov. 22, 1836, 1/2 mile NE Cherry Lake Post Office, Madison Co. NE 1/4 E 1/2 NW 1/4 Sect. 3 Tp. 2 R. 9, north and east.

**6072. HANKINS, Dennis**
Nov. 22, 1836, 1 1/2 miles ENE Cherry Lake, Madison Co. E 1/2 SE 1/4 Sect. 10 Tp. 2 R. 9, north and east.

**6073. HANKINS, Dennis**
Nov. 22, 1836, 1 mile E by S Cherry Lake, Madison Co. W 1/2 NW 1/4 Sect. 15 Tp. 2 R. 9, north and east.

**6074. HANKINS, Dennis**
Nov. 22, 1836, 2 1/2 miles ENE Cherry Lake Post Office, Madison Co. W 1/2 SW 1/4 Sect. 2 Tp. 2 R. 9, north and east.

**6075. HANKINS, Dennis**
Nov. 22, 1836, 1/2 mile N and E Cherry Lake, Madison Co. W 1/2 NE 1/4 and E 1/2 SE 1/4 Sect. 9 Tp. 2 R. 9, north and east. Patent for this acknowledged before **Thomas J. HODSON**, Register, Dec. 17, 1845. Signed **Dennis HANKINS**.

**6076. HANKINS, Dennis**
Nov. 22, 1836, 2 miles NE Cherry Lake Post Ofice, Madison Co. W 1/2 NE 1/4 and W 1/2 SE 1/4 Sect. 4 Tp. 2 R. 9, north and east.

**6077. HANKINS, Dennis**
Nov. 22, 1836, 4 miles ENE Cherry Lake Post Office, Madison Co. W 1/2 SW 1/4 Sect. 1 Tp. 2 R. 9, north and east.

**6078. HANKINS, Dennis**
Nov. 22, 1836, 2 miles NE Cherry Lake, Madison Co. W 1/2 SE 1/4 and NE 1/4 SE 1/4 Sect. 3 Tp. 2 R. 9, north and east.

**6166. HANKINS, Dennis**
Dec. 8, 1836, 2 miles E by S Cherry Lake Post Office, Madison Co. W 1/2 NW 1/4 Sect. 14 Tp. 2 R. 9, north and east.

**6221. HANKINS, Dennis**
Dec. 15, 1836, 1 mile N Cherry Lake, Madison Co. NW 1/4 Sect. 4 Tp. 2 R. 9, north and east.

**6818. HANKINS, Dennis**
Mar. 16, 1837, 1 mile NE Cherry Lake, Madison Co. W 1/2 NW 1/4 Sect. 10 Tp. 2 R. 9, north and east.

**4375. HANKINS,(?) Gideon**
May 20, 1833, 2 1/4 miles NNW of Greensboro, Gadsden Co. NW 1/4 SW 1/4 Sect. 32 Tp. 3 R. 5, north and west.

**5754. HANKINS, William**
July 4, 1836, 1/4 mile W of Ocklocknee, Leon Co. SE 1/4 SW 1/4 Sect. 25 Tp. 1 R. 2, north and west.

**3791. HANLEY, (Housley/Hemley) Ranon**
Dec. 11, 1830, 3 miles E by N Roy, Gadsden Co. NW 1/4 Sect. 3 Tp. 2 R. 6, north and west.

**3792. HANLEY, (Housley/Hemley) Ranson**
Dec. 11, 1830, 5 miles ENE Roy, Gadsden Co. W 1/2 SW 1/4 Sect. 34 Tp. 3 R. 6, north and west.

**3790. HANLEY, (Housley/Hemley) Ranson**
(No date given) c. 2 miles NW Roy, Liberty Co. Lot No. 3 Sect. 3 Tp. 2 R. 7, north and west.

**3186. HANNION, Henry**
Dec. 28, 1829, c. 3/4 mile S Ocheesee, Calhoun Co. Lot No. 3 Fractional Sect. 5 Tp. 2 R. 7, north and west.

**2873. HANNUM, Henry**
July 6, 1829, c. 1 mile S Ocheesee, Calhoun Co. Lot No. 5 Sect. 5 Tp. 2 R. 7, north and west.

**3161. HANSHAW, Thomas**
Dec. 10, 1829, 4 miles E Stringer, Leon Co. W 1/2 SE 1/4 Sect. 19 Tp. 3 R. 4, north and east.

**535. HARBOR, Littlebury**
May 30, 1831, Monticello, Jefferson Co. W 1/2 SW 1/4 Sect. 34 Tp. 2 R. 5, north and east.

**6854. HARBOUR, Littleberry**
March 8, 1837, 6 miles ENE Monticello, Jefferson Co. SE 1/4 Sect. 13 Tp. 2 R. 5, north and east.

**6856. HARBOUR, Littleberry**
March 8, 1837, 4 1/2 miles E by N Monticello, Jefferson Co. W 1/2 NE

1/4 Sect. 24 Tp. 2 R. 5, north and east.

**6857. HARBOUR, Littleberry**
March 8, 1837, 4 1/2 miles E Monticello, Jefferson Co. E 1/2 SW 1/4 and W 1/2 SE 1/4 Sect. 23 Tp. 2 R. 5, north and east.

**4669. HARBOUR, S. B.**
Dec. 2, 1834, 1 1/2 miles E of Monticello, Jefferson Co.(Leon?) NW 1/4 NW 1/4 Sect. 28 Tp. 2 R. 5, north and east.

**1274. HARDGROVE, Abraham**
(DUP) April 13, 1827, 3 miles S Felkel, Leon Co. W 1/2 NW 1/4 Sect. 22 Tp. 2 R. 2, north and east.

**203. HARDIN, Martin**
(DUP) (Assignee of **Jordan SMITH**) Dec. 30, 1826, 4 miles SW Greenwood, Jackson Co. SW 1/4 Sect. 4 Tp. 5 R. 10, north and west.

**204. HARDIN, Martin**
(DUP) (Assignee of **David SPEARS**) Dec. 30, 1826, 4 miles SW Greenwood, Jackson Co. SE 1/4 Sect. 4 Tp. 5 R. 10, north and west.

**205. HARDIN, Martin**
(DUP) (Assignee of **Sarah HARDIN**) Dec. 30, 1826, 2 miles SW Greenwood, Jackson Co. E 1/2 SE 1/4 Sect. 5 Tp. 5 R. 10, north and west.

**206. HARDIN, Martin**
(Assignee of **Sarah HARDIN**) Dec. 30, 1826, 6 miles N Marianna, Jackson Co. E 1/2 SE 1/4 Sect. 5 Tp. 5 R. 10, north and west.

**207. HARDIN, Martin**
(Assignee of **Ben MOODY**) Dec. 30, 1826, 5 miles N Marianna, Jackson Co. NW 1/4 Sect. 9 Tp. 5 R. 10, north and west.

**210. HARDIN, Martin**
(Assignee of **Robt. IRVING**) Dec. 30, 1826, 4 miles SW Greenwood, Jackson Co. NW 1/4 Sect. 10 Tp. 5 R. 10, north and west.

**211. HARDIN, Martin**
(Assignee of **Mih'l HUDSON**) Dec. 30, 1826, 5 miles N Marianna, Jackson Co. SW 1/4 Sect. 9 Tp. 5 R. 10, north and west.

**212. HARDIN, Martin**
(Assignee of **Cete HICKS**) Dec. 30, 1826, 4 miles SW Greenwood, Jackson Co. NE 1/4 E 1/2 Sect. 9 Tp. 5 R. 10, north and west.

**213. HARDIN, Martin**
(Assignee of **Amos ACOCK**) Dec. 30, 1826, 5 miles SW Greenwood, Jackson Co. SE 1/4 E 1/2 Sect. 9 Tp. 5 R. 10, north and west.

**4290. HARDISON, Winifred**
Jan. 31, 1833, 8 miles NE of Stringer, Jefferson Co. NW 1/4 SE 1/4 Sect. 33 Tp. 3 R. 1, north and east.

**817. HARDY, Allen**
(Of Fla.) Dec. 4, 1826, at Miccosukee, Leon Co. E 1/2 SE 1/4 Sect. 14 Tp. 2 R. 3, north and east.

**2086. HARDY, Theophilus**
Nov. 1, 1827, 3 miles SW Alma, Jefferson Co. W 1/2 SE 1/4 Sect. 4 Tp. 2 R. 4, north and east.

**2081. HARDY, Thomas**
Oct. 22, 1827, 2 miles ESE Alma, Jefferson Co. E 1/2 NW 1/4 Sect. 4 Tp. 2 R. 4, north and east.

**4366. HARDYMAN, Thomas**
June 5, 1833, 1 mile NNW of Monticello, Jefferson Co. SE 1/4 NW 1/4 Sect. 23 Tp. 2 R. 4, north and east.

**4725. HARDYMAN, Thomas**
Dec. 19, 1834, 1 mile NW of Monticello, Jefferson Co. SW 1/4 SW 1/4 Sect. 23 Tp. 2 R. 4, north and east.

**6247. HARDYMAN, Thomas**
Dec. 19, 1836, 3 miles N by W Monticello, Jefferson Co. E 1/2 SE 1/4 Sect. 1 Tp. 2 R. 4, north and east.

**8820. HARE, Mary**
Sept. 29, 1845, 2 1/4 miles NNW Steaphead, Gadsden Co. NE 1/4 NW 1/4 Sect. 13 Tp. 2 R. 7, north and west.

**8637. HARE, Wiles**
Feb. 9, 1844, 1 1/2 miles SW by S Ray, Liberty Co. SW 1/4 NE 1/4 Sect. 13 Tp. 2 R. 7, north and west.

**5859. HARISON, Thomas**
Sept. 23, 1836, 1 mile SE of Darsey, Gadsden Co. NW 1/4 NW 1/4 and NW 1/4 NE 1/4 Sect. 12 Tp. 3 R. 2, north and west.

**4175. HARLEY, Catherine**
June 4, 1832, 2 miles NW of San Helena, Gadsden Co. NE 1/4 SW 1/4 Sect. 9 Tp. 1 R. 1, south and west. Transferred to **George B. LUCAS**, (no date).

**8245. HARLEY, Edmond A.**
Mar. 3, 1840, 1 1/4 miles NNE Gadsden, Gadsden Co. Lot No. 3 and 4 Sect. 11 Tp. 1 R. 2, north and west.

**8241. HARLEY, Edmund A.**
Feb. 29, 1840, 1 mile N Gadsden, Gadsden Co. S 1/2 Sect. 10 Tp. 1 R. 2, north and west.

**1896. HARLEY, James**
June 9, 1827, at Helena, Leon Co. Lot No. 6 Sect. 23 Tp. 1 R. 2, north and west.

**2564. HARLEY, Jas. and Jos. F. C.**
Dec. 12, 1828, 2 miles ESE of Wadesboro, Jefferson Co. W 1/2 NE 1/4 Sect. 25 Tp. 2 R. 2, north and east.

**2631. HARLEY, Jas. and Jos F. C.**
Jan. 16, 1829, 3 miles N Wadesboro, Leon Co. E 1/2 SE 1/4 Sect. 24 Tp. 2 R. 3, north and east.

**4648. HARLEY, Joseph**
Oct. 24, 1834, 4 1/2 miles SE by S of Centerville, Leon Co. SW 1/4 NE 1/4 Sect. 21 Tp. 2 R. 2, north and east.

**4683. HARLEY, Joseph**
Dec. 5, 1834, 1 mile SSE of Centerville, Leon Co. E 1/2 SW 1/4 Sect. 21 Tp. 2 R. 2, north and east.

**4469. HARLEY, Joseph**
Dec. 7, 1833, 3 miles E by S of Centerville, Leon Co. E 1/2 SW 1/4 Sect. 22 Tp. 2 R. 2, north and east.

**5303. HARLEY, Joseph**
Dec.3, 1835, 2 3/4 miles E by S of Centerville, Jefferson Co. SE 1/4 NW 1/4 Sect. 21 Tp. 2 R. 2, north and east.

**HARLEY, Joseph F. C. see James HARLEY, #2564 and 2631**

**2316. HARLEY, Joshua**
March 20, 1828, at Gadsden, Gadsden Co. W 1/2 SE 1/4 Sect. 9 Tp. 1 R. 2, north and west.

**91. HARLEY, Joshua**
Dec. 11, 1826, at Midway Station, Gadsden Co. NE 1/4 Sect. 9 Tp. 1 R. 2, north and west.

**6263. HARLEY, Joshua**
Dec. 21, 1836, 1/2 mile S Lake Jackson Station, Leon Co. SW 1/4 Sect. 9 Tp. 1 R. 2, north and west.

**6292. HARLEY, Joshua**
Dec. 23, 1836, 3 miles SW Lake Jackson Station, Leon Co. NE 1/4 SW 1/4 Sect. 10 Tp. 1 R. 2, north and west.

**8702. HARVEY, John C.**
Oct. 4, 1844, 3 miles SSE Greenwood, Jackson Co. SW 1/4 SW 1/4 Sect. 3 Tp. 5 R. 9, north and west.

**8703. HARVEY, John C.**
Oct. 4, 1844, 4 miles SSE Greenwood, Jackson Co. E 1/2 NW 1/4 Sect. 10 Tp. 5 R. 9, north and west.

**7226. HARRELL, John J.**
Jan. 15, 1838, 5 miles SE by S Dills, Jefferson Co. E 1/2 NW 1/4 Sect. 14 Tp. 2 R. 6, north and east.

**7609. HARRELL, John J. A.**
Aug. 21, 1838, 3 miles SSE Dills, Jefferson Co. SW 1/4 SE 1/4 Sect. 2 Tp. 2 R. 6, north and east.

**8490. HARRELL, John J. A.**
June 17, 1841, 3/4 miles S Dills, Jefferson Co. SW 1/4 SW 1/4 Sect. 6 Tp. 2 R. 6, north and east.

**89. HARRELL, Moses**
Dec. 7, 1826, 1 mile SW Concord Post Office, Gadsden Co. SW 1/4 Sect. 18 Tp. 3 R. 2, north and west.

**7261. HARRIS, James N.**
Jan. 20, 1838, 2 1/2 miles SE Myrick, Madison Co. E 1/2 SE 1/4 Sect. 9 Tp. 1 R. 7, south and east.

**7262. HARRIS, James N.**
Jan. 20, 1838, 2 1/2 miles SE Myrick, Madison Co. W 1/2 SW 1/4 Sect. 10 Tp. 1 R. 7, south and east.

**4772. HARRIS, John**
Jan. 14, 1835, 1 mile W of Copeland, Leon Co. W 1/2 SE 1/4 Sect. 31 Tp. 3 R. 2, north and east.

**4773. HARRIS, John**
Jan. 14, 1835, 1 1/4 miles W of Copeland, Leon Co. E 1/2 SW 1/4 Sect. 31 Tp. 3 R. 2, north and east.

**4203. HARRIS, Levi**
Aug. 21, 1832, 1/4 mile S of McClellan, Jefferson Co. NW 1/4 SW 1/4 Sect. 15 Tp. 1 R. 5, north and east.

**85. HARRIS, William**
(Of Alabama) May 18, 1825, about 3 miles NW of Midway Station, Leon Co. E 1/2 NE 1/4 Sect. 25 Tp. 2 R. 1, north and west. (Marked "Mobile" on back, probably former site of land office.)

**86. HARRIS, William**
(Of Alabama) May 18, 1825, about 2

miles N of Lake Jackson Station, Leon Co. (Marked "Mobile" on the back). W 1/2 NE 1/4 Sect. 25 Tp. 2 R. 1, north and west.

**87. HARRIS, William**
(Of Ala.) May 18, 1825, 2 miles N of Lake Jackson Station, Leon Co. (Marked "Mobile" on the back). E 1/2 NW 1/4 Sect. 23 Tp. 2 R. 1, north and west.

**88. HARRIS, William**
(Of Ala.) May 18, 1825, 2 miles N of Lake Jackson Station, Leon Co. (Marked "Mobile" on the back). W 1/2 NW 1/4 Sect. 25 Tp. 2 R. 1, north and west.

**89. HARRIS, William**
May 18, 1825, 1 mile N of Lake Jackson Station, Leon Co. Lot No. 1 in Fractional Sect. 26 Tp. 2 R. 1, north and west. ( Marked "Mobile" on the back).

**90. HARRIS, William** May 18, 1825, a peninsula in Lake Jackson, Leon Co. Lot 2 in Fractional Sect. 26 Tp. 2 R. 1, north and west. (Marked "Mobile" on the back.)

**91. HARRIS, William**
(Of Ala.) May 18, 1825, about 1 mile N Lake Jackson Station, bordering the Lake. Lot 3 Fractional Sect. 26 Tp. 2 R. 1, north and west. (Marked "Mobile" on the back).

**92. HARRIS, William**
(Of Ala.) May 18, 1825, 3 miles NE of Lake Jackson Station, Leon Co. Lot No. 4 Fractional Sect. 26 Tp. 2 R. 1, north and west. (Back marked "Mobile").

**93. HARRIS, William**
(Of Ala.) May 18, 1825, 2 miles N of Lake Jackson Station, Leon Co. Lot No. 5 Fractional Sect. 26 Tp. 2 R. 1, north and west. (Mobile) 103.5 acres.

**94. HARRIS, William**
May 18, 1825, near Lake Jackson Station, Leon Co. Lot 6 in Fractional Sect. 26 Tp. 2 R. 1, north and west. (Mobile) 80 acres.

**418. HARRIS, William**
(Of Ala.) May 31, 1825, 7 miles N Tallahassee, Leon Co. SE 1/4 Sect. 25 Tp. 2 R. 1, north and west.

**419. HARRIS, William**
(Of Ala.) May 31, 1825, 6 miles E Tallahassee, Leon Co. E 1/2 NE 1/4 Sect. 10 Tp. 1 R. 1, south and east.

**420. HARRIS, William**
(Of Ala.) May 31, 1825, 5 miles ESE Tallahassee, Leon Co. E 1/2 SE 1/4 Sect. 10 Tp. 1 R. 1, south and east.

**421. HARRIS, William**
(Of Ala.) May 31, 1825, 5 miles ESE of Tallahassee, Leon Co. W 1/2 SW 1/4 Sect. 11 Tp.1 R. 1, south and east.

**422. HARRIS, William**
(Of Ala.) May 31, 1825, 8 miles N Tallahassee, Leon Co. NE 1/4 Sect. 24 Tp. 2 R. 1, north and west.

**423. HARRIS, William**
May 31, 1825, 8 miles N Tallahassee, Leon Co. E 1/2 SW 1/4 Sect. 25 Tp. 2 R. 1, north and west.

**443. HARRIS, William**
(Of Ala.) June 1, 1825, 8 miles N Tallahassee, Leon Co. SE 1/4 Sect. 24 Tp. 2 R. 1, north and west.

**172. HARRIS, William**
Feb. 12, 1852, 6 miles SSW of Guildford, Union Co. W 1/2 NW 1/4 Sect. 17 Tp. 5 R. 18, south and east. Patent delivered May 3, 1856.

**8639. HARRISON, Robert H.**
Feb. 12, 1844, 4 1/2 miles SW Greenboro, Gadsden Co. NE 1/4 NE 1/4 Sect. 34 Tp. 3 R. 6, north and east.

**8850. HARRISON, Robert Henry**
Dec. 2, 1845, 2 1/2 miles NNE Dills, Jefferson Co. NE 1/4 NW 1/4 Sect. 34 Tp. 3 R. 6, north and west.

**7815. HARRISON, Thomas**
Jan. 14, 1839, 1 1/2 miles S Florence, Gadsden Co. E 1/2 SE 1/4 Sect. 14 Tp. 3 R. 2, north and west.

**8058. HARRISON, Thomas**
Aug. 24, 1839, 2 miles W Concord, Gadsden Co. W 1/2 SW 1/4 Sect. 14 Tp. 3 R. 2, north and west.

**1457. HARRISON, W. D.**
(DUP) May 22, 1827, 2 1/2 miles ESE Sawdust, Gadsden Co. W 1/2 SE 1/4 Sect. 21 Tp. 2 R. 4, north and west.

**1458. HARRISON, W. D.**
(DUP) May 22, 1827, 2 miles ESE Sawdust, Gadsden Co. W 1/2 SE 1/4 Sect. 26 Tp. 2 R. 4, north and west.

**1459. HARRISON, W. D.**

May 22, 1827, 2 miles ESE Sawdust, Gadsden Co. E 1/2 SW 1/4 Sect. 267 Tp. 2 R. 4, north and west.

**4838. HART, David**
Jan. 31, 1835, 3 3/4 miles N of Monticello, Jefferson Co. W 1/2 NE 1/4 Sect. 1 Tp. 2 R. 4, north and east.

**5601. HART, David**
April 18, 1836, 4 miles N by W of Monticello, Jefferson Co. NE 1/4 NE 1/4 Sect. 1 Tp. 2 R. 4, north and east.

**6087. HART, David B.**
Nov. 24, 1836, 1/2 mile W Alma, Jefferson Co. Lot No. 7 Fractional Sect. 36 Tp. 3 R. 4, north and east. 80 acres.

**2830. HART, Edwin**
May 20, 1829, 1 1/2 miles NE Cay, Jefferson Co. E 1/2 NW 1/4 Sect. 26 Tp. 1 R. 3, south and east. Transferred Dec. 29, 1829, to **Andrew N. JOHNSON**.

**2831. HART, Edwin**
May 20, 1829, 3/4 miles Cay, Jefferson Co. E 1/2 SW 1/4 Sect. 26 Tp. 1 R. 3, south and east. Transferred Dec. 29, 1829, to **Andrew N. JOHNSON**.

**2843. HART, Edwin**
June 6, 1829, 1 1/4 miles NE Cay, Jefferson Co. W 1/2 SE 1/4 Sect. 26 Tp. 1 R. 3, south and east. Transferred to **Andrew N. JOHNSON** on Dec. 29, 1829.

**6414. HART, Isaiah**
Jan. 4, 1837, 2 miles SE Alma, Jefferson Co. W 1/2 NW 1/4 Sect. 6 Tp. 2 R. 5, north and east.

**6516. HART, Isaiah**
Jan. 10, 1837, 4 miles NNW Monticello, Jefferson Co. SE 1/4 NE 1/4 Sect. 1 Tp. 2 R. 4, north and east.

**4182. HART, James L.**
July 7, 1832, at Wadesboro, Leon Co. SW 1/4 SW 1/4 Sect. 1 Tp. 1 R. 2, north and east.

**6335. HART, James L.**
Dec. 28, 1836, 1 mile W by S Wadesboro, Jefferson Co. NW 1/4 SW 1/4 Sect. 1 Tp. 1 R. 2, north and east.

**8497. HART, James M.**
Sept. 6, 1841, 6 3/4 miles W by S Dills, Jefferson Co. SW 1/4 SW 1/4 Sect. 6 Tp. 2 R. 5, north and east.

**8429. HART, John J.**
Dec. 14, 1840, 5 miles N Monticello, Jefferson Co. S 1/2 Lot No. 5 Sect. 25 Tp. 3 R. 4, north and east.

**4709. HART, John L.**
Dec. 15, 1834, at Midway, Gadsden Co. SW 1/4 NW 1/4 Sect. 9 Tp. 1 R. 2, north and east.

**5555. HART, John S.**
Mar. 25, 1836, 1/2 mile N of Wadesboro, Leon Co. SE 1/4 SE 1/4 Sect. 36 Tp. 2 R. 2, north and east.

**6368.**

**6369. HART, John S.**

**6370.** Dec. 31, 1836, c. 3 miles NE Wadesboro, Leon Co. W 1/2 SW 1/4 Sect. 28, E 1/2 NE 1/4 Sect. 32, and W 1/2 NW 1/4 Sect. 33 Tp. 2 R.3, north and east. (**HART** deposed before **I. ATKINSON**, J. P. of Leon County, that he had lost these receipts, Sworn Jan. 22, 1845.

**3119. HART, Marshall**
Nov. 14, 1829, 2 1/2 miles SE Fincher, Leon Co. W 1/2 SW 1/4 Sect. 29 Tp. 3 R. 4, north and west.

**3834. HART, Marshall**
Jan. 7, 1831, 3 miles NW Alma, Leon Co. E 1/2 SW 1/4 Sect. 20 Tp. 3 R. R. 4, north and east.

**HART, Marshall see Josiah EVERETT**

**3418. HART, Wm. Watkins**
Feb. 22, 1830, 2 miles WNW Wadesboro, Leon Co. W 1/2 SE 1/4 Sect. 35 Tp. 2 R. 2, north and east.

**5248. HARTLEY, Emanuel Preedeneia**
Nov. 13, 1885, 1/2 mile N by W Loretty, Duval Co. Lots 4 and 5 Sect. 9 Tp. 4S R. 27E.

**719. HARVEY, Elijah**
(Of Fla.) June 19, 1826, 1/2 mile E Wetumpka, Jefferson Co. E 1/2 NE 1/4 Sect. 35 Tp. 1 R. 4, north and east.

**720. HARVEY, Elijah**
(OF Fla.) June 19, 1826, 2 miles ESE Wetumpka, Jefferson Co. W 1/2 NE 1/4 Sect. 1 Tp. 1 R. 4, south and east. Transferred to **Robert GAMBLE**, Feb. 21, 1827.

**721. HARVEY, Elijah**
(Of Fla.) June 19, 1826, 2 miles SSE Waukenah, Jefferson Co. W 1/2 (?) Sect. 14 Tp. 1 R. 4, south and east. Transferred to **Robert GAMBLE**, Feb. 21, 1827.

**722, HARVEY, Elijah**
(Of Fla.) June 19, 1826, 2 miles SSE Waukenah, Jefferson Co. W 1/2 SE 1/4 Sect. 11 Tp. 1 R. 4, south and east. Transferred to **Robt. GAMBLE**, Feb. 21, 1827. Teste: **Wm. P. DUVAL**.

**724. HARVEY, Elijah**
(Of Fla.) July 5, 1826, 2 miles S Waukenah, Jefferson Co. E 1/2 NW 1/4 Sect. 14 Tp. 1 R. 4, south and east. Transferred to **Robt. GAMBLE**, July 21, 1827.

**739. HARVEY, Elijah**
(Of Fla.) Aug. 20, 1826, 1/2 mile ESE Nash, Jefferson Co. W 1/2 NE 1/4 Sect. 36 Tp. 1 R. 4, north and east.

**1158. HARVEY, Elijah**
(DUP) Feb. 21, 1827, at Nash Post Office, Jefferson Co. E 1/2 SW 1/4 Sect. 25 Tp. 1 R. 4, north and east.

**1337. HARVEY, Elijah**
May 7, 1827, 1 mile SW Waukenah, Jefferson Co. E 1/2 NE 1/4 Sect. 9 Tp. 1 R. 4, south and east.

**2588. HARVEY, Elijah**
Dec. 27, 1828, 2 1/2 miles W Waukenah, Jefferson Co. E 1/2 SE 1/4 Sect. 6 Tp. 1 R. 4, south and east.

**2595. HARVEY, Elijah**
Dec. 31, 1828, 3 miles WSW Waukenah, Jefferson Co. E 1/2 NE 1/4 Sect. 7 Tp. 1 R. 4, south and east.

**760. HARVEY, Elijah**
(Of Fla.) Sept. 15, 1826, at Monticello, Jefferson Co. W 1/2 NW 1/4 Sect. 10 Tp. 1 R. 4, north and east.

**9219. HARVEY, James J.**
April 14, 1891, 2 1/2 miles NE Jane Jay, Polk Co. SW 1/4 NE 1/4 and SE 1/4 NW 1/4 Sect. 30 Tp. 32S R. 25E

**HARVEY, John C.** see #8702, 8703

**723. HARVEY, Michael**
(Of Fla.) June 19, 1826, 2 miles ESE Waukenah, Jefferson Co. E 1/2 SE 1/4 Sect. 9 Tp. 1 R. 4, south and east.

**1157. HARVEY, Michael**
(DUP) Feb. 21, 1827, 2 miles SW Waukenah, Jefferson Co. W 1/2 SE 1/4 Sect. 9 Tp. 1 R. 4, south and east.

**8548. HARVEY, Sarah**
July 21, 1842, 4 miles SE Greenwood, Jackson Co. NW 1/4 NW 1/4 Sect. 10 Tp. 5 R. 9, north and west.

**7666. HARVEY, William H.**
Oct. 5, 1838, 2 1/2 miles NNE Marianna, Jackson Co. NW 1/4 Sect. 36 Tp. 5 R. 10, north and west.

**891. HARVILLE, John E.**
Jan. 27, 1851, 5 1/2 miles W by N Ocala Junction, Marion Co. NE 1/4 NE 1/4 Sect. 1 Tp. 15 R. 20 and N 1/2 NW 1/4 NW 1/4 NE 1/4 Sect. 6 Tp. 15 R. 21, south and east.

**4173. HAVIS, John**
June 2, 1832, 4 miles NNW of Blackcreek, Leon Co. NW 1/4 SW 1/4 Sect. 5 Tp. 2 R. 2, north and east.

**4600. HAVIS, John**
July 29, 1834, 2 miles S of Iamonia, Leon Co. SE 1/4 NE 1/4 Sect. 31 Tp. 3 R. 2, north and east.

**4601. HAVIS, John**
July 29, 1834, 1 mile NNE of Felkel, Leon Co. SE 1/4 NW 1/4 Sect. 31 Tp. 3 R. 2, north and east.

**4364. HAWKINS, Gideon**
May 20, 1833, 1 mile S of Hardaway, Jefferson Co. SW 1/4 NW 1/4 Sect. 32 Tp. 3 R. 5, north and west.

**8094. HAWKINS, Gideon**
Sept. 24, 1839, 1 1/2 miles Greensober, Gadsden Co. E 1/2 SW 1/4 Sect. 32 Tp. 3 R. 5, north and west.

**613. HAWKINS, Howell Sharpe**
Feb. 4, 1848, c. 10 miles NW Orange Park, Clay Co. SW 1/4 NE 1/4 Sect. 3 Tp. 4 R. 14, south and east. Patent delivered March 7, 1855.

**1758. HAWKINS, Howell Sharpe**
Mar. 7, 1853, 2 miles E of Pine Mount, Suwannee Co. SE 1/4 SE 1/4 Sect. 3 Tp. 4 R. 14, south and east.

**1803. HAWKINS, Howell Sharpe**
April 1, 1853, 2 1/2 miles E of Pinemount, Suwannee Co. SW 1/4 NW 1/4 Sect. 2, SE 1/4 NE 1/4 Sect. 3 Tp. 4 R. 14, south and east.

**1804. HAWKINS, Howell Sharpe**
April 1, 1853, 4 miles E of Pinemount, Suwannee Co. NE 1/4 SW 1/4 Sect. 2 Tp. 4 R. 14, south and east.

**1811. HAWKINS, Howell Sharpe**
April 4, 1853, 1 3/4 miles E of Pinemount, Suwannee Co. NE 1/4 NE 1/4 Sect. 3 Tp. 4 R. 14, south and east.

**1880. HAWKINS, Howell Sharpe**
June 4, 1853, 3 1/2 miles E of Pinem-

ount, Suwannee Co. SW 1/4 SW 1/4 Sect. 2 Tp. 4 R. 14, south and east.

**4794. HAWKINS, Howell Sharpe**
Sept. 6, 1858, 2 miles SSE of Pinemount, Suwannee Co. N 1/2 NE 1/4 Sect. 10 Tp. 4 R. 14, south and east.

**173. HAWKINS, Mathew B.**
Sept. 8, 1845, 2 1/4 miles NW Falmouth, Suwannee Co. SE 1/4 SE 1/4 Sect. 17 Tp. 4 R. 12, south and east.

**165. HAWKINS, Thomas**
July 30, 1845, 3 1/2 miles NE Bass, Columbia Co. NE 1/4 NE 1/4 Sect. 20 Tp. 4 R. 17, south and east.

**3628. HAWKINS, Whithuss J.**
Oct. 8, 1830, 4 miles SSE Chattahoochee, Gadsden Co. W 1/2 SW 1/4 Sect. 22 Tp. 3 R. 3, north and west.

**4065. HAWKINS, Whitehurst I.**
Aug. 20, 1831, 3 miles SW Mears Spur, Gadsden Co. W 1/2 NE 1/4 Sect. 23 Tp.3 R. 6, north and west.

**8744. HAWKINS, Whitehurst J.**
Dec. 16, 1844, 4 miles E by S Rockbluff, Liberty Co. E 1/2 NW 1/4 W 1/2 NE 1/4 Sect. 33 Tp. 2 R. 6, north and west.

**8503. HAWKINS, William**
Sept. 25, 1841, 1 mile SW Ockipocknee, Leon Co. NE 1/4 NW 1/4 Sect. 36 Tp. 1 R. 2, north and west.

**373. HAWTHORN, Kedar**
April 25, 1846, c. 1 1/2 miles NE Millwood, Marion Co. W 1/2 NW 1/4 and W 1/2 SW 1/4 Sect. 35 Tp. 12 R. 21, south and east.

**374. HAWTHORN, Kedar**
April 25, 1846, c. 2 miles NE Millwood, Marion Co. SE 1/4 NW 1/4 Sect. 35 Tp. 12 R. 21, south and east.

**389. HAWTHORN, Kedar**
May 4, 1846, c. 2 miles NE Millwood, Marion Co. E 1/2 SW 1/4 Sect. 35 Tp. 12 R. 21, south and east.

**7224. HAY, Jacob**
Jan. 12, 1838, 10 miles E by S Stringer, Jefferson Co. Lot No. 1 Fractional Sect. 24 Tp. 3 R. 4, north and east.

**8742. HAY, Jacob**
Dec. 16, 1844, 1 1/4 miles SW San Helena, Leon Co. SE 1/4 SW 1/4 Sect. 19 Tp. 1 R. 1, north and west.

**8743. HAY, Jacob**
Dec. 16, 1844, 1 1/4 miles SW San Helena, Leon Co. SW 1/4 SW 1/4 Sect. 19 Tp. 1 R. 1, north and west.

**347. HAYLEY, Holaday**
(Assignee of **Joseph SINGLETON**) April 16, 1827, 5 miles SSW Campbellton, Jackson Co. SE 1/4 Sect. 23 Tp. 6 R. 12, north and west.

**391. HAYS, Benj.**
(Assignee of **R. THOMPSON** and **W. DONALD**, assignee of **Mark WILLIAMS**) March 5, 1827, 3 miles W Campbellton, Jackson Co. SW 1/4 Sect. 34 Tp. 7 R. 12, north and west.

**397. HAYS, Benj.**
May 5, 1827, 5 miles E Graceville, Jackson Co. W 1/2 SE 1/4 Sect. 33 Tp. 7 R. 12, north and west.

**398. HAYS, Benj.**
(Assignee of **Jas. CHASON**) May 5, 1827, 3 miles SW Campbellton, Jackson Co. SW 1/4 Sect. 2 Tp. 6 R. 12, north and west.

**2543. HAYS, Benj.**
(And Co.) Nov. 12, 1828, 1 mile S Campbellton, Jackson Co. W 1/2 SE 1/4 Sect. 2 Tp. 6 R. 12, north and west. See **John LYNCH**

**395. HAYS, John**
May 5, 1827, 5 miles E Graceville, Jackson Co. NW 1/4 Sect. 4 Tp. 6 R. 12, north and west.

**2295. HASY, Robert**
Oct. 26, 1853, rest was illegible as to Range.

**2698. HAYWARD, Richard**
Jan. 30, 1829, 1/2 mile N Lake Jackson Station, Leon Co. E 1/2 NE 1/4 Sect. 31 Tp. 2 R. 1, north and west.

**5538. HAYWARD, Richard**
Mar. 14, 1836, 2 miles SW by S of Tallahassee, Leon Co. NW 1/4 NW 1/4 Sect. 11 Tp. 1 R. 1, south and west.

**6386. HAYWARD, Richard**
Jan. 3, 1837, 5 1/2 miles N Shelton, Dixie Co. NW 1/4 Sect. 13 Tp. 11 R. 10, south and east.

**6387. HAYWARD, Richard**
Jan. 3, 1837, 4 1/2 miles NW Whelton, Dixie Co. Scct. 21 Tp. 11 R. 10, south and east.

**6388. HAYWARD, Richard**

Jan. 3, 1837, 5 1/2 miles N Shelton, Dixie Co. NE 1/4 Sect. 14 Tp. 11 R. 10, south and east.

**6389. HAYWARD, Richard**
Jan. 3, 1837, 5 1/4 miles NNW Shelton, Dixie Co. Sect. 15 Tp. 11 R. 10, south and east.

**6390. HAYWARD, Richard**
Jan. 3, 1837, 6 miles N Shelton, Dixie Co. S 1/2 Sect. 11 Tp. 11 R. 10, south and east.

**6391. HAYWARD, Richard**
Jan. 3, 1837, 6 miles N by W Shelton, Dixie Co. S 1/2 Sect. 10 Tp. 11 R. 10, south and east.

**6392. HAYWARD, Richard**
Jan. 3, 1837, 6 miles NNW Shelton, Dixie Co. S 1/2 Sect. 9 Tp. 11 R. 10, south and east.

**6393. HAYWARD, Richard**
Jan. 3, 1837, 5 miles NW Shelton, Dixie Co. N 1/2 Sect. 22 Tp. 11 R. 10, south and east.

**6394. HAYWARD, Richard**
Jan. 3, 1837, 5 miles NW Shelton, Dixie Co. N 1/2 Sect. 28 Tp. 11 R. 10, south and east.

**6395. HAYWARD, Richard**
Jan. 3, 1837, 7 miles S by W Jena, Dixie Co. N 1/2 Sect. 1 Tp. 11 R. 9, south and east.

**6396. HAYWARD, Richard**
Jan. 3, 1837, 6 miles S by W Jena, Dixie Co. Sect. 36 Tp. 10 R. 9, south and east.

**6397. HAYWARD, Richard**
Jan. 3, 1837, 5 miles SSW Jena, Dixie Co. S 1/2 Sect. 25 Tp. 10 R. 9, south and east.

**6398. HAYWARD, Richard**
Jan. 3, 1837, 1 1/4 miles WNW Jena, Dixie Co. S 1/2 NE 1/4 Sect. 36 Tp. 9 R. 9, south and east.

**6339. HAYWARD, Richard**
Jan. 3, 1837, c. 1 mile SW Stephensville, Taylor Co. Lot No. 6 Fractional Sect. 25 Tp. 9 R. 9, south and east.

**6400. HAYWARD, Richard**
Jan. 3, 1837, c. 9 miles WNW Stephensville, Taylor Co. S 1/2 Sect. 34 Tp. 8 R. 8, south and east.

**6401. HAYWARD, Richard**
Jan. 3, 1837, 8 miles S by E Thelma, Taylor Co. Lots No. 6 and 7 Sect. 32 Tp. 8 R. 8, south and east.

**6402. HAYWARD, Richard**
Jan. 3, 1837, 8 1/4 miles SSE Thelma, Taylor Co. S 1/2 Sect. 33 Tp. 8 R. 8, south and east.

**6403. HAYWARD, Richard**
Jan. 3, 1837, 7 miles WNW Stephensville, Taylor Co. S 1/2 NE 1/4 Sect. 36 Tp. 8 R. 8, south and east.

**6404. HAYWARD, Richard**
Jan. 3, 1837, 7 1/4 miles WNW Stephensville, Taylor Co. (?)1/2 Sect. 35 Tp. 8 R. 8, south and east.

**6405. HAYWARD, Richard**
Jan. 3, 1837, c. 11 miles WNW Stephensville, Taylor Co. Lots No. 1, 2, and 3 Fractional Sect. 4 Tp. 9 R. 8, south and east.

**6406. HAYWARD, Richard**
Jan. 3, 1837, 7 1/2 miles WNW Stephensville, Taylor Co. N 1/2 Sect. 1 Tp. 9 R. 8, south and east.

**6407. HAYWARD, Richard**
Jan. 3, 1837, 9 miles W by N Stephensville, Taylor Co. Lots No. 1, 2, 3, and 4 Fractional Sect. 3 Tp. 8 R. 8, south and east.

**6408. HAYWARD, Richard**
Jan. 3, 1837, 9 miles W by N Stephensville, Taylor Co. N 1/2 Sect. 2 Tp. 9 R. 8, south and east.

**6476. HAYWARD, Richard**
Jan. 9, 1837, 9 miles S by E Jena, Dixie Co. NE 1/4 Sect. 13 Tp. 11 R. 9, south and east.

**6477. HAYWARD, Richard**
Jan. 9, 1837, c. 2 miles SW Stephensville, Taylor Co. Lots No. 1 and 2 Sect. 26 Tp. 9 R. 9, south and east.

**6478. HAYWARD, Richard**
Jan. 9, 1837, c. 1 1/2 miles SSW Stephensville, Taylor Co. Lot No. 3 Fractional Sect. 25 Tp. 9 R. 9, south and east.

**6479. HAYWARD, Richard**
Jan. 9, 1837, 5 miles WNW Stephensville, Taylor Co. NW 1/4 W 1/2 SW 1/4 Sect. 9 Tp. 9 R. 9, south and east.

**6480. HAYWARD, Richard**
Jan. 9, 1837, 5 miles ESE Stephensville, Taylor Co. SE 1/4 Sect. 8 Tp. 9 R. 9, south and east.

**6481. HAYWARD, Richard**
Jan. 9, 1837, 4 miles WNW Stephens-

ville, Taylor Co. E 1/2 SE 1/4 Sect. 9 Tp. 9 R. 9, south and east.

**6482. HAYWARD, Richard**
Jan. 9, 1837, 7 1/2 miles NNE Shelton, Dixie Co. Sect. 8 Tp. 11 R. 10, south and east.

**6537. HAYWARD, Richard**
Jan. 14, 1837, c. 6 miles S by W Jena, Dixie Co. Lots No. 1 and 7 Fractional Sect. 35 Tp. 10 R. 9, south and east.

**6538. HAYWARD, Richard**
Jan. 14, 1837, 6 1/2 miles WNW Stephensville, Taylor Co. NW 1/4 Sect. 6 Tp. 9 R. 9, south and east.

**6539. HAYWARD, Richard**
Jan. 14, 1837, 4 1/2 miles ENE Jena, Dixie Co. E 1/2 SE 1/4 Sect. 26 Tp. 10 R. 9, south and east.

**6540. HAYWARD, Richard**
Jan. 14, 1837, c. 7 1/2 miles SSW Jena, Dixie Co. Lot No. 1 Fractional Sect. 2 Tp. 11 R. 9, south and east.

**242. HEARD, Benjamin Wilkinson**
Jan. 2, 1846, c. 2 1/2 miles N Shady, Marion Co. Lot No. 2 and E 1/2 SW 1/4 Sect. 1 Tp. 16 R. 21, south and east.

**243. HEARD, Benjamin Wilkinson**
Jan. 2, 1846, 3 miles SW Santos, Marion Co. NW 1/4 Sect. 17 Tp. 16 R. 22, south and east.

**244. HEARD, Benjamin Wilkinson**
Jan. 2, 1846, 1 mile W Santos, Marion Co. SW 1/4 NW 1/4 and SW 1/4 Sect. 5 Tp. 16 R. 22, south and east.

**245. HEARD, Benjamin Wilkinson**
Jan. 2, 1846, c. 2 miles NW Santos, Marion Co. SW 1/4 NW 1/4 and SW 1/4 SE 1/4 Sect. 5 Tp. 16 R. 22, south and east.

**246. HEARD, Benjamin Wilkinson**
Jan. 2, 1846, c. 2 miles N Shady, Marion Co. E 1/2 SE 1/4 Sect. 11 Tp. 16 R. 21, south and east.

**247. HEARD, Benjamin Wilkinson**
Jan. 2, 1846, 4 1/2 miles NW Shady, Marion Co. Lot No. 1 Fractional Sect. 7 Tp. 16 R. 22, south and east.

**378. HEARD, Benjamin Wilkinson**
April 28, 1846, 1 1/4 miles N Shady, Marion Co. W 1/2 SE 1/4 Sect. 11 Tp. 16 R. 21, south and east.

**380. HEARD, Benjamin Wilkinson**
(Of Ga.) April 28, 1846, 1 1/2 miles N Shady, Marion Co. W 1/2 NE 1/4 Sect. 11 Tp. 16 R. 21, south and east.

**381. HEARD, Benjamin Wilkinson**
(Of Ga.) April 28, 1846, c. 2 miles SW Ocala, Marion Co. W 1/2 NW 1/4 and SW 1/4 Sect. 26 Tp. 15 R. 21, south and east.

**5995. HEARD, Elizabeth**
Nov. 10, 1836, 3 miles NNW of Dills, Jefferson Co. W 1/2 SE 1/4 Sect. 27 Tp. 3 R. 5, north and east.

**7520. HEARD, Elizabeth**
July 9, 1838, 2 1/2 miles NNW Dills, Jefferson Co. N 1/2 SW 1/4 Sect. 27 Tp. 3 R. 5, north and east.

**773. HEARD, Falkner**
Dec. 13, 1850, 1 mile NW Shady, Marion Co. NE 1/4 SW 1/4 Sect. 11 Tp. 16 R. 21, south and east. Patent delivered April 21, 1856.

**877. HEARD, Falkner**
May 22, 1851, 1 mile N Shady, Marion Co. Ne 1/4 NE 1/4 Sect. 14 Tp. 16 R. 21, south and east. Patent delivered April 21, 1856.

**8705. HEARN, Lawrence H.**
Oct. 4, 1844, 2 miles E Greenwood, Jackson Co. W 1/2 SW 1/4 Sect. 34 Tp. 6 R. 9, north and west.

**7772. HEASTMAN, William**
Dec. 18, 1889, 1 mile W by S Citra, Marion Co. S 1/2 NW 1/4 Sect. 32 Tp.12S R. 22E.

**4934. HEAT, Jas. H.**
April 13, 1835, 1/2 mile NNW of Felkel, Leon Co. NW 1/4 SW 1/4 Sect. 33 Tp. 3 R. 2, north and east.

**4935. HEAT, Jas. H.**
April 13, 1835, 3/4 mile NW of Felkel, Leon Co. W 1/2 SE 1/4 Sect. 33 Tp. 3 R. 2, north and east.

**1155. HEATH, Samuel S.**
Feb. 7, 1852, 1 3/4 miles NE of Conner, Marion Co. Lot No. 9 Sect. 25 Tp. 14 R. 23, south and east. Patent delivered Jan. 17, 1857.

**2129. HEIR, Thomas**
(Of Fla.) Dec. 5, 1827, 3 miles SW Centerville, Leon Co. E 1/2 Se 1/4 Sect. 27 Tp. 2 R. 1, north and east.

**HEKING, A. L. see John GADSDEN**

**5855. HELLERY, John**
Sept. 19, 1836, 3 1/4 miles E by S of

Fincher, Jefferson Co. SE 1/4 NE 1/4 Sect. 20 Tp. 3 R. 4, north and east.

**2051. HELVENSTON, Simeon**
Aug. 12, 1853, 1 mile S of Elmwood, Marion Co. E 1/2 SE 1/4 Sect. 27 Tp. 13 R. 19, south and east. Patent delivered June 13, 1856.

**2125. HELVENSTON, Simeon**
Aug. 30. 1853, 1 mile W of Fort McCoy, Marion Co. NW 1/4 SW 1/4 Sect. 4 Tp. 13, R. 20, south and east. Patent delivered June 13, 1856.

**6131. HENDERSON, David A.**
Dec. 2, 1836, 2 miles WSW Cherry Lake, Madison Co. W 1/2 NW 1/4 Sect. 7 Tp. 2 R. 9, north and east. "Sold to **Wyche**. (Signed) E. **SUMMERLIN**".

**7862. HENDERSON, David A.**
Feb. 12, 1839, 1/2 mile NNE Chipola, Calhoun Co. E 1/2 NW 1/4 Sect. 34 Tp. 2 R. 9, north and east.

**7312. HENDERSON, Duncan**
Feb. 19, 1838, 2 miles SE by S Eucheeanna, Walton Co. NW 1/4 NW 1/4 Sect. 28 Tp. 2 R. 18, north and west.

**HENDERSON, Jasper M. see Appleton ROSSETTER**

**6423. HENDERSON, Samuel**
Jan. 4, 1837, 2 1/2 miles NW Cherry Lake, Madison Co. E 1/2 NW 1/4 Sect. 1 Tp. 2 R. 8, north and east.

**6223. HENDERSON, Samuel T.**
Dec. 15, 1836, 3 miles WNW Cherry Lake, Madison Co. SW 1/4 and W 1/2 NW 1/4 Sect. 1 Tp. 2 R. 8, north and east.

**6224. HENDERSON, Samuel T.**
Dec. 15, 1836, 3 miles WNW Cherry Lake, Madison Co. E 1/2 SE 1/4 Sect. 2 Tp. 2 R. 8, north and east.

**7834. HENDERSON, Samuel T.**
Jan. 24, 1839, 1/2 mile N Calhoun, Madison Co. W 1/2 NW 1/4 Sect. 12 Tp. 1 R. 9, north and east.

**7835. HENDERSON, Samuel T.**
Jan. 24, 1839, 1/4 mile N by W Calhoun, Madison Co. E 1/2 NE 1/4 Sect. 11 Tp. 1 R. 9, north and east.

**8808. HENDERSON, Williams**
May 7, 1881, 2 3/4 miles W by S Roberts, Escambia Co. NE 1/4 SW 1/4 Sect. 34 Tp. 1N R. 31W.

**2304. HENDRY, John M.**
Oct. 28, 1853, 1 mile E of Highland, Clay Co. W 1/2 NW 1/4 and W 1/2 SW 1/4 Sect. 5 Tp. 11 R. 23, south and east. Patent delivered Sept. 14, 1874.

**2305. HENDRY, John M.**
Oct. 28, 1853, 1 mile W of Oakton, Putnam Co. Lots No. 1, 12, 13, 14, 15, 25, and 26 Sect. 6 Tp. 11 R. 23, south and east.

**2364. HENDRY, John M.**
Nov. 27, 1853, 1 mile S of Oakton, Putnam Co. Lot No. 3 Sect. 6 Tp. 11 R. 23, south and east. Patent delivered Sept. 14, 1874. No. of Certificate of patent delivered 4294 instead of 2364.

**4593. HENLEY, Ambrose**
July 5, 1834, 1 mile W of Hermitage, Gadsden Co. NW 1/4 SE 1/4 Sect. 36 Tp. 4 R. 6, north and west.

**HERCULES, R. see Matthew J. ALLEN**

**474. HERRINGTON, Harvey**
Feb. 1, 1830, at Milton, Santa Rosa Co. Lot No. 4 Sect. 13 Tp. 1 R. 28, north and west.

**762. HERRINGTON, Thomas**
(The heirs of **Thomas HERRINGTON**, deceased) Nov. 25, 1850, near Suwannee Valley, Columbia Co. Lot No. 1 NE 1/4 Sect. 15 Tp. 2 R. 16, south and east.

**5156. HESTER, Wilson**
Sept. 26, 1835, 1 1/4 miles NNW of St. Marks Junction, Leon Co. NW 1/4 NW 1/4 Sect. 14 Tp. 1 R. 1, south and west.

**5234. HEWS, Samuel**
Oct. 27, 1835, 2 1/2 miles SE by E of Centerville, Leon Co. NE 1/4 NE 1/4 Sect. 32 Tp. 2 R. 2, north and east.

**6333. HEXT, James H.**
Dec. 28, 1836, 1/4 mile SE Midway, Gadsden Co. NE 1/4 SE 1/4 Sect. 8 Tp. 1 R. 2, north and west. Patent delivered Mar. 30, 1869, next to **McBride**. Signed **Chas. MUNDEE**, Reg.

**586. HICKMAN, William H.**
Aug. 16, 1847, 1 mile W Orange Lake, Marion Co. NE 1/4 Sect. 30 Tp. 12 R. 21, south and east.

**2434. HICKMAN, Wm.**
June 27, 1828, 1 mile SE Comfort, Jackson Co. W 1/2 NW 1/4 Sect. 25

Tp. 3 R. 8, north and west.
**6228. HICKS, Reuben B.**
Dec. 16, 1836, 1 mile NE Midway, Gasdsden Co. W 1/2 SW 1/4 Sect. 32 Tp. 3 R. 2, north and west.
**6930. HICKS, Reuben B.**
March 22, 1837, 3 miles S by W Blountstown, Calhoun Co. E 1/2 SE 1/4 Sect. 8 Tp. 1 R. 8, south and west.
**6931. HICKS, Reuben B.**
Mar. 22, 1837, 2 miles SE Sharpestown, Calhoun Co. E 1/2 NE 1/4 and E 1/2 SE 1/4 Sect. 29 Tp. 1 R. 8, south and west.
**6932. HICKS, Reuben B.**
Mar. 22, 1837, 1 mile E Nut, Calhoun Co. E 1/2 NE 1/4 Sect. 17 Tp. 1 R. 8, south and west.
**8916. HICKS, Reuben B.**
Mar. 4, 1846, 2 1/2 miles SSE Sharpestown, Calhoun Co. W 1/2 NE 1/4 Sect. 29 Tp. 1 R. 8, south and west.
**8917. HICKS, Reuben B.**
Mar. 4, 1846, 1/2 mile SW Nut, Calhoun Co. E 1/2 SW 1/4 Sect. 17 Tp. 1 R. 8, south and west.
**4149. HICKS, Reuben C.**
Mar. 7, 1832, 1 3/4 miles NW of Midway, Gadsden Co. E 1/2 SE 1/4 Sect. 21 Tp. 2 R. 2, north and west.
**1406. HICKSON, John**
July 26, 1852, at Island Grove Station, Alachua Co. SE 1/4 SE 1/4 Sect. 34 Tp. 12 R. 21, south and east. Patent delivered June 27, 1857.
**1407. HICKSON, John**
July 26, 1852, 4 1/2 miles E of Proctor, Alachua Co. On S shore of Orange Lake, Lot 13, Sect.27 Tp. 12 R. 21, south and east.
**6310. HIELSE, Isaac**
Dec. 26, 1836, 3 miles WSW Parker, Escambia Co. Lots Nos. 1 and 2 Fractional Sect. 2 Tp. 2 R. 32, south and west.
**4943. HIERSHON, William**
April 25, 1835, Range direction omitted. SW 1/4 SE 1/4 Sect. 28 Tp. 2 R. 5.
**2560. HIGGINS, Daniel**
Dec. 6, 1828, 3 miles WSW of Miccosukee, Leon Co. W 1/2 NW 1/4 Sect. 18 Tp. 2 R. 3, north and east.
**4059. HIGH, Harmon**
Aug. 3, 1831, 3 1/4 miles SW of Capitola, Leon Co. E 1/2 SW 1/4 Sect. 34 Tp. 1 R. 3, north and east.
**5337. HIGH, Harmon**
Dec. 9, 1835, 2 3/4 miles N by W of Braswells, Jefferson Co. NW 1/4 NW 1/4 Sect. 5 Tp. 1 R. 4, south and east.
**6651. HIGH, Julius**
Jan. 24, 1837, 3 miles W by S Waukenah, Jefferson Co. W 1/2 NE 1/4 and SE 1/4 NW 1/4 Sect. 7 Tp.1 R. 4, south and east.
**7149. HIGH, Julius**
Dec. 16, 1837, 3 1/2 miles W Waukenah, Jefferson Co. NW 1/4 SE 1/4 Sect. 7 Tp. 1 R. 4, south and east.
**5488. HIGH, Norman**
Feb. 23, 1836, 1 1/2 miles N by W of Braswells, Jefferson Co. NE 1/4 NW 1/4 Sect. 5 Tp. 1 R. 4, south and east.
**2138. HIGHSMITH, Isaac**
Sept. 5, 1853, 5 miles NE of Double Sink, Levy Co. NE 1/4 SE 1/4 and SW 1/4 SE 1/4 Sect. 32 Tp. 11 R. 16, south and east. Patent delivered Mar. 12, 1875.
**2060. HILL, James H.**
Aug. 16, 1853, 4 miles W of Rideout, Clay Co. SW 1/4 NW 1/4 Sect. 4 Tp. 5 R. 24, south and east. Patent delivered July 7, 1857.
**2061. HILL, James H.**
Aug. 16, 1853, 6 miles W of Rideout, Clay Co. NE 1/4 NE 1/4 Sect. 5 Tp. 5 R. 23, south and east. Patent delivered July 7, 1857.
**3534. HILL, Moses**
June 2, 1830, 1 mile N Wacissa, Jefferson Co. W 1/2 SE 1/4 Sect. 30 Tp. 1 R. 4, south and east.
**4343. HILL, Moses**
April 3, 1833, 3/4 mile N of Wacissa, Jefferson Co. E 1/2 NW 1/4 Sect. 30 Tp. 1 R. 4, south and east.
**4450. HILL, Moses**
Nov. 6, 1833, 1 3/4 miles NE by E of Cay, Jefferson Co. SE 1/4 NE 1/4 Sect. 25 Tp. 1 R. 3, south and east.
**4451. HILL, Moses**
Nov. 6, 1833, 2 miles NNE of Cay, Jefferson Co. SW 1/4 NW 1/4 Sect. 30 Tp. 1 R. 4, south and east.
**86. HILL, Saphia**
Dec. 21, 1844, 5 miles SW Lynne,

Marion Co. W 1/2 SW 1/4 Sect. 25 Tp. 15 R. 23, south and east.

**87. HILL, Saphia**
Dec. 21, 1844, 5 1/2 miles SW Lynne, Marion Co. SE 1/4 Sect. 26 Tp. 15 R. 23, south and east.

**7317. HILL, Stacy B.**
Feb. 10, 1838, 2 miles W by N Marion, Hamilton Co. E 1/2 NW 1/4 Sect. 1 Tp. 1 R. 14, south and east.

**838. HINES, Henry**
Feb. 19, 1851, 2 1/2 miles SE Benton, Columbia Co. SW 1/4 SE 1/4 Sect. 4 Tp. 1 R. 17, south and east.

**1862. HINES, Henry**
May 17, 1853, 2 3/4 miles SE of Benton, Columbia Co. W 1/2 SW 1/4 Sect. 4 Tp. 1 R. 17, south and east.

**1874. HINES, Henry**
May 31, 1853, 2 1/2 miles SE of Benton, Columbia Co. S 1/2 NW 1/4 Sect. 4 Tp. 1 R. 17, south and east.

**2329. HINES, Robert R.**
Nov. 1, 1853, 2 1/4 miles SSE of Campville, Alachua Co. SW 1/4 SW 1/4 Sect. 2 Tp. 10 Tp. 22, south and east.

**2999. HINES, Robert R.**
Oct. 17, 1854, 2 miles W by N Campville, Alachua Co. SW 1/4 NE 1/4 Sect. 2 Tp. 10 R. 22, south and east.

**4022. HINES, William**
Dec. 21, 1855, 3 miles W of Bixford, Suwannee Co. W 1/2 SE 1/4 and E 1/2 SW 1/4 Sect. 33 Tp. 1 R. 13, south and east.

**2738. HINSON, Daniel M.**
Feb. 14, 1829, 1 1/2 miles E Jamieson, Gadsden Co. E 1/2 NE 1/4 Sect. 8 Tp. 3 R. 2, north and west.

**8097. HINSON, Daniel M.**
Sept. 27, 1839, 1 1/4 miles NNE Hinson, Gadsden Co. E 1/2 SW 1/4 Sect. 22 Tp. 3 R. 2, north and west.

**1429. HINSON, Mathew**
Aug. 10, 1852, 2 miles N Hawthorne, Alachua Co. SW 1/4 SW 1/4 Sect. 14 Tp. 10 R. 22, south and east. Patent delivered April 4, 1857.

**3438. HINTON, David M.**
Mar. 6, 1830, 1 3/4 miles E of Jamieson, Gadsden Co. W 1/2 NW 1/4 Sect. 9 Tp. 3 R. 2, north and west.

**599. HIRES, George Adam**
Nov. 29, 1847, 3 1/2 miles S Thomasville, Alachua Co. NW 1/4 NW 1/4 Sect. 12 Tp. 8 R. 19, south and east. Patent delivered April 28, 1858.

**2096. HIRES, George A.**
Aug. 22, 1853, 5 1/4 miles NE of Hague, Alachua Co. SE 1/4 NE 1/4 Sect. 11 Tp. 8 R. 19, south and east. Patent delivered July 7, 1857.

**1832. HIRES, George H.**
April 18, 1853, 4 miles SE Haynesworth, Alachua Co. S 1/2 Lot 4 Sect. 12 Tp. 8 R. 19, south and east. Patent delivered July 7, 1857.

**3867. HOGAN, Jesse W.**
(And **Robt. C. HURST**) Feb. 7, 1831, 2 miles SW Ashville, Jefferson Co. E 1/2 NW 1/4 Sect. 5 Tp. 2 R. 7, north and east. ( **HURST** relinquished his interest Nov. 9, 1831).

**7774. HOGAN, John F.**
Dec. 20, 1838, 1 mile W by N Dills, Jefferson Co. W 1/2 SE 1/4 Sect. 35 Tp. 3 R. 5, north and east.

**314. HOGG, Benj.**
Jan. 1, 1827, 7 miles NW Marianna, Jackson Co. NW 1/4 Sect. 15 Tp. 5 R. 11, north and west.

**2481. HOGG, Hatton M.**
Sept. 8, 1828, 3 1/2 miles S Welchton, Jackson Co. E 1/2 NW 1/4 Sect. 13 Tp. 5 R. 12, north and west.

**2482. HOGG, Hatton M.**
Sept. 8, 1828, 3 1/2 miles S Welchton, Jackson Co. W 1/2 NE 1/4 Sect. 13 Tp. 5 R. 12, north and west.

**179. HOGG, Jno.**
Dec. 29, 1826, 4 1/2 miles SSE Graceville, Jackson Co. E 1/2 NE 1/4 Sect. 23 Tp. 6 R. 12, north and west.

**389. HOGG, John**
May 5, 1827, 2 miles SW Jacob, Jackson Co. W 1/2 NE 1/4 Sect. 23 Tp. 6 R. 12, north and west.

**188. HOGG, Wm.**
(DUP) Dec. 29, 1826, 3 1/2 miles S Graceville, Jackson Co. W 1/2 NW 1/4 Sect. 24 Tp. 6 R. 12, north and west.

**390. HOGG, Wm.**
May 5, 1827, 1 mile SW Jacob, Jackson Co. E 1/2 NW 1/4 Sect. 24 Tp. 6 R. 12, north and west.

**HOLDER, Daniel** see **John Matthews MOTT, #277**

**200. HOLDER, Joseph**
Nov. 5, 1845, just SE Hampton, Bradford Co. W 1/2 NW 1/4 Sect. 29 Tp. 7 R. 21, south and east.

**1996. HOLDER, Joseph J. B.**
Aug. 1, 1853, 2 1/2 miles E Hague, Alachua Co. SW 1/4 SW 1/4 Sect. 24, N 1/2 Lot 1 Sect. 26 Tp. 8 R. 19, south and east. Patent delivered Jan. 27, 1857.

**354. HOLDER, Thomas Bell**
(DUP) April 4, 1846, 1/2 mile W Graham, Bradford Co. NW 1/4 NE 1/4 Sect. 25 Tp. 7 R. 20, south and east.

**2111. HOLDER, Thomas B.**
Aug. 23, 1853, 1 1/4 miles SW Cyril, Alachua Co. W 1/2 NE 1/4 Sect. 15 Tp. 8 R. 20, south and east. Patent delivered June 7, 1856.

**2129. HOLDER, Thomas B.**
Sept. 1, 1853, 1/2 mile W of Cyril, Alachua Co. NW 1/4 NW 1/4 Sect. 14 Tp. 8 R. 20, south and east. Patent delivered June 7, 1856.

**5711. HOLLAND, Caroline**
June 20, 1836, at Lawrence Switch, Leon Co. N 1/2 Lot No. 5 Fractional Sect. 23 Tp. 1 R. 2, north and west.

**3542. HOLLAND, Griffin W.**
June 22, 1830, 3 miles E Meridian, Leon Co. Lot No. 2 Sect. 22 Tp. 3 R. 1, north and east.

**4151. HOLLAND, Griffin W.**
Mar. 10, 1832, 1 mile E of Concord, Gadsden Co. E 1/2 SE 1/4 Sect. 15 Tp. 3 R. 1, north and east.

**4693. HOLLAND, G. U.**
Dec. 11, 1834, 4 miles W by S of Iamonia, Leon Co. NW 1/4 SE 1/4 Sect. 15 Tp. 3 R. 1, north and east.

**3201. HOLLAND, Jack**
Jan. 4, 1830, SE part of Centerville, Leon Co. E 1/2 SE 1/4 Sect. 24 Tp. 2 R. 1, north and east.

**7878. HOLLAND, James**
Feb. 20, 1839, 3 miles NNE Waco, Madison Co. SE 1/4 NW 1/4 Sect. 10 Tp. 1 R. 9, south and east.

**151. HOLLAND, John**
Dec. 28, 1828, 4 miles E Welchton, Jackson Co. SW 1/4 Sect. 28 Tp. 6 R. 11, north and west.

**56. HOLLAND, Lewis**
Nov. 9, 1826,(partial receipt) West 1/4 Sect. 33 Tp. 6 R.?, north and west.

**7759. HOLLAND, William**
Dec. 12, 1838, 1/2 mile W Ocklocknee, Leon Co. SW 1/4 SW 1/4 Sect. 25 Tp. 1 R. 2, north and west.

**2173. HOLLEMAN, Wm.**
Dec. 26, 1827, 2 miles ENE Sedalia, Gadsden Co. E 1/2 SE 1/4 Sect. 32 Tp. 2 R. 5, north and west.

**986, HOLLIDAY, Solomon F.**
Nov. 4, 1851, 2 1/2 miles S Candler, Marion Co. Lot No. 7 Sect. 12 Tp. 17 R. 23, south and east. Patent delivered May 8, 1858.

**987. HOLLIDAY, Solomon F.**
Nov. 4, 1851, 2 1/2 miles S Candler, Marion Co. Lot No. 6 Fractional Sect. 13 Tp. 17 R. 23, south and east. Patent delivered May 8, 1858.

**990. HOLLIDAY, Solomon F.**
Nov. 5, 1851, near Eastlake, Marion Co. Lot No. 1 Fractional Sect. 18 Tp. 17 R. 24, south and east. Patent delivered May 8, 1858.

**991. HOLLIDAY, Solomon F.**
Nov. 5, 1851, near Stanton, Marion Co. Lot No. 5 Sect. 19 Tp. 17 R. 24, south and east. Patent delivered May 8, 1858.

**113. HOLLINGER, L. B.**
Dec. 22, 1826, at Quincy, Gadsden Co. E 1/2 NE 1/4 Sect. 1 Tp. 2 R. 3, north and west.

**142. HOLLINGER, Littleberry**
(Heir of **S. HOLLINGER**) Dec. 27, 1827, 4 miles N Midway Station, Gadsden Co. SW 1/4 Sect. 21 Tp. 2 R. 2, north and west.

**4263. HOLLINSWORTH, John**
Dec. 30, 1832, 3 1/4 miles NW of Aucilla, Jefferson Co. W 1/2 NE 1/4 Sect. 5 Tp. 2 R. 6, north and east.

**5446. HOLLINGSWORTH, John**
Feb. 6, 1836, 3/4 mile E of Dill, Jefferson Co. E 1/2 NW 1/4 and E 1/2 SW 1/4 Sect. 5 Tp. 2 R. 6, north and east.

**7727. HOLLINGSWORTH, John**
Nov. 26, 1838, 2 miles N by E Steaphead, Gadsden Co. SW 1/4 SE 1/4 Sect. 5 Tp. 2 R. 6, north and east.

**8154. HOLLINGSWORTH, John**
Nov. 25, 1839, 2 miles SE Dills, Jefferson Co. E 1/2 SE 1/4 Sect. 5 Tp. 2 R. 6, north and east.

**2896. HOLLINGSWORTH, William**
July 7, 1829, 3 miles ESE Wadesboro, Jefferson Co. E 1/2 SW 1/4 Sect. 10 Tp. 1 R. 3, north and east.

**5232. HOLLINGSWORTH, William**
Oct. 23, 1835, 2 miles N by E of Lloyd, Jefferson Co. NE 1/4 NE 1/4 Sect. 15 Tp. 1 R. 3, north and east.

**5640. HOLLINGSWORTH, William**
May 2, 1836, 3 1/2 miles SSE of Miccosukee, Leon Co. NW 1/4 SE 1/4 Sect. 15 Tp. 1 R. 3, north and east.

**6183. HOLLINGSWORTH, William**
Dec. 10, 1836, just N Lloyd, Jefferson Co. E 1/2 NW 1/4 Sect. 15 Tp. 1 R. 3, north and east.

**7929. HOLLINGSWORTH, William**
April 3, 1838, 4 1/2 miles SSE Dills, Jefferson Co. NE 1/4 NE 1/4 Sect. 2 Tp. 2 R. 6, north and east.

**2428. HOLLINGSWORTH, William**
June 4, 1828, 3 miles W Moseley Hall, Madison Co. W 1/2 SW 1/4 Sect. 25 Tp. 1 R. 7, south and east.

**2429. HOLLINGSWORTH, William**
June 4, 1828, 3 1/4 miles W Moseley Hall, Madison Co. E 1/2 SE 1/4 Sect. 26 Tp. 1 R. 7, south and east.

**2591. HOLLINGSWORTH, William**
Dec. 20, 1828, 1/2 mile NW Moseley Hall, Madison Co. E 1/2 SW 1/4 Sect. 20 Tp. 1 R. 8, south and east.

**3804. HOLLINGSWORTH, William**
Dec. 21, 1830, 1 1/2 miles NE Lloyd, Jefferson Co. W 1/2 SW 1/4 Sect. 10 Tp. 1 R. 3, north and west.

**6184. HOLLINGSWORTH, William**
Dec. 10, 1836, 1 mile NNE Lloyd, Jefferson Co. E 1/2 SE 1/4 Sect. 9 Tp. 1 R. 3, north and east.

**6185. HOLLINGSWORTH, William**
Dec. 10, 1836, 1 mile NNE Lloyd, Jefferson Co. E 1/2 SE 1/4 Sect. 9 Tp. 1 R. 3, north and east.

**4857. HOLLOWAY, Richard L.**
Sept. 24, 1858, 2 1/2 miles SW of Cooper, Columbia Co. S 1/2 NW 1/4 and SW 1/4 and W 1/2 SE 1/4 Sect. 14 Tp. 5 R. 15, south and east.

**4858. HOLLOWAY, Russel H.**
Sept. 24, 1858, 2 1/2 miles SW Columbia, Columbia Co. E 1/2 Sect. 18 Tp. 5 R. 16, south and east.

**4048. HOLLOWAY, Susannah**
(Widow of **John T. HOLLOWAY**) July 9, 1883, 1/4 mile W Sparling, Polk Co. SE 1/4 SE 1/4 ( or Lot 6) Sect. 20, S 1/2 SW 1/4 and NE 1/4 SW 1/4 Sect. 21 Tp. 28S R. 24E.

**2247. HOLMES, Arthur F.**
(Of Fla.) Feb. 6, 1828, 5 1/2 miles SW Waukenah, Jefferson Co. W 1/2 NW 1/4 Sect. 19 Tp. 1 R. 4, north and east.

**6269. HOLMES, Arthur F.**
Dec. 22, 1836, 4 miles ESE El Destino, Jefferson Co. NW 1/4 NW 1/4 NE 1/4 NW 1/4 Sect.14 Tp. 1 R. 3, south and east.

**HOLMES, A. F.** see **Horatio M. GRAY**

**4812. HOLMES, Arthur T.**
Jan. 22, 1835, 2 1/4 miles E by S of El Destino, Jefferson Co. SW 1/4 NW 1/4 Sect. 14 Tp. 1 R. 3, south and east.

**4813. HOLMES, Arthur T.**
Jan. 22, 1835, 2 1/2 miles E by S of El Destino, Jefferson Co. SE 1/4 NW 1/4 Sect. 14 Tp. 1 R. 3, south and east.

**4814. HOLMES, Arthur T.**
Jan. 22, 1835, 2 1/2 miles S of El Destino, Jefferson Co. W 1/2 SW 1/4 Sect. 14 Tp. 1 R. 3, south and east.

**4815. HOLMES, Arthur T.**
Jan. 22, 1835, 2 3/4 miles E by S of El Destino, Jefferson Co. W 1/2 NE 1/4 Sect. 14 Tp. 1 R. 3, south and east.

**4082. HOLMES, Edgar Henry**
Sept. 16, 1831, 4 miles NNE El Destino, Jefferson Co. E 1/2 SE 1/4 Sect. 3 Tp. 1 R. 3, south and east.

**4878. HOLMES, Henry**
Mar. 2, 1835, 3 3/4 miles W by N of Facil, Hamilton Co. NW 1/4 SW 1/4 Sect. 24 Tp. 1 R. 4, south and east.

**5959. HOLMES, Henry**
Nov. 3, 1836, 10 miles E by N of Genoa, Hamilton Co. Lot No. 3 Fractional Sect. 1 Tp. 1 R. 16, south and east.

**HOLMES, Hugh** see **MILLS & PERRY, #456**

**2673. HOLMES, Richard**
Jan. 27, 1829, at Jacob, Jackson Co. E 1/2 NE 1/4 Sect. 13 Tp. 6 R. 12, north and west.

**4955. HOLT, James H.**
May 6, 1835, 1 mile S by W of Jamieson, Gadsden Co. SE 1/4 SW 1/4 Sect. 18 Tp. 3 R. 2, north and east.

**4370. HOLT, Nathan**
June 14, 1833, 1 mile N by E of Wadesboro, Leon Co. NW 1/4 SE 1/4 Sect. 30 Tp. 2 R. 3, north and east.

**4371. HOLT, Nathan**
June 14, 1833, 3/4 mile N by E of Wadesboro, Leon Co. NE 1/4 SW 1/4 Sect. 30 Tp. 2 E. 3, north and east.

**4388. HOLT, Nathan**
Aug. 16, 1833, 1 1/2 miles N by E of Wadesboro, Leon Co. SW 1/4 NE 1/4 Sect. 30 Tp. 2 R. 3, north and east.

**5301. HOLT, Nathan**
Dec. 2, 1835, 1 1/4 miles N of Wadesboro, Jefferson Co. W 1/2 SW 1/4 Sect. 30 Tp. 2 R. 3, north and east.

**5302. HOLT, Nathan**
Dec. 2, 1835, 1 1/2 miles N of Wadesboro, Jefferson Co. E 1/2 NW 1/4 Sect. 30 Tp. 2 R. 3, north and east.

**7259. HOLT, Nathan**
Jan. 19, 1838, 2 miles N by E Wadesboro, Jefferson Co. NE 1/4 SE 1/4 Sect. 30 Tp. 3 R. 3, north and east.

**5790. HOLTON, Thomas**
Aug. 2, 1836, 1 1/2 mile N by E of Steaphead, Gadsden Co. NW 1/4 NW 1/4 Sect. 7 Tp. 2 R. 6, south and east.

**4420. HOOKER, William B.**
Sept. 24, 1833, 6 miles S by E of Facil, Hamilton Co. Lot No. 1 Sect. 8 Tp. 2 R. 16, south and east.

**6849. HOOKER, William B.**
Mar. 7, 1837, 3 miles E by N White Springs, Hamilton Co. E 1/2 SE 1/4 Sect. 4 Tp. 2 R. 16, south and east.

**6750. HOOKER, William B.**
Feb. 6, 1837, c. 2 miles E White Springs, Hamilton Co. Lot No. 3 Fractional Sect. 9 Tp. 2 R. 16, south and east.

**6751. HOOKER, William B.**
Feb. 6, 1837, 2 miles E by N White Springs, Hamilton Co. SW 1/4 Sect. 4 Tp. 2 R. 16, south and east.

**5199. HOOPER, Joseph C.**
Feb. 17, 1860, 4 miles NE of Branford, Suwannee Co. SW 1/4 SW 1/4 Sect. 14 Tp. 6 R. 14, south and east. Patent delivered Nov. 6, 1870.

**455. HOOT, Henry Christopher**
Aug. 13, 1846, near Seffner, Hillsborough Co. SE 1/4 SE 1/4 Sect. 23, SW 1/4 SW 1/4 Sect. 24, and SE 1/4 SE 1/4 NW 1/4 SE 1/4 Sect. 26 Tp. 28 R. 20, south and east. Filed in office April 15, 1850, **Martin CUNNINGHAM**, Clerk.

**5116. HOPSON, Edmund I.**
July 27, 1835, 1 1/2 miles W of Iamonia, Gadsden Co. W 1/2 NW 1/4 Sect. 14 Tp. 3 R. 1, north and east.

**5100. HOPSON, Hardy C.**
July 23, 1835, 3 miles N by E of Meridian, Leon Co. E 1/2 NE 1/4 Sect. 15 Tp. 3 R. 1, north and east.

**5101. HOPSON, Hardy C.**
July 23, 1835, 2 1/2 miles W of Iamonia, Leon Co. NW 1/4 NE 1/4 Sect. 15 Tp. 3 R. 1, north and east.

**6031. HOPSON, Hardy C.**
Nov. 15, 1836, at Iamonia, Leon Co. NE 1/4 and E 1/2 NW 1/4 Sect. 18 Tp. 3 R. 2, north and east.

**60. HOPSON, John**
Nov. 13, 1826, c. 1/2 mile N Fairgrounds Post Office, Jackson Co. SE 1/4 Sect. 30 Tp. 5 R. 10, north and west.

**562. HOPSON, John**
Dec. 7, 1834, 2 1/2 miles W Leonards Siding, Calhoun Co. NE 1/4 NW 1/4 Sect. 17 Tp. 1 R. 9, north and west. Paid in bills from Central Bank of Florida.

**4057. HOPSON, Wm. G.**
Aug. 3, 1831, 1 1/4 miles E of Concord, Gadsden Co. E 1/2 NW 1/4 Sect. 15 Tp. 3 R. 1, north and east.

**2984. HOPSON, Zachariah**
( Of Ga.) Aug. 24, 1829, 1/2 mile SE Centerville, Leon Co. NW 1/4 Sect. 30 Tp. 2 R. 2, north and east.

**6067. HOPSON, Zachariah**
Nov. 21, 1836, 1 mile ENE Meridian, Leon Co. SW 1/4 SE 1/4 Sect. 17 Tp. 3 R. 2, north and east.

**7466. HORN, W. A.**
July 23, 1889, 1 mile E Argyle, Holmes Co. N 1/2 NW 1/4, NW 1/4 NE 1/4 and SW 1/4 NE 1/4 Sect. 34 Tp. 3N R. 18W.

**6784. HORNE, Eli**
Feb. 7, 1837, 1 1/2 miles NNW Indian

Ford Station, Rosa Co. Altered by Commissioners of the G. L. O. to a location 1 mile S Fentress (Red Rock Post Office) Station, Rosa Co. SE 1/4 SW 1/4 Sect. 27 Tp. 3 R. 27, north and west. Patent delivered to **Maj. WARD**, Oct. 26, 1846.

HORNE, Eli see Nicholas BAGGETT

**7723. HORNE, Henry E.**
Nov. 24, 1838, 2 miles SSW Concord, Gadsden Co. E 1/2 NE 1/4 Sect. 23 Tp. 3 R. 2, north and west.

**7724. HORNE, Henry E.**
Nov. 24, 1838, 1 3/4 miles SSW Concord, Gadsden Co. E 1/2 NW 1/4 Sect. 24 Tp. 3 R. 2, north and west.

**470. HORNE, Joab**
Jan. 15, 1830, 1 mile SE Laurel Hill, Okaloosa Co. SE 1/4 Sect. 8 Tp. 3 R. 23, north and west.

**96. HORT, Wm. P.**
(For the Heirs of **Martin NOLL**) Dec. 14, 1826, 5 miles NW Marianna, Jackson Co. NW 1/4 Sect. 19 Tp. 5 R. 10, north and west.

**97. HORT, Wm. P.**
(For **Warren NOLL**) Dec. 14, 1826, c. 5 miles NW Marianna, Jackson Co. SW 1/4 Sect. 17 Tp. 5 R. 10, north and west.

**98. HORT, Wm. P.**
Dec. 14, 1826, c. 5 miles NW Marianna, Jackson Co. SE 1/4 Sect. 18 Tp. 5 R. 10, north and west.

**739. HOTT, Richard Scrugs**
May 21, 1850, c. 4 1/2 miles SW New River, Bradford Co. Excess of the land contained in the E 1/2 SW 1/4 and N 1/2 SW 1/4 Sect. 33 Tp. 6 R. 20, south and east.

**6878. HOUCK, Conrad**
Mar. 10, 1837, 3/4 mile NE Centerville, Leon Co. E 1/2 SW 1/4 Sect. 18 Tp. 2 R. 2, north and east.

**6936. HOUCK, Conrad**
Mar. 23, 1837, 3/4 mile NE Centerville, Leon Co. E 1/2 NW 1/4 Sect. 18 Tp. 2 R. 2, north and east.

**4314. HOUCK, Daniel**
Feb.. 19, 1833, 2 miles SE Centerville, Leon Co. SW 1/4 SE 1/4 Sect. 30 Tp. 2 R. 2, north and east.

**5199. HOUCK, Daniel**
Oct. 12, 1835, 2 miles SE by S of Centerville, Leon Co. SW 1/4 SW 1/4 Sect. 30 Tp. 2 R. 2, north and east.

**5352. HOUCK, Daniel**
Dec. 18, 1835, 1 1/2 miles S by E of Centerville, Leon Co. SE 1/4 SW 1/4 Sect. 30 Tp. 2 R. 2, north and east.

**5517. HOUCK, Daniel L.**
Mar. 8, 1836, 1/4 mile SSW of Centerville, Leon Co. NW 1/4 SE 1/4 Sect. 30 Tp. 2 R. 2, north and east.

**4525. HOUCK, Gasper**
Jan. 20, 1834, 1 1/2 miles S by E of Centerville, Leon Co. NW 1/4 SE 1/4 Sect. 31 Tp. 2 R. 2, north and east.

**151. HOUSE, Cynthia C.**
June 9, 1845, just E Ocala, Marion Co. Lot No. 2 Sect. 17 Tp. 15 R. 22, south and east. "Recorded in Book "A" on page 51 in the clerk's office in Marion County Circuit Court on the 28th day of Nov., 1845. **John G. REARDON**, Clerk."

**8931. HOUSTON, Isaac T.**
April 6, 1846, 1/2 mile NNE Myrick, Madison Co. W 1/2 SE 1/4 E 1/2 SW 1/4 Sect. 33 Tp. 1 R. 7, north and east.

**376. HOWARD, Chas.**
May 3, 1827, 2 miles N Campbellton, Jackson Co. W 1/2 NW 1/4 Sect. 24 Tp. 7 R. 12, north and west.

**53. HOWARD, David**
Nov. 8, 1826, at Havana, Gadsden Co. SW 1/4 Sect. 28 Tp. 3 R. 2, north and west.

**4706. HOWARD, David**
Dec. 12, 1834, 1 mile E of Hinson, Gadsden Co. NW 1/4 SE 1/4 Sect. 27 Tp. 3 R. 2, north and west.

**4602. HOWARD, David**
Aug. 6, 1834, 3 miles NNW of Lake Jackson Station, Leon Co. NE 1/4 SW 1/4 Sect. 27 Tp. 3 R. 2, north and west.

**7553. HOWARD, George**
July 28, 1838, 5 miles W by S Oakdale, Jackson Co. SW 1/4 Sect. 31 Tp. 4 R. 10, south and west.

**7554. HOWARD, George**
July 28, 1838, 1 1/4 miles NNW Semsville, Jackson Co. E 1/2 NW 1/4 Sect. 6 Tp. 3 R. 10, north and west.

**7555. HOWARD, George**
July 28, 1838, 6 3/4 miles E Alford, Jackson Co. NE 1/4 SE 1/4 Sect. 36

Tp. 4 R. 11, north and west.

**7556. HOWARD, George**
July 28, 1838, 4 1/2 miles W by S Oakdale, Jackson Co. SE 1/4 NW 1/4 Sect. 31 Tp. 4 R. 10, north and west.

**5356. HOWARD, Peter**
Dec. 19, 1835, 1 mile N by W of Hinson, Gadsden Co. NW 1/4 NW 1/4 Sect. 22 Tp. 3 R. 2, north and west.

**54. HOWARD, Samuel**
Nov. 8, 1826, at Havana, Gadsden Co. W 1/2 NW 1/4 Sect. 33 Tp. 3 R. 2, north and west.

**124. HOWARD, Samuel**
Dec. 23, 1826, at Havana, Gadsden Co. E 1/2 NW 1/4 Sect. 33 Tp. 3 R. 2, north and west.

**8797. HOWARD, Wiley**
July 22, 1845, 1/2 mile SE Bond, Madison Co. NE 1/4 SW 1/4 NW 1/4 SE 1/4 Sect. 4 Tp. 2 R. 8, north and east.

**294. HOWELL, Joseph**
Jan. 27, 1846, 1/2 mile N Trapnell, Hillsborough Co. NE 1/4 SE 1/4 Sect. 10 Tp. 29 R. 22, south and east.

**5996. HOWREN, James C.**
Nov. 10, 1836, 2 miles SSW of Madison, Madison Co. E 1/2 SE 1/4 Sect. 31 Tp. 1 R. 9, north and east.

**6079. HOWREN, James E.**
Nov. 22, 1836, 4 miles WSW Madison, Madison Co. NE 1/4 SW 1/4 Sect. 31 Tp. 1 R. 9, north and east.

**1941. HUBBARD, Elijah**
June 25, 1827, 6 miles S by W Quincy, Gadsden Co. E 1/2 SE 1/4 Sect. 7 Tp. 2 R. 4, south and west.

**3015. HUBBARD, Elijah**
Sept. 5, 1829, 2 miles E by N Greensboro, Gadsden Co. E 1/2 SE 1/4 Sect. 2 Tp. 2 R. 5, north and west. Transferred to E. W. PITTMAN (no date).

**8032. HUBBARD, Elijah**
Aug. 15, 1839, (Illegible) Gadsden Co. NE 1/4 NE 1/4 and NW 1/4 NE 1/4 Sect. 22 Tp. 4 R. ?, north and west.

**7245. HUBBARD, William H.**
Jan. 16, 1838, 1 1/4 miles E Chattahoochee, Gadsden Co. NW 1/4 NW 1/4 Sect. 2 Tp. 3 R. 6, north and west.

**8719. HUBBARD, William H.**
Nov. 7, 1844, 1/4 mile SE Steaphead, Gadsden Co. NE 1/4 SW 1/4 Sect. 20 Tp. 2 R. 6, north and west.

**8153. HUDNALL, Willis**
Nov. 23, 1839, 4 miles NNW Chaires, Leon Co. SW 1/4 SW 1/4 Sect. 20 Tp. 3 R. 2, north and west.

**239. HUDSON, Asbury**
Dec. 30, 1826, 3 miles NE Graceville, Jackson Co. SW 1/4 Sect. 20 Tp. 7 R. 12, north and west.

**2741. HUGGINS, Daniel**
Feb. 17, 1829, 3 miles W Miccosukee, Leon Co. W 1/2 NE 1/4 Sect. 12 Tp. 2 R. 2, north and east.

**5201. HUGGINS, Daniel**
Oct. 12, 1835, 2 1/2 miles SE of Felkel, Leon Co. SE 1/4 SW 1/4 Sect. 12 Tp. 2 R. 2, north and east.

**4444. HUGH, Harmon**
Oct. 25, 1833, 3/4 mile N by W of Wadesboro, Leon Co. SE 1/4 SW 1/4 Sect. 36 Tp. 2 R. 2, north and west.

**4148. HULL, Henry R.**
Feb. 8, 1856, 1 1/2 miles SW of O'Brien, Suwannee Co. NW 1/4 SW 1/4 and SW 1/4 NW 1/4 Sect. 25, and SE 1/4 NE 1/4 Sect. 26 Tp. 5 R. 13, south and east.

**933. HULL, Joseph M.**
Aug. 22, 1851, 2 1/2 miles SW O'Brien, Suwannee Co. W 1/2 NW 1/4 Sect. 36 Tp. 5 R. 13, south and east. Patent delivered June 4, 1857.

**2280. HULL, Joseph M.**
Oct. 24, 1853, 4 miles SE of Padlock, Suwannee Co. W 1/2 NW 1/4 and NW 1/4 SW 1/4 and NW 1/4 NE 1/4 Sect. 28 Tp. 3 R. 14, south and east. Patent delivered July 22, 1853

**2499. HULL, Sarah**
Sept. 13, 1828, 5 miles S Chattahoochee, Gadsden Co. NE 1/4 Sect. 29 Tp. 3 R. 6, north and west.

**263. HULL, Thomas H.**
Jan. 1, 1827, 10 miles NW of Marianna, Jackson Co. NE 1/4 Sect. 3 Tp. 5 R. 11, north and west.

**5942. HULSE, Isaac**
Oct. 31, 1836, apparently in Perdido Bay, 3 miles S of the town of Lillian on the Alabama State line, Escambia Co. Fractional Sect. 6 Tp. 3 R. 32, south and west.

**5946. HULSE, Isaac**
Oct. 31, 1836, apparently in Baldwin Co., Alabama, 4 miles W by W of Parker, Escambia Co., Fla. Lot No. 2 Fractional Sect. 3 Tp. 2 R. 32, south and west.

**5947. HULSE, Isaac**
Oct. 31, 1836, 5 miles W by N of Gulf Beach, Escambia Co. Lot No. 3 Fractional Sect. 7 Tp. 3 R. 32, south and west.

**6030. HULSE, Isaac**
Nov. 15, 1836, c. 5 miles NW Lillian, Baldwin Co., Alabama. Lot No. 1 Fractional Sect. 3 Tp. 2 R. 32, south and west.

**520. HUMPHREYS, Benj.**
May 10, 1831, 3 miles W Fincher, Leon Co. E 1/2 NE 1/4 Sect. 17 Tp. 1 R. 3, north and east.

**5484. HUMPHRIES, Robert**
Feb. 22, 1836, 3 1/2 miles SSE of Centerville, Leon Co. E 1/2 SE 1/4 Sect. 27 Tp. 2 R. 2, north and east.

**5485. HUMPHRIES, Robert**
Feb. 22, 1836, 4 1/2 miles SSE of Centerville, Leon Co. NW 1/4 SW 1/4 Sect. 26 Tp. 2 R. 2, north and east.

**3245. HUNT, John**
Feb. 4, 1830, near Bagdad, Santa Rosa Co. Lot No. 3 Sect. 13 Tp. 1 R. 28, north and west.

**3428. HUNT, John**
Mar. 2, 1830, just N Milton, Santa Rosa Co. Lot No. 4 Sect. 11 Tp. 1 R. 28, north and west.

**3429. HUNT, John**
Mar. 2, 1830, N Milton, Santa Rosa Co. Lot No. 5 Sect. 11 Tp. 1 R. 28. north and west.

**3567. HUNT, John**
July 14, 1830, just S Bagdad, Santa Rosa Co. Lot No. 2 Sect. 14 Tp. 1 R. 28, north and west.

**4563. HUNT, John**
Mar. 25, 1834, 12 miles N of Milton, Santa Rosa Co. Lot No. 4 Sect. 2 Tp. 1 R. 28, north and west.

**3565. HUNT, John**
Aug. 3, 1830, near Banyan Siding, Santa Rosa Co. Lot No. 3 Fractional Sect. 2 Tp. 1 R. 28, north and west.

**4564. HUNT, John**
Mar. 25, 1834, 1 mile N by E of Milton, Santa Rosa Co. Lot No. 2 Sect. 24 Tp. 1 R. 28, north and west.

**4925. HUNT, John**
April 6, 1835, on this receipt the Range given was "30 Tp. 2 Sect. 44 (?)". Only 36 sections to a township - and even counting this way - it brings the 32.40 acres sold to him about 2 1/2 miles W of Pensacola in the middle of Pensacola Bay. There are no islands indicated.

**4926. HUNT, John**
April 7, 1835, R. 30 Tp. 2 Sect. 41, south and west.

**4927. HUNT, John**
April 7, 1835, Sect. 47 Tp. 2 R. 30, south and west.

**4928. HUNT, John**
April 7, 1835, Sect. 32 Tp. 2 R. 30, south and west. Note: According to sectional map (36 sections to the township) the above locations would be in the middle of Pensacola Bay, Escambia Co.- unless the system of marking off townships in 1835 in the above county differed radically from that of the present.

**4946. HUNT, John**
April 29, 1835, 1/2 mile SE of Delta, Escambia Co. Lot No. 1 Sect. 6 Tp. 2 R. 29, south and west.

**4947. HUNT, John**
April 29, 1835, Sect. 49 Tp. 2 R. 30, south and west.

**4948. HUNT, John**
April 29, 1835, Sect. 48 Tp. 2 R. 30, south and west.

**4949. HUNT, John**
April 29, 1835, Sect. 39 Tp. 2 R. 30, south and west.

**4950. HUNT, John**
April 29, 1835, Lot No. 2 Sect. 38 Tp. 2 R. 30, south and west.

**4951. HUNT, John**
April 29, 1835, Sect. 4 Tp. 2 R. 29, south and west. Note: According to the present system all the above locations seem to be in the middle of Pensacola Bay with no land indicated. (See note on #4925-4928.)

**5471. HUNT, John**
Feb. 18, 1836, 1 mile N of Milton, Santa Rosa Co. W 1/2 SE 1/4 Sect. 2 Tp. 1 R. 28, north and west.

**5472. HUNT, John**
Feb. 18, 1836, at Milton, Santa Rosa Co. W 1/2 NE 1/4 Sect. 11 Tp. 1 R. 28, north and west.

**5473. HUNT, John**
Feb. 18, 1836, at Milton, Santa Rosa Co. NW 1/4 Sect. 11 Tp. 1 R. 28, north and west.

**5474. HUNT, John**
Feb. 18, 1836, 2 1/4 miles S by W of Milton, Santa Rosa Co. NE 1/4 Sect. 23 Tp. 1 R. 28, north and west.

**5475. HUNT, John**
Fe. 18, 1836, 1/4 mile SW of Pinewood, Santa Rosa Co. SE 1/4 Sect. 23 Tp. 1 R. 28, north and west.

**5476. HUNT, John**
Feb. 18, 1836, 1/2 mile W of Pinewood, Santa Rosa Co. NW 1/4 Sect. 23 Tp. 1 R. 28, north and west.

**5477. HUNT, John**
Feb. 18, 1836, on St. Mary de Galves Bay, 4 miles SE of Pinewood, Santa Rosa Co. SE 1/4 Sect. 35 Tp. 1 R. 28, north and west.

**5478. HUNT, John**
Feb. 18, 1836, on St. Mary de Galves Bay, 4 miles SE Pinewood, Santa Rosa Co. NE 1/4 Sect. 35 Tp. 1 R. 28, north and west.

**5479. HUNT, John**
Feb. 18, 1836, 2 1/2 miles E by S of Milton, Santa Rosa Co. SE 1/4 Sect. 19 Tp. 1 R. 27, north and west.

**5547. HUNT, John**
Mar. 19, 1836, St. Mary de Galves Bay, Santa Rosa Co. Lot No. 2 Fractional Sect. 23 Tp. 1 R. 28, north and west.

**5547. HUNT, John**
(No date given) 4 1/2 miles N of Holley, Santa Rosa Co. W 1/2 SW 1/4 Sect. 24 Tp. 2 R. 28, north and west.

**5547. HUNT, John**
Mar. 19, 1836, in St Mary de Galves Bay, 3 miles NNE of Garcon Point, Santa Rosa Co. W 1/2 SW 1/4 Sect. 24 Tp. 2 R. 28, north and west.

**5551. HUNT, John**
Mar. 22, 1836, 1 1/2 miles E of Milton, Santa Rosa Co. W 1/2 NW 1/4 Sect. 18 Tp. 1 R. 27, north and west.

**5551. HUNT, John**
Mar. 22, 1836, 1 1/2 miles E by S of Milton, Santa Rosa Co. W 1/2 SW 1/4 Sect. 18 Tp. 1 R. 27, north and west.

**5676. HUNT, John**
May 21, 1836, 1/4 mile E of Bayou Siding, Santa Rosa Co. Lot No. 4 Fractional Sect. 35 Tp. 1 R. 28, north and west.

**5694. HUNT, John**
June 6, 1836, 1/2 mile NE of Milton, Santa Rosa Co. Lot No. 2 Fractional Sect. 2 Tp. 1 R. 28, north and west.

**5694. HUNT, John**
June 6, 1836, 1 3/4 miles SE of Pinewood, Santa Rosa Co. Lot No. 2 Fractional Sect. 25 Tp. 1 R. 28, north and west.

**5694. HUNT, John**
June 6, 1836, 2 miles SE of Robinson Point, Santa Rosa Co. E 1/2 NE 1/4 Sect. 26 Tp. 1 R. 28, north and west.

**5694. HUNT, John**
June 6, 1836, 2 3/4 miles SE of Robinson Point, Santa Rosa Co. Lot No. 2 Fractional Sect. 35 Tp. 1 R. 28, north and west.

**5695. HUNT, John**
June 6, 1836, 2 miles SSE of Robinson Point, Santa Rosa Co. Lot No. 1 Fractional Sect. 19 Tp. 1 R. 27, north and west.

**5759. HUNT, John**
July 8, 1836, 4 miles E by S of Pinewood, Santa Rosa Co. Lot No. 3 Fractional Sect. 24 Tp. 1 R. 28, north and west.

**5760. HUNT, John**
July 8, 1836, 2 1/2 miles E of Pinewood, Santa Rosa Co. Lot No. 3 Fractional Sect. 19 Tp. 1 R. 27, north and west.

**6039. HUNT, John**
Nov. 17, 1836, at Robinson Point, Santa Rosa Co. Lot No. 3 Fractional Sect. 25 Tp. 1 R. 28, north and west.

**6142. HUNT, John**
Dec. 5, 1836, c. 8 miles SSE Milton, Santa Rosa Co. Lots No. 1 and 2 Sect. 13 Tp. 1 R. 28, south and west. 160 acres.

**6143. HUNT, John**
Dec. 5, 1836, 2 1/2 miles SE Pine-

wood, Santa Rosa Co. Fractional Sect. 30 Tp. 1 R. 27, south and west.

**6144. HUNT, John**
Dec. 5, 1836, c. 2 miles SE Mulat, Santa Rosa Co. Lot No. 6 Fractional Sect. 1 Tp. 1 R. 28, south and west.

**7229. HUNT, John**
Jan. 15, 1838, 3 1/2 miles E Pinewood, Santa Rosa Co. Lot No. 1 Fractional Sect. 24 Tp. 1 R. 28, north and west.

**7230. HUNT, John**
Jan. 15, 1838, 1 mile E Millon, Santa Rosa Co. Lots No. 1 and 5 Fractional Sect. 10 Tp. 1 R. 28, north and west.

**7232. HUNT, John**
Jan. 15, 1838, 3 miles SE by E Robinson's Place, Santa Rosa Co. Fractional Sect. 31 Tp. 1 R. 27, north and west.

**7707. HUNT, John**
Nov. 15, 1838, 7 miles S by E Pinewood, Santa Rosa Co. Lot No. 5 Fractional Sect. 1 Tp. 1 R. 28, south and west.

**7952. HUNT, John**
May 11, 1839, 1/2 mile N Milton, Santa Rosa Co. Lot No. 6 Sect. 2 Tp. 1 R. 28, north and west.

**7953. HUNT, John**
May 11, 1839, 1 3/4 miles SW Coldwater, Santa Rosa Co. W 1/2 SW 1/4 Sect. 14 Tp. 2 R. 27, north and west.

**7954. HUNT, John**
May 11, 1839, 1 1/4 miles SW by S Coldwater, Santa Rosa Co. E 1/2 NE 1/4 E 1/2 NW 1/4 Sect. 15 Tp. 2 R. 27, north and west.

**7955. HUNT, John**
May 11, 1839, 1 1/2 miles SSW Coldwater, Santa Rosa Co. S 1/2 Sect. 15 Tp. 2 R. 27, north and west.

**7956. HUNT, John**
May 11, 1839, 1 mile SW by S Coldwater, Santa Rosa Co. NE 1/4 Sect. 21 Tp. 2 R. 27, north and west.

**7957. HUNT, John**
May 11, 1839, 1 mile SW Coldwater, Santa Rosa Co. W 1/2 NW 1/4 Sect. 22 Tp. 2 R, 27, north and west.

**8017. HUNT, John**
July 9, 1839, 4 miles E Pinewood, Santa Rosa Co. W 1/2 SW 1/4 Sect. 20 Tp. 1 R. 27, north and west.

**8018. HUNT, John**
July 9, 1829, 3 1/2 miles E by S Pinewood, Santa Rosa Co. Lot No. 2 Sect. (?) Tp. 1 R. 27, north and west.

**8019. HUNT, John**
July 9, 1839, 1 mile E Roeville, Santa Rosa Co. Lot No. 3 Sect. 23 Tp. 1 R. 28, north and west.

**8601. HUNT, John**
Sept. 5, 1843, 2 miles NNE Milton, Santa Rosa Co. NE 1/4 NE 1/4 Sect. 12 Tp. 1 R. 26, north and west.

**8725. HUNT, John**
Nov. 22, 1844, 4 miles S by W Batts, Santa Rosa Co. E 1/2 NWP E 1/2 SW 1/4 Sect. 3 Tp. 3 R. 28, north and west.

**4407. HUNT, John W.**
Sept. 6, 1833, 1 1/2 miles S by W Botts, Santa Rosa Co. W 1/2 NW 1/4 Sect. 3 Tp 3 R. 28, north and west.

**4408. HUNT, John W.**
Sept. 6, 1833, 2 miles SSW of Botts, Santa Rosa Co. E 1/2 SW 1/4 Sect. 4 Tp. 3 R. 28, north and west.

**4409. HUNT, John W.**
Sept. 6, 1833, 4 miles S by W of Botts, Santa Rosa Co. E 1/2 NW 1/4 Sect. 10 Tp. 3 R. 28, north and west.

**3238. HUNT, John Stanford**
Jan. 30, 1830, 2 miles W by S Wadesboro, Leon Co. E 1/2 SW 1/4 Sect. 2 Tp. 1 R. 2, north and east. (Copy from the official record by **M. J. ALLEN**, Rec. Jan. 30, 1838.)

**4499. HUNT, Thomas**
Jan. 16, 1857, 1/2 mile S of Houston, Suwannee Co. E 1/2 NE 1/4 Sect. 4 Tp. 3 R. 14, south and east. Patent delivered Aug. 19, 1869.

**4422. HUNT, William H.**
July 31, 1856, 2 1/2 miles NE McKinley, Columbia Co. SE 1/4 NE 1/4 and NE 1/4 SE 1/4 Sect. 8, SW 1/4 NW 1/4 and NW 1/4 SW 1/4 Sect. 9 Tp. 3 R. 16, south and east.

**3922. HUNTER, Adam**
March 24, 1831, c. 1 mile SW Midway, Gadsden Co. Lot No. 6 Sect. 7 Tp. 1 R. 2, north and west. Patent delivered March 30, 1869, **Chas. MUNDEE**, Reg.

**4458. HUNTER, Adam**
Nov. 13, 1833, 1/4 mile SW of Mid-

way, Gadsden Co. SE 1/4 SW 1/4 Sect. 8 Tp. 1 R. 2, north and west. Patent delivered March 30, 1869.

**4329. HUNTER, A. P.**
Mar. 19, 1833, 1 mile W of Cay, Jefferson Co. NW 1/4 NW 1/4 Sect. 32 Tp. 1 R. 3, south and east.

**5170. HUNTER, James**
Sept. 29, 1835, 1 mile S by W of Bradfordville, Leon Co. E 1/2 SW 1/4 Sect. 27 Tp. 2 R. 1, north and east.

**2483. HUNTER, J. M. G.**
Sept. 8, 1828, 3 miles WSW Lake Jackson Station, Leon Co. E 1/2 SE 1/4 Sect. 3 Tp. 1 R. 2, north and west.

**2484. HUNTER, J. M. G.**
Sept. 8, 1828, 1 mile NE Gadsden, Gadsden Co. E 1/2 NE 1/4 Sect. 10 Tp. 1 R. 2, north and west.

**4054. HUNTER, William A.**
Jan. 1, 1856, 5 miles E of Bass, Columbia Co. SW 1/4 NW 1/4 Sect. 34 Tp. 4 R. 17, south and east. Patent delivered Mar. 16, 1858.

**4055. HUNTER, William A.**
Jan. 1, 1850, 5 miles E of Bass, Columbia Co. W 1/2 NE 1/2 Sect. 34 Tp. 4 R. 17, south and east. Patent delivered Mar. 18, 1858.

**4056. HUNTER, William A.**
Jan. 1, 1856, 4 1/2 miles E of Bass, Columbia Co. SE 1/4 SW 1/4 Sect. 27 Tp. 4 R. 17 south and east Patent delivered Mar. 18, 1858

**4876. HUNTER, William A.**
Oct. 7, 1858, at Bass, Columbia Co. SW 1/4 NW 1/4 Sect. 36 Tp. 4 R. 16, south and east.

**5022. HUNTER, William A.**
May 11, 1859, 5 miles SE of Lake City, Columbia Co. SE 1/4 SE 1/4 Sect. 26 Tp. 4 R. 16, south and east.

**6584. HUNTER, William D.**
March 23, 1888, 2 1/2 miles SE Harlem, Putnam Co. S 1/2 SW 1/4 Sect. 26 Tp. 8S R. 25E.

**5398. HUNTER, William M.**
Jan. 13, 1836, 2 miles E of Jasper, Hamilton Co. W 1/2 NE 1/4 Sect. 4 Tp. 1 R. 14, north and east.

**7495. HUNTER, William M., Sr.**
June 20, 1838, touching NW corner Jasper, Hamilton Co. E 1/2 NW 1/4 Sect. 7 Tp. 1 R. 14, north and east.

**7665. HUNTER, William M., Jr.**
Oct. 5, 1838, 3 miles NNE Marion, Hamilton Co. SW 1/4 NW 1/4 Sect. 22 Tp. 1 R. 14, north and east.

**6841. HUNTER, Wm. M.**
March 6, 1837, 6 1/4 miles W by S Jasper, Hamilton Co. E 1/2 NW 1/4 Sect. 7 Tp. 1 R. 13, north and east.

**8254. HURD, Elizabeth**
Mar. 13, 1840, 4 3/4 miles NW Dills, Jefferson Co. E 1/2 NW 1/4 Sect. 27 Tp. 3 R. 5, north and east.

**7593. HURST, John**
Aug. 15, 1838, 4 miles NNW Calhoun, Madison Co. NE 1/4 SW 1/4 Sect. 5 Tp. 1 R. 9, north and east.

**HURST, Robert C. see Jesse W. HOGAN.**

**4166. HURST, Thomas**
Feb. 15, 1856, 1/2 miles SE of Houston, Suwannee Co. SE 1/4 NW 1/4 Sect. 3 Tp. 3 R. 14, south and east. Patent delivered Aug. 19, 1869.

**5796. HURST, William B.**
July 16, 1836, 2 miles NE Lamont, Jefferson Co. NW 1/4 NE 1/4 Sect. 13 Tp. 1 R. 5, south and east.

**2601. HURST, Wm. B.**
Jan. 6, 1829, 2 1/2 miles NE Alma, Jefferson Co. W 1/2 NW 1/4 Sect. 30 Tp. 3 R. 5, north and east.

**4990. HUTTO, Henry James**
June 12, 1835, 2 1/2 miles S of Miccosukee, Leon Co. W 1/2 NW 1/4 Sect. 30 Tp. 2 R. 3, north and east.

**7354. HUTTO, Isaac**
Feb. 27, 1838, 2 miles S Miccosukee, Leon Co. W 1/2 NW 1/4 Sect. 20 Tp. 2 R. 3, north and east.

**7355. HUTTO, Isaac**
Feb. 27, 1838, 3 1/2 miles N by E Wadesboro, Leon Co. NE 1/4 NE 1/4 Sect. 19 Tp. 2 R. 3, north and east.

**4871. HUSTERS, Wilson**
Feb. 18, 1835, 2 miles W of St. Marks Junction, Leon Co. NE 1/4 NE 1/4 Sect. 15 Tp. 1 R. 1, south and west.

**410. HUTSON, Aaron**
May 7, 1827, 3 miles WSW Campbellton, Jackson Co. E 1/2 SE 1/4 Sect. 3 Tp. 6 R. 12, north and west.

**4566. HYFRET, John**
Apr. 1, 1834, 2 1/2 miles S by E of Greenwood, Santa Rosa Co. SE 1/4 NW 1/4 Sect. 19 Tp. 5 R. 9, north and west.

\* I \*

**8263. INAMN (INMAN ?), Edward**
Mar. 26, 1840, 3 miles E by N Hinson, Gadsden Co. SW 1/4 NE 1/4 Sect. 26 Tp. 3 R. 2, north and west.

**6027. INNARARITY, Henry**
Nov. 15, 1836, c. 6 miles SW Pensacola, Escambia Co. Lot No. 1 Fractional Sect. 37 Tp. 2 R. 30, south and west.

**6028. INNARARITY, Henry**
Nov. 15, 1836, 1 1/2 miles N Indian Ford, Santa Rosa Co. W 1/2 SE 1/4 NE 1/4 NE 1/4 SE 1/4 Sect. 24 Tp. 3 R. 27, north and west.

**6029. INNARARITY, John**
Nov. 15, 1836, in Alabama, Baldwin Co. c. 3 miles N Lillian, Lot No. 1 Fractional Sect. 4 Tp. 2 R. 32, south and west.

**4254. IRVINE, John A.**
( Of Ga.) Mar. 19, 1856, 3 miles NNE Peterson, Suwannee Co. Lot No. 4 W 1/2 NW 1/4 Sect. 23 and N 1/2 of Lot No. 1 NE 1/4 NE 1/4 Sect. 22 Tp. 4 R. 11, south and east.

**4413. IRVINE, John A.**
July 25, 1856, 2 miles SW of Luraville, Columbia Co. S 1/2 NE 1/4 and NE 1/4 SE 1/4 Sect. 22 and NW 1/4 SW 1/4 Sect. 23 Tp. 4 R. 11, south and east.

**4692. IRVINE, John A.**
Dec. 2, 1857, 2 1/2 miles SSW of Luraville, Suwannee Co. SW 1/4 NE 1/4 and SW 1/4 SW 1/4 Sect. 23 Tp. 4 R. 11, south and east. Patent delivered Feb. 14, 1872.

**4192. IRVINE, John R.**
Aug. 6, 1832, 3 1/2 miles E of Capps, Jefferson Co. NW 1/4 SE 1/4 Sect. 3 Tp. 1 R. 5, south and east.

**4193. IRVINE, John R.**
Aug. 6, 1832, 4 miles SE of Capps, Jefferson Co. SW 1/4 NE 1/4 Sect. 10 Tp. 1 R. 5, south and east.

**4194. IRVINE, John R.**
Aug. 6, 1832, 4 1/2 miles SE of Capps, Jefferson Co. E 1/2 NE 1/4 Sect. 10 Tp. 1 R. 5, south and east.

**4255. IRVINE, Washington L.**
Mar. 19, 1856, 3 miles SW Luraville, Suwannee Co. N 1/2 NE 1/4 Sect. 23 Tp. 4 R. 11, south and east.

**357. IRWIN, Joseph**
April 23, 1827, 10 miles ENE of Malone, Jackson Co. E 1/2 SE 1/4 Sect. 17 Tp. 7 R. 8, north and west.

**358. IRWIN, Joseph (Jr.)**
( Assignee of **Joseph IRWIN, Sr.**) April 23, 1827, 11 miles ENE of Malone, Jackson Co. NE 1/4 SE 1/4 Sect. 22 Tp. 7 R. 8, north and west. Transferred from **Joseph IRWIN, Jr.** to **F. CARTER** on April 23, 1827.

**5177. IRWIN, Joseph**
Oct. 2, 1835, 9 miles NNE of Bascom, Jackson Co. NW 1/4 NE 1/4 Sect. 21 Tp. 7 R. 8, north and west.

**6173. IRWIN, Joseeph**
Dec. 9, 1836, 8 miles ENE Malone, Jackson Co. E 1/2 NW 1/4 Sect. 22 Tp. 7 R. 3, north and west.

**8310. IRWIN, Joseph**
April 29, 1840, 10 miles E Malone, Jackson Co. SE 1/4 SW 1/4 Sect. 15 Tp. 7 R. 8, north and west.

**8692. IRWIN, Joseph**
Sept. 19, 1844, 10 miles NNE Bascom, Jackson Co. E 1/2 NE 1/4 Sect. 20 Tp. 7 R. 8, north and west.

**8693. IRWIN, Freeman B.**
Sept. 19, 1844, 6 miles NNE Malone, Jackson Co. SW 1/4 SW 1/4 Sect. 24 Tp. 7 R. 9, north and west.

**2611. IVES, Washington M.**
Mar. 14, 1854, at Providence, Union Co. SW 1/4 NW 1/4 Sect. 5 Tp. 6 R. 18, south and east.

## * J *

**4114. JACKSON, Benjamin F.**
Jan. 18, 1856, 1 3/4 miles SSW of Cooper, Columbia Co. E 1/2 SW 1/4 Sect. 31 Tp. 4 R. 16, south and east. ( Endorsed by **A. B. HAGAN.**)

**36. JACKSON, Geo.**
Nov. 6, 1826, c. 2 miles NE Cottondale, Jackson Co. NW 1/4 Sect. 22 Tp. 5 R. 11, north and west.

**487. JACKSON, John**
Dec. 1, 1846, 1/2 mile W Oneco, Manatee Co. N 1/2 NE 1/4 Sect. 13 Tp. 34 R. 17, south and east.

**38. JACKSON, John B.**
Nov. 6, 1826, c. 3 miles NE Cottondale, Jackson Co. E 1/2 NE 1/4 Sect. 21 Tp. 5 R. 11, north and west.

**146. JACKSON, Wm. A.**
Dec. 27, 1826, 2 miles N of Cottondale, Jackson Co. SW 1/4 Sect. 15 Tp. 5 R. 11, noorth and west.

**4338. JACOBSON, ?**
April 2, 1833, 2 1/2 miles N of Wadesboro, Leon Co. SW 1/4 SW 1/4 Sect. 25 Tp. 2 R. 2, north and east.

**4064. JAMESON, Nathaniel A.**
Jan. 4, 1856, 2 miles E of Lake City, Columbia Co. S 1/2 SE 1/4 and SE 1/4 SW 1/4 Sect. 21 and NW 1/4 NE 1/4 Sect. 28 Tp. 6 R. 16, south and east. Patent delivered July 24, 1857.

**153. JAMESON, Robert**
( Of Ala.) May 19, 1825, 2 miles E Maxwell Spur, Leon Co. E 1/2 NE 1/4 Sect. 14 Tp. 1 R. 1, south and east.

**154. JAMESON, Robert**
( Of Ala.) May, 19, 1825, 1 mile E Tallahassee, Leon Co. E 1/2 NW 1/4 Sect. 5 Tp. 1 R. 1, south and east.

**155. JAMESON, Robert**
( Of Ala.) May 19, 1825, 1 mile S Perkins, Leon Co. W 1/2 NE 1/4 Sect. 5 Tp. 1 R. 1, south and east.

**157. JAMESON, Robert**
(SIC) ( Of Ala.) May 19, 1825, 2 miles SE Tallahassee, Leon Co. E 1/2 SW 1/4 Sect. 11 Tp. 1 R. 1, south and east.

**158. JAMESON, Robert**
( Of Ala.) May 19, 1825, 2 miles SE Tallahassee, Leon Co. W 1/2 SE 1/4 Sect. 11 Tp. 1 R. 1, south and east.

**163. JAMESON, Robert**
( Of Ala.) May 19, 1825, 1 mile SE Tallahassee, Leon Co. E 1/2 NW 1/4 Sect. 11 Tp. 1 R. 1, south and east.

**164. JAMESON, Robert**
( Of Ala.) May 19, 1825, 1 mile S Perkins Station, Leon Co. W 1/2 SE 1/4 Sect. 5 Tp. 1 R. 1, south and east.

**165. JAMESON, Robert**
( Of Ala.) May 19, 1825, 1 mile S Perkins Station, Leon Co. E 1/2 SW 1/4 Sect. 5 Tp. 1 R. 1, south and east.

**166. JAMESON, Robert**
( Of Ala.) May 19, 1825, 1 mile S Perkins Station, Leon Co. W 1/2 SW 1/4 Sect. 5 Tp. 1 R. 1, south and east.

**167. JAMESON, Robert**
(SIC) ( Of Ala.) May 19, 1826, 2 miles SE Tallahassee, Leon Co. E 1/2 SE 1/4 Sect. 5 Tp. 1 R. 1, south and east.

**1624. JAMESON, Robert (Jr.)**
(DUP) No. date. 2 1/2 miles NW Cottondale, Jackson Co. E 1/2 SE 1/4 Sect. 24 Tp. 3 R. 12, north and west. Transferred to **Chas. WILLIAMSON** on June 4, 1827.

**1625. JAMESON, Robert (Jr.)**
(DUP) May 26, 1827, 3 miles NW Cottondale, Jackson Co. W 1/2 SE 1/4 Sect. 24 Tp. 3 R. 12, north and west. Transferred to **Chas. WILLIAMSON** on June 4, 1827.

**3134. JAMISON, Humphrey**
Nov. 24, 1829, 4 miles N by E Bradfordville, Leon Co. E 1/2 NW 1/4 Sect. 2 Tp. 2 R. 1, north and east.

**1455. JAMISON, Robert**
May 22, 1827, 4 miles SW Quincy, Gadsden Co. W 1/2 SW 1/4 Sect. 15 TP. 2 R. 4, north and west. Transferred June 6, 1827, to **Robert W. WILLIAMS, (G. W. WARD,** Register).

**1456. JAMISON, Robert**
May 22, 1827, near Sawdust, Gadsden Co. Lot No. 4 Sect. 21 Tp. 2 R. 4, north and west. Transferred to **Robert W. WILLIAMS** on June 6, 1827. (**G. W. WARD**, Register)

**1698. JAMISON, Robert (Jr.)**
May 30, 1827, 3 1/2 miles W Greenwood, Jackson Co. W 1/2 NE 1/4

Sect. 34 Tp. 6 R. 10, north and west. Transferred June 4, 1827, to **Benj. CLEMENTS.**

**1699. JAMISON, Robert (Jr.)**
(DUP) May 30, 1827, 4 miles ESE Jacob, Jackson Co. W 1/2 SE 1/4 Sect. 21 Tp. 6 R. 11, north and west.

**1700. JAMISON, Robert (Jr.)**
(DUP) May 30, 1827, 4 1/2 miles SE Jacob, Jackson Co. E 1/2 SE 1/4 Sect. 21 Tp. 6 R. 11, north and west. Transferred to **Chas. WILLIAMSON** on June 4, 1827.

**1701. JAMISON, Robert (Jr.)**
(DUP) May 30, 1827, 5 miles ENE Welchton, Jackson Co. W 1/2 SW 1/4 Sect. 22 Tp. 6 R. 11, north and west. Transferred to **Charles WILLIAMSON** on June 4, 1827. (**G. W. WARD**, Register).

**1702. JAMISON, Robert (Jr.)**
May 30, 1827, 4 miles ENE Welchton, Jackson Co. E 1/2 NE 1/4 Sect. 28 Tp. 6 R. 11, north and west. Transferred to **Charles WILLIAMSON** on June 4, 1827.

**1703. JAMISON, Robert (Jr.)**
May 30, 1827, 3 miles E Welchton, Jackson Co. W 1/2 SE 1/4 Sect. 28 Tp. 6 R. 11, north and west. Transferred to **Charles WILLIAMSON** on June 4, 1827.

**1704. JAMISON, Robert (Jr.)**
May 30, 1827, 4 miles ENE Welchton, Jackson Co. E 1/2 SW 1/4 Sect. 21 Tp. 6 R. 11, north and west. Transferred to **Charles WILLIAMSON** on June 4, 1827.

**424. JAMISON, Robert**
( Of Ala.) May 31, 1825, 8 miles N Tallahassee, Leon Co. W 1/2 SW 1/4 Sect. 25 Tp. 2 R. 1, north and west.

**1210. JARMAN, Berry**
(DUP) Mar. 14, 1827, 1 mile W Meridian, Leon Co. E 1/2 NE 1/4 Sect. 24 Tp. 3 R. 1, north and west. Relinquished to **Chestney BOATRIGHT.**

**7411. JEFFERS, Henry L.**
Mar. 16, 1838, at Madison, Madison Co. W 1/2 SW 1/4 Sect. 27 Tp. 1 R. 9, north and east.

**7577. JEFFERS, Henry L.**
Aug. 8, 1838, at Madison, Madison Co. E 1/2 SW 1/4 Sect. 27 Tp. 2 R. 9, north and east.

**2723. JEFFORDS, John M.**
May 2, 1854, 2 1/2 miles SSW of Santos, Marion Co. NW 1/4 NW 1/4 Sect. 21 Tp. 16 R. 22, south and east.

**2978. JEFFORDS, John W.**
Oct. 14, 1854, 5 1/2 miles NNW Belleview, Marion Co. NE 1/4 NE 1/4 Sect. 20 Tp. 16 R. 22, south and east.

**6211. JENKINS, Moses**
Dec. 15, 1836, 5 miles ENE Campbellton, Jackson Co. E 1/2 SW 1/4 Sect. 21 Tp. 7 R. 11, north and west.

**6410. JENKINS, Rachel**
Jan. 3, 1837, 4 miles NE Champaign, Madison Co. NW 1/4 Sect. 24 Tp. 1 R. 1, south and east.

**6411. JENKINS, Rachel**
Jan. 3, 1837, 3 miles NW Champaign, Madison Co. NE 1/4 NE 1/4 Sect. 7 Tp. 1 R. 9, north and east.

**6412. JENKINS, Rachel**
Jan. 3, 1837, 3 miles NNE Champaign, Madison Co. NW 1/4 NW 1/4 Sect. 8 Tp. 1 R. 9, north and east.

**8342. JENNINGS, George**
June 16, 1840, 1 mile W by S Avoca, Hamilton Co. E 1/2 NW 1/4 W 1/2 NE 1/4 Sect. 28 Tp. 2 R. 12, north and east.

**8104. JENNINGS, Lawrence D.**
Oct. 1, 1839, 2 1/4 miles N Westlake, Hamilton Co. W 1/2 SW 1/4 NW 1/4 NW 1/4 Sect. 28 Tp. 2 R. 12, north and east.

**7710. JENNINGS, William F.**
Nov. 19, 1838, 2 1/2 miles N by E Westlake, Hamilton Co. W 1/2 NE 1/4 Sect. 27 Tp. 2 R. 12, north and east.

**6803. JENNINGS, Wm. T.**
Mar. 1, 1837, 4 1/2 miles SSW Jennings, Hamilton Co. NW 1/4 NW 1/4 Sect. 27 Tp. 2 R. 12, north and east.

**6804. JENNINGS, Wm. T.**
Mar. 1, 1837, 2 1/2 miles N by W Westlake, Hamilton Co. NE 1/4 SW 1/4 Sect. 28 Tp. 2 R. 12, north and east.

**4280. JERNIGAN, A.**
Jan. 22, 1833, 4 1/2 miles E by S of El

Destino, Jefferson Co. E 1/2 SW 1/4 Sect. 13 Tp. 1 R. 3, south and east.

**4626. JERNIGAN, Alexander**
Oct. 18, 18344, 5 miles SSE El Destino, Jefferson Co. SW 1/4 SW 1/4 Sect. 13 Tp. 1 R. 3, south and east.

**4627. JERNIGAN, Alexander**
Oct. 18, 1834, 5 1/4 miles SSE of El Destino, Jefferson Co. SW 1/4 SE 1/4 Sect. 13 Tp. 1 R. 3, south and east.

**7179. JERNIGAN, Alexander**
Jan. 1, 1838, 5 miles SSE El Destino, Jefferson Co. NW 1/4 SE 1/4 Sect. 13 Tp. 1 R. 3, south and east.

**7647. JERNIGAN, Alexander**
Sept. 19, 1838, 3 1/2 miles W Gadsden, Gadsden Co. NW 1/4 SW 1/4 Sect. 13 Tp. 1 R. 3, south and east.

**6617. JERNIGAN, Benjamin**
Jan. 20, 1837, c. 4 miles S Milton, Santa Rosa Co. Lot No. 6 Fractional Sect. 3 Tp. 1 R. 28, north and west. Transferred to **Sam'l C. RYAN** (no date), in presence of **Isaac R. RILEY**.

**5658. JERNIGAN, Blake**
May 7, 1836, at Pensacola, Escambia Co. SE 1/4 NW 1/4 Sect. 36 Tp. 2 R. 30, north and west.

**6005. JERNIGAN, Blake**
Nov. 14, 1836, 3 1/2 miles E Quinette, Santa Rosa Co. W 1/2 SW 1/4 Sect. 22 Tp. 2 R. 30, north and west.

**8894. JERNIGAN, Blake**
Jan. 29, 1846, 1 mile NNW Pinewood, Santa Rosa Co. NE 1/4 NW 1/4 Sect. 22 Tp. 1 R. 28, north and west.

**5680. JERNY, John S.**
May 24, 1836, 1/4 mile E of Facil, Hamilton Co. E 1/2 NW 1/4 Sect. 27 Tp. 1 R. 15, south and east.

**6718. JERRY, John L.**
Feb. 1, 1837, 1/2 mile NW Facil, Hamilton Co. W 1/2 NW 1/4 Sect. 27 Tp. 1 R. 15, south and east.

**7452. JERRY, John L.**
April 14, 1838, 1 1/4 miles S Genoa, Hamilton Co. NE 1/4 NW 1/4 Sect. 20 Tp. 1 R. 15, south and east.

**7453. JERRY, John L.**
April 14, 1838, 3/4 mile S by W Genoa, Hamilton Co. SE 1/4 SW 1/4 Sect. 17 Tp. 1 R. 15, south and east.

**8127. JERRY, John L.**
Nov. 1, 1839, at Facil, Hamilton Co. E 1/2 NE 1/4 Sect. 28 Tp. 1 R. 15, south and east.

**8168. JERRY, John L.**
Dec. 6, 1839, 2 3/4 miles N by W Lake Mesial (town), Bay Co. E 1/2 SW 1/4 Sect. 22 Tp. 1 R. 15, south and east.

**8562. JERRY, John L.**
Dec. 23, 1842, 4 miles N by E Genoa, Madison Co. E 1/2 SE 1/4 Sect. 28 Tp. 1 R. 15, south and east.

**8683. JERRY, John L.**
Aug. 10, 1844, 1 1/4 miles N by W Noles, Washington Co. W 1/2 NE 1/4 Sect. 28 Tp. 1 R. 15, south and east.

**3068. JOHN, Thomas**
Sept. 28, 1829, 2 miles E by S Centerville, Leon Co. E 1/2 NE 1/4 Sect. 19 Tp. 2 R. 2, north and east.

**5055. JOHN, Thomas**
Dec. 24, 1832, 2 1/2 miles SSE of Centerville, Leon Co. NW 1/4 SW 1/4 Sect. 28 Tp. 2 R. 2, north and east.

**5348. JOHN, Thomas**
Dec. 12, 1835, 3/4 mile E of Centerville, Leon Co. SW 1/4 NE 1/4 Sect. 20 Tp. 2 R. 2, north and east.

**5349. JOHN, Thomas**
Dec. 12, 1835, 3/4 mile E of Centerville, Leon Co. SE 1/4 NE 1/4 Sect. 20 Tp. 2 R. 2, north and east.

**252. JOHNS, Archibald Hardy**
Jan. 5, 1846, c. 4 miles NW Starke, Bradford Co. SE 1/4 SE 1/4 Sect. 23 Tp. 6 R. 21, south and east.

**1607. JOHNS, Archibald H.**
Jan. 4, 1853, 3 1/4 miles E of New River, Bradford Co. SW 1/4 NW 1/4 and NW 1/4 SW 1/4 Sect. 23 Tp. 6 R. 21, south and east. Patent delivered Nov. 13, 1856.

**921. JOHNS, Bussill**
Aug. 8, 1851, 2 miles N New River, Bradford Co. SW 1/4 SE 1/4 Sect. 35 Tp. 5 R. 20, south and east.

**2091. JOHNS, Cometius**
Aug. 22, 1853, 2 miles NW of Cyril, Alachua Co. NW 1/4 NE 1/4 Sect. 3 Tp. 8 R. 20, south and east.

**45061/2. JOHNS, Henry M.**
Illegible.

**2033. JOHNS, Henry M.**
Aug. 10, 1853, 4 miles W of Bay Lake (town), Marion Co. Lot No. 3 Sect. 7 Tp. 12 R. 23, south and east.

**2057. JOHNS, Isaac**
Aug. 15, 1853, 3/4 mile S of Atlas, Bradford Co. E 1/2 NW 1/4 and W 1/2 NE 1/4 Sect. 34 Tp. 7 R. 20, south and east.

**6871. JOHNS, Jeremiah**
Mar. 9, 1837, 2 miles SW Genoa, Hamilton Co. SE 1/4 SE 1/4 Sect. 13 Tp. 1 R. 14, south and east.

**6872. JOHNS, Jeremiah**
Mar. 9, 1837, 1 mile SW Genoa, Hamilton Co. NW 1/4 SW 1/4 Sect. 18 Tp. 1 R. 15, south and east.

**2065. JOHNS, Riley**
Aug. 16, 1853, 1 1/4 miles N of Taylor, Baker Co. SE 1/4 NW 1/4 and SW 1/4 NE 1/4 Sect. 27 Tp. 1 R. 20, north and east. Patent delivered Aug. 10, 1857.

**1007. JOHNS, Tarlton**
Nov. 18, 1851, 5 1/2 miles SE by S of Taylor, Baker Co. SE 1/4 NE 1/4 Sect. 28 and SW 1/4 SW 1/4 Sect. 35 Tp. 1 R. 20, north and east. Patent delivered Aug. 10, 1867.

**1011. JOHNS, Tarlton**
Nov. 18, 1851, 4 miles S of Taylor, Baker Co. SW 1/4 NW 1/4 Sect. 27 Tp. 1 R. 20, north and east. Patent delivered Aug. 10, 1867. Transferred to **Wiley JOHNS** Oct. 10, 1853.

**1012. JOHNS, Tarlton**
Nov. 18, 1851, at Taylor, Baker Co. NW 1/4 NW 1/4 Sect. 2 Tp. 1 R. 20, south and east. Patent delivered Aug. 10, 1867.

**1028. JOHNS, Tarlton**
Dec. 4, 1851, 4 miles S of Taylor, Baker Co. SE 1/4 SE 1/4 Sect. 34 Tp. 1 R. 20, north and east. Patent delivered Aug. 11, 1867.

**1098. JOHNS, Tarlton**
Jan. 15, 1852, 4 miles SW of Taylor, Baker Co. W 1/2 NE 1/4 Sect. 28 Tp. 1 R. 20, north and east. Transferred by **Tarlton JOHNS** Oct. 10, 1853. Patent delivered Sept. 10, ?

**2034. JOHNS, Tarlton**
Aug. 10, 1853, 1 1/4 miles N of Taylor, Baker Co. E 1/2 SE 1/4 Sect. 27 Tp. 1 R. 20, north and east. Patent delivered Aug. 10, 1857.

**2035. JOHNS, Tarlton**
Aug. 10, 1853, 1 1/2 miles N by W of Taylor, Baker Co. SE 1/4 SE 1/4 and W 1/2 SE 1/4 Sect. 28 Tp. 1 R. 20, north and east. Patent delivered Aug. 10, 1857.

**2036. JOHNS, Tarlton**
Aug. 10, 1853, 1 3/4 miles NNW of Taylor, Baker Co. W 1/2 SW 1/4 Sect. 28 and NE 1/4 SE 1/4 Sect. 29 Tp. 1 R. 20, north and east. Patent delivered Aug. 11, 1857.

**2037. JOHNS, Tarlton**
Aug. 10, 1853, 1 1/2 miles N by W of Taylor, Baker Co. SE 1/4 SW 1/4 Sect. 28 Tp. 1 R. 20, north and east. Patent delivered Aug. 11, 1857.

**2064. JOHNS, Tarlton**
Aug. 16, 1853, 1 1/2 miles N by W of Taylor, Baker Co. NE 1/4 SW 1/4 Sect. 28 Tp. 1 R. 20, north and east.

**2248. JOHNS, Tarlton**
Oct. 11, 1853, 2 miles N by W of Taylor, Baker Co. SW 1/4 NW 1/4 Sect. 28 Tp. 1 R. 20, north and east. Patent delivered Aug. 19, 1857.

**6975. JOHNS, Thomas**
Apr. 5, 1837, 2 miles E by N Centerville, Leon Co. NW 1/4 NE 1/4 Sect. 20 Tp. 2 R. 2, north and east.

**JOHNS, Wiley see Tarleton JOHNS, #1011**

**2276. JOHNSON, Adna**
Oct. 22, 1853, at McMeekin, Putnam Co. SW 1/4, SW 1/4 SE 1/4 Sect. 32 Tp. 10 R. 23, south and east. Patent dellivered Oct. 8, 1857.

**JOHNSON, Andrew M. see Edwin HART**

**2160. JOHNSON, Andrew N.**
Dec. 24, 1827, 2 miles SW Havana, Gadsden Co. W 1/2 SW 1/4 Sect. 4 Tp. 2 R. 2, north and west.

**8093. JOHNSON, Daniel**
Sept. 23, 1839, 1/4 mile SW Lake Jackson (town), Leon Co. NW 1/4 SW 1/4 Sect. 12 Tp. 1 R. 2, north and west.

**1041. JOHNSON, David**
Jan. 31, 1827, 4 miles SW El Destino, Leon Co. W 1/2 SE 1/4 Sect. 22 Tp. 1 R. 2, south and east.

**3493. JOHNSON, David**
April 22, 1830, 2 1/2 miles W Cody, Leon Co. W 1/2 NE 1/4 Sect. 27 Tp. 1 R. 2, south and east.

**3362. JOHNSON, Elijah**

Feb. 15, 1830, c. 2 miles N Lake Jackson, Leon Co. Lot No. 7 Fractional Sect. 19 Tp. 2 R. 1, north and west.

**4405. JOHNSON, Elijah**
Sept. 3, 1835, 1 1/4 miles N of Lake Jackson (town), Leon Co. NE 1/4 NE 1/4 Sect. 30 Tp. 2 R. 1, north and west.

**4434. JOHNSON, Elijah**
Oct. 14, 1833, 3 1/4 miles N of Lake Jackson (town), Leon Co. Lot No. 8 Sect. 19 Tp. 2 R. 2, north and west.

**8860. JOHNSON, Ezekiel C.**
Dec. 22, 1845, 3 miles W Greensboro, Gadsden Co. NW 1/4 NE 1/4 Sect. 11 Tp. 2 R. 6, north and west.

**254. JOHNSON, Green**
Mar. 25, 1846, 1 1/2 miles SW Houston, Suwannee Co. NW 1/4 NE 1/4 Sect. 5 Tp. 3 R. 14, south and east. Patent delivered Dec. 29, 1856.

**1128. JOHNSON, Green**
Jan. 27, 1852, 1/4 mile S of Houston, Suwannee Co. NE 1/4 NE 1/4 Sect. 5 Tp. 3 R. 14, south and east. Patent delivered Dec. 29, 1856.

**4020. JOHNSON, Green**
Dec. 19, 1855, 3 1/2 miles S of Houston, Fla.,Suwannee Co. N 1/2 NW 1/4 Sect. 5 and NE 1/4 NE 1/4 Sect. 6 Tp. 3 R. 14, south and west. (Duplicate copy)

**JOHNSON, Hezekiah** see **Appleton ROSSETTER**

**7036. JOHNSON, Hulda**
Aug. 23, 1837, 2 3/4 miles SE Dills, Jefferson Co. W 1/2 NW 1/4 Sect. 11 Tp. 2 R. 6, north and east.

**2804. JOHNSON, Isaiah**
April 14, 1829, 1 mile W Ocklocknee, Leon Co. W 1/2 NE 1/4 Sect. 26 Tp. 1 R. 2, north and west.

**7159. JOHNSON, Isaiah**
Dec. 19, 1837, 1/2 mile NNW Lake Jackson, Leon Co. SE 1/4 SW 1/4 Sect. 31 Tp. 2 R. 1, north and west.

**7711. JOHNSON, Isaiah**
Nov. 199, 1838, 1 mile W San Helena, Leon Co. W 1/2 NW 1/4 Sect. 24 Tp. 1 R. 2, north and west.

**8075. JOHNSON, Isaiah**
Sept. 18, 1839, 1 mile N Lawrence Switch, Leon Co. SE 1/4 NW 1/4 Sect. 24 Tp. 1 R. 2, north and west.

**8760. JOHNSON, Isaish (Jr.)**
Mar. 24, 1845, 2 miles NNW San Helena, Leon Co. SE 1/4 NW 1/4 Sect. 13 Tp. 1 R. 2, north and west.

**138. JOHNSON, Isham**
Dec. 26, 1826, 5 miles S of Havana, Gadsden Co. SW 1/4 Sect. 17 Tp. 2 R. 2, north and west.

**JOHNSON, Isham** see **Rebecca OAKES**

**2198. JOHNSON, Jeremiah**
( Of Fla.) Dec. 31, 1827, 3 miles WNW Waukenah, Jefferson Co. E 1/2 NW 1/4 Sect. 32 Tp. 1 R. 4, north and east.

**2527. JOHNSON, Jerry**
Oct. 20, 1828, 3 miles NW Waukenah, Jefferson Co. E 1/2 SW 1/4 Sect. 29 Tp. 1 R. 4, north and east.

**1755. JOHNSON, Jno. A.**
(DUP) June 4, 1827, 2 miles W Wadesboro, Leon Co. E 1/2 NW 1/4 Sect. 2 Tp. 1 R. 2, north and east.

**2223. JOHNSON, John A.**
Jan. 14, 1828, 2 miles W Wadesboro, Leon Co. W 1/2 NW 1/4 Sect. 25 Tp. 2 R. 2, north and east.

**1359. JOHNSON, John A.**
May 14, 1827, 2 miles W Wadesboro, Leon Co. W 1/2 SE 1/4 Sect. 2 Tp. 1 R. 2, north and east.

**4452. JOHNSON, John**
Nov. 7, 1833, 1/2 mile N of Cody, Jefferson Co. SE 1/4 SW 1/4 Sect. 19 Tp. 1 R. 3, south and east.

**4453. JOHNSON, John**
Nov. 7, 1833, 1/2 mile N by E of Cody, Jefferson Co. SE 1/4 SE 1/4 Sect. 19 Tp. 1 R. 3, south and east.

**6341. JOHNSON, John**
Dec. 28, 1836, 5 miles NNE Ancilla, Jefferson Co. W 1/2 SW 1/4 Sect. 23 Tp. 2 R. 6, north and east.

**396. JOHNSON, King**
May 5, 1827, 5 miles E Graceville, Jackson Co. NE 1/4 Sect. 4 Tp. 6 R. 12, north and west.

**8549. JOHNSON, Nancy**
Aug. 16, 1842, at Lake Jackson, Leon Co. SW 1/4 SW 1/4 Sect. 7 Tp. 1 R. 1, north and west.

**8550. JOHNSON, Nancy**
Aug. 16, 1842, 1 mile SW Lake Jackson (town), Leon Co. W 1/2 NW 1/4 Sect. 7 Tp. 1 R. 1, north and west.

**8551. JOHNSON, Nancy**
Aug. 16, 1842, 1 mile SW Lake Jackson (town), Leon Co. E 1/2 NE 1/4 Sect. 12 Tp. 1 R. 2, north and west.

**58. JOHNSON, Rachel**
April 29, 1844, 1 mile S Starr, Suwannee Co. NW 1/4 NE 1/4 Sect. 5 Tp. 3 R. 13, south and east.

**57. JOHNSON, Randal**
Nov. 10, 1826, near Florence, Gadsden Co. SW 1/4 Sect. 7 Tp. 2 R. 3, north and west.

**4508. JOHNSON, Randol**
Jan. 13, 1834, 2 1/4 miles E by S of Greensboro, Gadsden Co. NW 1/4 SE 1/4 Sect. 12 Tp. 2 R. 6, north and west.

**8371. JOHNSON, Robert D.**
April 16, 1852, 1/2 mile E by N Dills, Jefferson Co. SE 1/4 Sect. 31 Tp. 3 R. 6, north and east. This is a provisional receipt issued by **H. B. R. ANDREWS** in the county of Leon, to above named claimant, replacing original receipt which owner on oath declared to have been lost or mislaid by Land Office as it had never been in his possession.

**2971. JOHNSON, Samuel B.**
Oct. 13, 1854, 3 miles SSW of Atlas, Alachua Co. S 1/2 Lot No. 10 Sect. 31 Tp. 7 R. 20, south and east.

**8848. JOHNSON, Samuel R.**
Dec. 2, 1845, 2 1/4 miles NW Marion, Hamilton Co. NE 1/4 SW 1/4 Sect. 25 Tp. 1 R. 13, north and east.

**8849. JOHNSON, Samuel R.**
Dec. 2, 1845, 2 1/2 miles N by W Marion, Hamilton Co. SW 1/4 NE 1/4 Sect. 25 Tp. 1 R. 13, north and east.

**1125. JOHNSON, Samuel R.**
Jan. 24, 1852, at Alachua, Alachua Co. S 1/2 Lot 1 SE 1/4 Sect. 23 Tp. 8 R. 18, south and east. Patent delivered May 8, 1857.

**4348. JOHNSON, Samuel R.**
April 28, 1856, 1 mile S of Alachua, Alachua Co. SE 1/4 SW 1/4 Sect. 14 and E 1/2 NE 1/4 Sect. 23 Tp. 8 R. 18, South and east.

**6227. JOHNSON, William**
Dec. 16, 1836, 1/4 mile W Midway, Gadsden Co. E 1/2 SW 1/4 Sect. 32 Tp. 2 R. 2, north and west. "Patent delivered April 2, 1870."

**7037. JOHNSON, William**
Aug. 26, 1837, 2 1/2 miles S Concord, Gadsden Co. SW 1/4 NE 1/4 Sect. 31 Tp. 3 R. 1, north and west.

**7038. JOHNSON, William**
Aug. 28, 1837, 2 1/2 miles S by E Concord, Gadsden Co. SE 1/4 NE 1/4 Sect. 31 Tp. 3 R. 1, north and west.

**8219. JOHNSON, William**
Jan. 11, 1840, 4 1/2 miles SSE Juniper, Gadsden Co. SW 1/4 NW 1/4 Sect. 35 Tp. 2 R. 5, north and west.

**2957. JOHNSON, William**
Oct. 12, 1854, 1 mile N of McMeekin, Putnam Co. Lots No. 1, 2, and 3 Sect. 8 and Lots No. 12 and 13 Sect. 7 Tp. 10, R. 23, south and east. Patent delivered Aug. 27, 1874.
See **Patrick KERR**

**1205. JOHNSON, William C.**
April 3, 1877, 3/4 mile N Padlock Welborn, Suwannee Co. SE 1/4 NE 1/4 Sect. 12 Tp. 3S R. 13E.

**8726. JOHNSON, William S.**
Nov. 25, 1844, 3/4 mile SE Steaphead, Gadsden Co. NW 1/4 NW 1/4 Sect. 21 Tp. 2 R. 6, north and west.

**60. JOHNSON, William Thomas**
Aug. 7, 1844, 1 1/4 miles N Mattox, Duval Co. SW 1/4 SE 1/4 and SE 1/4 SW 1/4 Sect. 17 Tp. 2 R. 32, south and east.

**8013. JOHNSTON, Allen G.**
July 4, 1839, 1 mile NNE Octahatchee, Hamilton Co. W 1/2 NE 1/4 Sect. 12 Tp. 2 R. 11, north and east.

**111. JOHNSTON, Andrew N.**
Dec. 21, 1826, 2 miles S Havana, Gadsden Co. NW 1/4 Sect. 9 Tp. 2 R. 2, north and west.

**3232. JOHNSTON, Andrew N.**
Jan. 25, 1830, 2 miles SSE Lloyd, Jefferson Co. W 1/2 SE 1/4 Sect. 26 Tp. 1 R. 3, south and east.

**3233. JOHNSTON, Andrew N.**
Jan. 25, 1830, 1 1/2 miles SE Lloyd, Jefferson Co. W 1/2 NW 1/4 Sect. 26 Tp. 1 R. 2, south and east. Transferred to **C. W. STEPHENS** ( no date).

**5583. JOHNSTON, Andrew N.**
April 8, 1836, 3/4 mile N by E of Hinson, Gadsden Co. NE 1/4 Sect. 21

Tp. 3 R. 2, north and west.

**2442. JOHNSTON, Angus**
July 17, 1828, 5 miles NW Chaires, Leon Co. W 1/2 NW 1/4 Sect. 7 Tp. 1 R. 2, north and east.

**3865. JOHNSTON, Angus**
Jan. 29, 1831, 5 1/2 miles W Black Creek, Leon Co. E 1/2 NW 1/4 Sect. 7 Tp. 1 R. 2, north and east.

**3771. JOHNSTON, Geo. W.**
Dec. 1, 1830, 1 1/2 miles SSE Maysland, Madison Co. E 1/2 SE 1/4 Sect. 8 Tp. 2 R. 7, north and east.

**3772. JOHNSTON, Geo. W.**
Dec. 1, 1830, 1 1/2 miles W Maysland, Madison Co. E 1/2 Sect. 9 Tp. 2 R. 7, north and east.

**3808. JOHNSTON, Geo. W.**
Dec. 21, 1830, 1 mile SW Maysland, Madison Co. W 1/2 NW 1/4 Sect. 6 Tp. 2 R. 7, north and east.

**3809. JOHNSTON, Geo. W.**
Dec. 21, 1830, 1 1/2 miles WSW Ashville, Jefferson Co. W 1/2 NE 1/4 Sect. 1 Tp. 2 R. 6, north and east.

**3810. JOHNSTON, Geo. W.**
Dec. 21, 1830, 2 miles E Ashville, Jefferson Co. E 1/2 NW 1/4 Sect. 1 Tp. 2 R. 6, north and east.

**3811. JOHNSTON, Geo. W.**
Dec. 21, 1830, 3 miles W Bailey, Madison Co. W 1/2 NW 1/4 Sect. 21 Tp. 2 R. 7, north and east.

**2800. JOHNSTON, George M.**
At Maysland, Madison Co. W 1/2 Sect. 10 Tp. 2 R. 7, north and east. (No date)

**5345. JOHNSTON, Isham**
Dec. 11, 1835, 2 1/2 miles SE of Havana, Gadsden Co. NE 1/4 SW 1/4 Sect. 9 Tp. 2 R. 2, north and west.

**5346. JOHNSTON, Isham**
Dec. 11, 1835, 2 1/2 miles SE of Havana, Gadsden Co. NW 1/4 SW 1/4 Sect. 9 Tp. 2 R. 2, north and west. See **Isham JONES**.

**6123. JOHNSTON, Stephen**
Nov. 30, 1836, c. 1 1/2 miles N Pensacola, Escambia Co. Lot No. 7 Fractional Sect. 12 Tp. 2 R. 30, south and east. (79.75 acres). On reverse of this receipt is the notation: "Capt. ALEXANDER will please get the patent for this and send it to me, S. J.".

**2470. JOHNSTONE, Isham**
Aug. 27, 1828, 1 3/4 miles W Newport, Wakulla Co. E 1/2 NW 1/4 Sect. 27 Tp. 1 R. 3, south and east.

**2634. JOHNSTONE, Wm.**
Jan. 17, 1829, 1 mile N Wadesboro, Leon Co. W 1/2 NE 1/4 Sect. 30 Tp. 2 R. 2, north and west.

**2052. JONES, Anna Mary**
Aug. 13, 1853, 3 1/2 miles N of McKinley, Columbia Co. SE 1/4 NW 1/4 Sect. 5 Tp. 3 R. 16, south and east. Patent delivered Mar. 2, 1857.

**2132. JONES, Anna Mary**
Sept. 2, 1853, 3 1/4 miles SW of Winfield, Columbia Co. SE 1/4 SW 1/4 Sect. 32 Tp. 2 R. 16, south and east. Also Sw 1/4 NE 1/4 Sect. 5 Tp. 3 R. 16, south and east. Patent delivered Mar. 2, 1857.

**2117. JONES, Buckner**
Nov. 26, 1827, 4 miles E Campbellton, Jackson Co. NW 1/4 Sect. 34 Tp. 7 R. 11, north and west.

**451. JONES, Charles P.**
Jan. 13, 1829, 5 miles NW Rock Hill, Walton Co. NE 1/4 Sect. 29 Tp. 2 R. 19, north and west.

**JONES, Dixon see John LEWIS**

**8774. JONES, George**
April 17, 1845, 1/2 mile N El Destino, Leon Co. SE 1/4 NE 1/4 Sect. 12 Tp. 1 R. 2, south and east.

**8846. JONES, George**
Nov. 22, 1845, 1/2 mile E by S Wadesboro, Jefferson Co. W 1/2 Nw 1/4 Sect. 8 Tp. 1 R. 3, south and east.

**8847. JONES, George**
Nov. 22, 1845, 3 1/2 miles NNW Braswells, Jefferson Co. NE 1/4 NE 1/4 Sect. 7 Tp. 1 R. 3, south and east.

**8866. JONES, George**
Dec. 27, 1845, 1/4 mile NE El Destino, Jefferson Co. N 1/2 SE 1/4 SE 1/4 NE 1/4 Sect. 7 Tp. 1 R. 3, south and east.

**8867. JONES, George**
Dec. 27, 1845, 1 1/4 miles SE Wadesboro, Jefferson Co. NW 1/4 SW 1/4 Sect. 8 Tp. 1 R. 3, south and west.

**371. JONES, Isaiah**
May 2, 1827, 3 miles W Campbellton, Jackson Co. W 1/2 SW 1/4 Sect. 23 Tp. 7 R. 12, north and west.

**5346. JONES, Isham**
This is the same as **Isham JOHNSTON, #5346.**

**1665. JONES, James D.**
Jan. 26, 1853, 1 mile NW of Louise, Alachua Co. NW 1/4 NE 1/4 Sect. 32 Tp. 7 R. 21, south and east. Patent delivered Aug. 23, 1856.

**2666. JONES, James D.**
Mar. 27, 1854, 3 3/4 miles E of LaCrosse, Alachua Co. NE 1/4 NW 1/4 Sect. 32 Tp. 7 R. 21, south and east.

**2240. JONES, James M.**
Oct. 8, 1853, 2 1/4 miles W of Jefferson, Columbia Co. SW 1/4 SE 1/4 Sect. 22 Tp. 4 R. 17, south and east.

**2564. JONES, James M.**
Mar. 6, 1854, 4 3/4 miles E of Bass, Columbia Co. NW 1/4 NE 1/4 Sect. 27 Tp. 4 R. 17, south and east. Patent delivered Sept. 9, 1857.

**2591. JONES, James M.**
Mar. 9, 1854, 4 3/4 miles SW of Jefferson, Columbia Co. E 1/2 SW 1/4 Sect. 22 Tp. 4 R. 17, south and east. Patent delivered Sept. 19, 1857.

**2246. JONES, Jno. T. B.**
Feb. 6, 1828, 2 1/2 miles S by E Campbellton, Jackson Co. E 1/2 NW 1/4 Sect. 5 Tp. 6 R. 11, north and west.

**1197. JONES, John A.**
Feb. 21, 1852, 2 miles SE Alligator Pond, Columbia Co. SW 1/4 SE 1/4 Sect. 14 Tp. 4 R. 17, south and east. Patent delivered Mar. 17, 1858.

**1369. JONES, John**
March 5, 1878, 1/4 mile W Catawba, Santa Rosa Co. Lots No. 1 and 6 or E 1/2 NE 1/4 and E 1/2 SE 1/4 Sect. 4 Tp. 5N R. 28W.

**448. JONES, John E.**
Dec. 27, 1828, 5 miles NW Rock Hill, Walton Co. NW 1/4 Sect. 29 Tp. 2 R. 19, north and west.

**2597. JONES, Jonathan**
Jan. 1, 1829, 2 miles S Marianna, Jackson Co. W 1/2 SE 1/4 Sect. 15 Tp. 4 R. 10, north and west.

**1010. JONES, L. H.**
Jan. 26, 1827, 1 mile Midway, Gadsden Co. E 1/2 SW 1/4 Sect. 33 Tp. 2 R. 2, north and west.

**1013. JONES, L. H.**
Jan. 26, 1827, 2 miles SW Tallahassee, Leon Co. W 1/2 SE 1/4 Sect. 11 Tp. 1 R. 1, south and west.

**1035. JONES, L. H.**
(DUP) Jan. 30, 1827, 5 miles NNW of Lake Jackson Station, Gadsden Co. SW 1/4 Sect. 23 Tp. 2 R. 2, north and west.

**1090. JONES, L. H.**
Feb. 8, 1827, 1/2 mile S Havana, Gadsden Co. E 1/2 SE 1/4 Sect. 3 Tp. 2 R. 2, north and west.

**1093. JONES, L. H.**
Feb. 8, 1827, 2 miles SSE Havana, Gadsden Co. E 1/2 SW 1/4 Sect. 2 Tp. 2 R. 2, north and west.

**1094. JONES, L. H.**
Feb. 8, 1827, 1/2 mile S Havana, Gadsden Co. W 1/2 NW 1/4 Sect. 3 Tp. 2 R. 2, north and west.

**1095. JONES, L. H.**
Feb. 8, 1827, 12 miles S Havana, Gadsden Co. W 1/2 NE 1/4 Sect. 3 Tp. 2 R. 2, north and west.

**1097. JONES, L. H.**
Feb. 8, 1827, 1 mile SSE Havana, Gadsden Co. W 1/2 NW 1/4 Sect. 2 Tp. 2 R. 2, north and west.

**1106. JONES, L. H.**
Feb. 9, 1827, 1 mile N Midway, Gadsden Co. W 1/2 SW 1/4 Sect. 33 Tp. 2 R. 2, north and west.

**1107. JONES. L. H.**
Feb. 9, 1827, 1 mile N Midway, Gadsden Co. E 1/2 SW 1/4 Sect. 33 Tp. 2 R. 2, north and west.

**1114. JONES, L. H.**
(DUP) Feb. 12, 1827, 2 miles NNE Rose, Leon Co. W 1/2 NE 1/4 Sect. 23 Tp. 1 R. 2, south and east.

**1121. JONES, L. H.**
(DUP) Feb. 13, 1827, 3 miles S Havana, Gadsden Co. W 1/2 NW 1/4 Sect. 15 Tp. 2 R. 2, north and west.

**1122. JONES, L. H.**
Feb. 13, 1827, 3 miles S Havana, Gadsden Co. E 1/2 SW 1/4 Sect. 15 Tp. 2 R. 2, north and west.

**1123. JONES, L. H.**
Feb. 13, 1827, 3 miles SW Havana, Gadsden Co. NE 1/4 Sect. 17 Tp. 2 R. 2, north and west.

**1138. JONES, L. H.**
(DUP) Feb. 17, 1827, 5 miles S Havana, Gadsden Co. W 1/2 SW 1/4 Sect. 26 Tp. 2 R. 2, north and west.

**1139. JONES, L. H.**
(DUP) Feb. 17, 1827, 3 miles S Havana, Gadsden Co. E 1/2 NE 1/4 Sect. 22 Tp. 2 R. 2, north and west.

**1150. JONES, L. H.**
(COPY) ( Of Ala.) Feb. 13, 1827, 4 miles SW Meridian, Leon Co. Lot No. 1 Fractional Sect. 35 Tp. 3 R. 1, north and west.

**1152. JONES, L. H.**
(COPY) ( Of Ala.) Feb. 20, 1827, 11 miles N Tallahassee, Leon Co. W 1/2 NW 1/4 Sect. 1 Tp. 2 R. 1, north and west.

**1165. JONES, L. H.**
Feb. 23, 1827, 1 mile W Chaires, Leon Co. W 1/2 NW 1/4 Sect. 27 Tp. 1 R. 2, north and east.

**864. JONES, Littleberry**
Jan. 16, 1827, 2 1/2 miles NNW Midway, Gadsden Co. W 1/2 SE 1/4 Sect. 30 Tp. 2 R. 2, north and west.

**866. JONES, Littleberry**
Jan. 16, 1827, 3 miles NW Midway, Gadsden Co. E 1/2 NW 1/4 Sect. 31 Tp. 2 R. 2, north and west.

**867. JONES, Littleberry**
Jan. 16, 1827, 3 miles NW Midway, Gadsden Co. W 1/2 NW 1/4 Sect. 31 Tp. 2 R. 2, north and west.

**868. JONES, Littleberry**
Jan. 16, 1827, 3 miles NW Midway, Gadsden Co. W 1/2 SE 1/4 Sect. 31 Tp. 2 R. 2, north and west.

**997. JONES, Littleberry H.**
Jan. 20, 1827, 6 miles SSW Havana, Gadsden Co. NW 1/4 Sect. 29 Tp. 2 R. 2, north and west.

**998. JONES, Littleberry H.**
Jan. 20, 1827, 6 miles SSW Havana, Gadsden Co. W 1/2 NE 1/4 Sect. 29 Tp. 2 R. 2, north and west.

**2555. JONES, Mathew**
Dec. 1, 1828, 3 miles NW Midway, Gadsden Co. W 1/2 SW 1/4 Sect. 30 Tp. 2 R. 2, north and west.

**2556. JONES, Mathew**
Dec. 1, 1828, 3 1/2 miles NW Midway, Gadsden Co. E 1/2 NW 1/4 Sect. 30 Tp. 2 R. 2, north and west.

**8242. JONES, Randle**
May 22, 1890, 2 1/4 miles NW Bass, Columbia Co. N 1/2 SE 1/4 Sect. 21 Tp. 4S R. 16E.

**180. JONES, Robert**
Dec. 29, 1826, 4 1/2 miles SSE Graceville, Jackson Co. E 1/2 SE 1/4 Sect. 23 Tp. 6 R. 12, north and west.

**1720. JONES, Robert**
May 31, 1827, 1/2 mile N Welchton, Jackson Co. E 1/2 NE 1/4 Sect. 26 Tp. 6 R. 12, north and west.

**6068. JONES, Robert R.**
Nov. 21, 1836, 4 1/2 miles E Monticello, Jefferson Co. W 1/2 SE 1/4 Sect. 25 Tp. 2 R. 5, north and east.

**8663. JONES, Robert R.**
Mar. 28, 1844, 1/2 mile N Dills, Jefferson Co. W 1/2 SW 1/4 Sect. 31 Tp.3 R. 6, north and east.

**8998. JONES, Robert**
Nov. 25, 1846, 3 miles NNW Dills, Jefferson Co. S 1/2 NE 1/4 Sect. 34 Tp. 3 R. 5, north and east.

**6885. JONES, Seaborn**
Mar. 13, 1837, 4 1/2 miles E by N Monticello, Jefferson Co. SW 1/4 NW 1/4 Sect. 24 Tp. 2 R. 5, north and east.

**7722. JONES, Seaborn**
Nov. 23, 1838, 1/4 mile SE Dills, Jefferson Co. NW 1/4 SE 1/4 Sect. 6 Tp. 2 R. 6, north and east.

**7726. JONES, Seaborn**
Nov. 26, 1838. 1/2 mile S Dills, Jefferson Co. SE 1/4 Sect. 6 Tp. 2 R. 6, north and east.

**8532. JONES, Seaborn**
Mar. 8, 1842, 1 mile SW Dills, Jefferson Co. NE 1/4 SW 1/4 Sect. 6 Tp. 2 R. 6, north and east.

**1766. JONES, Thomas F.**
Mar. 10, 1853, 4 1/2 miles SE Providence, Union Co. NW 1/4 NE 1/4 Sect. 12 Tp. 6 R. 18, south and east. Patent delivered Aug. 21, 1856.

**9737. JORDAN, Hartwell**
Dec. 14, 1891, 2 miles NE Svea, Walton Co. Lots No. 1, 2 and 3 Sect. 29 Tp. 6N R. 21W.

**JORDAN, Ratford see Phillip ROSE**

**2692. JORDAN, Samuel**
Jan. 29, 1829, 4 miles W Alma, Leon Co. W 1/2 NE 1/4 Sect. 31 Tp. 3 R. 4,

north and east.

**3138. JORDAN, Samuel**
Nov. 30, 1829, 2 miles WNW Alma, Leon Co. E 1/2 SE 1/4 Sect. 28 Tp. 3 R. 4, north and east.

**5636. JORDAN, Samuel**
April 30, 1836, 5 1/4 miles NNW of Dills, Jefferson Co. NW 1/4 NW 1/4 Sect. 29 Tp. 3 R. 5, north and east.

**4098. JOURDAN, Daniel M.**
Sept. 17, 1831, 3 1/2 miles SE Florence, Gadsden Co. W 1/2 SE 1/4 Sect. 8 Tp. 2 R. 2, north and west.

**4353. JOYCE, Daniel**
April 30, 1856, 5 miles NW High Springs, Alachua Co. Lot No. 1 Sect. 35 Tp. 7 R. 16, south and east. Patent delivered Feb. 22, 1857.

**2218. JOYNER, Joseph**
( Of Fla.) Jan. 10, 1828, 2 1/2 miles WSW Alma, Leon Co. E 1/2 NE 1/4 Sect. 9 Tp. 2 R. 3, north and east.

**6948. JUNERARITY, John**
Oct. 31, 1836, 6 miles E by S of Yniestra, across Escambia Bay, Escambia Co. Fractional Sect. 26 Tp. 2 R. 29, south and west.

## * K *

**2347. KEEN, Elizabeth**
Nov. 3, 1853, 3 1/2 miles NNW of Suwannee Valley, Columbia Co. SW 1/4 SW 1/4 Sect. 20 Tp. 2 R. 17, south and east.

**8052. KEISEY, William**
Aug. 21, 1839, S by E Dills, Jefferson Co. SW 1/4 NW 1/4 and NW 1/4 SE 1/4 Sect. 7 Tp. 2 R. 6, north and east.

**8102. KEITH, Jehu W.**
Oct. 1, 1839, 1/2 mile W Caryville, Holmes Co. Lot No. 4 Sect. 2 Tp. 4 R. 16, north and west.

**8374. KEITH, Jehu W.**
July 24, 1840, 8 miles E by S Prosperity, Holmes Co. SE 1/4 NW 1/4 Sect. 25 Tp. 5 R. 13, north and west.

**8375. KEITH, Jehu W.**
July 24, 1840, 7 miles E by S Prosperity, Holmes Co. SE 1/4 NW 1/4 Sect. 26 Tp. 5 R. 16, north and west.

**4085. KEMP, Peter**
Oct. 5, 1831, 2 1/2 miles NE Wadesboro, Leon Co. W 1/2 SE 1/4 Sect. 32 Tp. 2 R. 3, north and east. (Duplicate)

**356. KENNEDY, James**
April 23, 1827, 5 miles SW Fanlaw, Leon Co. NW 1/4 Sect. 17 Tp. 3 R. 2, south and east.

**4323. KENNEDY, James**
Mar. 14, 1833, 1/2 mile S of Roeville, Santa Rosa Co. NW 1/4 SW 1/4 Sect. 25 Tp. 2 R. 28, north and west. Transferred to **Reuben N. BARROW** (no date).

**4470. KENNEDY, James**
Dec. 10, 1833, 2 1/2 miles NNW of Coldwater, Santa Rosa Co. SE 1/4 NW 1/4 Sect. 5 Tp. 2 R. 27, north and west.

**4843. KENNEDY, William M.**
Sept. 11, 1858, 2 miles NE Lexington, Alachua Co. SE 1/4 NE 1/4 Sect. 22 Tp. 9 R. 17, south and east. Patent delivered Aug. 4, 1862.

**8415. KEMP, George W.**
Nov. 4, 1840, 2 1/2 miles E by N Hinson, Gadsden Co. NW 1/4 NW 1/4 Sect. 25 Tp. 3 R. 2, north and west.

**6968. KENNERLY, Sherod W.**
Apr. 1, 1837, 1 mile W Lamont, Jefferson Co. E 1/2 NE 1/4 Sect. 28 Tp. 1 R. 5, south and east.

**16. KENT, Jesse**
Sept. 16, 1826, (location not given). SW 1/4 Sect. 7 Tp. 5 R. 10, north and west. Received from **Jesse KENT** $200.07 1/2 (marked pre-emption).

**8369. KENT, Jesse**
July 18, 1840, 2 miles NNE Blountstown, Calhoun Co. SE 1/4 Sect. 22 Tp. 1 R. 8, north and west.

**262. KENT, Marmaduke**
Jan. 1, 1827, 5 miles NE of Marianna, Jackson Co. SE 1/4 Sect. 7 Tp. 5 R. 10, north and west.

**312. KENT, Marmaduke**
Jan. 1, 1827, 7 miles W of Greenwood, Jackson Co. NE 1/4 Sect. 30 Tp. 6 R. 11, north and west. Transferred to **R. C. ALLEN** through his attorney, **R. W. WILLIAMS** from **Marmaduke KENT** on Jan. 13, 1827. Transferred from **R. C. ALLEN** to **L. R. OVERTON** on Jan. 13, 1827.

**39. KENT, Wm.**
Nov. 6, 1826, c. 4 miles SW Greenwood, Jackson Co. NE 1/4 Sect. 18 Tp. 5 R. 10, north and west. Transferred Nov. 7, 1826, to **Richard C. ALLEN & Co.** by **NICHOLA**, atty. in fact for **Wm. KENT**.

**3540. KERR, Patrick**
June 17, 1830, 2 miles WSW Old Town, Dixie Co. W 1/4 SW 1/4 Sect. 22 Tp. 10 R. 13, south and east.

**3812. KERR, Patrick**
Dec. 21, 1830, 4 miles WSW Bradfordville, Leon Co. SE 1/4 Sect. 30 Tp. 2 R. 1, north and east. Transferred Jan. 1, 1830, to **William A. CARR**, (G. W. WARD, reg)

**3882. KERR, Patrick**
Feb. 22, 1831, 4 miles NE Cay, Jefferson Co. E 1/2 SE 1/4 Sect. 25 Tp. 1 R. 3, south and east. Transferred to **Job FREEMAN** on April 25, 1832, and the patent for it is ordered to be delivered to him. Teste: **Jno. A. FRANKLIN**.

**3914. KERR, Patrick**
Mar. 12, 1831, 5 miles WSW Aucilla, Jefferson Co. E 1/2 SE 1/4 Sect. 26 Tp. 1 R. 5, south and east.

**3920. KERR, Patrick**
March 23, 1831, 3 miles NE Lamont, Jefferson Co. E 1/2 SE 1/4 Sect. 13 Tp. 1 R. 5, south and east. Transferred Jan. 19, 1833, to **William JOHNSON**, Teste: **Henry BOND**.

**6541. KERR, Patrick**
Jan. 14, 1837, 2 1/2 miles NNW Eridu, Madison Co. W 1/2 NW 1/4 Sect. 1 Tp. 2 R. 5, south and east.

**6542. KERR, Patrick**
Jan. 14, 1837, 3 miles N by W Eridu, Madison Co. W 1/2 SW 1/4 Sect. 36 Tp. 1 R. 5, south and east.

**1903. KERR, William**
June 11, 1827, 4 miles W Tallahassee, Leon Co. W 1/2 SW 1/4 Sect. 33 Tp. 1 R. 1, north and west.

**1904. KERR, William**
June 11, 1827, 2 miles W by S Tallahassee, Leon Co. W 12 NW 1/4 Sect. 3 Tp. 1 R. 1, south and west.

**1939. KERR, William**
June 23, 1827, c. 11 miles N Tallahassee, Leon Co. Lot No. 3 Sect. 12 Tp. 2 R. 1, north and west.

**2059. KERR, William**
(of Ireland) Sept. 13, 1827, 1 1/2 miles E Lake Jackson Station, Leon Co. W 1/2 NW 1/4 Sect. 4 Tp. 1 R. 1, north and west.

**2060. KERR, William**
(of Ireland) Sept. 13, 1827, 1 mile E Lake Jackson Station, Leon Co. E 1/2 NE 1/4 Sect. 5 Tp. 1 R. 1, north and west.

**2340. KERR, William**
April 14, 1828, c. 2 miles E Lake Jackson Station, Leon Co. Lot No. 1 Sect. 33 Tp. 2 R. 1, north and west.

**2374. KERR, William**
May 9, 1828, 2 miles N Centerville, Leon Co. E 1/2 SW 1/4 Sect. 12 Tp. 2 R. 1, north and east.

**2505. KERR, William**
Sept. 29, 1828, at Lawrence Switch, Gadsden Co. Lot No. 5 Sect. 22 Tp. 1 R. 2, north and west. (37 1/2 acres)

**2506. KERR, William**
Sept. 29, 1828, 1 mile SW Lawrence Switch, Gadsden Co. E 1/2 NE 1/4 Sect. 27 Tp. 1 R. 2, north and west.

**2507. KERR, William**
Sept. 29, 1828, 1 mile SW Lawrence Switch, Gadsden Co. W 1/2 NE 1/4 Sect. 27 Tp. 1 R. 2, north and west.

**2508. KERR, William**
Sept. 29, 1828, Ockloknee River across from Lawrence Switch, Leon Co. Lot No. 1 Sect. 23 Tp. 1 R. 2, north and west.

**2509. KERR, William**
Sept. 29, 1828, opposite Lawrence Switch, Leon Co. Lot No. 2 Sect. 23 Tp. 1 R. 2, north and west.

**2510. KERR, William**
Sept. 29, 1828, 3 miles W by S Gadsden, Gadsden Co. Lot No. 8 Sect. 21 Tp. 1 R. 2, north and west.

**2526. KERR, William**
(of Ireland) Oct. 18, 1828, 1/2 mile SW Gadsden, Gadsden Co. Lot No. 6 Fractional Sect. 22 Tp. 1 R. 2, north and west.

**2776. KERR, William**
Mar. 7, 1829, 3 miles W Black Creek, Leon Co. W 1/2 SW 1/4 Sect. 9 Tp. 1 R. 2, north and east.

**2974. KERR, William**
(and **Patrick KERR**) Aug. 4, 1829, 8 miles SSW Chattahoochee, Jackson Co. W 1/2 NW 1/4 Sect. 36 Tp. 3 R. 7, north and west.

**3348. KERR, William**
Feb. 13, 1830, 1/2 mile SE Old Town, Dixie Co. E 1/2 NE 1/4 Sect. 23 Tp. 10 Tp. 13, south and east. Transferred to **Jas. W. DABNEY** on Feb. 14, 1830.

**3350. KERR, William**
Feb. 13, 1830, just SW Old Town, Dixie Co. E 1/2 NW 1/4 Sect. 23 Tp. 10 R. 13, north and west. Transferred to **Jas. W. DABNEY** on Feb. 14, 1830.

**3351. KERR, William**
Feb. 13, 1830, 1 1/2 miles SW Old Town, Dixie Co. E 1/2 SW 1/4 Sect. 22 Tp. 10 Tp. 13, south and east.

**3352. KERR, William**
Feb. 13, 1830, 2 miles SW Old Town, Dixie Co. W 1/2 NW 1/4 Sect. 22 Tp. 10 Tp. 13, south and east.

**3353. KERR, William**
Feb. 13, 1830, 1 mile SW Old Town, Dixie Co. E 1/2 NE 1/4 Sect. 22 Tp. 10 R. 13, south and east.

**3354. KERR, William**
Feb. 13, 1830, 2 miles SE Old Town, Dixie Co. W 1/2 NE 1/4 Sect. 22 Tp.

10 R. 13, south and east.

**3355. KERR, William**
Feb. 13, 1830, 2 miles SE Old Town, Dixie Co. Lot No. 1 Fractional Sect. 25 Tp. 10 R. 13, south and east.

**3356. KERR, William**
Feb. 13, 1830, 1/2 mile S Old Town, Dixie Co. W 1/2 NE 1/4 Sect. 23 Tp. 10 R. 13, south and east. Transferred to **Wm. BAILE** on Feb. 16, 1830.

**3378. KERR, William**
Feb. 16, 1830, 3 miles NNW Lamont, Jefferson Co. W 1/2 NE 1/4 Sect. 15 Tp. 1 R. 5, south and east.

**3380. KERR, William**
Feb. 16, 1830, 1 1/2 miles SW Old Town, Dixie Co. E 1/2 SE 1/4 Sect. 22 Tp. 10 R. 13, south and east.

**3381. KERR, William**
Feb. 16, 1830, 2 miles N Eridu, Madison Co. N 1/2 NE 1/4 Sect. 1 Tp. 2 R. 5, south and east.

**3382. KERR, William**
Feb. 16, 1830, 2 miles N by W Eridu, Madison Co. W 1/2 NW 1/4 Sect. 1 Tp. 2 R. 5, south and east.

**3385. KERR, William**
Feb. 16, 1830, 2 miles N Lamont, Jefferson Co. E 1/2 NW 1/4 Sect. 15 Tp. 1 R. 5, south and east.

**3384. KERR, William**
Feb. 16, 1830, 5 miles NW Lamont, Jefferson Co. E 1/2 SW 1/4 Sect. 18 Tp. 1 R. 5, south and east.

**3407. KERR, William**
Feb. 16, 1830, 1 mile S Mandalay, Taylor Co. E 1/2 NW 1/4 Sect. 30 Tp. 4 R. 4, south and east.

**3408. KERR, William**
Feb. 16, 1830, 1 mile S Mandalay, Taylor Co. W 1/2 NE 1/4 Sect. 30 Tp. 4 R. 4, south and east.

**3465. KERR, William**
Mar. 27, 1830, 2 miles SSW Old Town, Dixie Co. E 1/2 NE 1/4 Sect. 27 Tp. 10 R. 13, south and east. Received Treasury Scrip dated May 30, 1829, in favor of **Alex'r MACOMB**. (Treasury Scrip No. 64)

**3466. KERR, William**
March 27, 1830, 2 1/2 miles SW Old Town, Dixie Co. E 1/2 NW 1/4 Sect. 27 Tp. 10 R. 13, south and east. Received Treasury Scrip dated May 30, 1829, in favor of **Alex'r MACOMB**. Treasury Scrip No. 65.

**3467. KERR, William**
March 27, 1830, 1 1/2 miles SW Old Town, Dixie Co. E 1/2 SW 1/4 Sect. 22 Tp. 10 R. 13, south and east. Pd. with Treasury Scrip No. 66 issued to **Alex'r MACOMB**, May 30, 1829.

**3468. KERR, William**
March 29, 1830, 2 miles SW Old Town, Dixie Co. W 1/2 SE 1/4 Sect. 22 Tp. 10 R. 13, south and east. Pd. in Scrip issued to **Edgar MACOMB**, dated May 30, 1829.

**3478. KERR, William**
April 16, 1830, 2 miles SW Old Town, Dixie Co. E 1/2 NE 1/4 Sect. 21 Tp. 10 R. 13, south and east. Received in payment Cert. 77, dated May 30, 1829, in favor of **Alex'r MACOMB**, survivor of Edgar and Macomb.

**4596. KERR, William**
July 8, 1834, 1 1/2 miles NNE of Perkins, Leon Co. NE 1/4 SE 1/4 Sect. 30 Tp. 1 R. 2, north and east.

**2048. KERSEY, William**
Aug. 27, 1827, c. 3 miles NE Bradfordville, Leon Co. Lot No. 6 Fractional Sect. 12 Tp. 2 R. 1, north and west.

**4998. KERSEY, William**
June 15, 1835, 2 miles S of Dill, Jefferson Co. W 1/2 NE 1/4 Sect. 18 Tp. 2 R. 6, north and east.

**6241. KERSEY, William**
Dec. 19, 1836, 1 mile SW Ashville, Jefferson Co. SW 1/4 SE 1/4 Sect. 7 Tp. 2 R. 6, north and east.

**7531. KERSEY, William**
July 12, 1838, 3/4 mile S Dills, Jefferson Co. E 1/2 NW 1/4 Sect. 7 Tp. 2 R. 6, north and east.

**7532. KERSEY, William**
July 12, 1838, 2 3/4 miles W by W (?) Bradfordville, Leon Co. SE 1/4 SE 1/4 Sect. 18 Tp. 2 R. 6, north and east.

**8471. KETCHUM, William Scott**
Feb. 26, 1841, 2 1/2 miles SSE Myrick, Madison Co. W 1/2 NE 1/4 Sect. 3 Tp. 1 R.7, south and east.

**8472. KETCHUM, William Scott**
Feb. 26, 1841, 2 miles SSE Myrick, Madison Co. W 1/2 NW 1/4 Sect. 3 Tp. 1 R. 7, south and east.

**8473. KETCHUM, William Scott**

Feb. 26, 1841, 1 mile SSE Myrick, Madison Co. E 1/2 SW 1/4 Sect. 4 Tp. 1 R. 7, south and east.

**8474. KETCHUM, William Scott**
Feb. 26, 1841, 1 mile S by W Myrick, Madison Co. E 1/2 SE 1/4 Sect. 6 Tp. 1 R. 7, south and east.

**8475. KETCHUM, William Scott**
Feb. 26, 1841, 1 1/4 miles S by W Myrick, Madison Co. E 1/2 NE 1/4 Sect. 7 Tp. 1 R. 7, south and east.

**8478. KETCHUM, William Scott**
Mar. 1, 1841, 1/4 mile NW Myrick, Madison Co. W 1/2 SE 1/4 Sect. 31 Tp. 1 R. 7, north and east.

**8479. KETCHUM, William Scott**
Mar. 1, 1841, at Myrick, Madison Co. W 1/2 SW 1/4 Sect. 32 Tp. 1 R. 7, north and east.

**6748. KEYSER, Charles C.**
Feb. 6, 1837, 4 miles ESE Moline, Santa Rosa Co. E 1/2 NW 1/4 E 1/2 SW 1/4 Sect. 9 Tp. 2 R. 3, north and west. East of Escambia River.

**8720. KEYSER, Charles C.**
Nov. 12, 1844, 1 mile SW Fentresa, Santa Rosa Co. W 1/2 NE 1/4 Sect. 23 Tp. 3 R. 27, north and west.

**8481. KICKINSON, Samuel A.**
March 17, 1841, 4 1/2 miles W St. Marks Junction, Leon Co. SW 1/4 SW 1/4 Sect. 17 Tp. 1 R. 1, south and west.

**400. KILBEE, Lucy**
May 5, 1827, 5 miles WSW Greenwood, Jackson Co. NW 1/4 Sect. 4 Tp. 5 R. 10, north and west.

**244. KILBEE, Wm. T.**
Dec. 30, 1826, 6 miles NE of Cottondale, Jackson Co. NW 1/4 Sect. 23 Tp. 5 R. 10, north and west. Transfers: **Wm. T. KILBEE** to **Jacob ROBINSON**, Feb. 14, 1827.

**360. KILBEE, Wm. T.**
(Assignee of **Isham BAZZELL**) Apr. 23, 1827, 12 miles ESE Malone, Houston Co., Alabama. Lot No. 1 Fractional Sect. 23 Tp. 7 R. 8, north and west. Transferred from **W. T. KILBEE** to **F. CARTER**, April 23, 1827.

**405. KILBEE, Wm. T.**
(Assignee of **Jno. C. CARTER**) May 7, 1827, 6 miles ENE Marianna, Jackson Co. SW 1/4 Sect. 28 Tp. 5 R. 9,

north and west.

**359. KILBEE, Wm. T.**
(Assignee of **John ALLEN**) April 23, 1827, 10 miles ENE Malone, Houston Co., Alabama. Lot No. 1 Fractional Sect. 14 Tp. 7 R. 8, north and west. Transferred to **F. CARTER**, April 23, 1827.

**1607. KILBEE, Wm. T.**
May 25, 1827, 4 miles SW Greenwood, Jackson Co. W 1/2 NE 1/4 Sect. 35 Tp. 5 R. 10, north and west. Transferred to **Geo. POYTHRESS**, July 28, 1827.

**2796. KILBEE, Wm. T.**
March 31, 1829, 4 miles NE Marianna, Jackson Co. E 1/2 NW 1/4 Sect. 25 Tp. 5 R. 10, north and west.
See **James PATTERSON** and **George T. WARD**

**1890. KING, Benj.**
June 9, 1827, 1 1/2 miles E Felkel, Leon Co. W 1/2 NE 1/4 Sect. 2 Tp. 2 R. 2, north and east.

**1891. KING, Benj.**
June 9, 1827, 2 miles ENE Felkel, Leon Co. W 1/2 SW 1/4 Sect. 36 Tp. 3 R. 2, north and east. (On back," $142.25 paid over to **L. B. SKUGGS**.")

**8769. KING, S. D.**
April 13, 1845, 2 3/4 miles SE Havana, Gadsden Co. NE 1/4 SW 1/4 Sect. 12 Tp. 2 R. 2, north and west.

**5483. KING, William**
Feb. 22, 1836, 2 miles W of Cherrylake, Madison Co. W 1/2 SW 1/4 Sect. 7 Tp. 2 R. 9, north and east.

**127. KING, Wm. R.**
(of Ala.) May 19, 1825, at St. Marks Junction, Leon Co. E 1/2 NW 1/4 Sect. 13 Tp. 1 R. 1, south and east.

**128. KING, Wm. R.**
(of Alabama) May 19, 1825, at St. Marks Junction, Leon Co. W 1/2 NE 1/4 Sect. 13 Tp. 1 R. 1, south and east.

**129. KING, Wm. R.**
(of Alabama) May 19, 1825, at St. Marks Junction, Leon Co. E 1/2 NE 1/4 Sect. 13 Tp. 1 R. 1, south and east.

**130. KING, Wm. R.**
(of Alabama) May 19, 1825, at St. Marks Junction, Leon Co. W 1/2 NW 1/4 Sect. 13 Tp. 1 R. 1, south and east.

**141. KING, Wm. R.**
(of Alabama) May 19, 1825, 2 miles SE Tallahassee, Leon Co. E 1/2 SE 1/4 Sect. 11 Tp. 1 R. 1, south and east.

**142. KING, Wm. R.**
(of Alabama) May 19, 1825, 1 mile SE Tallahassee, Leon Co. W 1/2 NW 1/4 Sect. 11 Tp. 1 R. 1, south and east.

**2115. KIRKLAND, Mitchell**
Aug. 24, 1853, 4 miles N by E Hague, Alachua Co. N 1/2 Lot No. 3 Sect. 19 Tp. 8 R. 20, south and east. Patent delivered Dec. 3, 1856.

**2410. KIRKLAND, Mitchell**
Feb. 21, 1854, 4 1/2 miles SSW of Cyril, Alachua Co. S 1/2 Lot No. 8 Sect. 18 Tp. 8 R. 20, south and east. Patent delivered Dec. 3, 1856.

**2751. KIRKLAND, Moses**
Feb. 19, 1829, at Havana, Gadsden Co. W 1/2 SW 1/4 Sect. 27 Tp. 3 R. 2, north and west. Transferred Jan. 22, 1830, to **Redding BLOUNT ( Reddin BLUNT)**. Teste: **R. N. MORGAN** and **Wm. LOTT**.

**4937. KIRKLAND, Moses**
April 17, 1835, 1 1/2 miles NE of Hinson, Gadsden Co. SW 1/4 NW 1/4 Sect. 22 Tp. 3 R. 2, north and west.

**4052. KIRKLAND, Moses**
July 28, 1831, 3 miles NE of Smith Creek, Wakulla Co. W 1/2 SE 1/4 Sect. 13 Tp. 3 R. 2, north and west. Transferred to **John RIGGINS**, June 24, 1835.

**8119. KIRKLAND, Moses**
Oct. 18, 1839, 1/4 mile E by N Havana, Gadsden Co. NE 1/4 SW 1/4 Sect. 35 Tp. 3 R. 2, north and west.

**8944. KIRKSEY, James**
June 1, 1846, 4 miles N by W Scanlon, Jefferson Co. W 1/2 NW 1/4 Sect. 35 Tp. 3 R. 4, south and east.

**8945. KIRKSEY, James**
June 1, 1846, 4 1/2 miles N by W Scanlon, Jefferson Co. E 1/2 SE 1/4 Sect. 27 Tp. 3 R. 4, south and east.

**8946. KIRKSEY, James**
June 1, 1846, 5 miles N by E Scanlon, Jefferson Co. W 1/2 SW 1/4 Sect. 26 Tp. 3 R. 4, south and east.

**8947. KIRKSEY, James**
June 1, 1846, 3 3/4 miles N by W Scanlon, Jefferson Co. NE 1/4 Sect. 36 Tp. 3 R. 4, south and east.

**8948. KIRKSEY, James**
June 1, 1846, 5 miles N by W Scanlon, Jefferson Co. N 1/2 SW 1/4 Sect. 34 Tp. 3 R. 4, south and west.

**8949. KIRKSEY, James**
June 6, 1846, 4 3/4 miles N by W Scanlon, Jefferson Co. SW 1/4 SW 1/4 Sect. 27 Tp. 3 R. 4, south and east.

**1537. KITE, James**
Dec. 3, 1852, at New River, Bradford Co. NW 1/4 SW 1/4 Sect. 14 Tp. 6 R. 20, south and east.

**1972. KITTLES, Thomas C.**
July 25, 1853, 3 miles E of Adam, Alachua Co. Lots 6, 7 and 10 Sect. 27 Tp. 11 R. 18, south and east. Patent delivered Oct. 2, 1858.

**2313. KITTRELL, Thos.**
March 18, 1828, 3 miles SE Greensboro, Gadsden Co. W 1/2 NW 1/4 Sect. 23 Tp. 2 R. 5, north and west.

**2851. KNIGHTON, Milly**
June 19, 1829, 2 miles S Quincy, Gadsden Co. E 1/2 NW 1/4 Sect. 19 Tp. 2 R. 3, north and west.

**2852. KNIGHTON, Milly**
June 19, 1829, 2 miles S Quincy, Gadsden Co. W 1/2 NE 1/4 Sect. 19 Tp. 2 R. 3, north and west.

**2627. KNIGHTON, Thomas**
Jan. 15, 1829, 2 1/2 miles ENE Quincy, Gadsden Co. W 1/2 SW 1/4 Sect. 3 Tp. 3 R. 3, north and west.

**2693. KNIGHTON, Thomas**
Jan. 30, 1829, 2 miles NE Greensboro, Gadsden Co. E 1/2 NW 1/4 Sect. 4 Tp. 2 R. 3, north and west.

**2694. KNIGHTON, Thomas**
Jan. 30, 1829, 2 miles NE Quincy, Gadsden Co. E 1/2 SW 1/4 Sect. 33 Tp. 3 R. 3, north and west.

**2695. KNIGHTON, Thomas**
Jan. 30, 1829, 2 1/2 miles NW Quincy, Gadsden Co. E 1/2 NW 1/4 Sect. 33 Tp. 3 R. 3, north and west.

**2696. KNIGHTON, Thomas**
Jan. 30, 1829, 2 miles ESE Quincy, Gadsden Co. W 1/2 SW 1/4 Sect. 3 Tp. 2 R. 3, north and west.

**3982. KNIGHTON, Thomas**
June 10, 1831, 2 1/2 miles E Quincy,

Gadsden Co. NW 1/4 Sect. 10 Tp. 2 R. 3, north and west.

**3983. KNIGHTON, Thomas**
June 11, 1831, 2 miles SW Miccouskee, Leon Co. W 1/2 SW 1/4 Sect. 17 Tp. 2 R. 3, north and east.

**8317. KNOBLOCK, James**
May 12, 1840, 1 mile NNE Dills, Jefferson Co. NE 1/4 Sect. 31 Tp. 3 R. 6, north and east.

**7021. KORNBAW, Daniel**
June 24, 1837, 1 mile NNE Centerville, Leon Co. SE 1/4 NE 1/4 Sect. 18 Tp. 2 R. 2, north and east.

**6974. KORNLAW, Daniel**
April 5, 1837, 1 mile NE Centerville, Leon Co. W 1/2 NE 1/4 Sect. 18 Tp. 2 R. 2, north and east.

**4315. KRAMMEL, Lloyd**
Feb. 21, 1833, 3/4 mile N of Monticello, Jefferson Co. SW 1/4 NE 1/4 Sect. 24 Tp. 2 R. 4, north and east.

\* L \*

**8561. LACQUAY, Pauline A.**
(Widow of **Jefferson D. LACQUAY**)
Aug. 22, 1890, 1 3/4 miles Wanamake, Gilchrist Co. SW 1/4 SW 1/4 Sect. 5 and N 1/2 NE 1/4 Sect. 7 and NW 1/4 NW 1/4 Sect. 8 Tp. 7S R. 15E.

**8680. LACY, Claburn**
Aug. 3, 1844, 7 1/2 miles NNW Washington, Washington Co. NW 1/4 SE 1/4 Sect. 5 Tp. 3 R. 12, north and west.

**2099. LACY, Claiborne**
(of Fla.) Nov. 12, 1827, 3 miles ESE Everett, Washington Co. E 1/2 SW 1/4 Sect. 14 Tp. 3 R. 13, north and west.

**2668. LAING, Charles**
Jan. 26, 1829, 3 1/4 miles N Havana, Gadsden Co. W 1/2 SW 1/4 Sect. 11 Tp. 3 R. 2, north and west.

**2669. LAING, George H.**
Jan. 26, 1829, 4 miles E Havana, Gadsden Co. E 1/2 SE 1/4 Sect. 7 Tp. 3 R. 1, north and west.

**4291. LAING, Cornelius**
Jan. 31, 1833, 1 mile SW of Darsey, Gadsden Co. NE 1/4 SW 1/4 Sect. 11 Tp. 3 R. 2, north and west.

**4292. LAING, Cornelius**
Jan. 31, 1833, 1 1/4 miles SW of Darsey, Gadsden Co. SW 1/4 NW 1/4 Sect. 11 Tp. 3 R. 2, north and west.

**6181. LAING, William H.**
Dec. 10, 1836, 3 miles NE Havana, Gadsden Co. SE 1/4 SE 1/4 Sect. 14 Tp. 3 R. 2, north and west.

**4658. LAING, Willis**
Nov. 6, 1834, 2 1/4 miles W of Midway, Gadsden Co. NE 1/4 SE 1/4 Sect. 11 Tp. 1 R. 3, south and east. Sold to **O. H. GADSDEN** Dec. 21, 1836.

**8754. LAMB, Edward J.**
Mar. 7, 1845, 1/2 mile NE Rockbluff, Liberty Co. NE 1/4 SE 1/4 Sect. 24 Tp. 2 R. 7, north and west.

**8755. LAMB, Edward J.**
Mar. 7, 1845, 3/4 mile NW Rockbluff, Liberty Co. NE 1/4 SW 1/4 Sect. 23 Tp. 2 R. 7, north and west.

**8779. LAMB, Isaac N.**
May 23, 1845, 3/4 mile SW Greenville, Madison Co. NW 1/4 NW 1/4 Sect. 28 Tp. 1 R. 7, north and east.

**7602. LAMB, Jared**
Aug. 16, 1838, 3 1/2 miles N Champaign, Madison Co. NE 1/4 SE 1/4 Sect. 35 Tp. 2 R. 8, north and east.

**792. LANCASTER, Joseph B.**
(of Fla.) Oct. 31, 1826, 3 miles SSW of Perkins Station, Leon Co. W 1/2 SE 1/4 Sect. 10 Tp. 1 R. 1, south and east.

**793. LANCASTER, Joseph B.**
(of Fla.) Oct. 31, 1826, 3 miles SSW Perkins Station, Leon Co. E 1/2 SW 1/4 Sect. 10 Tp. 1 R. 1, south and east.

**6483. LANDERS, Lewis**
Jan. 9, 1837, 3 miles NNW Wadesboro, Leon Co. W 1/2 NE 1/4 Sect. 23 Tp. 2 R. 2, north and east.

**18. LANE, Joseph R.**
Sept 22, 1826, just E of Norum, Washington Co. SE 1/4 Sect. 10 Tp. 2 R. 15, north and west. 159.69 acres. Rec'd $199.61 1/4. **R. K. CALL**, Receiver. On reverse side: Above transferred to **R. C. ALLEN & CO.**, Sept. 22, 1826. (Signed **Jos. Rhea LANE**.)

**6116. LANG, Cornelius**
Nov. 30, 1836, 1 mile SW Darsey, Gadsden Co. W 1/2 NE 1/4 Sect. 11 Tp. 3 R. 2, north and west.

**4083. LANG, David A.**
Sept. 16, 1831, 1/4 mile N of Lake Jackson Station, Leon Co. E 1/2 NE 1/4 Sect. 7 Tp. 3 R. 1, north and west.

**6118. LANG, George H.**
Nov. 30, 1836, 1/2 mile E Concord, Gadsden Co. NW 1/4 NW 1/4 Sect. 17 Tp. 3 R. 1, north and west.

**6117. LANG, Robt. A.**
Nov. 30, 1836, 1/2 mile SW Darsey, Gadsden Co. SE 1/4 NE 1/4 Sect. 11 Tp. 3 R. 2, north and west.

**4866. LANG, Willis**
Feb. 14, 1835, 2 1/4 miles N of Cay, Jefferson Co. E 1/2 NE 1/4 Sect. 14 Tp. 1 R. 3, south and east.

**2053. LANG, Wm.**
Sept. 9, 1827, 3 miles NE Havana, Gadsden Co. W 1/2 NW 1/4 Sect. 24 Tp. 3 R. 2, north and west.

**8402. LANGFORD, Thomas**
Sept 4, 1840, 1 mile NW Calhoun,

Madison Co. E 1/2 NW 1/4 Sect. 11 Tp. 1 R. 9, north and east.

**278. LANGSTON, Seth S.**
Jan. 1, 1827, 6 miles NW Marianna, Jackson Co. SE 1/4 Sect. 4 Tp. 5 R. 11, north and west.

**8379. LANIER, Andrew J.**
Aug. 4, 1840, 3 miles NE Calhoun, Madison Co. NE 1/4 NW 1/4 Sect. 10 Tp. 1 R. 9, south and east.

**1213. LANIER, Agustus H.**
No date. Gadsden Co. Affidavit in lieu of receipt, sworn before **Samuel H. DUVAL**, J. P. of Leon County.

**8585. LANIER, Gibon S.**
April 20, 1843, 3 miles WNW Calhoun, Madison Co. NW 1/4 NE 1/4 Sect. 8 Tp. 1 R. 9, south and east.

**8559. LANIER, Gibson S.**
Oct. 14, 1842, 3 miles W by N Calhoun, Madison Co. NE 1/4 NE 1/4 Sect. 8 Tp. 1 R. 9, south and east.

**LANIER, Hannah** see **George LITTLE, #31**

**2513. LANIER, Miles**
Feb. 27, 1854, 3 1/4 miles NNE of Bass, Columbia Co. W 1/2 NW 1/4 and W 1/2 SW 1/4 Sect. 18 Tp. 4 R. 17, south and east. Patent delivered April 2, 1858.

**2514. LANIER, Miles**
Feb. 27, 1854, 2 miles S by W of Bass, Columbia Co. E 1/2 NE 1/4 Sect. 13 Tp. 4 R. 16, south and east. Patent delivered April 2, 1858.

**348. LAPSLEY, John W.**
Mar. 16, 1846, c. 3 1/2 miles NE Ocala, Marion Co. SW 1/4 Sect. 34 Tp. 16 R. 22, south and east. On the back of receipt: "Please deliver the patent for the within described land to Messer. **PAYNE** and child. **J. W. LAPSLEY**." Patent delivered May 15, 1852.

**341. LAPSLEY, John W.**
Mar. 16, 1854, 4 miles W Belleview, Marion Co. SE 1/4 Sect. 33 Tp. 16 R. 22, south and east.

**343. LAPSLEY, John W.**
Mar. 16, 1854, 1 1/4 miles NNE Shady, Marion Co. Lot No. 1 NW 1/4 Sect. 18 Tp. 16 R. 22, north and east.

**6648. LASTINGER, Andrew**
Jan. 24, 1837, 2 miles N by E Centerville, Leon Co. NW 1/4 SW 1/4 Sect. 7 Tp. 2 R. 2, north and east.

**6188. LASTINGER, David**
Dec. 12, 1836, 3 miles NNW Monticello, Jefferson Co. Lot No. 1 Fractional Sect. 14 Tp. 2 R. 4, north and east.

**6189. LASTINGER, David**
Dec. 12, 1836, 3 miles N by W Monticello, Jefferson Co. Lot No. 1 Fractional Sect. 11 Tp. 2 R. 4, north and east. See **Francis TOWLE**

**2750. LASTINGER, John**
Feb. 19, 1829, at Monticello, Jefferson Co. E 1/2 SE 1/4 Sect. 24 Tp. 2 R. 4, north and east.

**6168. LASTINGER, William**
Dec. 9, 1836, 3 miles E by N Alma, Jefferson Co. SW 1/4 NE 1/4 Sect. 29 Tp. 3 R. 5, north and east.

**1354. LASTINGER, William**
May 11, 1827, 5 1/2 miles N Monticello, Jefferson Co. E 1/2 SW 1/4 Sect. 29 Tp. 3 R. 5, north and east.

**6187. LASTINGER, William**
Dec. 12, 1836, 3 miles NE Alma, Jefferson Co. SW 1/4 NW 1/4 and SW 1/4 SW 1/4 Sect. 29 Tp. 3 R. 5, north and east.

**1778. LAVINUS, John W.**
June 5, 1827, 3 miles NE Lake Jackson Station, Leon Co. Lot No. 1 Fractional Sect. 28 Tp. 2 R. 1, north and west.

**1855. LAVINUS, John W.**
June 5, 1827, 1/2 mile N by E Lake Jackson Station, Leon Co. Lot No. 1 Fractional Sect. 32 Tp. 2 R. 1, north and west. Transferred to **Rowe HARRIS**, June 7, 1827. **G. W. WARD**, Reg.

**2573. LAVINUS, John W.**
Dec. 19, 1828, c. 1 1/2 miles N Lake Jackson, Leon Co. Lot No. 3 Sect. 29 Tp. 2 R. 1, north and west.

**2817. LAVINUS, John W.**
May 7, 1829, c. 2 miles NE Lake Jackson, Leon Co. Lot No. 5 Sect. 29 Tp. 2 R. 1, north and west.

**LAW, Br---** and **LAW** see **Jas. B. WEBB**

**2636. LAW, Dan'l M.**
Jan. 19, 1829, 1/4 mile E Eucheanna, Walton Co. W 1/2 NE 1/4 Sect. 34 Tp. 2 R. 18, north and west. ( Possible **Dan'l McLAIN**?)

**6850. LAW, Joseph E.**

Mar. 7, 1837, 1 mile E Jasper, Hamilton Co. SE 1/4 NE 1/4 and NW 1/4 SE 1/4 Sect. 4 Tp. 1 R. 14, north and east.

**6348. LAYTON, Willis**
Dec. 30, 1836, 1/2 mile N Stringer, Leon Co. SW 1/4 NE 1/4 Sect. 21 Tp. 3 R. 3, north and east.

**4631. LEA, John William**
Oct. 22, 1834, 3 miles NNW of Bradfordville, Leon Co. W 1/2 NW 1/4 Sect. 8 Tp. 2 R. 1, north and east.

**4916. LEA, John William**
Mar. 31, 1835, 3 1/2 miles NW of Perkins, Leon Co. E 1/2 NW 1/4 Sect. 8 Tp. 2 R. 1, north and east.

**8183. LEA, John William**
Dec. 26, 1829, 4 miles NW Bradfordville, Leon Co. W 1/2 NE 1/4 Sect. 7 Tp. 2 R. 1, north and east.

**7356. LEA, John William**
Feb. 27, 1838, 2 1/2 miles N by E Dills; Jefferson Co. W 1/2 NE 1/4 Sect. 1 Tp. 2 R. 5, north and east.

**7357. LEA, John William**
Feb. 27, 1838, 1/4 mile NNW Dills, Jefferson Co. W 1/2 SE 1/4 Sect. 36 Tp. 3 R. 5, north and east.

**7283. LEA, John William**
Jan. 31, 1838, 3/4 mile N by W Dills, Jefferson Co. E 1/2 SW 1/4 Sect. 36 Tp. 3 R. 5, north and east.

**7284. LEA, John William**
Jan. 31, 1838, 3/4 mile W Dills, Jefferson Co. E 1/2 NW 1/4 Sect. 1 Tp. 2 R. 5, north and east.

**7359. LEA, John William**
Feb. 27, 1838, at Dills, Jefferson Co. E 1/2 NE 1/4 Sect. 1 Tp. 2 R. 5, north and east.

**3240. LEA, John William**
Feb. 1, 1830, 3 miles NW Bradfordville, Leon Co. W 1/2 NE 1/4 Sect. 8 Tp. 2 R. 1, north and east. "This Certificate was paid for in scrip paid to **Alex MACOMB**, survivor of **Edgar MACOMB**, issued May 30, 1829.

**5339. LEA, John William**
Dec. 10, 1835, 3 miles N by W of Bradfordville, Leon Co. W 1/2 NW 1/4 Sect. 9 Tp. 2 R. 1, north and east.

**5827. LEA, John Wnss.**
Sept. 5, 1836, 2 1/2 miles W of Cherrylake (town), Madison Co. E 1/2 SE 1/4 Sect. 12 Tp. 2 R. 8, north and east.

**4527. LEALMAN, Eliza B.**
Mar. 6, 1857, 2 1/2 miles NNE Padlock, Suwannee Co. NW 1/4 NE 1/4 Sect. 9 Tp. 3 R. 14, south and east.

**5516. LeBARON, Charles**
Mar. 8, 1836, 2 miles W of Bohemia, Escambia Co. Fractional Sect. 47 Tp. 1 R. 30, south and west.

**5520. LeBARON, Charles**
Mar. 10, 1836, 6 miles SE of Pensacola, Escambia Co. Lot No. 10 Fractional Tp. 3 R. 29, south and west.

**9506. Le BARRON, Charles**
Oct. 13, 1841, 3 1/2 miles NNE Olive, Escambia Co. W 1/2 SW 1/4 Sect. 13 Tp. 2 R. 30, south and west.

**5575. LEDWITH, Michael**
April 5, 1836, 5 1/2 miles SSE Centerville, Leon Co. NE 1/4 SW 1/4 Sect. 26 Tp. 2 R. 2, north and east.

**582. LEDWITH, Michael**
July 29, 1847, near Bradenton, Manatee, Co. NE 1/4 SW 1/4 Sect. 25 Tp. 34 R. 17, south and east.

**6375. LEE, Charles**
Jan. 2, 1837, at Hamburg, Madison Co. NW 1/4 SE 1/4 Sect. 14 Tp. 2 R. 8, north and east.

**7241. LEE, Charles**
Jan. 16, 1838, 1/4 mile NE Hamburg, Madison Co. NE 1/4 NW 1/4 Sect. 14 Tp. 2 R. 8, north and east.

**8045. LEE, Diley**
Aug. 17, 1839, 3 miles SE Facil, Hamilton Co. SW 1/4 SE 1/4 Sect. 36 Tp. 1 R. 15, south and east.

**4505. LEE, Jesse**
Jan. 7, 1834, 1 3/4 miles NE by E Jasper, Hamilton Co. W 1/2 NW 1/4 Sect. 17 Tp. 1 R. 14, north and east.

**4747. LEE, Jim**
Dec. 27, 1834, 3/4 miles S of Jasper, Hamilton Co. NE 1/4 SW 1/4 Sect. 8 Tp. 1 R. 14, north and east.

**4138. LEE, John**
Feb. 19, 1832, at Facil, Hamilton Co. NE 1/4 Sect. 27 Tp. 1 R. 15, south and east.

**8046. LEE, John**
Aug. 17, 1839, 2 miles SE Genoa, Hamilton Co. SE 1/4 SW 1/4 Sect. 15 Tp. 1 R. 15, south and east.

**8882. LEE, John**
Jan. 24, 1846, 1 1/2 miles SE Genoa, Hamilton Co. NE 1/4 SW 1/4 Sect. 15 Tp. 1 R. 15, south and east.

**LEE, John** see **William LEE, #4506.**

**3197. LEE, John Williams**
( No date) 4 miles NW Bradfordville, Leon Co. E 1/2 NE 1/4 Sect. 7 Tp. 2 R. 1, north and east.

**3835. LEE, William**
Jan. 7, 1831, 3 miles SE Centerville, Leon Co. W 1/2 NW 1/4 Sect. 33 Tp. 2 R. 2, north and east.

**4506. LEE, William**
(and **John LEE**) Jan. 7, 1834, 1/4 mile NNE Suwannee, Suwannee Co. NE 1/4 Sect. 18 Tp. 1 R. 14, north and east.

**5235. LEE, William**
Oct. 27, 1835, 2 1/2 miles SE by E Centerville, Leon Co. SE 1/4 NE 1/4 Sect. 32 Tp. 2 R. 2, north and east.

**8918. LEIGH, James (Jr.)**
Mar. 5, 1846, 1 1/4 miles SSE Jennings, Hamilton Co. SE 1/4 NW 1/4 Sect. 7 Tp. 2 R. 13, north and east.

**3486. LEMDY(?), James**
Apr. 21, 1830, 3 miles NE Wadesboro, Leon Co. E 1/2 NW 1/4 Sect. 28 Tp. 2 R. 3, north and east.

**5358. LEMMON, James**
Dec. 22, 1835, 2 miles S of Chaires, Leon Co. NE 1/4 NE 1/4 Sect. 12 Tp. 1 R. 2, south and east.

**6148. LEONARD, Alexander H.**
( Guardian for **Claude KING**) Sept. 13, 1887, 2 miles Kingsford, Polk Co. SE 1/4 NE 1/4 and SW 1/4 NE 1/4; also NW 1/4 SE 1/4 and NE 1/4 SW 1/4 Sect. 35 Tp. 29S R. 24E.

**7244. LESLY, Leroy G.**
Jan. 16, 1838, 3 miles SW by W Cherrylake, Madison Co. W 1/2 SE 1/4 Sect. 19 Tp. 2 R. 9, north and east.

**3494. LESTER, John**
April 22, 1830, at Bradfordville, Leon Co. E 1/2 SW 1/4 Sect. 22 Tp. 2 R. 1, north and east.

**3803. LESTER, William**
Dec. 16, 1830, 4 miles WSW Roeville, Santa Rosa Co. SE 1/4 Sect. 28 Tp. 2 R. 1, north and east.

**3874. LESTER, William**
Feb. 7, 1831, at Bradfordville, Leon Co. E 1/2 NE 1/4 Sect. 21 Tp. 2 R. 1, north and east.

**3945. LESTER, William**
Apr. 11, 1831, at Bradfordville, Leon Co. E 1/2 NW 1/4 Sect. 22 Tp. 2 R. 1, north and east.

**3946. LESTER, William**
Apr. 11, 1831, 1/2 mile S Bradfordville, Leon Co. E 1/2 NW 1/4 Sect. 27 Tp. 2 R. 1, north and east.

**5508. LESTER, William**
Mar. 3, 1836, 5 3/4 miles N by E of Tallahassee, Leon Co. W 1/2 SE 1/4 Sect. 20 Tp. 2 R. 1, north and west.

**7818. LESTER, William**
Jan. 15, 1839, 6 miles W Bradfordville, Leon Co. SW 1/4 NE 1/4 Sect. 22 Tp. 2 R. 1, north and east.

**3919. LESTER, Witwirm**
March 23, 1831, at Bradfordville, Leon Co. W 1/2 SE 1/4 Sect. 22 Tp. 2 R. 1, north and east.

**527. LEVER, William**
May 20, 1831, 3 miles N Cherrylake, Madison Co. E 1/2 NE 1/4 Sect. 32 Tp. 3 R. 9, north and east.

**528. LEVER, William**
May 20, 1831, at Lovett, Madison Co. W 1/2 NW 1/4 Sect. 33 Tp. 3 R. 9, north and east.

**2444. LEVINUS, Jno. W.**
July 21, 1828, c. 2 miles N Lake Jackson Station, Leon Co. Lot No. 6 Sect. 29 Tp. 2 R. 1, north and west.

**3102. LEVY, Alfred**
Nov. 2, 1829, 2 1/2 miles W Tallahassee, Leon Co. W 1/2 NE 1/4 Sect. 4 Tp. 1 R. 1, south and west.

**4187. LEVY, Alfred**
July 16, 1832, 2 1/2 miles E of Tallahassee, Leon Co. NE 1/4 SW 1/4 Sect. 4 Tp. 1 R. 1, south and west.

**5801. LEVY, Alfred**
Aug. 18, 1836, 4 1/2 miles W of Tallahassee, Leon Co. SW 1/4 SE 1/4 Sect. 5 Tp. 1 R. 1, south and west.

**5831. LEVY, Alfred**
Sept. 6, 1836, 5 1/4 miles W of Tallahassee, Leon Co. NW 1/4 SE 1/4 Sect. 5 Tp. 1 R. 1, south and west.

**5848. LEVY, Almon**
Sept. 14, 1836, at Midway, Gadsden Co. NW 1/4 NE 1/4 Sect. 8 Tp. 1 R. 1, south and west.

**5121. LEVY, Parker**
July 31, 1835, 3 miles SW of Tallahassee, Leon Co. NW 1/4 SW 1/4 Sect. 9 Tp. 1 R. 1, south and west.

**7439. LEVY, Parker**
April 5, 1838, 4 1/4 miles W by S Tallahassee, Leon Co. NE 1/4 SE 1/4 Sect. 8 Tp. 1 R. 1, south and west.

**7671. LEVY, Robert**
Oct. 13, 1838, 3 3/4 miles W by S Tallahassee, Leon Co. NE 1/4 SE 1/4 Sect. 5 Tp. 1 R. 1, south and west.

**6701. LEWIS, John**
Jan. 30, 1837, c. 3 miles S Marina, Hamilton Co. Lot No. 6 Fractional Sect. 17 Tp. 1 R. 14, south and east.

**6702. LEWIS, John**
Jan. 10, 1837, c. 4 miles S Marina, Suwannee Co. Lot No. 1 Fractional Sect. 20 Tp. 1 R. 14, south and east.

**6760. LEWIS, John**
Feb. 7, 1837, 3 miles WSW Jasper, Hamilton Co. W 1/2 NW 1/4 and W 1/2 SW 1/4 Sect. 12 Tp. 1 R. 13, south and east.

**7895. LEWIS, John**
Feb. 27, 1839, 6 miles W by N Jamieson, Gadsden Co. SE 1/4 NE 1/4 Sect. 6 Tp. 3 R. 3, north and west. Transferred to **Dixon JONES** Aug. 6, 1839. Transferred to **James D. DICKENS** Nov. 15, 1839. Transferred to **E. J. THOMAS** Jan. 29, 1840.

**6816. LEWIS, John**
Mar. 1, 1837, c. 3 miles S Marina, Hamilton Co. Lot No. 1 Fractional Sect. 17 Tp. 1 R. 14, south and east.

**6848. LEWIS, John**
Mar. 7, 1837, c. 3 miles S Marina, Hamilton Co. Lot No. 3 Fractional Sect. 17 Tp. 1 R. 14, south and east.

**6927. LEWIS, John**
Mar. 20, 1837, c. 2 miles S Marina, Hamilton Co. Lot No. 7 Fractional Sect. 7 Tp. 1 R. 14, south and east.

**6973. LEWIS, John**
Apr. 5, 1837, 5 miles W Marina, Hamilton Co. SW 1/4 W 1/2 SE 1/4 Sect. 32 Tp. 1 R. 13, north and east.

**6993. LEWIS, John**
Apr. 13, 1837, 5 miles W Marina, Hamilton Co. E 1/2 SE 1/4 Sect. 32 Tp. 1 R. 13, north and east.

**6994. LEWIS, John**
Apr. 13, 1837, c. 2 miles S Marina, Hamilton Co. Lot No. 6 Fractional Sect. 7 Tp. 1 R. 14, south and east.

**2239. LEWIS, Jno. P.**
(of Fla.) Jan. 29, 1828, 5 miles E Alford, Jackson Co. E 1/2 SW 1/4 Sect. 35 Tp. 4 R. 11, north and west.

**7805. LEWIS, John W.**
(and **Isaac L. BATTLE**) Jan. 9, 1839, 4 1/2 miles NNW Greenwood, Jackson Co. E 1/2 NE 1/4 Sect. 28 Tp. 6 R. 10, north and west.

**21. LEWIS, Joseph**
Oct. 20, 1826, just north Cottondale, Jackson Co. SW 1/4 Sect. 14 Tp. 5 R. 11, north and west. Rec'd $200.35 for 160.36 acres. **R. K. CALL**, Receiver. On reverse side: Above transferred to **Joseph RUSS** Oct. 20, 1826. (Signed) **Joseph LEWIS**.

**2134. LEWIS, Romeo**
(of Fla.) Dec. 11, 1827, 4 miles E Myrick, Madison Co. E 1/2 SE 1/4 Sect. 1 Tp. 1 R. 7, south and east.

**2135. LEWIS, Romeo**
(of Fla.) Dec. 11, 1827, 6 miles E by S Myrick, Madison Co. E 1/2 NE 1/4 Sect. 12 Tp. 1 R. 7, south and east.

**2149. LEWIS, Romeo**
Dec. 12, 1827, at Moseley Hall, Madison Co. E 1/2 NE 1/4 Sect. 29 Tp. 1 R. 8, south and east.

**2150. LEWIS, Romeo**
Dec. 12, 1827, 3 1/2 miles NNE Moseley Hall, Madison Co. E 1/2 SE 1/4 Sect. 6 Tp. 1 R. 8, south and east.

**2151. LEWIS, Romeo**
Dec. 12, 1827, 3 miles N Moseley Hall, Madison Co. E 1/2 NE 1/4 Sect. 7 Tp. 1 R. 8, south and east.

**2152. LEWIS, Romeo**
Dec. 12, 1827, 4 miles NNW Moseley Hall, Madison Co. W 1/2 NE 1/4 Sect. 7 Tp. 1 R. 8, south and east.

**2153. LEWIS, Romeo**
Dec. 12, 1827, 4 miles NNW Moseley Hall, Madison Co. W 1/2 NW 1/4 Sect. 7 Tp. 1 R. 8, south and east.

**2154. LEWIS, Romeo**
Dec. 12, 1827, 5 miles NNW Moseley Hall, Madison Co. W 1/2 SE 1/4 Sect. 6 Tp. 1 R. 8, south and east.

**2155. LEWIS, Romeo**
Dec. 12, 1827, 5 miles NNW Moseley

Hall, Madison Co. W 1/2 SW 1/4 Sect. 6 Tp. 1 R. 8, south and east.

**2156. LEWIS, Romeo**
Dec. 12, 1827, 3 miles NW Moseley Hall, Madison Co. E 1/2 SW 1/4 Sect. 18 Tp. 1 R. 8, south and east.

**2157. LEWIS, Romeo**
(of Fla.) Dec. 12, 1827, 3 miles NW Moseley Hall, Madison Co. W 1/2 SE 1/4 Sect. 18 Tp. 1 R. 8, south and east.

**2158. LEWIS, Romeo**
(of Fla.) Dec. 12, 1827, 5 miles WSW Madison, Madison Co. W 1/2 NW 1/4 Sect. 1 Tp. 1 R. 8, south and east. Transferred to **J. G. SEARCY**, Feb. 23, 1827(?)

**2618. LEWIS, Romeo**
Jan. 13, 1829, 2 1/2 miles ENE Sneads, Jackson Co. Lot No. 4 Sect. 30 Tp. 4 R. 6, north and west.

**2619. LEWIS, Romeo**
Jan. 13, 1829, 1 mile W of Chattahoochee, Jackson Co. Lot No. 1 Sect. 31 Tp. 4 R. 6, north and west.

**2620. LEWIS, Romeo**
Jan. 13, 1829, 1 mile W Chattahoochee, Jackson Co. Lot No. 2 Sect. 31 Tp. 4 R. 6, north and west.

**2664. LEWIS, Romeo**
Jan. 26, 1829, 4 miles NE Moseley Hall, Madison Co. W 1/2 SE 1/4 Sect. 20 Tp. 1 R. 8, south and east.

**2665. LEWIS, Romeo**
Jan. 26, 1829, 3 1/2 miles NE Moseley Hall, Madison Co. W 1/2 SW 1/4 Sect. 21 Tp. 1 R. 8, south and east.

**2666. LEWIS, Romeo**
Jan. 26, 1829, 4 miles NNE Moseley Hall, Madison Co. W 1/2 NE 1/4 Sect. 29 Tp. 1 R. 8, south and east.

**2671. LEWIS, Romeo**
Jan. 26, 1829, 1/2 mile NE Steaphead, Gadsden Co. E 1/2 NE 1/4 Sect. 17 Tp. 2 R. 6, north and west. Transferred May 21, 1829, to **J. F. I. WILSON**.

**2679. LEWIS, Romeo**
Jan. 27, 1829, 2 miles NW Chattahoochee, Jackson Co. Lot No. 2 Sect. 30 Tp. 4 R. 6, north and west.

**2680. LEWIS, Romeo**
Jan. 27, 1829, c. 1 mile W Chattahoochee, Jackson Co. Lot No. 4 Sect. 31 Tp. 4 R. 6, north and west.

**2681. LEWIS, Romeo**
Jan. 23, 1829, 2 miles WNW Sawdust, Gadsden Co. E 1/2 NE 1/4 Sect. 19 Tp. 2 R. 4, north and west. Assigned to **H. W. PATTESON** Dec. 7, 1829, and to **Jesse YON**, Dec. 17, 1836.

**3000. LEWIS, Romeo**
Aug. 29, 1829, 5 miles SW El Destino, Leon Co. E 1/2 SW 1/4 Sect. 21 Tp. 1 R. 2, south and east.

**3284. LEWIS, Romeo**
Feb. 10, 1830, 3 miles N Lamont, Jefferson Co. W 1/2 SE 1/4 Sect. 11 Tp. 1 R. 5, south and east.

**3285. LEWIS, Romeo**
Feb. 10, 1830, 3 miles NNE Lamont, Jefferson Co. E 1/2 SE 1/4 Sect. 11 Tp. 1 R. 5, south and east.

**4624. LEWIS, Romeo**
Oct. 14, 1834, 1/2 mile N of Corey, Leon Co. NE 1/4 SW 1/4 Sect. 20 Tp. 1 R. 2, south and east.

**4625. LEWIS, Romeo**
Oct. 14, 1834, 1/2 mile N by E of Corey, Leon Co. NW 1/4 SE 1/4 Sect. 20 Tp. 1 R. 2, south and east.

**6623. LEWIS, Romeo**
(and **Richard C. ALLEN**) Jan. 21, 1837, 2 miles SE Sadler, Taylor Co. NE 1/4 W 1/2 SE 1/4 Sect. 1 Tp. 7 R. 7, south and east.

**6624. LEWIS, Romeo**
(and **Richard C. ALLEN**) Jan. 21, 1837, 5 miles SE by E Greenville, Madison Co. NW 1/4 W 1/2 NE 1/4 Sect. 6 Tp. 1 R. 8, south and east.

**6625. LEWIS, Romeo**
(and **Richard C. ALLEN**) Jan. 12, 1837, 4 miles NW Moseley Hall, Madison Co. S 1/2 Sect. 7 Tp. 1 R. 8, south and east.

**6626. LEWIS, Romeo**
(and **Richard C. ALLEN**) Jan. 21, 1837, 4 miles NNW Moseley Hall, Madison Co. W 1/2 NE 1/4 Sect. 12 Tp. 1 R. 7, south and east.

**6627. LEWIS, Romeo**
(and **Richard C. ALLEN**) Jan. 21, 1837, 3 1/2 miles NW Moseley Hall, Madison Co. E 1/2 SE 1/4 Sect. 12 Tp. 1 R. 7, south and east.

**2275. LEWIS, Seth P.**
Feb. 26, 1828, 3 miles E Alford, Jackson Co. W 1/2 NW 1/4 Sect. 4

Tp. 3 R. 11, north and west.
**3106. LEWIS, Seth P.**
Nov. 3, 1829, 1/4 mile S Norum, Washington Co. W 1/2 NE 1/4 Sect. 18 Tp. 2 R. 15, north and west.
**LEWIS, Wiley see Reuben CLOUD**
**182. LEWIS, William**
Dec. 29, 1826, 3 miles S of Graceville, Jackson Co. W 1/2 SE 1/4 Sect. 13 Tp. 6 R. 12, north and west.
**4936. LING, Daniel T.**
(and **E. BLACK**) April 13, 1835, 3 miles SE Stringer, Jefferson Co. W 1/2 SW 1/4 Sect. 32 Tp. 5 R. 4, north and east.
**6248. LINGO, Daniel T.**
Dec. 19, 1836, 3 miles NW Alma, Leon Co. NW 1/4 Sect. 29 Tp. 3 R. 4, north and east.
**6249. LINGO, Daniel T.**
Dec. 19, 1836, 4 miles WNW Alma, Leon Co. E 1/2 NE 1/4 Sect. 30 Tp. 3 R. 4, north and east.
**6302. LINGO, Daniel T.**
Dec. 24, 1836, 3 miles WNW Alma, Jefferson Co. W 1/2 NW 1/4 Sect. 28 Tp. 3 R. 4, north and east.
**6465. LINGO, Daniel T.**
Jan. 9, 1837, 3 miles WNW Alma, Jefferson Co. W 1/2 NW 1/4 Sect. 8 Tp. 2 R. 5, north and east.
**6466. LINGO, Daniel T.**
Jan. 9, 1837, 5 miles W by N Alma, Jefferson Co. W 1/2 NE 1/4 Sect. 30 Tp. 3 R. 4, north and east.
**6382. LINGO, Daniel T.**
Jan. 3, 1837, 2 1/2 miles NW Alma, Jefferson Co. E 1/2 NE 1/4 Sect. 29 Tp. 3 R. 4, north and east.
**8148. LINGO, Daniel T.**
Nov. 19, 1839, 1 mile E Copeland, Jefferson Co. SW 1/4 SE 1/4 Sect. 33 Tp. 3 R. 4, north and east.
**7708. LINTON, Hamden**
Nov. 16, 1838, 1 1/2 miles SE Champaign, Madison Co. W 1/2 SE 1/4 Sect. 25 Tp. 1 R. 8, north and east.
**8247. LINTON, Hamden S.**
Mar. 3, 1840, 1/4 mile E Greenville, Madison Co. NW 1/4 W 1/2 NE 1/4 Sect. 20 Tp. 1 R. 7, north and east.
**8277. LINTON, Hampden S.**
Mar. 31, 1840, 4 miles SSE Greenville, Madison Co. W 1/2 NW 1/4 Sect. 26 Tp. 1 R. 7, north and east.
**8278. LINTON, Hampden S.**
Mar. 31, 1840, 1/2 mile SW Greenville, Madison Co. E 1/2 SE 1/4 Sect. 20 Tp. 1 R. 7, north and east.
**5972. LINTON, Thomas J.**
Nov. 5, 1836, 1/4 mile E of Spray, Madison Co. SE 1/4 Sect. 23 Tp. 1 R. 7, north and east.
**5973. LINTON, Thomas J.**
Nov. 5, 1836, 2 1/4 miles E of Greenville, Madison Co. E 1/2 SW 1/4 Sect. 24 Tp. 1 R. 7, north and east.
**6023. LINTON, Thomas J.**
Nov. 15, 1836, 5 miles ESE Greenville, Madison Co. W 1/2 NE 1/4 Sect. 30 Tp. 1 R. 8, north and east.
**6103. LINTON, Thomas J.**
Nov. 29, 1836, 4 1/2 miles E Greenville, Madison Co. W 1/2 Sect. 20 Tp. 1 R. 8, north and east.
**6104. LINTON, Thomas J.**
Nov. 29, 1836, 4 miles E by S Greenville, Madison Co. NE 1/4 E 1/2 SE 1/4 Sect. 19 Tp. 1 R. 8, north and east.
**6105. LINTON, Thomas J.**
Nov. 29, 1836, 3 1/2 miles E Greenville, Madison Co. E 1/2 SE 1/4 Sect. 13 Tp. 1 R. 7, north and east.
**6013. LINTON, Thomas J.**
Nov. 15, 1836, 3 miles NE Greenville, Madison Co. SE 1/4 Sect. 10 Tp. 1 R. 7, north and east.
**6014. LINTON, Thomas J.**
Nov. 15, 1836, 3 miles E Greenville, Madison Co. E 1/2 NE 1/4 Sect. 24 Tp. 1 R. 7, north and east.
**6015. LINTON, Thomas J.**
Nov. 15, 1836, 3 miles ESE Greenville, Madison Co. E 1/2 NW 1/4 and W 1/2 NE 1/4 Sect. 25 Tp. 1 R. 7, north and east.
**6016. LINTON, Thomas J.**
Nov. 15, 1836, 2 1/2 miles E Greenville, Madison Co. E 1/2 NE 1/4 Sect. 26 Tp. 1 R. 7, north and east.
**6020. LINTON, Thomas J.**
Nov. 15, 1836, 3 1/4 miles E Greenville, Madison Co. NW 1/4 W 1/2 SW 1/4 Sect. 18 Tp. 1 R. 8, north and east.
**6021. LINTON, Thomas J.**
Nov. 15, 1836, 3 1/4 miles E Greenville, Madison Co. NW 1/4 Sect. 19

Tp. 1 R. 8, north and east.
**6022. LINTON, Thomas J.**
Nov. 15, 1836, 3 1/2 miles E by S Greenville, Madison Co. E 1/2 SW 1/4 and W 1/2 SE 1/4 Sect. 19 Tp. 1 R. 8, north and east.
**7127. LINTON, Thomas J.**
Dec. 6, 1837, 1/4 mile E Spray, Madison Co. NE 1/4 Sect. 10 Tp. 1 R. 7, north and east.
**7709. LINTON, Thomas J.**
Nov. 16, 1838, 3 1/2 miles SSE Hamburg, Madison Co. E 1/2 SW 1/4 and NE 1/4 SE 1/4 Sect. 19 Tp. 1 R. 9, north and east.
**170. LIPPERER (ZIPPERER ?), Solomon**
Aug. 15, 1845, 5 miles N Falmouth, Suwannee Co. NW 1/4 SE 1/4 Sect. 2 Tp. 1 R. 12, south and east. Patent delivered Aug. 15, 1856.
**4491. LIPSCOMB, James T.**
Dec. 26, 1833, 3 1/2 miles W by N Tallahassee, Leon Co. SW 1/4 NE 1/4 Sect. 33 Tp. 1 R. 1, north and west.
**7065. LIPSCOMB, James Thornton**
Oct. 23, 1837, 4 miles SW Norfleet, Leon Co. NW 1/4 SW 1/4 Sect. 4 Tp. 1 R. 1, south and west.
**7418. LIPSCOMB, John**
Mar. 22, 1838, 1 mile SSW Moseley Hall, Madison Co. E 1/2 NW 1/4 and W 1/2 SE 1/4 Sect. 32 Tp. 1 R. 8, south and east.
**7419. LIPSCOMB, John**
Mar. 22, 1838, 1 3/4 miles SSW Moseley Hall, Madison Co. SW 1/4 Sect. 32 Tp. 1 R. 9, south and east.
**8203. LIPSCOMB, John**
Jan. 4, 1840, at Moseley Hall, Madison Co. W 1/2 SW 1/4 Sect. 29 Tp. 1 R. 8, south and east.
**8665. LIPSCOMB, John**
Mar. 18, 1844, 2 1/2 miles S by W Ellaville, Madison Co. Lots No. 1 and 4 Sect. 34 Tp. 1 R. 11, south and east.
**8667. LIPSCOMB, John**
Mar. 18, 1844, 1 1/4 miles SSW Ellaville, Madison Co. E 1/2 SE 1/4 Sect. 27 Tp. 1 R. 11, south and east.
**8668. LIPSCOMB, John**
Mar. 18, 1844, 1 1/2 miles SSW Ellaville, Madison Co. N 1/2 Lots No. 2 and 3 Sect. 34 Tp. 1 R. 11, south and east.
**8876. LIPSCOMB, John**
Jan. 17, 1846, 3 miles NNE Moseley Hall, Madison Co. W 1/2 SW 1/4 Sect. 18 Tp. 1 R. 8, south and east.
**4313. LIPSCOMB, John**
April 8, 1856, 3 miles W Dickert, Suwannee Co. S 1/2 NE 1/4 and SE 1/4 NW 1/4 Sect. 10 Tp. 2 R. 12, south and east.
**4314. LIPSCOMB, John**
April 18, 1856, 3 1/4 miles W Dickert, Suwannee Co. N 1/2 NE 1/4 and NE 1/4 NW 1/4 Sect. 10 Tp. 2 R. 12, south and east.
**31. LITTLE, George**
Nov. 2, 1826, near Quincy, Gadsden Co. SW 1/4 Sect. 20 Tp. 2 R. 2, north and west. Transferred same day to **Hannah LANIER.**
**3249. LITTLE, George**
Feb. 4, 1830, 1 1/2 miles S Florence, Gadsden Co. E 1/2 SW 1/4 Sect. 11 Tp. 2 R. 3, north and west.
**284. LITTLE, John**
Jan. 1, 1827, 1 mile S of Cory, Gadsden Co. E 1/2 NW 1/4 Sect. 12 Tp. 2 r. 3, north and west.
**6475. LITTLE, John**
(SIC)Jan. 17, 1837, 1 mile SSE Florence, Gadsden Co. NW 1/4 NE 1/4 Sect. 12 Tp. 2 R. 3, north and west.
**2077. LITTLE, Thomas**
Oct. 11, 1827, 5 miles SSE Florence, Gadsden Co. W 1/2 SW 1/4 Sect. 19 Tp. 2 R. 2, north and west.
**417. LITTLETON, Thomas**
(Assignee of **G. R. WILLIAMS**) Nov. 28, 1827, 2 miles N Haywood, Jackson Co. Fractional Sect. 28 Tp. 2 R. 7, north and west.
**441. LITTLETON, Thomas**
Dec. 23, 1828, 3 miles NNW Haywood, Gadsden Co. Lot No. 5 Sect. 29 Tp. 6 R. 7, north and west.
**7255. LITTLETON, Thomas**
Jan. 17, 1838, 4 miles NNW Haywood, Jackson Co. Lot No. 2 Fractional Sect. 19 Tp. 6 R. 7, north and west.
**7257. LITTLETON, Thomas**
Jan. 17, 1838, 4 miles NNW Haywood, Jackson Co. Lot No. 5 Fractional Sect. 19 Tp. 6 R. 7, north and west.
**2826. LIVINGSTON, Susan**

July 21, 1854, 5 miles SE by S Oakton, Alachua Co. SE 1/4 NE 1/4 Sect. 24 Tp. 11 R. 23, south and east. Patent delivered Sept. 28, 1859.

**4633. LIVINGSTON, Thomas**
Oct. 23, 1834, 2 miles SSW of Champaign, Leon Co. NW 1/4 SW 1/4 Sect. 28 Tp. 1 R. 8, north and east.

**4634. LIVINGSTON, Thomas**
Oct. 23, 1834, 1 mile SSW Champaign, Leon Co. SW 1/4 SW 1/4 Sect. 27 Tp. 1 R. 8, north and east.

**4635. LIVINGSTON, Thomas**
Oct. 23, 1834, 3 miles SSW Champaign, Leon Co. W 1/2 SE 1/4 Sect. 33 Tp. 1 R. 8, north and east.

**4636. LIVINGSTON, Thomas**
Oct. 23, 1834, 1 1/4 miles W of Champaign, Leon Co. W 1/2 SE 1/4 Sect. 22 Tp. 1 R. 8, north and east.

**4637. LIVINGSTON, Thomas**
Oct. 23, 1834, 1 mile SSW of Champaign, Leon Co. W 1/2 SE 1/4 Sect. 27 Tp. 1 R. 8, north and east.

**4670. LIVINGSTON, Thomas**
Dec. 3, 1834, 3 1/4 miles SSE of Greenville, Madison Co. S 1/2 Sect. 25 Tp. 1 R. 7, north and east.

**4803. LIVINGSTON, Thomas**
Jan. 21, 1835, at Cherrylake (town), Madison Co. W 1/2 SW 1/4 Sect. 10 Tp. 2 R. 9, north and east.

**4804. LIVINGSTON, Thomas**
Jan. 21, 1835, 1/2 mile N of Cherrylake (town), Madison Co. E 1/2 NW 1/4 Sect. 10 Tp. 2 R. 9, north and east.

**4805. LIVINGSTON, Thomas**
Jan. 21, 1835, 1 1/2 miles SSE Greenville, Madison Co. NE 1/4 Sect. 27 Tp. 1 R. 7, north and east.

**4806. LIVINGSTON, Thomas**
Jan. 21, 1835, 1/2 mile SE of Cherrylake, Madison Co. W 1/2 NE 1/4 Sect. 10 Tp. 2 R. 9, north and east.

**4807. LIVINGSTON, Thomas**
Jan. 21, 1835, 1 1/2 miles S by E of Greenville, Madison Co. SW 1/4 Sect. 27 Tp. 1 R. 7, north and east.

**4808. LIVINGSTON, Thomas**
Jan. 21, 1835, 1 mile S Greenville, Madison Co. SE 1/4 Sect. 28 Tp. 2 R. 7, north and east.

**4809. LIVINGSTON, Thomas**
Jan. 21, 1835, 1 1/4 miles S by E of Greenville, Madison Co. NW 1/4 Sect. 34 Tp. 1 R. 7, north and east.

**6100. LIVINGSTON, Thomas**
Nov. 28, 1836, 1 mile SW Champaign, Madison Co. SW 1/4 Sect. 22 Tp. 1 R. 8, north and east.

**6150. LIVINGSTON, Thomas**
Dec. 5, 1836, c. 4 miles SE by S Westlake, Hamilton Co. Lot No. 5 Fractional Sect. 35 Tp. 1 R. 12, north and east.

**6151. LIVINGSTON, Thomas**
Dec. 5, 1836, 1 mile W Champaign, Madison Co. E 1/2 NW 1/4 Sect. 22 Tp. 1 R. 8, north and east.

**6152. LIVINGSTON, Thomas**
Dec. 5, 1836, 3 miles SW Champaign, Madison Co. E 1/2 SE 1/4 and W 1/2 SE 1/4 Sect. 28 Tp. 1 R. 8, north and east.

**6808. LIVINGSTON, Thomas**
Mar. 1, 1837, 1/2 mile NE Eridu, Madison Co. W 1/2 NE 1/4 and E 1/2 NW 1/4 Sect. 7 Tp. 2 R. 6, south and east.

**6809. LIVINGSTON, Thomas**
Mar. 1, 1837, 1 mile N by E Eridu, Madison Co. N 1/2, E 1/2 SW 1/4 Sect. 6 Tp. 2 R. 6, south and east.

**6810. LIVINGSTON, Thomas**
Mar. 1, 1837, 1 mile N Eridu, Madison Co. W 1/2 SW 1/4 Sect. 6 Tp. 2 R. 6, south and east.

**6982. LIVINGSTON, Thomas**
Apr. 13, 1837, 4 miles W Madison Co. W 1/2 SW 1/4 Sect. 25 Tp. 1 R. 8, north and east.

**7221. LIVINGSTON, Thomas**
Jan. 12, 1838, 1 1/2 miles W Champaign, Madison Co. E 1/2 SE 1/4 Sect. 21 Tp. 1 R. 8, north and east.

**7676. LIVINGSTON, Thomas**
Oct. 18, 1838, 2 miles SW Champaign, Madison Co. NW 1/4 SW 1/4 Sect. 27 Tp. 1 R. 8, north and east.

**7843. LIVINGSTON, Thomas**
Jan. 29, 1839, 2 miles SW Champaign, Madison Co. E 1/2 NE 1/4 Sect. 33 Tp. 1 R. 8, north and east.

**7842. LIVINGSTON, Thomas**
Jan. 29, 1839, 2 miles SSW Champaign, Madison Co. E 1/2 NE 1/4 and E 1/2 SE 1/4 Sect. 28 Tp. 1 R. 8, north and east.

**8258. LIVINGSTON, Thomas**
Mar. 29, 1840, 4 miles E by S Bailey, Madison Co. E 1/2 NW 1/4 Sect. 28 Tp. 1 R. 8, north and east.

**8560. LIVINGSTON, Thomas**
Oct. 22, 1842, 2 miles SW Ellaville, Madison Co. E 1/2 NE 1/4 Sect. 33 Tp. 1 R. 11, south and east.

**3923. LIVINGSTON, T.**
March 24, 1831, 4 miles W Madison, Madison Co. E 1/2 SE 1/4 Sect. 26 Tp. 1 R. 8, north and east.

**3924. LIVINGSTON, T.**
March 16, 1834, 5 miles W Madison, Madison Co. W 1/2 NW 1/4 Sect. 35 Tp. 1 R. 8, north and east.

**4638. LIVINGSTON, William**
Oct. 23, 1834, 1 1/4 miles E of Champaign, Leon Co. SE 1/4 SE 1/4 Sect. 19 Tp. 1 R. 9, north and east.

**4639. LIVINGSTON, William**
Oct. 23, 1834, 2 1/2 miles W of Madison, Madison Co. NE 1/4 NE 1/4 Sect. 30 Tp. 1 R. 9, north and east.

**4642. LIVINGSTON, William**
Oct. 23, 1834, 2 1/2 miles W by N Madison, Madison Co. W 1/2 NW 1/4 Sect. 30 Tp. 1 R. 9, north and east.

**4643. LIVINGSTON, William**
Oct. 23, 1834, 2 3/4 miles W of Madison, Madison Co. E 1/2 SW 1/4 Sect. 30 Tp. 1 R. 9, north and east.

**4985. LOCKEY, Joseph B.**
June 2, 1835, at Dalkeith, Gulf Co. Lot No. 1 Sect. 28 Tp. 5 R. 9, south and west.

**8527. LOEB, Bernard**
Feb. 5, 1842, 1 1/2 miles NNE Monticello, Jefferson Co. S 1/2 SW 1/4 Sect. 21 Tp. 2 R. 5, north and east.

**2885. LOFTIN, Jeremiah**
July 7, 1829, 2 miles SSE Millspring, Jackson Co. W 1/2 SE 1/4 Sect. 20 Tp. 3 R. 7, north and west.

**2886. LOFTIN, Jeremiah**
July 7, 1829, 1 1/2 miles S Millspring, Jackson Co. E 1/2 NE 1/4 Sect. 29 Tp. 3 R. 7, north and west.

**2887. LOFTIN, Jeremiah**
July 7, 1829, 1 1/2 miles S Millspring, Jackson Co. W 1/2 NE 1/4 Sect. 29 Tp. 3 R. 7, north and west.

**553.** See entry 554.

**554. LOFTIN, William M.**
( And **Peter W. GAUTIER, Sr., Wylie P. Clark, John R. W. CLARK, John W. CAMPBELL**, heirs of **JOHN CLARK**, deceased.) Dec. 1, 1834, 1/2 mile W of Panama City, Bay Co. Lot No. 5 Sect. 6 Tp. 4 R. 14, south and west. 86 1/2 acres. Conveyed July 26, 1835, to **A. B. BLACKWELL**, 20 5/8 acres of **W. M. LOFTIN**'s interest, balance later to **WATSON** by **W. M. LOFTIN**, by **BLACKWELL** and **WATSON** to the trustees of the St. Andrews Bay Land Co. **GAUTIER** and **CLARK** interest also conveyed by **GAUTIER** and the heirs of **CLARK** to the St. Andrews Bay Land Co. Labelled "U. S. Receipt for the Allen Pre-emption." and "Pre-emption under the Act of 1826."

**7060. LOFTIN, William M.**
Nov. 10, 1837, 2 1/2 miles NNE Parker, Bay Co. E 1/2 SE 1/4 Sect. 8 Tp. 4 R. 13, south and west.

**5244. LOFTIN, William M.**
Nov. 5, 1835, 5 1/2 miles SE of Smith Creek, Wahulla Co. W 1/2 NW 1/4 Sect. 12 Tp. 4 R. 14, south and west.

**5245. LOFTIN, William M.**
Nov. 5, 1835, 4 1/2 miles SE of Smith Creek, Wakulla Co. W 1/2 SW 1/4 Sect. 13 Tp. 4 R. 14, south and west.

**LOGATREE, Jno** see **Jno. LOTT, #378**

**298. LLOYD, Richard**
Jan. 1, 1827, 3 miles W of Quincy, Gadsden Co. SW 1/4 Sect. 3 Tp. 2 R. 4, north and west.

**3032. LONDAY, Mathew**
Aug. 13, 1827, 12 miles N Miccosukee, Leon Co. E 1/2 NW 1/4 Sect. 4 Tp. 2 R. 3, north and east.

**1202. LONG, Henry**
(DUP) March 12, 1827, 2 1/2 miles E Felkel Post Office, Leon Co. W 1/2 SE 1/4 Sect. 1 Tp. 2 R. 2, north and east.

**2466. LONG, Henry**
Aug. 23, 1828, 3 miles WNW Miccosukee, Leon Co. E 1/2 SE 1/4 Sect. 1 Tp. 2 R. 2, north and east.

**4160. LONG, Henry**
April 9, 1832, 2 miles W of Felkel, Leon Co. E 1/2 SW 1/4 Sect. 1 Tp. 2 R. 2, north and east.

**2040. LONG, James**
Aug. 11, 1853, 3 miles S Taylor, Baker

Co. SE 1/4 SE 1/4 Sect. 20 Tp. 1 R. 20, south and east. Patent delivered May 31, 1869.

**2622. LONG, Reading**
Jan. 4, 1854, 5 1/2 miles ESE Fort White, Suwannee Co. NW 1/4 SE 1/4 Sect. 6 Tp. 7 R. 17, south and east. Patent delivered June 26, 1869.

**1839. LONG, Redding**
April 22, 1853, 2 1/4 miles NW of Traxlen, Alachua Co. NE 1/4 SE 1/4 Sect. 6 Tp. 7 R. 17, south and east.

**1994. LONG, Redding**
July 30, 1853, 4 miles SSE of Fort White, Columbia Co. S 1/2 Lot No. 1 E 1/2 NE 1/4 Sect. 6 Tp. 7 R. 17, south and east.

**7185. LONG, Richard**
Jan. 4, 1838, 2 miles SE Monticello, Jefferson Co. NE 1/4 SE 1/4 and SW 1/4 SE 1/4 Sect. 32 Tp. 1 R. 4, north and east.

**7186. LONG, Richard**
Jan. 4, 1838, 1 1/4 miles W Waukenah, Jefferson Co. NW 1/4 NE 1/4 Sect. 5 Tp. 1 R. 4, south and east.

**3551. LONG, Richard H.**
July 5, 1830, at Fairgrounds Station, Jackson Co. E 1/2 SE 1/4 Sect. 32 Tp. 5 R. 10, north and west.

**3598. LONG, Richard H.**
Aug. 23, 1830, 6 miles N by E Marianna, Jackson Co. W 1/2 NE 1/4 Sect. 11 Tp. 5 R. 10, north and west.

**3599. LONG, Richard H.**
Aug. 23, 1830, 3 miles SW Greenwood, Jackson Co. E 1/2 NW 1/4 Sect. 11 Tp. 5 R. 10, north and west.

**4880. LONG, Richard H.**
Mar. 5, 1835, 2 miles SSW of Greenwood, Jackson Co. E 1/2 SW 1/4 Sect. 2 Tp. 5 R. 10, north and west.

**4881. LONG, Richard H.**
Mar. 5, 1835, 2 1/2 miles SSW of Greenwood, Jackson Co. W 1/2 SE 1/4 Sect. 2 Tp. 5 R. 10, north and west.

**5009. LONG, Richard H.**
June 19, 1835, 2 miles SSW of Greenwood, Jackson Co. W 1/2 SW 1/4 Sect. 2 Tp. 5 R. 10, north and west.

**5222. LONG, Richard H.**
Oct. 15, 1835, 4 miles SW of Greenwood, Jackson Co. E 1/2 SE 1/4 Sect. 3 Tp. 5 R. 10, north and west.

**5276. LONG, Richard H.**
Nov. 20, 1835, 3 1/4 miles S by W of Greenwood, Jackson Co. NW 1/4 SW 1/4 Sect. 12 Tp. 5 R. 10, north and west.

**5427. LONG, Richard H.**
Jan. 29, 1836, 2 1/2 miles SSW of Greenwood, Jackson Co. W 1/2 NW 1/4 Sect. 2 Tp. 5 R. 10, north and west.

**5566. LONG, Richard H.**
(and **James WATSON**) Mar. 31, 1836, 1 mile N Mill Bayou, Bay Co. W 1/2 NE 1/4 and E 1/2 NW 1/4 Sect. 13 Tp. 3 R. 14, south and west.

**5603. LONG, Richard H.**
April 19, 1836, 4 miles SW of Greenwood, Jackson Co. W 1/2 SE 1/4 Sect. 3 Tp. 5 R. 10, north and west.

**5604. LONG, Richard H.**
April 19, 1836, 4 1/2 miles SW of Greenwood, Jackson Co. W 1/2 NW 1/4 Sect. 11 Tp. 5 R. 10, north and west.

**5605. LONG, Richard H.**
April 19, 1836, 2 1/4 miles SW of Greenwood, Jackson Co. E 1/2 NW 1/4 Sect. 2 Tp. 5 R. 10, north and west.

**5608. LONG, Richard H.**
April 20, 1836, 1 1/4 miles E of Fairgrounds, Jackson Co. W 1/2 SW 1/4 Sect. 33 Tp. 5 R. 10, north and west.

**6162. LONG, Richard H.**
Dec. 7, 1836, 1 mile E Panama City, Bay Co. SE 1/4 Sect. 4 Tp. 4 R. 14, south and west.

**6437. LONG, Richard H.**
Jan. 5, 1837, 3 miles NW Marianna, Jackson Co. SW 1/4 NE 1/4 Sect. 32 Tp. 5 R. 10, north and west.

**6585. LONG, Richard H.**
(and **Jesse H. WHITE** and **Jas. WATSON**) Jan. 18, 1837, 1 mile W St. Andrews, Bay Co. Lot No. 1 Fractional Sect. 34 Tp. 3 R. 15, south and west.

**6587. LONG, Richard H.**
(and **Jesse H. White** and **Jas. Watson**) Jan. 18, 1837, c. 1/2 mile NW St. Andrews, Bay Co. Lots No. 1 and 2 Fractional Sect. 26 Tp. 3 R. 15, south and west.

**6622. LONG, Richard H.**
Jan. 21, 1837, 1/4 mile SE Greenwood, Jackson Co. W 1/2 NW 1/4 Sect. 6 Tp. 5 R. 9, north and west.

**6660. LONG, Richard H.**
Jan. 25, 1837, 1/2 mile SE Greenwood, Jackson Co. NE 1/4 NW 1/4 Sect. 6 Tp. 5 R. 9, north and west.

**6827. LONG, Richard H.**
Mar. 2, 1837, 5 miles NE Marianna, Jackson Co. W 1/2 SE 1/4 Sect. 13 Tp. 5 R. 10, north and west.

**6828. LONG, Richard H.**
Mar. 2, 1837, 3/4 mile SE Greenwood, Jackson Co. NW 1/4 NE 1/4 Sect. 6 Tp. 5 R. 9, north and west.

**6586. LONG, Richard H.**
(and Jesse H. WHITE and Jas. WATSON) Jan. 18, 1837, just W St. Andrews, Bay Co. Lot No. 4 Fraction Sect. 35 Tp. 3 R. 15, south and west.

**8790. LONGWORTH, Eliza F.**
July 1, 1845, 1/2 mile W Roy, Liberty Co. NW 1/4 SW 1/4 Sect. 2 Tp. 2 R. 7, north and west.

**8791. LONGWORTH, Eliza F.**
July 1, 1845, 1 3/4 miles SW Roy, Liberty Co. NW 1/4 SW 1/4 Sect. 11 Tp. 2 R. 7, north and west.

**5627. LORIMER, James H. T.**
April 27, 1836, 3 1/4 miles W of Black Creek, Leon Co. E 1/2 SE 1/4 Sect. 8 Tp. 1 R. 2, north and east.

**6282. LOTT, Jesse**
Dec. 23, 1836, 5 miles NE Marianna, Jackson Co. SW 1/4 NE 1/4 Sect. 24 Tp. 5 R. 10, north and west.

**8395. LOTT, Jesse**
Aug. 21, 1840, 4 miles NNE Durham, Calhoun Co. SE 1/4 Sect. 14 Tp. 1 R. 8, north and west.

**378. LOTT, Jno.**
(Assignee of Jno. LOGATHREE) May 3, 1827, 4 miles W Greenwood, Jackson Co. SE 1/4 Sect. 34 Tp. 6 R. 10, north and west.

**6230. LOTT, Luke**
Dec. 16, 1836, 4 miles W Greenwood, Jackson Co. SE 1/4 NE 1/4 Sect. 33 Tp. 6 R. 10, north and west.

**6283. LOTT, Luke**
Dec. 23, 1836, 4 miles W Greenwood, Jackson Co. E 1/2 NW 1/4 and W 1/2 NE 1/4 Sect. 33 Tp. 6 R. 10, north and west.

**7648. LOTT, Luke**
Sept. 20, 1838, 4 3/4 miles N by W Greenwood, Jackson Co. E 1/2 NE 1/4 Sect. 32 Tp. 6 R. 10, north and west.

**7649. LOTT, Luke**
Sept. 20, 1838, 3 3/4 miles N by W Greenwood, Jackson Co. W 1/2 NW 1/4 Sect. 33 Tp. 6 R. 10, north and west.

**8349. LOTT, Luke**
June 18, 1840, 4 miles E Leonard's Siding, Calhoun Co. NE 1/4 Sect. 15 Tp. 1 R. 8, north and west.

**4657. LOTT, Maddison**
Nov. 5, 1834, 3/4 mile E of Hinson, Gadsden Co. NE 1/4 SW 1/4 Sect. 27 Tp. 3 R. 2, north and west.

**58. LOTT, Robert A.**
Nov. 13, 1826, 2 miles N Ellis Post Office, Jackson Co. SW 1/4 Sect. 34 Tp. 6 R. 10, north and west.

**8346. LOTT, Sarah**
June 18, 1840, 3 miles NNE Blountstown, Calhoun Co. SW 1/4 Sect. 14 Tp. 1 R. 8, north and west.

**215. LOVE, Alex.**
Dec. 30, 1826, 2 miles W Quincy, Gadsden Co. SE 1/4 Sect. 4 Tp. 2 R. 4, north and west.

**1823. LOVE, Alex.**
June 5, 1827, 4 miles W Quincy, Gadsden Co. E 1/2 SW 1/4 Sect. 4 Tp. 2 R. 4, north and west.

**4131. LOVE, Archibald**
Feb. 1, 1832, 1 1/2 miles S of Gretna, Gadsden Co. E 1/2 NE 1/4 Sect. 33 Tp. 3 R. 4, north and west.

**287. LOVE, Daniel**
Jan. 1, 1827, 7 miles NW of Quincy, Gadsden Co. NW 1/4 Sect. 36 Tp. 3 R. 4, north and west.

**6066. LOVE, Daniel**
Nov. 21, 1836, 4 miles E Mt. Pleasant, Gadsden Co. W 1/2 SE 1/4 Sect. 23 Tp. 3 R. 4, north and west.

**75. LOVE, John C.**
Nov. 27, 1826, at Greta, Gadsden Co. NE 1/4 Sect. 27 Tp. 3 R. 4, north and west.

**2380. LOVE, John C.**
May 17, 1828, 3 miles W Quincy, Gadsden Co. E 1/2 NE 1/4 Sect. 4 Tp.

2 R. 4, north and west.

**63. LOWE, John Wesley**
Oct. 19, 1844, 3 1/2 miles W by N Falmouth, Suwannee Co. E 1/2 NW 1/4 and NW 1/4 NE 1/4 Sect. 19 Tp. 1 R. 12, south and east.

**8265. LOWRY, James**
Mar. 28, 1840, 1 mile N by W Ellis, Jackson Co. W 1/2 SW 1/4 Sect. 4 Tp. 6 R. 10, north and west.

**8266. LOWRY, James**
Mar. 28, 1840, 1 3/4 miles N by W Ellis, Jackson Co. E 1/2 SE 1/4 Sect. 32 Tp. 7 R. 10, north and west.

**8267. LOWRY, James**
Mar. 28, 1840, 6 miles NNW Malone, Jackson Co. W 1/2 NE 1/4 and W 1/2 SE 1/4 Sect. 21 Tp. 7 R. 10, north and west.

**8268. LOWRY, James**
Mar. 28, 1840, 4 miles NNW Malone, Jackson Co. W 1/2 NW 1/4 and SW 1/4 SW 1/4 Sect. 27 Tp. 7 R. 10, north and west.

**8269. LOWRY, James**
Mar. 28, 1840, 5 3/4 miles W by N Malone, Jackson Co. E 1/2 NW 1/4 and W 1/2 NE 1/4 Sect. 28 Tp. 7 R. 10, north and west.

**8270. LOWRY, James**
Mar. 28, 1840, 4 1/4 miles W Malone, Jackson Co. E 1/2 SE 1/4 and E 1/2 SW 1/4 Sect. 33 Tp. 7 R. 10, north and west.

**8271. LOWRY, James**
Mar. 28, 1840, 4 3/4 miles NNW Malone, Jackson Co. W 1/2 SW 1/4 and W 1/2 SE 1/4 Sect. 28 Tp. 7 R. 10, north and west.

**8272. LOWRY, James**
Mar. 28, 1840, 4 1/2 miles W by N Malone, Jackson Co. NW 1/4 E 1/2 NE 1/4 Sect. 33 Tp. 7 R. 10, north and west.

**8273. LOWRY, James**
Mar. 28, 1840, 3 1/2 miles W Malone, Jackson Co. W 1/2 SW 1/4 Sect. 34 Tp. 7 R. 10, north and west.

**8274. LOWRY, James**
Mar. 28, 1840, 7 1/2 miles W by N Malone, Jackson Co. W 1/2 NW 1/4 Sect. 29 Tp. 7 R. 10, north and west.

**8275. LOWRY, James**
Mar. 28, 1840, 5 miles N by W Ellis, Jackson Co. W 1/2 NW 1/4 Sect. 20 Tp. 7 R. 10, north and west.

**8283. LOWRY, James**
Apr. 14, 1840, 4 1/2 miles N by W Ellis, Jackson Co. SE 1/4 Sect. 30 Tp. 7 R. 10, north and west.

**8284. LOWRY, James**
Apr. 14, 1840, 8 miles W by N Malone, Jackson Co. E 1/2 NE 1/4 and E 1/2 SE 1/4 Sect. 19 Tp. 7 R. 10, north and west.

**8285. LOWRY, James**
April 14, 1840, 7 miles NNW Malone, Jackson Co. E 1/2 NE 1/4 Sect. 30 Tp. 7 R. 10, north and west.

**8286. LOWRY, James**
April 14, 1840, 7 1/4 miles W by N Malone, Jackson Co. W 1/2 NE 1/4 Sect. 31 Tp. 7 R. 10, north and west.

**2734. LUCAR, Charles**
Feb. 14, 1829, 3 miles E Centerville, Leon Co. E 1/2 NE 1/4 Sect. 21 Tp. 2 R. 2, north and east.

**2735. LUCAR, Charles**
Feb. 14, 1829, 3 miles E Centerville, Leon Co. W 1/2 SW 1/4 Sect. 22 Tp. 2 R. 2, north and east.

**LUCAS, George B. see Catherine HARLEY, #4175**

**4599. LYME, Daniel**
July 9, 1857, 2 miles SE of McCrae, Clay Co. SE 1/4 NE 1/4 and N 1/2 SE 1/4 Sect. 9 Tp. 8 R. 21, south and east. Patent delivered Jan. 22, 1863.

**471. LYNCH, James**
Oct. 21, 1846, near Dunnellon, Marion Co. NW 1/4 Sect. 30 Tp. 16 R. 19, south and east. Patent delivered Dec. 14, 1856.

**90. LYNCH, John**
(SIC) Dec. 11, 1826, 5 miles SE Graceville, Jackson Co. NW 1/4 Sect. 11 Tp. 6 R. 12, north and west.

**2255. LYNCH, John**
Feb. 12, 1828, 3 miles WSW Campbellton, Jackson Co. E 1/2 SW 1/4 Sect. 4 Tp. 6 R. 12, north and west. Transferred Aug. 14, 1828, to **Benj. HAYS** for $100. Testes: **John HAYS** and **Elizabeth Ann LYNCH**.

**4422. LYTRELL, John A.**
Sept. 25, 1833, 2 1/2 miles S of Greenwood, Jackson Co. NW 1/4 SW 1/4 Sect. 17 Tp. 5 R. 9, north and west.

## * M *

**3079. MACINNIS, Daniel**
Oct. 6, 1829, 1 mile N Florence, Gadsden Co. W 1/2 SE 1/4 Sect. 25 Tp. 3 R. 3, north and west.

**1258. MACOMB, David B.**
(DUP) April 9, 1827, 4 1/2 miles SE Tallahassee, Leon Co. E 1/2 NW 1/4 Sect. 15 Tp. 1 R. 1, south and east.

**5161. MADDUX, John P.**
Sept. 29, 1835, 2 miles S Greenwood, Jackson Co. E 1/2 NW 1/4 Sect. 8 Tp. 5 R. 9, north and west. Transferred to **Thomas GODWIN** and **Marmaduke DICKSON** Jan. 21, 1837.

**5892. MADDUX, John P.**
Oct. 7, 1836, 1 3/4 miles SSE Greenwood, Jackson Co. W 1/2 NE 1/4 Sect. 8 Tp. 5 R. 9, north and west. Transferred to **Thomas GODWIN** and **Marmaduke DIXKSON** Jan. 21, 1837.

**3629. MAGUIER, Peter**
Oct. 9, 1830, just SW Lamont, Jefferson Co. E 1/2 NW 1/4 Sect. 26 Tp. 1 R. 5, south and east.

**4321. MAGUIER, Peter**
Mar. 4, 1833, (information illegible for location)

**7246. MAINOR, John**
March 22, 1889, 2 1/4 miles SE Paxton, Okaloosa Co. NE 1/4 Sect. 12 Tp. 5N R. 21W.

**4265. MALHERB, Paul De**
Jan. 1, 1833, 3 miles NE El Destino, Jefferson Co. SW 1/4 SW 1/4 Sect. 4 Tp. 1 R. 3, south and east.

**489. MALLARD, Daniel**
Oct. 9, 1830, at Dills, Jefferson Co. E 1/2 SW 1/4 Sect. 11 Tp. 2 R. 6, north and east.

**533. MALLARD, Daniel**
May 30, 1831, 3 miles W Ashville, Jefferson Co. E 1/2 NE 1/4 Sect. 35 Tp. 3 R. 6, north and east.

**5546. MALLARD, Daniel**
Mar. 18, 1836, 4 1/2 miles E Monticello, Jefferson Co. NW 1/4 SW 1/4 Sect. 25 Tp. 2 R. 5, north and east.

**364. MALONE, Green**
April 17, 1846, 1 1/2 miles SW Crystal River, Citrus Co. E 1/2 SW 1/4 and W 1/2 SE 1/4 Sect. 29 Tp. 18 R. 17, south and east. Delivered to **R. J. PITTMAN**, April 4, 1868.

**6172. MALONE, John W.**
Dec. 10, 1839, 1 1/2 miles SW Quincy, Gadsden Co. E 1/2 NE 1/4 Sect. 14 Tp. 2 R. 4, north and west.

**2931. MALONEY, John**
July 9, 1829, just S Butler, Jackson Co. Lot 5 Sect. 33 Tp. 5 R. 7, north and west. (155.5 acres)

**2932. MALONEY, John**
July 9, 1829, just S Butler, Jackson Co. Lot No. 1 Sect. 33 Tp. 5 R. 7, north and west.

**2933. MALONEY, John**
July 9, 1829, just S Butler, Jackson Co. Lot No. 2 Sect. 33 Tp. 5 R. 7, north and west.

**2874. MALPHURS, William**
Aug. 15, 1854, 1 1/2 miles SW Bellamy, Alachua Co. Lots No. 5 and 6 Sect. 2 Tp. 9 R. 20, south and east. Patent delivered Oct. 17, 1857.

**2805. MANDALL, Addison**
April 20, 1829, 2 1/2 miles NE Marianna, Jackson Co. E 1/2 NE 1/4 Sect. 35 Tp. 5 R. 10, north and west.

**8698. MANER, Henry C.**
Sept. 28, 1844, at Watson, Liberty Co. Lot No. 5 Sect. 32 Tp. 2 R. 7, north and west.

**8699. MANER, Henry C.**
Sept. 28, 1844, 1/2 mile NNW Watson, Liberty Co. W 1/2 SW 1/4 Sect. 28 Tp. 2 R. 7, north and west.

**2604. MANER, Wm.**
(of S. Carolina) Jan. 12, 1829, 3 miles W Midway, Gadsden Co. Lot No. 3 Sect. 2 Tp. 1 R. 3, north and west.

**2605. MANER, Wm.**
(DUP) (of S. C.) Jan. 12, 1829, c. 3 miles W Midway, Gadsden Co. Lot No. 4 Sect. 2 Tp. 1 R. 3, north and west.

**2610. MANER, Wm.**
(of S. C.) Jan. 12, 1829, c. 2 1/2 miles WSW Midway, Gadsden Co. Lot No. 1 Sect. 12 Tp. 1 R. 3, north and west.

**2611. MANER, Wm.**
(of S. C.) Jan. 12, 1829, c. 2 1/2 miles WSW Midway, Gadsden Co. Lot No. 2 Sect. 12 Tp. 1 R. 3, north and west.

**2612. MANER, Wm.**
(of S. C.) Jan. 12, 1829, c. 2 1/2 miles

WSW Midway, Gadsden Co. Lot No. 3 Sect. 12 Tp. 1 R. 3, north and west.

**3013. MANER, Wm.**
Sept. 5, 1829, 2 miles NW Sawdust, Gadsden Co. E 1/2 NW 1/4 Sect. 19 Tp. 2 R. 4, north and west.

**3014. MANER, Wm.**
Sept 5, 1829, 1 3/4 miles NW Sawdust, Gadsden Co. W 1/2 NE 1/4 Sect. 19 Tp. 2 R. 4, north and west.

**5748. MANING, Martha**
July 1, 1836, 2 3/4 miles NNE Chumuckla, Santa Rosa Co. NE 1/4 NE 1/4 Sect. 7 Tp. 3 R. 29, north and west.

**5957. MANN, John W.**
Nov. 1, 1836, 5 3/4 miles W Tallahassee, Leon Co. E 1/2 NW 1/4 Sect. 6 Tp. 1 R. 1, south and west.

**8112. MANN, John W.**
Oct. 8, 1839, 2 1/2 miles E by N Havana, Gadsden Co. W 1/2 NW 1/4 SE 1/4 NW 1/4 Sect. 36 Tp. 3 R. 2, north and west.

**7269. MANN, John W.**
July 23, 1838, 5 1/2 miles SSE Iamonia, Leon Co. W 1/2 NE 1/4 Sect. 24 Tp. 3 R. 2, north and west.

**7705. MANN, John W.**
Nov. 15, 1838, 2 1/2 miles S by W Concord, Jackson Co. E 1/2 SW 1/4 Sect. 30 Tp. 3 R. 1, north and west.

**7706. MANN, William A.**
Nov. 15, 1838, 1/2 mile SW Concord, Jackson Co. SW 1/4 NE 1/4 Sect. 25 Tp. 3 R. 2, north and west.

**MANNER, Wm. see Alex CAMERON**

**788. MANNING, Benjamin**
(of Fla.) Oct. 16, 1826, 12 miles N Tallahassee, Leon Co. W 1/2 NE 1/4 Sect. 5 Tp. 2 R. 2, north and east.

**197. MANNING, Benjamin**
Dec. 29, 1826, 3 miles N Monticello, Jefferson Co. Lot No. 1 Fractional Sect. 17 Tp. 2 R. 4, north and east.

**2337. MANNING, Benjamin**
April 10, 1828, 2 miles W Copeland, Leon Co. E 1/2 SW 1/4 Sect. 31 Tp. 3 R. 1, north and east.

**3151. MANNING, Benjamin**
Dec. 5, 1829, c. 3 1/2 miles SW Alma, Leon Co. Lot No. 1 Sect. 8 Tp. 2 R. 4, north and east.

**5440. MANNING, Benjamin**
Dec. 5, 1836, 1 1/4 miles S by W Iamonia, Leon Co. NW 1/4 Sect. 27 Tp. 3 R. 2, north and east.

**5441. MANNING, Benjamin**
Feb. 5, 1836, 1 1/2 miles S by W Iamonia, Leon Co. W 1/2 SW 1/4 Sect. 20 Tp. 3 R. 2, north and east.

**5442. MANNING, Benjamin**
Feb. 5, 1836, 2 1/2 miiles SSW Iamonia, Leon Co. W 1/2 NE 1/4 Sect. 29 Tp. 3 R. 2, north and east.

**5527. MANNING, Benjamin**
Mar. 10, 1836, 1 mile E by N Meridian, Leon Co. W 1/2 SW 1/4 and NW 1/4 SW 1/4 Sect. 17 Tp. 3 R. 2, north and east.

**6171. MANNING, Benjamin**
Dec. 9, 1836, 2 1/4 miles S by E Iamonia, Leon Co. S 1/2 Sect. 29 Tp. 3 R. 2, north and east.

**6172. MANNING, Benjamin**
Dec. 9, 1836, 1 mile S by E Iamonia, Leon Co. E 1/2 SE 1/4 Sect. 18 Tp. 3 R. 2, north and east.

**6474. MANNING, Benjamin**
Jan. 9, 1837, 2 miles NE Alma, Jefferson Co. E 1/2 NE 1/4 Sect. 30 Tp. 3 R. 5, north and east.

**6844. MANNING, Benjamin**
Mar. 7, 1837, 3 miles NE Alma, Jefferson Co. NE 1/4 NW 1/4 Sect. 29 Tp. 3 R. 5, north and east.

**2813. MANNING, Benjamin**
May 2, 1829, 5 miles W Alma, Leon Co. W 1/2 SW 1/4 Sect. 31 Tp. 3 R. 4, north and east.

**2818. MANNING, Benjamin**
May 8, 1829, 2 1/2 miles SSW Monticello, Jefferson Co. E 1/2 NW 1/4 Sect. 1 Tp. 1 R. 4, north and east.

**2819. MANNING, Benjamin**
May 8, 1829, 4 miles W by S Alma, Leon Co. W 1/2 NW 1/4 Sect. 6 Tp. 2 R. 4, north and east.

**6499. MANNING, Benjamin and Joseph**
Jan. 19, 1837, 5 miles NNE Monticello, Jefferson Co. W 1/2 NW 1/4 and W 1/2 SW 1/4 Sect. 33 Tp. 3 R. 5, north and east.

**6502. MANNING, Benjamin and Joseph**
Jan. 19, 1837, 3 miles E Alma, Jefferson Co. E 1/2 NE 1/4 and W 1/2 NW 1/4 Sect. 32 Tp. 3 R. 5, north and east.

**6503. MANNING, Benjamin and Joseph**
Jan. 19, 1837, 2 1/2 miles NNW

Greensboro, Gadsden Co. E 1/2 SE 1/4 and E 1/2 NE 1/4 Sect. 31 Tp. 3 R. 5, north and east.

**6600. MANNING, Benjamin and Joseph**
Jan. 19, 1837, 3 miles N by E Monticello, Jefferson Co. Sect. 5 Tp. 2 R. 5, north and east.

**6601. MANNING, Benjamin and Joseph**
Jan. 19, 1837, 4 miles NNW Monticello, Jefferson Co. S 1/2 Sect. 32 Tp. 3 R. 5, north and east.

**6604. MANNING, Benjamin and Joseph**
Jan. 19, 1837, 4 1/2 miles W Dills, Jefferson Co. W 1/2 NW 1/4 Sect. 4 Tp. 2 R. 5, north and east.

**6605. MANNING, Benjamin and Joseph**
Jan. 19, 1837, 3 1/4 miles N Monticello, Jefferson Co. E 1/2 NE 1/4 NE 1/4 SE 1/4 Sect. 6 Tp. 2 R. 5, north and east.

**6646. MANNING, Benjamin and Joseph**
Jan. 24, 1837, 2 miles E Alma, Jefferson Co. W 1/2 NE 1/4 and E 1/2 SW 1/4 Sect. 31 Tp. 3 R. 5, north and east.

**6647. MANNING, Benjamin and Joseph**
Jan. 24, 1837, 2 miles E Alma, Jefferson Co. NW 1/4 SW 1/4 Sect. 31 Tp. 3 R. 5, north and east.

**5828. MANNING, Druey**
Sept. 6, 1836, 6 miles SSW Coldwater, Santa Rosa Co. SE 1/4 NE 1/4 Sect. 7 Tp. 2 R. 29, north and west.

**6725. MANNING, Joseph**
Feb. 1, 1837, 3 miles NW Monticello, Jefferson Co. Lot No. 6 Fractional Sect. 15 Tp. 2 R. 4, north and east.
(See **Benjamin MANNING**)

**3862. MANNING, Reuben**
Jan. 26, 1831, 2 miles S Iamonia, Leon Co. E 1/2 NE 1/2 Sect. 30 Tp. 3 R. 2, north and east.

**4305. MANNING, Reuben**
Feb. 9, 1833, 2 miles S Iamonia, Leon Co. E 1/2 NW 1/4 Sect. 30 Tp. 3 R. 2, north and east.

**4306. MANNING, Reuben**
Feb. 9, 1833, 1 3/4 miles S Iamonia, Leon Co. W 1/2 NE 1/4 Sect. 30 Tp. 3 R. 2, north and east.

**4339. MANNING, Reuben**
April 3, 1833, 6 miles W Copeland, Leon Co. W 1/2 SW 1/4 Sect. 31 Tp. 3 R. 2, north and east.

**4340. MANNING, Reuben**
April 3, 1833, 1 mile S Iamonia, Leon Co. SE 1/4 SE 1/4 Sect. 19 Tp. 3 R. 2, north and east.

**4341. MANNING, Reuben**
April 3, 1833, 3/4 mile S Iamonia, Leon Co. SW 1/4 SE 1/4 Sect. 19 Tp. 3 R. 2, north and east.

**6169. MANNING, Reuben**
Dec. 9, 1836, 2 miles S Iamonia, Leon Co. S 1/2 Sect. 30 Tp. 3 R. 2, north and east.

**6170. MANNING, Reuben**
Dec. 9, 1836, 1 mile S Iamonia, Leon Co. NE 1/4 SE 1/4 and NW 1/4 SE 1/4 Sect. 19 Tp. 3 R. 2, north and east.

**2708. MARER, Wm.**
Feb. 4, 1829, c. 2 miles W Lake Jackson Station, Gadsden Co. Lot No. 2 Tp. 1 R. 3, north and west.

**8092. MARGAN, Marcellus**
Sept. 21, 1839, 3 miles NE Hinson, Gadsden Co. E 1/2 NE 1/4 SW 1/4 NE 1/4 Sect. 22 Tp. 3 R. 2, north and east.

**8815. MARIN, John**
Sept. 20, 1845, 7 1/2 miles E by N Fincher, Jefferson Co. NW 1/4 NE 1/4 Sect. 12 Tp. 2 R. 4, south and east.

**8884. MARION, Nathaniel P.**
Jan. 26, 1846, 3/4 mile W by S Marion, Hamilton Co. W 1/2 NW 1/4 Sect. 6 Tp. 1 R. 14, south and east.

**8885. MARION, Nathaniel P.**
Jan. 26, 1846, 1/4 mile W Marion, Hamilton Co. SW 1/4 SW 1/4 Sect. 31 Tp. 1 R. 14, north and east.

**7946. MARKS, Joseph D.**
April 27, 1839, 1/4 mile W Buck Horn, Taylor Co. NW 1/4 NW 1/4 Sect. 4 Tp. 1 R. 4, south and east.

**102. MARSHAL, Mathew**
Dec. 19, 1826, 2 miles W Campbellton, Jackson Co. E 1/2 NE 1/4 Sect. 35 Tp. 7 R. 12, north and west. On the back of the receipt is written "$100 to pay for the other half of the named quota."

**2338. MARSHALL, Daniel**
April 11, 1828, 2 1/2 miles W Ellis, Jackson Co. W 1/2 NW 1/4 Sect. 7 Tp. 16 R. 10, north and west.

**2056. MARSHALL, Joseph**
Sept. 9, 1827, 2 miles N Havana, Gadsden Co. E 1/2 SW 1/4 Sect. 15

Tp. 3 R. 2, north and west.

**2339. MARSHALL, Isaac Hamilton**
April 11, 1828, 2 1/2 miles W Ellis, Jackson Co. E 1/2 NW 1/4 Sect. 7 Tp. 6 R. 10, north and west

**658. MARTIN, Alexander**
Aug. 9, 1848, 3 1/2 miles NE Houston, Suwannee Co. SE 1/4 NW 1/4 Sect. 20 Tp. 2 R. 15, south and east. Patent delivered April 19, 1855.

**4944. MARTIN, Alexander H.**
Jan. 26, 1859, at Luraville, Suwannee Co. SE 1/4 NE 1/4 Sect. 18 Tp. 4 R. 12, south and east.

**355. MARTIN, Emanuel Henry**
(SIC) March 25, 1846, 1 mile SW Burbank, Marion Co. NW 1/4 NW 1/4 Sect. 17 Tp. 13 R. 23, south and east.

**4575. MARTIN, Gibson**
May 15, 1834, 2 miles S by E Greenwood, Jackson Co. E 1/2 SW 1/4 Sect. 18 Tp. 5 R. 9, north and west.

**4580. MARTIN, Gibson**
May 31, 1834, 2 1/4 miles S Greenwood, Jackson Co. SW 1/4 NE 1/4 Sect. 18 Tp. 5 R. 9, north and west. Transferred to **Edward BRYAN** May 26, 1835; sworn before **Peter SIMONS**, Justice of Peace, Jackson Co.

**5167. MARTIN, Gipson(?)**
Sept. 29, 1835, 3 1/4 miles S by E Greenwood, Jackson Co. NE 1/4 SE 1/4 Sect. 17 Tp. 5 R. 9, north and west.

**5168. MARTIN, Gipson(?)**
Sept. 29, 1835, 3 miles S by E Greenwood, Jackson Co. SE 1/4 NE 1/4 Sect. 17 Tp. 5 R. 9, north and west.

**5289. MARTIN, Gipson(?)**
Nov. 28, 1835, 6 1/2 miles W Dellwood, Jackson Co. W 1/2 NW 1/4 Sect. 19 Tp. 5 R. 9, north and west. Transferred to **Elijah BRYAN**, Aug. 20, 1836; sworn before **Thomas M. BUSH**, Nov. 21, 1836, Jackson Co.

**5870. MARTIN, Gipson(?)**
Sept. 30, 1836, 3 miles SSE Greenwood, Jackson Co. NE 1/4 NE 1/4 Sect. 17 Tp. 5 R. 9, north and west.

**982. MARTIN, Henry E.**
Nov. 4, 1851, 2 miles NW Burbank, Marion Co. W 1/2 SW 1/4 Sect. 6 Tp. 14 R. 23, south and east.

**4552. MARTIN, Jackson**
Feb. 18, 1834, 7 miles SSE Fentress, Santa Rosa Co. W 1/2 NE 1/4 Sect. 23 Tp. 3 R. 26, north and west.

**45. MARTIN, John**
Nov. 8, 1826, SW Mt. Pleasant, Gadsden Co. NE 1/4 Sect. 25 Tp. 3 R. 4, north and west.

**1807. MARTIN, John**
(DUP) June 5, 1827, 1 1/2 miles N Quincy, Gadsden Co. W 1/2 NW 1/4 Sect. 30 Tp. 3 R. 3, north and west.

**1808. MARTIN, John**
(DUP) June 5, 1827, 3 miles N Quincy, Gadsden Co. W 1/2 SW 1/4 Sect. 19 Tp. 3 R. 3, north and west.

**5290. MARTIN, John P.**
Nov. 28, 1835, 5 miles W by N Dellwood, Jackson Co. NW 1/4 SE 1/4 Sect. 17 Tp. 5 R. 9, north and west. Transferred to **Gipson MARTIN** on Aug. 20, 1836.

**5291. MARTIN, John P.**
Nov. 28, 1835, 2 3/4 miles S by W Greenwood, Jackson Co. NE 1/4 SE 1/4 Sect. 13 Tp. 5 R. 10, north and west.

**5868. MARTIN, John P.**
Sept. 30, 1836, 1 3/4 miles S Greenwood, Jackson Co. E 1/2 SW 1/4 Sect. 8 Tp. 6 R. 9, north and west.

**3008. MARTIN, John Sinclair**
Sept. 3, 1829, 2 miles N Mt. Pleasant, Gadsden Co. W 1/2 NW 1/4 Sect. 6 Tp. 3 R. 4, north and west.

**4933. MARTIN, R. T.**
April 11, 1835, 4 1/2 miles W by S Campbellton, Jackson Co. NE 1/4 SW 1/4 Sect. 5 Tp. 6 R. 12, north and west.

**9042. MASBY, Wiley**
Feb. 9, 1891, 5 miles (?) Shady, Marion Co. W 1/2 NE 1/4 Set. 30 Tp. 16S R. 21E.

**5660. MASHBURN, Samuel**
May 9, 1836, 3 1/4 miles S Havana, Gadsden Co. SE 1/4 NE 1/4 Sect. 23 Tp. 2 R. 2, north and west.

**7367. MASHBURN, William**
Mar. 1, 1838, 3 miles SE by S Florence, Gadsden Co. NE 1/4 NE 1/4 Sect. 23 Tp. 2 R. 2, north and west.

**4297. MATHENY, John**
Feb. 6, 1833, 1 1/2 miles NNE Corey,

Leon Co. NW 1/4 SE 1/4 Sect. 21 Tp. 1 R. 2, south and east.

**2987. MATHERS, Solomon E.**
Aug. 25, 1829, 1 mile S Monticello, Jefferson Co. E 1/2 SW 1/4 Sect. 31 Tp. 2 R. 5, north and east.

**4069. MATHERS, Solomon E.**
Aug. 23, 1831, 1/4 mile N McLellan, Jefferson Co. E 1/2 SW 1/4 Sect. 10 Tp. 1 R. 5, north and east.

**4070. MATHERS, Solomon E.**
Aug. 22, 1831, 1/4 mile NNE McLellan, Jefferson Co. E 1/2 SE 1/4 Sect. 10 Tp. 1 R. 5, north and east.

**4071. MATHERS, Solomon E.**
Aug. 22, 1831, at McLellan, Jefferson Co. W 1/2 NE 1/4 Sect. 15 Tp. 1 R. 5, north and east.

**7849. MATHERS, Solomon E.**
Feb. 4, 1829, 1/2 mile NE by N McClellan, Jefferson Co. SE 1/4 SW 1/4 Sect. 11 Tp. 1 R. 5, north and east.

**4202. MATHERS, William H.**
Aug. 20, 1832, 1 mile N McClellan, Jefferson Co. SW 1/4 SW 1/4 Sect. 10 Tp. 1 R. 5, north and east.

**1551. MATHEWS, C. L.**
(DUP) May 24, 1827, 5 miles ENE Marianna, Jackson Co. W 1/2 NE 1/4 Sect. 31 Tp. 5 R. 9, north and west. Transferred to **Chas. WILLIAMSON**, June 4, 1827.

**1582. MATHEWS, C. L.**
May 25, 1827, 4 miles NNE Marianna, Jackson Co. E 1/2 NE 1/4 Sect. 23 Tp. 5 R. 10, north and west. Transferred to **Malcolm GILCHRIST**, June 4, 1827. **(G. W. WARD, Reg.)**

**1585. MATHEWS, C. L.**
May 25, 1827, 3 1/2 miles NNE Marianna, Jackson Co. W 1/2 NE 1/4 Sect. 23 Tp. 5 R. 10, north and west. Transferred to **Malcolm GILCHRIST**, June 4, 1827. **(G. W. WARD, Reg.)**

**1587. MATHEWS, C. L.**
(DUP) May 25, 1827, 2 miles NE Marianna, Jackson Co. E 1/2 NW 1/4 Sect. 35 Tp. 3 R. 10, north and west. Tranferred to **Malcolm GILCHRIST**, June 4, 1827. **(G. W. WARD, Reg.)**

**3452. MATHEWS, Henry**
Oct. 11, 1882, 2 miles N by E Melrose, Putnam Co. E 1/2 NW 1/4 Sect. 6 Tp. 9S R. 23E.

**2157. MATHEWS, John**
Sept. 7, 1853, 2 1/2 miles SW Ellerslie, Pasco Co. NW 1/4 SW 1/4 Sect. 21 Tp. 25 R. 21, north and east.

**2158. MATHEWS, John**
Sept. 7, 1853, 6 miles SSW Dukes, Union Co. SW 1/4 NE 1/4 Sect. 22 Tp. 6 R. 18, south and east. Patent delivered April 10, 1858.

**4631. MATHEWS, John E.**
Sept. 4, 1857, 3 1/2 miles E Fort White, Columbia Co. SW 1/4 and W 1/2 SE 1/4 SW 1/4 NW 1/4 Sect. 30 ; and NW 1/4 NW 1/4 Sect. 31 Tp. 6 R. 17, north and east.

**4778. MATHEWS, John E.**
Sept. 4, 1858, 7 miles WNW Lake City Junction, Columbia Co. SW 1/4 NW 1/4 Sect. 31 Tp. 6 R. 17, south and east. Patent delivered Sept. 4, 1865.

**2536. MATTAIN, Lewis**
Mar. 3, 1854, 4 miles E Rixford, Suwannee Co. NW 1/4 SW 1/4 Sect. 11 Tp. 2 R. 14, south and east. Patent delivered Oct. 8, 1869.

**2735. MATTAIR, Lewis**
May 4, 1854, 2 miles SSE Rixford, Suwannee Co. NE 1/4 SE 1/4 Sect. 4 Tp. 2 R. 14, south and east. Patent delivered Oct. 8, 1869.

**8598. MATTHEWS, Charles**
Sept. 5, 1843, 1 mile SSE Greenwood, Jackson Co. W 1/2 NE 1/4 Sect. 5 Tp. 5 R. 9, north and west.

**174. MATTHEWS, Francis**
Sept. 17, 1845, at Homosassa Springs, Citrus Co. SE 1/4 NW 1/4 Sect. 27 Tp. 19 R. 17, south and east.

**167. MATTHEWS, John**
Aug. 1, 1845, 8 miles W Worthing Springs, Alachua Co. W 1/2 NW 1/4 Sect. 30 Tp. 6 R. 18, south and east.

**210. MATTHEWS, John**
Nov. 14, 1845, c. 1 mile NE Homsassa Springs, Citrus Co. SE 1/4 NE 1/4 and SW 1/4 NW 1/4 Sect. 22 Tp. 19 R. 17, south and east.

**6742. MATTHIS, Bunyan**
Feb. 6, 1837, 3 miles W Genoa, Hamilton Co. W 1/2 NW 1/4 Sect. 10 Tp. 1 R. 14, south and east.

**697. MATTOX, Elijah**
Dec. 26, 1849, 4 miles E by S Bass,

Columbia Co. SE 1/4 SE 1/4 Sect. 33 Tp. 4 R. 17, south and east.

**2334. MATTOX, Elijah**
Nov. 2, 1853, 3 1/2 miles N by W Mason, Columbia Co. SE 1/4 SE 1/4 Sect. 4 Tp. 5 R. 17, south and east.

**4066. MATTOX, Elijah**
Jan. 5, 1856, 1 mile S Lulu, Union Co. SW 1/4 SW 1/4 and SE 1/4 NE 1/4 Sect. 3; E 1/2 NW 1/4 and SE 1/4 NE 1/4 Sect. 4 Tp. 5 R. 17, south and east.

**2316. MATTOX, Elijah H.**
Oct. 30, 1853, 2 3/4 miles N Mason, Columbia Co. SW 1/4 SW 1/4 Sect. 3 and NE 1/4 NE 1/4 Sect. 10 Tp. 3 R. 17, south and east.

**2458. MATTOX, Elijah H.**
Feb. 23, 1854, 5 miles SW Bass, Columbia Co. NW 1/4 NW 1/4 Sect. 34 and SW 1/4 SE 1/4 Sect. 33 Tp. 4 R. 17, south and east. Patent delivered Mar. 18, 1858.

**2459. MATTOX, Elijah H.**
Feb. 23, 1854, 3 3/4 miles N by W Mason, Columbia Co. NW 1/4 SE 1/4 and NW 1/4 NW 1/4 Sect. 4 Tp. 5 R. 17, south and east. Patent delivered June 19, 1857.

**2739. MATTOX, Elijah H.**
May 5, 1854, 4 3/4 miles SSE Bass, Columbia Co. E 1/2 NW 1/4 Sect. 34 Tp. 4 R. 17, south and east. Patent delivered Mar. 18, 1858.

**4513. MATTOX, Hampton**
Jan. 14, 1834, 1 mile NW Felkel, Leon Co. SE 1/4 SW 1/4 Sect. 33 Tp. 3 R. 2, north and east.

**4514. MATTOX, Hampton**
Jan. 14, 1834, 1 1/4 miles NW Felkel, Leon Co. SW 1/4 SW 1/4 Sect. 33 Tp. 3 R. 2, north and east.

**5597. MATTOX, Hampton**
April 16, 1836, 2 1/2 miles NNE Centerville, Leon Co. SW 1/4 NE 1/4 Sect. 15 Tp. 2 R. 2, north and east.

**5638. MATTOX, Hampton**
April 30, 1836, 4 1/2 miles N Miccosukee, Jefferson Co. E 1/2 NE 1/4 Sect. 9 Tp. 2 R. 2, north and east.

**6326. MATTOX, Hampton**
Dec. 27, 1836, 1 1/2 miles NNW Felkel, Leon Co. NW 1/4 Sect. 33 Tp. 3 R. 2, north and east.

**6327. MATTOX, Hampton**
Dec. 27, 1836, 1 1/2 miles NNW Felkel, Leon Co. W 1/2 SW 1/4 Sect. 28 Tp. 3 R. 2, north and east.

**2579. MAULAIN, Wm. J.**
Dec. 23, 1828, 1828, 3 miles NE Marianna, Jackson Co. SE 1/4 Sect. 24 Tp. 5 R. 10, north and west.

**2580. MAULAIN, Wm. J.**
Dec. 23, 1828, 4 miles NE Marianna, Jackson Co. E 1/2 NE 1/4 Sect. 24 Tp. 5 R. 10, north and west.

**2581. MAULAIN, Wm. J.**
Dec. 23, 1828, 2 1/2 miles NE Marianna, Jackson Co. E 1/2 SE 1/4 Sect. 26 Tp. 5 R. 10, north and west.

**2811. MAULDEN, Wm. J.**
April 28, 1829, 2 miles NNE Marianna, Jackson Co. W 1/2 SE 1/4 Sect. 26 Tp. 5 R. 10, north and west.

**3050. MAULDEN, Wm. J.**
Sept. 17, 1829, 3 miles NE Marianna, Jackson Co. NE 1/4 Sect. 26 Tp. 5 R. 10, north and west.

**3222. MAYO, HOWEL**
Jan. 21, 1830, 4 miles W by N Alma, Leon Co. E 1/2 SW 1/4 Sect. 29 Tp. 3 R. 4, north and west. Paid in scrip issued to **Alex. MACOMB**, survivor of Edgar & Macomb, dated May 30, 1829.

**1042. MAYO, James**
Feb. 1, 1827, 4 miles SE Quincy, Gadsden Co. E 1/2 NW 1/4 Sect. 22 Tp. 2 R. 3, north and west.

**1043. MAYO, James**
Feb. 1, 1827, 4 miles SW Quincy, Gadsden Co. W 1/2 NE 1/4 Sect. 22 Tp. 2 R. 3, north and west.

**2945. MAYO, James**
July 20, 1829, 3 miles SE Quincy, Gadsden Co. E 1/2 NE 1/4 Sect. 21 Tp. 2 R. 3, north and west.

**6721. MAYO, James**
Feb. 1, 1837, 3 miles SE Quincy, Gadsden Co. W 1/2 NE 1/4 Sect. 21 Tp. 2 R. 3, north and west.

**8988. MAYO, James**
Nov. 4, 1846, 2 1/4 miles N Watson, Liberty Co. Lot No. 6 E 1/2 SE 1/4 Sect. 17 Tp. 2 R. 7, north and west.

**2291. MAYO, Jas.**
March 10, 1828, 4 1/2 miles SE Quincy, Gadsden Co. E 1/2 SW 1/4

Sect. 22 Tp. 2 R. 3, north and west.

**2345. MAYO, Richard**
April 14, 1828, 2 miles WSW Dills, Jefferson Co. W 1/2 SE 1/4 Sect. 2 Tp. 2 R. 5, north and east.

**260. MAYO, Stephen**
Jan. 28, 1829, 3 miles WNW Dills, Jefferson Co. E 1/2 NE 1/4 Sect. 34 Tp. 3 R. 5, north and east.

**7841. MAYS, Dennett H.**
Jan. 29, 1839, 1 mile W by N Bond, Madison Co. NW 1/4 Sect. 5 Tp. 2 R. 8, north and east.

**8091. MAYS, Dennett H.**
Sept. 21, 1839, 3 miles SSW Bond, Madison Co. NW 1/4 Sect. 7 Tp. 2 R. 8, north and east.

**5374. MAYS, Dennis H.**
Dec. 30, 1835, 1 mile NNW Champaign, Madison Co. SW 1/4 Sect. 15 Tp. 1 R. 8, south and east.

**4952. MAYS, James B.**
Probably April 29, 1835, 2 miles SW Champaign, Madison Co. W 1/2 SW 1/4 Sect. 33 Tp. 1 R. 8, south and east.

**5250. MAYS, James B.**
Nov. 6, 1835, 1 mile SE Moseley Hall, Madison Co. SE 1/4 NE 1/4 Sect. 33 Tp. 1 R. 8, south and east.

**5251. MAYS, James B.**
Nov. 6, 1835, 1 mile S by W Moseley Hall, Madison Co. NE 1/4 SE 1/4 Sect. 32 Tp. 1 R. 8, south and east.

**4960. MAYS, Richard I.**
May 18, 1825, 5 1/2 miles N Woods, Liberty Co. E 1/2 SW 1/4 Sect. 26 Tp. 1 R. 7, south and east.

**4960. MAYS, Richard I.**
May 18, 1835, 2 1/2 miles NW Sirmans, Madison Co. E 1/2 SW 1/4 Sect. 26 Tp. 1 R. 7, south and east.

**4961. MAYS, Richard I.**
May 18, 1835, 2 1/2 miles NW Sirmans, Madison Co. E 1/2 SE 1/4 Sect. 27 Tp. 1 R. 7, south and east.

**4962. MAYS, Richard I.**
May 18, 1835, at Sirmans, Madison Co. W 1/2 NW 1/4 Sect. 23 Tp. 1 R. 7, south and east.

**4963. MAYS, Richard I.**
May 18, 1835, at Sirmans, Madison Co. W 1/2 SW 1/4 Sect. 23 Tp. 1 R. 7, south and east.

**5285. MAYS, Richard I.**
Nov. 26, 1835, 1/4 mile NW Sirmans, Madison Co. E 1/2 SE 1/4 Sect. 35 Tp. 1 R. 7, south and east.

**5614. MAYS, Richard I.**
April 22, 1836, 1 mile N by E Sirmans, Madison Co. E 1/2 NW 1/4 Sect. 36 Tp. 1 R. 7, south and east.

**6499. MAYS, Richard J.**
(No date) 5 miles ESE Waco, Madison Co. E 1/2 SW 1/4 and NW 1/4 SW 1/4 Sect. 36 Tp. 1 R. 7, south and east.

**6500. MAYS, Richard J.**
Jan. 10, 1837, 1 mile W Sirmans, Madison Co. SE 1/4 NW 1/4 Sect. 35 Tp. 1 R. 7, south and east.

**7249. MAYS, Richard J.**
Jan. 17, 1838, 3 miles SE by S Myrick, Madison Co. W 1/2 SW 1/4 Sect. 14 Tp. 1 R. 7, south and east.

**7250. MAYS, Richard J.**
Jan. 17, 1838, 3 miles N by E Sirmans, Madison Co. E 1/2 NW 1/4 and W 1/2 NE 1/4 Sect. 23 Tp. 1 R. 7, south and east.

**7251. MAYS, Richard J.**
Jan. 17, 1838, 3 3/4 miles W Moseley Hall, Madison Co. E 1/2 SW 1/4 Sect. 26 Tp. 1 R. 7, south and east.

**7252. MAYS, Richard J.**
Jan. 17, 1838, 3 3/4 miles SE by S Myrick, Madison Co. E 1/2 SE 1/4 Sect. 22 Tp. 1 R. 7, south and east.

**7253. MAYS, Richard J.**
Jan. 17, 1838, 1/2 mile SW Shady Grove, Madison Co. E 1/2 SW 1/4 Sect. 35 Tp. 1 R. 7, south and east.

**7435. MAYS, Richard J.**
April 4, 1838, 2 1/2 miles NNE Champaign, Madison Co. E 1/2 SW 1/4 Sect. 7 Tp. 1 R. 9, north and east.

**7436. MAYS, Richard J.**
April 4, 1838, 3 miles NNE Champaign, Madison Co. NW 1/4 Sect. 7 Tp. 1 R. 9, north and east.

**7437. MAYS, Richard J.**
April 4, 1838, 1 3/4 miles NNE Champaign, Madison Co. NE 1/4 Sect. 18 Tp. 1 R. 9, north and east.

**7563. MAYS, Richard J.**
Aug. 4, 1838, 1 3/4 miles W Bond, Madison Co. SW 1/4 Sect. 1 Tp. 2 R. 7, north and east.

**7564. MAYS, Richard J.**

Aug. 4, 1838, 3 miles W Hamburg, Madison Co. W 1/2 Sect. 18 Tp. 2 R. 8, north and east.

**7565. MAYS, Richard J.**
Aug. 4, 1838, 1 mile NNE Bailey, Madison Co. NE 1/4 Sect. 13 Tp. 2 R. 7, north and east.

**7566. MAYS, Richard J.**
Aug. 4, 1838, 1 1/2 miles E Maysland, Madison Co. E 1/2 NW 1/4 Sect. 12 Tp. 2 R. 7, north and east.

**7567. MAYS, Richard J.**
Aug. 4, 1838, 1 3/4 miles NNE Bailey, Madison Co. W 1/2 SE 1/4 Sect. 13 Tp. 2 R. 7, north and east.

**7568. MAYS, Richard J.**
Aug. 4, 1838, 1/4 mile NNE Bailey, Madison Co. E 1/2 NE 1/4 Sect. 24 Tp. 2 R. 7, north and east.

**7569. MAYS, Richard J.**
Aug. 4, 1838, 1/4 mile N Bailey, Madison Co. E 1/2 NW 1/4 Sect. 24 Tp. 2 R. 7, north and east.

**7570. MAYS, Richard J.**
Aug. 4, 1838, 2 1/4 miles E Bailey, Madison Co. W 1/2 SW 1/4 Sect. 24 Tp. 2 R. 7, north and east.

**7571. MAYS, Richard J.**
Aug. 4, 1838, 1/4 mile N by E Bailey, Madison Co. SE 1/4 SE 1/4 Sect. 13 Tp. 2 R. 7, north and east.

**7581. MAYS, Richard J.**
Aug. 10, 1838, 1 mile N by E Dennett, Madison Co. NW 1/4 Sect. 26 Tp. 2 R. 7, north and east.

**7582. MAYS, Richard J.**
Aug. 10, 1838, 1 1/4 miles N by E Dennett, Madison Co. NE 1/4 Sect. 27 Tp. 2 R. 7, north and east.

**7586. MAYS, Richard J.**
Aug. 10, 1838, 2 1/2 miles W Hamburg, Madison Co. W 1/2 SE 1/4 Sect. 18 Tp. 2 R. 8, north and east.

**7587. MAYS, Richard J.**
Aug. 10, 1838, 2 1/4 miles W by N Hamburg, Madison Co. E 1/2 NE 1/4 Sect. 18 Tp. 2 R. 8, north and east.

**7598. MAYS, Richard J.**
Aug. 15, 1838, 1/4 mile SW Bailey, Madison Co. W 1/2 SE 1/4 and E 1/2 SW 1/4 Sect. 23 Tp. 2 R. 7, north and east.

**7599. MAYS, Richard J.**
Aug. 15, 1838, 1/2 mile NNW Bailey, Madison Co. W 1/2 SW 1/4 Sect. 23 Tp. 2 R. 7, north and east.

**8056. MAYS, Richard J.**
Aug. 24, 1839, 1 1/4 miles SE Bailey, Madison Co. E 1/2 SE 1/4 Sect. 25 Tp. 2 R. 7, north and east.

**8057. MAYS, Richard J.**
Aug. 24, 1839, 2 miles SE by S Bailey, Madison Co. W 1/2 SW 1/4 Sect. 30 Tp. 2 R. 8, north and east.

**8142. MAYS, Richard J.**
Nov. 15, 1839, 2 miles E by S Dennett, Madison Co. W 1/2 NE 1/4 Sect. 36 Tp. 2 R. 7, north and east.

**8165. MAYS, Richard J.**
Dec. 5, 1839, at Dennett, Madison Co. NW 1/4 Sect. 34 Tp. 2 R. 7, north and east.

**8202. MAYS, Richard J.**
Jan. 4, 1840, 2 miles SSE Bailey, Madison Co. E 1/2 NE 1/4 Sect. 30 Tp. 2 R. 8, north and east.

**8606. MAYS, Richard J.**
Nov. 30, 1843, 2 miles W by N Bond, Madison Co. E 1/2 NW 1/4 Sect. 6 Tp. 2 R. 8, north and east.

**8655. MAYS, Richard J.**
May 15, 1844, 3 1/2 miles W Maysland, Madison Co. NE 1/4 Sect. 7 Tp. 2 R. 8, north and east.

**8926. MAYS, Richard J.**
Mar. 26, 1846, 2 miles E Maysland, Madison Co. W 1/2 NE 1/4 Sect. 12 Tp. 2 R. 7, north and east.

**4870. MAYS, Richard T.**
Feb. 18, 1835, 2 miles SW Greenville, Madison Co. W 1/2 SE 1/4 Sect. 26 Tp. 1 R. 7, south and east.

**5541. MAYS, Richard T.**
Mar. 17, 1836, 2 miles NNW Moseley Hall, Madison Co. SW 1/4 Sect. 17 Tp. 1 R. 8, south and east.

**5541. MAYS, Richard T.**
Mar. 17, 1836, 1/4 mile N Moseley Hall, Madison Co. E 1/2 NW 1/4 Sect. 20 Tp. 1 R. 8, south and east.

**5541. MAYS, Richard T.**
Mar. 17, 1836, 2 1/4 miles NNW Moseley Hall, Madison Co. E 1/2 NE 1/4 Sect. 18 Tp. 1 R. 8, south and east.

**6508. MAYS, Rhydon G.**
Jan. 10, 1837, 1 mile SW Moseley Hall, Madison Co. W 1/2 NW 1/4 Sect. 32 Tp. 1 R. 8, south and east.

**7420. MAYS, Rhydon G.**
Mar. 22, 1838, 2 miles SW by S Moseley Hall, Madison Co. NW 1/4 SE 1/4 Sect. 31 Tp. 1 R. 8, south and east.

**McARON, Wm. J.** see **Adam FORTUNE**

**123. McARTHUR, Alexander**
Dec. 23, 1826, 5 miles N Quincy, Gadsden Co. W 1/2 NW 1/4 Sect. 14 Tp. 3 R. 3, north and west.

**119. McARTHUR, Catherine**
Dec. 23, 1826, at Littman Station, Gadsden Co. SE 1/4 Sect. 5 Tp. 2 R. 3, north and west. Transferred to **Jesse GORE**, Dec. 23, 1826.

**82. McARTHUR, Peter**
Dec. 1, 1826, 3 miles W Jamieson Post Office, Gadsden Co. NE 1/4 Sect. 9 Tp. 3 R. 3, north and west.

**56. McAULAY, Angus**
April 18, 1844, 3 1/2 miles E Padlock, Suwannee Co. SE and SW quarters Sect. 21 Tp. 3 R. 14, south and east.

**4194. McAULAY, Angus**
Feb. 23, 1856, 2 1/2 miles SE Padlock, Suwannee Co. SW 1/4 SE 1/4 Sect. 21 Tp. 3 R. 14, south and east.

**4195. McAULAY, Angus**
Feb. 23, 1856, 2 miles SE Padlock, Suwannee Co. NW 1/4 SE 1/4 Sect. 20 Tp. 3 R. 14, south and east.

**1522. McBRIDE, Burrell**
(DUP) May 23, 1827, 3 miles ESE Hermitage, Gadsden Co. E 1/2 NW 1/4 Sect. 1 Tp. 3 R. 5, north and west.

**1523. McBRIDE, Burrell**
May 23, 1827, 3 miles E Hermitage, Gadsden Co. W 1/2 NE 1/4 Sect. 1 Tp. 3 R. 5, north and west.

**5585. McBRIDE, Burwell**
April 8, 1836, at Waukenah, Jefferson Co. W 1/2 SE 1/4 Sect. 3 Tp. 1 R. 4, south and east.

**5586. McBRIDE, Burwell**
April 8, 1836, at Waukenah, Jefferson Co. E 1/2 SW 1/4 Sect. 3 Tp. 1 R. 4, south and east.

**5587. McBRIDE, Burwell**
April 8, 1836, 1/2 mile SSE Waukenah, Jefferson Co. NE 1/4 NE 1/4 Sect. 10 Tp. 1 R. 4, south and east. On the back of the above receipt is written: The within two hundred acres, is situated in Jefferson County, Florida, touching the Public Government Road from Tallahassee to Savanna River and whereon **McMURRAY** in his lifetime built 14 negro houses.

**6191. McBRIDE. Burwell**
Dec. 12, 1836, 1 mile SSE Waukenah, Jefferson Co. W 1/2 NW 1/4 Sect. 11 Tp. 1 R. 4, south and east.

**6458. McBRIDE, Burwell**
Jan. 9, 1837, 1/2 mile E Waukenah, Jefferson Co. E 1/2 NE 1/4 Sect. 4 Tp. 1 R. 4, south and east.

**6459. McBRIDE, Burwell**
Jan. 9, 1837, just S Waukenah, Jefferson Co. NW 1/4 SW 1/4 Sect. 4 Tp. 1 R. 4, south and east.

**1880. McBRIDE, David S.**
June 8, 1827, 1 mile W Midway, Leon Co. E 1/2 SE 1/4 Sect. 6 Tp. 1 R. 2, north and west.

**1995. McBRIDE, David S.**
(DUP) July 10, 1827, 1/2 mile NW Midway, Leon Co. W 1/2 NW 1/4 Sect. 5 Tp. 1 R. 2, north and west.

**3547. McBRIDE, David S.**
June 26, 1830, 1 mile W Midway, Gadsden Co. W 1/2 SE 1/4 Sect. 6 Tp. 1 R. 2, north and west.

**3938. McBRIDE, David S.**
Apr. 6, 1831, 3 1/2 miles S by E Centerville, Leon Co. E 1/2 SW 1/4 Sect. 6 Tp. 1 R. 2, north and west.

**168. McBRIDE, Joseph**
Dec. 29, 1826, 1 mile E Midway Station, Gadsden Co. W 1/2 SW 1/4 Sect. 4 Tp. 4 R. 2, north and west.

**1109. McBRIDE, Joseph**
(DUP) Feb. 9, 1827, 5 miles SSE Quincy, Gadsden Co. E 1/2 SE 1/4 Sect. 29 Tp. 2 R. 3, north and west. Transferred to **Thomas A. STRAIN** (?) on Feb. 13, 1827.

**2700. McBRIDE, Joseph**
Feb. 2, 1829, 1/2 mile W Midway, Gadsden Co. E 1/2 SW 1/4 Sect. 5 Tp. 1 R. 2, north and west.

**6594. McBRIDE, Joseph**
Jan. 18, 1837, 1/4 mile NW Midway, Gadsden Co. E 1/2 NW 1/4 Set. 5 Tp. 1 R. 2, north and west.

**6594. McBRIDE, Joseph**
Jan. 18, 1837, just NW Midway, Gadsden Co. E 1/2 NW 1/4 Sect. 5 Tp. 1 R. 2, north and west. Sworn to be

lost before **R. J. HACKLEY**, J. P. of Leon Co. and signed, "**Joseph McBRIDE**, Jan. 18, 1837." This is an Affidavit to the loss of Receipt No. 6594.

**127. McCALL, Howard**
(DUP) Dec. 23, 1826, 4 miles S Quincy, Gadsden Co. Lot No. 2 Fractional Sect. 3 Tp. 1 R. 3, north and west.

**130. McCALL, Jesse**
Dec. 23, 1826, at Havana, Gadsden Co. SW 1/4 Sect. 32 Tp. 2 R. 3, north and west.

**McCALL, Jesse** see **Sherrod McCALL**

**5878. McCALL, John**
Oct. 3, 1836, 4 1/4 miles W Tallahassee, Leon Co. NE 1/4 SW 1/4 Sect. 5 Tp. 1 R. 1, south and west.

**129. McCALL, Sherod**
(DUP) Dec. 23, 1826, 4 miles NW Midway Station, Gadsden Co. NW 1/4 Sect. 32 Tp. 2 R. 3, north and west.

**4163. McCALL, Sherod**
April 14, 1832, 7 miles SW Mears Spur, Gadsden Co. W 1/2 SW 1/4 Sect. 32 Tp. 3 R. 6, north and west.

**2606. McCALL, Sherrod**
Jan. 12, 1829, 4 miles W Midway, Gadsden Co. Lot No. 3 Sect. 3 Tp. 1 R. 3, north and west.

**2607. McCALL, Sherrod**
Jan. 12, 1829, 4 1/2 miles W Midway, Gadsden Co. Lot No. 1 Sect. 4 Tp. 1 R. 3, north and west. Paid off by **Jesse McCALL** at 2.50 cents per acre, reserving widow's dower."

**894. McCALL, Wm.**
Jan. 17, 1827, 3 miles SSE Quincy, Gadsden Co. E 1/2 SW 1/4 Sect. 20 Tp. 2 R. 3, north and west.

**895. McCALL, Wm.**
Jan. 17, 1827, 3 miles SSE Quincy, Gadsden Co. W 1/2 SE 1/4 Sect. 20 Tp.2 R. 2, north and west.

**896. McCall, Wm.**
Jan. 17, 1827, 3 miles SSE Quincy, Gadsden Co. E 1/2 SE 1/4 Sect. 20 Tp. 2 R. 3, north and west.

**1083. McCALL, Wm.**
Feb. 5, 1827, 4 1/4 miles SSE Quincy, Gadsden Co. W 1/2 NE 1/4 Sect. 29 Tp. 2 R. 3, north and west.

**3473. McCALL, Wm. B.**
April 8, 1830, c. 4 miles W Midway, Gadsden Co. Lot No. 1 Fractional Sect. 3 Tp. 1 R. 3, north and west. Pd. with Treasury Cert. No. 59 dated May 30, 1829, in favour of **Alex'r MACOMB**, survivor of Edgar and Macomb. Amt. $100.

**316. McCALL, Wm. B.**
Sept. 11, 1839, 3 miles SW Gadsden Co. Lot No. 3 Sect. 23 Tp. 1 R. 2, north and west.

**8207. McCALLUM, William W.**
Jan. 7, 1840, 1 1/4 miles NNW Redbay, Walton Co. NE 1/4 SE 1/4 Sect. 36 Tp. 2 R. 18, north and west.

**665. McCARTHY, Fones**
Oct. 13, 1848, 1/2 mile N Orange Springs, Marion Co. SW 1/4 NW 1/4 Sect. 24 Tp. 11 R. 23, south and east.

**2047. McCARTY, Wm. M.**
Aug. 25, 1827, 1 mile W Maxwell's Spur, Leon Co. E 1/2 NW 1/4 Sect. 14 Tp. 1 R. 1, south and west.

**2049. McCARTY, Wm. M.**
Aug. 27, 1827, 3 miles SSW Tallahassee, Leon Co. W 1/2 NE 1/4 Sect. 14 Tp. 1 R. 1, south and west.

**430. McCASKILL, Alexander**
Dec. 16, 1828, 2 1/2 miles NE Eucheanna, Walton Co. SW 1/4 Sect. 25 Tp. 2 R. 18, north and west.

**2643. McCASKILL, Alexander**
Jan. 19, 1829, 3 miles NE Eucheanna, Walton Co. E 1/2 NW 1/4 Sect. 24 Tp. 2 R. 18, north and west.

**429. McCASKILL, Finley**
(Jr.) Dec. 16, 1828, 3 miles NE Eucheanna, Walton Co. SW 1/4 Sect. 13 Tp. 2 R. 18, north and west.

**2644. McCASKILL, Finley**
Jan. 19, 1829, 1 1/2 miles E Eucheanna, Walton Co. W 1/2 NE 1/4 Sect. 36 Tp. 2 R. 18, north and west.

**2645. McCASKILL, Finley**
Jan. 19, 1829, 1 1/4 miles E Eucheanna, Walton Co. E 1/2 NW 1/4 Sect. 36 Tp. 2 R. 18, north and west.

**2646. McCASKILL, Finley**
Jan. 19, 1829, 2 1/2 miles E Eucheanna, Walton Co. E 1/2 NE 1/4 Sect. 36 Tp. 2 R. 18, north and west.

**3239. McCASKILL, Margaret**
Feb. 1, 1830, 2 miles ESE Rock Creek,

Okaloosa Co. E 1/2 NW 1/4 Sect. 9 Tp. 5 R. 25, north and west. Transferred Aug. 28, 1830, to **Richmond T. McDAVID**; teste: **Geo. SEVELD**, J. P.

**431. McCASKILL, Peter**
Dec. 16, 1828, 2 1/2 miles NE Eucheanna, Walton Co. E 1/2 NW 1/4 Sect. 25 Tp. 2 R. 18, north and west.

**4797. McCELLAN, George**
Sept. 6, 1858, 3/4 mile NNW McAlpin, Suwannee Co. SE 1/4 NE 1/4 Sect. 12 Tp. 4 R. 13, south and east.

**7023. McCELLAN, Henry Y.**
July 8, 1837, 1 1/2 miles W Nash, Jefferson Co. SW 1/4 SW 1/4 Sect. 27 Tp. 1 R. 4, north and east.

**5399. McCLARY, John Oneal**
Feb. 12, 1886, 4 miles S by W Old Town, Dixie Co. SW 1/4 SW 1/4 Sect. 3; SE 1/4 SE 1/4 Sect. 4; NE 1/4 NE 1/4 Sect. 9; and NW 1/4 NW 1/4 Sect. 10 Tp. 11S R. 13E.

**5078. McCLELLAN, Andrew**
July 15, 1835, 1 1/2 miles SSE Moseley Hall, Madison Co. W 1/2 NE 1/4 Sect. 34 Tp. 1 R. 8, south and east.

**5079. McCLELLAN, Andrew**
July 15, 1835, 1 1/4 miles SSE Moseley Hall, Madison Co. W 1/2 NW 1/4 Sect. 34 Tp. 1 R. 8, south and east.

**5141. McCLELLAN, Andrew**
Aug. 20, 1835, 2 miles SE Moseley Hall, Madison Co. SW 1/4 NE 1/4 Sect. 33 Tp. 1 R. 8, south and east.

**5142. McCLELLAN, Andrew**
Aug. 20, 1835, 1 1/2 miles SE Moseley Hall, Madison Co. SE 1/4 NW 1/4 Sect. 33 Tp. 1 R. 8, south and east.

**4907. McCLELLAN, John W.**
Dec. 2, 1858, 2 1/2 miles E Rossburg, Suwannee Co. NW 1/4 NE 1/4 and E 1/2 NW 1/4 and S 1/2 SE 1/4 Sect. 4 Tp. 4 R. 13, south and east. Patent delivered Jan. 7, 1864.

**4877. McCLELLAN, Charles**
Feb. 28, 1835, 2 1/2 miles W Nash, Jefferson Co. NE 1/4 NE 1/4 Sect. 28 Tp. 1 R. 4, north and east.

**94. McCLELLAN, Susan**
Dec. 23, 1844, 4 3/4 miles S Ringgold, Hernando Co. NW 1/4 NE 1/4 Sect. 1 Tp. 22 R. 18, south and east. Patent delivered June 24, 1845.

**2465. McCORMICK, Abner H.**
Feb. 23, 1854, 3 miles NNW Millwood, Marion Co. NE 1/4 NE 1/4 Sect. 4 Tp. 13 R. 21, south and east. Patent delivered Mar. 16, 1857.

**2542. McCORMICK, Abner H.**
Mar. 4, 1854, 5 miles W Millwood, Marion Co. SE 1/4 SW 1/4 Sect. 4 Tp. 13 R. 21, south and east. Patent delivered Feb. 22, 1860.

**2878. McCORMICK, Abner H.**
Aug. 18, 1854, 3/4 mile S Proctor, Marion Co. NW 1/4 SW 1/4 Sect. 4 Tp. 13 R. 21, south and east. Patent delivered Oct. 17, 1857.

**4364. McCORMICK, Abner H.**
May 13, 1856, 2 miles W Citra, Marion Co. SE 1/4 SE 1/4 Sect. 33 Tp. 12 R. 21, south and east. Patent delivered 1860.

**McCORMICK, Abner H.** see **William CONE, #684.**

**2820. McCORMICK, Abner M.**
July 17, 1854, 3 1/2 miles S by E Proctor, Alachua Co. SW 1/4 SE 1/4 Sect. 33 Tp. 12 R. 21, south and east. Patent delivered July 22, 1860.

**300. McCORMICK, Jno.**
Jan. 1, 1827, 6 miles E Marianna, Jackson Co. E 1/2 SW 1/4 Sect. 5 Tp. 4 R. 9, north and west.

**2075. McCORMICK, Jno.**
Oct. 5, 1827, 3 miles E Marianna, Jackson Co. E 1/2 SW 1/4 Sect. 7 Tp. 4 R. 9, north and west.

**5953. McCORMICK, Paul**
Nov. 1, 1836, 3/4 mile S Inwood, Jackson Co. SE 1/4 Sect. 4 Tp. 3 R. 7, north and west.

**5954. McCORMICK, Paul**
Nov. 1, 1836, 3/4 mile E by S Inwood, Jackson Co. NE 1/4 Sect. 9 Tp. 3 R. 7, north and west.

**7479. McCORMICK, Paul**
May 30, 1838, 3 1/2 miles SSE Gaskin, Calhoun Co. SE 1/4 SE 1/4 Sect. 36 Tp. 3 R. 9, south and west.

**7652. McCORMICK, Paul**
Sept. 24, 1838, 2 miles SE Maysville, Calhoun Co. NE 1/4 SE 1/4 Sect. 36 Tp. 2 R. 9, south and west.

**841. McCORMICK, Paul**
Feb. 26, 1851, at Proctor, Marion Co. SW 1/4 SE 1/4 Sect. 28 Tp. 12 R. 21, south and east.

**1255. McCORMICK, Paul**
Mar. 16, 1852, at Island Grove Station, Alachua Co. Lot No. 10 Sect. 27 Tp. 12 R. 21, south and east.

**2286. McCORMICK, Paul**
Oct. 25, 1853, 3 miles NNW Citra, SSE shore of Orange Lake, Alachua Co. Lot No. 6 Sect. 27 Tp. 12 R. 21, south and east.

**2427. McCORMICK, Paul**
Feb. 21, 1854, 4 miles NE Millwood, Marion Co. NE 1/4 SE 1/4 Sect. 33 Tp. 12 R. 21, south and east.

**4296. McCORMICK, Paul**
Mar. 27, 1856, 1/2 mile W Oxford, Sumter Co. N 1/2 NW 1/4 and NW 1/4 NE 1/4; also SW 1/4 SW 1/4 Sect. 18 Tp. 18 R. 23, south and east.

**4297. McCORMICK, Paul**
Mar. 27, 1856, 7 miles WNW Oxford, Sumter Co. SW 1/4 SE 1/4 Sect. 7 Tp. 18 R. 23, south and east.

**4365. McCORMICK, Paul**
May 13, 1856, 2 1/2 miles SSE Oxford, Sumter Co. NW 1/4 SE 1/4 Sect. 7 Tp. 18 R. 23, south and east. Patent delivered Feb. 22, 1860.

**2254. McCOY, Asa**
(of Fla.) Feb. 11, 1827, 3 miles NE Wadesboro, Leon Co. W 1/2 SE 1/4 Sect. 28 Tp. 2 R. 3, north and east.

**128. McCULLOCH, Briant**
(SIC) Dec. 23, 1826, at Chattahoochee, Gadsden Co. SW 1/4 Sect. 4 Tp. 2 R. 6, north and west.

**321. McCULLOCH, John**
Feb. 17, 1827, 3 miles E Chattahoochee, Gadsden Co. Lot No. 1 Sect. 32 Tp. 4 R. 6, north and west.

**323. McCULLOCH, John**
March 16, 1827, 2 miles SE Chattahoochee, Gadsden Co. SE 1/4 Sect. 5 Tp. 3 R. 6, north and west.

**418. McCULLOCH, John**
(Assignee of **Wm. STILE**) Nov. 28, 1827, at Chattahoochee, Gadsden Co. W 1/2 NE 1/4 Sect. 33 Tp.4 R. 6, north and west.

**1895. McCULLOCH, John**
(DUP) June 9, 1827, 5 miles WNW Greensboro, Gadsden Co. SE 1/4 Sect. 35 Tp. 3 R. 6, north and west. Transferred to **John COLSON**, June 14, 1827.

**1905. McCULLOCH, John**
June 12, 1827, 5 1/2 miles NW Greensboro, Gadsden Co. W 1/2 NE 1/4 Sect. 35 Tp. 3 R. 6, north and west. Transferred June 14, 1827, to **John COLSON.**

**2015. McCULLOCH, John**
Aug. 4, 1827, 1 1/2 miles E Sneads, Jackson Co. NW 1/4 Sect. 3 Tp. 3 R. 6, north and west.

**4045. McCULLOH, John**
July 26, 1831, at River Junction, Gadsden Co. Lot No. 1 Sect. 5 Tp. 3 R. 6, north and west.

**2621. McCULLOCK, Jno.**
Jan. 13, 1829, at Chattahoochee, Gadsden Co. Lot No. 2 Sect. 32 Tp. 14 R. 6, north and west.

**4426. McDANIEL, Bartlett**
Oct. 6, 1833, 2 1/4 miles E Felkel, Leon Co. NW 1/4 SE 1/4 Sect. 7 Tp. 2 R. 2, north and east.

**4427. McDANIEL, Bartlett**
Oct. 6, 1833, 2 miles E Felkel, Leon Co. NE 1/4 SW 1/4 Sect. 7 Tp. 2 R. 2, north and east.

**2710. McDANIEL, Edward**
Feb. 5, 1829, 1/4 mile S Monticello, Jefferson Co. E 1/2 NW 1/4 Sect. 31 Tp. 2 R. 5, north and east.

**5764. McDANIEL, Elisha**
July 12, 1836, 3 miles SW Felkel, Leon Co. SE 1/4 NW 1/4 Sect. 7 Tp. 2 R. 2, north and east.

**6693. McDANIEL, William**
Jan. 30, 1837, 2 miles NNE Bradfordville, Leon Co. SW 1/4 NE 1/4 Sect. 7 Tp. 2 R. 2, north and east. Notation on back, "Included in Bond."

**7345. McDANIEL, William**
Feb. 22, 1838, 1 1/2 miles N by E Centerville, Leon Co. SW 1/4 SW 1/4 Sect. 7 Tp. 2 R. 2, north and east.

**8053. McDAVID, David A.**
Aug. 22, 1839, 5 miles SE Bolts, Santa Rosa Co. E 1/2 SE 1/4 Sect. 34 Tp. 4 R. 27, north and west. Transferred to **P. T. McDAVID** on Feb. 18, 1851.

**8230. McDAVID, David A.**
Feb. 24, 1840, 1/4 mile NNE Fentress, Santa Rosa Co. E 1/2 SE 1/4 Sect. 1 Tp. 3 R. 27, north and west. Transferred to **P. T. McDAVID** on Feb. 18, 1851.

**121. McDAVID, David A.**
Jan. 19, 1845, 3 miles SW Santos, Marion Co. SW 1/4 SW 1/4 Sect. 20 Tp. 16 R. 22, south and east. Transferred to **Allen GIBSON**, on Dec. 11, 1850. Patent delivered on July 15, 1858.

**292. McDAVID, Martha**
Jan. 26, 1846, 3 miles SW Santos, Marion Co. E 1/2 NE 1/4 Sect. 19 Tp. 16 R. 22, south and east. Sold Dec. 11, 1850. Patent delivered July 15, 1858.

**McDAVID, P. T.** see **David A. McDAVID**

**8796. McDAVID, R. T.**
July 22, 1845, 3 miles NNE Oak Grove, Okaloosa Co. NW 1/4 NE 1/4 Sect. 9 Tp. 5 R. 23, north and west.

**McDAVID, Richmond T.** see **Margaret McCASKILL**

**3899. McDONALD, Alexander**
Feb. 25, 1831, 4 1/4 miles NNE Monticello, Jefferson Co. W 1/2 NW 1/4 Sect. 9 Tp. 1 R. 5, south and east.

**3900. McDONALD, Alexander**
Feb. 25, 1831, 4 miles NNW Monticello, Jefferson Co. W 1/2 SW 1/4 Sect. 2 Tp. 2 R. 5, south and east.

**3901. McDONALD, Alexander**
Feb. 25, 1831, 4 miles NE Monticello, Jefferson Co. NE 1/4 Sect. 10 Tp. 2 R. 5, south and east.

**4139. McDONALD, Alexander**
Feb. 16, 1832, 2 1/4 miles NW Redoak, Taylor Co. E 1/2 NW 1/4 Sect. 9 Tp. 2 R. 5, south and east.

**4140. McDONALD, Alexander**
Feb. 16, 1832, 2 miles NW Redoak, Taylor Co. W 1/2 NE 1/4 Sect. 9 Tp. 2 R. 5, south and east.

**8535. McDONALD, Angus**
Mar. 31, 1842, 1/2 mile SW Redbay, Walton Co. W 1/2 NE 1/4 Sect. 8 Tp. 2 R. 17, north and west.

**432. McDONALD, Angus**
Dec. 16, 1828, 2 miles NE Eucheanna, Walton Co. E 1/2 NE 1/4 Sect. 26 Tp. 2 R. 18, north and west.

**564. McDONALD, Archibald**
Jan. 31, 1834, 4 miles W Miller's Ferry, Walton Co. E 1/2 SW 1/4 Sect. 14 Tp. 2 R. 17, north and west.

**8732. McDONALD, Archibald D.**
Dec. 2, 1844, 1/4 mile N Steaphead, Gadsden Co. SE 1/4 NW 1/4 Sect. 17 Tp. 2 R. 6, north and west.

**8634. McDONALD, Daniel K.**
Feb. 5, 1844, 1 1/4 miles SE Eucheeanna, Walton Co. NW 1/4 SE 1/4 Sect. 35 Tp. 2 R. 18, north and west.

**5931. McDONALD, James H.**
Oct. 27, 1836, 1/4 mile N by E Fecil, Hamilton Co. E 1/2 NW 1/4 and W 1/2 NE 1/4 Sect.22 Tp. 1 R. 15, south and east.

**4055. McDONALD, John**
Aug. 2, 1831, 1 1/4 miles SW Lamont, Jefferson Co. W 1/2 NE 1/4 Sect. 35 Tp. 1 R. 5, south and east.

**4056. McDONALD, John**
Aug. 2, 1831, 1/4 mile W Lamont, Jefferson Co. E 1/2 SE 1/4 Sect. 28 Tp. 1 R. 5, south and east.

**8529. McDONALD, John K.**
Feb. 10, 1842, 1 1/2 miles SSW Redbay, Walton Co. NW 1/4 Sect. 7 Tp. 2 R. 17, north and west.

**2640. McDONALD, Lauchlin**
Jan. 19, 1829, 1/2 mile SE Eucheanna, Walton Co. W 1/2 SE 1/4 Sect. 34 Tp. 2 R. 18, north and west.

**8544. McDONALD, Mary**
June 6, 1842, 4 1/2 miles NNW Redbay, Walton Co. W 1/2 SW 1/4 Sect. 14 Tp. 2 R. 17, north and west.

**433. McDONALD, Peter**
Dec. 16, 1828, 2 miles NNE Eucheanna, Walton Co. E 1/2 SW 1/4 Sect. 23 Tp. 2 R. 18, north and west.

**8521. McDONALD, Peter K.**
Jan. 24, 1842, 2 miles SSE Redbay, Walton Co. NW 1/4 Sect. 8 Tp. 2 R. 17, north and west.

**1662. McDOWEL, Jno.**
May 29, 1827, just NW Nash, Jefferson Co. NE 1/4 Sect. 20 Tp. 1 R. 4, north and east. Assigned to Messrs. **CUTHBERT** and **MANNY** (no date).

**1663. McDOWEL, Jno.**
May 29, 1827, 3 miles SW Bradwell's Station, Jefferson Co. W 1/2 NW 1/4 Sect. 29 Tp. 1 R. 4, north and east. Patent assigned to Messrs. **CUTHBERT** and **MANNY** (no date).

**2348. McDOWEL, Jno.**
April 23, 1828, 4 miles WNW Waukenah, Jefferson Co. NW 1/4 Sect. 31 Tp. 1 R. 4, north and east. Transferred

April 16, 1829, to **Dr. Sam PRIOLEAN.**
**2349. McDOWEL, Jno.**
April 23, 1828, 4 miles ENE Waukenah, Jefferson Co. E 1/2 SW 1/4 Sect. 31 Tp. 1 R. 4, north and east. Transferred April 16, 1829, to **Dr. Sam PRIOLEAN.**
**2350. McDOWEL, Jno.**
April 23, 1828, 3 1/2 miles W by N Waukenah, Jefferson Co. E 1/2 SE 1/4 Sect. 36 Tp. 1 R. 3, north and east.
**2807. McDOWEL, Jno.**
April 21, 1829, 1 mile SW Waukenah, Jefferson Co. E 1/2 NW 1/4 Sect. 4 Tp. 1 R. 4, south and east.
**696. McDOWEL, John**
(of Fla.) April 3, 1826, 2 miles S Fincher, Leon Co. W 1/2 NE 1/4 Sect. 24 Tp. 3 R. 3, north and east.
**733. McDOWEL, John**
(of Fla.) Aug. 2, 1826, 1 mile NE Stringer, Leon Co. W 1/2 SE 1/4 Sect. 24 Tp. 3 R. 3, north and east.
**4062. McDOWELL, John**
Aug. 15, 1831, 1 1/4 miles W by S Wacissa, Jefferson Co. E 1/2 NE 1/4 Sect. 28 Tp. 1 R. 3, south and east.
**1421. McELOY, George R.**
(of Ga.) May 21, 1827, 3 miles W Jamieson, Gadsden Co. W 1/2 SE 1/4 Sect. 10 Tp. 3 R. 3, north and west.
**2061. McELOY, Jno.**
Sept. 14, 1827, 2 miles SW Oakdale, Jackson Co. W 1/2 NE 1/4 Sect. 10 Tp. 3 R. 3, north and west.
**44. McELOY, Jno. C.**
Nov. 7, 1826, 3 miles W Jamieson Post Office, Gadsden Co. SW 1/4 Sect. 9 Tp. 3 R. 3, north and west. Transferred to **Benj. FOSCUE**, Nov. 7, 1826, by John McELOY.
**5393. McELRY, Noah**
Dec. 9, 1835, 1/4 mile S Lake Jackson ( town ), Leon Co. NW 1/4 SE 1/4 Sect. 6 Tp. 1 R. 1, north and west.
**5703. McELVEY, Noah**
June 11, 1836, 1/4 mile W Lake Jackson ( town ), Leon Co. W 1/2 NW 1/4 Sect. 6 Tp. 1 R. 1, north and west.
**7792. McELVY, John**
Dec. 3, 1839, 2 3/4 miles W Jamieson, Gadsden Co. E 1/2 NE 1/4 Sect. 10 Tp. 3 R. 3, north and west.
**8253. McELVY, Noah**

Mar. 12, 1840, 1 mile W Lake Jackson ( town ), Leon Co. Lot No. 1 Sect. 1 Tp. 1 R. 2, north and west.
**2151. McFALL, Andrew**
(and **Pickens CRESWELL**) Sept. 6, 1853, 2 miles NW Elmwood, Alachua Co. E 1/2 NW 1/4 Sect. 13 Tp. 13 R. 19, south and east. Patent delivered Mar. 18, 1857.
**4130. McFARLAND, Stander G.**
Jan. 31, 1832, 3 1/4 miles NNE Mount Pleasant, Gadsden Co. W 1/2 SE 1/4 Sect. 9 Tp. 3 R. 6, north and west.
**264. McFARLAND, Xanders G.**
Jan. 1, 1827, 7 miles NE Quincy, Gadsden Co. NE 1/4 Sect. 8 Tp. 3 R. 3, north and west. Transfers: **X. G. McFARLAND** to **L.** and **M. A. ARMISTEAD**, Jan. 1, 1827.
**3902. McFARLAND, Xanders G.**
Feb. 26, 1831, 2 miles S Ghattahoochee, Gadsden Co. E 1/2 SE 1/4 Sect. 9 Tp. 3 R. 6, north and west.
**222. McGAHAGIN, Joshua**
Dec. 5, 1845, 1 1/2 miles SW Shady, Marion Co. W 1/2 SW 1/4 Sect. 25 Tp. 16 R. 22, south and east.
**2034. McGEHEE, Jno.**
Aug. 15, 1827, 2 miles SSW Felkel, Leon Co. W 1/2 SW 1/4 Sect. 9 Tp. 2 R. 2, north and east.
**3813. McGEHEE, John C.**
Dec. 22, 1830, 2 1/4 miles W Moseley Hall, Madison Co. W 1/2 NE 1/4 Sect. 30 Tp. 1 R. 8, south and east.
**4644. McGEHEE, John C.**
Oct. 23, 1834, 2 1/4 miles NNW Moseley Hal, Madison Co. SE 1/4 SE 1/4 Sect. 24 Tp. 1 R. 7, south and east.
**4645. McGEHEE, John C.**
Oct. 23, 1834, 2 miles NNW Moseley Hall, Madison Co. SW 1/4 SE 1/4 Sect. 24 Tp. 1 R. 7, south and east.
**4646. McGEHEE, John C.**
Oct. 23, 1834, 2 miles W Moseley Hall, Madison Co. SE 1/4 Sect. 25 Tp. 1 R. 7, south and east.
**4647. McGEHEE, John C.**
Oct. 23, 1834, 2 1/4 miles W Moseley Hall, Madison Co. E 1/2 SW 1/4 Sect. 25 Tp. 1 R. 7, south and east.
**4964. McGEHEE, John C.**
May 18, 1835, 2 miles SW Madison,

Madison Co. E 1/2 NW 1/4 Sect. 5 Tp. 1 R. 9, south and east.

**4965. McGEHEE, John C.**
May 18, 1835, 1 mile W Waco, Madison Co. W 1/2 SW 1/4 Sect. 24 Tp. 1 R. 8, south and east.

**4966. McGEHEE, John C.**
May 18, 1835, 1 1/2 miles NW Waco, Madison Co. E 1/2 NE 1/4 Sect. 13 Tp. 1 R. 8, south and east.

**4315. McGEHEE, John C.**
April 8, 1856, 3 miles NW Falmouth, Suwannee Co. SW 1/4 SE 1/4 Sect. 20; NW 1/4 NE 1/4 Sect. 29 Tp. 1 R. 12, south and east.

**14. McGRIFF, Patrick**
Sept. 12, 1826, near W Lake Jackson, Gadsden Co. NW 1/4 Sect. 21 Tp. 2 R. 2, north and west. Rec'd From **Patrick McGRIFF**, $199.37 1/2 for 159.50 acres.

**857. McGRIFF, Patrick**
Jan. 16, 1827, 5 miles SSW Havana, Gadsden Co. W 1/2 NE 1/4 Sect. 21 Tp. 2 R. 2, north and west.

**945. McGRIFF, Patrick**
Jan. 19, 1827, 3 miles N Midway, Gadsden Co. SE 1/4 Sect. 21 Tp. 2 R. 2, north and west.

**7099. McGRIFF, William**
Nov. 18, 1837, 3 1/2 miles S Florence, Gadsden Co. SW 1/4 SW 1/4 Sect. 23 Tp. 2 R. 2, north and west.

**15. McGRIFF, Wm.**
Sept. 12, 1826, near W Lake Jackson, Gadsden Co. NW 1/4 Sect. 22 Tp. 2 R. 2, north and west. Rec'd from **Wm. McGRIFF**, $200.15 for 160.12 acres.

**5734. McINTOSH, John**
June 28, 1836, 3 1/4 miles S by W Myrick, Madison Co. W 1/2 SW 1/4 Sect. 19 Tp. 2 R. 7, south and east.

**678. McINTOSH, John Houston**
Feb. 12, 1849, 1 mile W Rideout, Clay Co. NE 1/4 NE 1/4 Sect. 1 Tp. 5 R. 24, south and east. Patent delivered July 19, 1856. Transferred April 24, 1857, to **George BRANNING**. Witness: **B. WILSON**.

**99. McINTOSH, John M.**
Dec. 28, 1844, near Martel, Marion Co. SE 1/4 SW 1/4 Sect. 18 Tp. 15 R. 20, south and east.

**2804. McINTOSH, John M.**

July 6, 1854, 1 1/2 miles SSW Ellzey, Levy Co. S 1/2 Sect. 5 Tp. 14 R. 15, south and east. Patent delivered July 18, 1857.

**3707. McINTYRE, Daniel**
Oct. 26, 1830, 1/2 mile NE Spray, Madison Co. SW 1/4 Sect. 2 Tp. 1 R. 7, north and east. Received in part, Cert. No. 154, dated May 30, 1829, issued to **Alex'r MACOMB**, survivor of Edgar and Macomb.

**3708. McINTYRE, Daniel**
Oct. 26, 1830, 1/2 mile SE Spray, Madison Co. SW 1/4 Sect. 11 Tp. 1 R. 7, north and east.

**3709. McINTYRE, Daniel**
Oct. 26, 1830, 1/4 mile E Spray, Madison Co. N 1/4 Sect. 11 Tp. 1 R. 7, north and east.

**8919. McINTYRE, George A.**
Mar. 5, 1846, 5 miles W by N Fowler, Jefferson Co. W 1/2 NE 1/4 Sect. 12 Tp. 1 R. 6, north and east.

**172. McIVER, Jno.**
(of Fla.) May 19, 1825, 2 miles S Perkins Station, Leon Co. W 1/2 SW 1/4 Sect. 8 Tp. 1 R. 1, south and east.

**478. McIVER, John**
June 1, 1825, 2 miles E Maxwell's Spur, Leon Co. E 1/2 NW 1/4 Sect. 17 Tp. 1 R. 1, south and east.

**5989. McJUNKINS, Aquilla**
Nov. 8, 1836, 6 1/4 miles N by W Quincy, Gadsden Co. E 1/2 SW 1/4 Sect. 13 Tp. 3 R. 4, north and west.

**McKAY, Chas. see Wm. DONALD**

**7743. McKENZIE, Alexander**
Dec. 1, (no date), 1 mile S by W Havana, Gadsden Co. SW 1/4 SW 1/4 Sect. 3 Tp. 2 R. 2, north and west.

**72. McKENZIE, Allen**
(SIC) Nov. 24, 1826, near Mt. Pleasant, Gadsden Co. E 1/2 NE 1/4 Sect. 23 Tp. 3 R. 4, north and west.

**295. McKENZIE, Allen**
Jan. 1, 1827, 5 miles NW Quincy, Gadsden Co. W 1/2 NW 1/4 Sect. 19 Tp. 3 R. 3, north and west.

**318. McKENZIE, Daniel**
(Sr.) Feb. 3, 1827, 1 mile NE Quincy, Gadsden Co. W 1/2 NW 1/4 Sect. 35 Tp. 3 R. 3, north and west.

**2760. McKENZIE, Daniel**
Feb. 24, 1829, 3 miles ENE Quincy,

Gadsden Co. E 1/2 NW 1/4 Sect. 35 Tp. 3 R. 3, north and west.

**220. McKENZIE, Dan'l B.**
(DUP) (Assignee of **Thos. DORSEY, Senr.**), Dec. 30, 1826, at Florence, Gadsden Co. SW 1/4 Sect. 6 Tp. 2 R. 3, north and west. Transferred to **Aquilla BRUTON**, 14th April, 1827. Witness: **Ferdinand Mullen Allen McKENZIE.** Sworn before **C. A. ROBINSON**, Clerk G. C. C., **H. M. McNEILE**, Deputy Clerk.

**221. McKENZIE, Duncan**
(DUP) Dec. 30, 1826, 5 miles SE Quincy, Gadsden Co. NW 1/4 Sect. 17 Tp. 2 R. 3, north and west. Tranferred Dec. 30, 1826, to **Godfrey STEPHENS.**

**4281. McKENZIE, James C.**
Jan. 23, 1833, 3/4 mile N Florence, Gadsden Co. SW 1/4 SW 1/4 Sect. 35 Tp. 3 R. 3, north and west.

**514. McKINSTRY, John**
Feb. 2, 1847, near Irvine, Marion Co. SW 1/4 SW 1/4 Sect. 36 Tp. 12 R. 20, south and east.

**7731. McKINZIE, Alexander**
Nov. 29, 1838, 1 mile S Havana, Gadsden Co. W 1/2 NW 1/4 and NE 1/4 NW 1/4 Sect. 10 Tp. 2 R. 2, north and west.

**1286. McKINNEY, James F. B.**
Mar. 10, 1852, 2 miles NE New River ( town ), Bradford Co. SW 1/4 NW 1/4 Sect. 1 Tp.6 R. 20, south and east. Patent delivered Feb. 14, 1862.

**1287. McKINNEY, James F. B.**
Mar. 10, 1852, 2 1/4 miles NE New River ( town ), Bradford Co. NE 1/4 SE 1/4 Sect. 1 Tp. 6 R. 20, south and east. Patent delivered Feb. 2, 1857.

**2198. McKINNEY, James F. B.**
Sept. 24, 1853, 2 miles S by E Raiford, Union and Bradford Co. SW 1/4 SW 1/4 Sect. 23; NE 1/4 SE 1/4 and SW 1/4 SE 1/4 Sect. 28 Tp. 5 R. 21, south and east. Patent delivered Feb. 2, 1857.

**2200. McKINNEY, James F. B.**
Sept. 23, 1853, 7 miles NNE Saxton, Bradford Co. SE 1/4 SE 1/4 Sect. 28 Tp. 5 R. 21, south and east. Patent delivered Feb. 2, 1857.

**2641. McKINNON, John L.**
Jan. 19, 1829, 3/4 mile SSW Eucheanna, Walton Co. E 1/2 NW 1/4 Sect. 4 Tp. 1 R. 18, north and west.

**2642. McKINNON, John L.**
Jan. 19, 1829, 3/4 mile SW Wucheanna, Walton Co. W 1/2 NW 1/4 Sect. 4 Tp. 1 R. 18, north and west.

**4550. McKINNON, Lauchlin L.**
Feb. 18, 1834, 2 miles WSW Redbay, Walton Co. E 1/2 SE 1/4 Sect. 6 Tp. 2 R. 17, north and west.

**4551. McKINNON, Lauchlin L.**
Feb. 18, 1834, 1 3/4 miles WSW Redbay, Walton Co. W 1/2 SW 1/4 Sect. 5 Tp. 2 R. 17, north and west.

**8546. McKINNON, Lauchlin L.**
June 20, 1842, 1/2 mile W by S Redbay, Walton Co. E 1/2 SW 1/4 Sect. 5 Tp. 2 R. 17, north and west.

**514. McKINSTRY, John**
Feb. 2, 1847, near Irvine, Marion Co. SW 1/4 SW 1/4 Sect. 36 Tp. 12 R. 20, south and east.

**8751. McKINZIE, Alexander**
March 6, 1845, 1 1/2 miles S by W Concord, Gadsden Co. NW 1/4 SW 1/4 Sect. 19 Tp. 3 R. 1, north and west.

**1921. McKINZIE, Allen**
June 18, 1827, 5 miles NE Gretna, Gadsden Co. E 1/2 SE 1/4 Sect. 13 Tp. 3 R. 4, north and west.

**2637. McLAIN, Daniel**
Jan. 17, 1829, at Eucheanna, Walton Co. E 1/2 SE 1/4 Sect. 34 Tp. 2 R. 18, north and west.

**2638. McLANE, John**
Jan. 17, 1829, 1/2 mile N Eucheanna, Walton Co. E 1/2 SW 1/4 Sect. 27 Tp. 2 R. 18, north and west.

**2639. McLEAN, John**
Jan. 19, 1829, 1/2 mile N Eucheanna, Walton Co. E 1/2 SW 1/4 Sect. 27 Tp. 2 R. 18, north and west.

**6880. McLAIN, John**
March 10, 1837, 1 mile NNW Eucheanna, Walton Co. SW 1/4 NE 1/4 Sect. 28 Tp. 2 R. 18, north and west.

**2707. McLAUCHLIN, Daniel**
Feb. 4, 1829, 3 miles WNW Quincy, Gadsden Co. E 1/2 SW 1/4 Sect. 34 Tp. 3 R. 4, north and west.

**2847. McLAUGHLIN, Neil**
June 9, 1829, 6 miles WNW Green-

sboro, Gadsden Co. E 1/2 SW 1/4 Sect. 26 Tp. 3 R. 6, north and west.

**427. McLEAN, Daniel**
(Assignee of **John FLOKS**), Dec. 10, 1828, 1 mile E Eaucheanna, Walton Co. W 1/2 NE 1/4 Sect. 35 Tp. 2 R. 18, north and west.

**8242. McLEAN, Daniel M.**
Feb. 29, 1840, 1 mile SE Eucheanna, Walton Co. E 1/2 SW 1/4 Sect. 35 Tp. 2 R. 18, north and west.

**8237. McLEAN, Daniel S.**
Feb. 28, 1840, 1 mile NE Eucheanna, Walton Co. E 1/2 NE 1/4 Sect. 35 Tp. 2 R. 18, north and west.

**428. McLEAN, Donald**
Dec. 10, 1828, 1 mile N Eucheanna, Walton Co. SE 1/4 Sect. 27 Tp. 2 R. 18, north and west.

**2672. McLEAN, Hugh**
Jan. 27, 1829, 6 1/2 miles SSW DeFuniak Springs, Walton So. W 1/2 SE 1/4 Sect. 20 Tp. 2 R. 19, north and west.

**8915. McLELLAND, John**
March 3, 1846, 5 miles NW Indian Ford, Santa Rosa Co. W 1/2 SW 1/4 Sect. 20 Tp. 3 R. 27, north and west.

**305. McLENNON, Catherine**
Jan. 1, 1827, 5 miles W Redbay, Walton Co. SW 1/4 Sect. 3 Tp. 1 R. 18, north and west.

**440. McLENNON, Lauchlin**
Jan. 13, 1829, 1 mile SW Eucheanna, Walton Co. NE 1/4 Sect. 4 Tp. 1 R. 18, north and west.

**8206. McLEOD, Alexander**
Jan. 7, 1840, 3 miles NNE Rockhill, Walton Co. NE 1/4 NW 1/4 Sect. 5 Tp. 1 R. 18, north and west.

**150. McLEOD, Alexander**
June 9, 1845, c. 2 miles NE Ocala, Marion Co. SW 1/4 SE 1/4 Sect. 9 Tp. 15 R. 22, south and east. Transferred to **Daniel GOINS**, June 11, 1847, **J. H. HARDEN**, Justice of the Peace. Patent delivered Jan. 31, 1859.

**330. McLEOD, Alexander**
Feb. 27, 1846, 3 miles NE Ocala, Marion Co. SE 1/4 SE 1/4 Sect. 9 Tp. 15 R. 22, south and east. Transferred to **Daniel GOINS**, June 11, 1847. Teste: **J. H. HARRISON**, Justice of the Peace. Patent delivered Jan. 31, 1859.

**2561. McLEOD, Norman**
Dec. 9, 1828, 2 miles WNW Braswell, Jefferson Co. E 1/2 NE 1/4 Sect. 7 Tp. 1 R. 4, north and east. Transferred to **William GORMAN**, Dec. 15, 1828.

**1015. McLEOD, Norman A.**
Nov. 24, 1851, 1 1/4 miles SE Lynne, Marion Co. W 1/2 NW 1/4 Sect. 15 Tp. 20 R. 24, south and east. Transferred to **Thomas PIE**, Feb. 21, 1854. Sworn to before **Wm. G. HALE**, J. P. of Sumter Co. Patent delivered Sept. 15, 1871.

**1216. McLEOD, Norman A.**
Feb. 26, 1852, 3 miles SW Okahumpka, Lake Co. NE 1/4 SW 1/4 and NW 1/4 SE 1/4 Sect. 9 Tp. 20 R. 24, south and east. Transferred to **Thomas PYE**, Feb. 21, 1864. Sworn to before **William G. HALL**, J. P. of Sumter Co. Patent delivered Sept. 15, 1871.

**8735. McLEON, Neil**
Dec. 5, 1844, 3 1/2 miles NNW Rockhill, Walton Co. NE 1/4 NE 1/4 Sect. 32 Tp. 2 R. 19, north and west.

**434. McLONG, John**
(Assignee of **Joshua ENGLAND**) Dec. 22, 1828, 2 1/2 miles ESE Norum, Washington Co. NE 1/4 Sect. 10 Tp. 2 R. 15, north and west.

**219. McMILLAN, Alex**
(DUP) Dec. 30, 1826, at Florence, Gadsden Co. NE 1/4 Sect. 6 Tp. 2 R. 3, north and west. Transferred to **William HOLLAMAN**, Dec. 30, 1826. Transferred to **Robert FORT** of Georgia, May 18, 1827.

**7328. McMILLAN, Daniel W.**
Feb. 13, 1838, 2 miles ESE Bluff Springs, Escambia Co. N 1/2 Lot No. 6 Sect. 28 Tp. 5 R. 30, north and west.

**4396. McMILLAN, Duncan**
Aug. 23, 1833, 2 1/2 miles W Greensboro, Gadsden Co. SE 1/4 SW 1/4 Sect. 12 Tp. 2 R. 6, north and west.

**4397. McMILLAN, Duncan**
Aug. 23, 1833, 2 1/2 miles W Greensboro, Gadsden Co. SE 1/4 NW 1/4 Sect. 12 Tp. 2 R. 6, north and west.

**2039. McMILLAN, Elisabeth**
Aug. 21, 1827, 2 miles E by N Greensboro, Gadsden Co. W 1/2 SE 1/4 Sect. 2 Tp. 2 R. 3, north and west.

**3992. McMILLAN, John**
June 24, 1831, 1 mile SW Union, Walton Co. E 1/2 NW 1/4 Sect. 18 Tp. 3 R. 5, north and west.

**4282. McMILLAN, John**
Jan. 23, 1833, 1/2 mile NE Mears Spur, Gadsden Co. NE 1/4 SW 1/4 Sect. 13 Tp.3 R. 6, north and west.

**6474. McMILLAN, John**
(DUP) Jan. 17, 1837, 1/2 mile W Hardaway, Gadsden Co. SE 1/4 NW 1/4 Sect. 19 Tp. 3 R. 5, north and west.

**6475. McMILLAN, John**
Jan. 17, 1837, 5 miles SE Chattahoochee, Gadsden Co. E 1/2 NE 1/4 Sect. 13 Tp. 3 R. 6, north and west.

**8729. McMILLAN, John**
Dec. 2, 1844, 1/2 mile S Mears Spur, Gadsden Co. W 1/2 SW 1/4 Sect. 18 Tp. 3 R. 5, north and west.

**5450. McMILLAN, John I./J.**
Jan. 9, 1836, 6 miles SE Stringer, Jefferson Co. W 1/2 SE 1/4 Sect. 5 Tp. 2 R. 4, north and east.

**5494. McMILLAN, John I./J.**
Feb. 25, 1836, 6 1/2 miles NNW Stringer, Jefferson Co. SW 1/4 Sect. 5 Tp. 2 R. 4, north and east.

**125. McMILLAN, Mary**
Dec. 23, 1826, 5 miles N Quincy, Gadsden Co. W 1/2 SW 1/4 Sect. 11 Tp. 3 R. 3, north and west.

**6776. McMILLAN, Neill**
Feb. 7, 1837, 3 miles SE Century, Santa Rosa Co. East of Escambia River. NW 1/4 NW 1/4 Sect. 23 Tp. 5 R. 30, north and west.

**6865. McMILLAN, Neill**
March 8, 1837, c. 2 miles N by W McDavid, Escambia Co. Lot 2 Fractional Sect. 10 Tp. 4 R. 31, north and west.

**4570. McNATTY, William**
April 9, 1834, 5 miles NNW Greenwood, Jackson Co. E 1/2 SE 1/4 Sect. 28 Tp. 6 R. 10, north and west.

**186. McNEALY, William**
(DUP) Dec. 29, 1826, 2 miles WNW Greenwood, Jackson Co. E 1/2 SE 1/4 Sect. 29 Tp. 6 R. 10, north and west.

**187. McNEALY, William**
Dec. 29, 1826, 3 miles WNW Greenwood, Jackson Co. W 1/2 SW 1/4 Sect. 28 Tp. 6 R. 10, north and west.

**6291. McNEALY, William**
Dec. 23, 1836, 5 1/2 miles W Greenwood, Jackson Co. NE 1/4 NW 1/4 Sect. 32 Tp. 6 R. 10, north and west.

**7098. McNEALY, William**
Nov. 17, 1837, 5 miles S by W Ellis, Jackson Co. E 1/2 NE 1/4 Sect. 29 Tp. 6 R. 10, north and west.

**7864. McNEALY, William**
Feb. 12, 1839, 5 1/2 miles W Greenwood, Jackson Co. W 1/2 SE 1/4 Sect. 29 Tp. 6 R. 10, north and west.

**2443. McNEELEY, Wm.**
July 21, 1828, 5 miles WNW Greenwood, Jackson Co. W 1/2 NE 1/4 Sect. 28 Tp. 6 R. 10, north and west.

**509. McNEIL, Hector**
June 6, 1825, 2 miles W Tallahassee, Leon Co. E 1/2 SE 1/4 Sect. 34 Tp. 1 R. 1, north and west.

**294. McNEILL, Hector**
Jan. 1, 1827, 5 miles W Quincy, Gadsden Co. NE 1/4 Sect. 1 Tp. 2 R. 4, north and west.

**1925. NcNEILLY, William**
(DUP) June 18, 1827, 5 miles WNW Greenwood, Jackson Co. W 1/2 NW 1/4 Sect. 28 Tp. 6 R. 10, north and west.

**2031. McNELLY/McNEELY, Wm.**
Aug. 13, 1827, 4 1/2 miles W by N Greenwood, Jackson Co. W 1/2 SE 1/4 Sect. 28 Tp. 6 R. 10, north and west.

**4548. McPHALL, John**
Feb. 13, 1834, SSW Mears Spur, Gadsden Co. SE 1/4 SW 1/4 Sect. 25 Tp. 3 R. 6, north and west.

**4085. McPHATTER, Archibald**
Sept. 17, 1831, 1 1/2 miles SSW Mears Spur, Gadsden Co. E 1/2 NE 1/4 Sect. 28 Tp. 3 R. 6, north and west.

**8438. McPHATTER, Archibald**
Dec. 29, 1840, 3 1/4 miles W by N Greensboro, Gadsden Co. SW 1/4 SE 1/4 Sect. 2 Tp. 2 R. 6, north and west.

**2834. McPHERSON, Neil**
May 26, 1829, 1/2 mile E Union, Holmes Co. W 1/2 NW 1/4 Sect. 33 Tp. 4 R. 18, north and west.

**7035. McQUAGGE, Daniel**
Aug. 18, 1837, 1/4 mile S Marianna,

Jackson Co. NW 1/4 SW 1/4 Sect. 10 Tp. 4 R. 10, north and west.

**7964. McQUAGGE, Daniel**
May 16, 1839, at Marianna, Jackson Co. E 1/2 NE 1/4 Sect. 15 Tp. 4 R. 10, north and west.

**7999. McQUAGGE, Daniel**
June 26, 1839, at Marianna, Jackson Co. E 1/2 SE 1/4 Sect. 10 Tp. 4 R. 10, north and west.

**2650. McQUAIG, Duncan**
Jan. 19, 1829, 4 1/2 miles SSW Ponce de Leon, Walton Co. E 1/2 SE 1/4 Sect. 12 Tp. 2 R. 18, north and west.

**422. McQUEEN, Malcolm**
Nov. 22, 1828, 2 miles S Ponce de Leon, Walton Co. NE 1/4 Sect. 18 Tp. 3 R. 17, north and west.

**6490. McRAE, Archibald**
Jan. 10, 1837, 1/2 mile SW Jasper, Hamilton Co. W 1/2 NW 1/4 Sect. 8 Tp. 1 R. 14, north and east.

**6840. McRAE, Archibald**
Mar. 6, 1837, 1 mile S Jasper, Hamilton Co. SE 1/4 SW 1/4 Sect. 8 Tp. 1 R. 14, north and east.

**7274. McRAE, Archibald**
Jan. 26, 1838, 3/4 mile W Jasper, Hamilton Co. E 1/2 SE 1/4 Sect. 5 Tp. 1 R. 14, south and east.

**7303. McRAE, Archibald**
Feb. 7, 1838, 2 miles SE by S Marion, Hamilton Co. E 1/2 SE 1/4 Sect. 8 Tp. 1 R. 14, south and east.

**7371. McRAE, Archibald**
Mar. 1, 1838, 1/2 mile SSE Marion, Hamilton Co. SE 1/4 NE 1/4 Sect. 5 Tp. 1 R. 14, south and east.

**7496. McRAE, Archibald**
June 20, 1838, 2 miles SSE Marion, Hamilton Co. E 1/2 NW 1/4 Sect. 4 Tp. 1 R. 14, south and east.

**5654. McRAE, Colin C.**
May 6, 1836, 2 1/4 miles NE Gretna, Gadsden Co. E 1/2 NE 1/4 Sect. 13 Tp. 3 R. 4, north and west.

**3725. McRAE, Joseph**
Feb. 12, 1883, 3/8 mile N Lake City, Columbia Co. SE 1/4 NW 1/4 Sect. 19 Tp. 6S R. 16E.

**3533. McRAENG, Daniel**
May 28, 1830, 2 1/2 miles W Alma, Leon Co. W 1/2 SW 1/4 Sect. 33 Tp. 3 R. 4, north and east. Transferred to

**Henry C. WHEELER and Wm. GARRETT**, Jan. 7, 1831.

**5090. McSEMORE, John**
July 23, 1835, 9 miles NNW Indian Pass, on St. Joseph's Bay, Gulf Co. Lot No. 1 Tp. 9 R. 12, south and west.

**2986. McSWEEN, Sween**
Aug. 25, 1829, 1/2 mile E Eucheanna, Walton Co. W 1/2 SW 1/4 Sect. 35 Tp. 2 R. 18, north and west.

**1785. MEARS, David J.**
Feb. 25, 1880, 2 miles NE Ocheesee, Calhoun Co. N 1/2 SW 1/4 and S 1/2 NW 1/4 Sect. 11 Tp. 2N R. 8W.

**5993. MENNEN, Asa**
Nov. 9, 1836, 1 mile S Lake Jackson, Leon Co. E 1/2 NE 1/4 Sect. 7 Tp. 1 R. 1, north and west.

**5994. MENNEN, Asa**
Nov. 9, 1836, 3/4 mile SE Havana, Gadsden Co. W 1/2 NE 1/4 Sect. 13 Tp. 1 R. 2, north and west.

**7860. MERRITT, Ethrington J.**
Feb. 11, 1839, at Oakdale, Jackson Co. NE 1/4 SW 1/4 Sect. 25 Tp. 4 R. 10, north and west.

**6453. MERSHON, William**
Jan. 7, 1837, 4 miles WNW Dills, Jefferson Co. SE 1/4 SW 1/4 Sect. 28 Tp. 3 R. 5, north and east.

**7615. MICKLIN, Launnu**
Aug. 24, 1838, 1 mile W by N White Springs, Hamilton Co. E 1/2 NW 1/4 Sect. 1 Tp. 3 R. 15, south and east.

**2654. MICKLER, Mathews**
Mar. 23, 1854, 2 1/4 miles NNW Burke's Mill, Suwannee Co. SE 1/4 NE 1/4 Sect. 6 Tp. 3 R. 15, south and east.

**2655. MICKLER, Mathews**
Mar. 23, 1854, 3 miles NNE Houston, Suwannee Co. SE 1/4 NE 1/4 Sect. 25 Tp. 2 R. 14, south and east.

**5919. MICKLER, Mathews**
Oct. 24, 1836, 2 3/4 miles NE Genoa, Hamilton Co. NW 1/4 NW 1/4 Sect. 34 Tp. 1 R. 15, south and east.

**8276. MILES, James**
Mar. 30, 1840, 4 miles N McDavid, Escambia Co. NW 1/4 SW 1/4 Sect. 2 Tp. 4 R. 31, north and west.

**8805. MILLER, Andrew J.**
Aug. 22, 1845, 2 miles W Concord, Gadsden Co. NW 1/4 NW 1/4 Sect.

14 Tp. 3 R. 1, north and west.

**8980. MILLER, Andrew J.**
Oct. 17, 1846, 2 1/2 miles S Concord, Gadsden Co. SW 1/4 NW 1/4 Sect. 31 Tp. 3 R. 1, north and west.

**3858. MILLER, Benjamin**
Jan. 21, 1831, 2 miles W Hamburg, Madison Co. W 1/2 NW 1/4 Sect. 17 Tp. 2 R. 8, north and east.

**7025. MILLER, Ebenezer G.**
Aug. 9, 1837, 4 miles W Midway, Gadsden Co. NE 1/4 NW 1/4 and NW 1/4 NE 1/4 Sect. 15 Tp. 3 R. 1, north and west.

**2686. MILLER, Francis P.**
Jan. 28, 1829, 2 1/2 miles E Stringer, Leon Co. W 1/2 NE 1/4 Sect. 26 Tp. 3 R. 3, north and east.

**3212. MILLER, Francis P.**
Jan. 16, 1830, 2 miles NE Havana, Gadsden Co. E 1/2 NE 1/4 Sect. 26 Tp. 3 R. 3, north and east. Paid in scrip issued to **Alex. MACOMB**, survivor of Edgar and Macomb.

**457. MILLER, Francis P.**
Nov. 12, 1833, 1 mile S Finch, Jefferson Co. E 1/2 SE 1/4 Sect. 23 Tp. 3 R. 3, north and east.

**5332. Miller, Francis P.**
Dec. 8, 1835, 2 miles NE Stringer, Jefferson Co. W 1/2 SE 1/4 Sect. 23 Tp. 3 R. 3, north and east.

**5588. MILLER, Henry**
April 9, 1836, 1 1/4 miles N Wadesboro, Leon Co. SE 1/4 SW 1/4 Sect. 30 Tp. 2 R. 3, north and east.

**5809. MILLER, Henry T.**
Aug. 24, 1836, 2 miles N by E Wadesboro, Leon Co. E 1/2 NE 1/4 Sect. 30 Tp. 2 R. 3, north and east.

**3857. MILLER, Irwin**
Jan. 21, 1831, 1 1/4 miles N Meridian, Leon Co. E 1/2 SE 1/4 Sect. 7 Tp. 1 R. 3, north and east.

**5336. MILLER, Irwin**
Dec. 9, 1835, 3 miles NE Stringer, Jefferson Co. NW 1/4 NE 1/4 Sect. 7 Tp. 1 R. 3, north and east.

**5649. MILLER, Irwin**
May 3, 1836, 3 1/4 miles NW Lloyd, Jefferson Co. NW 1/4 SW 1/4 Sect. 8 Tp. 1 R. 3, north and east.

**6334. MILLER, Irwin**
Dec. 28, 1836, 1 1/2 miles SSE Wadesboro, Jefferson Co. SW 1/4 SW 1/4 Sect. 8 Tp. 1 R. 3, north and east.

**3236. MILLER, Humphrey D.**
Jan. 28, 1830, 1/2 mile NE Stringer, Leon Co. W 1/2 NW 1/4 Sect. 22 Tp. 3 R. 3, north and east. Certificate No. 73, dated May 30, 1829 in favour of **Alex MACOMB**, for $100. received for the within."

**4782. MILLER, Humphrey D.**
Jan. 19, 1835, 3 miles NE Fanlew, Jefferson Co. SE 1/4 SE 1/4 Sect. 21 Tp. 3 R. 3, north and east.

**5243. MILLER, Humphrey D.**
Nov. 3, 1835, 1 mile N Stringer, Jefferson Co. W 1/2 SE 1/4 Sect. 21 Tp. 3 R. 3, north and east.

**4043. MILLER, Jas. R.**
July 23, 1831, 1 mile SE Stringer, Leon Co. W 1/2 NW 1/4 Sect. 27 Tp. 3 R. 3, north and east.

**4521. MILLER, Jas. R.**
Jan. 18, 1834, 1 1/2 miles NNE Stringer, Leon Co. NE 1/4 SW 1/4 Sect. 22 Tp. 3 R. 3, north and east.

**1973. MILLER, Joseph**
June 30, 1827, 2 miles NE Quincy, Gadsden Co. W 1/2 NE 1/4 Sect. 32 Tp. 3 R. 3, north and west.

**2327. MILLER, Joseph**
April 1, 1828, 1/2 mile W Copeland, Leon Co. W 1/2 NW 1/4 Sect. 32 Tp. 3 R. 3, north and east.

**2630. MILLER, Joseph**
Jan. 16, 1829, at Copeland, Leon Co. E 1/2 NE 1/4 Sect. 32 Tp. 3 R. 3, north and east.

**3137. MILLER, Joseph**
Nov. 28, 1829, 1 mile W Alma, Leon Co. E 1/2 SW 1/4 Sect. 33 Tp. 3 R. 4, north and east.

**3437. MILLER, Joseph**
March 5, 1830, just W Copeland, Leon Co. SE 1/4 Sect. 32 Tp. 3 R. 3, north and east.

**3859. MILLER, Joseph**
Jan. 21, 1831, 1 mile W Copeland, Leon Co. E 1/2 NE 1/4 Sect. 31 Tp. 3 R. 3, north and east.

**5533. MILLER, Joseph**
Mar. 11, 1836, 1/4 mile E Copeland, Jefferson Co. W 1/2 NE 1/4 Sect. 31 Tp. 3 R. 3, north and east.

**7395. MILLER, John**

Mar. 6, 1838, 2 1/2 miles SSE Myrick, Madison Co. SW 1/4 Sect. 2 Tp. 1 R. 7, south and east.

**1969. MILLER, John S.**
June 28, 1827, 2 miles SSE Capitola, Jefferson Co. SW 1/4 Sect. 31 Tp. 1 R. 3, north and east.

**1979. MILLER, John S.**
July 2, 1827, 6 1/2 miles SW Monticello, Jefferson Co. W 1/2 SW 1/4 Sect. 4 Tp. 1 R. 4, north and east.

**1980. MILLER, John S.**
July 2, 1827, 6 1/2 miles SW Monticello, Jefferson Co. E 1/2 SE 1/4 Sect. 5 Tp. 1 R. 4, north and east.

**8441. MILLER, Levi F.**
Jan. 4, 1841, at Norum, Washington Co. SE 1/4 SE 1/4 Sect. 7 Tp. 2 R. 15, north and west.

**1579. MILLER, Mathew**
Dec. 20, 1852, 2 miles W Dukes, Union Co. NE 1/4 NE 1/4 Sect. 18 Tp. 6 R. 19, south and east. Patent delivered Oct. 10, 1856.

**7922. MILLER, Nathaniel**
March 15, 1839, 1/4 mile SW norum, Washington Co. NE 1/4 NE 1/4 Sect. 18 Tp. 2 R. 15, north and west.

**8662. MILLER, Nathaniel**
Aug. 3, 1844, 4 1/2 miles W by N Vernon, Washington Co. SW 1/4 SE 1/4 Sect. 6 Tp. 2 R. 14, north and west.

**8442. MILLER, Sara**
Jan. 4, 1841, 1/4 mile NE Norum, Washington Co. SE 1/4 NW 1/4 Sect. 7 Tp. 2 R. 15, north and west.

**8443. MILLER, William L.**
Jan. 4, 1841, 1/4 mile SW Norum, Washington Co. SW 1/4 SW 1/4 Sect. 7 Tp. 2 R. 15, north and west.

**6301. MILLIN, Humphrey D.**
Dec. 24, 1836, 3/4 miles NNE Stringer, Leon Co. NE 1/4 SE 1/4 Sect. 21 Tp. 3 R. 3, north and east.

**2253. MILLS, Archibald**
(of Fla.) Feb. 11, 1828, 5 miles NNE Wadesboro, Leon Co. E 1/2 NW 1/4 Sect. 21 Tp. 2 R. 3, north and east.

**2365. MILLS, Archibald**
Feb. 20, 1854, 1/2 mile W Standard, Marion Co. NW 1/4 SE 1/4 Sect. 19 Tp. 14 R. 20, south and east. Patent delivered Aug. 7, 1857.

**1388. MILLS, Charles C.**
(of Ga.) May 19, 1827, 1/2 mile S Capitola, Jefferson Co. W 1/2 SE 1/4 Sect. 19 Tp.1 R. 3, north and east. Transcribed from the original record in ther Register of Receipts, Tallahassee, Florida.

**1389. MILLS, Charles C.**
(of Ga.) May 19, 1827, 2 miles E Capitola, Jefferson Co. SW 1/4 Sect. 29 Tp. 1 R. 3, north and east. Transcribed from the original record in the office of the Receiver at Tallahassee, Jan. 15, 1834. (Signed L. READ)

**1390. MILLS, Charles C.**
(of Ga.) May 19, 1827, 5 miles E Capitola, Jefferson Co. W 1/2 NE 1/4 Sect. 30 Tp. 1 R. 3, north and east. Transcript from original record in the office of the Receiver at Tallahassee. (Signed L. READ)

**2352. MILLS, David**
April 24, 1828, 5 miles N Havana, Gadsden Co. E 1/2 NE 1/4 Sect. 10 Tp. 3 R. 2, north and west.

**4468. MILLS, David**
Dec. 5, 1833, 3 1/2 miles SSE Iamonia, Leon Co. NW 1/4 NE 1/4 Sect. 10 Tp. 3 R. 2, north and east.

**5933. MILLS, David**
Oct. 27, 1836, 6 1/2 miles N by E Round Lake (town), Jackson Co. NW 1/4 NW 1/4 Sect. 11 Tp. 3 R. 2, north and west.

**7784. MILLS, David**
Dec. 29, 1838, 1 mile SSW Darsey, Gadsden Co. SW 1/4 NE 1/4 Sect. 10 Tp. 3 R. 2, north and west.

**6418. MILLS, Elizabeth**
Jan. 4, 1837, 1/2 mile W Madison, Madison Co. NW 1/4 W 1/2 NE 1/4 Sect. 29 Tp. 1 R. 9, north and east.

**5519. MILLS, Gideon**
Mar. 10, 1836, 1 1/2 miles N by E Wadesboro, Leon Co. NW 1/4 NE 1/4 Sect. 30 Tp. 2 R. 3, north and east.

**8807. MILLS, Gideon**
Aug. 26, 1845, 2 3/4 miles N by E Monticello, Madison Co. Nw 1/4 SW 1/4 Sect. 8 Tp. 2 R. 5, south and east.

**4982. MILLS, Henry I.**
May 25, 1835, 3 miles S Miccosukee, Jefferson Co. W 1/2 SE 1/4 Sect. 29 Tp. 2 R. 3, north and east.

**5535. MILLS, Henry I.**
Mar. 14, 1836, 7 miles E Centerville, Leon Co. W 1/2 SW 1/4 Sect. 19 Tp. 2 R. 3, north and east.

**7158. MILLS, James A.**
Dec. 19, 1837, 2 miles N Wadesboro, Leon Co. SE 1/4 SE 1/4 Sect. 30 Tp. 2 R. 3, north and east.

**2356. MILLS, Jas.**
April 30, 1828, 7 miles E by N Marianna, Jackson Co. SE 1/4 Sect. 28 Tp. 5 R. 9, north and west.

**2357. MILLS, Jas.**
April 30, 1828, 6 1/2 miles E by N Marianna, Jackson Co. NW 1/4 Sect. 28 Tp. 5 R. 9, north and west.

**2319. MILLS, Jane**
(Widow) March 24, 1828, 2 miles E Copeland, Jefferson Co. W 1/2 NW 1/4 Sect. 35 Tp. 3 R. 3, north and east.

**4542. MILLS, Jonathan**
Feb. 7, 1834, 2 1/2 miles N by E Felkel, Leon Co. E 1/2 NW 1/4 Sect. 6 Tp. 2 R. 2, north and east.

**456. MILLS & PERRY**
(Assignee of **Hugh HOLMES**) June 22, 1829, 1 mile S Ocheesee, Calhoun Co. Lot No. 7 Sect. 7 Tp. 2 R. 7, north and west. (Also Register's Receipt of Application of same date.)

**460. MILLS & PERRY**
(Assignee of **John GILSTRAP**) June 22, 1829, 3 miles WSW Roy, Liberty Co. Lot 1 Fractional Sect. 8 Tp. 2 R. 7, north and west. Transferred to **William TONEY**, July 7, 1829. (With this is a Register's Application Receipt signed by **G. W. WARD**, Reg.)

**460. MILLS & PERRY**
(Assignee of **Jas. WILLIAMS**) June 22, 1829, 3 miles ENE Ocheesee, or WNW Roy, Liberty Co. Lot No. 7 Fractional Sect. 33 Tp. 2 R. 7, north and west. Transferred from **MILLS & PERRY** to **William TONEY**, July 7, 1829.

**461. MILLS & PERRY**
(Assignee of **David KING**) June 22, 1829, 3 miles W Roy, Liberty Co. Lot No. 2 Fractional Sect. 4 Tp. 2 R. 7, north and west. Transferred to **William TONEY**, July 7, 1829.

**462. MILLS & PERRY**
(Assignee of **James WILLIAMS**) June 22, 1829, 2 miles NE Ocheesee, Jackson Co. Lot No. 7 Sect. 33 Tp. 3 R. 7, north and west. Transferred to **William TONEY**, July 7, 1829. Also Register's Receipt.
See **DAVID THOMAS** and **Ivory B. PERRY**

**3587. MILLS, Reuben**
Aug. 11, 1830, 11 miles N Tallahassee, Leon Co. W 1/2 SE 1/4 Sect. 1 Tp. 2 R. 1, north and west.

**112. MILLS, Thos.**
Dec. 22, 1826, 4 miles N Lake Jackson Station, Gadsden Co. NE 1/4 Sect. 18 Tp. 2 R. 2, north and west.

**8765. MILLS, William C.**
March 29, 1845, 1 mile SE Darsey, Gadsden Co. SW 1/4 NW 1/4 Sect. 12 Tp. 3 R. 2, north and west.

**6749. MILLS, Wm. J.**
Feb. 6, 1837, 2 miles SE Perkins, Leon Co. SW 1/4 Sect. 1 Tp. 1 R. 13, south and east.

**MILTON, John** see **James L. FINLEY, #8486**

**2824. MIMFORD, Wm.**
May 14, 1829, 1/2 mile E Copeland, Leon Co. E 1/2 SW 1/4 Sect. 34 Tp. 3 R. 3, north and east.

**7606. MIMS, James**
Aug. 18, 1838, 4 1/2 miles SSE Westlake, Hamilton Co. W 1/2 Lot No. 1 Sect. 17 Tp. 1 R. 13, north and east.

**7607. MIMS, James**
Aug. 18, 1838, 4 1/2 miles SSE Westlake, Hamilton Co. N 1/2 Lot No. 2 Sect. 17 Tp. 1 R. 13, north and east.

**2118. MITCHELL, Isaac W.**
(of Fla.) Nov. 27, 1827, 4 1/2 miles N Bradfordville, Leon Co. Lot No. 6 Sect. 34 Tp. 3 R. 1, north and east.

**2797. MITCHELL, Isaac W.**
April 1, 1829, 4 miles N by W Bradfordville, Leon Co. Lot No. 5 Sect. 33 Tp. 3 R. 1, north and east.

**2798. MITCHELL, Isaac W.**
April 1, 1829, 4 miles N by W Bradfordville, Leon Co. Lot No. 3 Sect. 33 Tp. 3 R. 1, north and east.

**3805. MITCHELL, Isaac W.**
Dec. 21, 1830, 5 miles WNW Bradfordville, Leon Co. W 1/2 SE 1/4

Sect. 7 Tp. 2 R. 1, north and east.
**3806. MITCHELL, Isaac W.**
Dec. 21, 1830, 4 3/4 miles WNW Bradfordville, Leon Co. E 1/2 SW 1/4 Sect. 7 Tp. 2 R. 1, north and east.

**3538. MITCHELL, N. H.**
June 6, 1830, 1 mile NE Vernon, Washington Co. E 1/2 NW 1/4 Sect. 25 Tp. 3 R. 15, north and west.

**5794. MITCHELL, Nicholas H.**
Aug. 12, 1836, 1 mile N Macon, Wahington Co. SE 1/4 NW 1/4 Sect. 9 Tp. 2 R. 14, north and west.

**7278. MITCHELL, Nicholas**
Jan. 29, 1838, 2 miles NNE Cook, Bay Co. W 1/2 NE 1/4 Sect. 13 Tp. 4 R. 13, south and west.

**3218. MITCHELL, Samuel**
Jan. 18, 1830, 3 miles WSW Norum, Washington Co. W 1/2 SW 1/4 Sect. 13 Tp. 2 R. 16, north and west.

**4673. MITCHELL, Samuel H.**
Dec. 4, 1834, 1 mile NW Macon, Washington Co. W 1/2 SE 1/4 Sect. 9 Tp. 2 R. 14, north and west.

**674. MITCHELL, Samuel H.**
Dec. 4, 1834, 1 mile NW Macon, Washington Co. E 1/2 SE 1/4 Sect. 9 Tp. 2 R. 14, north and west.

**4845. MITCHELL, Samuel H.**
Feb. 6, 1835, 3 miles SW Enconfino, Bay Co. E 1/2 NW 1/4 Sect. 9 Tp. 1 R. 13, south and west.

**4051. MOAT, David**
July 28, 1831, 1 1/4 miles SE Marion, Hamilton Co. W 1/2 SW 1/4 Sect. 4 Tp. 1 R. 14, south and east. Transferred to **John G. SMITH**, Aug. 26, 1833.

**5261. MOBLEY, John**
Nov. 12, 1835, 1 1/4 miles S by W Marion, Hamilton Co. W 1/2 SE 1/4 Sect. 1 Tp. 1 R. 13, south and east.

**5262. MOBLEY, John**
Nov. 12, 1835, 1 1/4 miles SW Marion, Hamilton Co. SE 1/4 NE 1/4 Sect. 1 Tp. 1 R. 13, south and east.

**6893. MOBLEY, John**
March 14, 1837, 1 mile WSW Marina, Hamilton Co. NE 1/4 NE 1/4 Sect. 1 Tp. 1 R. 13, south and east.

**7738. MOBLEY, William**
Dec. 1, 1838, 3 miles SE Bellville, Hamilton Co. E 1/2 NE 1/4 Sect. 4 Tp. 2 R. 11, north and east.

**2042. MOLT, Abraham, Sr.**
Aug. 23, 1827, 2 miles S Monticello, Jefferson Co. W 1/2 SW 1/4 Sect. 6 Tp. 1 R. 5, north and east.

**8099. MONROE, George**
Sept. 28, 1839, 3 3/4 miles N Midway, Gadsden Co. E 1/2 NW 1/4 Sect. 17 Tp. 2 R. 1, north and west.

**8315. MONROE, Thomas S.**
May 5, 1840, 1 mile SW Jamieson, Gadsden Co. S 1/2 NE 1/4 Sect. 13 Tp. 2 R. 3, north and west.

**MONROE, Wm. P.** see **James STRINGFELLOW**

**3150. MONSON, Asa**
Dec. 5, 1829, 2 1/2 miles W Ocklocknee, Leon Co. W 1/2 NW 1/4 Sect. 27 Tp. 1 R. 2, north and west.

**55. MONTAGUE, Frances**
Feb. 26, 1874, 2 1/2 miles S Harwood, Flagler Co. Lot No. 3 Sect. 34 Tp. 13 and Lot No. 1 Sect. 3 Tp. 14 R. 32, south and east. Commented Homestead Emty. No. 4689. Filed In Clerk's office for Board Oct. 26th and recorded the same date 26th day of October, 1874 in Book "B" on page 261. **John W. DICKINS**, Clerk.

**734. MONTFORD, John C.**
(of Fla.) Aug. 8, 1826, 3 miles ENE Centerville, Leon Co. E 1/2 NW 1/4 Sect. 17 Tp. 3 R. 2, north and east.

**2072. MONTFORD, John C.**
Oct. 4, 1827, 1 mile SSE Miccosukee, Leon Co. W 1/2 SE 1/4 Sect. 10 Tp. 2 R. 3, north and east.

**3842. MONTFORD, John C.**
April 20, 1830, 2 miles SSW Miccosukee, Leon Co. W 1/2 SE 1/4 Sect. 17 Tp. 2 R. 3, north and west.

**3985. MONTFORD, John C.**
June 15, 1831, 2 miles SW Miccosukee, Leon Co. W 1/2 SW 1/4 Sect. 17 Tp. 2 R. 3, north and east.

**5630. MONTFORD, John C.**
April 28, 1836, at Fincher, Jefferson Co. E 1/2 SW 1/4 Sect. 17 Tp. 2 R. 3, north and east.

**7181. MONTFORD, John C.**
Jan. 1 1838, 2 miles S Miccosukee, Jefferson Co. E 1/2 NW 1/4 Sect. 20 Tp. 2 R. 3, north and east.

**1279. MONTFORD, John E.**

(DUP) April 16, 1827, 1 mile SW Miccosukee, Leon Co. W 1/2 NE 1/4 Sect. 17 Tp. 2 R. 3, north and east.
**2261. MONTFORD, Wm.**
Feb. 16, 1828, 4 miles E by N Quincy, Gadsden Co. W 1/2 SE 1/4 Sect. 34 Tp. 3 R. 3, north and east.
**1932. MOODY, Benjamin**
June 23, 1827, 5 miles W Tallahassee, Leon Co. E 1/2 NW 1/4 Sect. 3 Tp. 1 R. 1, south and west.
**4001. MOODY, Benjamin**
July 12, 1831, 2 1/4 miles W Tallahassee, Leon Co. E 1/2 SE 1/4 Sect. 3 Tp. 1 R. 1, south and west.
**4172. MOODY, Benjamin**
May 29, 1832, 1 1/4 miles SW Tallahassee, Leon Co. N 1/2, E 1/2 NE 1/4 Sect. 10 Tp. 1 R. 1, south and west.
**5623. MOODY, Benjamin**
April 25, 1836, 2 1/2 miles W Tallahassee, Leon Co. W 1/2 NW 1/4 Sect. 4 Tp. 1 R. 1, south and west.
**5777. MOODY, Benjamin**
July 19, 1836, 3 1/2 miles W Tallahassee, Leon Co. SE 1/4 NE 1/4 Sect. 5 Tp. 1 R. 1, south and west.
**967. MOODY, Benjamin**
Oct. 11, 1851, c. 2 miles NW Dukes, Union Co. NE 1/4 NE 1/4 Sect. 17 Tp. 6 R. 19, south and east. Patent delivered Dec. 4, 1850 (?)
**1739. MOODY, Benjamin**
Mar. 1, 1853, 2 3/4 miles SE Providence, Union Co. NE 1/4 SW 1/4 Sect. 14 Tp. 6 R. 18, south and east. Patent delivered Oct. 4, 1856.
**1740. MOODY, Benjamin**
Mar. 1, 1853, 2 3/4 miles SE Providence, Union Co. NW 1/4 NE 1/4 Sect. 23 Tp. 6 R. 18, south and east. Patent delivered Oct. 4, 1856.
**2214. MOODY, Benjamin**
Sept. 29, 1853, 3 1/2 miles SE Dukes, Union Co. SE 1/4 NE 1/4 and NE 1/4 SE 1/4 Sect. 19 Tp. 6 R. 19, south and east. Patent delivered Oct. 4, 1856.
**2405. MOODY, Benjamin**
Feb. 21, 1854, 3 miles SSW Dukes, Union Co. W 1/2 SW 1/4 Sect. 23 Tp. 6 R. 18, south and east. Patent delivered Oct. 4, 1856.
**2810. MOODY, Benjamin**
July 10, 1854, 2 1/2 miles SW Dukes, Union Co. S 1/2 SE 1/4 Sect. 19 Tp. 6 R. 19, south and east. Patent delivered Oct. 4, 1856.
**2423. MOODY, John B.**
Feb. 21, 1854, 1/2 miles N Dukes, Union Co. SE 1/4 NE 1/4 Sect. 17 Tp. 6 R. 19, south and east. Patent delivered Sept. 24, 1857.
**8997. MOORE, Columbus F.**
Jan. 23, 1891, 2 miles NW Mutual, Gilchrist Co. NE 1/4 Sect. 10 Tp. 9S R. 16E.
**1140. MOORE, George**
(DUP) Feb. 17, 1827, 2 miles NW Centerville, Leon Co. SW 1/4 Sect. 11 Tp. 2 R. 1, south and east.
**1923. MOORE, George**
June 18, 1827, 2 miles N Bradfordville, Leon Co. E 1/2 SE 1/4 Sect. 10 Tp. 2 R. 1, north and east.
**1924. MOORE, George**
June 18, 1827, 2 1/2 miles N Bradfordville, Leon Co. W 1/2 NE 1/4 Sect. 9 Tp. 2 R. 1, north and east.
**2759. MOORE, George**
Feb. 24, 1829, 1 mile NNW Bradfordville, Leon Co. W 1/2 NW 1/4 Sect. 14 Tp. 2 R. 1, north and east.
**6337. MOORE, Hardy**
Dec. 28, 1836, c. 3 miles NE Alma, Jefferson Co. Lots No. 3 and 5, & 6 Fractional Sect. 24 Tp. 3 R. 4, north and east.
**8940. MOORE, Hiddar M.**
April 29, 1846, 4 1/2 miles SSE Bloxan, Wakulla Co. SE 1/4 NW 1/4 Sect. 28 Tp. 1 R. 3, south and east.
**5833. MOORE, James**
Sept. 7, 1836, 4 miles S by W Quincy, Gadsden Co. NW 1/4 NW 1/4 and NE 1/4 NW 1/4 Sect. 24 Tp. 2 R. 4, north and east.
**8147. MOORE, James**
Nov. 19, 1839, 3 miles NNW Monticello, Jefferson Co. Lot No. 4 Sect. 14 Tp. 2 R. 4, north and east.
**2776. MOORE, John**
March 10, 1829, 4 miles SSW Miccosukee, Leon Co. E 1/2 SW 1/4 Sect. 11 Tp. 2 R. 2, north and east.
**2781. MOORE, John**
March 11, 1829, 4 1/2 miles W Miccosukee, Leon Co. E 1/2 SE 1/4

Sect. 10 Tp. 2 R. 2, north and east.
**7153. MOORE, John**
Dec. 18, 1837, 3 miles SW Dills, Jefferson Co. E 1/2 NW 1/4 Sect. 14 Tp. 2 R. 5, north and east.
**4607. MOORE, Joseph**
Aug. 19, 1834, 1 mile SE Centerville, Leon Co. W 1/2 SE 1/4 Sect. 26 Tp. 2 R. 1, north and east.
**4608. MOORE, Joseph**
Aug. 19, 1834, 1 1/4 miles SE Centerville, Leon Co. E 1/2 SW 1/4 Sect. 16 Tp. 2 R. 1, north and east.
**4609. MOORE, Joseph**
Aug. 19, 1834, 1 1/4 miles S by E Centerville, Leon Co. NE 1/4 SE 1/4 Sect. 16 Tp. 2 R. 1, north and east.
**7576. MOORE, Joseph**
Aug. 6, 1838, 1 mile SSW Hamburg, Madison Co. E 1/2 SW 1/4 Sect. 9 Tp. 2 R. 8, north and east.
**5176. MOORE, Kiddar M.**
Oct. 1, 1835, 1/4 mile SE Fincher, Leon Co. W 1/2 NW 1/4 SSect. 24 Tp. 3 R. 3, north and east.
**6836. MOORE, Kiddar M.**
Mar. 4, 1837, 1 mile W Miccosukee, Leon Co. SW 1/4 NW 1/4 Sect. 8 Tp. 2 R. 3, north and east.
**2366. MOORE, Leon**
May 8, 1828, 1 mile NW Miccosukee, Leon Co. E 1/2 SW 1/4 Sect. 5 Tp. 2 R. 3, north and east.
**2131. MOORE, Levi**
(of Fla.) Dec. 7, 1828, 1 mile SW Copeland, Leon Co. W 1/2 NW 1/4 Sect. 5 Tp. 2 R. 3, north and east.
**4464. MOORE, Levi**
Dec. 2, 1833, 1/2 mile S Copeland, Leon Co. SW 1/4 SW 1/4 Sect. 5 Tp. 2 R. 3, north and east.
**5470. MOORE, Levi**
Feb. 18, 1836, 2 1/2 miles NW Fincher, Leon Co. NW 1/4 SW 1/4 Sect. 5 Tp. 2 R. 3, north and east.
**8968. MOORE, Luke**
Aug. 14, 1846, 4 miles SW O'Brian, Suwannee Co. Lot No. 3 Sect. 35 Tp. 5 R. 13, south and east.
**2103. MOORE, Thomas**
Nov. 14, 1827, 3 miles S Meridian, Leon Co. W 1/2 NW 1/4 Sect. 6 Tp. 2 R. 1, north and east.
**2105. MOORE, Thomas**
Nov. 16, 1827, 3 miles SW Meridian, Leon Co. Lot No. 3 Sect. 36 Tp.3 R. 1, north and west.
**2123. MOORE, Thomas**
(of Ga.) Dec. 4, 1827, 4 miles S by W Meridian, Leon Co. E 1/2 NE 1/4 Sect. 1 Tp. 2 R. 1, north and west.
**7114. MOORE, Thomas**
Nov. 27, 1837, 3 1/2 miles W Tallahassee, Leon Co. NW 1/4 NW 1/4 Sect. 32 Tp. 1 R. 1, north and west.
**MOORE, William B. see Thos. P. RANDOLPH**
**212. MORGAN, Ephraim Preston**
Nov. 17, 1845, c. 3 1/2 miles NE McKinley, Columbia Co. SE 1/4 NW 1/4 Sect. 10 Tp. 3 R. 16, south and east.
**521. MORGAN, Ephraim Preston**
Feb. 11, 1847, 3 miles NE McKinley, Columbia Co. NW 1/4 SW 1/4 Sect. 10 Tp. 3 R. 16, south and east. Patent delivered Mar. 3, 1875.
**8314. MORGAN, Marcellus**
May 2, 1840, 2 miles NNE Hinson, Gadsden Co. SW 1/4 NW 1/4 Sect. 15 Tp. 1 R. 2, north and west.
**8932. MORING, John S.**
April 6, 1846, 1/4 mile S Gadsden, Gadsden Co. NE 1/4 SW 1/4 Sect. 15 Tp. 1 R. 2, north and west.
**4658. MORISON, Daniel**
Oct. 19, 1857, 1 mile SW Grove Park, Alachua Co. SE 1/4 Sect. 25 Tp. 10 R. 22, south and east.
**513. MORRIS, Edwin**
May 2, 1831, 4 miles NW Ashville, Jefferson Co. W 1/2 SE 1/4 Sect. 25 Tp. 3 R. 6, north and east.
**514. MORRIS, Edwin**
May 2, 1831, 1/2 mile N Ashville, Jefferson Co. W 1/2 NE 1/4 Sect. 32 Tp. 3 R. 7, north and east.
**8857. MORRIS, Elizabeth A.**
Dec. 17, 1845, 3 miles W by N Greensboro, Gadsden Co. E 1/2 SE 1/4 Sect. 2 Tp. 2 R. 6, north and west.
**7689. MORRIS, James D.**
(and **Lemuel R. SESSIONS**) Oct. 27, 1838, 3 miles W Sirmans, Madison Co. NE 1/4 NE 1/4 Sect. 6 Tp. 2 R. 7, north and east.
**7701. MORRIS, Jonathan**
Nov. 18, 1838, 1/2 mile S Marianna,

Jackson Co. NE 1/4 SE 1/4 Sect. 9 Tp. 4 R. 10, north and west.

**8753. MORRIS, Jonathan**
Mar. 6, 1845, 6 1/2 miles E by N Wansan, Washington Co. SW 1/4 NE 1/4 Sect. 25 Tp. 3 R. 13, north and west.

**507. MORRIS, John E. B.**
(MORRIP?) April 26, 1831, at Lovett, Madison Co. W 1/2 NE 1/4 Sect. 33 Tp. 3 R. 7, north and east. (Preemption Act of 1830).

**508. MORRIS, John E. B.**
(MORRIP?) Apr. 26, 1831, at Lovett, Madison Co. E 1/2 NW 1/4 Sect. 33 Tp. 3 R. 7, north and east.

**5720. MORRIS, John E. B.**
June 24, 1836, 2 3/4 miles SE Bond, Madison Co. W 1/2 SW 1/4 Sect. 11 Tp. 2 R. 8, north and east.

**5724. MORRIS, John E. B.**
June 24, 1836, 2 1/2 miles SE Bond, Madison Co. W 1/2 SW 1/4 Sect. 12 Tp. 2 R. 8, north and east.

**5744. MORRIS, John E. B.**
June 30, 1836, 1 mile E by N Hamburg, Madison Co. NE 1/4 NW 1/4 Sect. 13 Tp. 2 R. 8, north and east.

**5745. MORRIS, John E. B.**
June 30, 1836, 1 1/4 miles NNE Hamburg, Madison Co. SE 1/4 SE 1/4 Sect. 11 Tp. 2 R. 8, north and east.

**8434. MORRIS, John E. B.**
Dec. 23, 1840, 1 mile NNE Ashville, Jefferson Co. SE 1/4 Sect. 29 Tp. 3 R. 7, north and east.

**454. MORRISON, Allen**
Jan. 19, 1829, 5 miles SSW Ponce de Leon, Walton Co. E 1/2 NW 1/4 Sect. 18 Tp. 3 R. 17, north and west.

**726. MORRISON Daniel**
April 1, 1850, at Oakton, Putnam Co. SW 1/4 NE 1/4 Sect. 36 Tp. 10 R. 22, south and east.

**2298. MORRISON, Daniel**
Oct. 1853, 1/2 mile E Hawthorne, Alachua Co. S 1/2 SW 1/4 Sect. 25 Tp. 3 R. 2, south and east.

**2227. MORTAN, Marcellus**
Jan. 15, 1828, at Hinson, Gadsden Co. E 1/2 SW 1/4 Sect. 21 Tp. 3 R. 2, north and west.

**2226. MORTAN, Richard**
(of Fla.) Jan. 15, 1828, at Hinson, Gadsden Co. W 1/2 SE 1/4 Sect. 21 Tp. 3 R. 2, north and west.

**5497. MORTON, Jackson**
Mar. 1, 1836, 1/2 mile NNW Fentress, Santa Rosa Co. E 1/2 NE 1/4 Sect. 12 Tp. 3 R. 27, north and west.

**5906. MORTON, Jackson**
Oct. 18, 1836, 1 1/2 miles N by W Fentress, Santa Rosa Co. E 1/2 NE 1/4 Sect. 1 Tp. 3 R. 27, north and west.

**5907. MORTON, Jackson**
Oct. 18, 1836, 2 miles N by W Fentress, Santa Rosa Co. SE 1/4 Sect. 36 Tp. 4 R. 27, north and west.

**3363. MORTON, William**
Feb. 14, 1830, 1 mile E Roseville, Santa Rosa Co. E 1/2 SE 1/4 Sect. 19 Tp. 2 R. 27, north and west.

**3364. MORTON, William**
Feb. 14, 1830, 1 1/4 miles E Roseville, Santa Rosa Co. W 1/2 SW 1/4 Sect. 20 Tp. 2 R. 27, north and west.

**3419. MORTON, William**
Feb. 22, 1830, just S Roseville, Santa Rosa Co. NE 1/4 Sect. 25 Tp. 2 R. 28, north and west.

**3420. MORTON, William**
Feb. 22, 1830, just E Roseville, Santa Rosa Co. SW 1/4 Sect. 19 Tp. 2 R. 27, north and west.

**2931. MOSEBY, Mathew B.**
Oct. 2, 1854, 3/4 mile S Wannee, Gilchrist Co. SE 1/4 SW 1/4 Sect. 17 Tp. 9 R. 14, south and east.

**8289. MOSELEY, Alexander**
April 14, 1840, 1 3/4 miles W Calhoun, Madison Co. W 1/2 NW 1/4 Sect. 15 Tp. 1 R. 9, north and east.

**8569. MOSELEY, Alexander**
Jan. 6, 1843, 2 miles SSW Champaign, Madison Co. W 1/2 NE 1/4 Sect. 28 Tp. 1 R. 9, north and east.

**8530. MOSELEY, Jennet**
Feb. 15, 1842, 1 mile W Champaign, Madsion Co. E 1/2 SE 1/4 Sect. 22 Tp. 1 R. 8, north and east.

**8240. MOSELEY, Lewis M.**
Feb. 29, 1840, 1 mile W Champaign, Madison Co. NE 1/4 SW 1/4 Sect. 27 Tp. 1 R. 8, north and east.

**8085. MOSELEY, William A.**
Sept. 19, 1839, 1 1/2 miles S Champaign, Madison Co. SE 1/4 SE 1/4

Sect. 27 Tp. 1 R. 8, north and east.

**4848. MOSLEY, Henry H.**
Sept. 13, 1858, 5 miles NE McAlpin, Suwannee Co. NE 1/4 Sect. 24 Tp. 4 R. 14, south and east.

**1502. MOTES, Zachariah**
Nov. 8, 1852, 1/2 mile E Mannville, Putnam Co. NE 1/4 SE 1/4 Sect. 13 Tp. 10 R. 24, south and east. Patent delivered Nov. 27, 1857.

**5810. MOTT, Abraham**
Aug. 24, 1836, 3/4 mile W Madison, Madison Co. NE 1/4 NW 1/4 Sect. 33 Tp. 1 R. 9, north and east.

**277. MOTT, John Matthews**
Jan. 17, 1846, 2 miles NW Thomasville, Alachua Co. NW 1/4 NW 1/4 Sect. 15 Tp. 7 R. 19, south and east. Transferred to **Daniel HOLDER**, Aug. 14, 1846.

**6355. MOTT, Paul**
Dec. 30, 1836, 2 miles WSW Copeland, Jefferson Co. NE 1/4 NW 1/4 Sect. 6 Tp. 2 R. 3, north and east.

**1031. MOTT, William**
Dec. 6, 1851, 1/2 mile W Thomasville, Alachua Co. SE 1/4 SW 1/4 Sect. 23 Tp. 7 R. 19, south and east. Patent delivered Nov. 28, 1856.

**4827. MOUNTFORD, John C.**
Jan. 26, 1835, 2 miles S Miccosukee, Leon Co. W 1/2 SW 1/4 Sect. 20 Tp. 2 R. 3, north and east.

**4828. MOUNTFORD, John C.**
Jan. 26, 1835, 1 1/2 miles S Miccosukee, Leon Co. SE 1/4 SE 1/4 Sect. 17 Tp. 2 R. 3, north and east.

**4829. MOUNTFORD, John C.**
Jan. 26, 1835, 1 1/2 miles S by E Miccosukee, Leon Co. W 1/2 NE 1/4 Sect. 20 Tp. 2 R. 3, north and east.

**2050. MUNDEN, John B.**
Sept. 1, 1827, 3 miles N Lake Jackson, Leon Co. E 1/2 SE 1/4 Sect. 17 Tp. 2 R. 1, north and west.

**3523. MUNROE, Thomas**
May 22, 1830, 3 miles NW Old Town, Dixie Co. E 1/2 SE 1/4 Sect. 4 Tp. 10 R. 13, south and east.

**3524. MUNROE, Thomas**
May 22, 1830, 3 1/2 miles NW Old Town, Dixie Co. E 1/2 NE 1/4 Sect. 4 Tp. 10 R. 13, south and east.

**3525. MUNROE, Thomas**
May 22, 1830, 3 miles NNW Old Town, Dixie Co. W 1/2 NW 1/4 Sect. 3 Tp. 10 R. 13, south and east.

**4591. MUNSON, Asa**
July 5, 1834, 5 miles S by W Tallahassee, Leon Co. SW 1/4 SE 1/4 Sect. 26 Tp. 1 R. 1, south and west.

**4592. MUNSON, Asa**
July 5, 1834, 4 3/4 miles S by W Tallahassee, Leon Co. NE 1/4 NW 1/4 Sect. 26 Tp. 1 R. 1, south and west.

**4660. MUNSON, Asa**
Nov. 10, 1834, 1/4 mile W Ocklocknee, Leon Co. W 1/2 SW 1/4 Sect. 26 Tp. 1 R. 2, north and west.

**5755. MUNSON, Asa**
July 4, 1836, 1 mile SSE Ocklocknee, Leon Co. E 1/2 NE 1/4 Sect. 30 Tp. 1 R. 1, north and west.

**5902. MUNSON, Asa**
Oct. 14, 1836, 1/4 mile N Ocklocknee, Leon Co. E 1/2 NW 1/4 Sect. 30 Tp. 1 R. 1, north and west.

**6008. MUNSON, Asa**
Nov. 14, 1836, 1 1/2 miles NW San Helena, Leon Co. E 1/2 NE 1/4 Sect. 13 Tp. 1 R. 2, north and west.

**6962. MUNSON, Asa**
Mar. 30, 1837, 3 miles SW Tallahassee, Leon Co. SW 1/4 SE 1/4 Sect. 9 Tp. 1 R. 1, south and west.

**6963. MUNSON, Asa**
Mar. 30, 1837, 5 miles S by W Tallahassee, Leon Co. W 1/2 NE 1/4 and NW 1/4 SE 1/4 Sect. 26 Tp. 1 R. 1, south and west.

**2445. MURAT, Achille**
July 21, 1828, 2 miles ENE El Destino, Jefferson Co. E 1/2 SW 1/4 Sect. 4 Tp. 1 R. 3, south and east.

**2578. MURAT, Achille**
Dec. 22, 1828, 3 miles SE El Destino, Jefferson Co. NW 1/4 Sect. 21 Tp. 1 R. 3, south and east.

**2832. MURAT, Achille**
May 22, 1829, 2 miles N Cay, Jefferson Co. W 1/2 SE 1/4 Sect. 22 Tp. 1 R. 3, south and east.

**2833. MURAT, Achille**
May 22, 1829, 2 miles N Cay, Jefferson Co. E 1/2 NE 1/4 Sect. 22 Tp. 1 R. 3, south and east.

**2839. MURAT, Achille**

June 3, 1829, 3 1/4 miles ESE El Destino, Jefferson Co. E 1/2 SE 1/4 Sect. 15 Tp. 1 R. 3, south and east.

**2840. MURAT, Achille**
June 3, 1829, 4 1/4 miles ESE El Destino, Jefferson Co. W 1/2 NW 1/4 Sect. 23 Tp. 1 R. 3, south and east.

**3113. MURAT, Achille**
(of Fla.) Nov. 8, 1829, 3/4 miles ENE El Destino, Jefferson Co. E 1/2 NE 1/4 Sect. 8 Tp. 1 R. 3, south and east.

**3503. MURAT, Achille**
May 5, 1830, 3 miles SE El Destino, Jefferson Co. W 1/2 NE 1/4 Sect. 22 Tp. 1 R. 3, south and east.

**3504. MURAT, Achille**
May 5, 1830, 3 miles NW Wacissa, Jefferson Co. W 1/2 SW 1/4 Sect. 23 Tp. 1 R. 3, south and east.

**3505. MURAT, Achille**
May 5, 1830, 3 1/2 miles SE El Destino, Jefferson Co. W 1/2 NW 1/4 Sect. 22 Tp. 1 R. 3, south and east.

**3580. MURAT, Achille**
July 21, 1830, 1 mile NE Eridu, Madison Co. E 1/2 NE 1/4 Sect. 7 Tp. 2 R. 6, south and east.

**3581. MURAT, Achille**
July 21, 1830, 1 1/4 miles NE Eridu, Madison Co. W 1/2 SW 1/4 Sect. 8 Tp. 2 R. 6, south and east.

**3582. MURAT, Achille**
July 21, 1830, 1 mile E Eridu, Madison Co. W 1/2 NW 1/4 Sect. 8 Tp. 1 R. 6, south and east.

**3583. MURAT, Achille**
July 21, 1830, 3/4 mile E Eridu, Madison Co. E 1/2 SE 1/4 Sect. 7 Tp. 2 R. 6, south and east.

**4455. MURAT, Achille**
Nov. 11, 1833, 1 mile SSW Lloyd, Jefferson Co. NE 1/4 SW 1/4 Sect. 21 Tp. 1 R. 3, south and east.

**5080. MURAT, Achille**
July 16, 1835, 2 miles N by W Cay, Jefferson Co. E 1/2 SE 1/4 Sect. 22 Tp. 1 R. 3, south and east.

**5081. MURAT, Achille**
July 16, 1835, 2 miles N Cay, Jefferson Co. E 1/2 NW 1/4 Sect. 23 Tp. 1 R. 3, south and east.

**5082. MURAT, Achille**
July 16, 1835, 2 1/2 miles N Cay, Jefferson Co. W 1/2 SE 1/4 Sect. 15 Tp. 1 R. 3, south and east.

**5083. MURAT, Achille**
July 16, 1835, 2 1/2 miles N by W Cay, Jefferson Co. E 1/2 SW 1/4 Sect. 15 Tp. 1 R. 3, south and east.

**5084. MURAT, Achille**
July 16, 1835, 2 1/2 miles NNW Cay, Jefferson Co. NW 1/4 SW 1/4 Sect. 21 Tp. 1 R. 3, south and east.

**5118. MURAT, Achille**
July 29, 1835, 8 miles W by S Sirmans, Madison Co. E 1/2 NW 1/4 Sect. 8 Tp. 2 R. 6, south and east.

**5119. MURAT, Achille**
July 29, 1835, 7 miles W Sirmans, Madison Co. W 1/2 SW 1/4 Sect. 5 Tp. 2 R. 6, south and east.

**5259. MURAT, Achille**
Nov. 12, 1835, 1/2 mile N Lloyd, Jefferson Co. NE 1/4 Sect. 15 Tp. 1 R. 3, south and east.

**MURAT, Achille see James GADSDEN**

**4437. MURPHEY, John**
Oct. 20, 1856, 2 1/4 miles NW Luraville, Suwannee Co. SE 1/4 SW 1/4 Sect. 15 Tp. 4 R. 11, south and east.

**78. MURPHY, James L.**
Nov. 29, 1826, c. 4 miles SW Dellwood, Jackson Co. E 1/2 SE 1/4 Sect. 31 Tp. 5 R. 9, north and west. Indorsed to Miles (?) SIMS (no date).

**79. MURPHY, James L.**
Nov. 29, 1826, 3 miles NW Cypress Station, Gadsden Co. NW 1/4 Sect. 5 Tp. 4 R. 9, north and west. Assigned Sept. 20, 1827, to **James W. EXUM** and **James P. LOVE**.

**299. MURPHY, James S.**
Jan. 1, 1827, 7 miles E Marianna, Jackson Co. SW 1/4 Sect. 32 Tp. 5 R. 9, north and west. Transfer: **J. S. MURPHY**

**MURPHY, John see William BELLAMY**

**5553. MURRAY, Barns H.**
Mar. 25, 1836, 5 1/2 miles E Centerville, Leon Co. NW 1/4 SE 1/4 Sect. 26 Tp. 2 R. 2, north and east.

**Murray----- see CUTHBERT & MURRAY**

**5111. MURRELL, Daniel**
July 25, 1835, 1 1/4 miles SSE Moseley Hall, Madison Co. NE 1/4 NW 1/4 Sect. 34 Tp. 1 R. 8, south and east.

**5112. MURRELL, Daniel**

July 25, 1835, 1 mile SE Moseley Hall, Madison Co. SE 1/4 SE 1/4 Sect. 33 Tp. 1 R. 8, south and east.

**5066. MURRELL, Joseph E.**
July 10, 1835, 2 miles W West Pensacola, Escambia Co. Lot No. 1 Fractional Sect. 18 Tp. 2 R. 30, south and west.

**5067. MURRELL, Joseph E.**
July 10, 1835, 2 miles W West Pensacola, Escambia Co. Lot No. 2 Fractional Sect. 18 Tp. 2 R. 30, south and west.

**6580. MURRELL, Joseph E.**
Jan. 17, 1837, c. 1 mile N Pensacola, Escambia Co. Lots No. 2, 3, 4 and 5 Fractional Sect. 12 Tp. 2 R. 30, south and west. Indorsed on the back "C. BARON".

**6581. MURRELL, Joseph E.**
Jan. 17, 1837, N part of Pensacola, Escambia Co. Lots No. 1, 2, and 3 Fractional Sect. 14 Tp. 2 R. 3, south and west. Indorsed on the back "C. BARON".

**6639. MURRELL, Joseph E.**
Jan. 24, 1837, c. 1 mile N Pensacola, Escambia Co. E 1/2 NE 1/4 and E 1/2 SW 1/4 Sect. 13 Tp. 2 R. 3, south and west. Indorsed on back "C. LeBARON".

**2589. MYRICK, Adam**
(of No. Carolina) Dec. 29, 1828, 3/4 mile SE Monticello, Jefferson Co. E 1/2 NW 1/4 Sect. 32 Tp. 2 R. 5, north and east.

**2590. MYRICK, Adam**
Dec. 29, 1828, 3/4 mile SE Monticello, Jefferson Co. W 1/2 NE 1/4 Sect. 32 Tp. 2 R. 5, north and east.

**3978. MYRICK, Adam**
May 38, 1831, 3 1/2 miles E by S Greenville, Madison Co. W 1/2 SW 1/4 Sect. 19 Tp. 1 R. 18, north and east. On reverse side, "Madison City, Cherry Lake Land."

**3979. MYRICK, Adam**
May 28, 1831, 2 miles NE Cherry Lake Post Office, Madison Co. E 1/2 SW 1/4 Sect. 3 Tp. 2 R. 9, north and east. On reverse side, "Madison City, Cherry Lake Lands."

**5021. MYRICK, L.**
July 7, 1835, 2 1/2 miles NNW Moseley Hall, Madison Co. E 1/2 SE 1/4 Sect. 18 Tp. 1 R. 18, south and east.

**5022. MYRICK, L.**
July 7, 1835, 2 1/4 miles NNW Moseley Hall, Madison Co. W 1/2 NE 1/4 Sect. 18 Tp. 1 R. 8, south and east.

**5023. MYRICK, L.**
July 7, 1835, 1 3/4 miles NNW Moseley Hall, Madison Co. W 1/2 NW 1/4 Sect. 20 Tp. 1 R. 8, south and east.

**5024. MYRICK, L.**
July 7, 1835, 1 3/4 miles NNW Moseley Hall, Madison Co. E 1/2 NW 1/4 Sect. 18 Tp. 1 R. 8, south and east.

**5025. MYRICK, L.**
July 7, 1835, 1 1/2 miles NNW Moseley Hall, Madison Co. W 1/2 SW 1/4 Sect. 20 Tp. 1 R. 8, south and east.

\* N \*

**7659. NALE, James**
Oct. 5, 1838, 1 mile NNE Maysville, Calhoun Co. NE 1/4 NE 1/4 Sect. 25 Tp. 2 R. 9, south and west.

**7660. NALE, James**
Oct. 5, 1838, 3/4 mile NNE Maysville, Calhoun Co. NE 1/4 SW 1/4 Sect. 24 Tp. 2 R. 9, south and west.

**8936. NALL, James**
April 17, 1846, 1 1/4 miles E by S Maysville, Calhoun Co. E 1/2 NE 1/4 Sect. 36 Tp. 2 R. 9, south and west.

**3620. NEALE, Benj. A.**
Sept. 26, 1830, 1/2 mile W Rock Bluff, Gadsden Co. W 1/2 NE 1/4 Sect. 23 Tp. 25 R. 7, north and west. Transferred Feb. 27, 1833, to **Leonard H. CASH.**

**2895. NEALY, Mary**
July 7, 1829, 4 miles E Capitola, Jefferson Co. E 1/2 SE 1/4 Sect. 23 Tp. 1 R. 3, north and east.

**6289. NEALY, Wm. W.**
Dec. 23, 1836, 6 miles W by N Wadesboro, Jackson Co. E 1/2 SW 1/4 Sect. 29 Tp. 6 R. 10, north and west.

**2201. NEELEY, Mary**
(of Fla) Dec. 31, 1827, 4 miles W by S Gadsden, Gadsden Co. W 1/2 SE 1/4 Sect. 23 Tp. 1 R. 3, north and east.

**8416. NEEL, William M. C.**
Nov. 7, 1840, 10 miles N Haywood, Jackson Co. N 1/2 Lot No. 2 Sect. 36 Tp. 7 R. 8, north and west.

**5836. NELLSON, Charles A.**
Sept. 8, 1836, 1 1/4 miles E Rhode's Spur, Leon Co. W 1/2 SW 1/4 Sect. 4 Tp. 2 R. 1, south and east.

**5837. NELLSON, Charles A.**
Sept. 8, 1836, 1 1/2 miles E Rhodes Spur, Leon Co. E 1/2 SE 1/4 Sect. 5 Tp. 2 R. 1, south and east.

**4845. NEWBERN/NEWBIRN, William C.**
Sept. 11, 1858, 3/4 mile W by N Guilford, Union Co. NW 1/4 NE 1/4 and NE 1/4 NW 1/4 Sect. 28 Tp. 5 R. 18, south and east.

**4927. NEWBERN/NEWBIRN, William C.**
Jan. 4, 1859, 2 miles NE Providence, Union Co. NE 1/4 NE 1/4 Sect. 28 Tp. 5 R. 18, south and east.

**4994. NEWBERN/NEWBIRN, William C.**
Mar. 17, 1859, 4 1/2 miles SSE Guilford, Union Co. SE 1/4 SE 1/4 Sect. 20 Tp. 5 R. 18, south and east.

**4995. NEWBERN/NEWBIRN, William C.**
Mar. 17, 1859, 2 miles NNE Providence, Union Co. SE 1/4 NE 1/4 Sect. 28 Tp. 5 R. 18, south and east.

**937. NEWTON, Isaac**
Aug. 25, 1851, near Martel, Marion Co. E 1/2 SW 1/4 and W 1/2 NE 1/4 Sect. 14 Tp. 15 R. 20, south and east. Pre-emption Act, Sept. 4, 1841, Newnansville.

**4870. NEWTON, William F.**
Oct. 1, 1858, 3 miles N Lake City Junction, Columbia Co. N 1/2 SE 1/4 Sect. 6 Tp. 6 R. 16, south and east.

**2809. NIBLACK, John**
Oct. 20, 1853, 3 1/2 miles SE Bass, Columbia Co. S 1/2 NW 1/4 and N 1/2 SW 1/4 Sect. 5 Tp. 5 R. 17, south and east.

**2638. NIBLACK, John**
Mar. 18, 1854, 3 1/2 miles S by W Lulu, Columbia Co. SE 1/4 SE 1/4 Sect. 36 Tp. 4 R. 17, south and east.

**4217. NIBLACK, T.**
Mar. 1, 1856, 2 3/4 miles NNE Bass, Columbia Co. SW 1/4 NE 1/4 Sect. 19 Tp. 4 R. 17, south and east.

**6778. NICHOLSON, Agnes W.**
Feb. 7, 1837, 3 miles NNE McDavid, Santa Rosa Co. West of Escambia River. NW 1/4 SW 1/4 Sect. 7 Tp. 4 R. 30, north and west.

**8235. NICHOLSON, Angus W.**
Feb. 27, 1840, 4 1/2 miles NNE McDavid, Santa Rosa Co. SW 1/4 SW 1/4 Sect. 8 Tp. 4 R. 30, north and west.

**8457. NICHOLSON, James**
Feb. 11, 1851, 1 1/4 miles E Florence, Gadsden Co. NE 1/4 Sect. 6 Tp. 2 R. 2, north and west. The above is a duplicate of original receipt, which was lost or mislaid, and sworn to before **H. R. W. ANDREWS**, Registrar in Leon Co.

**103. NICHOLSON, Malcom**
Dec. 19, 1826, 2 miles W Havana, Gadsden Co. NE 1/4 Sect. 31 Tp. 3 R. 2, north and west.

**879. NICHOLSON, Malcom**
Jan. 16, 1827, 2 1/2 miles W Havana, Gadsden Co. W 1/2 SE 1/4 Sect. 31 Tp. 3 R. 2, north and west.

**878. NICHOLSON, Malcom**
(DUP) Jan. 16, 1827, 3 miles W Havana, Gadsden Co. E 1/2 NW 1/4 Sect. 31 Tp. 3 R. 2, north and west.

**1055. NICHOLSON, Malcom**
Feb. 2, 1827, 3 miles W Havana, Gadsden Co. W 1/2 SW 1/4 Sect. 31 Tp. 3 R. 2, north and west.

**2329. NICHOLSON, Malcom**
April 5, 1828, 1 1/2 miles W by S Havana, Gadsden Co. E 1/2 SE 1/4 Sect. 31 Tp. 3 R. 2, north and west.

**5387. NICHOLSON, Malcom**
Jan. 5, 1836, 1 mile E by N Florence, Gadsden Co. E 1/2 SW 1/4 Sect. 31 Tp. 3 R. 2, north and west.

**5388. NICHOLSON, Malcom**
Jan. 5, 1836, 3/4 mile SE Florence, Gadsden Co. SE 1/4 SE 1/4 Sect. 36 Tp. 3 R. 3, north and west.

**6536. NICHOLSON, Malcom**
Jan. 14, 1837, 1 mile W Hinson, Gadsden Co. SE 1/4 NE 1/4 Sect. 30 Tp. 3 R. 2, north and west.

**2148. NIX, John T.**
Jan. 3, 1881, 1 mile NW Slavia, Seminole Co. N 1/2 NW 1/4 and W 1/2 NE 1/4 Sect. 19 Tp. 21S R. 31E.

**8670. NIXON, Thomas D.**
April 18, 1844, 1/2 mile S Roy, Liberty Co. NW 1/4 SW 1/4 Sect. 13 Tp. 2 R. 7, north and west.

**8829. NIXON, Thomas D.**
Sept. 28, 1845, 3/4 mile S Roy, Liberty Co. W 1/2 NW 1/4 Sect. 13 Tp. 2 R. 7, north and west.

**5212. NOBLES, William**
Oct. 13, 1836, 9 miles SSW Bascom, Jackson Co. Lot No. 3 Sect. 1 Tp. 6 R. 8, north and west.

**4283. NORTON, Lewis**
Jan. 23, 1833, 3 miles SSW Madison, Madison Co. SE 1/4 NE 1/4 Sect. 31 Tp. 1 R. 9, north and east.

**4284. NORTON, Lewis**
Jan. 23, 18933, 2 3/4 miles SSW Madison, Madison Co. SW 1/4 NW 1/4 Sect. 32 Tp. 1 R. 9, north and east.

**2426. NUTALL, Wm. B.**
June 3, 1828, 1 mile SE Wadesboro, Jefferson Co. E 1/2 SW 1/4 Sect. 5 Tp. 1 R. 3, south and east.

**3878. NUTT, William B.**
Feb. 7, 1831, 3 miles W Waukenah, Jefferson Co. E 1/2 NE 1/4 Sect. 6 Tp. 1 R. 4, south and east.

**NUTTAH, Mary W.** see **Rebecca ALKMAN**

**3411. NUTTALL, William B.**
Feb. 17, 1830, 1 mile NNE Mandalay, Taylor Co. E 1/2 SW 1/4 Sect. 8 Tp. 4 R. 4, south and east.

**2423. NUTTALL, William B.**
May 27, 1828, at Wadesboro, Leon Co. E 1/2 NE 1/4 Sect. 6 Tp. 1 R. 3, north and east.

**3107. NUTTALL, William B.**
Nov. 6, 1829, c. 4 miles W Stephensville, Taylor Co. Lot No. 1 Sect. 21 Tp. 9 R. 9, south and east.

**3108. NUTTALL, William B.**
Nov. 6, 1829, c. 4 miles W Stephensville, Taylor Co. Lot No. 7 Sect. 21 Tp. 9 R. 9, south and east.

**3395. NUTTALL, William B.**
Feb. 16, 1830, 4 miles N by E Mandalay, Jefferson Co. W 1/2 SW 1/4 Sect. 32 Tp. 3 R. 4, south and east. Transferred to **James GADSDEN**, March 16, 1830.

**3457. NUTTALL, William B.**
Mar. 16, 1830, 2 1/2 miles N Mandalay, Taylor Co. E 1/2 NW 1/4 Sect. 7 Tp. 4 R. 4, south and east.

**4664. NUTTALL, William B.**
Nov. 20, 1834, 2 1/4 miles S by E Jewell, Libery Co. W 1/2 NW 1/4 Sect. 7 Tp. 4 R. 4, south and east.

**4665. NUTTALL, William B.**
Nov. 20, 1834, 2 1/4 miles S by E Jewell, Liberty Co. W 1/2 SW 1/4 Sect. 7 Tp. 4 R. 4, south and east.

\* O \*

**994. OAKES, Rebecca**
Jan. 22, 1827, 2 miles SSE Havana, Gadsden Co. W 1/2 SW 1/4 Sect. 2 Tp. 2 R. 2, north and west.

**3306. OAKES, Rebecca**
Feb. 13, 1830, 2 1/2 miles E Cody, Jefferson Co. W 1/2 NW 1/4 Sect. 27 Tp. 1 R. 3, south and east.

**3415. OAKES, Rebecca**
Feb. 18, 1830, 1 mile N Cay, Jefferson Co. E 1/2 NE 1/4 Sect. 27 Tp. 1 R. 3, south and east.

**5188. OCAIN, Daniel**
Oct. 5, 1835, 2 miles N by E Centerville, Leon Co. E 1/2 SE 1/4 Sect. 7 Tp. 2 R. 2, north and east.

**7083. OCAIN, Daniel**
Nov. 10, 1837, 1 3/4 miles NNE Centerville, Leon Co. W 1/2 SW 1/4 Sect. 8 Tp. 2 R. 2, north and east.

**7084. OCAIN, Daniel**
Nov. 11, 1837, 1 1/2 miles NNE Centerville, Leon Co. NE 1/4 SW 1/4 Sect. 8 Tp. 2 R. 2, north and east.

**1502. ODOM, Godfrey**
**1503?**
Nov. 8, 1852, 3 miles NW Dukes, Union Co. E 1/2 SE 1/4 Sect. 13 Tp. 6, R. 18, south and east. Patent delivered Oct. 4, 1856.

**1509. ODOM, Godfrey**
Nov. 13, 1852, 3 miles SSW Dukes, Union Co. SE 1/4 NE 1/4 Sect. 24 Tp. 6 R. 18, south and east.

**2404. ODOM, Godfrey**
Feb. 21, 1854, 2 3/4 miles SSW Dukes, Union Co. S 1/2 NW 1/4 Sect. 24 Tp. 6 R. 18, south and east. Patent delivered Oct. 4, 1856.

**96. ODOM, James**
Dec. 26, 1844, 7 1/2 miles SW Long Branch, Clay Co. NW 1/4 SE 1/4 Sect. 32 Tp. 6 R. 24, south and east.

**1998. OGILVIE, James**
July 17, 1827, 4 miles NE Newport, Wakulla Co. SE 1/4 Sect. 8 Tp. 3 R. 2, south and east.

**1999. OGILVIE, James**
July 17, 1827, 4 1/2 miles NE Newport, Wakulla Co. W 1/2 NE 1/4 Sect. 8 Tp. 3 R. 2, south and east.

**2008. OGILVIE, James**
July 20, 1827, 7 miles E Wakulla, Wakulla Co. E 1/2 NE 1/4 Sect. 8 Tp. 3 R. 2, south and east.

**2106. OGILVIE, James**
(of New Orleans) Nov. 19, 1827, 4 1/2 miles W Wakulla, Wakulla Co. W 1/2 SE 1/4 Sect. 5 Tp. 3 R. 2, south and east.

**2107. OGILVIE, James**
Nov. 19, 1827, 5 miles E Vereen, Wakulla Co. W 1/2 NE 1/4 Sect. 5 Tp. 3 R. 2, south and east.

**2174. OGILVIE, James**
(of New Orleans) Dec. 26, 1827, 5 1/2 miles E Wakulla, Wakulla Co. E 1/2 SE 1/4 Sect. 5 Tp. 3 R. 2, south and east.

**2175. OGILVIE, James**
Dec. 26, 1827, 6 miles E Wakulla, Wakulla Co. E 1/2 NE 1/4 Sect. 5 Tp. 3 R. 2, south and east.

**2195. OGDEN, Josiah W.**
(of Fla.) Dec. 31, 1827, 2 miles SE Iamonia, Leon Co. W 1/2 SE 1/4 Sect. 20 Tp. 1 R. 2, north and east.

**4122. OLIVER, James**
Jan. 20, 1822, 1/4 mile N Lawrence Switch, Gadsden Co. W 1/2 SE 1/4 Sect. 24 Tp. 1 R. 2, north and west.

**`3132. OLIVER, Jas.**
Nov. 23, 1829, 1/2 mile N Ocklocknee, Leon Co. E 1/2 SE 1/4 Sect. 24 Tp. 1 R. 2, north and west.

**7044. OLIVER, Nancy**
Sept. 19, 1837, 1 mile W Ocklocknee, Leon Co. SE 1/4 NE 1/4 Sect. 35 Tp. 1 R. 2, north and west.

**4018. OLLIFF, Joseph**
Dec. 18, 1855, 1 1/2 miles E Pinemount, Suwannee Co. SW 1/4 SW 1/4 Sect. 3 and NW 1/4 NW 1/4 Sect. 10 Tp. 4 R. 14, south and east.

**4784. OLLIFF, Joseph**
Sept. 6, 1858, 4 1/2 miles SE McAlpin, Suwannee Co. E 1/2 NW 1/4 and SW 1/4 NW 1/4 and N 1/2 SW 1/4 Sect. 10 Tp. 4 R. 14, south and east.

**373. ONEAL, Henry**
(Assignee of **J. MOSES** and **J. SMITH**, Assignee of **A. ROACH**) May 3, 1827, 1 mile N Campbellton, Jackson Co. NE 1/4 Sect. 26 Tp. 7 R. 12, north and west.

**374. ONEAL, Henry**
(Assignee of **J. MOSES** and **J. SMITH**, Assignee of **A. ROACH**) May 3, 1827, 1 mile N Campbellton, Jackson Co. NE 1/4 Sect. 26 Tp. 7 R. 12, north and west.

**6754. ONEAL, Henry**
Feb. 6, 1837, 4 miles NW Campbellton, Geneva Co., Ala. E 1/2 NW 1/4 Sect. 23 Tp. 7 R. 12, north and west.

**8115. O'NEAL, Henry**
Oct. 15, 1839, 2 miles N by W Campbellton, Jackson Co. (Part in Geneva Co., Alabama) W 1/2 NW 1/4 Sect. 23 Tp. 7 R. 12, north and west.

**6560. ONEIL, Catton B.**
Jan. 16, 1837, 1 mile S by E Bailey, Madison Co. SE 1/4 E 1/2 SW 1/4 Sect. 24 Tp. 2 R. 7, north and east.

**3077. O'NEIL, Colton**
Oct. 3, 1829, 1/2 mile NE Cay, Jefferson Co. E 1/2 SE 1/4 Sect. 27 Tp. 1 R. 3, south and east.

**5204. O'NEEL, Daniel**
Oct. 12, 1835, 1 mile NW Collins, Franklin Co. Lot No. 2 Sect. 1 Tp. 6 R. 6, north and west.

**5205. O'NEEL, Daniel**
Oct. 12, 1835, 1 1/4 miles N Collins, Franklin Co. E 1/2 NE 1/4 Sect. 2 Tp. 6 R. 8, north and west.

**6174. O'NEIL, Daniel**
Dec. 9, 1836, 9 1/2 miles NNW Haywood, Jackson Co. NW 1/4 NE 1/4 Sect. 2 Tp. 6 R. 8, north and west.

**2701. ORMAN & YOUNG**
Feb. 2, 1829, 2 miles W Greenwood, Jackson Co. E 1/2 SW 1/4 Sect. 35 Tp. 6 R. 10, north and west.

**2702. ORMAN & YOUNG**
Feb. 2, 1829, 2 1/4 miles W by N Greenwood, Jackson Co. E 1/2 NW 1/4 Sect. 35 Tp. 6 R. 10, north and west.

**OSBORN, James V. see Henry PENNY, #4424**

**1584. OSTEEN, Elias**
Dec. 24, 1852, 2 1/2 miles NW Dukes, Union Co. SW 1/4 SW 1/4 and NW 1/4 NW 1/4 Sect. 8 Tp. 6 R. 19, south and east. Patent delivered Aug. 2, 1856.

**4475 1/2. OSTEEN, John**
Nov. 9, 1856, 4 1/2 miles NW Dukes, Union Co. NE 1/4 SE 1/4 Sect. 11 Tp. 1 R. 18, south and east. Excess payment on entry No. 3028

**1840. OSTEEN, William**
April 22, 1853, 4 1/4 miles ESE Fort White, Columbia Co. NW 1/4 SE 1/4 Sect. 21 Tp. 6 R. 18, south and east.

**5296. OVERSTREET, Eliza**
Dec. 1, 1835, 1 1/2 miles N Lake Jackson (town), Leon Co. NE 1 /4 Sect. 29 Tp. 2 R. 1, north and east.

**5297. OVERSTREET, Eliza**
Dec. 1, 1835, 1 1/4 miles N Lake Jackson (town), Leon Co. E 1/2 SE 1/4 Sect. 29 Tp. 2 R. 1, north and east. See **Henry B. OVERSTREET, #3455**

**3080. OVERSTREET, E. B.**
Oct. 6, 1829, 3 miles WSW Bradfordville, Leon Co. SW 1/4 Sect. 29 Tp. 2 R. 1, north and east. Bought with the funds of **Eliza BRENAN**, of Charleston, S.C., and transferred to her Nov. 3, 1839, by **Edwin B. OVERSTREET**. Witnesses: **James LITTLE** and **Ann FOX**.

**3081. OVERSTREET, E. B.**
Oct. 6, 1829, 3 miles WSW Bradfordville, Leon Co. W 1/2 NE 1/4 Sect. 29 Tp. 2 R. 1, north and east. Transferred as was **3080**.

**6779. OVERSTREET, George E.**
Feb. 7, 1837, c. 3 1/2 miles SE Westlake, Hamilton Co. Lot No. 3 Fractional Sect. 24 Tp. 1 R. 12, north and east.

**3455. OVERSTREET, Henry B.**
(for **Eliza OVERSTREET**) March 15, 1830, 2 miles SW Bradfordville, Leon Co. E 1/2 NW 1/4 Sect. 29 Tp. 2 R. 1, north and east. "Received Leon Co., Florida,, June 10, 1830, of **Mrs. Eliza OVERSTREET**, one hundred dollars, being in full for the within names 1/4 of Section 29, Township 2 Range one. "**H. B. OVERSTREET**, Trustee for **Eliza OVERSTREET**."

**5136. OVERSTREET, Silas**
Aug. 18, 1835, 2 1/4 miles NW Pinetta, Madison Co. SE 1/4 SE 1/4 Sect. 3 Tp. 2 R. 9, north and east.

**5137. OVERSTREET, Silas**
Aug. 18, 1835, 2 miles S by W Pinetta, Madison Co. NW 1/4 SW 1/4 Sect.

11 Tp. 2 R. 9, north and east.

**5773. OVERSTREET, Silas**
July 16, 1836, 1 1/4 miles W Cherrylake (town), Madison Co. E 1/2 SW 1/4 Sect. 7 Tp. 2 R. 9, north and east.

**5843. OVERSTREET, Silas**
Sept. 12, 1836, 1 mile W Cherrylake, Madison Co. W 1/2 SE 1/4 Sect. 7 Tp. 2 R. 9, north and east.

**7207. OVERSTREET, Silas**
Jan. 10, 1838, 2 miles S by W Jasper, Hamilton Co. E 1/2 SW 1/4 Sect. 18 Tp. 1 R. 14, north and east.

**7264. OVERSTREET, Silas**
Jan. 22, 1838, 2 1/2 miles SSE Hamberg, Madison Co. SE 1/4 NW 1/4 and SW 1/4 NE 1/4 Sect. 13 Tp. 2 R. 8, north and east.

**5125. OVERSTREET, Silas S.**
Aug. 5, 1835, 5 miles NW Shady Grove, Madison Co. NW 1/4 Sect. 11 Tp. 2 R. 9, south and east.

**6128. OVERSTREET, Silas S.**
Dec. 2, 1836, 1 mile NW Shady Grove, Madison Co. E 1/2 NE 1/4 and SE 1/4 SE 1/4 Sect. 14 Tp. 2 R. 7, south and east.

**6129. OVERSTREET, Silas S.**
Dec. 2, 1836, 2 miles SSE Maysland, Madison Co. W 1/2 NW 1/4 and W 1/2 SW 1/4 Sect. 14 Tp. 2 R. 7, north and east.

**6225. OVERSTREET, Silas S.**
Dec. 15, 1836, 5 miles SW Cherry Lake, Madison Co. W 1/2 SW 1/4 and W 1/2 SE 1//4 Sect. 26 Tp. 2 R. 8, north and east.

**OWENS, Hastings E. see Whitman H. OWENS**

**1913. OWENS, Joshua**
(DUP) June 15, 1827, c. 1 mile W Midway, Gadsden Co. Lot No. 5 Sect. 7 Tp. 1 R. 2, north and west.

**1914. OWENS, Joshua**
(DUP) Jun 15, 1827, c. 1 mile W Midway, Gadsden Co. Lot No. 4 Sect. 7 Tp. 1 R. 2, north and west.

**5270. OWENS, Whitman**
(Georgia) Nov. 20, 1835, 8 miles N by W Haywood, Jackson Co. W 1/2 SE 1/4 Sect. 13 Tp. 6 R. 8, north and west.

**5271. OWENS, Whitman**
(Georgia) Nov. 20, 1835, 8 miles N by W Haywood, Jackson Co. W 1/2 NE 1/4 Sect. 13 Tp. 6 R. 8, north and west. Transferred to **Hastings E. OWENS**, April 26, 1848.

**5272. OWENS, Whitman**
(Georgia) Nov. 20, 1835, 8 1/4 miles N by W Haywood, Jackson Co. E 1/2 SW 1/4 Sect. 13 Tp. 6 R. 8, (?south) and west. Transferred to **Hastings E. OWENS**, April 26, 1848.

**5274. OWENS, Whitman**
(Georgia) Nov. 20, 1835, 2 1/4 miles NNW Haywood, Jackson Co. Lot No. 2 Sect. 18 Tp. 6 R. 7, north and west. Transferred to **Hastings E. OWENS**, April 26, 1848.

**5275. OWENS, Whitman**
(Georgia) Nov. 20, 1835, 4 1/2 miles N by W Haywood, Jackson Co. NW 1/4 NE 1/4 Sect. 24 Tp. 6 R. 8, north and west. Transferred to **Hastings E. OWENS**, April 26, 1848.

**5914. OWENS, Whitman**
Oct. 21, 1836, 7 miles N by W Haywood, Jackson Co. E 1/2 SE 1/4 Sect. 13 Tp. 6 R. 8, north and west. Transferred to **Hastings E. OWENS**, April 26, 1848, owner being then located in Barham (Barbour ?) County, Alabama.

**OVERTON, L. R. see Marmaduke KENT, #312**
SE 1/4 Sect. 11 Tp. 5 R. 12, north and west.

\* P \*

**7193. PADGETT, Elijah**
Jan. 4, 1838, 1 mile SW Rock Creek, Jackson Co. NE 1/4 NW 1/4 Sect. 30 Tp. 3 R. 9, north and west.

**7386. PADGETT, James T.**
Mar. 6, 1838, 1 1/4 miles NNW Baker's Mill, Hamilton Co. NW 1/4 NW 1/4 Sect. 18 Tp. 2 R. 14, north and east.

**7219. PADGETT, John**
Jan. 12, 1838, 3 1/2 miles S by W Marianna, Jackson Co. SW 1/4 SW 1/4 Sect. 26 Tp. 4 R. 10, north and west.

**7220. PADGETT, John**
Jan. 12, 1838, 1 mile W Oakdale, Jackson Co. W 1/2 NW 1/4 Sect. 35 Tp. 4 R. 10, north and west.

**8845. PADGETT, Margaret**
Nov. 22, 1845, 4 1/2 miles SE by S Westlake, Hamilton Co. NE 1/4 NE 1/4 Sect. 27 Tp. 1 R. 12, north and east.

**2628. PAGE, John B.**
Jan. 14, 1829, 3/4 mile W Waukenah, Jefferson Co. W 1/2 NE 1/4 Sect. 4 Tp. 1 R. 4, south and east.

**4342. PAGE, John B.**
April 3, 1833, 1 mile N Wacissa, Jefferson Co. SW 1/4 SW 1/4 Sect. 30 Tp. 1 R. 4, south and east.

**6057. PAGE, John B.**
Nov. 19, 1836, 3 miles E Cay, Jefferson Co. NE 1/4 SE 1/4 Sect. 31 Tp. 1 R. 4, south and east.

**6421. PAGE, John B.**
Jan. 4, 1837, 3 miles ENE Cay, Jefferson Co. NW 1/4 SW 1/4 Sect. 30 Tp. 1 R. 4, south and east.

**8378. PAGE, Thomas**
Aug. 3, 1840, at Madison, Madison Co. SE 1/4 NW 1/4 Sect. 34 Tp. 1 R. 9, north and east.

**4868. PAGETT, Elijah**
Feb. 16, 1835, 1/4 mile W Oakdale, Jackson Co. SE 1/4 SW 1/4 Sect. 26 Tp. 4 R. 10, north and west.

**2208. PAINTER, Thomas**
(Florida) Dec. 31, 1827, 2 miles E Juniper, Gadsden Co. W 1/2 NW 1/4 Sect. 33 Tp. 2 R. 5, north and west.

**4298. PAINTER, Thomas**
Feb. 6, 1833, 3 miles SSE Jumper, Gadsden Co. SE 1/4 NW 1/4 Sect. 33 Tp. 2 R. 5, north and west.

**3179. PALMER, Martin**
Dec. 23, 1829, 1 mile E Monticello, Jefferson Co. E 1/2 NE 1/4 Sect. 29 Tp. 2 R. 5, north and east.

**3180. PALMER, Martin**
Dec. 23, 1829, 1 1/4 miles SE Monticello, Jefferson Co. E 1/2 SE 1/4 Sect. 29 Tp. 2 R. 5, north and east.

**5905. PALMER, Martin**
Oct. 17, 1836, 1 1/4 miles NNW Monticello, Jefferson Co. Lot No. 1 Fractional Sect. 23 Tp. 2 R. 4, north and east.

**2647. PANSI, Richard**
Jan. 10, 1829, 3 miles E by N Wadesboro, Leon Co. E 1/2 SE 1/4 Sect. 34 Tp. 2 R. 3, north and east.

**196. PARAMORE, Jno.**
(DUP) Dec. 29, 1826, Florence, Gadsden Co. SW 1/4 Sect. 5 Tp. 2 R. 3, north and west.

**2176. PARAMORE, Jno.**
(Florida) Dec. 28, 1827, 3 miles ESE Quincy, Gadsden Co. W 1/2 SE 1/4 Sect. 9 Tp. 2 R. 3, north and west.

**2177. PARAMORE, Jno.**
Dec. 28, 1827, 2 miles E Quincy, Gadsden Co. W 1/2 NE 1/4 Sect. 9 Tp. 2 R. 3, north and west.

**2178. PARAMORE, Jno.**
Dec. 28, 1827, 2 miles E Quincy, Gadsden Co. E 1/2 SE 1/4 Sect. 4 Tp. 2 R. 3, north and west.

**2209. PARAMORE, Jno.**
(Florida) Dec. 31, 1827, 2 1/2 miles E Quincy, Gadsden Co. E 1/2 NE 1/4 Sect. 9 Tp. 2 R. 3, north and west.

**1418. PARAMORE, Stephen**
May 21, 1827, 2 1/2 miles NNE Quincy, Gadsden Co. E 1/2 SW 1/4 Sect. 29 Tp. 3 R. 3, north and west.

**1865. PARAMORE, Stephen**
June 6, 1827, at Cory 1 1/2 miles E Quincy, Gadsden Co. W 1/2 NW 1/4 Sect. 33 Tp. 3 R. 3, north and west.

**28. PARAMORE, Wm./Wm. H.**
Nov. 1, 1826, near Quincy, Gadsden Co. NW 1/4 Sect. 32 Tp. 3 R. 3, north and west. (Pre-emption).

**1419. PARAMORE, Wm./Wm. H.**

May 21, 1827, 1 1/2 miles NE Quincy, Gadsden Co. E 1/2 SW 1/4 Sect. 32 Tp. 3 R. 3, north and west.

**1909. PARISH, Richard**
(DUP) June 13, 1827, 4 miles NE Wadesboro, Leon Co. W 1/2 NW 1/4 Sect. 27 Tp. 2 R. 3, north and east.

**1938. PARISH, Richard**
June 23, 1827, 4 miles NE Wadesboro, Leon Co. W 1/2 SW 1/4 Sect. 22 Tp. 2 R. 3, north and east.

**648. PARISH, Richard**
(of Florida) Jan. 13, 1826, 1 mile S Miccosukee, Leon Co. W 1/2 SW 1/4 Sect. 15 Tp. 2 R. 3, north and east.

**2427. PARISH, Richard**
June 3, 1828, 3 1/2 miles NE Wadesboro, Leon Co. E 1/2 NW 1/4 Sect. 27 Tp. 2 R. 3, north and east.

**2439. PARISH, Richard**
July 12, 1828, 5 1/2 miles E Wadesboro, Leon Co. W 1/2 SW 1/4 Sect. 36 Tp. 2 R. 3, north and east.

**2514. PARISH, Richard**
Oct. 8, 1828, 4 miles ENE Wadesboro, Leon Co. W 1/2 SW 1/4 Sect. 35 Tp.2 R. 3, north and east.

**3009. PARISH, Richard**
Sept. 3, 1829, 2 miles SE Wadesboro, Leon Co. W 1/2 SE 1/4 Sect. 8 Tp. 1 R. 3, north and east.

**3061. PARISH, Richard**
Sept. 23, 1829, 2 1/2 miles ENE Wadesboro, Leon Co. E 1/2 SE 1/4 Sect. 33 Tp. 2 R. 3, north and east.

**3566. PARISH, Richard**
July 13, 1830, 5 1/2 miles W Wadesboro, Jefferson Co. W 1/2 SE 1/4 Sect. 36 Tp. 2 R. 3, north and east.

**3597. PARISH, Richard**
Aug. 23, 1830, 3 miles NW Braswell, Jefferson Co. W 1/2 NW 1/4 Sect. 32 Tp. 2 R. 4, north and east.

**3768. PARISH, Richard**
Nov. 30, 1830, 3 1/2 miles E by N Wadesboro, Leon Co. W 1/2 NE 1/4 Sect. 36 Tp. 2 R. 3, north and east.

**3769. PARISH, Richard**
Nov. 30, 1830, 2 1/2 miles E Wadesboro,, Leon Co. E 1/2 NE 1/4 Sect. 4 Tp. 1 R. 3, north and east.

**3847. PARISH, Richard**
Jan. 13, 1831, 2 miles E Wadesboro, Leon Co. W 1/2 NE 1/4 Sect. 4 Tp. 1 R. 3, north and east.

**3987. PARISH, Richard**
June 17, 1831, 4 miles E Wadesboro, Jefferson Co. E 1/2 NE 1/4 Sect. 2 Tp. 1 R. 3, north and east.

**6320. PARISH, Richard**
Dec. 27, 1836, 4 1/2 miles E Wadesboro, Jefferson Co. W 1/2 SW 1/4 Sect. 1 Tp. 1 R. 3, north and east.

**6497. PARISH, Richard**
Jan. 10, 1837, 2 miles E Wadesboro, Leon Co. NW 1/4 SE 1/4 Sect. 4 Tp. 1 R. 3, north and east.

**6824. PARISH, Richard**
Mar. 2, 1837, 2 miles NE Eridu, Madison Co. NE 1/4 E 1/2 NW 1/4 E 1/2 SW 1/4 Sect. 5 Tp. 2 R. 6, south and east.

**6825. PARISH, Richard**
Mar. 2, 1837, 2 miles N Eridu, Madison Co. W 1/2 NW 1/4 Sect. 5 Tp. 2 R. 6, south and east.

**6823. PARISH, Richard**
Mar. 2, 1837, near Lamont, Jefferson Co. W 1/2 NE 1/4 Sect. 26 Tp. 1 R. 5, south and east.

**6508. PARISH, Richard C.**
Jan. 20, 1837, c. 3 miles W by N Lamont, Jefferson Co. Lots No. 2 and 3 Fractional Sect. 19 Tp. 1 R. 5, south and east.

**3965. PARISH, Richard C.**
May 10, 1831, 2 miles SE Wadesboro, Jefferson Co. E 1/2 SE 1/4 Sect. 8 Tp. 1 R. 3, north and east.

**6232. PARISH, Richard C.**
Dec. 17, 1836, just N Alma, Leon Co. Lots No. 2 and 3 Fractional Sect. 26 Tp. 3 R. 4, south and east.

**6448. PARISH, Richard C.**
Jan. 6, 1837, 1/2 mile S Alma, Jefferson Co. Lot No. 2 Fractional Sect. 2 Tp. 2 R. 4, north and east.

**6509. PARISH, Richard C.**
Jan. 20, 1837, 1 1/2 miles S Lamont, Jefferson Co. W 1/2 NE 1/4 Sect. 35 Tp. 1 R. 5, south and east.

**6510. PARISH, Richard C.**
Jan. 20, 1837, 3 miles NW Lamont, Jefferson Co. SW 1/4 Sect. 17 Tp. 1 R. 5, south and east.

**6511. PARISH, Richard C.**
Jan. 20, 1837, 3 1/4 miles NW Lamont, Jefferson Co. W 1/2 SE 1/4 Sect.

18 Tp. 1 R. 5, south and east.
**6549. PARISH, Richard C.**
Jan. 14, 1837, just SE Dills, Jefferson Co. SE 1/4 Sect. 6 Tp. 2 R. 6, south and east.
**6550. PARISH, Richard C.**
Jan. 14, 1837, 1/2 mile NW McClellan, Jefferson Co. E 1/2 NW 1/4 and NW 1/4 SW 1/4 Sect. 9 Tp.1 R. 5, north and east.
**6551. PARISH, Richard C.**
Jan. 14, 1837, 1/2 mile NE Drifton, Jefferson Co. NE 1/4 SE 1/4 Sect. 8 Tp. 1 R. 5, north and east.
**6607. PARISH, Richard C.**
Jan. 20, 1837, at Drifton, Jefferson Co. W 1/2 SW 1/4 Sect. 8 Tp. 1 R. 5, north and east.
**1621. PARISH, William C.**
Jan. 7, 1853, 1 1/4 miles W Dukes, Union Co. NE 1/4 NW 1/4 Sect. 20 Tp. 6 R. 19, south and east. Patent delivered Feb. 2, 1857.
**8370. PARKER, Alias**
June 18, 1840, 4 miles NNE Blountstown, Calhoun Co. NE 1/4 Sect. 14 Tp. 1 R. 8, north and west.
**348. PARKER, John**
April 16, 1827, 7 miles NNW Cottondale, Jackson Co. W 1/2 SE 1/4 Sect. 27 Tp. 6 R. 11, north and west.
**4162. PARKER, Richard H.**
Feb. 12, 1856, 1 1/2 miles NE Haynesworth, Alachua Co. N 1/2 SE 1/4 Sect. 33 Tp. 7 R. 19, south and east. Patent delivered June 22, 1857.
**4940. PARKER, Richard H.**
Jan. 19, 1859, 1/2 mile NW Haynesworth, Alachua Co. NE 1/4 NW 1/4 Sect. 34 Tp. 7 R. 19, south and east. Endorsed by **James PARKER** and **Berry PARKER**.
**2136. PARKER, William**
Sept. 5, 1853, 2 miles NW Santa Fe, Alachua Co. SE 1/4 NE 1/4 Sect. 14 Tp. 7 R. 19, south and east. Patent delivered Nov. 10, 1856.
**1775. PARKHILL, John**
June 4, 1827, 2 miles NNE Chaires, Leon Co. SE 1/4 Sect. 14 Tp. 1 R. 2, north and east.
**1776. PARKHILL, John**
June 4, 1827, 1 3/4 miles N Chaires, Leon Co. E 1/2 SW 1/4 Sect. 14 Tp. 1 R. 2, north and east.
**1777. PARKHILL, John**
June 4, 1827, 2 miles ENE Chaires, Leon Co. E 1/2 NE 1/4 Sect. 14 Tp. 1 R. 2, north and east.
**1859. PARKHILL, John**
June 5, 1827, 1 mile SW Black Creek, Leon Co. W 1/2 NE 1/4 Sect. 14 Tp. 1 R. 1, north and east.
**1860. PARKHILL, John**
June 6, 1827, 1 1/4 miles SW Black Creek, Leon Co. E 1/2 NW 1/4 Sect. 14 Tp. 1 R. 2, north and east.
**2273. PARKHILL, John**
Feb. 25, 1828, 2 1/2 miles N Chaires, Leon Co. W 1/2 NW 1/4 Sect. 14 Tp. 1 R. 2, north and east.
**7516. PARKHILL, John**
July 7, 1838, 1/4 mile SE Champaign, Madison Co. W 1/2 NW 1/4 Sect. 28 Tp. 1 R. 9, north and east.
**7517. PARKHILL, John**
July 7, 1838, 1 mile SSW Calhoun, Madison Co. E 1/2 SE 1/4 Sect. 15 Tp. 1 R. 9, north and east.
**7518. PARKHILL, John**
July 7, 1838, 2 miles S Chipola, Calhoun Co. E 1/2 NW 1/4 Sect. 15 Tp. 1 R. 9, north and east.
**7519. PARKHILL, John**
July 7, 1838, 2 miles S by E Chipola, Calhoun Co. W 1/2 NE 1/4 Sect. 15 Tp. 1 R. 9, north and east.
**7638. PARKHILL, John**
Sept. 13, 1838, 1 mile SSE Chaires, Leon Co. SW 1/4 Sect. 25 Tp. 1 R. 2, north and east.
**7639. PARKHILL, John**
Sept. 13, 1838, at Chaires, Leon Co. E 1/2 SE 1/4 Sect. 26 Tp. 1 R. 2, north and east.
**7640. PARKHILL, John**
Sept. 13, 1838, 1/4 mile E Chaires, Leon Co. W 1/2 NW 1/4 Sect. 36 Tp. 1 R. 2, north and east.
**7641. PARKHILL, John**
Sept. 13, 1838, at Chaires, Leon Co. E 1/2 NE 1/4 Sect. 35 Tp. 1 R. 2, north and east.
**2322. PARKHILL, Samuel**
March 29, 1828, 3 miles W by N Wadesboro, Leon Co. W 1/2 SW 1/4 Sect. 34 Tp. 2 R. 2, north and east.
**2330. PARKHILL, Samuel**

April 5, 1828, 2 miles W Wadesboro, Leon Co. SW 1/4 Sect. 35 Tp. 2 R. 2, north and east.

**2724. PARKHILL, Samuel**
Feb. 11, 1829, 2 1/2 miles W Wadesboro, Leon Co. E 1/2 NW 1/4 Sect. 3 Tp. 1 R. 2, north and east.

**3588. PARKHILL, Samuel**
Aug. 16, 1830, 4 miles SE Centerville, Leon Co. W 1/2 SE 1/4 Sect. 33 Tp. 2 R. 2, north and east.

**3795. PARKHILL, Samuel**
Dec. 13, 1830, 5 miles SE Centerville, Leon Co. E 1/2 SE 1/4 Sect. 33 Tp. 2 R. 2, north and east.

**2692. PARKS, Clark D.**
April 22, 1854, 4 miles E Bass, Columbia Co. NE 1/4 SW 1/4, SE 1/4 NW 1/4 and SW 1/4 SW 1/4 Sect. 27 Tp. 4 R. 17, south and east. Patent delivered June 1, 1857.

**2693. PARKS, Clark D.**
April 22, 1854, 3 miles E Bass, Columbia Co. N 1/2 NE 1/4 and SW 1/4 SE 1/4 Sect. 28 Tp. 4 R. 17, south and east.

**2695. PARKS, Clark D.**
April 29, 1854, 3 miles N by E Bass, Columbia Co. NW 1/4 NW 1/4 Sect. 27 Tp. 4 R. 17, south and east. Patent delivered June 1, 1857.

**2755. PARKS, Clark D.**
May 31, 1854, 2 1/2 miles SSE Bass, Columbia Co. E 1/2 SW 1/4 and W 1/2 SE 1/4; SE 1/4 NW 1/4; SW 1/4 NE 1/4 and SE 1/4 SE 1/4 Sect. 32 Tp. 4 R. 17, south and east. Patent delivered June 1, 1857.

**2756. PARKS, Clark D.**
May 31, 1854, 4 miles SSE Bass, Columbia Co. NW 1/4 NE 1/4 Sect. 5 Tp. 5 R. 17, south and east. Patent delivered June 1, 1857.

**2760. PARKS, Clark D.**
June 6, 1854, 3 1/4 miles SE Bass, Columbia Co. NE 1/4 NW 1/4 and NE 1/4 NE 1/4 Sect. 5 Tp. 5 R. 17, south and east. Patent delivered June 1, 1857.

**2950. PARKS, Clark D.**
Oct. 11, 1854, 3 3/4 miles N by W Mason, Columbia Co. S 1/2 NE 1/4 Sect. 5 and SW 1/4 NW 1/4 Sect. 4 Tp. 5 R. 17, south and east.

**2951. PARKS, Clark D.**
Oct. 11, 1854, 4 1/2 miles SE Bass, Columbia Co. S 1/2 SW 1/4 Sect. 33 Tp. 4 R. 17, south and east.

**2952. PARKS, Clark D.**
Oct. 11, 1854, 3 3/4 miles E Bass, Columbia Co. NE 1/4 SW 1/4 Sect. 28 Tp. 4 R. 17, south and east.

**4362. PARKS, Mark D.**
May 11, 1856, 3 1/2 miles SE Bass, Columbia Co. NE 1/4 NW 1/4 Sect. 32 Tp. 4 R. 17, south and east.

**1517. PARKS, Wm.**
May 14, 1827, 2 miles SE Simsville, Jackson Co. E 1/2 NE 1/4 Sect. 14 Tp. 3 R. 10, north and west.

**4901. PARRAMORE, Redden W.**
(And **Gissett WILLIS**) Mar. 20, 1835, 5 1/2 miles E by N Leonton, Jefferson Co. NE 1/4 Sect. 5 Tp. 2 R. 5, south and east.

**4902. PARRAMORE, Redden W.**
(And **Gissett WILLIS**) Mar. 20, 1835, 6 1/2 miles E by N Leonton, Jefferson Co. W 1/2 NE 1/4 Sect. 4 Tp. 2 R. 5, south and east.

**4903. PARRAMORE, Redden W.**
(And **Gissett WILLIS**) Mar. 20, 1835, 6 1/2 miles E by N Leonton, Jefferson Co. E 1/2 SW 1/4 Sect. 4 Tp. 2 R. 5, south and east.

**4904. PARRAMORE, Redden W.**
(and **Gissett WILLIS**) Mar. 20, 1835, 6 3/4 miles E by N Leonton, Jefferson Co. E 1/2 NW 1/4 Sect. 3 Tp. 2 R. 5, south and east.

**4905. PARRAMORE, Redden W.**
(and **Gissett WILLIS**) Mar. 20, 1835, 6 3/4 miles E by N Leonton, Jefferson Co. E 1/2 SW 1/4 Sect. 3 Tp. 2 R. 5, south and east.

**4909. PARRAMORE, Redden W.**
(and **Gissett WILLIS**) Mar. 21, 1835, 5 1/2 miles E by N Leonton, Jefferson Co. E 1/2 NW 1/4 Sect. 5 Tp. 2 R. 5, south and east.

**4913. PARRAAMORE, Redden W.**
(and **Jesse H. WILLIS**) Mar. 24, 1835, 5 1/2 miles E by N Leonton, Jefferson Co. W 1/2 SW 1/4 Sect. 3 Tp. 2 R. 5, south and east.

**4914. PARRAMORE, Redden W.**
(and **Jesse H. WILLIS**) Mar. 24, 1835, 7 1/2 miles E by N Leonton,

Jefferson Co. SE 1/4 Sect. 4 Tp. 2 R. 5, south and east.

**5282. PARRAMORE, Redden W.**
(and **Jesse H. WILLIS**) Nov. 24, 1835, 6 1/2 miles E by S Leonton, Jefferson Co. W 1/2 SW 1/4 Sect. 4 Tp. 2 R. 5, south and east.

**5283. PARRAMORE, Redden H.**
(and **Jesse H. WILLIS**) Nov. 24, 1835, 8 1/2 miles E by S Leonton, Jefferson Co. W 1/2 SE 1/4 Sect. 2 Tp. 2 R. 5, south and east.

**5284. PARRAMORE, Redden H.**
(and **Jesse H. WILLIS**) Nov. 24, 1835, 8 1/2 miles E by S Leonton, Jefferson Co. E 1/2 SW 1/4 Sect. 2 Tp. 2 R. 5, south and east.

**4235. PARRISH, George**
Oct. 22, 1832, at Stringer, Jefferson Co. SW 1/4 NW 1/4 Sect. 28 Tp. 3 R. 3, north and east.

**5269. PARRISH, Richard**
April 28, 1836, 1 1/2 miles E Wadesboro, Jefferson Co. SE 1/4 NW 1/4 Sect. 4 Rp. 1 R. 3, north and east.

**811. PARROT, John**
Jan. 22, 1851, 3 1/2 miles S Benton, Columbia Co. SE 1/4 NW 1/4 Sect. 17 Tp. 1 R. 17, south and east. Patent delivered April 26, 1856.

**2650. PARROTT, John**
Mar. 21, 1854, 5 miles S by W Benton, Columbia Co. N 1/2 SW 1/4 Sect. 17 Tp. 1 R. 17, south and east.

**539. PARSONS, John**
Mar. 3, 1847, near Citra, Marion Co. Lot 5 Sect. 22 and N 1/2 NE 1/4 Sect. 27 Tp. 12 R. 22, south and east. Filed March 1, 1855.

**864. PARSONS, John**
April 11, 1851, near Crystal River, Citrus Co. Lot No. 4 Fractional Sect. 21 Tp. 18 R. 17, south and east. Patent delivered at Tampa Land Office, Feb. 5, 1859, **Jesse CARTER**, Register. Date of patent May 1, 1855. Recorded in Vol. 2, page 270.

**1143. PARSONS, John**
Jan. 31, 1852, 2 3/4 miles NE Gulf Hammock, Levy Co. W 1/2 NE 1/4 and SE 1/4 Sect. 36 Tp. 14 R. 15, south and east.

**1161. PARSONS, John**
Feb. 10, 1852, 1/2 mile N Gulf Hammock, Levy Co. SE 1/4 SE 1/4, SW 1/4 NE 1/4, NE 1/4 SW 1/4 Sect. 36 Tp. 14, R. 15, south and east.

**5818. PARTRIDGE, Henry**
Aug. 31, 1836, 1 1/4 miles E by S Stringer, Jefferson Co. W 1/2 NE 1/4 Sect. 34 Tp. 3 R. 3, north and east.

**5154. PARTRIDGE, John N.**
Sept. 24, 1835, 1/2 mile S Fincher, Leon Co. NW 1/4 Sect. 23 Tp. 3 R. 3, north and east.

**5155. PARTRIDGE, John N.**
Sept. 25, 1/2 mile S Fincher, Leon Co. SE 1/4 NE 1/4 Sect. 23 Tp. 3 R. 3, north and east.

**8996. PASS, William C.**
Nov. 24, 1846, 9 3/4 miles E by S Genoa, Hamilton Co. SE 1/4 NE 1/4 Sect. 13 Tp. 1 R. 16, south and east.

**3234. PATRICK, John F.**
Jan. 26, 1830, at San Helena, Leon Co. SW 1/4 Sect. 17 Tp. 1 R. 1, north and west. "Received on this section a certificate dated May 30, 1829, of the Secretary of the Treasury in favour of **Alex. MACOMB**, No. 38, for $100."

**3936. PATRICK, John F.**
April 4, 1831, at San Helena, Leon Co. E 1/2 SE 1/4 Sect. 17 Tp. 1 R. 1, north and west.

**PATTESON, H. W. see Romeo LEWIS, #2681**

**2115. PATTERSON, David**
(of Fla.) Nov. 26, 1827, 3 miles ESE Quincy, Gadsden Co. W 1/2 SW 1/4 Sect. 10 Tp. 2 R. 3, north and west.

**PATTERSON, H. W. see Romeo LEWIS**

**344. PATTERSON, James**
(Assignee of **John ROBINSON**) April 14, 1827, 3 miles NW Greenwood, Jackson Co. NE 1/4 Sect. 27 Tp. 6 R. 10, north and west. Transferred from **James PATTERSON** to **W. T. KILBEE**, Feb. 19, 1829.

**385. PATTERSON, James**
(Assignee of **James O. BAXTER**) May 4, 1827, 4 miles WNW Greenwood, Jackson Co. NW 1/4 Sect. 27 Tp. 6 R. 10, north and west.

**386. PATTERSON, James**
May 4, 1827, 10 miles E Malone, Jackson Co. NW 1/4 Sect. 35 Tp. 7 R. 8, north and west.

**2116. PATTERSON, James**

Nov. 26, 1827, 3 miles WNW Greenwood, Jackson Co. W 1/2 SE 1/4 Sect. 27 Tp. 6 R. 10, north and west.

**2449. PATTERSON, James**
Aug. 1, 1828, 4 miles W by N Greenwood, Jackson Co. E 1/2 SW 1/4 Sect. 27 Tp. 6 R. 10, north and west. Assigned to **Wm. T. KILBEE**, Feb. 18, 1829. Assigned to heirs of **Robert FLOURNOY**, deceased, Feb. 19, 1829.

**2532. PATTERSON, James**
Oct. 28, 1828, 4 miles W by S Greenwood, Jackson Co. NE 1/4 Sect. 3 Tp. 5 R. 10, north and west.

**8394. PATTERSON, James**
Aug. 21, 1840, 4 miles NNE Blountstown, Calhoun Co. SW 1/4 Sect. 24 Tp. 1 R. 8, north and west.

**4135. PATTERSON, John**
Feb. 6, 1832, 5 miles E by S Monticello, Jefferson Co. E 1/2 SE 1/4 Sect. 22 Tp. 2 R. 5, north and east.

**4136. PATTERSON, John**
Feb. 6, 1832, at Greenville, Madison Co. E 1/2 NE 1/4 Sect. 21 Tp. 1 R. 7, north and east.

**2882. PATTERSON, Joseph**
July 7, 1829, 1/2 mile S Grand Ridge, Jackson Co. E 1/2 SW 1/4 Sect. 5 Tp. 3 R. 7, north and west.

**2883. PATTERSON, Joseph**
July 7, 1829, 3/4 mile S Grand Ridge, Jackson Co. W 1/2 SW 1/4 Sect. 5 Tp. 3 R. 7, north and west.

**2884. PATTERSON, Joseph**
July 7, 1829, 2 miles S Grand Ridge, Jackson Co. W 1/2 NW 1/4 Sect. 8 Tp. 3 R. 7, north and west.

**4697. PATTERSON, Samuel**
Dec. 11, 1834, 2 miles S by W Bluff Springs, Escambia Co. Lot No. 1 Sect. 36 Tp. 5 R. 31, north and west.

**4698. PATTERSON, Samuel**
Dec. 11, 1834, 2 1/4 miles S by W Bluff Springs, Escambia Co. Lot No. 6 Sect. 36 Tp. 5 R. 31, north and west.

**5099. PATTERSON, Samuel**
July 23, 1835, 2 1/2 miles SSW Bluff Springs, Escambia Co. Lot No. 1 Fractional Sect. 26 Tp. 5 R. 31, north and west.

**5453. PATTERSON, Samuel**
Feb. 11, 1836, 2 miles SSW Bluff Springs, Escambia Co. Lots Nos. 5 and 8 Sect. 26 Tp. 5 R. 31, north and west.

**6176. PATTERSON, Solomon**
Dec. 9, 1836, 1/4 mile N Sneads, Jackson Co. NE 1/4 NW 1/4 Sect. 35 Tp. 4 R. 7, north and west.

**387. PATTERSON, William**
(Assignee of **J. TRUSSELL**) May 4, 1827, 10 miles E Malone, Jackson Co. W 1/2 SE 1/4 Sect. 35 Tp. 7 R. 8, north and west.

**1833. PATTERSON, William**
June 5, 1827, 10 miles NNW Haywood, Jackson Co. Lot No. 7 Sect. 35 Tp. 7 R. 8, north and west.

**5036. PATTISON, John**
Oct. 22, 1832, at Greenville, Madison Co. NW 1/4 SE 1/4 Sect. 21 Tp. 1 R. 7, north and east.

**6937. PATTISON, John**
Mar. 24, 1837, at Greenville, Madison Co. SW 1/4 NW 1/4 and NW 1/4 SW 1/4 Sect. 21 Tp. 1 R. 7, north and east.

**4288. PATTISON, William R.**
Jan. 29, 1833, at Greenville, Madison Co. NE 1/4 NW 1/4 Sect. 21 Tp. 1 R. 7, north and east.

**4289. PATTISON, William R.**
Jan. 29, 1833, at Greenville, Madison Co. SW 1/4 SW 1/4 Sect. 21 Tp. 1 R. 7, north and east.

**8068. PAYNE, Isham**
Sept. 4, 1839, 4 miles E Norum, Washington Co. NW 1/4 SE 1/4 Sect. 12 Tp. 2 R. 15, north and west.

**PAYNE & Child** see **John W. LAPSLEY, #348**

**PAYTHROP, George** see **Nathan WILLIAMSON**

**4938. PAYTON, Edward W.**
April 23, 1835, (location omitted) E 1/2 NW 1/4 Sect. 31 Tp. 5 R. 9, (direction omitted).

**4197. PEACOCK, Calvin**
Feb. 23, 1856, 3 1/2 miles NNW Luraville, Suwannee Co. S 1/2 SE 1/4 Sect. 10 Tp. 4 R. 11, south and east.

**2258. PEACOCK, Eli**
Feb. 15, 1828, 4 miles E Campbellton, Jackson Co. E 1/2 SE 1/4 Sect. 33 Tp. 7 R. 11, north and west.

**4380. PEACOCK, John W.**
June 5, 1856, 2 1/2 miles SW Campville, Alachua Co. Excess on Entry No.

3369 for N 1/2 NW 1/4 Sect. 26 Tp. 10 R. 22, south and east.

**339. PEACOCK, Timothy**
April 12, 1827, 5 miles E Campbellton, Jackson Co. W 1/2 NE 1/4 Sect. 34 Tp. 7 R. 11, north and west.

**1611. PEARCE, James W.**
Jan. 6, 1853, 1 mile W Jefferson, Columbia Co. N 1/2 SE 1/4 Sect. 24 Tp. 4 R. 17, south and east. Patent delivered Mar. 21, 1857.

**1928. PEARCE, James W.**
July 8, 1853, at Lulu, Columbia Co. NE 1/4 SE 1/4 Sect. 32 SW 1/4 NW 1/4 Sect. 33 Tp. 4 R. 18, south and east. Patent delivered Mar. 21, 1857.

**2991. PEARCE, John D.**
Oct. 16, 1854, 1 mile SE Lulu, Columbia Co. E 1/2 SE 1/4 Sect. 34 Tp. 4 R. 18, south and east.

**1721. PEARCE, Samuel J.**
Feb. 19, 1853, 3 miles SW Hawthorne, Alachua Co. Lot 2 Sect. 31 Tp. 10 R. 22, south and east. Transferred to **S. B. ATKINS**, Jan. 13, 1855.

**1736. PEARCE, Samuel J.**
Feb. 26, 1853, 5 1/2 miles W Jefferson, Columbia Co. SE 1/4 NE 1/4 Sect. 11 Tp. 4 R. 17, south and east. Patent delivered Sept. 9, 1857.

**572. PEARSON, John William**
Feb. 2, 1847, 2 1/4 miles SW Orange Springs, Marion Co. SW 1/4 NW 1/4 Sect. 2 Tp. 12 R. 23, south and east.

**629. PEARSON, John William**
March 6, 1848, c. 5 miles NE Brooksville, Hernando Co. SW 1/4 SW 1/4 Sect. 25 Tp. 21 R. 19, south and east.

**653. PEARSON, John William**
July 12, 1848, at Orange Springs, Marion Co. SW 1/4 SE 1/4 Sect. 36 Tp. 11 R. 23, south and east.

**752. PEARSON, John William**
Nov. 16, 1850, 2 1/2 miles SE Kenwood, Putnam Co. NW 1/4 NW 1/4 Sect. 25 and NE 1/4 NE 1/4 Sect. 26 Tp. 11 R. 24, south and east.

**660. PEARSON, John William**
Aug. 19, 1848, 3/4 mile S Orange Springs, Marion Co. NE 1/4 SW 1/4 and SW 1/4 SW 1/4 Sect. 36 Tp. 11 R. 23, south and east.

**768. PEARSON, John William**
Dec. 4, 1850, c. 2 miles W Orange Springs, Marion Co. Lot No. 11 Fractional Sect. 5 Tp. 12 R. 24, south and east.

**821. PEARSON, John W.**
Feb. 6, 1851, c. 2 miles SE Kenwood, Putnam Co. SW 1/4 SE 1/4 Sect. 23 Tp. 11 R. 24, south and east.

**2761. PEARSON, John W.**
June 7, 1854, 5 1/2 miles SSE Oakton, Alachua Co. SE 1/4 SE 1/4 Sect. 25 Tp. 11 R. 23, south and east. Patent delivered (no date).

**2762. PEARSON, John W.**
June 7, 1854, 3 miles SE Johnson, Alachua Co. SW 1/4 SW 1/4 Sect. 30 Tp. 11 R. 24, south and east. Patent delivered (no date).

**2887. PEARSON, John W.**
Aug. 23, 1854, 3/4 mile N Emathla, Marion Co. SE 1/4 and SE 1/4 NE 1/4 Sect. 3 Tp. 14 R. 20, south and east. Patent delivered (no date).

**2467. PEARSON, Sam'l M.**
Aug. 25, 1828, 1 1/4 miles WSW Dills, Jefferson Co. E 1/2 SE 1/4 Sect. 2 Tp. 2 R. 5, north and east.

**573. PEARSON, Sarah Martha**
Feb. 2, 1847, 2 3/4 miles SW Orange Springs, Marion Co. SE 1/4 NE 1/4 Sect. 3 Tp. 12 R. 23, south and east.

**PEEBLES, Dudley see Henry PEEBLES, #465**

**1103. PEEBLES, H. & D.**
Feb. 9, 1827, 3 miles NW Midway, Gadsden Co. W 1/2 NE 1/4 Sect. 36 Tp. 2 R. 3, north and west.

**1104. PEEBLES, H. & D.**
Feb. 9, 1827, 3 miles NW Midway, Gadsden Co. E 1/2 NW 1/4 Sect. 36 Tp. 2 R. 3, north and west.

**1105. PEEBLES, H. & D.**
Feb. 9, 1827, 5 miles WNW Midway, Gadsden Co. E 1/2 SE 1/4 Sect. 34 Tp. 2 R. 3, north and west.

**1828. PEEBLES, H. & D.**
June 5, 1827, 5 miles ESE Greensboro, Gadsden Co. Lot No. 1 Sect. 18 Tp. 2 R. 4, north and west.

**1829. PEEBLES, H. & D.**
June 5, 1827, 6 1/2 miles ESE Campbellton, Jackson Co. E 1/2 SE 1/4 Sect. 11 Tp. 6 R. 11, north and west.

**1830. PEEBLES, H. & D.**
June 5, 1827, 5 miles E Jacob, Jackson

Co. E 1/2 NE 1/4 Sect. 14 Tp. 6 R. 11, north and west.

**1897. PEEBLES, H. & D.**
June 11, 1827, 5 miles S Florence, Gadsden Co. W 1/2 SE 1/4 Sect. 25 Tp. 2 R. 3, north and west.

**1993. PEEBLES, H. & D.**
July 10, 1827, 7 miles SE Quincy, Gadsden Co. W 1/2 SW 1/4 Sect. 36 Tp. 2 R. 3, north and west.

**2207. PEEBLES, Henry & Dudley**
(of Fla.) Dec. 31, 1827, 2 1/2 miles WNW Midway, Gadsden Co. E 1/2 SW 1/4 Sect. 36 Tp. 2 R. 3, north and west.

**2219. PEEBLES, Henry & Dudley**
(of Fla.) Jan. 10, 1828, 2 miles W Sawdust, Gasden Co. Lot No. 6 Fractional Sect. 18 Tp. 2 R. 4, north and west.

**465. PEEBLES, Henry & Dudley**
(Assignee of **Thomas RICHARD**) June 22, 1829, 2 miles S Ocheesee, Calhoun Co. Lot 1 Sect. 18 Tp. 2 R. 7, north and west. (Register's Certificate) Applied for through **John TUNSTALL**.

**466. PEEBLES, Henry & Dudley**
(Assignee of **John G. RICHARD**) June 22, 1829, 1 mile S Ocheesee, Calhoun Co. Lot 2 Sect. 7 Tp. 2 R. 7, north and west. Register's receipt.

**467. PEEBLES, Henry & Dudley**
(Assignee of **John RICHARD**) June 22, 1829, 2 miles S Ocheesee, Calhoun Co. Lot 3 Sect. 18 Tp. 2 R. 7, north and west. Applied for through **John TUNSTALL**. (Register's Certificate.

**468. PEEBLES, Henry & Dudley**
(Assignee of **John G. RICHARDS**) June 22, 1829, 1 mile S Ocheesee, Calhoun Co. Lot 1 Fractional Sect. 7 Tp. 2 R. 7 north and west. (Register's Certificate and Receiver's Receipt of same place.)

**469. PEEBLES, Henry & Dudley**
(Assignee of **M. G. RICHARDS**) June 22, 1829, 1 mile S Ocheesee, Calhoun Co. Lot 2 Fractional Sect. 7 Rp. 2 R. 2, north and west. Receiver's Receipt signed by **R. K. CALL**.

**898. PEEBLES, Henry**
Jan. 17, 1827, 4 miles ESE Quincy, Gadsden Co. E 1/2 NE 1/4 Sect. 26 Tp. 2 R. 3, north and west.

**899. PEEBLES, Henry**
Jan. 17, 1827, 4 miles ESE Quincy, Gadsden Co. W 1/2 NE 1/4 Sect. 26 Tp. 2 R.3, north and west.

**900. PEEBLES, Henry**
Jan. 17, 1827, 5 miles ESE Quincy, Gadsden Co. W 1/2 NW 1/4 Sect. 26 Tp. 2 R. 3, north and west.

**901. PEEBLES, Henry**
Jan. 17, 1827, 5 miles ESE Quincy, Gadsden Co. W 1/2 NW 1/4 Sect. 26 Tp. 2 R. 3, north and west.

**902. PEEBLES, Henry**
Jan. 17, 1827, 5 miles ESE Quincy, Gadsden Co. W 1/2 SW 1/4 Sect. 26 Tp. 2 R. 3, north and west.

**903. PEEBLES, Henry**
Jan. 17, 1827, 5 miles ESE Quincy, Gadsden Co. E 1/2 SW 1/4 Sect. 26 Tp. 2 R. 3, north and west.

**904. PEEBLES, Henry**
(DUP) Jan. 17, 1827, 5 miles ESE Quincy, Gadsden Co. W 1/2 SE 1/4 Sect. 26 Tp. 2 R. 3, north and west.

**905. PEEBLES, Henry**
Jan. 17, 1827, 5 miles ESE Quincy, Gadsden Co. E 1/2 SE 1/4 Sect. 26 Tp. 2 R. 3, north and west.

**1446. PEEBLES, Henry**
May 22, 1827, 3 1/2 miles SSW Quincy, Gadsden Co. W 1/2 SE 1/4 Sect. 23 Tp. 2 R. 4, north and west.

**1447. PEEBLES, Henry**
May 22, 1827, 3 miles SSW Quincy, Gadsden Co. W 1/2 NE 1/4 Sect. 23 Tp. 2 R. 4, north and west.

**1448, PEEBLES, Henry**
May 22, 1827, 3 1/2 miles SSW Quincy, Gadsden Co. E 1/2 NW 1/4 Sect. 23 Tp. 2 R. 4, north and west.

**1471. PEEBLES, Henry**
May 23, 1827, 1/2 mile W Mear's Spur, Gadsden Co. E 1/2 NW 1/4 Sect. 13 Tp. 3 R. 6, north and west.

**1472. PEEBLES, Henry**
(DUP) May 23, 1827, at Mear's Spur, Gadsden Co. W 1/2 NE 1/4 Sect. 13 Tp. 3 R. 6, north and west.

**1553. PEEBLES, Henry**
(DUP) May 24, 1827, 2 miles NW Simsville, Jackson Co. E 1/2 SW 1/4 Sect. 1 Tp. 3 R. 10, north and west. Transferred to **William BANKS**, June 20, 1827. (**G. W. WARD**, Register).

**948. PEEBLES, Henry W.**
Jan. 19, 1827, 5 miles SE Quincy, Gadsden Co. E 1/2 NE 1/4 Sect. 27 Tp. 2 R. 3, north and west. Transferred to **John BOYD**, Jan. 20, 1827.

**954. PEEBLES, Henry W.**
Jan. 20, 1827, 5 miles SW Quincy, Gadsden Co. E 1/2 NE 1/4 Set. 28 Tp. 2 R. 3, north and west.

**955. PEEBLES, Henry W.**
Jan. 20, 1827, 5 miles SSE Quincy, Gadsden Co. W 1/2 NE 1/4 Sect. 28 Tp. 2 R. 3, north and west.

**956. PEEBLES, Henry W.**
Jan. 20, 1827, 8 miles SE Quincy, Gadsden Co. E 1/2 NE 1/4 Sect. 25 Tp. 2 R. 3, north and west.

**957. PEEBLES, Henry W.**
Jan. 20, 1827, 6 miles SE Quincy, Gadsden Co. E 1/2 NW 1/4 Sect. 27 Tp. 2 R. 3, north and west.

**958. PEEBLES, Henry W.**
Jan. 20, 1827, 5 miles SE Quincy, Gadsden Co. W 1/2 NW 1/4 Sect. 27 Tp. 2 R. 3, north and west.

**959. PEEBLES, Henry W.**
Jan. 20, 1827, 5 miles SSE Quincy, Gadsden Co. W 1/2 SW 1/4 Sect. 27 Tp. 2 R. 3, north and west.

**960. PEEBLES, Henry W.**
Jan. 20, 1827, 7 miles SE Quincy, Gadsden Co. W 1/2 Sect. 25 Tp. 2 R. 3, north and west.

**961. PEEBLES, Henry W.**
Jan. 20, 1827, 8 miles SE Quincy, Gadsden Co. E 1/2 SW 1/4 Sect. 30 Tp. 2 R. 3, north and west.

**962. PEEBLES, Henry W.**
Jan. 20, 1827, 5 miles SE Quincy, Gadsden Co. W 1/2 SW 1/4 Sect. 29 Tp. 2 R. 2, north and west.

**2220. PEEBLES, Henry W.**
(of Fla.) Jan. 10, 1828, 3/4 mile N Sawdust, Gadsden Co. W 1/2 NE 1/4 Sect. 22 Tp. 2 R. 4, north and west. Transferred Jan. 12, 1828, to **Jesse GREGORY**.

**8643. PELLUS, John G.**
Feb. 21, 1844, 1/4 mile N Dills, Jefferson Co. E 1/2 SW 1/4 Sect. 31 Tp. 3 R. 6, north and east.

**917. PELOM/PELHAM, Levi**
Aug. 4, 1851, Raiford, Union Co. N 1/2 NW 1/4 Sect. 20 and S 1/2 SW 1/4 Sect. 17 Tp. 5 R. 21, south and east.

**237. PELOT, John Cooper**
Dec. 24, 1845, c. 3 1/2 miles E Live Oak, Suwannee Co. W 1/2 Sect. 21 Tp. 2 R. 14, south and east.

**3361. PENDAVIS, James**
Jan. 8, 1855, 4 1/2 miles S by W Holder, Citrus Co. (Cancelled). Lot No. 5 and 6 Sect. 4 Tp. 8 R. 18, south and east. Purchase Money Order to be refunded.

**647. PENKINS, Lewis**
May 18, 1848, c. 3 miles SE Ringgold, Hernando Co. E 1/2 SE 1/4 and NW 1/4 SE 1/4 Sect. 20 Tp. 21 R. 19, south and west.

**8935. PENNINGTON, Henry**
April 16, 1846, 1 1/4 miles N by W Baker's Mill, Hamilton Co. E 1/2 SW 1/4 Sect. 8 Tp. 2 R. 14, north and east.

**4424. PENNY Henry**
Oct. 3, 1833, 1 mile NNE Vernon, Washington Co. NE 1/4 SE 1/4 Sect. 25 Tp. 3 R. 15, north and west. Transferred to **John WITHERS**, May 9, 1834. Transferred to **Charles T. PORTER**, Sept. 24, 1836. Transferred to **James V. OSBORN**, Aug. 12, 1838. Transferred to **S. L. ROCHE**, Mar. 28, 1839.

**5650. PENNY, Henry**
May 4, 1836, on Key in Gulf, 1/2 mile S of Camp Walton, Okaloosa Co. Fractional Sect. 24 Tp. 2 R. 24, south and west.
See **Charles HAIRE**

**4111. PENNY, John**
Jan. 17, 1856, 3 miles SSW Hodgson, Levy Co. Lots No. 1 and 2 Sect. 10 Tp. 12 R. 18, south and east.

**4332. PENNY, John**
April 15, 1856, 2 miles W Raleigh, Levy Co. Lot No. 4 Sect. 10 Tp. 12 R. 18, south and east.

**PENNY, Thomas** see **John G. GAMBLE**

**2054. PEPPER, Solomon**
Sept. 9, 1827, 2 1/2 miles Havana, Gadsden Co. E 1/2 NE 1/4 Sect. 25 Tp. 3 R. 2, north and west.

**34. PERKINS, Elijah**
Nov. 4, 1826, near Florence, Gadsden Co. SE 1/4 Sect. 30 Tp. 3 R. 2, north and west.

**5571. PERKINS, Epaminondas D. U.**
June 11, 1886, bordering NE corner Winter Garden, Orange Co. NW 1/4 SW 1/4 Sect. 13; and N 1/2 SE 1/4 and NE 1/4 SW 1/4 Sect. 14 Tp. 22S R. 27E.

**9794. PERKINS, Isaac**
Jan. 20, 1892, 6 miles SE Bascom, Jackson Co. NW 1/4 Sect. 28 Tp. 6N R. 8W

**457. PERRY, Benj. F.**
(Assignee of **Henry KIMBRO**) June 22, 1829, 3 miles NW Ocheesee, Jackson Co. Lot No. 1 Fractional Sect. 33 Tp. 3 R. 7, north and west. (Also Register's receipt of Application of same date.)

**458. PERRY, Benj. F.**
(Assignee of **Henry KIMBRO**) June 22, 1829, 3 miles NE Ocheesee, Gadsden Co. Lot 2 Fractional Sect. 33 Tp. 3 R. 7, north and west. Transferred to **Robert W. -------**, June 2, 1829. Transferred to **William TONEY**, July --, 1829. (Also Register's Receipt for same.) Pre-emption.

**459. PERRY, Benj. F.**
(Assignee of **Adam KIMBRO**) June 22, 1829, 8 miles SW Chattahoochee, Gadsden Co. Lot No. 4 Fractional Sect. 26, Tp. 3 T. 7, north and west. Transferred from **B. J. PERRY** to **R. W. WILLIAMS**, June 22, 1829. Transferred from **R. W. WILLIAMS** to **MILLS & PERRY**, July 7, 1829, Receiver's receipt.

**2860. PERRY, Benj. F.**
July 6, 1829, 1 mile NW Watson, Liberty Co. Lot No. 4 Sect. 30 Tp. 2 R. 7, north and west.

**2861. PERRY, Benj. F.**
July 6, 1829, 1 mile NW Watson, Liberty Co. Lot No. 3 Sect. 30 Tp. 2 R. 7, north and west.

**2892. PERRY, Benj. F.**
July 7, 1829, 3 miles S by E Millspring, Jackson Co. Lot No. 2 Sect. 34 Tp. 3 R. 7, north and west.

**3260. PERRY, Burwell G.**
Feb. 8, 1830, 2 miles NE Midway, Gadsden Co. W 1/2 NE 1/4 Sect. 34 Tp. 2 R. 2, north and west.

**3261. PERRY, Burwell G.**
Feb. 8, 1830, 1 3/4 miles NE Midway, Gadsden Co. W 1/2 SE 1/4 Tp. 2 R. 2, north and west.

**PERRY, Burrell G.** see **John D. BOWEN, #3869**

**2888. PERRY, Ivory B.**
July 7, 1829, 1 1/2 miles SW Millspring, Jackson Co. W 1/2 NE 1/4 Sect. 19 Tp. 3 R. 7, north and west.

**2889. PERRY, Ivory B.**
July 7, 1829, 1 mile SW Millspring, Jackson Co. W 1/2 NW 1/4 Sect. 20 Tp. 3 R. 7, north and west.

**2890. PERRY, Ivory B.**
July 7, 1829, near Millspring, Jackson Co. E 1/2 NE 1/4 Sect. 29(?) Tp. 3 R. 7, north and west. (This was Sect. 9, 19, or 29). Transferred July 7, 1829, to Mills & Perry, (**G. W. WARD**, Register).

**3070. PERRY, Ivy B.**
Sept 30, 1829, 1 1/2 miles SE Ocheesee, Calhoun Co. Lot No. 2 Fractional Sect. 8 Tp. 2 R. 7, north and west.

**PERRY(Mills & Perry)** see **David THOMAS** and **Ivy B. Perry**

**169. PETERSON, Malcolm**
Aug. 7, 1845, 2 miles SW Oxford, Sumter Co. SE 1/4 NE 1/4 Sect. 24 Tp. 22 R. 18, south and east. Patent delivered Oct. 13, 1854.

**6834. PETTUS, John G.**
Mar. 3, 1837, at Dills, Jefferson Co. E 1/2 NW 1/4 NW 1/4 NE 1/4 Sect. 6 Tp. 2 R. 6, north and east.

**7492. PEURIFOY, Tilman D.**
June 11, 1838, 1 mile N by W Lamont, Jefferson Co. W 1/2 NW 1/4 Sect. 22 Tp. 1 R. 5, south and east.

**5652. PEYTON, Edward**
May 5, 1836, 3 miles NE Marianna, Jackson Co. NW 1/4 SW 1/4 Sect. 25 Tp. 2 R. 10, north and west.

**5653. PEYTON, Edward**
May 5, 1836, 3 1/4 miles NE Marianna, Jackson Co. SE 1/4 SE 1/4 Sect. 25 Tp. 5 R. 10, north and west.

**4339. PEYTON, Joseph**
Jan. 8, 1884, 1 3/4 miles ENE Hardeetown, Levy Co. E 1/2 NE 1/4 Sect. 30 Tp. 11S R. 15E.

**7299. PHEITTER, Archibald**
Feb. 5 1838, 4 1/4 miles SSW Mears Spur, Gadsden Co. E 1/2 SE 1/4 Sect. 28 Tp. 3 R. 6, north and west.

**3612. PHILIPS, Hillary**
Sept 14, 1830, 2 1/2 miles E Centerville, Leon Co. W 1/2 NW 1/4 Sect. 21 Tp. 2 R. 3, north and east.

**2062. PHILIPS, Patrick**
Aug. 16, 1853, 4 miles E Eaton, NE shore Santa Fe Lake, Bradford Co. SW 1/4 NW 1/4 Sect. 36 Tp. 8 R. 22, south and east.

**2063. PHILIPS, Patrick**
Aug. 16, 1853, 2 1/4 miles SW Lake Geneva Station, Clay Co. N 1/2 Lot No. 4 Sect. 31 Tp. 8 R. 23, south and east.

**266. PHILIPS, Nancy**
Jan. 1, 1827, 8 miles NE Graceville, Jackson Co. E 1/2 SE 1/4 Sect. 20 Tp. 7 R. 12, north and west.

**537. PHINIZY, John**
(of Ga.) July 21, 1825, 3 miles NNE Tallahassee, Leon Co. Lot No. 1 Sect. 14 Tp. 1 R. 1, north and west. Sold to H. F. Seminary.

**540. PHINIZY, John**
(of Ga.) July 21, 1825, 3 miles N Tallahassee, Leon Co. Lot No. 6 Sect. 14 Tp. 1 R. 1, north and west.

**3878. PICKENS, James M.**
Feb. 17, 1831, 5 miles NW Bradfordville, Leon Co. E 1/2 SE 1/4 Sect. 6 Tp. 2 R. 1, north and east.

**5467. PICKETT, Asa**
Feb. 15, 1836, 4 1/2 miles SE Jumper, Gadsden Co. NE 1/4 SE 1/4 Sect. 34 Tp. 2 R. 5, north and west.

**PIE/PYE, Thomas see Norman A. McLEOD**

**8843. PIERSON, John**
Nov. 18, 1845, 1 1/4 miles SW Jasper, Hamilton Co. N 1/2 SE 1/4 Sect. 12 Tp. 1 R. 13, north and east.

**286. PIGG, John**
Jan. 1, 1827, 10 miles SE Marianna, Jackson Co. E 1/2 SW 1/4 Sect. 19 Tp. 3 R. 9, north and west.

**1746. PINKSTON, John S.**
Mar. 3, 1853, at Worthington Springs, Alachua Co. NE 1/4 NW 1/4 Sect. 28 Tp. 6 R. 19, south and east. Patent delivered June 25, 1856.

**1769. PINKSTON, John S.**
Mar. 11, 1853, 5 miles SE by S Providence, Union Co. N 1/2 NE 1/4 Sect. 29 Tp. 6 R. 19, south and east. Patent delivered June 25, 1856.

**1770. PINKSTON, John S.**
Mar. 11, 1853, 4 1/2 miles E Providence, Union Co. N 1/2 NE 1/4 Sect. 29 Tp. 6 R. 19, south and east. Patent delivered June 25, 1856.

**1771. PINKSTON, John S.**
Mar. 11, 1853, 2 miles W by S Dukes, Union Co. SW 1/4 SW 1/4 Sect. 19 Tp. 6 R. 19, south and east; and SE 1/4 SE 1/4 Sect. 25 Tp. 6 R. 18, south and east. Patent delivered June 25, 1856.

**2213. PILES, James W.**
Sept 28, 1853, 7 3/4 miles W Thaggard, Marion Co. NE 1/4 SW 1/4 Sect. 5 and NW 1/4 NE 1/4 Sect. 8 Tp. 17 R. 22, south and east. Patent delivered June 25, 1858.

**2436. PILES, James W.**
Feb. 22, 1854, 2 miles NNE Santos, Marion Co. NE 1/4 NE 1/4 and SW 1/4 NE 1/4 Sect. 9 Tp. 16 R. 22, south and east. Patent delivered Dec. 23, 1856.

**8948. PIPPEN, Ennis**
Oct. 19, 1846, 2 1/2 miles NNE Macon, Washington Co. SE 1/4 NE 1/4 Sect. 13 Tp. 2 R. 14, north and west.

**4231. PEPPEN, Solomon**
Oct. 16, 1832, 2 1/4 miles E Hinson, Gadsden Co. NE 1/4 SE 1/4 Sect. 25 Tp. 3 R. 2, north and west.

**450. PITMAN, Isaac**
Dec. 29, 1828, 6 miles E Barkers, Holmes Co. Lot No. 3 Sect. 21 Tp. 6 R. 16, north and west.

**4385. PITTMAN, James F.**
Aug. 14, 1833, 3 miles E Greensboro, Gadsden Co. SE 1/4 NW 1/4 Sect. 12 Tp. 2 R. 6, north and west.

**2851. PITTS, Joshua**
July 29, 1854, 1 3/4 miles NNW Santa Fe, Alachua Co. SE 1/4 SE 1/4 Sect. 7 Tp. 7 R. 19, south and east. Transferred to **Richard and Co.** (no date).

**4659. PITWORTH, Joseph**
Nov. 6, 1834, 4 miles N Tallahassee, Leon Co. SW 1/4 NW 1/4 Sect. 11 Tp. 1 R. 1, south and west.

**3814. PLATT, David**
Dec. 22, 1830, 1 mile E Cherry Lake,

Madison Co. SE 1/4 Sect. 10 Tp. 2 R. 9, north and east.

**3815. PLATT, David**
Dec. 15, 1830, 1 mile E Cherry Lake, Madison Co. E 1/2 SW 1/4 Sect. 10 Tp. 2 R. 9, north and east.

**4048. PLATT, David**
July 27, 1831, 3 1/2 miles E Centerville, Leon Co. NE 1/4 Sect. 10 Tp. 2 R. 8, north and east.

**4431. PLATT, William**
Oct. 11, 1833, 7 miles E Stringer, Leon Co. Lot No. 1 Sect. 25 Tp. 3 R. 4, north and east.

**1002. PLAYER, Boney**
Jan. 25, 1827, 4 miles SW Quincy, Gadsden Co. W 1/2 SW 1/4 Sect. 21 Tp. 2 R. 3, north and west. Transferred to **Homer GEE**, Feb. 1, 1827.

**1208. POITEVINT, John**
(DUP) March 13, 1827, 1 mile SSW Miccosukee, Leon Co. E 1/2 NE 1/4 Sect. 17 Tp. 2 R. 3, north and east.

**1209. POITEVINT, John**
(DUP) Mar. 13, 1827, 1 mile SW Miccosukee, Leon Co. W 1/2 SE 1/4 Sect. 8 Tp. 2 R. 3, north and east.

**6838. POLEGE(TOLEGE), John G.**
Mar. 6, 1837, 2 miles N By W Westlake, Hamilton Co. SE 1/4 SW 1/4 and SW 1/4 SE 1/4 Sect. 28 Tp. 2 R. 12, north and east.

**3723. POLLOCK, John**
Oct. 29, 1830, 1/2 mile N Wadesboro, Leon Co. W 1/2 NW 1/4 Sect. 31 Tp. 2 R. 3, north and east.

**3724. POLLOCK, John**
Oct. 29, 1830, just N Wadesboro, Leon Co. W 1/2 SW 1/4 Sect. 31 Tp. 2 R. 3, north and east.

**6441. PONDER, Ann**
Jan. 5, 1837, 2 1/2 miles E Iamonia, Leon Co. NW 1/4 W 1/2 NE 1/4 Sect. 15 Tp. 3 R. 2, north and east.

**6442. PONDER, Ann**
Jan. 5, 1837, 2 1/4 miles E Iamonia, Leon Co. NW 1/4 SW 1/4 and NE 1/4 SW 1/4 Sect. 15 Tp. 3 R. 2, north and east.

**6951. PONDER, Ann**
Mar. 30, 1837, 3 miles E Iamonia, Leon Co. E 1/2 NE 1/4 Sect. 15 Tp. 2 R. 2, north and east.

**3520. PONDER, Hezekiah**
May 19, 1830, 1 mile SSE Waco, Madison Co. W 1/2 SE 1/4 Sect. 29 Tp. 1 R. 9, south and east.

**2807. PONDER, Benj. F.**
Dec. 8, 1881, 3/4 mile NE Lee, Madison Co. E 1/2 SE 1/4 Sect. 2 Tp. 1S R. 10E.

**5360. PONDER, William C.**
Dec. 28, 1835, 1/2 mile N Felkel, Leon Co. W 1/2 NW 1/4 Sect. 34 Tp. 3 R. 2, north and east.

**5361. PONDER, William C.**
Dec. 28, 1835, 1/2 mile N Felkel, Leon Co. E 1/2 NW 1/4 Sect. 34 Tp. 3 R. 2, north and east.

**5362. PONDER, William C.**
Dec. 28, 1835, 1 mile N by E Felkel, Leon Co. W 1/2 NW 1/4 Sect. 35 Tp. 3 R. 2, north and east.

**5363. PONDER, William C.**
Dec. 28, 1835, 1/2 mile N Felkel, Leon Co. NE 1/4 NW 1/4 Sect. 34 Tp. 3 R. 2, north and east.

**5364. PONDER, William C.**
Dec. 28, 1835, 3/4 mile W by E Felkel, Leon Co. NW 1/4 NE 1/4 Sect. 34 Tp. 3 R. 2, north and east.

**7105. PONDER, William C.**
Nov. 21, 1837, 4 3/4 miles NNE Felkel, Leon Co. E 1/2 NW 1/4 Sect. 25 Tp. 3 R. 2, north and east.

**1341. PONDER, Wm. G.**
May 8, 1827, 3 miles E Iamonia, Leon Co. W 1/2 SE 1/4 Sect. 15 Tp. 3 R. 2, north and east.

**2167. PONDER. Wm. G.**
Dec. 24, 1827, 2 miles N Wadesboro, Leon Co. W 1/2 SE 1/4 Sect. 19 Tp. 2 R. 3, north and east.

**2479. PONDER, Wm. G.**
Aug. 30, 1828, 3 miles SW Miccosukee, Leon Co. W 1/2 SW 1/4 Sect. 18 Tp. 2 R. 3, north and east.

**3568. PONDER, Wm. G.**
July 19, 1830, 3 miles N by E Moseley Hall, Madison Co. W 1/2 SW 1/4 Sect. 10 Tp. 1 R. 8, south and east.

**3569. PONDER, Wm. G.**
July 19, 1830, 2 1/2 miles N by E Moseley Hall, Madison Co. W 1/2 SE 1/4 Sect. 10 Tp. 1 R. 8, south and east.

**3570. PONDER, Wm. G.**
July 19, 1830, 3 miles N Moseley Hall, Madison Co. W 1/2 SE 1/4 Sect. 9

Tp. 1 R. 8, south and east.

**3571. PONDER, Wm. G.**
July 19, 1830, 2 1/2 miles NE Moseley Hall, Madison Co. E 1/2 NW 1/4 Sect. 15 Tp. 1 R. 8, south and east.

**3713. PONDER, Wm. G.**
Oct. 26, 1830, 2 miles E by S Lovett, Madison Co. E 1/2 NE 1/4 Sect. 1 Tp. 2 R. 7, north and east.

**4155. PONDER, Wm. G.**
Mar. 27, 1832, 4 miles W Copeland, Leon Co. W 1/2 SW 1/4 Sect. 32 Tp. 3 R. 2, north and east.

**4167. PONDER, Wm. G.**
May 3, 1832, 1 1/4 miles W Felkel, Leon Co. W 1/2 SE 1/4 Sect. 5 Tp. 2 R. 2, north and east.

**4661. PONDER, Wm. G.**
Nov. 15, 1834, 1 1/4 miles W Bond, Madison Co. W 1/2 SW 1/4 Sect. 6 Tp. 2 R. 8, north and east.

**5816. PONDER, Wm. G.**
Aug. 31, 1836, 1 1/4 miles NE Felkel, Leon Co. E 1/2 NW 1/4 Sect. 35 Tp. 3 R. 2, north and east.

**6284. PONDER, Wm. G.**
Dec. 23, 1836, 2 miles N by W Felkel, Leon Co. E 1/2 SE 1/4 and E 1/2 SW 1/4 Sect. 28 Tp. 3 R. 2, north and east.

**6285. PONDER, Wm. G.**
Dec. 23, 1836, 4 miles NE Wadesboro, Leon Co. W 1/2 SW 1/4 Sect. 27 Tp. 3 R. 2, north and east.

**6469. PONDER, Wm. G.**
Jan. 9, 1837, 3 miles WNW Copeland, Leon Co. W 1/2 SW 1/4 Sect. 24 Tp. 3 R. 2, north and east.

**6470. PONDER, Wm. G.**
Jan. 9, 1837, 3 1/4 miles WNW Copeland, Leon Co. W 1/2 SE 1/4 Sect. 26 Tp. 3 R. 2, north and east.

**6471. PONDER, Wm. G.**
Jan. 9, 1837, 4 miles E by S Iamonia, Leon Co. E 1/2 SE 1/4 Sect. 23 Tp. 3 R. 2, north and east.

**6923. PONDER, Wm. G.**
Mar. 18, 1837, 1 mile E Havana, Gadsden Co. W 1/2 NE 1/4 Sect. 35 Tp. 3 R. 2, north and west.

**6924. PONDER, Wm. G.**
Mar. 18, 1837, 3 1/4 miles W by N Copeland, Leon Co. E 1/2 SE 1/4 Sect. 26 Tp. 3 R. 2, north and east.

**7077. PONDER, Wm. G.**
Nov. 6, 1837, 2 3/4 miles NNW Copeland, Jefferson Co. W 1/2 NW 1/4 and W 1/2 SW 1/4 Sect. 25 Tp. 3 R. 2, north and east.

**2100. PONDER, Wm. P.**
Nov 13, 1827, 3 miles N Wadesboro, Leon Co. E 1/2 NW 1/4 Sect. 19 Tp. 2 R. 3, north and east.

**8609. POPE, Harriet**
Oct. 13, 1843, 1/4 mile SE Sneads, Jackson Co. NE 1/4 SW 1/4 Sect. 35 Tp. 4 R. 7, north and west.

**POPE, John B. see Thomas RANDALL**

**35. POPE, John M.**
Nov. 6, 1826, c. 2 miles NE Cottondale, Jackson Co. SE 1/4 Sect. 22 Tp. 5 R. 11, north and west. (Pre-emption)

**2021. POPE, John M.**
Aug. 10, 1827, 3 miles E by S Marianna, Jackson Co. E 1/2 NE 1/4 Sect. 12 Tp. 4 R. 10, north and west.

**2022. POPE, John M.**
Aug. 10, 1827, 3 1/2 miles ESE Marianna, Jackson Co. E 1/2 SE 1/4 Sect. 12 Tp. 14 R. 10, north and west.
**#2021** and **#2022** tranferred Feb. 16, 1828, to **Beverage Nowland**. Witnesses: **L. M. STONE** and **M. G. HANSON**, who were sworn in before **Joseph W. RUSS**, Justice of Peace, Jackson Co. sworn Mar. 12, 1828.

**2190. POPE, Thomas H.**
(of Fla.) Dec. 31, 1827, 2 miles WSW Black Creek, Leon Co. W 1/2 NE 1/4 Sect. 15 Tp. 1 R. 2, north and east.

**2212. POPE, Thomas H.**
(of Fla.) Jan. 9, 1828, 3 miles WNW Capitola, Leon Co. E 1/2 SW 1/4 Sect. 15 Tp. 1 R. 2, north and east.

**149. POPE, William S.**
Dec. 27, 1826, 2 miles NE Cottondale, Jackson Co. NE 1/4 Sect. 22 Tp. 5 R. 11, north and west.

**2616. POPE, William S.**
Jan. 13, 1829, 3 miles NE Sneads, Jackson Co. Lot No. 1 Sect. 19 Tp. 4 R. 6, north and west.

**2617. POPE, William S.**
Jan. 13, 1829, 2 1/2 miles ENE Sneads, Jackson Co. Lot No. 1 Sect. 30 Tp. 4 R. 6, north and west.

**2723. POPE, William S.**
Feb. 11, 1829, 2 miles W Chattahoochee, Jackson Co. Lot No. 5 Sect. 31

Tp. 4 R. 6, north and west.

**2910. POPE, Thomas H.**
July 8, 1829, 1 1/2 miles NW Sneads, Jackson Co. W 1/2 NW 1/4 Sect. 27 Tp. 4 R. 7, north and west.

**2911. POPE, William S.**
July 8, 1829, 3 miles NNW Sneads, Jackson Co. Lot No. 1 Sect. 15 Tp. 4 R. 7, north and west. Transferred to **Benj. PERRY**, July 8, 1829; retransferred to **Frederick TOWLE**, July 8, 1829. (**G. W. WARD**, Register).

**2918. POPE, William S.**
July 9, 1829, 5 miles NNW Haywood, Jackson Co. Lot No. 1 Sect. 7 Tp. 6 R. 7, north and west.

**2919. POPE, William S.**
July 9, 1829, 4 miles NNW Haywood, Jackson Co. Lot No. 1 Sect. 18 Tp. 6 R. 7, north and west.

**2922. POPE, William S.**
July 9, 1829, 5 miles NNW Haywood, Jackson Co. E 1/2 NE 1/4 Sect. 13 Tp. 6 R. 8, north and west.

**5372. POPE, William S.**
Dec. 29, 1835, 1 3/4 miles N Inwood, Jackson Co. NE 1/4 Sect. 25 Tp. 4 R. 7, north and west.

**5373. POPE, William S.**
Dec. 29, 1835, 1 1/4 miles NE Sneads, Jackson Co. NE 1/4 NW 1/4 Sect. 25 Tp. 4 R. 7, north and west.

**5692. POPE, William S.**
June 3, 1836, 1 mile E by N Sneads, Jackson Co. NW 1/4 SE 1/4 Sect. 25 Tp. 4 R. 7, north and west.

**7769. POPE, William S.**
(with **John, Henry, Elizabeth**, and **Margaret POPE**) Dec. 19, 1838, 3 miles N by E Inwood, Jackson Co. E 1/2 NE 1/4 Sect. 28 Tp. 4 R. 7, north and west.

**8930. POPPELL, Henry D.**
April 4, 1846, 2 1/2 miles SW Hawkins, Liberty Co. NE 1/4 Sect. 31 Tp. 1 R. 6, north and east.

**8259. POPPELL, John**
Mar. 20, 1840, 5 miles N by E Champaign, Madison Co. NE 1/4 SW 1/4 Sect. 31 Tp. 1 R. 6, north and east.

**7644. POPPELL, John W.**
Sept. 18, 1838, 3 3/4 miles N by E Champaign, Madison Co. SW 1/4 SW 1/4 Sect. 6 Tp. 1 R. 9, north and east.

**6572. POPPELL, Nathan W.**
Jan. 17, 1837, 3/4 mile E Concord, Gadsden Co. SW 1/4 SE 1/4 Sect. 17 Tp. 3 R. 1, north and west.

**8856. POPPELL, Nathan Ward**
Dec. 13, 1845, 4 1/2 miles NNE Monticello, Jefferson Co. SE 1/4 NW 1/4 Sect. 14 Tp. 2 R. 5, south and east.

**PORTER, Charles T.** see **Henry PENNY, #4424**

**8366. PORTER, Joel**
June 30, 1840, 2 miles E Flower's Still, Calhoun Co. Lots No. 1 and 2 Sect. 3 Tp. 1 R. 8, south and west.

**8812. POSEY, Martha**
Sept. 13, 1845, 4 miles E Macon, Washington Co. NE 1/4 SE 1/4 Sect. 15 Tp. 2 R. 13, north and west.

**8873. POSEY, Martha**
Jan. 10, 1846, 6 miles E Macon, Washington Co. NW 1/4 SE 1/4 Sect. 15 Tp. 2 R. 13, north and west.

**7762. POTTER, Celia**
Dec. 15, 1838, 3 miles NNW Macon, Washington Co. NE 1/4 SE 1/4 Sect. 8 Tp. 2 R. 14, north and west.

**3221. POTTER, Levi**
Jan. 21, 1830, 3 miles ENE Vernon, Washington Co. E 1/2 NW 1/4 Sect. 19 Tp. 3 R. 14, north and west. Paid in scrip issued to **Alex. MACOMB**, surviving partner of the firm of **EDGAR & MACOMB**, dated May 30, 1829.

**5780. POTTER, Levi**
July 22, 1836, 2 1/4 miles NNW Macon, Washington Co. W 1/2 NW 1/4 Sect. 8 Tp. 2 R. 14, north and west.

See **William STAPLE, #546**

**4672. POTTER, Lin**
Dec. 4, 1834, 2 3/4 miles NNW Macon, Washington Co. E 1/2 NW 1/4 Sect. 8 Tp. 2 R. 14, north and west.

**4414. POTTER, Robert**
Sept. 16, 1833, 3 1/4 miles SSE Everett, Washington Co. E 1/2 NW 1/4 Sect. 14 Tp. 3 R. 13, north and west.

**972. POUCHIER, John C.**
Oct. 16, 1851, c. 3 1/2 miles SW O'Brien, Suwannee Co. N 1/2 Lot No. 7 Sect. 27 Tp. 5 R. 13, south and east. Transferred Oct. 29, 1857, to **Nathan-**

iel BRYAN. In presence of **Daniel HALL** and **L. B. DAVIS**, Justice of the Peace.

**2541. POWELL, Benjamin N.**
Mar. 4, 1854, 1/2 mile NE Hawthorne, Alachua Co. NE 1/4 NE 1/4 and W 1/2 NE 1/4 Sect. 35 Tp. 10 R. 22, south and east. Patent delivered Mar. 31, 1857.

**4344. POWELL, Coleman**
April 7, 1833, 1 1/4 miles E Felkel, Leon Co. SE 1/4 SE 1/4 Sect. 2 Tp. 2 R. 2, north and east.

**4345. POWELL, Coleman**
April 9, 1833, 1 mile E Felkel, Leon Co. SW 1/4 SE 1/4 Sect. 2 Tp. 2 R. 2, north and east.

**5620. POWELL, Coleman**
April 23, 1836, 5 1/4 miles E Stringer, Jefferson Co. E 1/2 NW 1/4 Sect. 33 Tp. 3 R. 3, north and east.

**6219. POWELL, Coleman**
Dec. 15, 1836, 2 1/2 miles W Alma, Leon Co. W 1/2 NW 1/4 Sect. 33 Tp. 3 R. 4, north and east.

**4606. POWELL, Immiah**
Aug. 16, 1834, 2 1/2 miles NNW Chaires, Leon Co. NE 1/4 SE 1/4 Sect. 21 Tp. 1 R. 2, south and east.

**2500. POWELL, Jeremiah**
Sept. 23, 1828, at Capitola, Leon Co. E 1/2 SE 1/4 Sect. 30 Tp. 1 R. 3, north and east.

**3088. POWELL, Jeremiah**
Oct. 22, 1829, 1/2 mile SW Capitola, Leon Co. W 1/2 SW 1/4 Sect. 29 Tp. 1 R. 3, north and east.

**3089. POWELL, Jeremiah**
Oct. 22, 1829, 3 miles E Capitola, Leon Co. W 1/2 SE 1/4 Sect. 36 Tp. 1 R. 3, north and east.

**4251. POWELL, Jeremiah**
Dec. 18, 1832, 10 miles W by S Nash, Jefferson Co. E 1/2 NW 1/4 Sect. 32 Tp. 1 R. 3, north and east.

**4252. POWELL, Jeremiah**
Dec. 18, 1832, 1 1/2 miles S Capitola, Jefferson Co. E 1/2 SW 1/4 Sect. 32 Tp. 1 R. 3, north and east.

**4801. POWELL, Jeremiah**
Jan. 21, 1835, 4 miles SSW Lloyd, Jefferson Co. W 1/2 NE 1/4 Sect. 32 Tp. 1 R. 3, north and east.

**4802. POWELL, Jeremiah**
Jan. 21, 1835, 4 1/2 miles SSW Lloyd, Jefferson Co. W 1/2 SE 1/4 Sect. 32 Tp. 1 R. 3, north and east.

**5238. POWELL, Jeremiah**
Oct. 28, 1835, 3/4 mile E Chaires, Leon Co. NE 1/4 Sect. 36 Tp. 1 R. 2, north and east.

**5239. POWELL, Jeremiah**
Oct. 29, 1835, at Capitola, Leon Co. W 1/2 NE 1/4 Sect. 30 Tp. 1 R. 3, north and east.

**5298. POWELL, Jeremiah**
Dec. 1, 1835, 1 1/2 miles NW Lloyd, Jefferson Co. E 1/2 NW 1/4 Sect. 9 Tp. 1 R. 3, north and east.

**5299. POWELL, Jeremiah**
Dec. 1, 1835, 1 1/4 miles NW Lloyd, Jefferson Co. E 1/2 SW 1/4 Sect. 9 Tp. 1 R. 3, north and east.

**5300. POWELL, Jeremiah**
Dec. 1, 1835, 3 miles SW Lloyd, Jefferson Co. W 1/2 SW 1/4 Sect. 33 Tp. 1 R. 3, north and east.

**5713. POWELL, Jeremiah**
June 20, 1836, 1/2 mile S Capitola, Leon Co. SW 1/4 NW 1/4 Sect. 31 Tp. 1 R. 3, north and east.

**6226. POWELL, Jeremiah**
Dec. 16, 1836, 1/2 mile NW Wadesboro, Leon Co. W 1/2 SE 1/4 Sect. 36 Tp. 1 R. 2, north and east.

**6303. POWELL, Jeremiah**
Dec. 24, 1836, at El Destino, Jefferson Co. NE 1/4 NW 1/4 Sect. 7 Tp. 1 R. 3, south and east. On back of Receipt, "Land Scrip, 1836."

**6304. POWELL, Jeremiah**
Dec. 24, 1836, at El Destino, Jefferson Co. E 1/2 SW 1/4 and W 1/2 SE 1/4 Sect. 6 Tp. 1 R. 3, south and east.

**6913. POWELL, Jeremiah**
Mar. 15, 1837, just NE Capitola, Leon Co. W 1/2 SE 1/4 Sect. 19 Tp. 1 R. 3, north and east. On back, "March, 1837, Land Scrip for one eighth."

**1801. POWELL, John**
April 1, 1853, 9 1/2 miles S by E Alton, Lafayette Co. Lot No. 6 S 1/2 Lot No. 7 Sect. 28 N 1/2 Lots No. 1 and 2 Sect. 33 Tp. 6 R. 12, south and east.

**5229. POWELL, John**
Feb. 13, 1860, 3 miles SE Ogden, Columbia Co. NE 1/4 NW 1/4 Sect.

32 Tp. 3 R. 15, south and east. Patent delivered Jan. 7, 1864.

**4267. POWELL, Nathan**
Jan. 4, 1833, 1 3/4 miles SE Rose, Leon Co. SW 1/4 NW 1/4 Sect. 34 Tp. 1 R. 2, south and east.

**3184. POWERS, John**
Dec. 28, 1829, 1/2 mile SE Darsey, Gadsden Co. E 1/2 NE 1/4 Sect. 12 Tp. 3 R. 2, north and west.

**8871. POYTHREES, James**
Jan. 9, 1846, 1/2 mile NW Steaphead, Gadsden Co. SE 1/4 NE 1/4 Sect. 12 Tp. 3 R. 2, north and west.

**POYTHRESS, Geo.** see **Wm. T. KILBEE, #1607**

**4135. PRESCOTT, Darling C.**
Jan. 31, 1856, 6 miles SW Guilford, Columbia Co. S 1/2 SW 1/4 Sect. 20 Tp. 5 R. 18, south and east. Transferred to **William C. NEWBURN**, July 1857.

**PRESCOTT, D. C.** see **James B COLE, #601**

**163. PRESSCOTT, Eli Warren**
July 18, 1845, c. 4 miles E Highland, Clay Co. E 1/2 SE 1/4 Sect. 27 Tp. 4 R. 23, south and east. Patent delivered May 17, 1836.

**4472. PREVATT, Celia A.**
(widow of **Barnett C. PREVATT**) Mar. 24, 1884, in Rocky, Levy Co. SW 1/4 NW 1/4 and NW 1/4 SW 1/4 Sect. 12 Tp. 13S R. 14E.

**4590. PREVATT, James D.**
July 4, 1834, 3/4 mile NNE Facil, Hamilton Co. W 1/2 SW 1/4 Sect. 23 Tp. 1 R. 15, south and east.

**7421. PREVATT, James D.**
Mar. 24, 1838, 1 mile N by E Facil, Hamilton Co. SW 1/4 NW 1/4 and NE 1/4 SW 1/4 Sect. 23 Tp. 1 R. 15, south and east.

**5600. PREVATT, James D.**
April 18, 1836, 1 3/4 miles E Facil, Hamilton Co. SW 1/4 NE 1/4 Sect. 26 Tp. 1 R. 15, south and east.

**8095. PREVATT, James D.**
Sept. 26, 1839, 2 miles N by W Noles, Washington Co. E 1/2 NW 1/4 Sect. 23 Tp. 1 R. 15, south and east.

**8096. PREVATT, James D.**
Sept. 26, 1839, 2 1/4 miles N by W Noles, Washington Co. NW 1/4 NW 1/4 Sect. 23 Tp. 1 R. 15, south and east.

**2552. PREVATT, James H.**
Mar. 4, 1854, 7 miles E Lake City Junction, Columbia Co. NE 1/4 NE 1/4 Sect. 20; Nw 1/4 SE 1/4 Sect. 21 Tp. 6 R. 17, south and east. Patent delivered Aug. 16, 1856.

**4913. PREVATT, Joseph F.**
Dec. 15, 1858, 1 mile N Newtown, Levy Co. NW 1/4 NW 1/4 Sect. 28 Tp. 11 R. 16, south and east. Patent delivered Jan. 22, 1875.

**1285. PREVATT, Thomas J.**
April 9, 1852, 2 1/2 miles NW Alachua, Alachua Co. NE 1/4 NE 1/4 Sect. 11 Tp. 8 R. 18, south and east. Patent delivered Aug. 19, 1856.

**2224. PREVATT, Valentine R.**
Oct. 3, 1853, 2 miles E Sharon, Clay Co. W 1/2 Lot No. 2 Sect. 7 Tp. 7 R. 22, south and east.

**4992. PREVATT, William J. D.**
Mar. 17, 1859, 4 1/2 miles SW Dukes, Union Co. NE 1/4 SW 1/4 Sect. 22 Tp. 6 R. 18, south and east.

**4993. PREVATT, William J. D.**
Mar. 17, 1859, 4 3/4 miles SW Dukes, Union Co. S 1/2 SW 1/4 Sect. 22 and SE 1/4 SE 1/4 Sect. 21 Tp. 6 R. 18, south and east.

**5104. PRICE, David W.**
Oct. 1, 1859, at Arno, Alachua Co. SE 1/4 NE 1/4 Sect. 36 Tp. 8 R. 17, south and east. Patent delivered Dec. 1, 1863.

**2550. PRICE, Joseph**
Mar. 4, 1854, 4 1/2 miles SE Jefferson, Columbia Co. N 1/2 NW 1/4 Sect. 22 Tp. 4 R. 17, south and east.

**470. PRICE, Spencer**
Oct. 16, 1846, c. 4 miles W Hodgson, Levy Co. W 1/2 NW 1/4 Sect. 28 Tp. 12 R. 18, south and east.

**1026. PRICE, Wm. D.**
Jan. 30, 1827, 2 miles E Rose, Jefferson Co. NE 1/4 Sect. 21 Tp. 1 R. 3, south and east.

**1027. PRICE, Wm. D.**
Jan. 30, 1827, 2 miles E Rose, Jefferson Co. W 1/2 SW 1/4 Sect. 15 Tp. 1 R. 3, south and east.

**1949. PRICE, Wm. D.**
June 25, 1827, 3 miles ENE Cody,

Jefferson Co. SW 1/4 Sect. 22 Tp. 1 R. 3, south and east.

**4086. PRICHARD, Robert S.**
(Coweta Co., Ga.) Jan. 11, 1856, 2 miles SSE Bass, Columbia Co. SE 1/4 and N 1/2 SE 1/4 and N 1/2 SW 1/4 Sect. 31 Tp. 4 R. 17, south and east. Patent delivered Feb. 6, 1902

**1433. PRIEST, Gabriel C.**
Aug. 16, 1852, 7 miles W Dungarvan, Alachua Co. SW 1/4 SE 1/4 Sect. 25 Tp. 12 R. 19, south and east. Patent delivered June 17, 1857.

**2181. PRIEST, Gabriel C.**
Sept 15, 1853, 1 mile SSE Hodgson, Levy Co. NE 1/4 SE 1/4 Sect. 31 Tp. 12 R. 19, south and east. Patent delivered June 22, 1864.

**2197. PRIGHAM, Emerald**
(of Fla.) Dec. 31, 1827, 6 miles E Capitola, Jefferson Co. W 1/2 SE 1/4 Sect. 25 Tp. 1 R. 3, north and east.

**4011. PRINGLE, Jackson**
Dec. 17, 1855, 4 miles W Brycerville, Duval Co. E 1/2 SW 1/4 Sect. 29 Tp. 1 R. 23, south and east. Patent delivered Nov. 14, 1864.

**6853. PRINGLE, John A.**
March 7, 1837, at Century, Escambia Co. and west of Escambia River. E 1/2 SE 1/4 Sect. 6 Tp. 5 R. 30, north and west.

**PRIOLEAU, Dr. Sam see Jno. McDOWEL**

**3890. PRIOLEAU, Samuel C.**
Feb. 23, 1831, 6 miles SW Lamont, Jefferson Co. SW 1/4 Sect. 5 Tp. 2 R. 5, south and east.

**3891. PRIOLEAU, Samuel C.**
Feb. 23, 1831, 6 miles SW Lamont, Jefferson Co. W 1/2 SE 1/4 Sect. 5 Tp. 2 R. 5, south and east.

**3892. PRIOLEAU, Samuel C.**
Feb. 23, 1831, 5 miles SW Lamont, Jefferson Co. W 1/2 NE 1/4 Sect. 8 Tp. 2 R. 5, south and east.

**3906. PRIOLEAU, Samuel C.**
Feb. 28, 1831, 5 miles SW Lamont, Jefferson Co. W 1/2 SE 1/4 Sect. 6 Tp. 2 R. 5, south and east.

**3907. PRIOLEAU, Samuel C.**
Feb. 28, 1831, 4 miles E Leonton, Jefferson Co. W 1/2 SE 1/4 Sect. 6 Tp. 2 R. 5, south and east.

**7791. PRITCHARD, Aaron**
Jan. 2, 1839, 2 1/2 miles N by E Wadesboro, Jefferson Co. NW 1/4 NW 1/4 Sect. 32 Tp. 2 R. 3, north and east.

**4208. PRIVLEAU, Francis C.**
(in pencil, 5008 in ink) Aug. 29, 1832, 1/4 mile E El Destino, Jefferson Co. W 1/2 NE 1/4 Sect. 7 Tp. 1 R. 3, south and east.

**4209. PRIVLEAU, Francis C.**
Aug. 29, 1832, at El Destino, Jefferson Co. SE 1/4 NW 1/4 Sect. 7 Tp. 1 R. 3, south and east.

**2842. PROILEAU, Sam'l C.**
June 4, 1829, 5 1/2 miles ENE El Destino, Jefferson Co. W 1/2 SE 1/4 Sect. 36 Tp. 1 R. 3, north and east.

**4399. PROMPHUAY, Silvanus**
Aug. 26, 1833, 1 mile S Iamonia, Leon Co. SW 1/4 SW 1/4 Sect. 18 Tp. 23 R. 2, north and east.

**4400. PROMPHUAY, Silvanus**
Aug. 26, 1833, 1 1/2 miles SSE Iamonia, Leon Co. E 1/2 SW 1/4 Sect. 17 Tp. 3 R. 2, north and east.

**4204. PUMPHREAY, Silvanus**
Aug. 23, 1832, 1 mile S Iamonia, S shore on arm extending N by E of Lake Iamonia, Leon Co. NE 1/4 NW 1/4 Sect. 19 Tp. 3 R. 2, north and east.

**7275. PURVIANCE, Henry E.**
Jan. 26, 1838, 2 miles SE Marion, Hamilton Co. NW 1/4 NE 1/4 Sect. 8 Tp. 1 R. 14, south and east.

**7276. PURVIANCE, Henry E.**
Jan.26, 1838, 1/4 mile SE Marion, Hamilton Co. SW 1/4 NW 1/4 and E 1/2 NW 1/4; SW 1/4 NE 1/4 Sect. 5 Tp. 1 R. 14, south and east.

**8824. PURVIANCE, Henry E.**
Sept. 23, 1845, 4 1/2 miles E by N White Springs, Hamilton Co. Lot No. 3 Sect. 2 Tp. 2 R. 16, south and east.

**8920. PURVIANCE, Henry E.**
Mar. 10, 1846, 5 miles E by N White Springs, Hamilton Co. Lot No. 4 W 1/2 NW 1/4 Sect. 2 Tp. 2 R. 16, south and east.

**4577. PYLES, Samuel R.**
June, 1857, 3 miles SE Wanamaker, Gilchrist Co. Lot No. 4 Sect. 21 Tp. 7 R. 18, south and east. Patent delivered Sept. 17, 1859.

**2437. PYLES, William**

Feb. 22, 1854, at Zuber, Marion Co. SE 1/4 NW 1/4 Sect. 23 Tp. 14 R. 21, south and east.

**381. PYKE, Wm. H.**
May 3, 1827, 6 miless NNW Haywood, Jackson Co. Lot No. 3 Sect. 12 Tp. 6 R. 8, north and west.

## * Q *

**QUAILES, D. M.** see **Robert GAMBLE, # 2263, 2264, 2265, and 2266**

**2310. QUARLES, Duncan M.**
Mar. 17, 1828, 1 1/2 miles NW Waukenah, Jefferson Co. E 1/2 NW 1/4 Sect. 33 Tp. 1 R. 4, north and east.

**727. QUARTERMAN, Robert Y.**
Apr. 4, 1850, near McIntosh, Marion Co. Lot No. 1 Fractional Sect. 19 Tp. 12 R. 21, south and east.

**4471. QUIN, James**
Dec. 10, 1833, 2 miles NNE Roeville, Santa Rosa Co. W 1/2 SE 1/4 Sect. 34 Tp. 2 R. 28, north and west.

**4617. QUIN, James**
Oct. 3, 1834, 1 1/4 miles W by N Milton, Santa Rosa Co. NE 1/4 SE 1/4 Sect. 34 Tp. 2 R. 28, north and west.

**4507. QUINN, James**
Jan. 7, 1834, 1 1/4 miles N Milton, Santa Rosa Co. E 1/2 NE 1/4 Sect. 34 Tp. 2 R. 28, north and west.

**8833. QUINN, James**
Nov. 4, 1845, 2 1/2 miles SW Roeville, Santa Rosa Co. NW 1/4 NE 1/4 Sect. 34 Tp. 2 R. 28, north and west.

**2552. QUINTACK, Wm.**
Nov. 25, 1828, 7 miles SE Quincy, Gadsden Co. Lot No. 2 Sect. 33 Tp. 2 R. 3, north and west.

## * R *

**3487. RAGSDALE, William**
April 21, 1830, 2 miles ENE Wadesboro, Leon Co. E 1/2 NW 1/4 Sect. 33 Tp. 2 R. 3, north and east.

**3623. RALPH, Moses**
Oct. 5, 1830, 5 miles NNW Bradfordville, Leon Co. W 1/2 NW 1/4 Sect. 5 Tp. 2 R. 1, north and east.

**2417. RAMSEY, Eli**
Feb. 21, 1854, 1 mile NW Martel, Marion Co. SE 1/4 NW 1/4 Sect. 14 Tp. 15 R. 20, south and east. Patent delivered Dec. 19, 1856.

**2654. RAMSEY, Henry G.**
Jan. 21, 1829, 4 1/2 miles S Mavis, Walton Co. W 1/2 NW 1/4 Sect. 18 Tp. 2 R. 19, north and west.

**8337. RAMSEY, James**
(and **Rachel DREW**) June 11, 1840, 2 miles N by E Dills, Jefferson Co. NW 1/4 Sect. 28 Tp. 3 R. 6, north and east. Patent delivered June 5, 1869.

**2109. RAMSEY, Nathan**
Nov. 20, 1827, 4 1/2 miles E by N Campbellton, Jackson Co. E 1/2 SW 1/4 Sect. 27 Tp. 7 R. 11, north and west.

**6980. RAMSEY, Nathan**
Apr. 12, 1837, 1 mile SW Aberdeen, Jackson Co. NE 1/4 SW 1/4 and SW 1/4 NW 1/4 Sect. 10 Tp. 4 R. 11, south and west.

**8540. RAMSEY, William V.**
March 6, 1842, 4 miles NE Dills, Jefferson Co. NE 1/4 Sect. 29 Tp. 3 R. 6, north and east.

**RANDALL, Asa R.** see **William C. CARUTHERS, #2349**

**John RANDALL** see **Irby ROBERTS, #1213**

**2583. RANDALL, Thomas**
Dec. 25, 1828, 1 mile NNE Wacissa, Jefferson Co. E 1/2 NW 1/4 Sect. 32 Tp. 1 R. 4, south and east.

**2584. RANDALL, Thomas**
Dec. 25, 1828, 1 1/2 miles NNE Wacissa, Jefferson Co. N 1/2 NE 1/4 Sect. 32 Tp. 1 R. 4, south and east.

**2997. RANDALL, Thomas**
Aug. 29, 1829, 2 miles NNW Wacissa, Jefferson Co. E 1/2 SW 1/4 Sect. 30 Tp. 1 R. 4, south and east. Transferred Dec. 28, 1829 to **John B. POPE**. Teste: **James HAWKINS**.

**3947. RANDALL, Thomas**
Apr. 11, 1831, 2 miles ENE Wacissa, Jefferson Co. W 1/2 SW 1/4 Sect. 35 Tp. 1 R. 4, south and east.

**6206. RANDALL, Thomas**
Dec. 13, 1836, 4 miles SW Lamont, Jefferson Co. W 1/2 NW 1/4 Sect. 9 Tp. 2 R. 5, south and east.
See **Wm. CANNON, #6884**

**7469. RANDALL, Thomas**
May 17, 1838, 2 miles S by W Lamont, Jefferson Co. E 1/2 SE 1/4 Sect. 33 Tp. 1 R. 5, south and east.

**7470. RANDALL, Thomas**
May 18, 1838, 1/4 mile SW Lamont, Jefferson Co. E 1/2 SW 1/4 Sect. 27 Tp. 1 R. 5, south and east.

**7471. RANDALL, Thomas**
May 18, 1838, 3 1/2 miles S Lamont, Jefferson Co. SW 1/4 Sect. 10 Tp. 2 R. 5, south and east.

**2967. RANDOLPH, Thomas E.**
Aug. 1, 1829, 3 miles ESE Centerville, Leon Co. W 1/2 NW 1/4 Sect. 28 Tp. 2 R. 2, north and east.

**2968. RANDOLPH, Thomas E.**
Aug. 1, 1829, 3 1/2 miles SE Centerville, Leon Co. W 1/2 SE 1/4 Sect. 28 Tp. 2 R. 2, north and east.

**2970. RANDOLPH, Thomas E.**
Aug. 1, 1829, 2 miles E Centerville, Leon Co. W 1/2 NW 1/4 Sect. 21 Tp. 2 R. 2, north and east.

**3052. RANDOLPH, Thomas P.**
(of Ga.) Sept. 19, 1829, 3 miles WSW Bradfordville, Leon Co. SW 1/4 Sect. 20 Tp. 2 R. 1, north and east. Transferred to **Joseph W. FIELD** of Leon Co.(no date). Transferred to **William B. MOORE** (no date). Transferred back to **Joseph W. FIELD**.

**3203. RANDOLPH, Thomas P.**
Jan. 6, 1830, 5 1/2 miles WSW Monticello, Jefferson Co. E 1/2 SW 1/4 Sect. 5 Tp. 1 R. 4, north and east.

**3510. RANDOLPH, Thomas P.**
(of Ga.) May 12, 1830, c. 3 miles NNW Braswell, Jefferson Co. Lot No. 5 Sect. 31 Tp. 2 R. 4, north and east.

**4154. RANDOLPH, Thomas P.**
Mar. 23, 1832, 1 mile W Drifton, Jefferson Co. E 1/2 NE 1/4 Sect. 13

Tp. 1 R. 4, north and east.
**4973. RANDOLPH, Thomas P.**
May 21, 1835, 2 1/2 miles N by W Braswell, Jefferson Co. NE 1/4 NE 1/4 Sect. 6 Tp. 1 R. 4, north and east.
**4974. RANDOLPH, Thomas P.**
May 21, 1835, 2 3/4 miles NNW Braswell, Jefferson Co. NW 1/4 NE 1/4 Sect. 8 Tp. 1 R. 4, north and east.
**813. RAULERSON, Herod**
Jan. 25, 1851, 5 1/2 miles S by E Benton, Columbia Co. NE 1/4 NW 1/4 and SW 1/4 NE 1/4 Sect. 28 Tp. 1 R. 17, south and east. Patent delivered May 23, 1856.
**1387. RAULERSON, William**
July 2, 1852, 9 miles WSW Ekal, Sumter Co. SE 1/4 SE 1/4 Sect. 20 Tp. 1 R. 21, north and east. Patent delivered July 14, 1857.
**996. RAULLISON, Nimrod**
Nov. 6, 1851, 3 miles NE Taylor, Baker Co. W 1/2 SE 1/4 Sect. 20 Tp. 1 R. 20, north and east. Transferred Jan. 6, 1851 to **Willis A. HODGES**. Witnesses: **Paul JOHNSON** and **Riley JONES**.
**68. RAULS, William**
Nov. 22, 1826, c. 3 miles SW Havana, Gadsden Co. NE 1/4 Sect. 15 Tp. 2 R. 2, north and west.
**69. RAULS, Seborn**
Nov. 22, 1826, 2 miles SW Havana, Gadsden Co. SE 1/4 Sect. 10 Tp. 2 R. 2, north and west.
**211. RAWLS, Cotton**
Nov. 17, 1845, c. 7 1/2 miles W Irvine, Marion Co. W 1/2 NE 1/4 and W 1/2 SE 1/4 Sect. 35 Fractional Tp. 12 R. 19, south and east.
**270. RAWLS, Cotton**
Jan. 8, 1846, near Homassassa Springs, Citrus Co. E 1/2 SE 1/4 E 1/2 SW 1/4 Sect. 21 Tp. 19 R. 16, south and east.
**271. RAWLS, Cotton**
Jan. 8, 1846, at Homassassa Springs, Citrus Co. Lot No. 2 Fractional Sect. 28 Tp. 19 R. 17, south and east.
**286. RAWLS, Cotton**
May 4, 1846, near Homassassa Springs, Citrus Co. NW 1/4 Sect. 33 and S 1/2 SW 1/4 Sect. 28 Tp. 19 R. 17, south and east.

**2374. RAWLS, Cotton**
Feb. 20, 1854, 1/2 mile NE Williston, Levy Co. N 1/2 NW 1/4 Sect. 36 Tp. 12 R. 18, south and east. Patent delivered Jan. 26, 1859.
**2726. RAWLS, Cotton**
May 2, 1854, 1/4 mile N Williston, Levy Co. NW 1/4 NE 1/4 Sect. 36 Tp. 12 R. 18, south and east. Patent delivered Jan. 26, 1859.
**4142. RAWLS, Cotton**
Feb. 4, 1856, at Hodgson, Levy Co. E 1/2 SE 1/4 Sect. 26 and SW 1/4 SW 1/4 Sect. 25 Tp. 12 R. 18, south and east. Patent delivered Jan. 26, 1859.
**4143. RAWLS, Cotton**
Feb. 4, 1856, at Hodgson, Levy Co. E 1/2 SE 1/4 Sect.25 Tp. 12 R. 18, south and east. Patent delivered Jan. 26, 1859.
**2226. RAWLS, John G.**
Oct. 3, 1853, on WNW shore of Pawsoffkee Lake, 6 miles W Monarch, Sumter Co. W 1/2 NE 1/4 Sect. 36 and SE 1/4 SW 1/4 and SW 1/4 SE 1/4 Sect. 25 Tp. 19 R. 22, south and east. Patent delivered Mar. 25, 1858.
**2277. RAWLS, John G.**
Oct. 22, 1853, 2 miles N Elmwood, Alachua Co. SW 1/4 SE 1/4 Sect. 3 Tp. 13 R. 19, south and east. Patent delivered March 5, 1858. (Mar. 25)
**2366. RAWLS, John G.**
Feb. 20, 1854, 3 1/2 miles NE Mason, Columbia Co. SW 1/4 NE 1/4 and SE 1/4 SW 1/4, and E 1/2 SW 1/4 Sect. 19 Tp. 5 R. 18, south and east. Patent delivered March 25, 1858.
**2367. RAWLS, John G.**
Feb. 20, 1854, 5 miles ENE Houston, Suwannee Co. W 1/2 SE 1/4 Sect. 12 Tp. 2 R. 14, south and east. Patent delivered Mar. 28, 1857.
**2612. RAWLS, John G.**
Mar. 14, 1854, 1 mile E Cadillac, Alachua Co. W 1/2 NW 1/4 Sect. 4 Tp. 9 R. 18, south and east. Patent delivered March 25, 1858.
**4311. RAWLS, John G.**
April 7, 1856, 3/4 mile SE East Alachua, Alachua Co. E 1/2 SW 1/4 and W 1/2 SE 1/4 Lot No. 2 Sect. 23 Tp. 8 R. 18, south and east.
**1038. RAWLS, Laban**

Jan. 30, 1827, 2 miles S Havana, Gadsden Co. W 1/2 SW 1/4 Sect. 10 Tp. 2 R. 2, north and west.

**941. RAWLS, Seborn**
Jan. 19, 1827, 3 miles S Havana, Gadsden Co. E 1/2 SW 1/4 Sect. 10 Tp. 2 R. 2, north and west.

**944. RAWLS, Seborn**
Jan. 19, 1827, 4 miles SSW Havana, Gadsden Co. E 1/2 NW 1/4 Sect. 15 Tp. 2 R. 2, north and west.

**1149. RAWLS, Seborn**
(DUP) Feb. 19, 1827, 2 miles S Havana, Gadsden Co. E 1/2 SE 1/4 Sect. 9 Tp. 2 R. 2, north and west.

**8956. RAYSON, John M.**
July 10, 1846, 6 miles E Capps, Jefferson Co. E 1/2 SE 1/4 Sect. 1 Tp. 1 R. 5, south and east.

**8957. RAYSON, John M.**
July 10, 1846, 5 1/2 miles NNE Lamont, Jefferson Co. W 1/2 NW 1/4 Sect. 7 Tp. 1 R. 6, south and east.

**8958. RAYSON, John M.**
July 10, 1846, 6 miles E by S Capps, Jefferson Co. SE 1/4 NE 1/4 Sect. 12 Tp. 1 R. 5, south and east.

**8959. RAYSON, John M.**
July 10, 1846, 5 miles NNE Lamont, Jefferson Co. NE 1/4 NW 1/4 Sect. 7 Tp. 1 R. 6, south and east.

**8962. RAYSON, John M.**
July 31, 1846, 4 1/2 miles NW Aucilla, Jefferson Co. W 1/2 SW 1/4 Sect. 6 Tp. 1 R. 6, south and east.

**8414. READ, David**
Oct. 26, 1840, 1 1/2 miles N by W Lake Jackson (town), Leon Co. SW 1/4 SW 1/4 Sect. 30 Tp. 2 R. 1, north and west.

**2245. READ, John**
(of Fla.) Feb. 5, 1828, 1 miles SSW Jamison, Gadsden Co. E 1/2 NE 1/4 Sect. 13 Tp. 3 R. 3, north and west.

**8997. REAVES, Rawlins L.**
Nov. 24, 1846, 6 3/4 miles NNW Dills, Jefferson Co. NW 1/4 SW 1/4 Sect. 30 Tp. 3 R. 5, north and east.

**2548. REDDING, Wade H.**
Mar. 4, 1854, 3/4 mile E Citra, Marion Co. NW 1/4 SW 1/4 Sect. 25 and NE 1/4 SE 1/4 Sect. 26 Tp. 12 R. 22, south and east.

**6316. REDDING, William H.**
Dec. 26, 1836, 1 mile SW Alma, Jefferson Co. Lot No. 1 Fractional Sect. 2 Tp. 2 R. 4, north and east.

**7372. REED, William M.**
Mar. 1, 1838, 2 miles N by Westlake, Madison Co. NE 1/4 SE 1/4 Sect. 27 Tp. 2 R. 12, north and east.

**7373. REED, William M.**
Mar. 1, 1838, 2 1/2 miles N by E Westlake, Madison Co. E 1/2 SW 1/4 and W 1/2 SE 1/4 Sect. 27 Tp. 2 R. 12, north and east.

**7932. REED, William M.**
Mar. 6, 1839, at Jasper, Hamilton Co. W 1/2 SE 1/4 Sect. 6 Tp. 1 R. 14, north and east.

**8925. REESE, Joseph**
Mar. 25, 1846, 1/4 mile SE Gadsden. Gadsden Co. NW 1/4 SE 1/4 Sect. 15 Tp. 1 R. 2, north and west.

**3445. REEVES, John W.**
Mar. 10, 1830, 2 1/2 miles N Lamont, Jefferson Co. E 1/2 NW 1/4 Sect. 14 Tp. 1 R. 5, south and east.

**5937. REGAN, John**
Oct. 29, 1836, 1 mile NNE Hinson, Gadsden Co. NW 1/4 NE 1/4 Sect. 22 Tp.3 R. 2, north and west.

**8771. REGISTER, Bartholomew**
April 11, 1845, 2 miles NE Miller's Ferry, Washington Co. Lot No. 9 Sect. 15 Tp. 2 R. 16, north and west.

**3801. REGISTER, Ezekiel**
Dec. 16, 1830, just SE Miller's Ferry, Washington Co. Lot No. 3 Sect. 28 Tp. 2 R. 16, north and west.

**8788. REGISTER, John**
June 23, 1845, 2 1/2 miles NNE Miller's Ferry, Washington Co. Lot No. 8 Sect. 15 Tp. 2 R. 16, north and west.

**1410. REGISTER, Samuel**
May 8, 1878, 2 miles SE Avoca, Hamilton Co. W 1/2 SE 1/4 and SE 1/4 SE 1/4 Sect. 13; and NE 1/4 1/4 Sect. 24 Tp. 2N R. 13E.

**7267. REICHERT, Jacob F.**
Jan. 23, 1838, 2 miles NE Monticello, Jefferson Co. NE 1/4 NW 1/4 Sect. 21 Tp. 2 R. 5, north and east.

**4600. Renfroe, Asabel P.**
July 14, 1857, 5 1/2 miles NW Worthington, Union Co. NW 1/4 SW 1/4 Sect. 22 Tp. 6 R. 18, south and east.

Patent delivered July 18, 1868.
**4634. RENFROE, Asabel P.**
(of Columbia) Sept. 9, 1857, 3 1/2 miles S by E Providence, Union Co. SW 1/4 NE 1/4 and NE 1/4 SE 1/4 Sect. 21 Tp. 6 R. 18, south and east. Purchase money ordered to be refunded Sept. 20, 1859.
**4772. RENFROE, Asabel P.**
Sept. 1, 1858, 4 miles NW Worthington Post Office, Union Co. SW 1/4 NW 1/4 Sect. 22 Tp.6 R. 18, south and east.
**529. RENFROE, Enoch**
May 30, 1831, 3 miles NE Dills, Jefferson Co. SW 1/4 Sect. 26 Tp. 3 R. 6, north and east. (Pre-emption Act of 1830).
**8525. RENFROE, Mitchel**
Jan. 31, 1842, 4 1/2 miles NNE Dills, Jefferson Co. NE 1/4 Sect. 26 Tp. 3 R. 6, north and east.
**5705. REVELS, John**
June 11, 1836, 3 1/4 miles NNE Champaign, Madison Co. SE 1/4 NE 1/4 and NE 1/4 SE 1/4 Sect. 6 Tp. 1 R. 9, north and east.
**7431. REVELS, John**
April 2, 1838, 2 3/4 miles NNE Champaign, Madison Co. W 1/2 SW 1/4 Sect. 5 Tp. 1 R. 9, north and east.
**7432. REVELS, John**
April 2, 1838, 3 miles NNE Champaign, Madison Co. SW 1/4 NW 1/4 Sect. 8 Tp. 1 R. 1, north and east.
**8003. REVELS, John**
Jan. 8, 1839, 5 miles NNW Calhoun, Madison Co. W 1/2 NW 1/4 Sect. 5 Tp. 1 R. 9, north and east.
**1728. REVELS, Owen**
Feb. 23, 1853, 3/4 mile NW Dukes, Union Co. SE 1/4 NW 1/4 and NE 1/4 SW 1/4 Sect. 19 Tp. 6 R. 19, south and east. Patent delivered Mar. 4, 1857.
**2189. REVELS, Owen**
Sept. 20, 1853, 3 miles SSW Dukes, Bradford Co. NE 1/4 NE 1/4 Sect. 24 Tp. 6 R. 18, south and east. Patent delivered Oct. 4, 1856.
**2554. REVELS, Owen**
Mar. 4, 1854, 1 1/4 miles E Providence, Columbia Co. E 1/2 NW 1/4 Sect. 4 Tp. 6 R. 18, south and east.

**6212. REVELS, Owen**
Dec. 15, 1836, 2 miles NE Champaign, Madison Co. NE 1/4 SE 1/4 Sect. 12 Tp. 1 R. 8, north and east. Transferred to **E. G. MAYS**, (no date).
**133. REVIER, Alex. M.**
Dec. 25, 1826, 3 miles SE Welchton Station, Jackson Co. SW 1/4 Sect. 3 Tp. 5 R. 11, north and west.
**2113. REVIER, Alex. M.**
(of Fla.) Nov. 22, 1827, 1 mile SSE Cottondale, Jackson Co. E 1/2 NE 1/4 Sect. 5 Tp. 4 R. 11, north and west.
**132. REVIER, Henry L.**
Dec. 25, 1826, 2 miles SE Welchton Station, Jackson Co. NW 1/4 Sect. 3 Tp. 5 R. 11, north and west. Transferred to **Alex. M. REVIER**, Dec. 25, 1826.
**3251. REYNOLDS, John**
Feb. 5, 1830, 4 miles W Tallahassee, Leon Co. W 1/2 SE 1/4 Sect. 31 Tp. 1 R. 1, north and west.
**5334. REYNOLDS, John**
Dec. 8, 1835, 1 mile NE Copeland, Jefferson Co. W 1/2 NE 1/4 Sect. 30 Tp. 3 R. 3, north and east.
**5335. REYNOLDS, John**
Dec. 8, 1835, 1 mile NE Copeland, Jefferson Co. W 1/2 SE 1/4 Sect. 30 Tp. 3 R. 3, north and east.
**1919. RHODEN, John**
July 2, 1853, 6 miles NW Knabbs Spur Station, Baker Co. E 1/2 NE 1/4 Sect. 36 Tp. 2 R. 20, south and east. Patent delivered Oct. 26, 1857.
**7507. RICHARD, Arthur**
June 30, 1838, 3 3/4 miles S by W Chipola, Calhoun Co. W 1/2 NE 1/4 Sect. 17 Tp. 1 R. 9, north and west.
**5732. RICHARDS, David T.**
June 24, 1836, 1 1/2 miles S Greenwood, Jackson Co. Lot No. 3 Fractional Sect. 7 Tp. 5 R. 9, south and west.
**5730. RICHARDS, Jackson N.**
June 24, 1836, 2 1/2 miles NW Dellwood, Jackson Co. Lot No. 3 Fractional Sect. 12, Tp. 6 R. 9, south and west.
**7459. RICHARDS, Jehew**
April 26, 1838, at Wewahitchka, Calhoun Co. W 1/2 NE 1/4 Sect. 25 Tp. 4 R. 10, south and west.

RICHARDS, John see Henry and Dudley PEOPLES, #467

**7477. RICHARDS, John G.**
May 28, 1838, 4 miles W Durham, Calhoun Co. SW 1/4 SE 1/4 Sect. 20 Tp. 1 R. 9, north and west. Transferred to **Stephen E. FARLEY**, Feb. 20, 1830(?).

**4710. RICHARDS, Stephen**
(Per **D. M. SHEFFIELD**) Dec. 16, 1834, 2 3/4 miles NNW Leonards Siding Station, Calhoun Co. W 1/2 SE 1/4 Sect. 8 Tp. 1 R. 9, north and west.

**4711. RICHARDS, Stephen**
(Per **D. M. SHEFFIELD**) Dec. 16, 1834, 2 1/2 miles NNW Leonards Siding Station, Calhoun Co. SE 1/4 SW 1/4 Sect. 8 Tp. 1 R. 9, north and west.

**4712, RICHARDS, Stephen**
(Per **D. M. SHEFFIELD**) Dec. 16, 1834, 2 3/4 miles NNW Leonards Siding Station, Calhoun Co. NW 1/4 NE 1/4 Sect. 8 Tp. 1 R. 9, north and west.

**5020. RICHARDS, Stephen**
July 3, 1835, 3 1/2 miles NNW Madison, Madison Co. SE 1/4 NW 1/4 Sect. 17 Tp. 1 R. 9, north and west.

**7478. RICHARDS, Stephen**
May 28, 1838, 1 1/4 miles SSW Chipola, Calhoun Co. SW 1/4 NE 1/4 and NE 1/4 SW 1/4 Sect. 8 Tp. 1 R. 9, north and west.

**509. RICHARDSON, James**
April 26, 1831, 1 mile W Lovett, Jefferson Co. E 1/2 NE 1/4 Sect. 33 Tp. 3 R. 7, north and east.

**510. RICHARDSON, James**
April 26, 1831, 1 mile W Lovett, Jefferson Co. W 1/2 SE 1/4 Sect. 33 Tp. 3 R. 7, north and east.

**2138. RICHARDSON, Samuel B.**
Dec. 12, 1827, 2 1/2 miles E by S Moseley Hall, Madison Co. W 1/2 NE 1/4 Sect. 35 Tp. 1 R. 8, south and east.

**2225. RICHARDSON, Samuel B.**
(of Fla.) Jan. 14, 1828, at Moseley Hall, Madison Co. W 1/2 SE 1/4 Sect. 26 Tp. 1 R. 8, south and east.

**2306. RICHARDSON, Samuel B.**
March 13, 1828, at Moseley Hall, Madison Co. W 1/2 NW 1/4 Sect. 28 Tp. 1 R. 8, south and east.

**4159. RICHARDSON, Samuel B.**
Mar. 31, 1832, 1 1/4 miles SW Moseley Hall, Madison Co. E 1/2 NE 1/4 Sect. 35 Tp. 1 R. 8, south and east.

**4170. RICHARDSON, Samuel B.**
May 14, 1832, 1 1/4 miles W Waco, Madison Co. W 1/2 SW 1/4 Sect. 25 Tp. 1 R. 8, south and east.

**5134. RICHARDSON, Samuel B.**
Aug. 17, 1835, 1 1/2 miles E Moseley Hall, Madison Co. W 1/2 NW 1/4 Sect. 26 Tp. 1 R. 8, south and east.

**5573. RICHARDSON, Samuel B.**
April 4, 1836, 3 1/4 miles SW by W Waco, Madison Co. E 1/2 SE 1/4 Sect. 26 Tp. 1 R. 8, south and east.

**6510. RICHARDSON, Samuel B.**
Jan. 10, 1837, 2 1/2 miles SE Moseley Hall, Madison Co. SW 1/4 SW 1/4 Sect. 35 Tp. 1 R. 8, south and east.

**4212. RICKS, John**
Sept. 6, 1832, 3 3/4 miles SSE Ocheesee, Calhoun Co. Lot No. 4 Sect. 1 Tp. 6 R. 8, north and west.

**4249. RIDAUGHT, David J.**
Mar. 15, 1856, 1 mile NNE Haynesworth, Alachua Co. SW 1/4 NE 1/4 Sect. 34 Tp. 7 R. 19, south and east. Patent delivered July 4, 1859.

RIGGINS, John see Moses KIRKLAND, #4052

**7853. RILEY, James R.**
Feb. 5, 1839, 1/2 mile N Milton, Santa Rosa Co. N 1/2 Lot No. 3 Fractional Sect. 3 Tp. 1 R. 28, north and west. Transferred to **Samuel W. KRYSER** (no date).

**4770. RIMES, John C.**
Aug. 30, 1858, 2 miles SW Dukes, Union Co. W 1/2 SE 1/4 Sect. 20 Tp. 6 R. 19, south and east. Patent delivered Aug. 6, 1869.

**1185. RIVERS, Abraham**
Feb. 16, 1852, 4 miles W Winfield, Columbia Co. NE 1/4 SE 1/4 Sect. 28 Tp. 2 R. 16, south and east.

**8012. RIVIERE, Armistead S.**
July 1, 1839, 1 3/4 miles W by N Aberdeen, Jackson Co. W 1/2 NW 1/4 Sect. 4 Tp. 4 R. 11, north and west.

**8400. RIVIERE, Henry L.**
Sept. 2, 1840, 1 mile SE Gainer, Bay

Co. N 1/2 NE 1/4 Sect. 23 Tp. 2 R. 13, south and west.

**1221. ROBARDS, Ransom J.**
Mar. 21, 1827, 5 miles NE Meridian, Leon Co. E 1/2 NE 1/4 Sect. 13 Tp. 3 R. 1, north and west.

**4346. ROBERTS, Abraham J.**
April 26, 1856, 4 1/2 miles NW Guilford, Union Co. SE 1/4 SE 1/4 Sect. 8 Tp. 5 R. 17, south and east.

**1108. ROBERTS, Arthur**
Jan. 20, 1852, 2 miles W Jefferson, Columbia Co. NW 1/4 NW 1/4 Sect. 23 Tp. 4 R. 17, south and east.

**1228. ROBERTS, Arthur**
Mar. 1, 1852, 3 1/4 miles SW Jefferson, Columbia Co. NW 1/4 SW 1/4 Sect. 23 Tp. 4 R. 17, south and east. Patent delivered Mar. 17, 1858.

**1193. ROBERTS, Asa**
Feb. 19, 1852, 3 miles NNW Jefferson, Columbia Co. E 1/2 NW 1/4 W 1/2 NE 1/4 Sect. 11 Tp. 4 R. 17, south and east.

**1213. ROBERTS, Irby**
Feb. 26, 1852, at Rutland, Sumter Co. NW 1/4 SW 1/4 and NW 1/4 NW 1/4 Sect. 32 Tp. 18 R. 21, south and east. Transferred to **Abigal S. BROWN**, Jan. 17, 1859. Transferred to **John RANDALL**, Jan. 8, 1875.

**2018. ROBERTS, John B.**
Aug. 8, 1827, 2 miles SW Greenwood, Jackson Co. SW 1/4 Sect. 1 Tp. 3 R. 10, north and west.

**2019. ROBERTS, John B.**
Aug. 8, 1827, 2 miles WSW Greenwood, Jackson Co. E 1/2 NE 1/4 Sect. 2 Tp. 5 R. 10, north and west.

**2111. ROBERTS, John B.**
(of Fla.) Nov. 20, 1827, 1 1/2 miles SW Greenwood, Jackson Co. W 1/2 NW 1/4 Sect. 1 Tp. 5 R. 10, north and west.

**3974. ROBERTS, John B.**
May 21, 1831, 2 1/2 miles SW Greenwood, Jackson Co. E 1/2 SE 1/4 Sect. 2 Tp. 5 R. 10, north and west.

**4188. ROBERTS, John B.**
July 17, 1832, 2 miles SW Greenwood, Jackson Co. SW 1/4 NE 1/4 Sect. 1 Tp. 5 R. 10, north and west.

**4762. ROBERTS, Mary**
Jan. 10, 1835, 2 1/4 miles SSW Greenwood, Jackson Co. W 1/2 NW 1/4 Sect. 2 Tp. 5 R. 10, north and west.

**5178. ROBERTS, Mary**
Sept. 2, 1835, 2 miles W Greenwood, Jackson Co. SE 1/4 SE 1/4 Sect. 35 Tp. 6 R. 10, north and west.

**5179. ROBERTS, Mary**
Oct. 2, 1835, 3/4 mile SE Greenwood, Jackson Co. NW 1/4 NE 1/4 Sect. 1 Tp. 5 R. 10, north and west.

**5180. ROBERTS, Mary**
Oct. 2, 1835, 1 1/2 miles W Malone, Jackson Co. NW 1/4 SW 1/4 Sect. 36 Tp. 6 R. 10, north and west.

**5220. ROBERTS, Mary**
Oct. 15, 1835, 1 3/4 miles W by N Greenwood, Jackson Co. NE 1/4 SE 1/4 Sect. 35 Tp. 6 R. 10, north and west.

**5221. ROBERTS, Mary**
Oct. 15, 1835, 1 1/2 miles W Greenwood, Jackson Co. E 1/2 SW 1/4 Sect. 36 Tp. 6 R. 10, north and west.

**5685. ROBERTS, Mary**
June 2, 1836, 2 1/4 miles NW Greenwood, Jackson Co. NW 1/4 Sect. 36 Tp. 6 R. 10, north and west.

**5686. ROBERTS, Mary**
June 2, 1836, 1 mile NW Greenwood, Jackson Co. SE 1/4 Sect. 26 Tp. 6 R. 10, north and west.

**5687. ROBERTS, Mary**
June 2, 1836, 2 miles NNW Greenwood, Jackson Co. NE 1/4 Sect. 36 Tp. 6 R. 10, north and west.

**5688. ROBERTS, Mary**
June 2, 1836, 1 mile NW Greenwood, Jackson Co. W 1/2 SE 1/4 Sect. 25 Tp. 6 R. 10, north and west.

**5689. ROBERTS, Mary**
June 2, 1836, 1 3/4 miles NNW Greenwood, Jackson Co. SW 1/4 Sect. 25 Tp. 6 R. 10, north and west.

**5690. ROBERTS, Mary**
June 2, 1836, 1 mile NW Greenwood, Jackson Co. W 1/2 NE 1/4 Sect. 36 Tp. 6 R. 10, north and west.

**5691. ROBERTS, Mary**
June 2, 1836, 1 mile W Greenwood, Jackson Co. W 1/2 SE 1/4 Sect. 36 Tp. 6 R. 10, north and west.

**5871. ROBERTS, Mary**
Sept. 30, 1836, 5 1/2 miles SSE Ellis,

Jackson Co. E 1/2 SE 1/4 Sect. 25 Tp. ? R. 10, north and west.

**5872. ROBERTS, Mary**
Sept. 30, 1836, 3/4 mile NW Greenwood, Jackson Co. E 1/2 SE 1/4 and E 1/2 NE 1/4 Sect. 36 Tp. 1 R. 10, north and west.

**5873. ROBERTS, Mary**
Sept. 30, 1836, 3/4 mile NNW Greenwood, Jackson Co. W 1/2 SW 1/4 Sect. 30 Tp. 1 R. 9, north and west.

**5874. ROBERTS, Mary**
Sept. 30, 1836, 1/2 mile NNW Greenwood, Jackson Co. W 1/2 SW 1/4 and W 1/2 NW 1/4 Sect. 31 Tp. 6 R. 9, north and west.

**8602. ROBERTS, Mary**
Sept. 11, 1843, 1/4 mile W Greenwood, Jackson Co. E 1/2 SW 1/4 Sect. 31 Tp. 6 R. 9, north and west.

**8966. ROBERTS, Mary**
Aug. 10, 1846, 1/2 mile N Greenwood, Jefferson Co. E 1/2 NW 1/4 and W 1/2 NE 1//4 Sect. 31 Tp. 6 R. 9, north and west.

**NONE. ROBERTS, Nathan M.**
Feb. 12, 1852, 2 1/4 miles E by N Guilford, Union Co. NW 1/4 SE 1/4 Sect. 33 Tp. 4 R. 19, south and east. (Note at bottom of receipt-"Rejected-content not given.")

**4978. Illegible**

**4886. Illegible**
Oct. 21, 1858, place illegible. Patent delivered Feb. 18, 1868.

**6207. ROBERTS, Ransom J.**
Dec. 14, 1836, 3 miles W by S Dills, Jefferson Co. SW 1/4 NW 1/4 and SW 1/4 SW 1/4 Sect. 2 Tp. 2 R. 5, north and west.

**7653. ROBERTS, Ransom J.**
Sept. 27, 1838, 2 3/4 miles SS? Dills, Jefferson Co. SW 1/4 NE 1/4 and NW 1/4 SW 1/4 Sect. 2 Tp. 2 R. 5, north and east.

**7930. ROBERTS, Wiley**
April 6, 1839, 1 mile NNW Hamburg, Madison Co. SE 1/4 NE 1/4 Sect. 15 Tp. 2 R. 8, north and east.

**6513. ROBERTS, Wiley**
Jan. 10, 1837, 3 1/2 miles S by W Moseley Hall, Madison Co. NE 1/4 NE 1/4 Sect. 15 Tp. 2 R. 8, north and east.

**2012. ROBERTS, Wm.**
Aug. 2, 1827, 1 mile NNE Meridian, Leon Co. E 1/2 NW 1/4 Sect. 17 Tp. 3 R. 1, north and east.

**485. ROBERTS, William F.**
Oct. 9, 1830, 3 miles W Cherry Lake, Madison Co. E 1/2 SW 1/4 Sect. 12 Tp. 2 R. 8, north and east.

**4164. ROBERTS, William F.**
April 30, 1832, 2 miles W Bond, Jefferson Co. E 1/2 SE 1/4 Sect. 32 Tp. 3 R. 6, north and west.

**4165. ROBERTS, William F.**
April 30, 1832, 3/4 mile E Hamburg, Madison Co. E 1/2 NE 1/4 Sect. 14 Tp. 2 R. 8, north and east.

**4166. ROBERTS, William F.**
April 30, 1832, 2 1/2 miles SE Bond, Jefferson Co. W 1/2 SE 1/4 Sect. 12 Tp. 2 R. 8, north and east.

**1173. ROBERTS, William H.**
Feb. 12, 1852, 6 miles SW Guilford, Union Co. NW 1/4 NE 1/4 Sect. 17 Tp. 5 R. 18, south and east. Patent delivered May 3, 1856.

**2641. ROBERTS, William H. T.**
Mar. 18, 1854, 2 miles NNE Lake City Junction, Columbia Co. SW 1/4 SE 1/4 Sect. 6 and NW 1/4 NE 1/4 Sect. 7 Tp. 6 R. 16, south and east. Patent delivered (no date).

**8776. ROBERTS, Wylie**
April 30, 1845, 1 1/4 miles E by S Hamburg, Madison Co. E 1/2 NW 1/4 Sect. 23 Tp. 2 R. 8,, north and east.

**148. ROBERTSON, Henry**
(of Tennessee) May 19, 1825, 2 miles S Perkins Station, Leon Co. S 1/2 SW 1/4 Sect. 8 Tp. 1 R. 1, south and east.

**175. ROBERTSON, Henry**
(of Tennessee) May 19, 1825, 1 mile S Perkins Station, Leon Co. W 1/2 NW 1/4 Sect. 5 Tp. 1 R. 1, south and east.

**1818. ROBERTSON, James R.**
April 7, 1853, 1/2 mile SS Hodgson, Levy Co. SE 1/4 SE 1/4 Sect. 31 Tp. 12 R. 19, south and east.

**1232. ROBINSON, Blake**
Mar. 4, 1852, 1 3/4 miles SSW Sparr, Marion Co. 18 acres and 60/100 of NW 1/4 Sect. 31 Tp. 13 R. 22, south and east.

**ROBINSON, Isaac see William H. ROB-**

INSON, #5784
ROBINSON, Jacob see Wm. T. KILBEE, #244
**477. ROBINSON, John G.**
Sept 20, 1830, 3 miles SSW Ashville, Jefferson Co. W 1/2 NW 1/4 Sect. 18 Tp. 2 R. 7, north and east. Purchased with scrip assigned to **Alexander MACOMB**, survivor of Edgar and Macomb, May 30, 1829.
**478. ROBINSON, John G.**
Sept 28, 1830, 3 miles SSE Ashville, Jefferson Co. W 1/2 SW 1/4 Sect. 18 Tp. 2 R. 7, north and east. Purchased with scrip assigned to **Alexander MACOMB**, survivor of Edgar and Macomb, May 30, 1829.
**3940. ROBINSON, John G.**
April 9, 1831, 3 miles SW Ashville, Jefferson Co. E 1/2 NW 1/4 Sect. 18 Tp. 2 R. 7, north and east.
**558. ROBINSON, John W.**
May 13, 1847, 3 miles NE Falmouth, Suwannee Co. NE 1/4 SE 1/4 Sect. 12 Tp. 1 R. 12, south and east. Patent delivered June 8, 1857.
**5582. ROBINSON, Jacob**
April 8, 1836, 1 1/4 miles E Fairgrounds, Jackson Co. E 1/2 SW 1/4 and W 1/2 SE 1/4 Sect. 33 Tp. 5 R. 10, north and west.
**912. ROBINSON, Jonathan**
Jan. 17, 1827, 5 miles S Quincy, Gadsden Co. Lot No. 5 Sect. 31 Tp. 2 R. 3, north and west.
**913. ROBINSON, Jonathan**
Jan. 17, 1827, 5 miles S Quincy, Gadsden Co. Lot No. 6 Sect. 31 Tp. 2 R. 3, north and west.
**914. ROBINSON, Jonathan**
Jan. 17, 1827, 5 miles S Quincy, Gadsden Co. Lot No. 7 Sect. 31 Tp. 2 R. 3, north and west.
**915. ROBINSON, Jonathan**
Jan. 17, 1827, 5 miles S Quincy, Gadsden Co. Lot No. 1 Sect. 32 Tp. 2 R. 3, north and west.
**916. ROBINSON, Jonathan**
Jan. 17, 1827, 5 miles S Quincy, Gadsden Co. Lot No. 2 Sect. 32 Tp. 2 R. 3, north and west.
**917. ROBINSON, Jonathan**
Jan. 17, 1827, 5 miles S Quincy, Gadsden Co. Lot No. 6 Sect. 32 Tp. 2 R. 3, north and west.
**1127. ROBINSON, Jonathan**
(DUP) Feb. 14, 1827, 6 miles SSE Quincy, Gadsden Co. Lot No. 5 Sect. 33 Tp. 2 R. 3, north and west.
**2024. ROBINSON, Jonathan**
Aug. 10, 1827, at Lawrence Switch, Leon Co. Lot No. 7 Fractional Sect. 23 Tp. 1 R. 2, north and west.
**2609. ROBINSON, Jonathan**
Jan. 12, 1829, 6 miles S Quincy, Gadsden Co. Lot No. 1 Sect. 6 Tp. 1 R. 3, north and west.
**2608. ROBINSON, Jonathan**
Jan. 12, 1829, 5 1/2 miles W Midway, Gadsden Co. Lot No. 1 Sect. 5 Tp. 1 R. 3, north and west.
**4105. ROBINSON, Jonathan**
Nov. 15, 1831, 5 miles NW Midway, Gadsden Co. W 1/2 NE 1/4 Sect. 34 Tp. 2 R. 3, north and west.
**5805. ROBINSON, Nicholas**
Aug. 22, 1836, 2 1/4 miles SE Lake Jackson (town), Leon Co. NW 1/4 NE 1/4 Sect. 19 Tp. 3 R. 1, north and west.
**5964. ROBINSON, Nicholas**
Nov. 3, 1836, 1/4 mile SW Concord, Gadsden Co. SE 1/4 SW 1/4 Sect. 18 Tp. 3 R. 1, north and west.
**5965. ROBINSON, Nicholas**
Nov. 3, 1836, 2 miles SE Concord, Gadsden Co. W 1/2 NW 1/4 Sect. 20 Tp. 3 R. 1, north and west.
ROBINSON, Robert see Joseph BUNEFAY
**5217. ROBINSON, William H.**
(and **Isaac ROBINSON**) Oct. 15, 1835, 5 3/4 miles SSW Dellwood, Washington Co. W 1/2 SW 1/4 Sect. 34 Tp. 5 R. 9, north and west.
**5218. ROBINSON, William H.**
(and **Isaac ROBINSON**) Oct. 15, 1835, 5 3/4 miles SSW Dellwood, Washington Co. W 1/2 NW 1/4 Sect. 34 Tp. 5 R. 9, north and west.
**5784. ROBINSON, William H.**
(and **Isaac ROBINSON**) July 28, 1836, 5 miles E Marianna, Jackson Co. NW 14 and W 1/2 NE 1/4 Sect. 3 Tp. 4 R. 9, north and west.
**5785. ROBINSON, William H.**
(and **Isaac ROBINSON**) July 28, 1836, 1 1/2 miles NW Grand Ridge, Jackson Co. W 1/2 SE 1/4 Sect. 21 Tp. 4

R. 8, north and west.
**2290. ROBINSON, William H.**
Mar. 20, 1828, 5 miles E Marianna, Jackson Co. NW 1/4 Sect. 4 Tp. 4 R. 9, north and west.
**2511. ROBINSON, William H.**
Sept. 29, 1828, 4 1/2 miles E Marianna, Jackson Co. NE 1/4 Sect. 4 Tp. 4 R. 9, north and west.
**2576. ROBINSON, William H.**
Dec. 22, 1828, 5 miles W Butler, Jackson Co. W 1/2 SW 1/4 Sect. 26 Tp. 5 R. 8, north and west.
See **Isaac ROBINSON**
**ROCHE, S.L.** see **Henry PENNY, #4424**
**511. ROGERS, Edwin**
May 2, 1831, 4 miles WNW Ashville, Jefferson Co. NW 1/4 Sect. 35 Tp. 3 R. 6, north and east.
**5678. ROGERS, Edwin**
May 23, 1836, 2 miles E Dills, Jefferson Co. NW 1/4 NE 1/4 and SE 1/4 SE 1/4 Sect. 3 Tp. 2 R. 6, north and east.
**1062. ROGERS, John**
Feb. 3, 1827, 5 miles SE Quincy, Gadsden Co. W 1/2 SE 1/4 Sect. 14 Tp. 2 R. 3, north and west.
**233. ROGERS, Lucius D.**
(and **Lonnie DOUGHTON**) Dec. ?, County ? ? of the NE 1/4 Sect. 11 Tp.? R. 16, south and east.
**234. ROGERS, Lucius D.**
(and **Lonnie DOUGHTON**) Dec. ? County ? ?of the SW 1/4 Sect. 1 Tp. ? R. 16, south and east.
**5240. ROGERSON, Edmund G.**
April 27, 1860, 10 miles NE White Springs, Columbia Co. S 1/2 SW 1/4 Sect. 30 Tp. 1 R. 17, south and east. Patent delivered Feb. 24, 1875.
**745. ROLLINS, Benjamin**
July 29, 1850, c. 2 1/2 miles SW Theressa, Alachua Co. Lot No. 2 Fractional Sect. 26 Tp. 8 R. 22, south and east.
**7752. RONEY, James**
Dec. 5, 1838, 3 miles NNE Monticello, Jefferson Co. E 1/2 NE 1/4 Sect. 17 Tp. 2 R. 5, south and east.
**2232. ROSE, Philip**
(of Fla.) Jan. 22, 1828, 2 1/2 miles W Welchton, Jackson Co. E 1/2 SW 1/4 Sect. 27 Tp. 16 R. 12, north and west.

Assigned to, **Ratford JORDAN**, April 6, 1829. Teste: **Benj. HOGG** and **Hector McNEILL**, J. P.
**5454. ROSS, Francis J.**
Feb. 11, 1836, at Jasper, Hamilton Co. SW 1/4 Sect. 8 Tp. 1 R. 14, south and east.
**5455. ROSS, Francis J.**
Feb. 11, 1836, at Jasper, Hamilton Co. E 1/2 SW 1/4 Sect. 8 Tp. 1 R. 14, south and east.
**5456. ROSS, Francis J.**
Feb. 11, 1836, 1 mile S Marion, Hamilton Co. W 1/2 SW 1/4 Sect. 5 Tp. 1 R. 14, south and east.
**5457. ROSS, Francis J.**
Feb. 11, 1836, 1 mile S Marion, Hamilton Co. SW 1/4 NE 1/4 Sect. 8 Tp. 1 R. 14, south and east.
**6738. ROSS, Francis J.**
Feb. 6, 1837, 1 1/2 miles SSE Marina, Hamilton Co. E 1/2 NE 1/4 Sect. 8 Tp. 1 R. 14, south and east.
**6739. ROSS, Francis J.**
Feb. 6, 1837, 2 miles SE Marina, Hamilton Co. E 1/2 NE 1/4 and SW 1/4 NE 1/4 Sect. 9 Tp. 1 R. 14, south and east.
**6873. ROSS, James L.**
Mar. 9, 1837, 2 1/2 miles WNW Avica, Hamilton Co. SE 1/4 SW 1/4 Sect. 8 Tp. 2 R. 13, north and east.
**414. ROSS, William B.**
Mar. 28, 1839, 1 mile SW Lake City, Columbia Co. E 1/2 NE 1/4 Sect. 35 Tp. 3 R. 16, south and east.
**21. ROSS, William B.**
Feb. 27, 1843, c. 1 mile SE Lake City, Columbia Co. NW 1/4 (?) and NE 1/4 SW 1/4 Sect. 36 Tp. 3 R. 16, south and east.
**6815. ROSSETTER, Appleton**
Mar. 1, 1837, c. 1/2 mile S Bellville, Hamilton Co. Lot No. 1 Fractional Sect. 6 Tp. 2 R. 11, north and east. Transferred Oct. 4, 1850, to **Jasper M. HENDERSON**. Signed by **Chas. COLLINS**, Atty. for **Sarah ATCHYESA**, **Robt. B. CLAYTON**, Atty. for **Sarah ROSSETTER** and **Payton P. SMITH**, and by **Hezekiah JOHNSTON**.
**7416. ROSSETTER, Appleton**
Mar. 19, 1838, 2 1/2 miles SE by S Bellville, Hamilton Co. W 1/2 NW

1/4 Sect. 5 Tp. 2 R. 11, north and east. Transferred to **Jasper M. HENDERSON**, Oct. 4, 1850.

**7905. ROSSETTER, Appleton**
Mar. 4, 1839, 1 mile SE Belleville, Hamilton Co. E 1/2 NW 1/4 and SW 1/4 NE 1/4 Sect. 5 Tp. 2 R. 11, north and east. Transferred to **Jasper M. HENDERSON**, Oct. 4, 1850.

**7906. ROSSETTER, Appleton**
Mar. 4, 1839, 1/2 mile NW Octahatchee, Hamilton Co. Lot No. 3 Sect. 6 Tp. 2 R. 11, north and east. Transferred to **Jasper M. HENDERSON**, Oct. 4, 1850.

**ROSSETTER, Sarah see Appleton ROSSETTER, #6815**

**4986. ROUNDTREE, John B.**
Mar. 15, 1859, 1 1/2 miles W Lake Butler Station, Union Co. S 1/2 NW 1/4 and SW 1/4 Sect. 36 Tp. 5 R. 19, south and east.

**5224. ROUNDTREE, John B.**
Mar. 14, 1860, 1 1/2 miles SSW Lake Butler (town), Union Co. SE 1/4 NE 1/4 Sect. 36 Tp. 5 R. 19, south and east. Patent delivered to **Hon. W. W. WILES**.

**3215. ROUSE, Canada**
Jan. 18, 1830, 3 miles N Wacissa, Jefferson Co. E 1/2 SW 1/4 Sect. 19 Tp. 1 R. 4, south and east.

**3216. ROUSE, Canada**
Jan. 18, 1830, 3 1/2 miles N Wacissa, Jefferson Co. W 1/2 NE 1/4 Sect. 19 Tp. 1 R. 4, south and east.

**3887. ROUSE, Canada**
Feb. 21, 1831, 5 miles SW Waukenah, Jefferson Co. W 1/2 SE 1/4 Sect. 19 Tp. 1 R. 4, south and east.

**8465. ROUSE, Daniel W.**
July 23, 1890, 8 miles E by N Orlando, Orange Co. S 1/2 SW 1/4 Sect. 20 and NW 1/4 SW 1/4 Sect. 29 Tp. 22S, R. 31E.

**5622. ROUSE, Isaac**
April 25, 1836, 4 1/4 miles NW Monticello, Jefferson Co. Lots No. 1 and 2 Fractional Sect. 15 Tp. 2 R. 4, north and east.

**7000. ROUSE, Isaac**
April 19, 1837, 3 1/4 miles NW Monticello, Jefferson Co. Lot No. 3 Fractional Sect. 15 Tp. 2 R. 4, north and east.

**317. ROUSSEAU, William H.**
Feb. 12, 1846, 2 miles E Pine Mount, Suwannee Co. SW 1/4 SW 1/4 Sect. 4 Tp. 4 R. 14, south and east.

**750. ROUSSEAU, William H.**
Nov. 1, 1850, c. 4 miles SW Wellborn, Suwannee Co. E 1/2 NW 1/4 Sect. 35 Tp. 3 R. 14 , south and east. Patent delivered July 12, 1856.

**8596. ROWELL, Caleb**
Aug. 23, 1843, 1/4 miles S Ashville, Jefferson Co. NW 1/4 SE 1/4 Sect. 5 Tp. 2 R. 7, north and east.

**8907. ROWELL, Henry**
Feb. 18, 1846, 2 miles N by E Dills, Jefferson Co. SE 1/4 Sect. 19 Tp. 3 R. 6, north and east.

**506. ROWELL, William**
April 26, 1831, at Lovett, Madison Co. SW 1/4 Sect. 34 Tp. 3 R. 7, north and east.

**8814. ROWELL, William (Sr.)**
Sept. 17, 1845, 4 3/4 miles E by N Leonton, Jefferson Co. E 1/2 NW 1/4 Sect. 8 Tp. 2 R. 5, south and east.

**355. ROWLAND, William**
April 8, 1846, 2 1/2 miles NE Live Oak, Suwannee Co. W 1/2 SE 1/4 Sect. 17 Tp. 2 R. 14, south and east.

**5543. ROYAL, Wilson**
Mar. 17, 1836, 11 miles N by W Haywood, Jackson Co. NE 1/4 NE 1/4 Sect. 34 Tp. 7 R. 8, north and west.

**388. ROYALS, Wilson**
May 5, 1827, at Haywood, Jackson Co. Lot No. 1 Sect. 4 Tp. 5 R. 7, north and west.

**6521. RUNNELS, John**
Jan. 12, 1837, 2 miles NW Copeland, Leon Co. NE 1/4 NE 1/4 Sect. 19 Tp. 3 R. 3, north and east.

**6522. RUNNELS, John**
Jan. 12, 1837, 2 miles WNW Copeland, Leon Co. E 1/2 NW 1/4 and E 1/2 SW 1/4 Sect. 30 Tp. 3 R. 3, north and east.

**837. RUSHING, Francis Eliza**
Jan. 10, 1827, 3 miles ENE Monticello, Jefferson Co. Lot No. 5 Sect. 27 Tp. 2 R. 4, north and east.

**4129. RUSHING, Francis Eliza**
Jan. 26, 1832, 1 3/4 miles N Monticel-

lo, Jefferson Co. E 1/2 SE 1/4 Sect. 18 Tp. 2 R. 5, north and east.

**8877. RUSK, Hugh**
Jan. 19, 1846, 2 miles NNW Butler, Jackson Co. Lot No.8 Sect. 20 Tp. 5 R. 7, north and west.

**164. RUSS, Jas. B.**
(SIC) (The heirs of) Dec. 28, 1826, 5 miles NE Cottondale, Jackson Co. SW 1/4 Sect. 5 Tp. 5 R. 11, north and west.

**5877. RUSS, John G.**
Oct. 3, 1836, 4 1/4 miles SSE Norum, Washington Co. NE 1/4 NE 1/4 Sect. 22 Tp. 2 R. 15, north and west.

**165. RUSS, Joseph**
(SIC) Dec. 28, 1826, 2 miles NW Cottondale, Jackson Co. NW 1/4 Sect. 23 Tp. 5 R. 11, north and west.

**1854. RUSS, Joseph**
June 5, 1827, 1/2 mile SE Keysville, Jackson Co. W 1/2 SW 1/4 Sect. 15 Tp. 4 R. 11, north and west.

**RUSS, Joseph see Joseph LEWIS**

**167. RUSS, Masters**
Dec. 29, 1826, 2 miles SW Vernon, Washington Co. SW 1/4 Sect. 9 Tp. 2 R. 15, north and west.

**166. RUSS, Robert**
(SIC) Dec. 29, 1826, 1 1/2 miles S Vernon, Washington Co. SE 1/4 Sect. 8 Tp. 2 R. 15, north and west. (duplicated)

**447. RUSS, Robert**
(Assignee of **Fred LEWIS**) Dec. 27, 1828, 1 mile SE Norum, Washington Co. E 1/2 NW 1/4 Sect. 17 Tp. 2 R. 15, north and west.

**2674. RUSS, Robert**
Jan. 27, 1829, 1 mile E Norum, Washington Co. E 1/2 SW 1/4 Sect. 8 Tp. 2 R. 15, north and west.

**208. RUSS, Thos.**
Dec. 30, 1826, 5 miles NE Cottondale, Jackson Co. E 1/2 SE 1/4 Sect. 8 Tp. 5 R. 11, north and west.

**209. RUSS, Thos.**
Dec. 30, 1826, 3 miles N Cottondale, Jackson Co. W 1/2 SW 1/4 Sect. 9 Tp. 5 R. 11, north and west.

**194. RUSS, Wm.**
(DUP) Dec. 29, 1826, 5 miles NE Cottondale, Jackson Co. NE 1/4 Sect. 8 Tp. 5 R. 11, north and west.

**596. RUSSELL, Harry Caroline**
Oct. 29, 1847, c. 2 miles W Irvine, Marion Co. NE 1/4 NE 1/4 Sect. 34 Tp. 12 R. 20, south and east. Patent delivered May 21, 1856.

**2320. RUSSELL, Wm.**
Mar. 25, 1828, 2 1/2 miles E Wadesboro, Jefferson Co. W 1/2 NW 1/4 Sect. 3 Tp. 1 R. 3, north and east.

**31. RUSSEN, Sam**
Feb. 11, 1846, (no site given) Suwannee Co. Tp.3 R.14, containing three hundred and ninety-nine and 89/100 acres, the receipt for same being mislaid or lost. Signed **James BLUE**.

**6554. RUTGERS, Henry L.**
Jan. 16, 1837, 2 miles SW Aucilla, Jefferson Co. E 1/2 NE 1/4 Sect. 25 Tp. 1 R. 5, south and east.

**6555. RUTGERS, Henry L.**
Jan. 16, 1837, 3 miles SW Aucilla, Jefferson Co. E 1/2 SW 1/4 W 1/2 SE 1/4, E 1/2 NW 1/4 Sect. 25 Tp. 1 R. 5, south and east.

**7071. RUTGERS, Henry L.**
Oct. 27, 1837, 2 1/2 miles ESE Lamont, Jefferson Co. NW 1/4 SW 1/4 Sect. 25 Tp. 1 R. 5, south and east.

**773. RUTHERFORD, Franklin**
(of Fla.) Sept. 25, 1826, 1/2 mile W Meridian, Leon Co. W 1/2 NE 1/4 Sect. 24 Tp. 3 R. 1, north and west.

**774. RUTHERFORD, Franklin**
(of Fla.) Sept. 25, 1826, 1 mile W Meridian, Leon Co. NW 1/4 Sect. 24 Tp. 3 R. 1, north and west.

**3855. RUTHERFORD, Samuel**
Jan. 20, 1831, 1 1/2 miles SE Greenville, Madison Co. E 1/2 SE 1/4 Sect. 19 Tp. 1 R. 7, north and east.

**4511. RYALL, Zachner**
Jan. 14, 1834, 1/2 mile S Ocheesee, Calhoun Co. NE 1/4 SW 1/4 Sect. 7 Tp. 2 R. 2, north and west.

**4512. RYALL, Zachner**
Jan. 14, 1834, 1/2 mile S by E Ocheesee, Calhoun Co. NW 1/4 SE 1/4 Sect. 7 Tp. 2 R. 2, north and west.

**7137. RYALL, Zachius**
Dec. 12, 1837, 2 miles SE Florence, Gadsden Co. SW 1/4 SE 1/4 Sect. 7 Tp. 2 R. 2, north and west.

**RYAN, Samuel C. see Alexander & Benj. JERNIGAN. #4627 and 6617**

\* S \*

**8992. SALTONSTALL, Labon L.**
Nov. 13, 1846, 9 1/4 miles E by S Stringer, Jefferson Co. SW 1/4 SW 1/4 Sect. 35 Tp. 3 R. 4, north and east.

**1168. SANBURN, Ira**
(DUP) Feb. 25, 1827, 6 miles ESE Quincy, Gadsden Co. W 1/2 SE 1/4 Sect. 23 Tp. 2 R. 3, north and west.

**1169. SANBURN, Ira**
(DUP) Feb. 25, 1827, 5 1/2 miles ESE Quincy, Gadsden Co. W 1/2 NW 1/4 Sect. 24 Tp. 2 R. 3, north and west.

**1170. SANBURN, Ira**
(DUP) Feb. 25, 1827, 3 miles SSE Quincy, Gadsden Co. E 1/2 NE 1/4 Sect. 23 Tp. 2 R. 3, north and west.

**1171. SANBURN, Ira**
(DUP) Feb. 25, 1827, 5 miles SE Quincy, Gadsden Co. E 1/2 NW 1/4 Sect. 23 Tp. 2 R. 3, north and west.

**1172. SANBURN, Ira**
(DUP) Feb. 25, 1827, 5 miles SE Quincy, Gadsden Co. E 1/2 SW 1/4 Sect. 23 Tp. 2 R. 3, north and west. Transferred to **Titus FARN**, Feb. 27, 1827.

**1649. SANBURN, Ira**
(DUP) May 29, 18278, 6 miles NNW Haywood, Jackson Co. Lot No. 4 Sect. 12 Tp. 6 R. 8, north and west.

**1912. SANBURN, Ira**
June 14, 1827, 5 miles ESE Quincy, Gadsden Co. E 1/2 SW 1/4 Sect. 14 Tp. 2 R. 3, north and west.

**1996. SANBURN, Ira**
July 12, 1827, 1/2 mile SW Marianna, Jackson Co.. E 1/2 SE 1/4 Sect. 14 Tp. 2 R. 3, north and west.

**3083. SANBURN, Ira**
Oct. 14, 1829, 3/4 mile SW Quincy, Gadsden Co. W 1/2 SE 1/4 Sect. 12 Tp. 2 R. 4, north and west.

**8921. SANDERS, David W.**
Mar. 20, 1846, 2 1/2 miles E Spray, Madison Co. E 1/2 SE 1/4 Sect. 33 Tp. 1 R. 7, north and east.

**8922. SANDERS, David W.**
Mar. 20, 1846, 1 mile NNE Spray, Madison Co. E 1/2 NE 1/4 Sect. 3 Tp. 1 R. 7, south and east.

**4549. SANDERS, Elizabeth**
Feb. 13, 1834, 3/4 mile N by W McClellan, Jefferson Co. SE 1/4 SE 1/4 Sect. 9 Tp. 1 R. 5, north and east.

**4613. SANDERS, Elizabeth**
Sept. 24, 1834, 3 miles SSE Watson, Liberty Co. SE SE 1/4 NW 1/4 Sect. 22 Tp. 1 R. 7, north and east.

**4614. SANDERS, Elizabeth**
Sept. 24, 1834, 4 1/2 miles S by E Watson, Liberty Co. NE 1/4 SW 1/4 Sect. 22 Tp. 1 R. 7, north and east.

**4112. SANDERS, Ephraim**
Dec. 13, 1831, 1 1/4 miles W Felkel, Leon Co. E 1/2 NE 1/4 Sect. 5 Tp. 2 R. 2, north and east.

**8515. SANDERS, Henry G.**
Jan. 10, 1842, 2 miles NNE Dills, Jefferson Co. W 1/2 NE 1/4 Sect. 28 Tp. 3 R. 6, north and east.

**3133. SANDERS, John**
Nov. 24, 1829, 4 miles W Miccosukee, Leon Co. E 1/2 SE 1/4 Sect. 11 Tp. 2 R. 2, north and east.

**2110. SANDERS, Lewis**
(of Fla.) Nov. 20, 1827, 3 1/2 miles NNW Wadesboro, Leon Co. E 1/2 SE 1/4 Sect. 11 Tp. 2 R. 2, north and east.

**2685. SANDERS, Lewis**
Jan. 28, 1829, 3 miles SSE Havana, Gadsden Co. W 1/2 SE 1/4 Sect. 10 Tp. 2 R. 2, north and east.

**3458. SANDERS, Lewis**
Mar. 15, 1830, 4 miles WSW Miccosukee, Leon Co. W 1/2 SW 1/4 Sect. 13 Tp. 2 R. 2, north and east. "Received for the within Treasury Scrip, dated May 30, 1829, in favor of **Alex'r MACOMB**, survivor of Edgar and Macomb."

**4183. SANDERS, Lewis**
July 11, 1832, 1 1/4 miles SE Felkel, Leon Co. SE 1/4 NW 1/4 Sect. 14 Tp. 2 R. 2, north and east.

**4184. SANDERS, Lewis**
July 11, 1832, 2 3/4 miles SE Felkel, Leon Co. NE 1/4 SW 1/4 Sect. 14 Tp. 2 R. 2, north and east.

**5408. SANDERS, Lewis**
Jan. 15, 1836, 4 1/2 miles E Centerville, Leon Co. E 1/2 NE 1/4 Sect. 23 Tp. 2 R. 2, north and east.

**5409. SANDERS, Lewis**
Jan. 15, 1836, 4 3/4 miles E Centerville, Leon Co. E 1/2 NW 1/4 Sect. 23

Tp. 2 R. 2, north and east.
**6484. SANDERS, Lewis**
Jan. 9, 1837, 4 miles NW Wadesboro, Leon Co. SE 1/4 SW 1/4 Sect. 14 Tp. 2 R. 2, north and east.
**5615. SANDERS, Stephen**
April 23, 1836, 1 1/2 miles NW Felkel, Leon Co. W 1/2 SE 1/4 Sect. 32 Tp. 3 R. 2, north and east.
**7636. SANDERS, Washington J.**
Sept. 11, 1838, 1 mile N by W Dills, Jefferson Co. W 1/2 SE 1/4 Sect. 25 Tp. 3 R. 5, north and east.
**1970. SANDERSON, John P.**
July 23, 1853, 3 1/4 miles W Rideout, Clay Co. SE 1/4 NE 1/4 and NE 1/4 SE 1/4 Sect. 34 Tp. 4 R. 24, south and east. Transferred to **George C. TIPPINS**, July 28, 1854. Transferred by **George C. TIPPINS** to **Daniel N. YOUNGBLOOD**, May 21, 1855.
**1971. SANDERSON, John P.**
July 23, 1853, 3 miles NNW Rideout, Clay Co. SW 1/4 NW 1/4 and NW 1/4 SW 1/4 Sect. 35 Tp. 4 R. 24, south and east. Transferred To **George C. TIPPINS**, Feb. 28, 1854. Transferred by **George C. TIPPINS** to **Daniel N. YOUNGBLOOD**, May 21, 1855.
**8392. SANSOM, William**
Aug. 31, 1840, 2 miles ESE Selman, Calhoun Co. SW 1/4 Sect. 36 Tp. 2 R. 8, north and west.
**2867. SAPAR, Eliza Ann**
Aug. 10, 1854, 1 mile SW Alta, Alachua Co. SW 1/4 SW 1/4 Sect. 33 Tp. 7 R. 20, south and east. Patent delivered -----1857 (date incomplete).
**1102. SAPP, John**
(DUP) Feb. 8, 1827, 3 miles NNE Lake Jackson Station, Leon Co. Lot No. 1 Sect. 20 Tp. 2 R. 1, north and west. Transferred to **Thomas BROWN**, March 5, 1827.
**1183. SAPP, John**
Mar. 1, 1827, 3 miles NNE Lake Jackson Station, Leon Co. Lot No. 2 Sect. 20 Tp. 2 R. 1, north and west. Transferred to **Thos. BROWN**, March 5, 1827.
**1940. SAPP, John**
June 23, 1827, 5 miles SW Meridian, Leon Co. E 1/2 SE 1/4 Sect. 3 Tp. 2 R. 1, north and west.

**3880. SAPP, John**
Feb. 12, 1831, 5 1/4 miles NW Bradfordville, Leon Co. W 1/2 SW 1/4 Sect. 6 Tp. 2 R. 1, north and east.
**2333. SAPP, John**
Nov. 2, 1853, 1 1/4 miles SSW Dukes, Union Co. NE 1/4 NE 1/4 Sect. 23 Tp. 6 R. 19, south and east. Patent delivered Aug. 1, 1857.
**7188. SAPP, William**
Jan. 4, 1838, 4 miles E Bond, Madison Co. NW 1/4 SW 1/4 Sect. 6 Tp. 2 R. 9, north and east.
**8987. SASSER, Bryant**
Nov. 4, 1846, 3 3/4 miles NNW Betts, Washington Co. SE 1/4 NW 1/4 Sect. 5 Tp. 1 R. 12, north and east.
**2320. SASSER, John**
Oct. 31, 1853, 2 1/2 miles E Providence, Union Co. SW 1/4 SW 1/4 Sect. 34 Tp. 5 and NW 1/4 NW 1/4 Sect. 3 Tp. 6 R. 18, south and east. Patent delivered Jan. 1, 1856.
**8844. SASSER, John**
Nov. 19, 1845, 2 3/4 miles NNW Westlake, Hamilton Co. N 1/2 NE 1/4 and NE 1/4 NW 1/4 Sect. 5 Tp. 1 R. 12, north and east.
**2994. SASSER, John**
Sept. 8, 1854, 1 1/4 miles NNE Providence, Union Co. NE 1/4 SW 1/4 Sect. 34 Tp. 5 R. 18, south and east. Patent delivered May 1, 1858.
**320. SAULS, Daniel**
Feb. 5, 1827, 2 miles SW Alford, Jackson Co. SW 1/4 Sect. 5 Tp. 3 R. 12, north and west. Transferred from **Daniel SAULS** to **Jno. ROBINSON**, Feb. 6, 1827.
**833. SAUNDERS, Lewis**
Jan. 9, 1827, 2 miles SE Felkel, Leon Co. W 1/2 NE 1/4 Sect. 11 Tp. 2 R. 2, north and east.
**834. SAUNDERS, Lewis**
Jan. 9, 1827, 3 miles SSE Felkel, Leon Co. NE 1/4 Sect. 14 Tp. 2 R. 2, north and east.
**835. SAUNDERS, Lewis**
Jan. 9, 1827, 3 miles SSE Felkel, Leon Co. W 1/2 SE 1/4 Sect. 14 Tp. 2 R. 2, north and east.
**1631. SAUNDERS, James D.**
Jan. 10, 1853, 4 miles W Francis, Putnam Co. SE 1/4 SW 1/4 and SW

1/4 SE 1/4 Sect. 10 Tp. 10 R. 22, south and east. Patent delivered Aug. 4, 1857.

**1076. SAUNDERS, James Dickerson**
Jan. 2, 1851 (1852?), 2 miles SE Campville, Alachua Co. SE 1/4 NE 1/4 Sect. 10 Tp. 10 R. 22, south and east. Patent delivered April, 1857.

**4413. SAUNDERS, John**
Sept. 13, 1833, 1 1/2 mile SSE Felkel, Leon Co. SE 1/4 NW 1/4 Sect. 11 Tp. 2 R. 2, north and east.

**5206. SAUNDERS, John**
Oct. 12, 1835, 3 miles SE Felkel, Leon Co. SW 1/4 NW 1/4 Sect. 11 Tp. 2 R. 2, north and east.

**5536. SAUNDERS, Richard**
Mar. 14, 1836, 2 miles SSW Felkel, Leon Co. SE 1/4 SE 1/4 Sect. 5 Tp. 2 R. 2, north and east.

**7096. SAUNDERS, Richard**
Nov. 17, 1837, 1 1/4 miles W Felkel, Leon Co. NE 1/4 SE 1/4 and SE 1/4 SW 1/4 Sect. 5 Tp. 2 R. 2, north and east.

**4177. SAUNDERS, Stephen**
June 5, 1832, 3 3/4 miles N BY E Monticello, Jefferson Co. E 1/2 NW 1/4 Sect. 5 Tp. 2 R. 2, north and east.

**4688. SAUNDERS, Stephen**
Dec. 7, 1834, at Copeland, Leon Co. E 1/2 SE 1/4 Sect. 32 Tp. 3 R. 2, north and east.

**4986. SAUNDERS, Stephen**
June 3, 1835, 2 miles NNW Felkel, Leon Co. SE 1/4 SE 1/4 Sect. 32 Tp. 3 R. 2, north and east.

**5183. SAUNDERS, Stephen**
Oct. 3, 1835, 1 mile SW Felkel, Leon Co. NE 1/4 SW 1/4 Sect. 5 Tp. 2 R. 2, north and east.

**7104. SAUNDERS, Stephen**
Nov. 20, 1837, 4 1/2 miles NNW Chaires, Leon Co. SW 1/4 SW 1/4 Sect. 5 Tp. 2 R. 2, north and east.

**2752. SAUNDERS, William H. G.**
May 27, 1854, 1/4 mile SSW Atlas, Alachua Co. NW 1/4 NW 1/4 Sect. 32 Tp. 7 R. 20, south and east. Transferred to **L. M. BROWN**, June 22, 1859. Patent delivered July 4, 1859.

**4713. SAW, Peter W.**
Dec. 16, 1834, 1 mile E Jasperr, Hamilton Co. W 1/2 NW 1/4 Sect. 4 Tp. 1 R. 14, north and east.

**4714. SAW, Peter W.**
Dec. 16, 1834, 1/2 mile S Jasper, Hamilton Co. E 1/2 SE 1/4 Sect. 8 Tp. 1 R. 14, north and east.

**4715. SAW, Peter W.**
Dec. 16, 1834, 1 1/4 miles SE Jasper, Hamilton Co. NW 1/4 NW 1/4 Sect. 9 Tp. 1 R. 14, north and east.

**4716. SAW, Peter W.**
Dec. 16, 1834, 1 1/2 miles SE Jasper, Hamilton Co. NW 1/4 SW 1/4 Sect. 9 Tp. 1 R. 14, north and east.

**4734. SAW, Peter W.**
Dec. 23, 1834, 2 miles SSE Jasper, Hamilton Co. SW 1/4 SW 1/4 Sect. 9 Tp. 1 R. 14, north and east.

**4754. SAW, Peter W.**
Jan. 5, 1835, 3 miles SSE Marion, Hamilton Co. E 1/2 SW 1/4 Sect. 9 Tp. 1 R. 14, north and east.

**2740. SAWYER, William**
Nov. 10, 1881, 1 mile W Tavernier on Barnes Sound, (no county given). Lots No. 1 and 2 Sect. 33 and Lot 5 Sect. 28 Tp. 62S R. 38E.

**2840. SCARBOROUGH, Mathew**
Feb. 24, 1854, 4 miles NW Claymo, Bradford Co. NE 1/4 NW 1/4 Sect. 28 Tp. 6 R. 20, south and east. Patent delivered Feb. 17, 1857.

**7290. SCARLOCK, Sarah**
Feb. 1, 1838, 2 1/4 miles N Sneads, Jackson Co. Lot No. 4 Sect. 15 Tp. 4 R. 7, north and west.

**4276. SCOTT, Alexander**
Jan. 15, 1833, 3 1/4 miles E Capps, Jefferson Co. NE 1/4 SW 1/4 Sect. 3 Tp. 1 R. 5, south and east.

**4196. SCOTT, David**
Aug. 13, 1832, 2 miles N McClellan, Jefferson Co. W 1/2 NE 1/4 Sect. 3 Tp. 1 R. 5, south and east.

**4197. Scott, David**
Illegible

**4198. SCOTT, David**
Aug. 13, 1832, 3 1/4 miles SSE Capps, Jefferson Co. NW 1/4 NW 1/4 Sect. 2 Tp. 1 R. 5, south and east.

**4199. SCOTT, David**
Aug. 13, 1832, 3 1/4 miles E by N Capps, Jefferson Co. NE 1/4 NE 1/4 Sect. 3 Tp. 1 R. 5, south and east.

**4425. SCOTT, David**
Aug. 4, 1856, 1/4 mile E Bass, Columbia Co. N 1/2 SE 1/4 and N 1/2 SW 1/4 Sect. 25 Tp. 4 R. 16, south and east.

**6495. SCOTT, David**
Jan. 10, 1837, 3 1/2 miles E Capps, Jefferson Co. W 1/2 NW 1/4 Sect. 3 Tp. 1 R. 5, south and east.

**7550. SCOTT, David**
July 26, 1838, 3 3/4 miles NNE Lamont, Jefferson Co. SE 1/4 Sect. 12 Tp. 1 R. 5, south and east.

**2562. SCOTT, James**
Dec. 11, 1828, 3 miles ESE Wadesboro, Jefferson Co. W 1/2 NE 1/4 Sect. 10 Tp. 1 R. 3, north and east.

**3256. SCOTT, James**
Feb. 6, 1830, 4 miles N by W Wadesboro, Leon Co. W 1/2 NW 1/4 Sect. 11 Tp. 1 R. 3, north and east.

**4758. SCOTT, James**
Jan. 7, 1835, 1 mile N Lloyd, Jefferson Co. W 1/2 NW 1/4 Sect. 10 Tp. 1 R. 3, north and east.

**4759. SCOTT, James**
Jan. 7, 1835, 1 mile N by W Lloyd, Jefferson Co. NE 1/4 NW 1/4 Sect. 10 Tp. 1 R. 3, north and east.

**5792. SCOTT, James**
Aug. 8, 1836, 1 mile N by W Lloyd, Jefferson Co. SE 1/4 NW 1/4 Sect. 10 Tp. 1 R. 3, north and east.

**6640. SCOTT, James**
Jan. 24, 1837, 2 miles SSE lloyd, Jefferson Co. SE 1/4 SE 1/4 Sect. 26 Tp. 1 R. 3, north and east.

**6641. SCOTT, James**
Jan. 24, 1837, 2 1/2 miles SE Lloyd, Jefferson Co. NW 1/4 SW 1/4 Sect. 25 Tp. 1 R. 3, north and east.

**7030. SCOTT, James**
Aug. 15, 1837, 2 1/2 miles NNE Stringer, Jackson Co. SE 1/4 NE 1/4 Sect. 25 Tp. 1 R. 3, north and east.

**2541. SCOTT, John**
Nov. 11, 1828, at Ellis, Jackson Co. NW 1/4 Sect. 34 Tp. 6 R. 10, north and west.

**5683. SCOTT, Joseph**
May 30, 1836, 3 miles NNE Campbellton, Jackson Co. W 1/2 NW 1/4 Sect. 19 Tp. 7 R. 11, north and west.

**4104. SCOTT, Joseph B.**
Nov. 3, 1831, 1/2 mile S Inwood, Gadsden Co. E 1/2 SE 1/4 Sect. 5 Tp. 3 R. 7, north and west.

**2960. SCOTT, Reuben**
July 17, 1829, 4 1/2 miles ENE Millspring, Jackson Co. Lot No. 1 Sect. 12 Tp. 3 R. 7, north and east.

**2830. SCOTT, William W.**
July 24, 1854, 1/2 mile S by W West Alachua, Alachua Co. NW 1/4 NE 1/4 Sect. 34 Tp. 8 R. 18, south and east. Patent delivered May 25, 1858.

**2831. SCOTT, William W.**
July 24, 1854, at West Alachua, Alachuua Co. NW 1/4 NW 1/4 Sect. 34 Tp. 8 R. 18, south and east. Patent delivered Mar. 25, 1858.

**145. SCURLOCK, Joshua**
Dec. 27, 1826, at Glass Post Office, Jackson Co. NW 1/4 Sect. 2 Tp. 5 R. 12, north and west.

**1619. SCURLOCK, Joshua**
May 26, 1827, 2 miles SSW Welchton, Jackson Co. W 1/2 SW 1/4 Sect. 2 Tp. 5 R. 12, north and west.

**2787. SCURLOCK, Joshua**
March 16, 1829, 1 1/2 miles SW Welchton, Jackson Co. W 1/2 NE 1/4 Sect. 2 Tp. 5 R. 12, north and west.

**315. SCURLOCK, Prestley**
(the heirs of) Jan. 13, 1827, 8 miles W Greenwood, Jackson Co. SE 1/4 Sect. 32 Tp. 6 R. 11, north and west.

**200. SCURLOCK, Sam'l**
Dec. 30, 1826, 6 miles NE Cottondale, Jackson Co. NW 1/4 Sect. 5 Tp. 5 R. 11, north and west.

**577. SCURLOCK, Sarah**
June 16, 1838, 1 mile ESE Welchton, Jackson Co. SE 1/4 Sect. 35 Tp. 6 R. 12, north and west. (Pre-emption).

**6356. SCURLOCK, Sarah**
Dec. 30, 1836, 1 mile S Welchton, Jackson Co. E 1/2 NE 1/4 Sect. 2 Tp. 5 R. 12, north and west.

**6513. SCURLOCK, Sarah**
Jan. 20, 1837, 3 miles N Inwood, Jackson Co. W 1/2 SW 1/4 Sect. 17 Tp. 4 R. 7, north and west.

**183. SCURLOCK, Thos. J.**
Dec. 29, 1826, 6 miles NE Cottondale, Jackson Co. SE 1/4 Sect. 5 Tp. 5 R. 11, north and west.

**4892. SEABROOK, Thomas Wilkes**

Mar. 16, 1835, 1/2 mile E Capps, Jefferson Co. NE 1/4 SW 1/4 Sect. 6 Tp. 1 R. 5, south and east.

**8903. SEALEY, Stephen E.**
Feb. 16, 1846, 3 miles SW Mears Spur, Gadsden Co. SW 1/4 SW 1/4 Sect. 36 Tp. 4 R. 6, north and west.

**2670. SEARCY, Isham G.**
Jan. 26, 1829, 4 miles NE Moseley Hall, Madison Co. E 1/2 SE 1/4 Sect. 20 Tp. 1 R. 8, south and east.

**5027. SEARCY, Isham G.**
(and **Louis M. GOLDSBOROUGH**) July 8, 1835, St. George's Sound, 2 miles SSW Clower, Franklin Co. Lot No. 2 Fractional Sect. 27 Tp. 7 R. 4, south and west.

**5028. SEARCY, Isham G.**
(and **Louis M. GOLDSBOROUGH**) July 8, 1835, 1 mile N Port St. Joe, Gulf Co. Lot No. 11 Sect. 26 Tp. 7 R. 11, south and west.

**5029. SEARCY, Isham G.**
(and **Louis M. GOLDSBOROUGH**) July 8, 1835, 1 mile N Port St. Joe, Gulf Co. Lot No. 5 Fractional Sect. 26 Tp. 7 R. 11, south and west.

**5030. SEARCY, Isham G.**
(and **Louis M. GOLDSBOROUGH**) July 8, 1835, 1 mile N Port St. Joe, Gulf Co. Lot No. 14 Fractional Sect. 26 Tp. 7 R. 11, south and west.

**5031. SEARCY, Isham G.**
(and **LOUIS M. GOLDSBOROUGH**) July 8, 1835, 1 mile N Port St. Joe, Gulf Co. Lot No. 13 Sect. 26 Tp. 7 R. 11, south and west.

**5032. SEARCY, Isham G.**
(and **Louis M. GOLDSBOROUGH**) July 8, 1835, 1 mile N by W Port St. Joe., Gulf Co. Lot 4 Fractional Sect. 29 Tp. 7 R. 11, south and west.

**5033. SEARCY, Isham G.**
(and **Louis M. GOLDSBOROUGH**) July 8, 1835, 1 mile N Port St. Joe, Gulf Co. Lot No. 12 Sect. 26 Tp. 7 R. 11, south and west.

**5034. SEARCY, Isham G.**
(and **Louis M. GOLDSBOROUGH**) July 8, 1835, St. Joe Bay, 2 miles W by S Port St. Joe, Gulf Co. Fractional Sect. 12, Tp. 8 R. 11, south and west.

**5035. SEARCY, Isham G.**
(and **Louis M. GOLDSBOROUGH**) July 8, 1835, 1 mile W Niles, Gulf Co. Fractional Sect. 13, Tp. 8 R. 11, south and west.

**5036. SEARCY, Isham G.**
(and **Louis M. GOLDSBOROUGH**) July 8, 1835, 3 1/2 miles SSW Niles, Gulf Co. Fractional Sect. 24 Tp. 8 R. 11, south and west.

**5086. SEARCY, Isham G.**
July 22, 1835, Peninsula, St. Joseph's Bay, 8 miles E Niles, Gulf Co. Fractional Sect. 26 Tp. 8 R. 12, south and west.

**5087. SEARCY, Isham G.**
July 22, 1835, on St. Joseph's Bay, 9 miles W Indian Pass, Gulf Co. Fractional Sect. 17 Tp. 9 R. 11, south and west.

**5110. SEARCY, Isham G.**
July 25, 1835, 7 miles SSW Indian Pass, on isthmus, Bay Co. Lot No. 1 Sect. 20 Tp. 9 R. 11, south and west.

**SEARCY, J. G.** see **Romeo LEWIS, #2158**

**4090. SECKINGER, Josiah**
Jan. 12, 1856, 3 miles NW Martel, Marion Co. NE 1/4 NW 1/4 and NW 1/4 NE 1/4 Sect. 14 Tp. 15 R. 20, south and east.

**2161. SEIGLER, Marshall**
Sept. 8, 1853, 1 1/4 miles E Putnam Hall, Putnam Co. NE 1/4 NE 1/4 Sect. 5 Tp. 9 R. 24, south and east. Patent delivered Feb. 21, 1857.

**8993. SELLERS, Asbury**
Nov. 17, 1846, 1/4 mile SE Dellwood, Jackson Co. NW 1/4 NE 1/4 Sect. 29 Tp. 5 R. 8, north and west.

**2575. SELMAN, Eliza B.**
Mar. 6, 1854, 1 mile S Houston, Suwannee Co. SW 1/4 NE 1/4 and NE 1/4 SW 1/4 Sect. 4 Tp. 3 R. 14, south and east.

**77. SELPH, John**
Nov. 28, 1826, c. 3 miles NW Lake Jackson Post Office, Gadsden Co. NE 1/4 Sect. 20 Tp. 2 R. 2, north and west. Transferred to **James LANIER** by **John SELPH**, Nov. 28, 1826. Teste: **Geo. W. WARD.**

**2582. SELPH, John**
Dec. 23, 1828, 7 miles N Tallahassee, Leon Co. W 1/2 NW 1/4 Sect. 25 Tp. 2 R. 1, north and west.

**4899. SELPH, John**
Mar. 19, 1835, 1/4 mile SW Bradfordville, Leon Co. NE 1/4 SW 1/4 Sect. 23 Tp. 2 R. 1, north and east.

**5380. SELPH, John**
Jan. 2, 1836, 1/4 mile W Centerville, Leon Co. NW 1/4 SE 1/4 Sect. 23 Tp. 2 R. 1, north and east.

**8210. SENTERFIT, Jesse**
Jan. 8, 1840, 4 miles W by N Campton, Okaloosa Co. NE 1/4 SE 1/4 Sect. 29 Tp. 5 R. 23, north and west.

**6719. SESSIONS, Samuel R.**
Feb. 1, 1837, 1 1/2 miles E Bailey, Madison Co. NE 1/4 SW 1/4 and NW 1/4 SE 1/4 Sect. 19 Tp. 2 R. 8, north and east.

**7622. SEVER, Enoch**
Sept. 3, 1838, 3 1/2 miles NNE Champaign, Madison Co. S 1/2 NE 1/4 Sect. 5 Tp. 1 R. 9, north and east.

**8787. SEVER, Mary**
June 16, 1845, 1/4 mile NNW Bailey, Madison Co. SW 1/4 NW 1/4 Sect. 19 Tp. 2 R. 7, south and east.

**5021. SEVER, William**
Sept. 29, 1832(?), 1 1/4 miles NE Madison, Madison Co. SW 1/4 NE 1/4 Sect. 32 Tp. 3 R. 9, north and east.

**190. SEWN, John Williams**
Oct. 31, 1845, 4 1/2 miles NE Burkes Hill, Suwannee Co. NW 1/4 SE 1/4 Sect. 22 Tp. 2 R. 15, south and east.

**5305. SEYLE, Robert E.**
(no date) 1861, 3 miles NE McMeekin, Putnam Co. Lots No. 12, 14, 23, and 24 Sect. 18 Tp. 10 R. 23, south and east. Patent delivered Dec. 3, 1863.

**7114. SEYMOUR, Charles**
Feb. 12, 1889, 1 3/4 miles NE Centralia, Hernando Co. S 1/2 SE 1/4 and S 1/2 SW 1/4 Sect. 30 Tp. 21S, R. 18E.

**436. SHACKLEFORD, David James**
Dec. 22, 1828, 1 miles SW Norum, Washington Co. NE 1/4 Sect. 13 Tp. 2 R. 16, north and west.

**435. SHACKLEFORD, Nathon**
Dec. 22, 1828, 3 miles E Norum, Washington Co. W 1/2 NW 1/4 Sect. 10 Tp. 2 R. 15, north and west. Transferred from **N. SHACKLEFORD** to **Wm. J. WATSON**, Dec. 29, 1828.

**88. SHAIR, Daniel**
(SIC) Dec. 6, 1826, at Florence, Gadsden Co. NE 1/4 Sect. 32 Tp. 3 R. 3, north and west. Transferred May 2, 1827, to **Stephen PARAMORE**.

**4831. SHANDS, Sarah C.**
Sept. 8, 1858, 3/4 mile NW Columbia, Columbia Co. W 1/2 Sect. 4 Tp. 5 R. 16, south and east.

**457. SHARP, George Hammond**
Sept. 5 1846, 2 miles S LaCrosse, Alachua Co. E 1/2 SW 1/4 Sect. 3 Tp. 8 R. 18, south and east. Transferred July 8, 1855. Patent delivered to **Geo. BROWN** June 2, 1855.

**6454. SHATSTEES, Jas. M.**
Jan. 7, 1837, 2 miles SE Alma, Jefferson Co. E 1/2 NW 1/4 and W 1/2 NE 1/4 Sect. 6 Tp. 2 R. 5, north and east.

**2191. SHAW, Daniel**
(of Fla.) Dec. 31, 1827, 3 miles NE Quincy, Gadsden Co. W 1/2 NW 1/4 Sect. 28 Tp. 3 R. 3, north and west.

**2192. SHAW, Daniel**
(of Fla.) Dec. 31, 1827, 3 miles NNE Quincy, Gadsden Co. E 1/2 NE 1/4 Sect. 29 Tp. 3 R. 3, north and west.

**3427. SHAW, Daniel**
Mar. 1, 1830, 5 miles E Mt. Pleasant, Gadsden Co. W 1/2 SE 1/4 Sect. 13 Tp. 3 R. 4, north and west.

**663, SHEFFIELD, Bryant**
Sept. 28, (no year), near White Springs, Hamilton Co. Lot No. 8 Sect. 7 Tp. 2 R. 16, south and east.

**6504. SHEFFIELD, Bryant**
Jan. 10, 1827, 4 miles W by N Sirmans, Madison Co. SE 1/4 NE 1/4 Sect. 31 Tp. 1 R. 7, south and east.

**8033. SHEFFIELD, Bryant**
Aug. 15, 1839, 3 miles S by E Facil, Hamilton Co. Lot No. 3 Sect. 2 Tp. 2 R. 15, south and east.

**7422. SHEFFIELD, Bryant**
Mar. 24, 1838, 2 1/2 miles SE by S Facil, Hamilton Co. S 1/2 Lot No. 2 Sect. 2 Tp. 2 R. 15, south and east.

**7423. SHEFFIELD, Bryant**
Mar. 26, 1838, 3 miles S by E Facil, Hamilton Co. West Division Lot No. 5 Sect. 7 Tp. 2 R. 16, south and east.

**2737. SHEFFIELD, Florida**
May 5, 1854, 7 miles NNE Houston, Suwannee Co. NE 1/4 SE 1/4 Sect. 25 Tp. 2 R. 15, south and east.

**2821. SHEFFIELD, Pliny**

July 18, 1854, 2 1/4 miles S by E Mason, Columbia Co. SW 1/4 NW 1/4 Sect. 2 Tp. 6 R. 17, south and east. Patent delivered June 9, 1858.

**2938. SHEFFIELD, Pliny**
Oct. 9, 1854, 2 miles S Mason, Columbia Co. SW 1/4 NW 1/4 and W 1/2 SW 1/4 Sect. 2, E 1/2 SE 1/4, S 1/2 NE 1/4 and SE 1/4 NW 1/4 Sect. 3 Tp. 6 R. 17, south and east. Patent delivered Feb. 17, 1860.

**2736. SHEFFIELD, Texis**
May 5, 1854, 6 miles W Winfield, Columbia Co. SW 1/4 SW 1/4 Sect. 30 Tp. 2 R. 16, south and east. Patent delivered Feb. 7, 1857.

**3770. SHEHEE, Ayles B.**
Dec. 1, 1830, 1 mile SW Ashville, Jefferson Co. W 1/2 SW 1/4 Sect. 5 Tp. 2 R. 7, north and east.

**3959. SHEHEE, Ayles B.**
May 2, 1831, 3 miles W by S Ashville, Jefferson Co. E 1/2 NE 1/4 Sect. 3 Tp. 2 R. 6, north and east.

**4110. SHEHEE, Ayles B.**
Nov. 29, 1831, 2 1/2 miles NE By E Maysland, Madison Co. E 1/2 SE 1/4 Sect. 7 Tp. 2 R. 7, north and east.

**4726. SHEHEE, Ayles B.**
Dec. 19, 2 miles NNW Spray, Madison Co. SE 1/4 NE 1/4 Sect. 6 Tp. 2 R. 7, north and east.

**5459. SHEHEE, Ayles B.**
Feb. 12, 1836, 7 miles NNW Shady Grove, Madison Co. E 1/2 NW 1/4 Sect. 7 Tp. 2 R. 7, north and east.

**6678. SHEHEE, Ayles B.**
Jan. 26, 1837, 1 mile E Bailey, Madison Co. W 1/2 NE 1/4 Sect. 24 Tp. 2 R. 7, north and east.

**7718. SHEHEE, Ayles B.**
Nov. 23, 1838, at Ashvale, Jefferson Co. SW 1/4 NW 1/4 Sect. 5 Tp. 2 R. 7, north and east.

**7719. SHEHEE, Ayles B.**
Nov. 23, 1838, 1 mile S by W Ashvale, Jefferson Co. E 1/2 SE 1/4 Sect. 6 Tp. 2 R. 7, north and east.

**7720. SHEHEE, Ayles B.**
Nov. 23, 1838, 1 1/4 miles S by W Ashvale, Jefferson Co. W 1/2 NE 1/4 Sect. 7 Tp. 2 R. 7, north and east.

**4656. SHEHEE, Asler B.**
Nov. 1, 1834, 2 miles NNW Maysland, Madison Co. NW 1/4 NW 1/4 Sect. 5 Tp. 2 R. 7, north and east.

**8694. SHEHEE, Henry D.**
Sept. 20, 1844, 2 miles E Maysland, Madison Co. SE 1/4 NW 1/4 Sect. 5 Tp. 2 R. 7, north and east.

**3669. SHEHEE, John H.**
Oct. 13, 1830, 3/4 mile S Ashvale, Jefferson Co. W 1/2 SW 1/4 Sect. 5 Tp. 2 R. 7, north and east.

**3787. SHEHEE, John H.**
Dec. 9, 1830, 1 1/2 miles SE Lovett, Madison Co. W 1/2 SE 1/4 Sect. 6 Tp. 2 R. 7, north and east.

**7725. SHELFER, Council**
Nov. 24, 1838, 1 3/4 miles E by N Havana, Gadsden Co. NE 1/4 NW 1/4 Sect. 36 Tp. 3 R. 2, north and west.

**5258. SHELFER, Hardy H.**
Nov. 10, 1835, 2 3/4 miles S Florence, Gadsden Co. E 1/2 SE 1/4 Sect. 14 Tp. 2 R. 3, north and west.

**8107. SHELFER, Nathan A.**
Oct. 4, 1839, 2 1/2 miles NNE Havana, Gadsden Co. E 1/2 NE 1/4 Sect. 36 Tp. 3 R. 2, north and west.

**3237. SHELFER, Nathan H.**
Jan. 29, 1830, 5 1/2 miles SE Quincy, Gadsden Co. E 1/2 SE 1/4 Sect. 23 Tp. 2 R. 3, north and west.

**5397. SHELFER, Nathan H.**
Jan. 12, 1835, 1 1/4 miles S Concord, Gadsden Co. NW 1/4 SW 1/4 Sect. 30 Tp. 3 R. 1, north and west.

**7263. SHELFER, Nathan H.**
Jan. 18, 1838, 2 1/2 miles E Hinson, Gadsden Co. NW 1/4 SE 1/4 Sect. 25 Tp. 3 R. 2, north and west.

**7626. SHELFER, Nathan H.**
Sept. 6, 1838, 2 1/2 miles E Hinson, Gadsden Co. S 1/2 SE 1/4 Sect. 25 Tp. 3 R. 2, north and west.

**7696. SHELFER, Nathan H.**
Nov. 5, 1838, 2 1/2 miles E Hinson, Gadsden Co. E 1/2 SW 1/4 Sect. 25 Tp. 3 R. 2, north and west.

**8101. SHELFER, Nathan H.**
Sept. 30, 1839, 2 miles W Hinson, Gadsden Co. SW 1/4 SW 1/4 Sect. 30 Tp. 3 R. 1, north and west.

**SHEPARD, John S. see David THOMAS**

**3807. SHEPHERD, Asa**
Dec. 21, 1830, 5 miles SE Miccosukee,

Leon Co. E 1/2 SW 1/4 Sect. 19 Tp. 2 R. 3, north and east.

**8745. SHEPHERD, Zacheus**
Dec. 16, 1844, 3 1/2 miles SSE Rockbluff, Liberty Co. W 1/2 SE 1/4 Sect. 28 Tp. 2 R. 6, north and west.

**9215. SHEPPARD, Simon A.**
Mar. 9, 1891, 1 mile N by E Rock, Levy Co. NE 1/4 Sect. 2 Tp. 13S, R. 14E.

**8372. SHEROUSE, Godlief**
July 24, 1840, 3 miles W Macomb, Washington Co. SW 1/4 SE 1/4 Sect. 19 Tp. 2 R. 13, north and east.

**8373. SHEROUSE, Godlief**
July 24, 1840, 3 1/4 miles SE Macomb, Washington Co. NW 1/4 NE 1/4 Sect. 30 Tp. 2 R. 13, north and east.

**2686. SHINOSIN, John**
April 15, 1854, at Island Grove, Alachua Co. Lot No. 2 Fractional Sect. 15 Tp. 12 R. 22, south and east.

**8131. SIBLEY, Charles S.**
Nov. 8, 1839, 1 mile S Cherry Lake, Madison Co. NW 1/4 Sect. 21 Tp. 2 R. 9, north and east.

**2699. SIKES, David**
Jan. 31, 1829, 2 miles SE Centerville, Leon Co. E 1/2 SE 1/4 Sect. 30 Tp. 2 R. 2, north and east.

**534. SIKES, John**
May 30, 1831, 1 mile SW Mandalay, Jefferson Co. Lot No. 7 Sect. 24 Tp. 4 R. 3, north and east.

**7988. SIKES, John**
June 7, 1839, 5 miles N by E Graceville (Jackson Co., Fla.) Geneva Co., Alabama. S 1/2 Lot No. 5 Sect. 13 Tp. 7 R. 13, north and west.

**8124. SIKES, John**
Oct. 22, 1839, 2 miles N Campbellton, Jackson Co. (part of Geneva Co., Alabama) SE 1/4 NE 1/4 Sect. 24 Tp. 7 R. 13, north and west.

**514. SIMMONS, Henry F.**
June 9, 1825, 3 miles N Tallahassee, Leon Co. Lot No. 5 Sect. 14 Tp. 1 R. 1, north and west. **H. F. SIMMONS**, Assignee to **Walter SANDERS**, Dec. 15, 1825.

**2063. SIMMONS, Henry F.**
Sept. 17, 1827, 2 miles SSE Lake Jackson, Leon Co. E 1/2 SW 1/4 Sect. 8 Tp. 1 R. 1, north and west.

**2101. SIMMONS, Henry F.**
(of Fla.) Nov. 14, 1827, 1/2 mile SSE Lake Jackson, Leon Co. E 1/2 SW 1/4 Sect. 5 Tp. 1 R. 1, north and west.

**2102. SIMMONS, Henry F.**
Nov. 14, 1827, 1/4 mile S Lake Jackson Station, Leon Co. W 1/2 SE 1/4 Sect. 5 Tp. 1 R. 1, north and west.

**2523. SIMMONS, Henry F.**
Oct. 14, 1828, 1 mile S Lake Jackson Station, Leon Co. W 1/2 NW 1/4 Sect. 8 Tp. 1 R. 1, north and west.

**6929. SIMMONS, Henry F.**
March 21, 1837, 3 1/3 miles W by N Higgins, Gulf Co. W 1/2 SW 1/4 Sect. 25 Tp. 8 R. 11, south and west.

**6939. SIMMONS, Henry F.**
Mar. 25, 1837, 3 miles ?NW Higgins, Gulf Co. SW 1/4 NW 1/4 Fractional Sect. 25 Tp. 8 R. 11, south and west.

**8358. SIMMONS, Henry F.**
June 19, 1840, 2 miles E Douglas, Gulf Co. Lot No. 8 Sect. 12 Tp. 6 R. 9, south and west.

**5384. SIMMONS, Henry F.**
Jan. 2, 1836, 2 1/2 miles N by W Monticello, Jefferson Co. NW 1/4 NW 1/4 Sect. 36 Tp. 8 R. 11, south and west.

**5552. SIMMONS, Henry F.**
Mar. 23, 1836, 5 1/4 miles W by S Hines, Lefayette Co. NW 1/4 NW 1/4 Sect. 25 Tp. 8 R. 11, south and west.

**5554. SIMMONS, Henry F.**
Mar. 25, 1836, 2 1/4 miles NNW Higgins, Gulf Co. Lots No. 7 and 1 Fractional Sect. 25 and 36 Tp. 8 R. 12, south and west.

**2533. SIMMONS, Peter**
Oct. 28, 1828, 2 miles NE Marianna, Jackson Co. W 1/2 SW 1/4 Sect. 35 Tp. 6 R. 10, north and west.

**2542. SIMMONS, Peter**
Nov. 11, 1828, 6 miles E Welchton, Jackson Co. W 1/2 SE 1/4 Sect. 35 Tp. 6 R. 10, north and west.

**402. SIMMS, John**
May 5, 1827, 3 miles E Marianna, Jackson Co. NW 1/4 Sect. 6 Tp. 4 R. 9, north and west.

**273. SIMMS, Miles**
Jan. 1, 1827, 8 miles E Marianna,

Jackson Co. NE 1/4 Sect. 5 Tp. 4 R. 9, north and west. Transfer: **Miles SIMMS** to **James ECUM** and **James P. LOFEA**, Oct. 16, 1827.

**274. SIMMS, Miles**
Jan. 1, 1827, 1 mile W Marianna, Jackson Co. NE 1/4 Sect. 2 Tp. 4 R. 10, north and west.

**403. SIMMS, Miles**
(Assignee of **Mahala WILKINSON**) May 5, 1827, 2 miles ENE Marianna, Jackson Co. SW 1/4 Sect. 26 Tp. 5 R. 10, north and west. Transferred from **Miles SIMMS** to **Geo. POYTHSEYS**, June 14, 1827.
See **James S. MURPHY**. Also see **Miles SIMS**

**275. SIMMS, William**
Jan. 1, 1827, 8 miles NE Marianna, Jackson Co. SW 1/4 Sect. 30 Tp. 5 R. 9, north and west.

**2087. SIMMS, William**
Nov. 3, 1827, 1/2 mile SE Marianna, Jackson Co. E 1/2 SW 1/4 Sect. 10 Tp. 4 R. 10, north and west.

**2252. SIMONS, Henry P.**
Feb. 11, 1823, 1 1/2 miles SE Lake Jackson Station, Leon Co. E 1/2 SE 1/4 Sect. 5 Tp. 1 R. 1, north and west.

**1463. SIMONS, John**
Sept. 27, 1852, 3 miles SE Lukene, on one of the Islands of Cedar Key, Levy Co. Lot No. 1 Fractional Sect. 22 Tp. 15 R. 13, south and east.

**SIMPSON, Andrew J.** see **Joseph FORSYTH**, #4260.

**5126. SIMPSON, Lewis Thomas**
Nov. 18, 1829, 3 1/2 miles W Wadesboro, Leon Co. E 1/2 SW 1/4 Sect. 33 Tp. 2 R. 3, north and east.

**3998. SIMPSON, Robert**
July 7, 1831, 1 1/2 miles ESE Welchton, Jackson Co. E 1/2 SW 1/4 Sect. 21 Tp. 6 R. 11, north and west.

**2820. SIMS, Ambrosa**
May 11, 1829, 3 miles Crigler, Jackson Co. E 1/2 SW 1/4 Sect. 15 Tp. 4 R. 9, north and west.

**SIMS, Benj. D.** see **Edward T. SHEPARD** and **Richard GORMAN**

**84. SIMS, Jeremiah**
Dec. 1, 1826, 2 miles E Chipola Big Spring, Jackson Co. NW 1/4 Sect. 32 Tp. 5 R. 9, north and west.

**2133. SIMS, Jeremiah**
(of Fla.) Dec. 11, 1827, 2 miles E Marianna, Jackson Co. W 1/2 SW 1/4 Sect. 6 Tp. 4 R. 9, north and west.

**3665. SIMS, Jeremiah**
Oct. 12, 1830, 3 1/2 miles E Marianna, Jackson Co. E 1/2 SW 1/4 Sect. 6 Tp. 4 R. 9, north and west. Paid in Scrip issued to **Alex'r MACOMB**, dated May 30, 1829, $98.43.

**4264. SIMS, Jeremiah**
Dec. 31, 1832, 3 1/4 miles E by N Marianna, Jackson Co. NE 1/4 SE 1/4 Sect. 1 Tp. 4 R. 10, north and west.

**2624. SIMS, John**
Jan. 15, 1829, 3 miles SE Marianna, Jackson Co. W 1/2 SW 1/4 Sect. 7 Tp. 4 R. 9, north and west.

**2030. SIMS, Miles**
(of Fla.) Aug. 10, 1827, 1 mile E Marianna, Jackson Co. E 1/2 SE 1/4 Sect. 2 Tp. 14 R. 10, north and west.

**2360. SIMS, Miles**
May 2, 1828, in Marianna, Jackson Co. E 1/2 SW 1/4 Sect. 11 Tp. 4 R. 10, north and west.

**2361. SIMS, Miles**
May 2, 1828, 1/2 mile E Marianna, Jackson Co. W 1/2 NE 1/4 Sect. 11 Tp. 4 R. 10, north and west.

**3043. SIMS, Miles**
Sept. 16, 1828, 3/4 mile SE Oakdale, Jackson Co. W 1/2 SE 1/4 Sect. 36 Tp. 4 R. 10, north and west.

**3045. SIMS, Miles**
Sept. 16, 1829, 2 miles NNW Simsville, Jackson Co. W 1/2 NE 1/4 Sect. 1 Tp. 3 R. 10, north and west.

**3046. SIMS, Miles**
Sept. 16, 1829, 1 1/2 miles S Marianna, Jackson Co. W 1/2 NE 1/4 Sect. 14 Tp. 4 R. 10, north and west.

**3047. SIMS, Miles**
Sept. 16, 1829, 2 miles SSE Marianna, Jackson Co. E 1/2 SW 1/4 Sect. 14 Tp. 4 R. 10, north and west.

**3048. SIMS, Miles**
Sept. 16, 1829, 2 1/4 miles SE Marianna, Jackson Co. NW 1/4 Sect. 14 Tp. 4 R. 10, north and west.
See **Cornelius GRANTHAM** and **Miles SIMMS**

**7700. SIMS, William**

Nov. 8, 1838, 1 mile SE Oakdale, Jackson Co. SE 1/4 SE 1/4 Sect. 36 Tp. 4 R. 10, north and west.

**SINGLETARY, Benjamin see Ambrose COOK, #1013**

**2524. SINGLETARY, Brayton**
Oct. 14, 1828, 3 miles S Meridian, Leon Co. Lot No. 2 Sect. 31 Tp. 3 R. 1, north and east.

**5381. SINGLETARY, Brayton**
Jan. 2, 1836, 3/4 mile E Facil, Hamilton Co. W 1/2 NW 1/4 Sect. 26 Tp. 1 R. 15, south and east.

**5426. SINGLETARY, Brayton**
Jan. 27, 1836, 3/4 mile SE by S Facil, Hamilton Co. NE 1/4 SE 1/4 Sect. 27 Tp. 1 R. 15, south and east.

**6277. SINGLETARY, Brayton**
Dec. 22, 1836, 1/2 mile SW Facil, Hamilton Co. SE 1/4 SSE 1/4 Sect. 27 Tp. 1 R. 15, south and east.

**1160. SINGLETARY, Braxton**
(DUP) Feb. 22, 1827, 1 mile SW Meridian, Leon Co. E 1/2 SE 1/4 Sect. 24 Tp. 3 R. 1, north and west.

**4524. SINGLETARY, Brazton**
Jan. 18, 1834, 3 miles SE Havana, Gadsden Co. SE 1/4 SE 1/4 Sect. 12 Tp. 2 R. 2, north and west.

**SINGLETARY, Edward see Richard C. ALLEN**

**3424. SINGLETARY, Joseph**
Feb. 22, 1830, just N Wadesboro, Leon Co. E 1/2 SW 1/4 Sect. 31 Tp. 2 R. 3, north and east.

**3968. SINGLETARY, Nathaniel**
May 17, 1831, 1 mile N Centerville, Leon Co. E 1/2 SW 1/4 Sect. 13 Tp. 2 R. 1, north and east.

**5681. SINGLETARY, Nathaniel**
May 24, 1836, 1 mile NW Wadesboro, Leon Co. SE 1/4 SW 1/4 Sect. 36 Tp. 2 R. 2, north and east.

**SINGLETON, Joseph see Holaday HAYLEY**

**4068. SISTRUNK, David**
Aug. 22, 1831, 3/4 mile S by E Marion, Hamilton Co. E 1/2 SW 1/4 Sect. 9 Tp. 1 R. 14, south and east.

**7062. SISTRUNK, David**
Oct. 12, 1837, 1 mile SSE Marion,, Hamilton Co. NW 1/4 SE 1/4 Sect. 9 Tp. 1 R. 14, south and east.

**7362. SISTRUNK, David**
Feb. 28, 1838, 3 miles SE Goethe, Bay Co. SW 1/4 SE 1/4 SE 1/4 Sect. 9 Tp. 1 R. 14, south and east.

**37. SISTRUNK, Gasper**
July 15, 1843, 2 miles E Rixford, Suwannee Co. NW 1/4 SW 1/4 Sect. 33 Tp. 1 R. 14, south and east.

**716. SKAGGS, Lemuel B.**
(of Ga.) June 8, 1826, at Copeland Station, Leon Co. W 1/2 NE 1/4 Sect. 33 Tp. 3 R. 3, north and east.

**2548. SKAGGS, Lemuel B.**
Nov. 22, 1828, at Copeland, Leon Co. W 1/2 SW 1/4 Sect. 33 Tp. 3 R. 3, north and east.

**3127. SKAGGS, Lemuel B.**
Nov. 18, 1829, 1/2 mile SW Stringer, Leon Co. W 1/2 SE 1/4 Sect. 29 Tp. 3 R. 3, north and east.

**3128. SKAGGS, Lemuel B.**
Nov. 18, 1829, at Copeland, Leon Co. W 1/2 NW 1/4 Sect. 33 Tp. 3 R. 3, north and east.

**1072. SKAGGS, Samuel B.**
Feb. 5, 1827, 1/2 mile E Copeland, Leon Co. E 1/2 NE 1/4 Sect. 33 Tp. 3 R. 3, north and east.

**1073. SKAGGS, Samuel B.**
Feb. 5, 1827, at Copeland, Leon Co. E 1/2 NW 1/4 Sect. 33 Tp. 3 R. 3, north and east.

**5482. SKANNAL, Lloyd**
Feb. 22, 1836, 4 1/2 miles E Dills, Jefferson Co. E 1/2 NE 1/4 Sect. 1 Tp. 2 R. 6, north and east.

**5557. SKENNILLE, Lloyd**
Mar. 28, 1836, 4 miles E Dills, Jefferson Co. E 1/2 SW 1/4 Sect. 1 Tp. 2 R. 6, north and east.

**8879. SKINE, V. V.**
Jan. 22, 1846, 3/4 mile SSW Sneads, Jackson Co. NE 1/4 NW 1/4 Sect. 3 Tp. 3 R. 7, north and west.

**2098. SKIPPER, Charlotte**
(of Fla.) Nov. 12, 1827, 2 1/2 miles E Wadesboro, Jefferson Co. W 1/2 SW 1/4 Sect. 21 Tp. 1 R. 3, north and east.

**5740. SKIPPER, Gabriel**
June 30, 1836, 2 1/2 miles E by S Capitola, Jefferson Co. SE 1/4 NE 1/4 Sect. 33 Tp. 1 R. 3, north and east.

**1971. SKIPPER, Manua D.**
June 30, 1827, 2 miles SE Capitola, Jefferson Co. E 1/2 NE 1/4 Sect. 29

Tp. 1 R. 3, north and east.

**1972. SKIPPER, Manua D.**
June 30, 1827, 1 1/2 miles E Capitola, Jefferson Co. W 1/2 NW 1/4 Sect. 28 Tp. 1 R. 2, north and east.

**2425. SKIPPER, Marma D.**
May 28, 1828, 2 miles SW Dills, Jefferson Co. E 1/2 NW 1/4 Sect. 11 Tp. 2 R. 5, north and east.

**3512. SKIPPER, Marmaduke**
May 15, 1830, 1 1/2 miles SE Capitola, Jefferson Co. W 1/2 SW 1/4 Sect. 28 Tp. 1 R. 3, north and east.

**4278. SKIPPER, Marmaduke**
Jan. 22, 1833, 2 miles E by S Capitola, Jefferson Co. E 1/2 NW 1/4 Sect. 28 Tp. 1 R. 3, north and east.

**5963. SLADE, Jeremiah**
Nov. 3, 1836, 1 mile SSW Darsey, Gadsden Co. E 1/2 NW 1/4 Sect. 11 Tp. 3 R. 2, north and west.

**2256. SLADE, William**
Feb. 13, 1828, 5 miles NW Havana, Gadsden Co. W 1/2 NE 1/4 Sect. 19 Tp. 3 R. 2, north and west.

**3479. SLADE, William**
April 19, 1830, 1 1/2 miles SSW Jamieson, Gadsden Co. SE 1/4 Sect. 13 Tp. 3 R. 3, north and east. "Received on acct. of within Certificates No. 62 and 63, dated May 30, 1829, in favour of **Alex'r MACOMB**.

**3480. SLADE, William**
April 19, 1830, 2 miles S Jamieson, Gadsden Co. NW 1/4 Sect. 19 Tp. 3 R. 2, north and west. Received on acct. of the within Certificates No. 61 and 76 in favour of **Alex. MACOMB**. Dated May 30, 1829."

**5401. SLADE, William**
Jan. 14, 1836, 1 1/4 miles SW Jamieson, Hamilton Co. W 1/2 NE 1/4 Sect. 13 Tp. 3 R. 3, north and west.

**4096. SLATER, James**
Oct. 17, 1831, 2 1/4 miles W McClellan, Jefferson Co. NW 1/4 Sect. 34 Tp. 3 R. 5, north and east.

**7046. SLATER, James**
Sept. 23, 1837, 1 3/4 miles N by W Dills, Jefferson Co. E 1/2 NW 1/4 Sect. 25 Tp. 3 R. 5, north and east.

**6444. SLAUTER, John**
Jan. 6, 1837, 3 miles NNE Lamont, Jefferson Co. SE 1/4 SW 1/4 Sect. 12 Tp. 1 R. 5, south and east.

**4999. SLEDGE, Green**
June 15, 1835, 2 miles S by E Dill, Jefferson Co. W 1/2 SE 1/4 Sect. 17 Tp. 2 R. 6, north and east.

**8905. SLOAN, James M.**
Feb. 18, 1846, 3 3/4 miles N by E Dills, Jefferson Co. SW 1/4 Sect. 20 Tp. 3 R. 6, north and east.

**2935. SLOAN, William**
July 11, 1829, 2 miles NE Marianna, Jackson Co. SW 1/4 Sect. 36 Tp. 5 R. 10, north and west.

**2936. SLOAN, William**
July 11, 1829, 2 miles ENE Marianna, Jackson Co. E 1/2 SE 1/4 Sect. 35 Tp. 3 R. 10, north and west.

**8286. SMALL, Hercules F.**
Sept. 21, 1897, 2 miles NW Levon, Marion Co. NW 1/4 Sect. 20 Tp. 17S R. 22E.

**SMALLWOOD, J. see Martin DOLON, #8728**

**11. SMITH, Archibald**
(Jr.) Sept. 1, 1826, near Quincy, Gadsden Co. SW 1/4 Sect. 27 Tp. 3 R. 4, north and west. Received $201.92 1/2 for 161.54 acres. **R. K. CALL**, Receiver.

**236. SMITH, Archibald**
(DUP) (Sr.) Dec. 30, 1826, at Cretha Station, Gadsden Co. SE 1/4 Sect. 27 Tp. 3 R. 4, north and west.

**1820. SMITH, Archibald**
(DUP) (Jun'r) June 5, 1827, 5 miles NW Quincy, Gadsden Co. E 1/2 NE 1/4 Sect. 28 Tp. 3 R. 4, north and west.

**1821. SMITH, Archibald**
(DUP) (Jun'r) June 5, 1827, 2 miles SE Greensboro, Gadsden Co. E 1/2 NE 1/4 Sect. 15 Tp. 2 R. 5, north and west.

**1822. SMITH, Archibald**
(Jun'r) June 5, 1827, 2 miles SE Greensboro, Gadsden Co. E 1/2 NE 1/4 Sect. 15 Tp. 2 R. 5, north and west.

**2058. SMITH, Archibald**
(of Ga.) Sept. 10, 1827, 3 miles SSE Hermitage, Gadsden Co. W 1/2 SE 1/4 Sect. 10 Tp. 3 R. 5, north and west.

**5979. SMITH, Archibald**
(Sr.) Nov. 7, 1836, 1/4 mile NNE

Gretna, Gadsden Co. NW 1/4 NW 1/4 and NE 1/4 NW 1/4 Sect. 34 Tp. 3 R. 4, north and west.

**5980. SMITH, Archibald**
(Sr.) Nov. 7, 1836, at Gretna, Gadsden Co. W 1/2 NE 1/4 Sect. 28 Tp. 3 R. 4, north and west.

**5981. SMITH, Archibald**
(Sr.) Nov. 7, 1836, 2 1/4 miles N by W Mt. Pleasant, Gadsden Co. W 1/2 SW 1/4 Sect. 2 Tp. 3 R. 5, north and west.

**6065. SMITH, Archibald**
(Jr.) Nov. 21, 1836, 3 1/2 miles SE Mt. Pleasant, Gadsden Co. W 1/2 SE 1/4 Sect. 28 Tp. 3 R. 4, north and west.

**5350. SMITH, Daniel**
Sept. 15, 1836, 1 3/4 miles W Steaphead, Gadsden Co. NE 1/4 SW 1/4 Sect. 13 Tp. 2 R. 7, north and west.

**2737. SMITH, Daniel C.**
Feb. 21, 1829, 1 mile NW Pleasant, Gadsden Co. E 1/2 SW 1/4 Sect. 10 Tp. 3 R. 5, north and west.

**189. SMITH, David**
(DUP) Dec. 29, 1826, at Jamieson Station, Gadsden Co. E 1/2 SE 1/4 Sect. 1 Tp. 2 R. 3, north and west.

**1986. SMITH, David**
July 6, 1827, 1 mile E Florence, Gadsden Co. E 1/2 NW 1/4 Sect. 7 Tp. 2 R. 2, north and west.

**8855. SMITH, Edmund M.**
Dec. 13, 1845, 2 1/2 miles E Riversick, Washington Co. W 1/2 SW 1/4 Sect. 14 Tp. 1 R. 14, south and east.

**8199. SMITH, Elizabeth**
(widow of **William G. SMITH**) May 13, 1890, 2 miles NE Clearwater, Pinellas Co. N 1/2 SE 1/4 Sect. 36 Tp. 28S R. 15E.

**1050. SMITH, Gabriel**
Feb. 1, 1827, 5 miles SE Quincy, Gadsden Co. E 1/2 NW 1/4 Sect. 28 Tp. 2 R. 3, north and west.

**5729. SMITH, George Washington**
Aug. 2, 1836, 1 1/2 miles E Jasper, Hamilton Co. SE 1/4 SW 1/4 Sect. 13 Tp. 1 R. 14, south and east.

**6875. SMITH, George W.**
Mar. 10, 1837, just E Ellaville, Madison Co. Lot No. 2 Fractional Sect. 24 Tp. 1 R. 11, south and east.

**8746. SMITH, Henry**
Dec. 21, 1844, 1 mile S Littman, Gadsden Co. SW 1/4 SE 1/4 Sect. 3 Tp. 2 R. 3, north and west.

**6741. SMITH, James**
Feb. 6, 1837, 2 1/4 miles SE Marina, Hamilton Co. W 1/2 SW 1/4 Sect. 3 Tp. 1 R. 14, south and east.

**4956. SMITH, Isabelle**
May 10, 1835, 4 miles N McClellan, Jefferson Co. SW 1/4 SW 1/4 Sect. 23 Tp. 2 R. 5, north and east.

**4957. SMITH, Isabelle**
May 10, 1835, 4 miles NNW McClellan, Jefferson Co. NW 1/4 NW 1/4 Sect. 26 Tp. 2 R. 5, north and east.

**27. SMITH, John**
(Jr.) Oct. 27, 1826, near Quincy, Gadsden Co. NE 1/4 Sect. 34 Tp. 3 R. 4, north and west. (Pre-emption)

**152. SMITH, John**
(Senr.) Dec. 29, 1826, at Gretha Station, Gadsden Co. NW 1/4 Sect. 27 Tp. 3 R. 4, north and west.

**366. SMITH, John**
(Assignee of **L. BOYKEN**) Apr. 28, 1827, at Gretha, Gadsden Co. W 1/2 SW 1/4 Sect. 22 Tp. 3 R. 4, north and west.

**2040. SMITH, John**
(Sen'r.) Aug. 21, 1827, 2 miles ENE Greensboro, Gadsden Co. E 1/2 SW 1/4 Sect. 2 Tp. 2 R. 5, north and west.

**3953. SMITH, John**
April 18, 1831, 1/2 mile S Wadesboro, Leon Co. W 1/2 NW 1/4 Sect. 7 Tp. 1 R. 3, north and west.

**8710. SMITH, John**
Oct. 5, 1844, 1 1/4 miles NNE Jacob, Jackson Co. NE 1/4 NE 1/4 Sect. 12 Tp. 5 R. 12, north and west.

**4890. SMITH, John G.**
Mar. 16, 1835, 1 mile E Jasper, Hamilton Co. NE 1/4 SE 1/4 Sect. 4 Tp. 1 R. 14, south and east.

**4891. SMITH, John G.**
Mar. 16, 1835, 1 mile SW Marion, Hamilton Co. NE 1/4 SE 1/4 Sect. 4 Tp. 1 R. 14, south and east.

**8143. SMITH, John G.**
Nov. 15, 1839, 4 1/2 miles W by N Facil, Hamilton Co. W 1/2 Lot No. 3 Sect. 23 Tp. 1 R. 14, south and east.

**SMITH, Jordan** see **Martin HARDIN**,

#203
**1974. SMITH, Joseph**
June 30, 1827, 3 miles W Tallahassee, Leon Co. W 1/2 SW 1/4 Sect. 34 Tp. 1 R. 1, north and west.

**2736. SMITH, Joseph**
Feb. 14, 1829, 5 miles N Quincy, Gadsden Co. W 1/2 NW 1/4 Sect. 17 Tp. 3 R. 5, north and west.

**4161. SMITH, Joseph P.**
April 13, 1832, 1 mile SE Mears Spur, Gadsden Co. E 1/2 NE 1/4 Sect. 18 Tp. 3 R. 5, north and west.

**3136. SMITH, Lewis**
Nov. 28, 1829, 4 miles E Monticello, Jefferson Co. W 1/2 SW 1/4 Sect. 29 Tp. 2 R. 5, north and east.

**157. SMITH, Malcomb**
(DUP) Dec. 28, 1826, 3 miles W Quincy, Gadsden Co. NW 1/4 Sect. 3 Tp. 2 R. 4, north and west. Transferred to **Daniel McLAUCHLIN** of Florida, Dec. 28, 1826.

**4244. SMITH, Morris**
Nov. 14, 1832, 3 1/4 miles N by E Midway, Gadsden Co. SE 1/4 NW 1/4 Sect. 21 Tp. 2 R. 5, north and east.

**1726. SMITH, Nathan**
Feb. 22, 1853, 1/2 mile N Mason, Columbia Co. SE 1/4 SE 1/4 Sect. 22 Tp. 5 R. 17, south and east. Patent delivered (no date).

**2335. SMITH, Nathan**
(Sr.) Nov. 2, 1853, 1 mile W Mason, Columbia Co. SW 1/4 SW 1/4 Sect. 23 and NW 1/4 NW 1/4 Sect. 26 Tp. 5 R. 17, south and east. Patent delivered (no date).

**2262. SMITH, Noble**
Feb. 18, 1828, 3 1/2 miles S by W Meridian, Leon Co. E 1/2 SW 1/4 Sect. 1 Tp. 2 R. 1, north and west.

**4945. SMITH, Noble**
April 27, 1835, 9 miles E Genoa, Hamilton Co. Lot No. 5 Sect. 7 Tp. 1 R. 17, south and east.

**3255. SMITH, Patrick**
Feb. 6, 1830, 2 miles W by N Wadesboro, Leon Co. W 1/2 SW 1/4 Sect. 32 Tp. 2 R. 3, north and east.

**3838. SMITH, Patrick**
Jan. 10, 1831, 2 1/2 miles E by N Wadesboro, Leon Co. E 1/2 SE 1/4 Sect. 31 Tp. 2 R. 3, north and east.

**5069. SMITH, Patrick**
July 10, 1835, 5 miles SE Sawdust, Gadsden Co. SE 1/4 NE 1/4 Sect. 31 Tp. 2 R. 3, north and east.

**6619. SMITH, Patrick**
Jan. 20, 1837, 1 mile NE Wadesboro, Leon Co. SW 1/4 NW 1/4 Sect. 32 Tp. 2 R. 3, north and east.

**SMITH, Peyton P. see Appleton ROSSETTER**

**4944. SMITH, Philoman**
April 27, 1835, 9 miles E Genoa, Hamilton Co. Lot No. 7 Sect. 7 Tp. 1 R. 17, south and east.

**176. SMITH, Powell**
Dec. 29, 1826, 4 miles NE Graceville, Jackson Co. SW 1/4 Sect. 22 Tp. 7 R. 12, north and west.

**5530. SMITH, Simeon Alexander**
Mar. 11, 1836, 3 1/2 miles SSW Dills, Jefferson Co. NW 1/4 Sect. 11 Tp. 2 R. 5, south and east.

**5531. SMITH, Simeon Alexander**
Mar. 11, 1836, 1 1/2 miles SSW Lamont, Jefferson Co. W 1/2 NE 1/4 Sect. 3 Tp. 2 R. 5, south and east.

**7935. SMITH, Simeon Alexander**
April 13, 1839, 5 miles NW Sadler, Taylor Co. N 1/2 Sect. 17 Tp. 6 R. 7, south and east.

**7936. SMITH, Simeon Alexander**
(of Ga.) April 13, 1839, 5 miles NNW Sadler, Taylor Co. SW 1/4 SW 1/4 and SE 1/4 Sect. 4 Tp. 6 R. 7, south and east.

**7937. SMITH, Simeon Alexander**
April 13, 1839, 6 miles NNW Sadler, Taylor Co. SE 1/4 SE 1/4, SW 1/4 Sect. 5 Tp. 6 R. 7, south and east.

**7938. SMITH, Simeon Alexander**
April 13, 1839, 6 miles NW Sadler, Taylor Co. E 1/2 NE 1/4 and E 1/2 SE 1/4 Sect. 7 Tp. 6 R. 7, south and east.

**7939. SMITH, Simeon Alexander**
April 13, 1839, 5 miles NNW Sadler, Taylor Co. W 1/2 Sect. 8 Tp. 6 R. 7, south and east.

**7940. SMITH, Simeon Alexander**
April 13, 1839, 5 miles NW Sadler, Taylor Co. N 1/2 Sect. 18 Tp. 6 R. 7, south and east.

**7941. SMITH, Simeon Alexander**
April 13, 1839, 4 1/2 miles NW

Sadler, Taylor Co. W 1/2 NE 1/4 and W 1/2 SE 1/4 Sect. 9 Tp. 6 R. 7, south and east.

**7942. SMITH, Simeon Alexander**
April 13, 1839, 4 1/2 miles NW Sadler, Taylor Co. E 1/2 NE 1/4 and E 1/2 SE 1/4 Sect. 9 Tp. 6 R. 7, south and east.

**1975. SMITH, Solomon**
June 30, 1827, in Monticello, Jefferson Co. W 1/2 SE 1/4 Sect. 30 Tp. 2 R. 5, north and east.

**2714. SMITH, Solomon**
Feb. 10, 1829, 2 miles NNW Wadesboro, Leon Co. E 1/2 SW 1/4 Sect. 29 Tp. 2 R. 5, north and east.

**2767. SMITH, Solomon**
Mar. 4, 1829, 1 mile E Monticello, Jefferson Co. W 1/2 NE 1/4 Sect. 29 Tp. 2 R. 5, north and east.

**155. SMITH, Wm.**
(DUP) Dec. 28, 1826, 5 miles NW Quincy, Gadsden Co. E 1/2 SE 1/4 Sect. 28 Tp. 3 R. 4, north and west.

**593. SMITH, William F.**
Oct. 29, 1847, c. 2 miles S Thomasville, Alachua Co. NE 1/4 and SW 1/4 SE 1/4 Sect. 36 Tp. 7 R. 19, south and east. Patent delivered April 28, 1855.

**2716. SMITH, Wm. T.**
Feb. 10, 1829, 2 1/2 miles S Centerville, Leon Co. W 1/2 SW 1/4 Sect. 6 Tp. 1 R. 2, north and east.

**1791. SMITHSON, George B.**
Mar. 28, 1853, 1 1/4 miles E Pine Mount, Suwannee Co. NW 1/4 SE 1/4 Sect. 5 Tp. 4 R. 14, south and east.

**1805. SMITHSON, George B.**
April 1, 1853, 3 miles SSW Lake City, Columbia Co. SE 1/4 SE 1/4 Sect. 34 Tp. 3 R. 16, south and east. Patent delivered Mar. 5, 1860.

**1833. SMITHSON, George B.**
April 20, 1853, 2 3/4 miles SE Lake City, Columbia Co. SW 1/4 SW 1/4 Sect. 25 Tp. 3 R. 16, south and east. Patent delivered Mar. 5, 1860.

**4190. SMYLIE, John M.**
July 25, 1832, 3/4 mile S Darsey, Gadsden Co. NE 1/4 SW 1/4 Sect. 12 Tp. 3 R. 2, north and west.

**476. SNEAD, Anderson**
Sept. 20, 1830, 4 miles WSW Ashville, Jefferson Co. W 1/2 SW 1/4 Sect. 11 Tp. 2 R. 6, north and east.

**4374. SNEAD, Anderson**
June 22, 1833, 5 miles SSE Dill, Jefferson Co. SW 1/4 NE 1/4 Sect. 10 Tp. 2 R. 6, north and east.

**6086. SNELL, Hamlin T.**
Nov. 22, 1836, c. 4 miles NE Grand Ridge, Jackson Co. Lots 5, 6, and 7 Sect. 15 Tp. 4 R. 7, north and west. (240 acres)

**8141. SNELL, Hamlin V.**
Nov. 14, 1839, 4 miles S by E Myson, Calhoun Co. SW 1/4 Sect. 33 Tp. 3 R. 9, south and west.

**4378. SNELL, Stephen W.**
July 17, 1833, 4 1/4 miles E by N Bradfordville, Leon Co. E 1/2 NW 1/4 Sect. 13 Tp. 2 R. 1, north and east.

**4379. SNELL, Stephen W.**
July 17, 1833, 3 3/4 miles E by N Bradfordville, Leon Co. SW 1/4 NW 1/4 Sect. 13 Tp. 2 R. 1, north and east.

**4380. SNELL, Stephen W.**
July 17, 1833, 3 3/4 miles E by N Bradfordville, Leon Co. NW 1/4 SW 1/4 Sect. 13 Tp. 2 R. 1, north and east.

**5984. SNELL, Stephen W.**
Nov. 7, 1836, 2 miles N by W Centerville, Leon Co. SW 1/4 SW 1/4 Sect. 13 Tp. 2 R. 1, north and east.

**6145. SNELL, Stephen W.**
Dec. 5, 1836, 2 miles NE Bradfordville, Leon Co. E 1/2 NE 1/4 Sect. 14 Tp. 2 R. 1, north and east.

**6380. SNELLING, Wm. F.**
Jan. 3, 1837, 5 miles NE by E Welchton, Jackson Co. E 1/2 NW 1/4 Sect. 27 Tp. 6 R. 11, north and west.

**6381. SNELLING, Wm. F.**
Jan. 3, 1837, 5 miles E by N Welchton, Jackson Co. W 1/2 SW 1/4 and S 1/2 NW 1/4 Sect. 26 Tp. 6 R. 11, north and west.

**6755. SNELLING, Wm. F.**
Feb. 6, 1837, 5 1/2 miles ENE Welchton, Jackson Co. W 1/2 SW 1/4 Sect. 23 Tp. 6 R. 11, north and west.

**7976. SNELLING, Wm. F.**
May 23, 1839, 4 1/2 miles E Welchton, Jackson Co. E 1/2 SW 1/4 Sect. 26 Tp. 6 R. 11, north and west.

**4439. SNOWDEN, George D.**
Oct. 22, 1833, 1/4 mile S Indian Ford,

Santa Rosa Co. SE 1/4 SW 1/4 Sect. 2 Tp. 2 R. 27, north and west.

**573. SOLOMON, William**
Nov. 13, 1874, 2 3/4 miles NE Rerdell, Sumter Co. N 1/2 SW 1/4 Sect. 15 Tp. 22(?) R. 22E.

**8579. SOREY, William**
Feb. 14, 1843, 2 1/2 miles N by W Greenwood, Jackson Co. NE 1/4 Sect. 25 Tp. 6 R. 10, north and west.

**8789. SOREY, William**
June 23, 1845, 2 1/2 miles NNW Miller's Ferry, Washington Co. SE 1/4 NW 1/4 Sect. 25 Tp. 6 R. 10, north and west.

**8967. SOREY, William**
Aug. 12, 1846, 3 3/4 miles NNW Greenwood, Jefferson Co. W 1/2 NW 1/4 Sect. 25 Tp. 6 R. 10, north and west.

**4581. SPAIN, David**
May 31, 1834, 2 1/4 miles NNW Greenwood, Jackson Co. E 1/2 NW 1/4 Sect. 26 Tp. 6 R. 10, north and west.

**1512. SPARKMAN, Lewis W.**
Nov. 16, 1852, 3 1/2 miles SE Campville, Alachua Co. NW 1/4 SE 1/4 Sect. 1 Tp. 10 R. 22, south and east. Patent delivered Dec. 14, 1856.

**4127. SPARKMAN, Peter**
Jan. 29, 1856, 2 miles SW Louise, Alachua Co. NW 1/4 SW 1/4 and SW 1/4 NW 1/4 Sect. 2 Tp. 8 R. 20, south and east.

**321. SPARKMAN, Simeon L.**
Feb. 21, 1846, 4 1/2 miles E Terra Ceia Junction, Manatee Co. SE 1/4 Sect. 1 Tp. 34 R. 18, south and east.

**589. SPARKMAN, Simeon L.**
Sept. 27, 1847, at Trapnell, Hillsborough Co. NW 1/4 SE 1/4 Sect. 15 Tp. 29 R. 22, south and east. Transferred to **John McCLAND** Oct. 24, 1849. Transferred to **N. K. SPARKNAN** Jan. 27, 1852. Patent delivered Jan. 1, 1854.

**696. SPARKMAN, Stephen**
(Jr.) Dec. 21, 1849, 3 miles SW Lulu, Columbia Co. SW 1/4 SE 1/4 Sect. 1 Tp. 5 R. 17, south and east. Patent delivered May 2, 1854.

**8492. SPARKS, Martin**
July 22, 1841, 6 1/4 miles N by W McClellan, Jefferson Co. SW 1/4 NW 1/4 Sect. 23 Tp. 2 R. 5, north and east.

**5869. SPEAR, David**
Sept. 30, 1836, 3 miles SSE Ellis, Jackson Co. NW 1/4 SW 1/4 and NE 1/4 SW 1/4 Sect. 23 Tp. 1 R. 10, north and west.
See **Martin HARDIN, #204**

**5392. SPEAR, James**
Oct. 5, 1838, 2 miles S by W Lake Jackson (town), Leon Co. SE 1/4 SW 1/4 Sect. 12 Tp. 1 R. 2, north and west.

**6011. SPEARS, Daniel**
Nov. 15, 1836, 4 miles NW Greenwood, Jackson Co. SE 1/4 Sect. 22 Tp. 6 R. 10, north and west.

**7989. SPEARS, Hugh**
June 15, 1839, 1/4 mile SE Aberdeen, Jackson Co. W 1/2 NE 1/4 and W 1/2 SE 1/4 Sect. 3 Tp. 4 R. 11, north and west.

**7990. SPEARS, Hugh**
June 15, 1839, 1 1/4 miles W Kynesville, Jackson Co. NE 1/4 SW 1/4 and NW 1/4 NE 1/4 Sect. 8 Tp. 4 R. 11, north and west.

**218. SPEARS, Wm.**
(DUP) Dec. 30, 1826, 3 miles SE Welchton Post Office, Jackson Co. NE 1/4 Sect. 12 Tp. 5 R. 11, north and west.

**261. SPEARS, Wm.**
(Sr.) Jan. 1, 1827, 12 miles NW Marianna, Jackson Co. NE 1/4 Sect. 13 Tp. 5 R. 11, north and west.

**2181. SPEER, David**
(of Fla.) Dec. 28, 1827, 2 1/2 miles W Greenwood, Jackson Co. W 1/2 NW 1/4 Sect. 35 Tp. 6 R. 10, north and west.

**580. SPEIGHTE, Thomas**
Aug. 4, 1825, 7 miles NW Tallahassee, Leon Co. E 1/2 NW 1/4 Sect. 9 Tp. 1 R. 1, north and west. 80 acres.

**581. SPEIGHTE, Thomas**
Aug. 4, 1825, 6 miles NW Tallahassee, Leon Co. W 1/2 NE 1/4 Sect. 9 Tp. 1 R. 1, north and west. 80.3 acres.

**6. SPEIGHTE, Thomas**
Aug. 28, 1826, near Florence, Gadsden Co. NW 1/4 Sect. 32 Tp. 3 R. 2, north and west. Rec'd $157.87/100 for 199.76 1/4 acres.

**880. SPEIGHTE, Thomas**
Jan. 16, 1827, 2 miles W Havana, Gadsden Co. E 1/2 SW 1/4 Sect. 32 Tp. 3 R. 2, north and west.

**1009. SPEIGHT, Thomas**
Jan. 25, 1827, 2 miles W Havana, Gadsden Co. W 1/2 SW 1/4 Sect. 32 Tp. 3 R. 2, north and west.

**1061. SPEIGHT, Thomas**
Feb. 3, 1827, 6 miles E Quincy, Gadsden Co. E 1/2 NE 1/4 Sect. 7 Tp. 2 R. 2, north and west.

**1076. SPEIGHT, Thomas**
Feb. 5, 1827, 2 miles W Havana, Gadsden Co. W 1/2 NE 1/4 Sect. 32 Tp. 3 R. 2, north and west.

**1296. SPEIGHT, Thomas**
April 21, 1827, 2 miles ESE Florence, Gadsden Co. W 1/2 NE 1/4 Sect. 7 Tp. 2 R. 2, north and west.

**1801. SPEIGHT, Thomas**
(DUP) June 5, 1827, 2 1/2 miles SSE Florence, Gadsden Co. W 1/2 SW 1/4 Sect. 7 Tp. 2 R. 2, north and west.

**3931. SPEIGHT, Thomas**
(and **M. NICHOLSON**) March 30, 1831, just S Chattahoochee, Gadsden Co. NE 1/4 Sect. 4 Tp. 3 R. 6, north and west.

See **Jesse STEPHENS, #156**

**4332. SPEIR, David**
Mar. 11, 1833, 2 3/4 miles SE Ellis, Jackson Co. SE 1/4 SW 1/4 Sect. 23 Tp. 6 R. 10, north and west.

**4412. SPENCE, Robert**
Sept. 7, 1833, 2 1/4 miles E by S Dill, Jefferson Co. SW 1/4 NE 1/4 Sect. 6 Tp. 2 R. 6, north and east.

**438. SPENCE, Samuel**
Dec. 22, 1828, 2 miles W Norum, Washington Co. NE 1/4 Sect. 14 Tp. 2 R. 16, north and west.

**2782. SPENCER, Samuel S.**
(No date) 3 miles NNE Bradfordville, Leon Co. E 1/2 SW 1/4 Sect. 8 Tp. 1 R. 2, north and east. Receipt for patent delivered Jan. 9, 1869.

**26. SPIER, David**
(Assignee) Oct. 26, 1826, 5 miles W Greenwood, Jackson Co. W 1/2 NW 1/4 Sect. 26 Tp. 6 R. 10, north and west. Pre-emption.

**5219. SPIER, David**
Oct. 15, 1835, 4 1/2 miles NW by N Greenwood, Jackson Co. SW 1/4 SW 1/4 Sect. 23 Tp. 6 R. 10, north and west.

**1099. STAFFORD, Ellis**
(DUP) Feb. 8, 1827, at Rose, Leon Co. W 1/2 NE 1/4 Sect. 25 Tp. 1 R. 2, south and east.

**1100. STAFFORD, Ellis**
Feb. 8, 1827, 1 mile NE Rose, Leon Co. W 1/2 SW 1/4 Sect. 24 Tp. 1 R. 2, south and east.

**2080. STAFFORD, Ellis**
Oct. 15, 1827, 1/4 mile NE Rose, Leon Co. E 1/2 NE 1/4 Sect. 26 Tp. 1 R. 2, south and east.

**2972. STAFFORD, Ellis**
Aug. 1, 1829, 6 miles E Woodville, Leon Co. W 1/2 SE 1/4 Sect. 7 Tp. 2 R. 2, south and east.

**391. STAFFORD, John Mercer**
May 5, 1846, 1 1/4 miles NNE Gulf Hammock, Levy Co. NE 1/4 E 1/2 and NW 1/4 Sect. 32 Tp. 14 R. 16, south and east.

**3850. STAFFORD, Richard**
Jan. 17, 1831, 3 miles S Meridian, Leon Co. E 1/2 SE 1/4 Sect. 6 Tp. 1 R. 2, north and east.

**8244. STAFFORD, William**
Mar. 2, 1840, 1 mile E Havana, Leon Co. W 1/2 SE 1/4 Sect. 2 Tp. 2 R. 2, north and west.

**1997. STAMELAND, John**
July 15, 1827, 6 miles N by E Monticello, Jefferson Co. W 1/2 SE 1/4 Sect. 29 Tp. 3 R. 5, north and east.

**989. STANALAND, Hugh**
Nov. 5, 1847, c. 2 miles S Thomasville, Alachua Co. NE 1/4 and SW 1/44 SE 1/4 Sect. 36 Tp. 7 R. 19, south and east. Patent delivered April 28, 1855.

**988. STANALAND, Samuel T.**
Nov. 5, 1851, 2 miles SE Lynne, Marion Co. Lot No. 4 Sect. 23 Tp. 15 R. 24, south and east. Patent delivered June 22, 1858.

**1907. STANALAND, Samuel T.**
June 20, 1853, 4 miles E Haynesworth, Alachua Co. Lot No. 1 Sect. 23 Tp. 15 R. 20, south and east. Patent delivered June 22, 1858.

**429. STANDLEY, Dicy**
June 12, 1846, near Cara, Marion Co. SE 1/4 SE 1/4 Sect. 15 and NE 1/4

SE 1/4 Sect. 22 and NW 1/4 SE 1/4 Sect. 23 Tp. 13 R. 20, south and east. Patent deliverd Mar. 6, 1856.

**7537. STANDLEY, George W.**
July 16, 1838, 2 miles S by W Dills, Jefferson Co. SW 1/4 SW 1/4 Sect. 13 Tp. 2 R. 5, north and east.

**8103. STANDLEY, George W.**
Oct. 1, 1839, 7 miles N by E McClellan, Jefferson Co. NW 1/4 SW 1/4 Sect. 13 Tp. 2 R. 5, north and east.

**422. STANDLEY, John Blackstone**
June 1, 1846, 2 miles NW Trenton, Gilchrist Co. NE 1/4 Sect. 5 and W 1/2 NW 1/4 Sect. 4 Tp. 10 R. 15, south and east. Patent delivered Feb. 9, 1856.

**428. STANDLEY, John Blackstone**
June 11, 1846, c. 2 miles NW Trenton, Gilchrist Co. W 1/2 NE 1/4 Sect. 4 Tp. 10 R. 15, south and east. Patent delivered Feb. 9, 1856.

**496. STANDLEY, John Blackston**
Jan. 1, 1847, 3 1/2 miles NW Trenton, Gilchrist Co. SE 1/4 NE 1/4 Sect. 29 Tp. 9 R. 15, south and east.

**427. STANDLEY, Liepha**
June 11, 1846, 1/2 mile NW Hague, Alachua Co. W 1/2 SE 1/4 Sect. 17 Tp. 8 R. 19, south and east.

**2109. STANDLEY, Seaborn I.**
Aug. 23, 1853, 1 1/4 miles SE Haynesworth, Alachua Co. S 1/2 Lot No. 5 Sect. 4 Tp. 8 R. 19, south and east. Patent delivered Oct. 10, 1857.

**578. STANDLEY, Zelpha**
July 29, 1847, 1 mile N Hague, Alachua Co. SW 1/4 SE 1/4 Sect. 8 and NW 1/4 NW 1/4 Sect. 17 Tp. 8 R. 19, south and east.

**579. STANDLEY, Zelpha**
July 29, 1847, 1 mile NW Hague, Alachua Co. NE 1/4 SW 1/4 Sect. 18 Tp. 8 R. 19, south and east.

**625. STANDLEY, Zelpha**
Feb. 2, 1848, at Alachua, Alachua Co. N 1/2 NE 1/4 Sect. 14 Tp. 8 R. 18, south and east.

**626. STANDLEY, Zelpha**
Feb. 27, 1848, 1/2 mile NE Burnettes Lake, Alachua Co. SW 1/4 NE 1/4 Sect. 7 Tp. 8 R. 19, south and east.

**633. STANDLEY, Zelpha**
Mar. 29, 1848, 1 mile NW Lexington, Alachua Co. NE 1/4 NW 1/4 Sect. 17 Tp. 9 R. 16, south and east.

**654. STANDLEY, Zelpha**
July 15, 1848, 2 1/2 miles NE Hague, Alachua Co. SW 1/4 NE 1/4 Sect. 14 Tp. 8 R. 19, south and east.

**530. STANDLY, Dicy**
Feb. 26, 1847, 1 mile SE Haynesworth, Alachua Co. SE 1/4 SE 1/4 Sect. 5 Tp. 8 R. 19, south and east. Patent delivered March 6, 1856. (see Dicy STANDLEY, #429)

**405. STANDLY, John Blackstone**
May 7, 1846, 2 miles NW Trenton, Gilchrist Co. NE 1/4 NW 1/4 Sect. 8 Tp. 10 R. 15, south and east. Patent delivered Feb. 9, 1856. (see **John Blackstone STANDLEY**)

**531. STANDLY, Thomas Cotton**
Feb. 26, 1847, 1 1/2 miles E Burnetts Lake, Alachua Co. NW 1/4 SE 1/4 Sect. 8 Tp. 8 R. 19, south and east. Patent delivered March 6, 1856.

**61. STAFFORD, John M.**
Sept. 6, 1844, 2 miles S Gulf Hammock, Levy Co. W 1/2 NW 1/4 and W 1/2 SE 1/4 Sect. 32 Tp. 14 R. 16, south and east. Patent delivered July 7, 1845.

**89. STAFFORD, John Mercer**
Dec. 21, 1844, 2 miles SE Gulf Hammock, Levy Co. W 1/2 SW 1/4 Sect. 33 Tp. 14 R. 16, south and east. Patent delivered July 7, 1845.

**114. STAFFORD, Joshua**
Jan. 6, 1845, just NW Homosassa Springs, Citrus Co. W 1/2 SE 1/4 Sect. 21 Tp. 19 R. 17, south and east. "Date of patent Jan. 19, 1846. Recorded Vol. 1, P. 71.". Delivered patent to **Joshua STAFFORD** July 2, 1857, **Jesse CARTER**, Register, Land Office, Tampa.

**115. STAFFORD, Joshua**
Jan. 6, 1845, just S Homosassa Springs, Citrus Co. NE 1/4 Sect. 33 Tp. 19 R. 17, south and east. Date of patent Jan. 19, 1845. Delivered patent to **Joshua STAFFORD**, Feb. 2, 1857. **Jesse CARTER**, Register, Land Office, Tampa.

**326. STAFFORD, Lafayette**
Feb. 25, 1846, near Montbrook, Levy Co. SW 1/4 SW 1/4 Sect. 26 and SE 1/4 SE 1/4 Sect. 27 Tp. 13 R. 18,

south and east. Patent delivered June 16, 1858.

**1254. STANLAND, Samuel T.**
Mar. 16, 1852, 3 miles SE Lynne, Marion Co. Lot No. 5 Sect. 23 Tp. 15 R. 24, south and east. Patent delivered June 22, 1858.

**3265. STANLEY, George W.**
Feb. 9, 1830, 4 miles E Monticello, Jefferson Co. E 1/2 SE 1/4 Sect. 25 Tp. 2 R. 5, north and east.

**3651. STANLEY, George W.**
Oct. 11, 1830, 4 1/2 miles S Dills, Jefferson Co. W 1/2 SW 1/4 Sect. 30 Tp. 2 R. 6, north and east.

**2866. STANLEY, Thomas C.**
Aug. 9, 1854, 1 mile SW Haynesworth, Alachua Co. S 1/2 Lot No. 6 Sect. 4 Tp. 8 R. 19, south and east. Patent delivered Oct. 10, 1854.

**4042. STANLEY, William**
July 20, 1831, 1/4 mile N McClellan, Jefferson Co. W 1/2 SE 1/4 Sect. 10 Tp. 1 R. 5, north and east.

**4080. STANLEY, William**
Sept. 10, 1831, 8 miles SE Dills, Jefferson Co. W 1/2 NW 1/4 Sect. 29 Tp. 2 R. 6, north and east.

**6297. STANLEY, William**
Dec. 24, 1836, 3 miles SSE Monticello, Jefferson Co. SW 1/4 NE 1/4 Sect. 36 Tp. 2 R. 5, north and east.

**8514. STANLEY, William**
Jan. 8, 1842, 3 1/4 miles E by S Greensboro, Gadsden Co. SE 1/4 SE 1/4 Sect. 11 Tp. 2 R. 5, north and east.

**546. STAPLE, William**
Nov. 26, 1834, at Coatsville, Holmes Co. NW 1/4 SE 1/4 Sect. 6 Tp. 2 R. 14, north and west. Sold to **Levi POTTER** March 20, 1835. Teste: **Thos. CARTER** and **Shelton BRYANT**.

**4671. STAPLE, William**
Dec. 4, 1834, 1 mile E Greenhead, Washington Co. W 1/2 SE 1/4 Sect. 7 Tp. 2 R. 14, north and west.

**3176. STAPLES, Wm.**
Dec. 22, 1829, 4 miles W Everett, Washington Co. W 1/2 NE 1/4 Sect. 10 Tp. 3 R. 14, north and west.

**6847. STAPLETON, Alexander**
March 7, 1837, 1/4 mile SE Facil, Hamilton Co. (Facil is 4 miles NW White Springs), W 1/2 SW 1/4 Sect. 26 Tp. 1 R. 15, south and east.

**8029. STAPLETON, Alexander**
Aug. 12, 1839, 3 miles N by W Noles, Washington Co. E 1/2 NW 1/4 Sect. 26 Tp. 1 R. 15, south and east.

**1235. STAPLETON, John**
(DUP) March 20, 1827, 5 miles WSW Monticello, Jefferson Co. E 1/2 SE 1/4 Sect. 32 Tp. 2 R. 4, north and east.

**1809. STAPLETON, William**
June 5, 1827, 5 miles WSW Monticello, Jefferson Co. E 1/2 SW 1/4 Sect. 33 Tp. 2 R. 4, north and east.

**1810. STAPLETON, William**
June 5, 1827, 6 miles WSW Monticello, Jefferson Co. W 1/2 NW 1/4 Sect. 4 Tp. 1 R. 4, north and east.

**1813. STAPLETON, William**
June 5, 1827, 5 miles SE Sawdust, Gadsden Co. E 1/2 SW 1/4 Sect. 2 Tp. 1 R. 4, north and west.

**1920. STAPLETON, William**
(DUP) June 18, 1827, at Graceville, Jackson Co. E 1/2 SE 1/4 Sect. 33 Tp. 7 R. 13, north and west.

**2020. STAPLETON, William**
Aug. 9, 1827, at Graceville, Jackson Co. W 1/2 SW 1/4 Sect. 34 Tp. 7 R. 13, north and west.

**7814. STARLING, Levi**
Jan. 14, 1839, 1/4 mile E Waco, Madison Co. S 1/2 SE 1/4 Sect. 20 Tp. 1 R. 9, south and east.

**8313. STARLING, Levi**
May 2, 1840, 2 miles NNW Madison, Madison Co. NW 1/4 SE 1/4 Sect. 20 Tp. 1 R. 9, south and east.

**591. STEIFEL, William Mantz**
Oct. 2, 1847, 3 1/2 miles W Belleview, Marion Co. SW 1/4 Sect. 33 Tp. 15 R. 22, south and east.

**8794. STELL, John N.**
July 18, 1845, 1 3/4 miles SSW Cox, Calhoun Co. E 1/2 SW 1/4 Sect. 7 Tp. 2 R. 5, north and west.

**8908. STELL, Thomas**
Feb. 20, 1846, 2 3/4 miles W by S Alliance, Calhoun Co. NW 1/4 NW 1/4 Sect. 16 Tp. 2 R. 9, north and west.

**6280. STEPHENS, Basreal G.**
Dec. 22, 1836, 4 miles ENE El Destino, Jefferson Co. NE 1/4 NW 1/4 Sect. 3 Tp. 1 R. 3, south and east.

**6455. STEPHENS, Bazzael G.**
Jan. 7, 1837, 3 miles S Lloyd, Jefferson Co. SW 1/4 SW 1/4 Sect. 34 Tp. 1 R. 3, north and east.

**401. STEPHENS, Benjamin**
May 5, 1827, 3 miles ENE Marianna, Jackson Co. E 1/2 SE 1/4 Sect. 36 Tp. 5 R. 10, north and east.

**4504. STEPHENS, Benjamin**
Jan. 6, 1834, 1/2 mile S Braswells, Jefferson Co. SE 1/4 NE 1/4 Sect. 28 Tp. 1 R. 4, north and east.

**7965. STEPHENS, Benjamin**
May 16, 1839, 2 miles E by N Cypress, Jackson Co. SW 1/4 NE 1/4 Sect. 23 Tp. 4 R. 9, north and west.

**4123. STEPHENS, Benjamin Joseph**
Jan. 25, 1832, 1 1/4 miles E Braswells, Madison Co. E 1/2 SW 1/4 Sect. 14 Tp. 1 R. 4, north and east.

**2848. STEPHENS, Clem W.**
June 12, 1829, 3 miles NW Wacissa, Jefferson Co. E 1/2 SE 1/4 Sect. 26 Tp. 1 R. 3, south and east.

**2214. STEPHENS, Clement**
(of Fla.) Jan. 10, 1828, 3 miles NW Wacissa, Jefferson Co. NE 1/4 Sect. 26 Tp. 1 R. 3, south and east.

**2215. STEPHENS, Clement**
(of Fla.) Jan. 10, 1828, 3 miles NW Wacissa, Jefferson Co. W 1/2 SW 1/4 Sect. 25 Tp. 1 R. 3, south and east.

**STEPHENS, C. W. see Andrew N. JOHNSON**

**1020. STEPHENS, Geofrey**
Jan. 29, 1827, 2 miles S Quincy, Gadsden Co. E 1/2 NW 1/4 Sect. 18 Tp. 2 R. 3, north and west.

**1245. STEPHENS, Godfoy**
(DUP) April 10, 1827, 1 mile S Quincy, Gadsden Co. W 1/2 NW 1/4 Sect. 18 Tp. 2 R. 3, north and west.

**192. STEPHENS, Godfrey**
(DUP) Dec. 29, 1826, 5 miles SE Quincy, Gadsden Co. NE 1/4 Sect. 18 Tp. 2 R. 3, north and west.

**2002. STEPHENS, Godfrey**
July 18, 1827, at Quincy, Gadsden Co. NW 1/4 Sect. 7 Tp. 2 R. 3, north and west. For the use of Gadsden County. See **Duncan McKENZIE, #221**

**4543. STEPHENS, Gore**
Jan. 7, 1834, 2 miles NNE Centerville, Leon Co. SE 1/4 NE 1/4 Sect. 8 Tp. 2 R. 2, north and east.

**5194. STEPHENS, James H.**
Feb. 9, 1860, 1 mile ENE Haynesworth, Alachua Co. NE 1/4 NE 1/4 Sect. 28 Tp. 7 R. 19, south and east.

**156. STEPHENS, Jesse**
(DUP) (Jr.) Dec. 28, 1836, 1 mile SE Havana, Gadsden Co. SW 1/4 Sect. 5 Tp. 2 R. 2, north and west. Transferred to **Thomas SPEIGHT**, Dec. 28, 1826.

**870. STEPHENS, Jesse**
Jan. 16, 1827, at Quincy, Gadsden Co. W 1/2 NE 1/4 Sect. 8 Tp. 3 R. 2, north and west.

**5591. STEPHENS, Jesse**
April 11, 1836, 2 miles N Round Lake, Jackson Co. SE 1/4 SW 1/4 and NW 1/4 SE 1/4 Sect. 12 Tp. 3 R. 2, north and west.

**5208. STEPHENS, John**
Oct. 13, 1835, 1/2 mile SW by S Capitola, Leon Co. E 1/2 SE 1/4 Sect. 32 Tp. 1 R. 3, north and east.

**5209. STEPHENS, John**
Oct. 13, 1835, 1 mile NNE El Destino, Jefferson Co. NW 1/4 NE 1/4 Sect. 5 Tp. 1 R. 3, south and east.

**6735. STEPHENS, John**
Feb. 4, 1837, 2 miles N Lloyd, Jefferson Co. SE 1/4 NW 1/4 Sect. 12 Tp. 1 R. 3, south and east.

**7861. STEPHENS, Richard**
Feb. 11, 1839, 5 miles W Rock Creek, Jackson Co. NE 1/4 SE 1/4 Sect. 20 Tp. 3 R. 10, north and west.

**2845. STEVENS, Clement W.**
June 8, 1829, 4 1/2 miles E Capitola, Jefferson Co. W 1/2 NW 1/4 Sect. 25 Tp. 1 R. 3, south and east.

**3208. STEVENS, Jesse**
Jan. 8, 1830, 1 1/4 miles SE Jamieson, Gadsden Co. E 1/2 SW 1/4 Sect. 8 Tp. 3 R. 2, north and west.

**7339. STEVENS, John**
Feb. 19, 1838, 1/4 mile N Rose, Leon Co. E 1/2 NE 1/4 Sect. 27 Tp. 1 R. 2, south and east.

**4348. STEVENS, Thomas H.**
April 13, 1833, 1/2 mile N Wacissa, Jefferson Co. NW 1/4 SE 1/4 Sect. 31 Tp. 1 R. 4, south and east.

**7739. STEWART, Ann**
Dec. 1, 1838, 2 3/4 miles W Jasper, Hamilton Co. NE 1/4 SW 1/4 Sect. 1

Tp. 1 R. 13, north and east.

**314. STEWART, Daniel McLaughling (Sr.)** Feb. 12, 1846, c. 5 miles W Dukes, Union Co. N 1/2 NE 1/4 Sect. 22 Tp. 6 R. 18, south and east. Patent delivered April 19, 1856.

**315. STEWART, Daniel McLaughling (Sr.)** July 12, 1846, c. 5 miles W Dukes, Union Co. W 1/2 SW 1/4 Sect. 14 Tp. 6 R. 18, south and east. Patent delivered Oct. 4, 1836(?).

**316. STEWART, Daniel McLaughling (Sr.)** Feb. 12, 1846, 3 miles SE Providence, Union Co. W 1/2 NW 1/4 Sect. 14 Tp. 6 R. 18, south and east. Patent delivered July 16, 1856.

**331. STEWART, Daniel McLaughling (Sr.)** Feb. 27, 1846, 6 miles NW Santa Fe, Alachua Co. E 1/2 NW 1/4 Sect. 33 Tp. 6 R. 18, south and east. Patent delivered Oct. 4, 1856.

**332. STEWART, Daniel McLaughling (Sr.)** Feb. 27, 1846, 5 1/2 miles W Dukes, Union Co. E 1/2 NW 1/4 Sect. 22 Tp. 6 R. 18, south and east. Patent delivered April 10, 1858.

**664. STEWART, Eliza Mary** Oct. 9, 1848, c. 5 miles SW Hildreth, Suwannee Co. Lot No. 1 Sect. 3 Tp. 7 R. 14, south and east.

**4618. STEWART, James** Oct. 8, 1834, 1/4 mile N Ocklocknee, Leon Co. Lot No. 2 Sect. 25 Tp. 2 R. 2, north and west.

**7620. STEWART, James J.** Sept 1, 1838, 2 1/2 miles NNW Westlake, Hamilton Co. S 1/2 SE 1/4 Sect. 32 Tp. 2 R. 12, north and east.

**984. STEWART, John L.** Nov. 4, 1851, 1 mile N Conner, Marion Co. E 1/2 NW 1/4 Sect. 26 Tp. 14 R. 23, south and east.

**7388. STEWART, Jonathan K.** Mar. 6, 1838, 2 1/2 miles SSE Avoca, Hamilton Co. E 1/2 NE 1/4 Sect. 26 Tp. 2 R. 13, north and east.

**7389. STEWART, Jonathan K.** Mar. 6, 1838, 3 miles SE by S Avoca, Hamilton Co. NW 1/4 NW 1/4 Sect. 25 Tp. 2 R. 13, north and east.

**4662. STEWART, John** Nov. 17, 1834, 1 mile W Miccosukee, Leon Co. NE 1/4 SW 1/4 Sect. 12 Tp. 2 R. 2, north and east.

**4730. STEWART, John** Dec. 20, 1834, 2 miles N by E Marion, Hamilton Co. NE 1/4 NW 1/4 Sect. 20 Tp. 1 R. 14, north and east.

**7966. STEWART, John** May 16, 1839, 3/4 mile S by W Marianna, Jackson Co. NE 1/4 SE 1/4 Sect. 15 Tp. 4 R. 10, north and west.

**623. ST. GEORGE, Edward** (of Ga.) Dec. 8, 1825, 3 miles SE Meridian, Leon Co. Lot No. 1 Sect. 27 Tp. 3 R. 1, north and east.

**624. ST. GEORGE, Edward** (of Ga.) Dec. 8, 1825, 3 1/2 miles N Bradfordville, Leon Co. Lot No. 2 Sect. 34 Tp. 3 R. 1, north and east.

**625. ST. GEORGE, Edward** (of Ga.) Dec. 8, 1825, 1 mile NE Meridian, Leon Co. W 1/2 SE 1/4 Sect. 17 Tp. 3 R. 1, north and east.

**626. ST. GEORGE, Edward** (of Ga.) Dec. 8, 1825, 1 mile NE Meridian, Leon Co. E 1/2 SW 1/4 Sect. 17 Tp. 3 R. 1, north and east.

**5960. STINSON, Sarah** Nov. 3, 1836, 2 3/4 miles SSE Inwood, Jackson Co. W 1/2 SW 1/4 Sect. 8 Tp. 3 R. 7, north and east.

**5481. STOCKTON, John N. C.** Feb. 20, 1836, at Midway, Gadsden Co. W 1/2 NE 1/4 Sect. 8 Tp. 1 R. 2, north and west.

**1947. STOKES, Burrel T.** July 16, 1853, 1/4 mile NE Hawthorne, Alachua Co. Lot No. 10 Sect. 27 Tp. 10 R. 18, south and east. Patent delivered Oct. 16, 1857.

**4250. STOKES, Burrel T.** Mar. 17, 1856, 1 mile SSE Half-Moon, Alachua Co. NW 1/4 SW 1/4 Sect. 30 Tp. 10 R. 18, south and east. Patent delivered (no date given).

**4251. STOKES, Burrel T.** Mar. 17, 1856, 1 1/4 miles SE Half-Moon, Alachua Co. S 1/2 NW 1/4 and NE 1/4 SW 1/4 Sect. 30 Tp. 10 R. 18, south and east. Patent delivered (no date given).

**2455. STOKES, William M.** Feb. 23, 1854, 2 1/2 miles W by S Southside, Marion Co. Lots No. 6 and 7 Sect. 20 Tp. 12 R. 20, south and east.

**382. STONE, Benjamin Isaiah**

April 28, 1846, 1 mile N Shady, Marion Co. SE 1/4 NE 1/4 Sect. 11 and NW 1/4 NE 1/4 Sect. 14 Tp. 16 R. 21, south and east.

**2872. STONE, David C.**
July 6, 1829, just SE Ocheesee, Calhoun Co. E 1/2 SE 1/4 Sect. 6 Tp. 2 R. 7, north and west. Transferred July 7, 1829, to **Seaton GRANTLAND**. Teste: **H. D. STONE**.

**49. STONE, Henry D.**
Nov. 8, 1826, near Jacob Post Office, Jackson Co. NE 1/2 Sect. 23 Tp. 5 R. 11, north and west.

**2897. STONE, Henry D.**
July 7, 1829, 2 miles SSW Millspring, Jackson Co. E 1/2 SW 1/4 Sect. 20 Tp. 3 R. 7, north and west. Transferred to **Seaton GRANTLAND**, July 7, 1829.

**2898. STONE, Henry D.**
July 7, 1829, 1 1/4 miles S Millspring, Jackson Co. E 1/2 NW 1/4 Sect. 29 Tp. 3 R. 7, north and west. Transferred July 7, 1829, to **Seaton GRANTLAND**.

**2899. STONE, Henry D.**
July 7, 1829, 2 miles S by E Millspring, Jackson Co. E 1/2 SW 1/4 Sect. 20 Tp. 3 R. 7, north and west. Transferred July 7, 1829, to **Seaton GRANTLAND**.

**8139. STONE, Henry D.**
Nov. 13, 1839, 4 1/2 miles E Henderson, Calhoun Co. SE 1/4 Sect. 13 Tp. 2 R. 8, north and west. Transferred to **Edwin G. BOOTH** on Nov. 14, 1839.

**8170. STONE, Henry D.**
Dec. 6, 1839, 5 1/2 miles E Henderson, Calhoun Co. SW 1/4 Sect. 13 Tp. 2 R. 8, north and west. Transferred to **Edwin G. BOOTH** on Dec. 6, 1839.

**8344. STONE, Henry D.**
June 17, 1840, 2 miles NNE Sink Creek, Jackson Co. NE 1/4 Sect. 27 Tp. 3 R. 9, south and west.

**199. STONE, Jas. M.**
(DUP) Dec. 30, 1826, 4 miles N Cottondale, Jackson Co. NW 1/4 Sect. 11 Tp. 5 R. 11, north and west. Transferred to **R. C. ALLEN** on Dec. 30, 1826 by **David THOMAS**, attorney in fact for **James M. STONE**.

**23. STONE, L. M.**
Oct. 23, 1826, c. 5 miles N Cottondale, Jackson Co. SE 1/4 Sect. 14 Tp. 5 R. 11, north and west. Above transferred to **R. C. ALLEN and Co.**, Oct. 24, 1826.

**42. STONE, L. M.**
(Assignee of **M. MARSHALL**) Nov. 7, 1826, 3 miles N Cottondale, Jackson Co. SW 1/4 Sect. 13 Tp. 5 R. 11, north and west. (Pre-emption) Assigned to **David THOMAS** by **L. M. STONE**, Nov. 8, 1826. Transferred to **John CLARK** by **David THOMAS**, Jan. 2, 1827, in the presence of **Geo. W. WARD**, Register.

**139. STONE, L. M.**
(Per **Sam'l DELK**) Dec. 26, 1826, 2 miles SE Welchton Station, Jackson Co. SE 1/4 Sect. 36 Tp. 3 R. 11, north and west. Transferred to **Sam'l R. OVERTON**, Dec. 26, 1826.

**455. STONE, L. M.**
(Assignee of **Stephen RICHARDS**) Apr. 28, 1829, 2 miles S Ocheesee, Liberty Co. Lot No. 7 Sect. 5 Tp. 2 R. 7, north and west. Transferred from **L. M. STONE** to **B. F. PERRY**, July 1, 1829. Transferred from **B. F. PERRY** to **Wm. TONEY**, July 7, 1829. Receiver's Receipt.

**6806. STORY, James**
Mar. 1, 1837, 6 miles SW Aucilla, Jefferson Co. SE 1/4 SW 1/4 Sect. 1 Tp. 1 R. 5, south and east. Indorsed to **Wm. ADAMS** on Mar. 2, 1837. Teste: **Cornelius BEAZLEY**.

**3010. STOWERS, Samuel**
Sept. 4, 1829, 3 miles ESE Marianna, Jackson Co. SE 1/4 Sect. 12 Tp. 4 R. 10, north and west.

**STOWERY, Samuel** see **Robert B. COBB**, #2326.

**STRAIN(?), Thomas A.** see **Joseph McBRIDE**.

**8055. STRICKLAND, Samuel**
Aug. 23, 1839, 3 3/4 miles NNW Greensboro, Gadsden Co. SE 1/4 SW 1/4 Sect. 2 Tp. 2 R. 6, north and west. Transferred to **Archibald McPATTER**, Dec. 23, 1840. Transferred back to **Sam'l STRICKLAND**, Sept. 16, 1843.

**7934. STRICKLAND, Vincent J.**
April 11, 1839, 4 3/4 miles E by N Leonton, Jefferson Co. E 1/2 SE 1/4 Sect. 6 Tp. 2 R. 5, south and east.

**8649. STRICKLAND, Vinson J.**

Feb. 28, 1844, 3 miles E Clia, Liberty Co. NE 1/4 NE 1/4 Sect. 7 Tp. 2 R. 5, south and east.

**749. STRICKLAND, William**
Aug. 19, 1850, near Graham, Bradford Co. SW 1/4 NE 1/4 Sect. 25 Tp. 7 R. 20, south and east. Patent delivered Nov. 13, 1856.

**1932. STRICKLAND, William**
June 8, 1853, 1 mile N Louise, Alachua Co. S 1/2 NW 1/4 Sect. 30 Tp. 7 R. 21, south and east. Patent delivered Nov. 13, 1856.

**1933. STRICKLAND, William**
June 8, 1853, 3 1/2 miles W Graham, Bradford Co. NE 1/4 NW 1/4 and SW 1/4 NW 1/4 Sect. 25 Tp. 7 R. 20, south and east. Patent delivered Nov. 13, 1856.

**1934. STRICKLAND, William**
July 8, 1853, 1 3/4 miles SW Graham, Bradford Co. NE 1/4 NE 1/4 Sect. 36 Tp. 7 R. 20, south and east. Patent delivered Nov. 13, 1856.

**5884. STRICTLAND, Vinson I.**
Oct. 5, 1836, 3 1/4 miles NNE Leonton, Jefferson Co. NE 1/4 SE 1/4 Sect. 1 Tp. 2 R. 4, south and east.

**6330. STRINGER, David C.**
Dec. 28, 1836, 4 miles ESE Wadesboro, Jefferson Co. NE 1/4 SE 1/4 Sect. 1 Tp. 2 R. 4, south and east.

**1173. STRINGFELLOW, James**
(DUP) Feb. 25, 1827, 4 1/2 miles N Lake Jackson Station, Leon Co. NE 1/4 Sect. 17 Tp. 2 R. 1, north and west. Sold to **Wm. P. MONROE**, Sept. 27, 1828.

**4836. STROMAN, Jacob**
Jan. 31, 1835, 1 1/4 miles N Centerville, Leon Co. SW 1/4 NE 1/4 Sect. 12 Tp.2 R. 1, north and east.

**4837. STROMAN, Jacob**
Jan. 31, 1835, 1 1/4 miles N by W Centerville, Leon Co. SE 1/4 NW 1/4 Sect. 12 Tp. 2 R. 1, north and east.

**6148. STROMAN, Jacob**
Dec. 5, 1836, 2 1/2 miles N Centerville, Leon Co. NW 1/4 NE 1/4 and NE 1/4 NW 1/4 Sect. 12 Tp. 2 R. 1, north and east.

**6149. STROMAN, Jacob**
Dec. 5, 1836, 2 1/2 miles N by W Centerville, Leon Co. W 1/2 NW 1/4 Sect. 12 Tp. 2 R. 1, north and east.

**4703. STUDSTILL, Emanuel**
Jan. 7, 1858, 1 mile N Judson, Levy Co. E 1/2 NE 1/4 Sect. 33 and W 1/2 NW 1/4 Sect. 34 Tp. 11 R. 15, south and east. Patent delivered 1876.

**5244. STUDSTILL, Emanuel**
May 14, 1860, 1 mile N Adam, Alachua Co. SE 1/4 SE 1/4 Sect. 28 Tp. 11 R. 15, south and east. Patent delivered Feb. 24, 1875.

**5847. SUMMERLIN, Elisha**
Sept. 14, 1836, 1 3/4 miles NW by N Cherrylake, Madison Co. NW 1/4 NW 1/4 Sect. 18 Tp. 2 R. 9, north and east.

**6130. SUMMERLIN, Elisha**
Dec. 23, 1836, 2 miles WSW Cherrylake, Madison Co. E 1/2 NW 1/4 Sect. 18 Tp. 2 R. 9, north and east.

**6544. SUMMERLIN, Elisha**
Jan. 14, 1837, 1/2 mile W Cherrylake, Madison Co. SW 1/4 SW 1/4 Sect. 8 Tp. 2 R. 9, north and east.

**7424. SUMMERLIN, Elisha**
Mar. 27, 1838, 1 mile N by W Cherrylake, Madison Co. W 1/2 SW 1/4 Sect. 5 Tp. 2 R. 9, north and east.

**7750. SUMMERLIN, Elisha**
Dec. 5, 1838, 1 mile NNW Cherrylake, Madison Co. W 1/2 NE 1/4 Sect. 7 Tp. 2 R. 9, north and east.

**8179. SUMMERLIN, Elisha**
Dec. 14, 1839, 1 mile NNW Cherrylake, Madison Co. NE 1/4 SE 1/4 Sect. 6 Tp. 2 R. 9, north and east.

**281. SUMMERLIN, Jacob**
(Jr.) Jan. 19, 1846, near Youmans, Hillsborough Co. SW 1/4 NW 1/4 and NE 1/4 SW 1/4 Sect. 5 Tp. 28 R. 22, south and east. Transferred Jan. 20, 1849 to **Perline HOLLINGSWORTH**. "Joseph HOWELL, (?) BROWN, Justice of the Peace. Acknowledged before me this the 20th day of Jan., 1849. **J. W. ROBARTS**, Clerk."

**4663. SUTTON, Andrew**
Nov. 18, 1834, 2 miles SSW Concord, Gadsden Co. SE 1/4 SE 1/4 Sect. 23 Tp. 3 R. 2, north and west.

**3786. SUTTON, Oliver**
Dec. 9, 1830, 4 1/2 miles WSW Ellis, Jackson Co. E 1/2 SE 1/4 Sect. 13 Tp.

6 R. 11, north and west.
**6743. SUTTON, Shaderach**
Feb. 6, 1837, 1 1/2 miles SSE Jasper, Hamilton Co. SW 1/4 SE 1/4 Sect. 9 Tp. 1 R. 14, north and east.
**6220. SUTTON, Shadrach**
Dec. 15, 1836, just southward Blountstown, Calhoun Co. Lots No. 9, 10, 11, and 12 Fractional Sect. 33 Tp. 1 R. 8, north and west.
**6231. SUTTON, Shadrach**
Dec. 16, 1836, 1/4 mile NW Selman, Calhoun Co. NE 1/4 NE 1/4 Sect. 28 Tp. 2 R. 8, north and west.
**7090. SUTTON, Shadrack**
Nov. 14, 1837, 1/2 mile SE Blountstown, Calhoun Co. Lot No. 4 Sect. 33 Tp. 2 R. 8, north and west.
**8353. SUTTON, Shadrack**
June 18, 1840, 1 1/4 miles E Flower's Still, Calhoun Co. Lots No. 6 and 7 Sect. 4 Tp. 1 R. 8, south and west.
**8354. SUTTON, Shadrack**
June 18, 1840, 3 1/2 miles E by S Selman, Calhoun Co. W 1/2 NW 1/4 Lots No. 1 and 2 Sect. 36 Tp. 2 R. 8, north and west.
**6843. SUTTON, Shederich**
Mar. 6, 1837, 1/2 mile SE Jasper, Hamilton Co. E 1/2 SE 1/4 Sect. 9 Tp. 1 R. 14, north and east.
**243. SUTTON, Theophilus**
(Heirs of) Dec. 30, 1826, 5 miles E Welchton, Jackson Co. NW 1/4 Sect. 32 Tp. 6 R. 11, north and wets.
**2568. SUTTON, Theophilus**
Dec. 16, 1828, 6 miles E by N Welchton, Jackson Co. E 1/2 NE 1/4 Sect. 25 Tp. 6 R. 11, north and west.
**2569. SUTTON, Theophilus**
Dec. 16, 1828, 7 1/2 miles E by N Welchton, Jackson Co. W 1/2 NW 1/4 Sect. 36 Tp. 6 R. 10, north and west.
**4587. SUVIS, Roneo**
June 23, 1834, 3 miles NNW Chattahoochee, Gadsden Co. Lot No. 5 Sect. 30 Tp. 4 R. 6, north and west.
**8939. SWAILS, James**
April 20, 1846, 3 1/4 miles NNW Betts, Washington Co. NW 1/4 SW 1/4 Sect. 28 Tp. 2 R. 12, north and west.
**9775. SWAIN, Robert**
Jan. 14, 1892, 1 3/4 miles SW Carleton, Putnam Co. Lots 1 and W 1/2 NE 1/4 Sect. 15 Tp. 10S R. 23E.
**2455. SWEET, Gasper**
Aug. 12, 1828, 3 miles ESE Sawdust, Gadsden Co. Lot No. 3 Sect. 36 Tp. 2 R. 4, north and west.
**4981. SWEET, Gasper**
May 23, 1835, 1/2 mile SW Mears Spur, Gadsden Co. SE 1/4 NW 1/4 Sect. 7 Tp. 3 R. 5, north and west.
**2939. SWEET, Gospero**
July 15, 1829, 2 miles S Vernon, Washington Co. NE 1/4 Sect. 11 Tp. 2 R. 15, north and west.
**2940. SWEET, Gospero**
July 15, 1829, 2 miles S Vernon, Washington Co. W 1/2 NE 1/4 Sect. 11 Tp. 2 R. 15, north and west.
**2944. SWEET, Gospero**
July 20, 1829, 1 1/2 miles S Vernon, Washington Co. E 1/2 NW 1/4 Sect. 11 Tp. 2 R. 15, north and west.
**3977. SWEET, Gospero**
May 27, 1831, 3 miles S Vernon, Washington Co. W 1/2 NE 1/4 Sect. 14 Tp. 2 R. 15, north and west.
**6805. SWILLEY, Calvin E.**
Mar. 1, 1837, 2 1/2 miles NNW Westlake, Hamilton Co. NE 1/4 SE 1/4 Sect. 29 Tp. 2 R. 12, north and east.
**5159. SYFRETT, John A.**
Sept. 28, 1835, 2 1/2 miles S by E Greenwood, Jackson Co. W 1/2 NE 1/4 Sect. 17 Tp. 5 R. 9, north and west.
**5492. SYFRETT, John A.**
Feb. 25, 1836, 5 1/4 miles W by N Dellwood, Jackson Co. NE 1/4 NW 1/4 Sect. 17 Tp. 5 R. 9, north and west.
**7791. SYFRETT, John A.**
Jan. 5, 1839, at Greenwood, Jackson Co. SE 1/4 Sect. 31 Tp. 6 R. 9, north and west.
**8965. SYFRETT, John A.**
Aug. 10, 1846, 1/2 mile N Greenwood, Jefferson Co. SE 1/4 NE 1/4 Sect. 31 Tp. 6 R. 9, north and west.
**913. SYKES, Guilford**
July 21, 1851, 1 mile NW Alachua, Alachua Co. SE 1/4 NE 1/4 Sect. 10 Tp. 8 R. 18, south and east.

**7560. SYLVESTER, Joseph H.**
July 31, 1838, 3/4 mile N Florence, Gadsden Co. SW 1/4 NE 1/4 Sect. 35 Tp. 3 R. 3, north and west.

**1891. SYMS, William**
June 14, 1853, 3/4 mile SE Lenkee Post Office, Alachua Co. NW 1/4 Sect. 30 Tp. 13 R. 20, south and east. Patent delivered Aug. 14, 1856.

## * T *

**4375. TAKEL, John**
June 26, 1833, 1 1/4 miles N Capitola, Jefferson Co. SW 1/4 SW 1/4 Sect. 17 Tp. 2 R. 2, north and east.

**140. TANNER, Jno.**
(The heirs of) Dec. 27, 1826, at Chattahoochee, Gadsden Co. NW 1/4 Sect. 33 Tp. 4 R. 6, north and west.

**2589. TANNER, Miles**
Mar. 8, 1854, 2 3/4 miles N by E Bass, Columbia Co. SE 1/4 Sect. 13 Tp. 4 R. 16, south and east. Patent delivered April 2, 1858.

**779. TAYLOR, Andrew**
(of Ga.) Oct. 5, 1826, at Stringer, Leon Co. W 1/2 NW 1/4 Sect. 26 Tp. 3 R. 3, north and east.

**1098. TAYLOR, Andrew**
Feb. 8, 1827, 2 miles E Stringer, Jefferson Co. E 1/2 NW 1/4 Sect. 26 Tp. 3 R. 3, north and west.

**1987. TAYLOR, Andrew**
(DUP) July 7, 1827, 1 mile E Stringer, Leon Co. E 1/2 NE 1/4 Sect. 27 Tp. 3 R. 3, north and east.

**3112. TAYLOR, Andrew**
Nov. 8, 1829, 2 1/2 miles WNW Stringer, Leon Co. E 1/2 SW 1/4 Sect. 23 Tp. 3 R. 3, north and east.

**3476. TAYLOR, Andrew**
April 9, 1830, 3 miles NE Copeland, Leon Co. W 1/2 SW 1/4 Sect. 23 Tp. 3 R. 3, north and east. Received for this property Treasury Cert. No. 67, dated May 30, 1829, in favour of **AAlex'r MACOMB**, survivor of **Edgar MACOMB**. $100.00.

**4115. TAYLOR, Andrew**
Dec. 21, 1831, 2 miles SW Finch, Leon Co. E 1/2 SE 1/4 Sect. 22 Tp. 3 R. 3, north and east.

**4489. TAYLOR, Andrew**
Dec. 24, 1833, 1 mile NNE Stringer, Leon Co. W 1/2 SW 1/4 Sect. 22 Tp. 3 R. 3, north and east.

**6158. TAYLOR, Andrew**
Dec. 6, 1836, 3/4 mile NE Stringer, Leon Co. SE 1/4 SW 1/4 Sect. 22 Tp. 3 R. 3, north and east.

**6319. TAYLOR, Benjamin F.**
Dec. 27, 1836, 3 miles NW Alma, Jefferson Co. NE 1/4 Sect. 21 Tp. 3 R. 4, north and east.

**8734. TAYLOR, George W.**
Dec. 4, 1844, 2 miles W by S Braswells, Jefferson Co. E 1/2 SE 1/4 Sect. 18 Tp. 1 R. 4, north and east.

**399. TAYLOR, Elizabeth Ann**
May 5, 1827, 2 miles SW Welchton, Jackson Co. E 1/2 SW 1/4 Sect. 2 Tp. 5 R. 12, north and west.

**144. TAYLOR, Herbert**
Dec. 27, 1826, 3 miles E Welchton, Jackson Co. SW 1/4 Sect. 33 Tp. 6 R. 11, north and west.

**5113. TAYLOR, John**
July 25, 1835, 1/4 mile S Mosely Hall, Madison Co. NE 1/4 NW 1/4 Sect. 33 Tp. 1 R. 8, south and east.

**5114. TAYLOR, John**
July 25, 1835, 1/4 mile SE Moseley Hall, Madison Co. NW 1/4 NE 1/4 Sect. 33 Tp. 1 R. 8, south and east.

**3124. TAYLOR, John L.**
Nov. 14, 1829, 1 mile S Fincher, Leon Co. E 1/2 NE 1/4 Sect. 24 Tp. 1 R. 3, north and east.

**2559. TAYLOR, Joseph**
Mar. 4, 1854, 1/4 mile N Safety Harbor, Hillsborough Co. S 1/2 NE 1/4 Sect. 4 Tp. 29 R. 16, south and east.

**2073. TAYLOR, May**
Oct. 4, 1827, 1 mile SW Miccosukee, Leon Co. E 1/2 SW 1/4 Sect. 8 Tp. 2 R. 3, north and east.

**6290. TAYLOR, Peter**
Dec. 23, 1836, 3 1/2 miles W by S Malone, Jackson Co. SW 1/4 SE 1/4 Sect. 3 Tp. 6 R. 10, north and west.

**8248. TAYLOR, Samuel W.**
Mar. 5, 1840, 2 miles N by W McDavid, Escambia Co. S 1/2 Lot No. 1 Sect. 10 Tp. 4 R. 31, north and west.

**2186. TAYLOR, Thomas**
(of Fla.) Dec. 31, 1827, at Miccosukee, Leon Co. W 1/2 NW 1/4 Sect. 9 Tp. 2 R. 3, north and east.

**2684. TAYLOR, Thomas**
Jan. 28, 1829, 1/2 mile W Miccosukee, Leon Co. E 1/2 NW 1/4 Sect. 9 Tp. 2 R. 3, north and east.

**5127. TAYLOR, Wesley R.**
Aug. 8, 1835, at Miccosukee, Jefferson

Co. SE 1/4 NW 1/4 Sect. 8 Tp. 2 R. 3, north and east.

**5770. TAYLOR, Wesley R.**
July 14, 1836, 3 1/4 miles N by W Cory, Gadsden Co. W 1/2 NE 1/4 Sect. 20 Tp. 3 R. 3, north and east.

**6095. TAYLOR, Wesley R.**
Nov. 26, 1836, 1/2 mile N Stringer, Leon Co. E 1/2 NW 1/4 Sect. 21 Tp. 3 R. 3, north and east.

**3205. TAYLOR, William**
Jan. 6, 1830, 5 1/2 miles W Wadesboro, Leon Co. E 1/2 SW 1/4 Sect. 6 Tp. 1 R. 2, north and east.

**125. TAYLOR, William**
Feb. 20, 1845, c. 3 miles SW Ringgold, Hernando Co. E 1/2 NW 1/4 Sect. 26 Tp. 21 R. 18, south and east.

**126. TAYLOR, William**
Feb. 20, 1845, c. 2 1/2 miles SW Ringgold, Hernando Co. E 1/2 SE 1/4 Sect. 22 Tp. 21 R. 18, south and east.

**2228. TAYLOR, William R.**
(Fla.) Jan. 16, 1828, 6 miles E Capitola, Jefferson Co. E 1/2 NW 1/4 Sect. 30 Tp. 1 R. 4, north and east.

**3110. TAYLOR, William R.**
Nov. 8, 1829, 2 miles W Braswells, Jefferson Co. W 1/2 SE 1/4 Sect. 18 Tp. 1 R. 4, north and east.

**4482. TAYLOR, William R.**
Dec. 18, 1833, 2 miles W by S Braswells, Jefferson Co. SE 1/4 SE 1/4 Sect. 13 Tp. 1 R. 3, north and east.

**7829. TAYLOR, William R.**
Jan. 24, 1839, 1 1/2 miles W by S Braswells, Jefferson Co. SW 1/4 SE 1/4 Sect. 13 Tp. 1 R. 3, north and east.

**8973. TAYLOR, William R.**
Aug. 29, 1846, 2 miles W Braswells, Jefferson Co. NW 1/4 SE 1/4 Sect. 13 Tp. 1 R. 3, north and east.

**2185. TEAGUE, Isaac G.**
(of Fla.) Dec. 31, 1827, at Monticello, Jefferson Co. E 1/2 SE 1/4 Sect. 25 Tp. 2 R. 4, north and east.

**3147. TEAGUE, Isaac G.**
Dec. 3, 1829, 2 miles W by S Dills, Jefferson Co. E 1/2 SW 1/4 Sect. 2 Tp. 2 R. 5, north and east.

**1256. TELLET, John**
Mar. 17, 1858, 2 miles SSW Mt. Carrie Station, Columbia Co. SE 1/4 NW 1/4 Sect. 4 Tp. 2 R. 18, south and east. Patent delivered Mar. 4, 1857.

**8311. TELLINGHOST, George W.**
May 1, 1840, 2 1/2 miles NNE Simsville, Jackson Co. E 1/2 NW 1/4 Sect. 10 Tp. 3 R. 9, north and west.

**1973. TERRELL, Reason S.**
July 25, 1853, 1 1/4 miles SE Campville, Alachua Co. SW 1/4 SE 1/4 Sect. 4 Tp. 10 R. 22, south and east. Patent delivered Oct. 2, 1858.

**538. TERRY, James L.**
Mar. 3, 1847, 4 1/2 miles N by W Ft. McCoy, Marion Co. SE 1/4 SE 1/4 Sect. 35 Tp. 12 R. 22, south and east.

**4076. TERRY, John L.**
Sept. 5, 1831, 1 1/2 miles S Genoa, Hamilton Co. W 1/2 NW 1/4 Sect. 20 Tp. 1 R. 15, south and east.

**2347. THEUS, Michael**
April 22, 1828, 2 1/2 miles SE Centerville, Leon Co. SW 1/4 Sect. 29 Tp. 2 R. 2, north and east.

**3509. THEUS, Samuel**
May 10, 1830, 2 miles ESE Centerville, Leon Co. W 1/2 NE 1/4 Sect. 21 TP. 2 R. 2, north and east. Transferred Aug. 3, 1835 to **John COOK**.

**4357. THEUS, Simeon**
May 1, 1833, 5 1/2 miles E El Destino, Jefferson Co. SW 1/4 NW 1/4 Sect. 12 Tp. 1 R. 3, south and east.

**6676. THEUS, Simeon**
Jan. 26, 1837, 2 1/2 miles NW Copeland, Leon Co. W 1/2 NE 1/4 and NE 1/4 NE 1/4 Sect. 24 Tp. 3 R. 2, north and east.

**2756. THEUS, Simon**
Feb. 24, 1829, 5 miles E El Destino, Jefferson Co. SW 1/4 Sect. 12 TP. 1 R. 3, south and east.

**3528. THEUS, William**
May 22, 1830, 1 1/2 miles E Centerville, Leon Co. W 1/2 SE 1/4 Sect. 20 Tp. 2 R. 2, north and east.

**7076. THEWS, Simeon**
Nov. 6, 1837, 6 miles E by S Iamonia, Leon Co. SE 1/4 NE 1/4 Sect. 24 Tp. 3 R. 2, north and east.

**115. THOMAS, David**
(of Tennessee) May 18, 1825, 2 miles N Lake Jackson Station, Leon Co. W 1/2 SW 1/4 Sect. 24 Tp. 2 R. 1, north and west. (Probably of Mobile Office. No mark on back).

**116. THOMAS, David**
(of Tennessee) May 18, 1825, 2 miles N Lake Jackson Station, Leon Co. E 1/2 SW 1/4 Sect. 24 Tp. 2 R. 1, north and west. (Probably of Mobile Office. No mark on back).

**134. THOMAS, David**
Dec. 25, 1826, 3 miles SE Welchton, Jackson Co. SE 1/4 Sect. 10 Tp. 5 R. 11, north and west. Transferred to **Robert L. WILLIAMS**, no date.

**1163. THOMAS, David**
(DUP) Feb. 22, 1827, 4 miles ESE Quincy, Gadsden Co. E 1/2 SE 1/4 Sect. 15 Tp. 2 R. 3, north and west.

**1470. THOMAS, David**
(DUP) May 22, 1827, 2 miles W Quincy, Gadsden Co. E 1/2 NW 1/4 Sect. 11 Tp. 2 R. 4, north and west. Transferred July 16, 1827, to **Robert FORBES**. (G. W. WARD, Reg.)

**1602. THOMAS, David**
May 25, 1827, 3 miles SW Greenwood, Jackson Co. E 1/2 NE 1/4 Sect. 11 Tp. 3 R. 10, north and west. Transferred June 6, 1827, to **Charles WILLIAMSON**

**1729. THOMAS, David**
(DUP) June 1, 1827, 2 1/2 miles SSW Moody, Wakulla Co. W 1/2 SW 1/4 Sect. 30 Tp. 2 R. 1, south and east. Transferred June 8, 1827, to **R. C. ALLEN & Co.**

**2136. THOMAS, David**
Dec. 11, 1827, 2 miles W Moseley Hall, Madison Co. E 1/2 NE 1/4 Sect. 25 Tp. 1 R. 7, south and east.

**2137. THOMAS, David**
Dec. 11, 1827, 2 1/2 miles W Moseley Hall, Madison Co. W 1/2 NE 1/4 Sect. 25 Tp. 1 R. 7, south and east.

**1246. THOMAS, David**
Dec. 12, 1827, 2 miles W Moseley Hall, Madison Co. E 1/2 NW 1/4 Sect. 30 Tp. 1 R. 8, south and east.

**2147. THOMAS, David**
Dec. 12, 1827, 2 miles WNW Moseley Hall, Madison Co. W 1/2 NW 1/4 Sect. 30 Tp. 1 R. 8, south and east.

**2148. THOMAS, David**
Dec. 12, 1827, 1 1/2 miles W Moseley Hall, Madison Co. E 1/2 SW 1/4 Sect. 30 Tp. 1 R. 8, south and east.

**2205. THOMAS, David**
(of Fla.) Dec. 31, 1827, 2 miles NW Midway, Gadsden Co. E 1/2 SE 1/4 Sect. 25 Tp. 2 R. 3, north and west.

**2206. THOMAS, David**
Dec. 31, 1827, 1/4 mile NW Midway, Gadsden Co. W 1/2 NE 1/4 Sect. 5 Tp. 1 R. 2, north and west.

**2874. THOMAS, David**
July 6, 1829, c. 3 miles S Ocheesee, Calhoun Co. Lot No. 4 Sect. 18 Tp. 2 R. 7, north and west. Transferred July 6, 1829, to **Henry D. STONE**. (G. W. WARD, Register). Transferred July 7, 1829, to **Seaton GRANTLAND**.

**2876. THOMAS, David**
July 6, 1829, 4 miles WSW Roy, Liberty Co. Lot No. 3 Sect. 20 Tp. 2 R. 7, north and west. Transferred July 21, 1829, to **John S. SHEPARD. G. W. WARD**, Register.

**2879. THOMAS, David**
July 6, 1829, 3 miles SW Roy, Liberty Co. Lot No. 4 Sect. 17 Tp. 2 R. 7, north and west. Transferred July 21, 1829, to **John S. SHEPARD. G. W. WARD**, Register.

**2880. THOMAS, David**
July 6, 1829, 1 mile SE Ocheesee, Calhoun Co. Lot No. 4 Sect. 8 Tp. 2 R. 7, north and west. Transferred July 21, 1829, to **John S. SHEPARD. G. W. WARD**, Register.

**2881. THOMAS, David**
July 6, 1829, c. 3 miles SW Roy, Liberty Co. Lot No. 3 Sect. 17 Tp. 2 R. 7, north and west.

**2891. THOMAS, David**
July 7, 1829, 3 miles S by E Millspring, Jackson Co. Lot No. 1 Sect. 34 Tp. 3 R. 7, north and west. Transferred to **MILLS & PERRY**, July 7, 1829. G. W. WARD, Register.

**2908. THOMAS, David**
July 7, 1829, 2 miles SE Millspring, Jackson Co. Lot No. 1 Sect. 26 Tp. 3 R. 7, north and west.

**2909. THOMAS, David**
July 7, 1829, 2 miles SE Millspring, Jackson Co. E 1/2 NE 1/4 Sect. 25 Tp. 3 R. 7, north and west.

**2913. THOMAS, David**
July 8, 1829, c. 1 mile S Butler, Jackson Co. Lot No. 2 Sect. 3 Tp. 4 R. 7, north and west.

**2914. THOMAS, David**
July 8, 1829, 2 miles S Butler, Jackson Co. Lot No. 1 Sect. 10 Tp. 4 R. 7, north and west.

**2915. THOMAS, David**
July 8, 1829, c. 2 miles S Butler, Jackson Co. Lot No. 4 Sect. 10 Tp. 4 R. 7, north and west.

**2916. THOMAS, David**
(of Fla.) July 8, 1829, c. 3/4 mile S Butler, Jackson Co. Lot No. 1 Sect. 3 Tp. 4 R. 7, north and west.

**2950. THOMAS, David**
July 21, 1829, 3 miles N Watson, Liberty Co. Lot No. 2 Sect. 17 Tp. 2 R. 7, north and west. Transferred July 21, 1829, to **John S. SHEPARD**. **G. W. WARD**, Register.

**2951. THOMAS, David**
July 21, 1829, 3 miles N Watson, Liberty Co. Lot No. 5 Sect. 17 Tp. 2 R. 7, north and west. Transferred July 21, 1829, to **John S. SHEPARD**.

**2877. THOMAS, David**
July 6, 1829, 3 miles SW Roy, Liberty Co. Lot No. 4 Sect. 17 Tp. 2 R. 7, north and west. Transferred July 21, 1829, to **John S. SHEPARD**. **G. W. WARD**, Register.

**2954. THOMAS, David**
July 23, 1829, 2 miles S by E Butler, Jackson Co. Lot No. 2 Sect. 10 Tp. 4 R. 7, north and west.

**2955. THOMAS, David**
July 23, 1829, 2 miles S Butler, Jackson Co. Lot No. 2 Sect. 15 Tp. 4 R. 7, north and west.

**2956. THOMAS, David**
July 23, 1829, 2 miles S Butler, Jackson Co. Lot No. 3 Sect. 10 Tp. 3 R. 7, north and west.

**3297. THOMAS, David**
Feb. 10, 1830, 1 1/2 miles N Mandalay, Taylor Co. E 1/2 NE 1/4 Sect. 7 Tp. 4 R. 4, south and east. Transferred Feb. 23, 1830, to **Wm. B. NUTTALL**. **G. W. WARD**, Register.

**3298. THOMAS, David**
Feb. 10, 1830, 1 1/2 miles N Mandalay, Jefferson Co. W 1/2 NE 1/4 Sect. 7 Tp. 4 R. 4, south and east. Transferred Feb. 23, 1830, to **Wm. B. NUTTALL**.

**3299. THOMAS, David**
Feb. 10, 1830, 1 1/2 miles N Mandalay, Jefferson Co. E 1/2 SW 1/4 Sect. 7 Tp. 4 R. 4, south and east. Transferred Feb. 23, 1830, to **Wm. B. NUTTALL**

**3300. THOMAS, David**
Feb. 10, 1830, 1 mile N Mandalay, Taylor Co. W 1/2 SE 1/4 Sect. 7 Tp. 4 R. 4, south and east. Transferred to **Wm. B. NUTTALL**, on Feb. 23, 1830.

**3301. THOMAS, David**
Feb. 10, 1830, 1 mile N Mandalay, Taylor Co. E 1/2 SE 1/4 Sect. 7 Tp. 4 R. 4, south and east. Transferred Feb. 23, 1830, to **Wm. B. NUTTALL**. **G. W. WARD**, Register.

**3357. THOMAS, David**
Feb. 13, 1830, 1/2 mile NW Old Town, Dixie Co. E 1/2 SE 1/4 Sect. 10 Tp. 10, R. 13, south and east. $1.97 per acre. Transferred Feb. 16, 1830, to **Wm. BAILEY**. **G. W. WARD**, Register.

**3358. THOMAS, David**
Feb. 13, 1830, a part of Old Town, Dixie Co. Lot No. 5 Sect. 13 Tp. 10 R. 13, south and east. $4.00 per acre.

**3359. THOMAS, David**
Feb. 13, 1830, in Old Town, Dixie Co. W 1/2 NE 1/4 Sect. 14 Tp. 14 R. 13, south and east. $2.80 per acre. Transferred Feb. 16, 1830, to **Wm. BAILEY**.

**3360. THOMAS, David**
Feb. 16, 1830, 3/4 mile SW Old Town, Dixie Co. E 1/2 NW 1/4 Sect. 23 Tp. 10 R. 13, south and east. $3.75 per acre.

**3361. THOMAS, David**
Feb. 13, 1830, 3/4 mile S Old Town, Dixie Co. E 1/2 SE 1/4 Sect. 23 Tp. 10 R. 13, south and east. Transferred Feb. 16, 1830, to **Wm. BAILEY**.

**3400. THOMAS, David**
Feb. 10, 1830, 2 1/2 miles N Mandalay, Taylor Co. W 1/2 NW 1/4 Sect. 5 Tp. 4 R. 4, south and east. Transferred to **Wm. B. NUTTALL**, Feb. 23, 1830.

**3402. THOMAS, David**
Feb. 10, 1830, 1 mile N by E Mandalay, Taylor Co. W 1/2 SW 1/4 Sect. 8 Tp. 4 R. 4, south and east. Transferred Feb. 23, 1830, to **Wm. B. NUTTALL**.

**3403. THOMAS, David**
Feb. 10, 1830, 1 1/2 miles N Mandalay, Taylor Co. W 1/2 NW 1/4 Sect. 8

Tp. 4 R. 4, south and east. Transferred Feb. 23, 1830, to **Wm. B. NUTTALL**.

**3404. THOMAS, David**
Feb. 10, 1830, 2 miles N Mandalay, Taylor Co. W 1/2 SE 1/4 Sect. 6 Tp. 4 R. 4, south and east. Transferred Feb.23, 1830, to **Wm. B. NUTTALL**.

**3405. THOMAS, David**
Feb. 10, 1830, 2 miles N Mandalay, Taylor Co. W 1/2 SW 1/4 Sect. 5 Tp. 4 R. 4, south and east. Transferred Feb. 23, 1830, to **Wm. B. NUTTALL**. See **Cornelius GRANTHAM, #242**.

**7189. THOMAS, Edward J.**
Jan. 4, 1838, 3 1/2 miles N by W Fincher, Leon Co. E 1/2 SE 1/4 Sect. 6 Tp. 3 R. 3, north and west.

**8125. THOMAS, Edward J.**
Oct. 22, 1839, 4 1/2 miles W by N Fincher, Jefferson in Grady Co., Alabama. NW 1/4 SE 1/4 Sect. 6 Tp. 3 R. 3, north and west.

**THOMAS, E. J.** see **John LEWIS, #7895**

**1673. THOMAS, Isom B.**
Jan. 28, 1853, 1 mile SSW of 30 Mile Siding Station, Alachua Co. SE 1/4 NW 1/4 Sect. 34 Tp. 8 R. 18, south and east. Patent delivered May 27, 1856.

**143. THOMAS, Jno. D.**
Dec. 27, 1826, 7 miles W Jacob Station, Jackson Co. E 1/2 NW 1/4 Sect. 18 Tp. 6 R. 11, north and west. Transferred Dec. 27, 1826, to **Benj. FOSCUE**.

**8393. THOMAS, John F. O.**
Aug. 21, 1840, 3 1/2 miles NNE Blountstown, Calhoun Co. Lots No. 1, 2 and 3 Sect. 24 Tp. 1 R. 8, north and west.

**4028. THOMAS, Jonathan**
July 16, 1831, N shore Lake Jackson, Leon Co. Lot No. 2 Sect. 28 Tp. 2 R. 4, north and west.

**5820. THOMAS, Mary Ann**
Sept. 1, 1836, 3 miles SW Tallahassee, Leon Co. NE 1/4 NW 1/4 Sect. 15 Tp. 1 R. 1, south and west.

**8893. THOMAS, Mary**
Jan. 29, 1846, 1 3/4 miles E by S Gaskin, Calhoun Co. NW 1/4 Sect. 24 Tp. 2 R. 9, south and west.

**32. THOMAS, Robert**
Nov. 4, 1826, near Havana, Gadsden Co. NW 1/4 Sect. 29 Tp. 3 R. 2, north and west.

**235. THOMAS, William**
Dec. 23, 1845, c. 4 miles NE Belmore, Clay Co. SW 1/4 NW 1/4 Sect. 32 Tp. 6 R. 24, south and east.

**672. THOMAS, William**
Dec. 27, 1848, c. 5 miles NW Belmore, Clay Co. SE 1/4 NE 1/4 Sect. 31 Tp. 6 R. 24, south and east.

**2402. THOMAS, William**
Feb. 21, 1854, 5 1/2 miles NE Belmore, Clay Co., SW 1/4 NE 1/4 and SE 1/4 NW 1/4 Sect. 31 Tp. 6 R. 24, south and east. Patent delivered Jan 27, 1857.

**8752. THOMAS, William**
Mar. 6, 1845, 1 1/2 miles S Roy, Liberty Co. S 1/2 SW 1/4 Sect. 13 Tp. 2 R. 7, north and west.

**97. THOMAS, William Henry**
Dec. 26, 1844, c. 6 1/2 miles SW Long Branch, Clay Co. SW 1/4 SW 1/4 Sect. 28 Tp. 6 R. 24, south and 4 east. Patent delivered July 24, 1857, to **Wm. H. THOMAS**.

**2088. THOMAS, William H.**
Aug. 22, 1853, 4 3/4 miles NNW Sharon, Clay Co. W 1/2 NE 1/4 Sect. 2 Tp. 7 R. 24, south and east. Patent delivered Mar. 20, 1903, was sent to **Drucilla THOMAS**, Belmore, Fla.

**7625. THOMAS, William M.**
Sept. 6, 1838, 1/2 mile NNE Bond, Madison Co. NE 1/4 NW 1/4 and NW 1/4 NE 1/4 Sect. 3 Tp. 2 R. 8, north and east.

**8476. THOMAS, William M.**
Feb. 26, 1841, 1 1/2 miles NNE Bond, Madison Co. SE 1/4 NW 1/4 Sect. 3 Tp. 2 R. 8, north and east.

**8477. THOMAS, William M.**
Feb. 26, 1841, 1 3/4 miles E by N Bond, Madison Co. SW 1/4 NE 1/4 Sect. 3 Tp. 2 R. 8, north and east.

**8763. THOMAS, William M.**
Mar. 26, 1845, 5 1/2 miles SE Dills, Jefferson Co. W 1/2 SE 1/4 Sect. 21 TP. 2 R. 6, south and east.

**8764. THOMAS, William M.**
Mar. 26, 1845, 5 miles N by W Aucilla, Jefferson Co. E 1/2 NE 1/4 and E 1/2 SE 1/4 Sect. 28 Tp. 2 R. 6, south and east.

**2290. THOMPSON, Jeremiah**
Oct. 26, 1853, 1 1/2 miles SE Maxville, Clay Co. SW 1/4 NW 1/4 Sect. 4 Tp. 4 R. 23, south and east.

**1162. THOMPSON, Samuel B.**
Feb. 10, 1852, 1 3/4 miles NW McMeekin, Marion Co. Lots 3 and 4 Sect. 19 Tp. 10 R. 23, south and east. Patent delivered Feb. 12, 1852.

**1909. THOMPSON, Samuel B.**
June 21, 1853, 4 1/2 miles E Haynesworth, Alachua Co. SE 1/4 SW 1/4 Sect. 36 Tp. 7 R. 19, south and east. Patent delivered June 21, 1853.

**2658. THOMPSON, Samuel B.**
Mar. 24, 1854, 2 miles SSE LaCrosse, Alachua Co. NW 1/4 SW 1/4 Sect. 36 Tp. 7 R. 19, south and east. Patent delivered July 7, 1857.

**2740. THOMPSON, Samuel B.**
May 6, 1854, 2 1/2 miles E LaCrosse, Bradford Co. N 1/2 Lot No. 10 and N 1/2 Lot No. 11 Sect. 31 Tp. 7 R. 20, south and east. Patent delivered July 7, 1857.

**2832. THOMPSON, Samuel B.**
July 24, 1854, 3 1/2 miles W Middleburg, Clay Co. SE 1/4 SW 1/4 and NW 1/4 SW 1/4 Sect. 9 Tp. 5 R. 24, south and east.

**2833. THOMPSON, Samuel B.**
July 24, 1854, 6 miles W Rideout, Clay Co. SE 1/4 NW 1/4 Sect. 4 Tp. 5 R. 24, south and east.

**4642. THOMPSON, Samuel B.**
Mar. 14, 1856, 1 3/4 miles E Haynesworth, Alachua Co. NE 1/4 SE 1/4 Sect. 35 Tp. 7 R. 19, south and east. Patent delivered April 28, 1858.

**4243. THOMPSON, Samuel B.**
Mar. 14, 1856, 1 1/2 miles E Haynesworth, Alachua Co. N 1/2 Lot No. 4 Sect. 31 Tp. 7 R. 30, south and east. Patent delivered April 28, 1858.

**3005. THOMPSON, William**
Sept. 2, 1829, 2 miles S by E Centerville, Leon Co. W 1/2 SW 1/4 Sect. 31 Tp. 2 R. 2, north and east.

**4316. THOMPSON, William**
Feb. 22, 1833, 1 1/2 miles N Wadesboro, Leon Co. Ne 1/4 SE 1/4 Sect. 36 Tp. 2 R. 2, north and east.

**4373. THOMPSON, William**
June 22, 1833, 2 miles S by E Centerville, Leon Co. SW 1/4 NW 1/4 Sect. 31 Tp. 2 R. 2, north and east.

**4466. THOMPSON, William**
Dec. 2, 1833, 1 mile SSE Bradfordville, Leon Co. SE 1/4 SE 1/4 Sect. 26 Tp. 2 R. 1, north and east.

**4546. THOMPSON, William**
Feb. 10, 1834, 2 miles N Blackcreek, Leon Co. SE 1/4 NE 1/4 Sect. 36 Tp. 2 R. 2, north and east.

**4547. THOMPSON, William**
Feb. 10, 1834, 3 miles S by E Centerville, Leon Co. NW 1/4 NW 1/4 Sect. 31 Tp. 2 R. 2, north and east.

**4689. THOMPSON, William**
Dec. 9, 1834, 2 3/4 miles S Centerville, Leon Co. SE 1/4 SE 1/4 Sect. 36 Tp. 2 R. 1, north and east.

**5173. THOMPSON, William**
Sept. 30, 1835, 1 3/4 miles E Perkins, Leon Co. SE 1/4 NW 1/4 Sect. 31 Tp. 2 R. 2, north and east.

**1585. THORNTON, Reddick R.**
Dec. 25, 1852, 2 1/2 miles SSW Dukes, Union Co. NE 1/4 NW 1/4 Sect. 29 Tp. 6 R. 19, south and east.

**1600. THORNTON, Reddick R.**
Jan. 1, 1853, 6 miles SSE Guilford, Union Co. NW 1/4 NW 1/4 Sect. 34 Tp. 5 R. 18, south and east.

**2811. THORNTON, Reddick R.**
July 10, 1854, 1 3/4 miles SW Dukes, Union Co. S 1/2 SW 1/4 Sect. 20 Tp. 6 R. 19, south and east. Patent delivered Oct. 29, 1856.

**4472. THURMAN, Josiah**
Dec. 4, 1856, 3 1/2 miles W Mason, Columbia Co. NW 1/4 Sect. 29 Tp. 5 R. 17, south and east.

**377. TILLIS, Richard**
April 27, 1846, c. 3 1/2 miles W Suwannee, Suwannee Co. E 1/2 NE 1/4 Sect. 21 and W 1/2 NW 1/4 Sect. 22 Tp. 1 R. 13, south and east. Patent delivered July 29, 1856.

**4215. TILLIS, Richard**
Feb. 29, 1856, 4 miles W Rixford, Suwannee Co. NE 1/4 NE 1/4 NE 1/4 Sect. 28 Tp. 1 R. 13, south and east. Patent delivered Aug. 20, 1858.

**2166. TILLIS, Thomas**
Sept. 13, 1853, at Louise, Alachua Co. S 1/2 NW 1/4 Sect. 31 Tp. 7 R. 21, south and east.

**1962. TILTON, Nehemiah**
June 28, 1827, 1 1/2 mile SE Capitola, Jefferson Co. W 1/2 NW 1/4 Sect. 32 Tp. 1 R. 3, north and east.

**451. TIPPERERE (ZIPPERERE ?), Solomon**
Aug. 7, 1846, 4 1/2 miles SW Westlake, Hamilton Co. Lot No. 7 Fractional Sect. 35 Tp. 1 R. ?, north and east.

**580 TISON, Louisa Jane**
July 29, 1847, 1 mile SE Traxler, Alachua Co. SW 1/4 NE 1/4 Sect. 21 Tp. 7 R. 18, south and east. Patent delivered Jan. 8, 1853.

**6709. TISON, William A.**
May 6, 1888, 4 miles N by E Wellborn, Suwannee Co. SW 1/4 SW 1/4 Sect. 32 Tp. 3S, R. 16 E.

**TOLEGE, John C. see John G. PELEGE**

**440. TOMPKINS, James**
July 8, 1846, near Lochloosa, Alachua Co. Lot No. 12 Sect. 22 Tp. 11 R. 22, south and east.

**2375. TOMPKINS, James**
Feb. 20, 1854, 1 1/4 miles SW Lockloosa, Alachua Co. Lot No. 1 Sect. 33 Tp. 11 R. 22, south and east. Patent delivered Sept. 17, 1856.

**492. TOMPKINS, John**
Dec. 11, 1846, 1 mile SW Summerfield, Marion Co. SE 1/4 Sect. 24 Tp. 17 R. 22, south and east.

**649. TOMPKINS, John**
May 19, 1849, 2 miles SW Summerfield, Marion Co. NE 1/4 SW 1/4 Sect. 24 Tp. 17 R. 22, south and east.

**1129. TOMPKINS, John**
Jan. 27, 1852, 2 1/2 miles SE Thaggard, Marion Co. N 1/2 SW 1/4 Sect. 30 Tp. 17 R. 23, south and east.

**1547. TOMLINSON, Levin**
Dec. 7, 1852, 7 miles WNW Macclenny, Baker Co. SW 1/4 E 1/2, SE 1/4 NW 1/4, NE 1/4 SW 1/4, NW 1/4 SE 1/4 Sect. 7 Tp. 2 R. 21, south and east.

**2859. TONEY, Wm.**
(of S. C.) July 6, 1829, 1 1/2 miles E Ocheessee, Calhoun Co. Lot No. 1 Sect. 5 Tp. 2 R. 7, north and west.

**2893. TONE, Wm.**
July 7, 1827, 3 1/2 miles S Millspring, Jackson Co. Lot No. 6 Sect. 33 Tp. 3 R. 7, north and west.

**2894. TONEY, Wm.**
July 7, 1829, 3 1/2 miles S Millspring, Jackson Co. Lot No. 5 Sect. 33 Tp. 3 R. 7, north and west.

**TONEY, William see MILLS & PERRY and L. M. STONE, #455**

**3185. TONEY, Wm.**
Dec. 28, 1829, 2 miles NE Ocheesee, Gadsden Co. SE 1/4 Sect. 32 Tp. 3 R. 7, north and west.

**8081. TOOKE, William L.**
Sept. 19, 1839, 1 1/4 miles E Hamburg, Madison Co. E 1/2 SW 1/4 Sect. 13 Tp. 2 R. 8, north and east.

**8082. TOOKE, William L.**
Sept. 19, 1839, 1 3/4 miles E Hamburg, Madison Co. NW 1/4 SE 1/4 Sect. 13 Tp. 2 R. 3, north and east.

**4763. TORT, Isaac**
Jan. 10, 1835, 7 1/2 miles SSW Greenwood, Jackson Co. W 1/2 NE 1/4 Sect. 56 Tp. 5 R. 10, north and west. Transferred to **Edward BALLAMY**, Jan. 2, 1836.

**4764. TORT, Isaac**
Jan. 10, 1835, 7 3/4 miles SSW Greenwood, Jackson Co. E 1/2 NW 1/4 Sect. 5 Tp. 5 R. 10, north and west.

**4765. TORT, Isaac**
Jan. 10, 1835, 7 3/4 miles SW Greenwood, Jackson Co. E 1/2 SW 1/4 Sect. 5 Tp. 5 R. 10, north and west. Transferred to **Edward C. BELLAMY**, Jan. 2, 1836.

**4766. TORT, Isaac**
Jan. 10, 1835, 7 1/2 miles SW Greenwood, Jackson Co. W 1/2 SE 1/4 Sect. 5 Tp. 5 R. 10, north and west. Transferred to **Edward C. BELLAMY**, Jan. 2, 1836.

**327. TOUCHSTON, Richard**
April 6, 1827, 1/2 mile SW Campbellton, Jackson Co. NE 1/4 Sect. 5 Tp. 6 R. 12, north and west.

**4818. TOUCHSTONE, Stephen**
Jan. 24, 1835, 1/2 miles SW Concord, Gadsden Co. SW 1/4 SE 1/4 Sect. 19 Tp. 3 R. 1, north and west.

**4819. TOUCHSTONE, Stephen**
Jan. 24, 1835, 1 1/2 miles S Meridian, Leon Co. SE 1/4 SW 1/4 Sect. 19 Tp. 3 R. 1, north and west.

**2488. TOULE, Frederick**
Sept. 10, 1828, 1 mile N Bradfordville, Leon Co. W 1/2 NE 1/4 Sect. 15 Tp. 2 R. 1, north and west.

**2422. TOWERS, Francis**
May 27, 1828, 4 1/2 miles Nw Marianna, Jackson Co. W 1/2 SW 1/4 Sect. 30 Tp. 5 R. 10, north and west.

**2536. TOWLE, Francis**
Nov. 3, 1828, 3 miles NNW Monticello, Jefferson Co. Lot No. 2 Sect. 14 Tp. 2 R. 4, north and east. Transferred Nov. 10, 1828, to **David LASTINGER**.

**2452. TOWLE, Frederick**
Aug. 8, 1828, 1/2 mile W Ocklocknee, Leon Co. E 1/2 NE 1/4 Sect. 26 Tp. 1 R. 2, north and west.

**2998. TOWLE, Frederick**
Aug. 28, 1829, 3 miles W Waukenah, Jefferson Co. W 1/2 NW 1/4 Sect. 7 Tp. 1 R. 4, south and east.

**4079. TOWLE, Frederick**
Sept. 8, 1831, 4 1/2 miles NNE Monticello, Jefferson Co. E 1/2 NE 1/4 Sect. 24 Tp. 2 R. 5, north and east.

**2531. TOWLE, Frederick**
Oct. 27, 1828, 1 mile SW Oakdale, Jackson Co. E 1/2 SW 1/4 Sect. 35 Tp. 4 R. 10, north and west.

**TOWLE, Simon see Cosam T. BARTLETT**

**5677. TOWNSEND, Allen**
May 21, 1836, 3/4 mile E Alliance, Calhoun Co. NE 1/4 NE 1/4 Sect. 15 Tp. 2 R. 9, north and east.

**6119. TOWNSEND, Allen**
Nov. 30, 1836, 3 miles SSE Cherry Lake Post Office, Madison Co. E 1/2 SW 1/4 Sect. 22 Tp. 2 R. 9, north and east.

**6120. TOWNSEND, Allen**
Nov. 30, 1836, 3 miles S by E Cherry Lake Post Office, Madison Co. E 1/2 SE 1/4 Sect. 21 Tp. Tp. 2 R. 9, north and east.

**6222. TOWNSEND, Allen**
Dec. 15, 1836, 2 miles E by S Bailey, Madison Co. SW 1/4 SW 1/4 Sect. 22 Tp. 2 R. 9, north and east.

**7204. TOWNSEND, Allen**
Jan. 10, 1838, 5 1/2 miles E by N Hanson, Hamilton Co. W 1/2 SW 1/4 Sect. 25 Tp. 2 R. 10, north and east.

**7505. TOWNSEND, Allen**
Jan. 10, 1838, 5 1/2 miles E Hanson, Hamilton Co. E 1/2 SE 1/4 Sect. 26 Tp. 2 R. 10, north and east.

**7534. TOWNSEND, Allen**
July 12, 1838, 3 1/2 miles NNW Hanson, Madison Co. W 1/2 NW 1/4 Sect. 23 Tp. 2 R. 9, north and east.

**7535. TOWNSEND, Allen**
July 12, 1838, 3 3/4 miles NNW Hanson, Madison Co. E 1/2 SE 1/4 Sect. 15 Tp. 2 R. 9, north and east.

**7630. TOWNSEND, Allen**
Sept. 7, 1838, 1 3/4 miles SW Pinetta, Madison Co. W 1/2 SW 1/4 Sect. 14 Tp. 2 R. 9, north and east.

**8295. TOWNSEND, Allen**
April 21, 1840, 2 miles SE Cherrylake (town), Madison Co. W 1/2 NW 1/4 Sect. 22 Tp. 2 R. 9, north and east.

**1814. TOWNSEND, Asa**
June 5, 1827, 4 miles SSE Sawdust, Gadsden Co. W 1/2 NE 1/4 Sect. 4 Tp. 1 R. 4, north and west.

**5278. TOWNSEND, Asa**
Nov. 20, 1835, 1 1/4 miles S by W Cherrylake (town), Madison Co. E 1/2 SW 1/4 Sect. 20 Tp. 2 R. 9, north and east.

**5279. TOWNSEND, Asa**
Nov. 21, 1835, 1/2 mile S Cherrylake (town), Madison Co. NE 1/4 SE 1/4 Sect. 20 Tp. 2 R. 9, north and east.

**5280. TOWNSEND, Asa**
Nov. 21, 1835, 1/2 mile S Cherrylake (town), Madison Co. NW 1/4 SE 1/4 Sect. 20 Tp. 2 R. 9, north and east.

**6449. TOWNSEND, Asa**
Jan. 6, 1837, in Havana, Gadsden Co. NE 1/4 SE 1/4 Sect. 34 Tp. 3 R. 2, north and west. Receipt for patent of the above land dated Nov. 25, 1846. Signed and sworn before **Thos. J. HODSON**, Register.

**6780. TOWNSEND, Benjamin**
Feb. 7, 1837, 5 1/2 miles E by S Hanson, Madison Co. NE 1/4 NW 1/4 Sect. 36 Tp. 2 R. 10, north and east.

**6781. TOWNSEND, Benjamin**
Feb. 7, 1837, 5 miles E Hanson, Madison Co. SE 1/4 SW 1/4 Sect. 25 Tp. 2 R. 10, north and east.

**7533. TOWNSEND, David R.**
July 12, 1838, 1 1/2 miles SSE Cherrylake (town), Madison Co. SW 1/4

Sect. 15 Tp. 2 R. 9, north and east.
**7623. TOWNSEND, David R.**
Sept. 7, 1838, 4 3/4 miles E Hanson, Madison Co. SW 1/4 SE 1/4 Sect. 25 Tp. 2 R. 10, north and east.
**7629. TOWNSEND, David R.**
Sept. 7, 1838, 5 1/2 miles SSE Hanson, Madison Co. NW 1/4 NE 1/4 Sect. 26 Tp. 2 R. 10, north and east.
**7713. TOWNSEND, David R.**
Nov. 20, 1838, 2 1/2 miles NNW Calhoun, Madison Co. NW 1/4 Sect. 2 Tp. 1 R. 9, north and east.
**7509. TOWNSEND, John**
July 5, 1838, 4 1/2 miles E by S Hanson, Madison Co. SW 1/4 SW 1/4 Sect. 36 Tp. 2 R. 10, north and east.
**1269. TOWNSEND, Isaac**
April 12, 1827, 2 miles W Drifton, Jefferson Co. W 1/2 NW 1/4 Sect. 14 Tp. 1 R. 4, north and east.
**2778. TOWNSEND, Isaac**
Mar. 10, 1829, 1/2 mile W Lutterlow, Leon Co. E 1/2 NW 1/4 Sect. 31 TP. 1 R. 4, south and east.
**2780. TOWNSEND, Isaac**
March 10, 1829, 1 mile N Wacissa, Jefferson Co. W 1/2 NE 1/4 Sect. 31 Tp. 1 R. 4, south and east.
**5242. TOWNSEND, Isaac**
Oct. 21, 1835, at Nash, Jefferson Co. E 1/2 NW 1/4 Sect. 25 Tp. 1 R. 4, north and east.
**6427. TOWNSEND, Isaac**
Jan. 4, 1837, 2 miles SW Drifton, Jefferson Co. E 1/2 SW 1/4 and W 1/2 SE 1/4 Sect. 24 Tp. 1 R. 4, north and east.
**2779. TOWNSEND, James S.**
March 10, 1829, 2 miles WNW Waukenah, Jefferson Co. E 1/2 SW 1/4 Sect. 32 Tp. 1 R. 4, north and east.
**2279. TOWNSEND, Jas. L.**
March 3, 1828, 1 1/2 miles W Waukenah, Jefferson Co. E 1/2 NE 1/4 Sect. 5 Tp. 1 R. 4, south and east.
**2293. TOWNSEND, Jas. L.**
March 11, 1828, 2 1/2 miles W by N Waukenah, Jefferson Co. SE 1/4 Sect. 31 Tp. 1 R. 4, north and east.
**2502. TOWNSEND, Jas. L.**
Sept. 23, 1828, 3 miles WNW Waukenah, Jeffeson Co. W 1/2 NE 1/4

Sect. 32 Tp. 1 R. 4, north and east.
**241. TOWNSEND, Jessie**
Dec. 20, 1826, 2 miles NE Havana, Gadsden Co. SE 1/4 Sect. 20 Tp. 3 R. 2, north and west.
**1268. TOWNSEND, John**
April 12, 1827, 6 miles WSW Monticello, Jefferson Co. E 1/2 NE 1/4 Sect. 5 Tp. 1 R. 4, north and east.
**3876. TOWNSEND, John**
Feb. 10, 1831, 6 miles SW Monticello, Jefferson Co. W 1/2 SE 1/4 Sect. 5 Tp. 1 R. 4, north and east.
**6694. TOWNSEND, John**
Jan. 30, 1837, 1 1/2 miles W by S Drifton, Jefferson Co. W 1/2 SE 1/4 Sect. 14 Tp. 1 R. 4, north and east.
**6695. TOWNSEND, John**
Jan. 30, 1837, 1 1/2 miles WSW Drifton, Jefferson Co. E 1/2 SE 1/4 Sect. 14 Tp. 1 R. 4, north and east.
**7744. TOWNSEND, John**
Dec. 3, 1838, 6 1/2 miles SSE Hanson, Madison Co. SE 1/4 NW 1/4 Sect. 36 Tp. 2 R. 10, north and east.
**7746. TOWNSEND, John**
Dec. 3, 1838, 6 1/2 miles SE by E Hanson, Madison Co. NW 1/4 SW 14 Sect. 36 Tp. 2 R. 10, north and east.
**8827. TOWNSEND, John A.**
Sept. 27, 1845, 3 1/2 miles N by W Walker Springs, Jefferson Co. N 1/2 NE 1/4 Sect. 21 Tp. 2 R. 5, south and east.
**1919. TOWNSEND, Light**
June 18, 1827, 3 1/2 miles E by S Lloyd, Jefferson Co. W 1/2 SW 1/4 Sect. 20 Tp. 1 R. 4, north and east. Sold March 10, 1828, and orderd patent delivered to **Messrs. CUTHBERT & MANNY.**
**2721. TOWNSEND, Light**
Feb. 10, 1829, 1/2 mile SW Waukenah, Jefferson Co. E 1/2 SE 1/4 Sect. 4 Tp. 1 R. 4, south and east.
**2363. TOWNSEND, Light**
May 3, 1828, 5 miles SW Monticello, Jefferson Co. W 1/2 SW 1/4 Sect. 4 Tp. 1 R. 4, south and east.
**2364. TOWNSEND, Light**
May 3, 1828, 1 mile W Waukenah, Jefferson Co. W 1/2 SE 1/4 Sect. 4 Tp. 1 R. 4, south and east.
**2948. TOWNSEND, Light T.**

July 21, 1829, 1 mile NE Monticello, Jefferson Co. E 1/2 NW 1/4 Sect. 20 Tp. 2 R. 5, north and east.

**2949. TOWNSEND, Light T.**
July 21, 1829, 1 1/4 miles NNE Monticello, Jefferson Co. E 1/2 NE 1/4 Sect. 2 Tp. 2 R. 5, north and east.

**2458. TOWNSEND, Moses**
Aug. 16, 1828, 1 mile N Dills, Jefferson Co. E 1/2 NE 1/4 Sect. 2 Tp. 2 R. 5, north and east.

**4461. TOWNSEND, Stapleton**
Nov. 28, 1833, 1 mile W Dill, Jefferson Co. NW 1/4 NE 1/4 Sect. 2 Tp. 2 R. 5, north and east.

**2942. TOWNSEND, Stephen**
July 18, 1829, 1 1/2 miles N Monticello, Jefferson Co. E 1/2 NE 1/4 Sect. 18 Tp. 2 R. 5, north and east.

**1978. TOWNSEND, Thomas**
July 2, 1827, 5 1/2 miles WSW Monticello, Jefferson Co. W 1/2 SE 1/4 Sect. 4 Tp. 1 R. 4, north and east.

**4171. TOWNSEND, Thomas L.**
May 21, 1832, 1/2 mile W Drifton, Jefferson Co. W 1/2 SW 1/4 Sect. 13 Tp. 1 R. 4, north and east.

**3286. TOWNSEND, Thomas R.**
Feb. 11, 1830, 4 miles E Alma, Jefferson Co. E 1/2 SE 1/4 Sect. 33 Tp. 3 R. 5, north and east.

**3093. TRAMMELL, Daniel**
Oct. 28, 1829, 3 miles SSW Greenwood, Jackson Co. SE 1/4 Sect. 12 Tp. 5 R. 10, north and west.

**2119. TRAMMELL, James J.**
(of Ga.) Nov. 29, 1827, 1 mile SSW Greenwood, Jackson Co. W 1/2 SW 1/4 Sect. 6 Tp. 5 R. 9, north and west.

**2120. TRAMMELL, James J.**
(of Ga.) Nov. 29, 1827, 1 1/2 miles SW Greenwood, Jackson Co. W 1/2 SE 1/4 Sect. 1 Tp. 5 R. 10, north and west.

**2549. TRAMMELL, James J.**
Nov. 24, 1828, 2 miles SSW Greenwood, Gadsden Co. E 1/2 NE 1/4 Sect. 12 Tp. 5 R. 10, north and west.

**3098. TRAMMELL, James J.**
Oct. 29, 1829, 1 1/2 miles SSW Greenwood, Jackson Co. E 1/2 SW 1/4 Sect. 6 Tp. 5 R. 9, north and west.

**4417. TRAMMELL, James J.**
Sept. 17, 1833, 3 1/4 miles S by W Greenwood, Jackson Co. E 1/2 SE 1/4 Sect. 18 Tp. 5 R. 9, north and west. Transferred to **Edward BRYON**, May 26, 1835.

**1234. TRESPEL, George H.**
April 9, 1852, 6 1/2 miles S Wilcox Junction Station, Levy Co. N 1/2 NE 1/4 Sect. 24 Tp. 11 R. 13, south and east. Patent delivered Mar. 25, 1864.

**5130. TRIPLETT, Martha P.**
Aug. 11, 1835, 2 miles NW Braswells, Jefferson Co. E 1/2 SE 1/4 Sect. 8 Tp. 1 R. 4, north and east.

**TRIPPE, Bryan see Chas. TRIPPE, #257**

**257. TRIPPE, Chas.**
Dec. 30, 1826, 9 miles E Marianna, Jackson Co. SE 1/4 Sect. 6 Tp. 4 R. 9, north and west. Transferred from **Chas. TRIPPE** to **Bryan TRIPPE**, Jan. 2, 1827.

**352. TRIPPE, Henry**
April 19, 1827, 3 miles E Welchton, Jackson Co. SW 1/4 Sect. 34 Tp. 6 R. 11, north and west.

**411. TRIPPE, Henry**
(Heir fo **Jno. T. J. TRIPPE**) May 7, 1827, 4 miles W Welchton, Jackson Co. E 1/2 SE 1/4 Sect. 33 Tp. 6 R. 11, north and west.

**8173 1/2. TRIPPE, Richard D.**
Dec. 11, 1839, 3 miles E Marianna, Jackson Co. NW 1/4 SE 1/4 Sect. 7 Tp. 4 R. 9, north and west.

**412. TRIPPE, Sarah**
(Assignee Of **Henry TRIPPE**) Heir of **Simeon TRIPPE**, May 7, 1827, 4 miles E Welchton, Jackson Co. E 1/2 NW 1/4 Sect. 34 Tp. 6 R. 11, north and west.

**101. TROTTE, James F.**
Dec. 15, 1826, 2 miles NE Midway Station, Gadsden Co. NW 1/4 Sect. 9 Tp. 1 R. 2, north and west.

**5679. TROTTER, James F.**
May 23, 1836, 1 1/2 miles NE Centerville, Leon Co. W 1/2 NE 1/4 and NE 1/4 NW 1/4 Sect. 17 Tp. 2 R. 2, north and east.

**4309. TROTTI, James F.**
Feb. 12, 1833, 2 miles NW Centerville, Leon Co. SE 1/4 NW 1/4 Sect. 17 Tp. 2 R. 2, north and east.

**5467. TROTTIE, James F.**
Feb. 13, 1836, 1 1/4 miles NNE

Centerville, Leon Co. W 1/2 SE 1/4 Sect. 17 Tp. 2 R. 2, north and east.

**7085. TROTTIE, James F.**
Nov. 11, 1837, 5 miles W Miccosukee, Leon Co. NW 1/4 SE 1/4 Sect. 8 Tp. 2 R. 2, north and east.

**5198. TRUELUCK, Joseph**
Oct. 12, 1835, 8 miles NNE Iamonia, Leon Co. W 1/2 SW 1/4 Sect. 12 Tp. 2 R. 2, north and east.

**4529. TRULL, William**
Jan. 27, 1834, 2 3/4 miles W Felkel, Leon Co. NW 1/4 NE 1/4 Sect. 6 Tp. 2 R. 2, north and east.

**3595. TRULUCK, Andrew**
Aug. 19, 1830, 1 1/2 miles E Stringer, Leon Co. E 1/2 NE 1/4 Sect. 30 Tp. 3 R. 3, north and east. Transferred Sept. 28, 1835, to **Shaderick ATKINSON**, signed and acknowledged before **Nathan Wm. BATTLE**, J. P. of Thomas Co., Georgia.

**2670. TRULUCK, Joseph**
April 1, 1854, 3 1/4 miles E Kingsley, Clay Co. E 1/2 SE 1/4 Sect. 12 Tp. 6 R. 23, south and east.

**8015. TUCKER, Barna**
July 8, 1839, 1 mile SW Concord, Gadsden Co. W 1/2 NW 1/4 Sect. 24 Tp. 3 R. 2, north and west.

**8016. TUCKER, Barna**
July 8, 1839, 2 miles SW Concord, Gadsden Co. NE 1/4 SE 1/4 Sect. 23 Tp. 3 R. 2, north and west.

**4998. TUCKER, John R. A.**
Mar. 28, 1859, 1 mile SE Guilford, Union Co. NW 1/4 NW 1/4 Sect. 36 Tp. 5 R. 19, south and east.

**5778. TUCKER, Lewis**
July 20, 1836, 5 miles E Campbellton, Jackson Co. Lot No. 2 Fractional Sect. 14 Tp. 7 R. 11, north and west.

**5779. TUCKER, Lewis**
July 20, 1836, 4 miles E Campbellton, Jackson Co. Lot Not. 2 Sect. 15 Tp. 7 R. 11, north and west.

**1889. TUCKER, Robert**
June 9, 1827, 1 mile W Copeland, Leon Co. W 1/2 SE 1/4 Sect. 27 Tp. 3 R. 3, north and east.

**TUCKER, Ware G.** see **Daniel BIRD**, #4310

**4958. TURNBULL, Theodore**
(Per **Miles BLAKE**) May 11, 1835, 2 miles S Miccosukee, Jefferson Co. E 1/2 SE 1/4 Sect. 20 Tp. 2 R. 3, north and east.

**8088. TURNBULL, Theodore**
Sept. 21, 1839, 1 mile W El Destino, Jefferson Co. W 1/2 NE 1/4 Sect. 28 Tp. 1 R. 3, south and east.

**8089. TURNBULL, Theodore**
Sept. 21, 1839, 3 miles NNW Cody, Jefferson Co. S 1/2 SW 1/4 Sect. 21 Tp. 1 R. 3, south and east.

**8090. TURNBULL, Theodore**
Sept. 21, 1839, 1 1/2 miles SW Cody, Jefferson Co. NW 1/4 NW 1/4 Sect. 28 Tp. 1 R. 3, south and east.

**8117. TURNBULL, Theodore**
Oct. 18, 18390, at Stringer, Jefferson Co. NE 1/4 NW 1/4 Sect. 28 Tp. 1 R. 3, south and east.

**8508. TURNBULL, Theodore**
Dec. 2, 1841, 1 1/2 miels NNE Cody, Jefferson Co. E 1/2 SE 1/4 Sect. 20 Tp. 1 R. 3, south and east.

**6445. TURNER, James**
Jan. 6, 1837, 3 miles WSW Miccosukee, Leon Co. SW 1/4 NE 1/4 Sect. 13 Tp. 2 R. 2, north and east.

**4872. TURNER, Jonas**
Feb. 19, 1835, 3 1/2 miles SSE Felkel, Leon Co. NE 1/4 NE 1/4 Sect. 13 Tp. 2 R. 2, north and east.

**4873. TURNER, Jonas**
Feb. 19, 1835, 3 1/2 miles SSE Felkel, Leon Co. NW 1/4 NE 1/4 Sect. 13 Tp. 2 R. 2, north and east.

**8208. TURNER, Joseph**
Jan. 7, 1840, 3/4 miles N Prosperity, Holmes Co. SW 1/4 SE 1/4 Sect. 15 Tp. 5 R. 17, north and west.

**4157. TURNER, Nathaniel**
Mar. 21, 1832, 1/2 mile W Copeland, Leon Co. W 1/2 SE 1/4 Sect. 31 Tp. 3 R. 3, north and east.

**5549. TURNER, Nathaniel**
Mar. 19, 1836, 2 1/4 miles N Quincy, Gadsden Co. SW 1/4 SW 1/4 Sect. 31 Tp. 3 R. 3, north and east.

**4239. TURNER, Thomas E.**
Nov. 7, 1832, 1 miles W Copeland, Leon Co. SW 1/4 NW 1/4 Sect. 6 Tp. 2 R. 3, north and east.

**5132. TURNER, Thomas E.**
Aug. 13, 1835, 1 1/4 miles W Copeland, Leon Co. E 1/2 SW 1/4 Sect. 36

Tp. 3 R. 2, north and east.

**6548. TURNER, Thomas**
Jan. 14, 1837, 2 miles WSW Copeland, Leon Co. NW 1/4 NW 1/4 Sect. 6 Tp. 2 R. 3, north and east.

**2234. TURNER, William**
(of Fla.) Jan. 25, 1828, 2 miles SW Miccosukee, Leon Co. E 1/2 NE 1/4 Sect. 18 Tp. 2 R. 3, north and west.

**2371. TURNER, William**
May 9, 1828, 2 miles W Miccosukee, Leon Co. W 1/2 SW 1/4 Sect. 7 Tp. 2 R. 2, north and west.

**2372. TURNER, William**
May 9, 1828, 3 miles N Wadesboro, Leon Co. W 1/2 NE 1/4 Sect. 19 Tp. 2 R. 3, north and east.

**2593. TURNER, William**
Dec. 29, 1828, 1 1/2 miles W Miccosukee, Leon Co. E 1/2 SE 1/4 Sect. 7 Tp. 2 R. 3, north and east.

**2744. TURNER, William**
Feb. 17, 1829, 2 1/2 miles WSW Copeland, Leon Co. NE 1/4 Sect. 1 Tp. 2 R. 2, north and east.

**3084. TURNER, William**
Oct. 17, 1829, 1 1/2 miles W Miccosukee, Leon Co. W 1/2 NE 1/4 Sect. 7 Tp. 2 R. 3, north and east.

**3092. TURNER, William**
Oct. 27, 1829, 2 miles SW Copeland, Leon Co. W 1/2 SW 1/4 Sect. 6 Tp. 2 R. 3, north and east.

**4921. TURNER, William**
April 4, 1835, 2 miles S by W Miccosukee, Jefferson Co. SE 1/4 NE 1/4 Sect. 19 Tp. 2 R. 3, north and east.

**4922. TURNER, William**
April 4, 1835, 1/4 mile NW Miccosukee, Jefferson Co. E 1/2 NE 1/4 Sect. 7 Tp. 2 R. 3, north and east.

**4923. TURNER, William**
April 4, 1835, at Miccosukee, Jefferson Co. W 1/2 SW 1/4 Sect. 8 Tp. 2 R. 3, north and east.

**7368. TURNER, William**
Mar. 1, 1838, 1 1/2 miles S by E Miccosukee, Leon Co. NE 1/4 SE 1/4 Sect. 17 Tp. 2 R. 3, north and east.

**8832. TWEED, Charles A.**
Oct. 29, 1845, 2 1/2 miles SW Roeville, Santa Rosa Co. SW 1/4 NE 1/4 Sect. 34 Tp. 2 R. 28, north and west.

**3851. TWITCHELL, Timothy**
Jan. 17, 1831, just W Bagdad Jct., Santa Rosa Co. Lot No. 3 Sect. 8 Tp. 1 R. 28, north and west.

**5469. TWITCHELL, Timothy**
Feb. 17, 1836, 2 1/4 miles W Milton, Santa Rosa Co. SE 1/4 Sect. 8 Tp. 1 R. 28, north and west.

**6774. TWITCHELL, Timothy**
Feb. 7, 1837, c. 3 miles S Milton, Santa Rosa Co. Lot No. 4 Fractional Sect. 5 Tp. 1 R. 28, north and west.

**6775. TWITCHELL, Timothy**
Feb. 7, 1837, c. 3 miles W Milton, Santa Rosa Co. Lot No. 2 Fractional Sect. 7 Tp. 1 R. 28, north and west.

\* U \*

**3086. ULMER, Paul**
Oct. 21, 1829, 2 miles NW Braswells, Leon Co. W 1/2 SW 1/4 Sect. 5 Tp. 1 R. 4, north and east.

**4694. ULMER, Paul**
Dec. 11, 1834, 1 mile NNE Waukenah, Leon Co. W 1/2 SW 1/4 Sect. 35 Tp. 1 R. 4, north and east. Transferred to **Charles Tullius ULMER**, Dec. 17, 1834.

**4695. ULMER, Paul**
Dec. 11, 1834, 1/2 mile E Waukenah, Leon Co. W 1/2 NW 1/4 Sect. 2 Tp. 1 R. 4, south and east. Transferred to **Charles Tulllius ULMER**, Dec. 17, 1834.

**5135. ULMER, Paul**
Aug. 17, 1835, 2 1/2 miles NW Braswells, Jefferson Co. W 1/2 SE 1/4 Sect. 7 Tp. 1 R. 4, north and east.

**6570. ULMER, Paul**
Jan. 16, 1837, 2 miles WNW Braswells, Jefferson Co. NE 1/4 SW 1/4 Sect. 7 Tp. 1 R. 4, north and east.

**8909. ULMER, Paul**
Feb. 20, 1846, 3 3/4 miles NNW Braswells, Jefferson Co. SE 1/4 NW 1/4 Sect. 8 Tp. 1 R. 4, north and east.

**ULMER, Charles Tullius see Paul ULMER**

**1587. UNDERWOOD, Fernando A.**
Dec. 27, 1852, 2 1/4 miles NNE High Springs, Alachua Co. SW 1/4 SW 1/4 Sect. 31 Tp. 7 R. 18, south and east. Patent delivered Aug. 13, 1857.

**2412. UNDERWOOD, Fernando A.**
Feb. 21, 1854, 2 1/4 miles E High Springs, Alachua Co. NW 1/4 NE 1/4 Sect. 6 Tp. 8 R. 18, south and east.

**2414. UNDERWOOD, Fernando A.**
Feb. 21, 1854, 2 1/2 miles E High Springs, Alachua Co. SE 1/4 SW 1/4 Sect. 31 Tp. 7 R. 18, south and east. Patent delivered Aug. 13, 1856.

**2593. UNDERWOOD, Fernando A.**
Mar. 9, 1854, 7 1/4 miles W Haynesworth, Alachua Co. SW 1/4 SE 1/4 Sect. 31 Tp. 7 R. 18, south and east. Patent delivered Aug. 13, 1856.

**569. UNDERWOOD, Fernando Arredondo**
June 24, 1847, 2 1/2 miles E High Springs, Alachua Co. NE 1/4 NE 1/4 Sect. 1 Tp. 8 R. 17, south and east.

## * V *

**8662. VANCE, Miles M.**
March 28, 1844, 2 miles W Marianna, Jackson Co. NE 1/4 SE 1/4 Sect. 6 Tp. 4 R. 10, north and west.

**5849. VANN, Heddar**
Sept. 14, 1836, 1/4 mile W Cherrylake (town), Gadsden Co. NE 1/4 NW 1/4 Sect. 6 Tp. 1 R. 1, north and west.

**8071. VANN, Nancy**
Sept. 12, 1839, 1 mile NW Lake Jackson, Leon Co. S 1/2 Lot No. 1 Sect. 36 Tp. 2 R. 2, north and west.

**1688. VANZANT, Garrett**
Feb. 1, 1853, 7 miles E Suwannee Valley Station, Columbia Co. SW 1/4 SW 1/4 Sect. 24 Tp. 2 R. 16, south and east. Patent delivered Sept. 16, 1856.

**8150. VARN, Frederick**
Nov. 20, 1839, 2 miles SE Jennings, Hamilton Co. NE 1/4 Sect. 13 Tp. 2 R. 12, north and west.

**8151. VARN, Frederick**
Nov. 21, 1839, 1 mile SE Jennings, Hamilton Co. W Division Lot No. 7 Sect. 12 Tp. 2 R. 12, north and east.

**8448. VARN, Frederick**
Jan. 7, 1841, 3 1/2 miles W by N Avoca, Hamilton Co. E 1/2 NW 1/4 Sect. 18 Tp. 2 R. 13, north and east.

**2097. VASS, Edmond B.**
(of Fla.) Nov. 12, 1827, 1/4 mile SW El Destino, Jefferson Co. W 1/2 SW 1/4 Sect. 7 Tp. 1 R. 3, south and east.

**2447. VASS, Edmond B.**
July 28, 1828, 1 mile SE El Destino, Jefferson Co. E 1/2 NW 1/4 Sect. 17 Tp. 1 R. 3, north and east.

**3440. VASS, Edmond B.**
March 8, 1830, in El Destino, Jefferson Co. E 1/2 SW 1/4 Sect. 7 Tp. 1 R. 3, south and east.

**3444. VASS, Edmond B.**
March 10, 1830, 1/2 mile S El Destino, Jefferson Co. NW 1/4 Sect. 18 Tp. 1 R. 3, south and east.

**4394. VASS, Edmond B.**
Aug. 22, 1833, 1 mile SE El Destino, Jefferson Co. SW 1/4 NW 1/4 Sect. 17 Tp. 1 R. 3, south and east.

**6419. VASS, Edmond B.**
Jan. 4, 1837, 1/2 mile S El Destino, Jefferson Co. E 1/2 NE 1/4 Sect. 18 Tp. 1 R. 3, south and east.

**6420. VASS, Edmond B.**
Jan. 4, 1837, 2 miles S El Destino, Jefferson Co. E 1/2 NW 1/4 and NW 1/4 NW 1/4 Sect. 19 Tp. 1 R. 3, south and east.

**7184. VASS, Edmond B.**
Jan. 3, 1838, 3 1/2 miles S Fanlew, Jefferson Co. W 1/2 NE 1/4 and W 1/2 SE 1/4 Sect. 19 Tp. 1 R. 3, south and east.

**7214. VASS, Edmond B.**
Jan. 11, 1838, at El Destino, Jefferson Co. W 1/2 NE 1/4 Sect. 13 Tp. 1 R. 2, south and east.

**7218. VASS, Edmond B.**
Jan. 12, 1838, at Capitola, Leon Co. NE 1/4 SW 1/4 Sect. 19 Tp. 1 R. 3, south and east.

**5772. VASSEUR, Eli**
July 15, 1836, at Galt City, Santa Rosa Co. E 1/2 NW 1/4 Sect. 15 Tp. 1 R. 28, north and west.

**1090. VICERS, Harris**
(DUP) Feb. 6, 1827, 3 miles NNE Lake Jackson Station, Leon Co. Lot No. 6 Sect. 20 Tp. 2 R. 1, north and west.

**118. VICKERS, Bryant**
Dec. 25, 1826, 1 mile NE Havana, Gadsden Co. SE 1/4 Sect. 29 Tp. 3 R. 2, north and west.

**7667. VICKERS, Bryant**
Oct. 5, 1838, 2 miles NNE Concord, Gadsden Co. E 1/2 NE 1/4 Sect. 17 Tp. 3 R. 1, north and west. This receipt is in the form of an application for a duplicate, applied for by alleged owner of above tract, Aug. 24, 1849, and sworn to by claimant before **H. R. W. ANDREWS**, Register of Leon Co.

**5019. VICKERS, Elizabeth**
(and **John G. GAMBLE**) July 1, 1835, 1/4 mile NNE Wacissa, Jefferson Co. E 1/2 SE 1/4 Sect. 36 Tp. 1 R. 3, south and east.

**2324. VICKERS, Hardy**
March 29, 1828, 2 miles NW Bradfordville, Leon Co. E 1/2 NE 1/4 Sect. 17 Tp. 2 R. 1, north and east.

**13. VICKERS, Hatcher**
Sept. 12, 1826, near L. Jackson (town),

Gadsden Co. SW 1/4 Sect. 29 Tp. 3 R. 2, north and west. Rec'd $200.38 3/4 for 160.31 acres. **R. K. CALL**, Receiver. By endorsement on back this was transferred Sept. 12, 1829, to **Thomas SPEIGHT** by Hatcher VICKERS.

**1927. VICKERS, James J.**
(DUP) June 18, 1827, 3 miles N Bradfordville, Leon Co. E 1/2 SW 1/4 Sect. 3 Tp. 2 R. 1, north and east.

**2383. VICKERS, James J.**
May 23, 3 miles N Centerville, Leon Co. E 1/2 NE 1/4 Sect. 10 Tp. 2 R. 1, north and east.

**3059. VICKERS, James J.**
Sept. 22, 1829, 2 miles N Bradfordville, Leon Co. W 1/2 NE 1/4 Sect. 10 Tp. 2 R. 1, north and east.

**3928. VICKERS, James J.**
March 20, 1831, 3 miles N Bradfordville, Leon Co. W 1/2 SE 1/4 Sect. 3 Tp. 2 R. 1, north and east.

**1957. VICKERS, James M.**
June 26, 1827, 3 miles N by W Bradfordville, Leon Co. E 1/2 NE 1/4 Sect. 4 Tp. 2 R. 1, north and east.

**1958. VICKERS, James M.**
June 26, 1827, 4 miles N Bradfordville, Leon Co. E 1/2 NW 1/4 Sect. 3 Tp. 2 R. 1, north and east.

**3143. VICKERS, James M.**
Dec. 1, 1829, 4 miles NNW Bradfordville, Leon Co. W 1/2 SW 1/4 Sect. 5 Tp. 2 R. 1, north and east.

**3145. VICKERS, James M.**
Dec. 3, 1829, 3 1/2 miles NNW Bradfordville, Leon Co. E 1/2 SW 1/4 Sect. 5 Tp. 2 R. 1, north and east.

**3182. VICKERS, James M.**
Dec. 26, 1829, 3 miles S Meridian, Leon Co. Lot No. 3 Fractional Sect. 31 Tp. 3 R. 1, north and east.

**5405. VICKERS, James M.**
Jan. 14, 1836, 2 1/2 miles S by E Meridian, Leon Co. NE 1/4 NW 1/4 Sect. 5 Tp. 2 R. 1, north and east.

**3502. VICKERS, James T.**
May 3, 1830, 2 miles NNE Bradfordville, Leon Co. W 1/2 NW 1/4 Sect. 11 Tp. 2 R. 1, north and east.

**2521. VICKERS, John L.**
Oct. 13, 1828, 2 1/2 miles SE Concord, Gadsden Co. W 1/2 SE 1/4 Sect. 24 Tp. 3 R. 1, north and west.

**7801. VICKERS, John L.**
Jan. 7, 1839, 1 1/4 miles N by W Meridian, Leon Co. W 1/2 SW 1/4 Sect. 24 Tp. 3 R. 1, north and west.

**7807. VICKERS, John L.**
Jan. 9, 1839, 2 1/2 miles E Hinson, Gadsden Co. NW 1/4 NW 1/4 Sect. 25 Tp. 3 R. 1, north and west.

**2029. VICKERS, Nathan**
Aug. 13, 1827, 3 miles NNW Bradfordville, Leon Co. W 1/2 SE 1/4 Sect. 3 Tp. 2 R. 1, north and east.

**3586. VICKERS, Nathan**
Aug. 3, 1830, 3 1/2 miles N by W Bradfordville, Leon Co. E 1/2 SW 1/4 Sect. 4 Tp. 2 R. 1, north and east.

**5403. VICKERS, Nathan**
Jan. 14, 1836, 2 1/2 miles S by E Meridian, Leon Co. W 1/2 NE 1/4 Sect. 5 Tp. 2 R. 1, north and east.

**5404. VICKERS, Nathan**
Jan. 14, 1836, 2 3/4 miles S by E Meridian, Leon Co. W 1/2 SE 1/4 Sect. 5 Tp. 2 R. 1, north and east.

**5410. VICKERS, Nathan**
Dec. 16, 1836, 3 miles NW Bradfordville, Leon Co. E 1/2 NE 1/4 Sect. 8 Tp. 2 R. 1, north and east.

**83. VICKERS, Young**
Dec. 1, 1826, 2 miles SW Havana, Gadsden Co. NE 1/4 Sect. 10 Tp. 2 R. 2, north and west. Transferred Dec. 1, 1826, to **Stephen BROWNING**. Teste: **G. W. WARD**, Register.

**494. VICKREY, Robert**
Oct. 25, 1830, 2 miles ENE Dills, Jefferson Co. W 1/2 SW 1/4 Sect. 33 Tp. 3 R. 6, north and east.

**5733. VINSANT, William**
June 27, 1836, 1/4 mile NE Hamburg, Madison Co. W 1/2 NE 1/4 Sect. 15 Tp. 2 R. 8, north and east.

* W *

**2089. WADKINS, Crawford**
Aug. 22, 1853, 2 3/4 miles W Hague, Alachua Co. N 1/2 Lot No. 1 Sect. 25 Tp. 8 R. 19, south and east. Patent delivered June 24, 1857.

**7037. WAITMAN, Thomas**
Dec. 31, 1888, 1 1/2 miles E Florahome, Putnam Co. NW 1/4 SE 1/4 and SW 1/4 NE 1/4 Sect. 6 Tp. 9S R. 25E.

**810. WALDON, George W. S.**
Jan. 22, 1851, 4 1/2 miles S Benton, Columbia Co. W 1/2 NW 1/4 Sect. 20 Tp. 1 R. 17, south and east. Patent delivered April 26, 1856.

**8795. WALKER, Ann J. C.**
July 21, 1845, 3 1/2 miles NNW Fowler, Madison Co. W 1/2 NW 1/4 Sect. 2 Tp. 1 R. 6, south and east.

**1593. WALKER, Ansel**
Dec. 29, 1852, 4 miles NE New River, Bradford Co. S 1/2 NW 1/4 Sect. 10 Tp. 6 R. 21, south and east. Patent delivered Nov. 24, 1856.

**1017. WALKER, B. G.**
Jan. 27, 1827, 2 miles ENE Centerville, Leon Co. E 1/2 SW 1/4 Sect. 17 Tp. 2 R. 2, north and east.

**1185. WALKER, Benj. G.**
(DUP) March 2, 1827, in Lake Hull, 7 miles NNE Tallahassee, Leon Co. E 1/2 SW 1/4 Sect. 33 Tp. 2 R. 1, north and east.

**9685. WALKER, Daniel**
Nov. 27, 1891, 2 miles S by W Lake Garfield, Polk Co. S 1/2 NE 1/4 Sect. 24 Tp. 30S R. 25E.

**62. WALKER, David**
Sept. 18, 1844, near White Springs, Columbia Co. W 1/2 NE 1/4 Sect. 27 Tp. 2 R. 16, south and east.

**1518. WALKER, Elias**
Nov. 25, 1852, at Winfield, Columbia Co. NE 1/4 SE 1/4 Sect. 26 Tp. 2 R. 16, south and east. Patent delivered Dec. 8, 1856.

**2469. WALKER, Elisha**
Aug. 27, 1828, 1 1/2 miles W Newport, Wakulla Co. W 1/2 NE 1/4 Sect. 27 Tp. 1 R. 3, south and east.

**7295. WALKER, Elisha**
Feb. 2, 1838, 1 1/2 miles E by N Felkel, Leon Co. NE 1/4 NE 1/4 Sect. 2 Tp. 2 R. 2, north and west.

**2121. WALKER, Elizabeth**
Aug. 29, 1853, 2 miles S Melrose, Alachua Co. Lot No. 4 Sect. 19 and Lots No. 2 and 5 Sect. 30 Tp. 9 R. 23, south and east. Patent delivered June 8, 1857.

**5739. WALKER, George K.**
June 29, 1836, 2 miles W Indian Pass, Gulf Co. Lot No. 1 Fractional Sect. 11 Tp.. 9 R. 11, south and west.

**4334. WALKER, Henry**
Mar. 23, 1833, 3 1/2 miles NE Stringer, Leon Co. NE 1/4 NE 1/4 Sect. 23 Tp. 3 R. 3, north and east.

**5186. WALKER, Henry**
Oct. 5, 1835, 1/2 mile S Fincher, Leon Co. W 1/2 NE 1/4 Sect. 23 Tp. 3 R. 3, north and east.

**1291. WALKER, Isham**
(Senior) April 18, 1827, 4 miles S Chaires, Leon Co. E 1/2 SE 1/4 Sect. 15 Tp. 1 R. 2, south and east.

**5903. WALKER, Isham**
Oct. 17, 1836, 5 miles W Hanson, Madison Co. E 1/2 NW 1/4 and W 1/2 NE 1/4 Sect. 30 Tp. 2 R. 9, north and east.

**5904. WALKER, Isham**
Oct. 17, 1836, 4 miles W Hanson, Madison Co. E 1/2 SW 1/4 and W 1/2 SE 1/4 Sect. 30 Tp. 2 R. 9, north and east.

**5983. WALKER, James**
Nov. 7, 1836, 4 miles S by E Dill, Jefferson Co. NE 1/4 SW 1/4 Sect. 20 Tp. 2 R. 6, north and east.

**6571. WALKER, James**
Jan. 16, 1837, 3 miles SSE Dills, Jefferson Co. W 1/2 NW 1/4 and NE 1/4 NW 1/4 Sect. 20 Tp. 2 R. 6, north and east.

**7559. WALKER, James**
July 30, 1838, 4 miles NNE McClellan, Gadsden Co. W 1/2 SE 1/4 Sect. 36 Tp. 2 R. 5, north and east.

**5430. WALKER, Jesse**
Feb. 1, 1836, 5 miles NNW Aucilla, Jefferson Co. E 1/2 SW 1/4 Sect. 29 Tp. 2 R. 6, north and east.

**6296. WALKER, Jesse**
Dec. 24, 1836, 3 1/2 miles S Dills,

Jefferson Co. W 1/2 SW 1/4 Sect. 29 Tp. 2 R. 6, north and east.

**7673. WALKER, Jesse**
Oct. 16, 1838, 5 1/2 miles NNE McClellan, Jefferson Co. E 1/2 SE 1/4 Sect. 30 Tp. 2 R. 6, north and east.

**9661. WALKER, Lucy**
(Nee **SHINGLES**) Nov. 16, 1891, 6 1/2 miles E Cocowitch, Marion Co. SE 1/4 Sect. 28 Tp. 16S R. 20E.

**237. WALKER, Richard**
(DUP) Dec. 30, 1826, 3 miles SE Florence, Gadsden Co. SW 1/4 Sect. 11 Tp. 2 R. 2, north and west. Transferred to **Davis S. BAGGS**, Dec. 30, 1826.

**5281. WALKER, Richard**
Nov. 21, 1835, 1 1/4 miles W by S Genoa, Hamilton Co. W 1/2 SE 1/4 Sect. 14 Tp. 1 R. 14, south and east.

**7546. WALKER, Richard**
July 23, 1838, 3 1/2 miles NNE Lamont, Jefferson Co. NE 1/4 SE 1/4 Sect. 12 Tp. 1 R. 3, south and east.

**8047. WALKER, Richard**
Aug. 19, 1839, 5 miles E El Destino, Jefferson Co. SW 1/4 NE 1/4 Sect. 12 Tp. 1 R. 3, south and east.

**1756. WALKER, Solomon**
(DUP) June 4, 1827, 1 mile WSW Black Creek, Leon Co. E 1/2 NW 1/4 Sect. 14 Tp. 1 R. 2, north and east.

**2648. WALKER, Solomon**
Jan. 19, 1829, 3 miles WSW Wadesboro, Leon Co. E 1/2 NW 1/4 Sect. 10 Tp. 1 R. 2, north and east.

**3139. WALKER, Solomon**
Nov. 30, 1829, just N Rose, Leon Co. E 1/2 NE 1/4 Sect. 26 Tp. 1 R. 2, south and east.

**4756. WALL, Perry G.**
Jan. 6, 1835, 2 miles S Marion, Hamilton Co. SE 1/4 SW 1/4 Sect. 5 Tp. 1 R. 14, north and east.

**4863. WALL, Perry G.**
Feb. 12, 1835, 2 1/2 miles N Marion, Hamilton Co. W 1/2 NW 1/4 Sect. 19 Tp. 1 R. 14, north and east.

**4864. WALL, Perry G.**
Feb. 12, 1835, 3 1/2 miles N by W Marion, Hamilton Co. E 1/2 NE 1/4 Sect. 24 Tp. 1 R. 13, north and east.

**489. WALL, Perry Green**
Dec. 8, 1846, 5 miles E Natal, Hernando Co. NE 1/4 NE 1/4 Sect. 24 Tp. 22 R. 18, south and east. Patent delivered Oct. 13, 1854.

**6811. WALLACE, James**
Mar. 1, 1837, 3 miles N by E Ericu, Madison Co. W 1/2 SW 1/4 Sect. 29 Tp. 1 R. 6, south and east.

**7380. WALLACE, James**
Mar. 2, 1838, 1 1/2 miles NNW Champaign, Madison Co. W 1/2 NE 1/4 Sect. 15 Tp. 1 R. 8, north and east.

**7836. WALLACE, James**
Jan. 25, 1839, 1 mile NNW Champaign, Madison Co. E 1/2 NW 1/4 Sect. 14 Tp. 1 R. 8, north and east.

**8989. WALLACE, James**
Nov. 6, 1846, 4 1/4 miles W by S Shady Grove, Taylor Co. SE 1/4 SW 1/4 Sect. 20 Tp. 2 R. 7, south and east.

**7527. WALLACE, William**
July 12, 1838, 5 miles W Dennelt, Madison Co. SE 1/4 SE 1/4 Sect. 34 Tp. 2 R. 8, north and east.

**7528. WALLACE, William**
July 12, 1838, 3 1/2 miles N Champaign, Madison Co. W 1/2 SW 1/4 Sect. 35 Tp. 2 R. 8, north and east.

**7529. WALLACE, William**
July 12, 1838, 4 1/2 miles NNW Champaign, Madison Co. NE 1/4 NE 1/4 Sect. 3 Tp. 1 R. 8, north and east.

**WALLENS, James M.** see **James GEIGER, #358.**

**3125. WARD, Geo. T.**
Nov. 16, 1829, c. 4 miles W Stephensville, Taylor Co. N 1/2 SW 1/4 Sect. 22 Tp. 9 R. 9, south and east.

**13. WARD, George W.**
May 16, 1825, near Lake Bradford, Leon Co. W 1/2 NE 1/4 Sect. 11 Tp. 1 R. 1, south and west. Rec'd of **Geo. W. WARD**, $120.80 for 80 1/4 acres. **R. K. CALL.**

**3412. WARD, George W.**
Feb. 17, 1830, just E Mandalay, Taylor Co. W 1/2 SW 1/4 Sect. 17 Tp. 4 R. 4, south and east.

**4721. WARD, George W.**
Dec. 16, 1834, 2 1/4 miles N by W Perkins, Leon Co. NE 1/4 SE 1/4 Sect. 22 Tp. 1 R. 1, south and east.

**4722. WARD, George W.**
Dec. 18, 1834, 2 miles N Perkins, Leon Co. NE 1/4 SW 1/4 Sect. 23 Tp. 1 R.

1, south and east.

**4723. WARD, George W.**
Dec. 18, 1834, 2 1/2 miles N by W Perkins, Leon Co. W 1/2 NE 1/4 Sect. 22 Tp. 1 R. 1, south and east.

**351. WARD, John**
(Assignee of **Mary WARD**) April 16, 1827, 3 miles SE Campbellton, Jackson Co. NE 1/4 Sect. 17 Tp. 6 R. 11, north and west.

**2010. WARD, William H.**
Aug. 6, 1853, at Brooker, Bradford Co. E 1/2 SW 1/4 Sect. 8 Tp. 7 R. 20, south and east. Patent delivered Sept. 15, 1857.

**2164. WARD, William N.**
Sept. 12, 1853, 1/2 mile E Brooker, Bradford Co. E 1/2 Lot No. 1 Sect. 18 Tp. 7 R. 20, south and east. Patent delivered Sept. 18, 1857.

**7573. WARE, Thompson**
Aug. 6, 1838, 5 1/2 miles SSW Dills, Jefferson Co. NE 1/4 Sect. 8 Tp. 2 R. 5, north and east.

**7574. WARE, Thompson**
Aug. 6, 1838, 1 1/2 miles N Monticello, Jefferson Co. E 1/2 NE 1/4 Sect. 17 Tp. 2 R. 5, north and east.

**7575. WARE, Thompson**
Aug. 6, 1838, 1 3/4 miles N Monticello, Jefferson Co. E 1/2 NW 1/4 Sect. 17 Tp. 2 R. 5, north and east.

**7654. WARE, Thompson**
Sept. 29, 1838, 3 1/2 miles N by E Monticello, Jefferson Co. E 1/2 SW 1/4 Sect. 9 Tp. 2 R. 5, north and east.

**7655. WARE, Thompson**
Sept. 29, 1838, 2 1/2 miles N by E Monticello, Jefferson Co. E 1/2 SW 1/4 Sect. 8 Tp. 2 R. 5, north and east.

**5138. WARING, Benjamin G.**
Aug. 19, 1835, 1 1/2 miles S by W Fincher, Leon Co. NW 1/4 Sect. 22 Tp. 3 R. 3, north and east.

**5139. WARING, Benjamin G.**
Aug. 19, 1835, 1/2 mile N Stringer, Leon Co. E 1/2 NE 1/4 Sect. 21 Tp. 3 R. 3, north and east.

**4119. WARING, Burford G.**
Jan. 3, 1832, 1 mile NE Stringer, Leon Co. NE 1/4 Sect. 22 Tp. 3 R. 3, north and east.

**7668. WARREN, Benjamin**
Oct. 9, 1838, 3 1/2 miles NNW Dills, Jefferson Co. NE 1/4 SE 1/4 Sect. 28 Tp. 3 R. 5, north and east.

**6124. WARREN, Elbert A.**
Dec. 1, 1836, 4 1/2 miles E by S Quincy, Gadsden Co. NE 1/4 SE 1/4 Sect. 11 Tp. 2 R. 3, north and west.

**4834. WARREN, Elbert A.**
Jan. 29, 1835, 1 mile W by S Florence, Leon Co. NW 1/4 SE 1/4 Sect. 11 Tp. 2 R. 3, north and west.

**2130. WARREN, Reuben**
(of Fla.) Dec. 7, 1827, 3 1/2 miles E Sawdust, Gadsden Co. E 1/2 NW 1/4 Sect. 30 Tp. 2 R. 3, north and west.

**8852. WASHBURN, Samuel**
Dec. 12, 1845, 3 miles N by W Lake Jackson (town), Leon Co. NE 1/4 NW 1/4 Sect. 24 Tp. 2 R. 2, north and west.

**6431. WASHINGTON, Henry**
Jan. 5, 1837, 1 mile SSW Stephensville, Taylor Co. Lot No. 5 Fractional Sect. 25 Tp. 9 R. 9, south and east. Deposition of **Henry WASHINGTON** in lieu of receipt, sworn Dec. 9, 1841, before **Robt. J. HACKLEY**, Register.

**6432. WASHINGTON, Henry**
Jan. 5, 1837, 2 miles S Clara, Taylor Co. W 1/2 SW 1/4 Sect. 15 Tp. 3 R. 10, south and east.

**6433. WASHINGTON, Henry**
Jan. 5, 1837, 2 miles S Clara, Taylor Co. W 1/2 NW 1/4 Sect. 22 Tp. 8 R. 10, south and east.

**5701. WATERS, Hezekiah M.**
June 10, 1836, 3 miles NNE Bond, Madison Co. SW 1/4 NE 1/4 Sect. 1 Tp. 2 R. 8, north and east.

**5758. WATERS, Hezekiah**
July 6, 1836, 2 1/2 miles NNE Hamburg, Madison Co. SE 1/4 NE 1/4 Sect. 2 Tp. 2 R. 8, north and east.

**6440. WATERS, Hezekiah**
Jan. 5, 1837, 2 miles W Cherry Lake Post Office, Madison Co. SE 1/4 NE 1/4 Sect. 12 Tp. 2 R. 8, north and east.

**4102. WATERS, H. M.**
Oct. 27, 1831, 3 1/2 miles SSE Bond, Madison Co. E 1/2 SE 1/4 Sect. 1 Tp. 2 R. 8, north and east.

**3856. WATKINS, Hartwell**
Jan. 21, 1831, 1 mile E Stringer, Leon Co. W 1/2 NE 1/4 Sect. 27 Tp. 3 R. 3, north and east.

**5618. WATKINS, Hartwell**
April 23, 1836, 6 miles SE Stringer, Jefferson Co. NE 1/4 SW 1/4 Sect. 33 Tp. 3 R. 4, north and east.

**5619. WATKINS, Hartwell**
April 23, 1836, 6 1/2 miles SE Stringer, Jefferson Co. W 1/2 NW 1/4 Sect. 34 Tp. 3 R. 4, north and east.

**707. WATKINS, John R.**
(of Fla.) April 20, 1826, 5 miles NNW Tallahassee, Leon Co. W 1/2 NW 1/4 Sect. 15 Tp. 1 R. 1, north and west.

**708. WATKINS, John R.**
(of Fla.) April 24, 1826, 2 miles E Helena, Leon Co. E 1/2 SE 1/4 Sect. 15 Tp. 1 R. 1, north and west.

**709. WATKINS, John R.**
(of Fla.) April 24, 1826, 2 miles E Helena, Leon Co. W 1/2 SE 1/4 Sect. 15 Tp. 1 R. 1, north and west.

**3309. WATSON, Alexander** Feb. 13, 1830, 3/4 mile N Old town, Dixie Co. E 1/2 NE 1/4 Sect. 11 Tp. 10 R. 13, south and east. Transferred Feb. 14, 1830, to **Wm. BAILEY.** (G.W. WARD, Reg.)

**3310. WATSON, Alexander**
Feb. 13, 1830, 3/4 mile N Old Town, Dixie Co. W 1/2 NE 1/4 Sect. 11 Tp. 10 R. 13, south and east. Transferred Feb. 14, 1830, to **Wm. BAILEY.**

**3311. WATSON, Alexander**
Feb. 13, 1830, 3/4 mile N Old Town, Dixie Co. E 1/2 SW 1/4 Sect. 11 Tp. 10 R. 13, south and east. Transferred Feb. 14, 1830, to **Wm. BAILEY.**

**3312. WATSON, Alexander**
Feb. 13, 1830, 1 mile NW Old Town, Dixie Co. W 1/2 NE 1/4 Sect. 10 Tp. 10 R. 13, south and east. Transferred Feb. 14, 1830, to **Wm. BAILEY.**

**3313. WATSON, Alexander**
Feb. 13, 1830, 1 mile NW Old Town, Dixie Co. E 1/2 NW 1/4 Sect. 10 Tp. 10 R. 13, south and east. Transferred to **Wm. BAILEY**, Feb. 14, 1830.

**3314. WATSON, Alexander**
Feb. 13, 1830, 1 1/2 miles WNW Old Town, Dixie Co. W 1/2 NW 1/4 Sect. 10 Tp. 10 R. 13, south and east. Transferred Feb. 14, 1830, to **Wm. BAILEY.**

**3315. WATSON, Alexander**
Feb. 13, 1830, 1 mile N Old Town, Dixie Co. W 1/2 SE 1/4 Sect. 2 Tp. 10 R. 13, south and east. Transferred to **Wm. BAILEY** on Feb. 14, 1830.

**3316. WATSON, Alexander**
Feb. 13, 1830, 1 mile N by E Old Town, Dixie Co. E 1/2 SE 1/4 Sect. 2 Tp. 10 R. 13, south and east. Transferred to **Wm. BAILEY** on Feb. 14, 1830.

**3318. WATSON, Alexander**
Feb. 13, 1830, c. 2 miles NE Old Town, Dixie Co. Lot No. 6 Fractional Sect. 1 Tp. 10 R. 13, south and east.Transferred Feb. 14, 1830, to **Wm. BAILEY.**

**3319. WATSON, Alexander**
Feb. 13, 1830, 2 miles N Old Town, Dixie Co. E 1/2 NE 1/4 Sect. 2 Tp. 10 R. 13, south and east. Transferred to **Wm. BAILEY** on Feb. 14, 1830.

**3320. WATSON, Alexander**
Feb. 13, 1830, 1 mile N Old Town, Dixie Co. E 1/2 SW 1/4 Sect. 2 Tp. 10 R. 13, south and east. Transferred to **Wm. BAILEY** on Feb. 14, 1830.

**3321. WATSON, Alexander**
Feb. 14, 1830, at Old Town, Dixie Co. E 1/2 NW 1/4 Sect. 14 Tp. 10 R. 13, south and east. At $6.00 per acre.

**3322. WATSON, Alexander**
Feb. 14, 1830, just W Old Town, Dixie Co. W 1/2 NW 1/4 Sect. 14 Tp. 10 R. 13, south and east. At $5.75 per acre.

**3323. WATSON, Alexander**
Feb. 14, 1830, just SW Old Town, Dixie Co. W 1/2 SW 1/4 Sect. 14 Tp. 10 R. 13, south and east. $4.75 per acre.

**3324. WATSON, Alexander**
Feb. 14, 1830, S part Old Town, Dixie Co. E 1/2 SW 1/4 Sect. 14 Tp. 10 R. 13, south and east. $4.00 per acre.

**3325. WATSON, Alexander**
Feb. 14, 1830, S part Old Town, Dixie Co. W 1/2 SE 1/4 Sect. 14 Tp. 10 R. 13, south and east. $5.00 per acre.

**3326. WATSON, Alexander**
Feb. 14, 1830, just SE Old Town, Dixie Co. E 1/2 SE 1/4 Sect. 14 Tp. 10 R. 13, south and east. $5.01 per acre.

**3327. WATSON, Alexander**
Feb. 14, 1830, 1/2 mile SW Old Town, Dixie Co. E 1/2 SW 1/4 Sect. 15 Tp. 20 R. 13, south and east. $3.90 per

acre.

**3328. WATSON, Alexander**
Feb. 14, 1830, 1/2 mile W Old Town, Dixie Co. W 1/2 NE 1/4 Sect. 15 Tp. 10 R. 13, south and east. $4.00 per acre.

**3329. WATSON, Alexander**
Feb. 14, 1830, 1 mile W Old Town, Dixie Co. W 1/2 SE 1/4 Sect. 5 Tp. 10 R. 13, south and east. $1.25 per acre.

**3330. WATSON, Alexander**
Feb. 14, 1830, 1/2 mile W Old Town, Dixie Co. E 1/2 SE 1/4 Sect. 15 Tp. 10 R. 13, south and east. $1.25 per acre.

**3331. WATSON, Alexander**
Feb. 13, 1830, 3/4 mile SW Old Town, Dixie Co. W 1/2 NW 1/4 Sect. 23 Tp. 10 R. 13, south and east. $4.00 per acre. Transferred Feb. 14, 1830, to **Wm. BAILEY.**

**3332. WATSON, Alexander**
Feb. 13, 1830, 1 mile SW Old Town, Dixie Co. W 1/2 SW 1/4 Sect. 23 Tp. 10 R. 13, south and east. $1.25 per acre. Transferred Feb. 14, 1830, to **Wm. BAILEY.**

**3333. WATSON, Alexander**
Feb. 13, 1830, c. 1 1/2 miles SE Old Town, Dixie Co. Lot No. 4 Fractional Sect. 24 Tp. 10 R. 13, south and east. Transferred Feb. 14, 1830, to **James W. DABNEY.**

**3334. WATSON, Alexander**
Feb. 13, 1830, c. 1 1/2 miles SE Old Town, Dixie Co. Lot No. 5 Fractional Sect. 24 Tp. 10 R. 13, south and east. Transferred to **Jas. W. DABNEY** on Feb. 14, 1830.

**3335. WATSON, Alexander**
Feb. 13, 1830, c. 1 1/2 miles SE Old Town, Dixie Co. Lot No. 6 Fractional Sect. 24 Tp. 10 R. 13, south and east. Transferred Feb. 14, 1830, to **Jas. W. DABNEY.**

**3336. WATSON, Alexander**
Feb. 13, 1830, 3/4 mile NW Old Town, Dixie Co. W 1/2 NW 1/4 Sect. 11 Tp. 10 R. 13, south and east. Transferred Feb. 14, 1830, to **Wm. BAILEY.**

**3337. WATSON, Alexander**
Feb. 14, 1830, 1/2 mile NW Old Town, Dixie Co. W 1/2 SW 1/4 Sect. 11 Tp. 10 R. 13, south and east. $3.99 per acre.

**3338. WATSON, Alexander**
Feb. 14, 1830, just NW Old Town, Dixie Co. E 1/2 SW 1/4 Sect. 11 Tp. 10 R. 13, south and east. $3.74 per acre.

**3339. WATSON, Alexander**
Feb. 13, 1830, just N Old Town, Dixie Co. W 1/2 SE 1/4 Sect. 11 Tp. 10 R. 13, south and east. Transferred Feb. 16, 1830, to **Wm. BAILEY.**

**3340. WATSON, Alexander**
Feb. 13, 1830, c. 1 mile NE Old Town, Dixie Co. Lot No. 4 Fractional Sect. 12 Tp. 10 R. 13, south and east. Transferred Feb. 14, 1830 to **Wm. BAILEY.**

**3341. WATSON, Alexander**
Feb. 14, 1830, just E Old Town, Dixie Co. Lot No. 7 Sect. 13 Tp. 10 R. 13, south and east.

**3342. WATSON, Alexander**
Feb. 14, 1830, 1 mile S Old Town, Dixie Co. W 1/2 SE 1/4 Sect. 23 Tp. 10 R. 13, south and east. Transferred Feb. 14, 1830, to **Jas. W. DABNEY.**

**3343. WATSON, Alexander**
Feb. 13, 1830, just SW Old Town, Dixie Co. Lot No. 3 Fractional Sect. 24 Tp. 10 R. 13, south and east. Transferred Feb. 14, 1830, to **James W. DABNEY.**

**3344. WATSON, Alexander**
Feb. 13, 1830, just SW Old Town, Dixie Co. Lot No. 7 Fractional Sect. 24 Tp. 10 R. 13, south and east. Transferred Feb. 14, 1830, to **James W. DABNEY.**

**3365. WATSON, Alexander**
Feb. 16, 1830, just E Old Town, Dixie Co. Lot No. 6 Sect. 13 Tp. 10 R. 13, south and east.

**4116. WATSON, Alexander**
(Jr.) Dec. 27, 1831, 2 miles E Old Town, Dixie Co. Lot No. 2 Sect. 13 Tp. 10 R. 13, south and east.

**6525. WATSON, Alexander**
Jan. 12, 1837, just E Old Town, Dixie Co. Lots No. 3 and 4 Fractional Sect. 13 Tp. 10 R. 13, south and east.

**4744. WATSON, James**
Dec. 26, 1834, 1/2 mile E Panama City, Bay Co. Lot No. 1 Sect. 15 Tp. 4

R. 14, south and west.

**4745. WATSON, James**
Dec. 26, 1834, at Millville, Bay Co. Lot No. 5 Sect. 15 Tp. 4 R. 14, south and west.

**5103. WATSON, James**
July 24, 1835, 1/4 NNW Panama City, Bay Co. N 1/2 Sect. 6 Tp. 4 R. 14, south and west.

**5104. WATSON, James**
July 24, 1835, 1/4 mile S Parker, Bay Co. Fractional Sect. 25 Tp. 4 R. 14, south and west.

**5105. WATSON, James**
July 24, 1835, 1/4 mile SE St. Andrew, Bay Co. Lots No. 1, 2 and 3 Sect. 1 Tp. 4 R. 15, south and west.

**5106. WATSON, James**
July 24, 1835, 1/2 mile W Millville Junction, Bay Co. Lot No. 6 Sect. 35 Tp. 3 R. 15, south and west.

**5107. WATSON, James**
July 24, 1835, 1 1/4 miles W St. Andrew, Bay Co. Lot No. 2 Sect. 34 Tp. 3 R. 15, south and west.

**5108. WATSON, James**
July 24, 1835, 1 1/2 miles W Millville Junction, Bay Co. Lot No. 5 Sect. 35 Tp. 3 R. 15, south and west.

**5109. WATSON, James**
July 24, 1835, at St. Andrew, Bay Co. W 1/2 SW 1/4 Sect. 36 Tp. 3 R. 15, south and west.

**5145. WATSON, James**
Aug. 22, 1835, 2 miles SE by E Wawahitchka, Gulf Co. Lot No. 1 Fractional Sect. 31 Tp. 4 R. 9, south and west.

**5146. WATSON, James**
Aug. 22, 1835, 2 miles SE by S Wewahitchka, Gulf Co. Lot No. 4 Fractional Sect. 31 Tp. 4 R. 9, south and west.

**5147. WATSON, James**
Aug. 22, 1835, 1 mile NNE Bayou George, Bay Co. SW 1/4 NE 1/4 Sect. 4 Tp. 3 R. 13, south and west.

**5148. WATSON, James**
Aug. 22, 1835, 2 miles SE by E Wewahitchka, Gulf Co. Lot No. 8 Fractional Sect. 31 Tp. 4 R. 9, south and west.

**5189. WATSON, James**
Oct. 6, 1835, 2 miles E St. Andrew, Bay Co. E 1/2 SE 1/4 Sect. 31 Tp. 3 R. 14, south and west.

**5190. WATSON, James**
Oct. 6, 1835, 2 miles E St. Andrew, Bay Co. SW 1/4 Sect. 32 Tp. 3 R. 14, south and west.

**5213. WATSON, James**
Oct. 15, 1835, 9 1/4 miles SE Riverside, Washington Co. W 1/2 SE 1/4 Sect. 27 Tp. 1 R. 13, north and west.

**5216. WATSON, James**
Oct. 15, 1835, 2 miles NNE Callaway, Bay Co. Fractional Sect. 27 Tp. 4 R. 13, south and west.

**5268. WATSON, James**
Nov. 19, 1835, 1 mile NNW Bayhead, Bay Co. Lot No. 2 Sect. 19 Tp. 2 R. 13, south and west.

**5606. WATSON, James**
April 20, 1836, 2 1/2 miles SSW Bayou George, Bay Co. E 1/2 SW 1/4 Sect. 4 Tp. 3 R. 13, south and west.

**5607. WATSON, James**
April 20, 1836, 1/4 mile SW Bayou George, Bay Co. W 1/2 SW 1/4 Sect. 3 Tp. 3 R. 13, south and west.

**6649. WATSON, James**
Jan. 24, 1837, 1 mile W Jacob, Jackson Co. W 1/2 NW 1/4 Sect. 13 Tp. 6 R. 12, north and west.

**6650. WATSON, James**
Jan. 24, 1837, 2 miles S by W Campbellton, Jackson Co. NW 1/4 W 1/2 SW 1/4 Sect. 12 Tp. 6 R. 12, north and west.

**6659. WATSON, James**
Jan. 25, 1837, 1 mile WNW Quincy, Gadsden Co. E 1/2 NE 1/4 Sect. 5 Tp. 4 R. 10, north and west.

**4502. WATSON, Leroy**
Jan. 21, 1857, 2 miles W Tioga, Alachua Co. SW 1/4 Sect. 5 Tp. 10 R. 18, south and east.

**5010. WATSON, Terrey B.**
June 20, 1835, 2 3/4 miles NW Cromanton, Bay Co. Lot No. 3 Sect. 15 Tp. 4 R. 14, south and west.

**5011. WATSON, Terrey B.**
June 20, 1835, 2 3/4 miles NW Cromanton, Bay Co. Lot No. 2 Fractional Sect. 15 Tp. 4 R. 14, south and west.

**5012. WATSON, Terrey B.**
June 20, 1835, 2 1/2 miles NW

Cromanton, Bay Co. Lot No. 4 Sect. 15 Tp. 4 R. 14, south and west.

**304. WATSON, Wm. J.**
Jan. 1, 1827, 8 miles W Greenwood, Jackson Co. NW 1/4 Sect. 29 Tp. 6 R. 11, north and west.

**2622. WATSON, Wm. J.**
Jan. 13, 1829, 1 1/2 miles SSW Vernon, Washington Co. E 1/2 SW 1/4 Sect. 3 Tp. 2 R. 15, north and west.
see **Wade H. DUBOSE**.

**3846. WATTERS, H. M.**
Jan. 13, 1831, 2 miles E Bond, Madison Co. W 1/2 SE 1/4 Sect. 1 Tp. 2 R. 8, north and east.

**8604. WATTS, Eleasusa**
Oct. 2, 1843, 1 mile SE Greenwood, Jackson Co. NE 1/4 NE 1/4 Sect. 5 Tp. 5 R. 9, north and west.

**1396. WATTS, Joseph B.**
May 21, 1827, 2 miles S Monticello, Jefferson Co. E 1/2 SW 1/4 Sect. 6 Tp. 1 R. 5, north and east. Transferred to **Abraham MOTT**, Aug. 25, 1827.

**2079. WATTS, Joseph B.**
Oct. 15, 1827, at Monticello, Jefferson Co. W 1/2 SE 1/4 Sect. 19 Tp. 2 R. 5, north and east.

**2112. WATTS, Joseph B.**
(of Fla.) Nov. 21, 1827, 4 miles S Quincy, Jackson Co. W 1/2 SE 1/4 Sect. 25 Tp. 2 R. 4, north and east.

**2365. WATTS, Joseph B.**
May 7, 1828, 1/2 mile SW Monticello, Jefferson Co. E 1/2 SW 1/4 Sect. 25 Tp. 2 R. 4, north and east.

**2711. WATTS, Joseph B.**
Feb. 5, 1829, in Monticello, Jefferson Co. E 1/2 NW 1/4 Sect. 29 Tp. 2 R. 5, north and east.

**2975. WATTS, Joseph B.**
Aug. 6, 1829, 1/2 mile N Monticello, Jefferson Co. W 1/2 NW 1/4 Sect. 19 Tp. 2 R. 5, north and east.

**2977. WATTS, Joseph B.**
Aug. 10, 1829, 1 mile SW Alma, Leon Co. E 1/2 NE 1/4 Sect. 24 Tp. 2 R. 4, north and east.

**3226. WATTS, Joseph B.**
Jan. 23, 1830, 2 miles SE Monticello, Jefferson Co. E 1/2 NE 1/4 Sect. 32 Tp. 2 R. 3, north and east.

**3227. WATTS, Joseph B.**
Jan. 23, 1830, 2 1/4 miles SE Monticello, Jefferson Co. E 1/2 SE 1/4 Sect. 32 Tp. 2 R. 5, north and east.

**3439. WATTS, Joseph B.**
March 6, 1830, 1/2 mile N Monticello, Jefferson Co. E 1/2 NW 1/4 Sect. 19 Tp. 2 R. 5, north and east.

**3656. WATTS, Joseph B.**
Oct. 11, 1830, 4 miles S by E Dills, Jefferson Co. E 1/2 NW 1/4 Sect. 29 Tp. 2 R. 6, north and east. Bought with Scrip No. 152, issued to **Alex'r MACOMB**, May 30, 1829.

**4120. WATTS, Joseph B.**
Jan. 7, 1832, 1 1/4 miles N Monticello, Jefferson Co. W 1/2 SE 1/4 Sect. 18 Tp. 2 R. 5, north and east.

**5091. WATTS, Joseph**
July 23, 1835, on peninsula on St. Joseph's Bay, 10 miles W of Indian Pass, Gulf Co. Lot No. 7 Fractional Sect. 36 Tp. 8 R. 12, south and west.

**5854. WATTS, Joseph**
Sept. 19, 1836, 1 mile SE Dills, Jefferson Co. E 1/2 SW 1/4 and W 1/2 SE 1/4 Sect. 20 Tp. 2 R. 5, north and east.

**7316. WATTS, Joseph**
Jan. 19, 1838, 4 miles W Jasper, Hamilton Co. E 1/2 NE 1/4 Sect. 11 Tp. 1 R. 13, north and east.

**8632. WATTS, Joseph**
Feb. 5, 1844, 1/2 mile E Ellaville, Madison Co. Lot No. 4 Sect. 4 Tp. 1 R. 11, south and east.

**8890. WATTS, Joseph**
Jan. 26, 1846, 1/4 mile N Ellaville, Madison Co. W 1/2 SE 1/4 Sect. 14 Tp. 1 R. 11, south and east.

**8891. WATTS, Tellespon J.**
Jan. 26, 1846, 1/4 mile N Ellaville, Madison Co. SE 1/4 SE 1/4 Sect. 14 Tp. 1 R. 11, north and east.

**2132. WATTS, Wm.**
(of Fla.) Dec. 8, 1827, 4 miles NE Wadesboro, Jefferson Co. W 1/2 SE 1/4 Sect. 22 Tp. 2 R. 3, north and east.

**5819. WEATHERINGTON, Frederick**
Aug. 31, 1836, 2 3/4 miles SSE Jumper, Gadsden Co. SE 1/4 NE 1/4 Sect. 34 Tp. 2 R. 5, north and west.

**510. WEATHERS, Benjamin**
Jan. 25, 1847, c. 1 mile NW Martel, Marion Co. SW 1/4 SW 1/4 Sect. 14 Tp. 15 R. 20, south and east. Patent

delivered May 1, 1854.

**1082. WEATHERS, Benjamin**
Jan. 6, 1852, 1/4 mile NNW Martel, Marion Co. N 1/2 NW 1/4 Sect. 23 Tp. 15 R. 20, south and east. Patent delivered (no date).

**1735. WEATHERS, Benjamin**
Jan. 26, 1853, 3 1/2 miles NW Martel, Marion Co. NW 1/4 SW 1/4 Sect. 14 Tp. 15 R. 20, south and east. Patent delivered (no date).

**59. WEBB, James**
Nov. 13, 1826, c. 4 miles N Cottondale, Jackson Co. SW 1/4 Sect. 10 Tp. 5 R. 11, north and west.

**260. WEBB, James**
Jan. 1, 1827, 8 miles NW Marianna, Jackson Co. SE 1/4 Sect. 9 Tp. 5 R. 11, north and west.

**383. WEBB, James**
(Assignee of **Samuel PINKHAM**) May 4, 1827, 2 miles WNW Campbellton, Jackson Co. NW 1/4 Sect. 35 Tp. 7 R. 12, north and west. Transferred from **James WEBB**, by purchase, to **T. I. BRYAN** (no date).

**2657. WEBB, Jas. B.**
Jan. 21, 1829, 1/2 mile S Campbellton, Jackson Co. W 1/2 SW 1/4 Sect. 1 Tp. 6 R. 12, north and west. Transferred Nov. 28, 182? to **BR---- & LAW**. Teste: **Eli PEACOCK**, **J. P. James C. DANIEL**.

**2081. WEEKS, Barnet C.**
Aug. 20, 1853, 7 miles ENE Fort White, Columbia Co. SW 1/4 NW 1/4 Sect. 27 Tp. 6 R. 17, south and east. Patent delivered Feb. 4, 1857.

**2155. WEEKS, James A.**
Sept. 6, 1853, 1 mile N Belmore, Clay Co. NW 1/4 SW 1/4 Sect. 11 Tp. 7 R. 24, south and east.

**2637. WEEKS, Levi R.**
Mar. 17, 1854, at Jefferson, Columbia Co. NE 1/4 SW 1/4 Sect. 18 Tp. 4 R. 18, south and east.

**2553. WEEKS, Sherod S.**
Mar. 4, 1854, 4 1/2 miles E Fort White, Columbia Co. SW 1/4 SE 1/4 Sect. 32 Tp. 6 R. 17, south and east. Patent delivered (no date).

**1809. WEEKS, Theophilus**
April 2, 1853, 9 1/2 miles NNE Fort White, Columbia Co. NE 1/4 SE 1/4 Sect. 23 Tp. 6 R. 17, south and east.

**14. WEISER, George W.**
July 25, 1873, near Paola, Seminole Co. SW 1/4 NW 1/4 Sect. 6 Tp. 20 R. 30, south and east. And NE 1/4 SE 1/4 and S 1/2 NE 1/4 and NW 1/4 NE 1/4 Sect. 1 Tp. 20 R. 29, south and east.

**507. WELLS, John**
Jan. 23, 1847, 3 miles NW Agnew, Marion Co. SW 1/4 SE 1/4 Sect. 31 Tp. 14 R. 21, south and east. Patent issued Nov. 24, 1854.

**7273. WEST, Arthur**
Jan. 26, 1838, 1 1/4 miles NNW Champaign, Madison Co. SW 1/4 NW 1/4 Sect. 14 Tp. 1 R. 8, north and east.

**4510. WEST, Charles B.**
Jan. 13, 1834, 1 3/4 miles N by E Centerville, Leon Co. SE 1/4 NE 1/4 Sect. 17 Tp. 2 R. 2, north and east.

**3140. WEST, Charles B.**
Dec. 1, 1829, 2 miles ENE Centerville, Leon Co. E 1/2 SE 1/4 Sect. 17 Tp. 2 R. 2, north and east.

**5342. WEST, Charles B.**
Dec. 11, 1835, 1 3/4 miles E Centerville, Leon Co. NE 1/4 NE 1/4 Sect. 20 Tp. 2 R. 2, north and east.

`**7926. WEST, Robert K.**
Mar. 21, 1839, 2 1/2 miles SE Jamieson, Gadsden Co. SE 1/4 SE 1/4 Sect. 17 Tp. 3 R. 2, north and west.

**WEST, Robt. K.** see **David DAVIDSON**

**296. WESTER, Elias**
Jan. 1, 1827, 5 miles NW Quincy, Gadsden Co. NW 1/4 Sect. 26 Tp. 2 R. 4, north and west.

**1468. WESTER, Elias**
May 22, 1827, 4 1/2 miles N Quincy, Gadsden Co. W 1/2 SW 1/4 Sect. 13 Tp. 3 R. 4, north and west.

**WESTEN/WESTER, Edmond P.** see **Henry COOK**

**WHEELER, Henry C.** see **Daniel McRAENG**

**47. WHIDDON, Bennett**
Nov. 8, 1826, near Gretha Post Office, Gadsden Co. SE 1/4 Sect. 35 Tp. 3 R. 4, north and west.

**1007. WHITTON, Elias**
Jan. 25, 1827, N edge of Concord, Gadsden Co. W 1/2 SW 1/4 Sect. 7

**1008. WHIDDON, Elias**
Jan. 25, 1827, 1 mile SE Darsey, Gadsden Co. W 1/2 NW 1/4 Sect. 7 Tp. 3 R. 1, north and west.

**2743. WHIDDON, Elias**
Feb. 17, 1829, 1 1/4 miles SE Darsey, Gadsden Co. E 1/2 NW 1/4 Sect. 7 Tp. 3 R. 1, north and west.

**4760. WHIDDON, Elias**
Jan. 7, 1835, 3 1/2 miles NNE Aucilla, Jefferson Co. SW 1/4 SW 1/4 Sect. 25 Tp. 1 R. 5, south and east.

**5936. WHIDDON, Elias**
Oct. 28, 1836, 2 3/4 miles SSE Concord, Gadsden Co. SW 1/4 SE 1/4 Sect. 20 Tp. 3 R. 1, north and west.

**8128. WHIDDON, Elias**
Nov. 4, 1839, 5 miles N Lake Jackson (town), Leon Co. NW 1/4 NW 1/4 Sect. 17 Tp. 2 R. 1, north and west.

**5853. WHIDDEN, Elizabeth**
Sept. 17, 1836, 2 miles S Concord, Gadsden Co. NW 1/4 NE 1/4 Sect. 30 Tp. 3 R. 1, north and west.

**5386. WHIDDON, Jeremiah**
Jan. 5, 1836, 2 miles S Concord, Gadsden Co. NE 1/4 NW 1/4 Sect. 30 Tp. 3 R. 1, north and west.

**8067. WHIDDON, Jeremiah**
Sept. 4, 1839, 1 mile SE Concord, Gadsden Co. E 1/2 SE 1/4 Sect. 24 Tp. 3 R. 2, north and west.

**48. WHIDDON, Mathew**
Nov. 8, 1826, near Gretha Post Office, Gadsden Co. NE 1/4 Sect. 35 Tp. 3 R. 4, north and west.

**136. WHIDDON, Sevier**
Dec. 26, 1826, at Mt. Pleasant, Gadsden Co. W 1/2 NW 1/4 Sect. 25 Tp. 3 R. 4, north and west.

**2801. WHIDDON, Sevier**
April 2, 1829, 2 miles SE Greensboro, Gadsden Co. W 1/2 NW 1/4 Sect. 14 Tp. 2 R. 5, north and west.

**76. WHITE, David L.**
Nov. 27, 1826, c. 3 miles NW Midway Post Office, Gadsden Co. NE 1/4 Sect. 31 Tp. 2 R. 3, north and west.

**2456. WHITE, David L.**
Aug. 12, 1828, 3 1/2 miles ESE Sawdust, Gadsden Co. W 1/2 SW 1/4 Sect. 30 Tp. 2 R. 3, north and west.

**4748. WHITE, David L.**
Dec. 30, 1834, 2 miles S by E Wewahitchka, Gulf Co. Lot No. 1 Sect. 31 Tp. 4 R. 9, south and west.

**4749. WHITE, David L.**
Dec. 30, 1834, 2 miles SSE Wewahitchka, Gulf Co. Lot No. 4 Sect. 31 Tp. 4 R. 9, south and west.

**3860. WHITE, Elijah**
Jan. 22, 1831, 1 mile E Centerville, Leon Co. W 1/2 NE 1/4 Sect. 19 Tp. 2 R. 2, north and east.

**4497. WHITE, Elijah**
Dec. 30, 1833, NE shore of Lake Jackson, Leon Co. W 1/2 SW 1/4 Sect. 26 Tp. 2 R. 1, north and east.

**4540. WHITE, Elijah**
Feb. 3, 1834, 1/2 mile SSE Centerville, Leon Co. NE 1/4 SE 1/4 Sect. 10 Tp. 2 R. 2, north and east.

**4816. WHITE, Elijah**
Jan. 22, 1835, 4 miles SSW Chaires, Leon Co. W 1/2 SE 1/4 Sect. 19 Tp. 2 R. 2, north and east.

**4911. WHITE, Elijah**
Mar. 24, 1835, 1/2 mile S Bradfordville, Leon Co. W 1/2 SE 1/4 Sect. 27 Tp. 2 R. 1, north and east.

**5448. WHITE, Elijah**
Feb. 8, 1836, 1 mile SW Centerville, Leon Co. NW 1/4 Sect. 26 Tp. 2 R. 1, north and east.

**6204. WHITE, Elijah**
Dec. 13, 1836, 1 mile S by E Centerville, Leon Co. SE 1/4 SE 1/4 Sect. 19 Tp. 2 R. 2, north and east.

**6205. WHITE, Elijah**
Dec. 13, 1836, 1 mile E Centerville, Leon Co. NW 1/4 SW 1/4 Sect. 20 Tp. 2 R. 2, north and east.

**7008. WHITE, Elijah**
May 6, 1837, 1/4 mile SSE Centerville, Leon Co. SW 1/4 SE 1/4 Sect. 18 Tp. 2 R. 2, north and east.

**1091. WHITE, Joseph M.**
Feb. 6, 1827, 2 miles W Monticello, Jefferson Co. E 1/2 SW 1/4 Sect. 26 Tp. 2 R. 4, north and east.

**1092. WHITE, Joseph M.**
(DUP) Feb. 6, 1827, 2 miles W Monticello, Jefferson Co. W 1/2 SE 1/4 Sect. 26 Tp. 2 R. 4, north and east.

**1223. WHITE, Joseph M.**
(DUP) Mar. 22, 1827, 1 mile W Monticello, Jefferson Co. W 1/2 SW 1/4 Sect. 25 Tp. 2 R. 4, north and east.

**2503. WHITE, Joseph M.**
Sept. 24, 1828, 3 miles SW Monticello, Jefferson Co. NW 1/4 Sect. 2 Tp. 1 R. 4, north and east.

**2504. WHITE, Joseph M.**
Sept. 24, 1828, 3 miles SW Monticello, Jefferson Co. E 1/2 NE 1/4 Sect. 2 Tp. 1 R. 4, north and east.

**2512. WHITE, Joseph M.**
Sept. 30, 1828, 2 miles SW Monticello, Jefferson Co. W 1/2 SW 1/4 Sect. 36 Tp. 2 R. 4, north and east.

**2800. WHITE, Joseph M.**
April 1, 1829, 4 miles WSW Monticello, Jefferson Co. E 1/2 SE 1/4 Sect. 34 Tp. 2 R. 3, north and east.

**3071. WHITE, Joseph M.**
Sept. 30, 1829, 2 miles WSW Monticello, Jefferson Co. W 1/2 NE 1/4 Sect. 34 Tp. 2 R. 4, north and east.

**3072. WHITE, Joseph M.**
Sept. 30, 1829, 6 1/2 miles NNE Tallahassee, Leon Co. W 1/2 NW 1/4 Sect. 1 Tp. 1 R. 4, north and east.

**3073. WHITE, Joseph M.**
Sept. 30, 1829, 3 miles SSE Monticello, Jefferson Co. E 1/2 SE 1/4 Sect. 2 Tp. 1 R. 4, north and east.

**3881. WHITE, Joseph M.**
Feb. 17, 1831, 2 miles SSW Monticello, Jefferson Co. W 1/2 NE 1/4 Sect. 1 Tp. 1 R. 4, north and east.

**4346. WHITE, Joseph M.**
April 10, 1833, 3 miles SW Monticello, Jefferson Co. W 1/2 SE 1/4 Sect. 2 Tp. 1 R. 4, north and east.

**4347. WHITE, Joseph M.**
April 10, 1833, 2 1/4 miles NW Monticello, Jefferson Co. W 1/2 NW 1/4 Sect. 26 Tp. 2 R. 4, north and east.

**6000. WHITE, Joseph M.**
Nov. 12, 1836, 1 mile E Bay Harbor, Bay Co. W 1/2 NW 1/4 and NE 1/4 NW 1/4 Sect. 13 Tp. 4 R. 14, south and west.

**6001. WHITE, Joseph M.**
Nov. 12, 1836, just E Bay Harbor, Bay Co. E 1/2 Sect.13 Tp. 4 R. 14, south and west.

**6002. WHITE, Joseph M.**
Nov. 12, 1836, 1 1/2 miles E Millville, Bay Co. SW 1/4 SE 1/4 NW 1/4 Sect. 12 Tp. 4 R. 14, south and west.

**6003. WHITE, Joseph M.**
Nov. 12, 1836, just SE Millville, Bay Co. S 1/2 Sect.11 Tp. 4 R. 14, south and west. Marked on back "St. Andrew's Patents issued."

**2013. WHITE, Thomas**
Aug. 3, 1827, at Capitola, Jefferson Co. SW 1/4 Sect. 30 Tp. 1 R. 3, north and east.

**2629. WHITE, Thomas**
Jan. 16, 1829, 1 mile S Capitola, Jefferson Co. E 1/2 NW 1/4 Sect. 31 Tp. 1 R. 3, north and east.

**4687. WHITE, Thomas**
Dec. 8, 1834, 1 1/2 miles S Capitola, Leon Co. W 1/2 NE 1/4 Sect. 3 Tp. 1 R. 3, north and east.

**1817. WHITE, Wm.**
(DUP) June 5, 1827, 1 mile N by W Kynesville, Jackson Co. W 1/2 SW 1/4 Sect. 3 Tp. 4 R. 11, north and west.

**1274. WHITE, William**
March 29, 1852, 1/4 mile W Hickman, Alachua Co. SE 1/4 NE 1/4 Sect. 34 Tp. 12 R. 20, south and east. Patent delivered May 21, 1856.

**4493. WHITAKER, Richard**
Dec. 26, 1833, 5 1/2 miles W by N Blackcreek, Leon Co. NW 1/4 NE 1/4 Sect. 5 Tp. 1 R. 2, north and east.

**93. WHITEHURST, Asa**
Dec. 23, 1844, 4 miles S Ringgold, Hernando Co. SE 1/4 SW 1/4 Sect. 36 Tp. 21 R. 18, south and east. Patent delivered June 24, 1845.

**333. WHITEHURST, Asa**
March 2, 1846, 5 miles E Centralia, Hernando Co. NE 1/4 NW 1/4 and SW 1/4 NE 1/4 Sect. 1 Tp. 22 R. 18, south and east.

**504. WHITEHURST, Asa**
Jan. 20, 1847, 5 miles E Centralia, Hernando Co. W 1/2 SW 1/4 Sect. 36 Tp. 21 R. 18, south and east.

**505. WHITEHURST, Asa**
Jan. 20, 1847, 5 miles E by S Centralia, Hernando Co. SE 1/4 NW 1/4 Sect. 1 Tp. 22 R. 18, south and east. On back of receipt: "Included in Grover Deed, P. W. Law." "D'd 9th January, 1855."

**7608. WHITEHURST, Daniel**
Aug. 18, 1838, 4 1/2 miles NNE Jasper, Hamilton Co. SW 1/4 SW 1/4

Sect. 4 Tp. 1 R. 14, north and east.
**521. WHITEHURST, Daniel S.**
May 20, 1831, at Jasper, Hamilton Co. SE 1/4 Sect. 5 Tp. 1 R. 14, north and east.
**7545. WHITEHURST, Daniel S.**
July 23, 1838, at Jasper, Hamilton Co. NE 1/4 NE 1/4 Sect. 5 Tp. 1 R. 14, north and east.
**646. WHITEHURST, Daniel Scott**
May 18, 1848, 3 miles SW Norman, Hernando Co. SE 1/4 NE 1/4 Sect. 7 and SW 1/4 NW 1/4 Sect. 8 Tp. 23 T. 19, south and east.
**4718. WHITEHURST, D. L.**
Dec. 16, 1834, at Jasper, Hamilton Co. SE 1/4 NE 1/4 Sect. 5 Tp. 1 R. 14, north and east.
**4041. WHITEHURST, Hillery**
July 20, 1831, at McClellan, Jefferson Co. E 1/2 NW 1/4 Sect. 15 Tp. 1 R. 5, north and east.
**5196. WHITEHURST, Hillery**
Feb. 13, 1860, at Buda, Alachua Co. S 1/2 NE 1/4 and N 1/2 SE 1/4 Sect. 31 Tp. 8 R. 17, south and east.
**5452. WHITEHURST, Hillery**
Feb. 10, 1836, 5 1/2 miles SE by E Dills, Jefferson Co. SW 1/4 NE 1/4 Sect. 29 Tp. 2 R. 6, north and east.
**7212. WHITEHURST, John**
Jan. 10, 1838, at Jasper, Hamilton Co. SW 1/4 SW 1/4 Sect. 5 Tp. 1 R. 14, north and east.
**7213. WHITEHURST, John**
Jan. 10, 1838, 1/4 mile W Jasper, Hamilton Co. SE 1/4 SE 1/4 Sect. 6 Tp. 1 R. 14, north and east.
**5595. WHITEHURST, Levi**
April 13, 1836, 4 1/2 miles W Ellis, Jackson Co. W 1/2 SE 1/4 Sect. 13 Tp. 6 R. 11, north and west.
**6690. WHITEHURST, Levi**
Jan. 30, 1837, 3 miles W by S Ellis, Jackson Co. E 1/2 NW 1/4 and E 1/2 SW 1/4 Sect. 13 Tp. 6 R. 11, north and west.
**6691. WHITEHURST, Levi**
Jan. 30, 1837, 4 miles WSW Ellis, Jackson Co. E 1/2 NW 1/4 Sect. 24 Tp. 6 R. 11, north and west.
**2202. WHITEHURST, Levy**
(of Fla.) Dec. 31, 1827, 6 miles E by N Campbellton, Jackson Co. E 1/2 NW 1/4 Sect. 26 Tp. 7 R. 11, north and west.
**2203. WHITEHURST, Levy**
(of Fla.) Dec. 31,1827, 6 1/4 miles E by N Campbellton, Jackson Co. W 1/2 SE 1/4 Sect. 26 Tp. 7 R. 11, north and west.
**2021. WHITFIELD, Benjamin M.**
Aug. 8, 1853, at Houston, Suwannee Co. NW 1/4 NW 1/4 Sect. 3 Tp. 3 R. 14, south and east. Patent delivered Aug. 19, 1869.
**2022. WHITFIELD, Benjamin M.**
Aug. 8, 1853, 5 miles SE Padlock, Suwannee Co. NE 1/4 SE 1/4 Sect. 33 Tp. 2 R. 14, south and east.
**473. WHITNELL, Jacob**
Jan. 30, 1830, at Robinson Point, Santa Rosa Co. Lot No. 1 Sect. 25 Tp. 1 R. 28, north and west.
**4967. WHITNER, B. F.**
May 18, 1835, 3 1/2 miles W by S Madison, Madison Co. E 1/2 NE 1/4 Sect. 36 Tp. 1 R. 8, north and east.
**5725. WHITNER, Benjamin F.**
June 24, 1836, 2 miles W Madison, Madison Co. SW 1/4 and W 1/2 SE 1/4 Sect. 29 Tp. 1 R. 9, north and east.
**5726. WHITNER, Benjamin F.**
June 24, 1836, 1 1/2 miles SSW Madison, Madison Co. E 1/2 NW 1/4 and NW 1/4 NE 1/4 Sect. 32 Tp. 1 R. 9, north and east.
**6099. WHITNER, Benjamin F.**
Nov. 28, 1836, 2 1/2 miles WSW Madison, Madison Co. W 1/2 SW 1/4 Sect. 32 Tp. 1 R. 9, north and east.
**6514. WHITNER, Benjamin F.**
Jan. 10, 1837, 1 1/2 miles SW Madison, Madison Co. E 1/2 NE 1/4 Sect. 32 Tp. 1 R. 9, north and east.
**6515. WHITNER, Benjamin F.**
Jan. 10, 1837, 4 1/2 miles W by S Madison, Madison Co. SE 1/4 NE 1/4 Sect. 35 Tp. 1 R. 8, north and east.
**6889. WHITNER, Benjamin F.**
Mar. 13, 1837, 1/2 mile SW Champaign, Madison Co. W 1/2 SW 1/4 Sect. 23 Tp. 1 R. 8, north and east.
**6890. WHITNER, Benjamin F.**
Mar. 13, 1837, 5 miles W Madison, Madison Co. E 1/2 SE 1/4 Sect. 17 Tp. 1 R. 8, north and east.
**6891. WHITNER, Benjamin F.**

Mar. 13, 1837, 5 miles E Greenville, Madison Co. E 1/2 SE 1/4 Sect. 17 Tp. 1 R. 8, north and east.
**6892. WHITNER, Benjamin F.**
Mar. 13, 1837, 2 miles W Madison, Madison Co. SE 1/4 Sect. 30 Tp. 1 R. 9, north and east.
**6971. WHITNER, Benjamin F.**
April 5, 1837, 4 miles SSW Champaign, Madison Co. W 1/2 NW 1/4 Sect. 3 TP. 1 R. 8, south and east. Note "Valued at nine dollars per acre."
**7987. WHITNER, benjamin F.**
June 6, 1839, 1/4 mile S by E Lake Jackson, Leon Co. E 1/2 SE 1/4 Sect. 7 Tp. 1 R. 1, north and east.
**3223. WIGGINS, George**
Jan. 21, 1830, 3 3/4 miles W by N Alma, Leon Co. W 1/2 SE 1/4 Sect. 29 Tp. 3 R. 4, north and east. Paid in scrip issued to **Alex. MACOMB**, survivor of Edgar and Macomb. Dated May 30, 1829.
**1046. WIGGINS, James A.**
Dec. 13, 1851, at Lake Weir (town), Marion Co. Lot No. 5 Sect. 5 Tp. 1 R. 24, south and east. Patent delivered May 8, 1858.
**4605. WIGGINS, Jesse**
Aug. 15, 1834, 2 miles W Bradfordville, Leon Co. SE 1/4 NE 1/4 Sect. 20 Tp. 2 R. 1, south and east.
**2535. WIGGINS, John**
Mar. 29, 1828, 2 1/2 miles E Centerville, Leon Co. W 1/2 SE 1/4 Sect. 21 Tp. 2 R. 2, north and east.
**3038. WIKOFF, Manuel G.**
Sept. 14, 1829, 2 1/2 miles W Bradfordville, Leon Co. NE 1/4 Sect. 19 Tp. 2 R. 1, north and east.
**4299. WILCOX, John**
Feb. 7, 1833, 3 miles SSE Florence, Gadsden Co. SW 1/4 SW 1/4 Sect. 9 Tp. 2 R. 2, north and west.
**4300. WILCOX, John**
Feb. 7, 1833, 3 1/2 miles SSE Florence, Gadsden Co. SE 1/4 SE 1/4 Sect. 8 Tp. 2 R. 2, north and west.
**193. WILDER, Hezekiah**
(DUP) Dec. 29, 1826, 2 miles S Florence, Gadsden Co. NE 1/4 Sect. 7 Tp. 2 R. 3, north and west.
**984. WILDER, Hezekiah**
(DUP) Jan. 22, 1827, 1 mile SE Quincy, Gadsden Co. SE 1/4 Sect. 8 Tp. 2 R. 3, north and west.
**1071. Wilder, Hezekiah**
Feb. 5, 1827, 3 miles SW Havana, Gadsden Co. E 1/2 SW 1/4 Sect. 8 Tp. 2 R. 3, north and west.
**5621. WILDER, Henson**
April 25, 1836, 3 3/4 miles SSE Dills, Jefferson Co. NW 1/4 SW 1/4 Sect. 1 Tp. 2 R. 6, north and west.
**397. WILDER, Isaac**
Nov. 1, 1830, 4 miles E Dills Post Office, Jefferson Co. SE 1/4 Sect. 34 Tp. 3 R. 6, north and east. (This number is corrected in pencil on the original to **497**.) Issued under the Pre-emption Act of 1830.
**888. WILDER, Hosea**
Jan. 17, 1827, 2 miles SE Quincy, Gadsden Co. W 1/2 SW 1/4 Sect. 9 Tp. 2 R. 3, north and west.
**889. WILDER, Hosea**
Jan. 17, 1827, 2 miles ESE Quincy, Gadsden Co. E 1/2 SW 1/4 Sect. 9 Tp. 2 R. 3, north and west.
**6928. WILDER, John M.**
March 20, 1837, 1 1/2 miles NE Octahatchee, Hamilton Co. SW 1/4 SW 1/4 and SW 1/4 SE 1/4 Sect. 1 Tp. 2 R. 11, north and east.
**9781. WILDER, John M.**
(One of the heirs for the heirs of **Andrew J. WILDER**, Decd.) Jan. 20, 1892, 1 1/2 miles N by W Jena, Dixie Co. S 1/2 SE 1/4 Sect. 30 and W 1/2 NE 1/4 Sect. 31 Tp. 9S R. 10E.
**2222. WILFORD, Abram**
(of Fla.) Jan. 14, 1826, 3 miles E Copeland, Leon Co. W 1/2 SE 1/4 Sect. 36 Tp. 3 R. 3, north and east.
**3848. WILFORD, Abram**
Jan. 14, 1831, c. 3 miles E Copeland, Leon Co. Lot No. 1 Sect. 1 Tp. 2 R. 3, north and east.
**1664. WILFORD, John**
(DUP) May 29, 1827, 2 1/2 miles E Stringer, Leon Co. W 1/2 NW 1/4 Sect. 25 Tp. 3 R. 3, north and east.
**6826. WILFORD, John**
Mar. 2, 1837, 1/2 mile NW Alma, Jefferson Co. E 1/2 Sect. 27 Tp. 3 R. 4, north and east.
**7617. WILKINSON, John**
Aug. 29, 1838, 1 mile NNE Bayou

Siding, Santa Rosa Co. SE 1/4 SW 1/4 Sect. 36 Tp. 2 R. 28, north and west.

**3164. WILKINSON, Milton S.**
Dec. 15, 1829, 2 miles E Greensboro, Gadsden Co. E 1/2 SW 1/4 Sect. 11 Tp. 2 R. 5, north and west.

**4968. WILKINSON, Peter**
May 18, 1835, 10 miles NNW Coldwater, Santa Rosa Co. SE 1/4 NE 1/4 Sect. 18 Tp. 4 R. 30, north and west.

**4969. WILKINSON, Peter**
May 18, 1835, 10 miles NNW Coldwater, Santa Rosa Co. SW 1/4 NW 1/4 Sect. 18 Tp. 4 R. 30, north and west.

**4061. WILKINSON, Richard**
Aug. 12, 1831, 1 1/2 miles SW Mears Spur, Gadsden Co. E 1/2 NE 1/4 Sect. 14 Tp. 3 R. 6, north and west.

**4132. WILKINSON, Richard**
Feb. 1, 1832, 1/2 mile W Mears Spur, Gadsden Co. W 1/2 NW 1/4 Sect. 13 Tp. 3 R. 6, north and west.

**5124. WILLEY, John A.**
Aug. 5, 1835, 1 1/2 miles SE Felkel, Leon Co. SW 1/4 Sect. 3 Tp. 2 R. 2, north and east.

**6063. WILLEY, John A.**
Nov. 19, 1836, 1 mile NW Felkel, Leon Co. NE 1/4 SW 1/4 Sect. 33 Tp. 3 R. 2, north and east.

**337. WILLIAMS, Andrew**
April 12, 1827, 4 miles SE Campbellton, Jackson Co. SE 1/4 Sect. 17 Tp. 6 R. 11, north and west.

**6062. WILLIAMS, Daniel**
Aug. 29, 1839, 4 1/2 miles N by E Graceville, Jackson Co. N 1/2 Lot No. 4 Sect. 13 Tp. 7 R. 13, north and west.

**5295. WILLIAMS, Daniel**
Dec. 1, 1835, 1 1/2 miles NW Lloyd, Jefferson Co. NW 1/4 NW 1/4 Sect. 8 Tp. 1 R. 3, north and east.

**6215. WILLIAMS, Daniel**
Dec. 15, 1836, 1 mile SE Wadesboro, Leon Co. NE 1/4 NW 1/4 Sect. 8 Tp. 1 R. 3, north and east.

**1519. WILLIAMS, Elijah Brown**
Nov. 25, 1852, 4 miles W Houston, Suwannee Co. NE 1/4 SE 1/4 Sect. 35 Tp. 2 R. 15, south and east. Patent delivered Jan. 22, 1870.

**8664. WILLIAMS, Glisson**
April 13, 1844, 3 3/4 miles SSE Calhoun, Madison Co. NW 1/4 NE 1/4 Sect. 20 Tp. 1 R. 10, south and east.

**WILLIAMS, G. R.** see **Thomas LITTLETON**

**3817. WILLIAMS, Henry**
Dec. 24, 1830, 4 miles SSE Centerville, Leon Co. E 1/2 NW 1/4 Sect. 32 Tp. 2 R. 2, north and east.

**3818. WILLIAMS, Henry**
Dec. 24, 1830, 3 miles SE Centerville, Leon Co. E 1/2 NW 1/4 Sect. 32 Tp. 2 R. 2, north and east.

**7984. WILLIAMS, Ira S.**
June 1, 1839, 4 1/2 miles NNE Graceville, Jackson Co. (State line) W 1/2 NE 1/4 Sect. 19 Tp. 7 R. 12, north and west.

**1306. WILLIAMS, James**
April 27, 1827, 3 miles SW El Destino, Leon Co. W 1/2 NW 1/4 Sect. 14 Tp. 1 R. 2, south and east.
See **MILLS & PERRY, #460**

**271. WILLIAMS, John**
Jan. 1, 1827, 8 miles NE Graceville, Jackson Co. W 1/2 SE 1/4 Sect. 20 Tp. 7 R. 12, north and west.

**4691. WILLIAMS, John**
Dec. 10, 1834, 3 1/4 miles W St. Marks Junction, Leon Co. NE 1/4 SW 1/4 Sect. 17 Tp. 1 R. 1, south and east.

**4743. WILLIAMS, John**
Dec. 24, 1834, 4 1/2 miles W St. Marks Junction, Leon Co. NE 1/4 SE 1/4 Sect. 18 Tp. 1 R. 1, south and east.

**7016. WILLIAMS, John**
June 6, 1837, 1/2 mile N Capitola, Leon Co. SE 1/4 SE 1/4 Sect. 19 Tp. 1 R. 3, north and east.

**7017. WILLIAMS, John**
June 6, 1837, 1 mile NNE Capitola, Leon Co. NW 1/4 SW 1/4 Sect. 20 Tp. 1 R. 3, north and east.

**4883. WILLIAMS, John T.**
Mar. 9, 1835, 4 1/2 miles N by W Lloyd, Jefferson Co. SE 1/4 NW 1/4 Sect. 32 Tp. 2 R. 3, north and east.

**8594. WILLIAMS, Joseph**
July 25, 1843, 1 1/2 miles W San Helena, Leon Co. NW 1/4 SE 1/4 Sect. 13 Tp. 1 R. 2, north and west.

**8768. WILLIAMS, Joseph**

April 1, 1845, 3 1/2 miles W San Helena, Leon Co. NE 1/4 SW 1/4 Sect. 13 Tp. 1 R. 2, north and west.

**4622. WILLIAMS, Kindreth**
Aug. 13, 1857, 2 1/4 miles W Luraville, Suwannee Co. N 1/2 NE 1/4 Sect. 15 Tp. 4 R. 11, south and east. Patent delivered Feb. 14, 1877.

**2739. WILLIAMS, Lewis**
Feb. 14, 1829, 3 1/2 miles NNE Wadesboro, Leon Co. W 1/2 NE 1/4 Sect. 28 Tp. 2 R. 3, north and east.

**2728. WILLIAMS, Lewis**
Feb. 11, 1829, 3 miles S by E Miccosukee, Leon Co. E 1/2 NE 1/4 Sect. 28 Tp. 2 R. 3, north and east.

**4245. WILLIAMS, Lorit**
Mar. 14, 1856, 4 3/4 miles NW Oxford, Sumter Co. SW 1/4 SW 1/4 Sect. 9 and SE 1/4 SW 1/4 and SW 1/4 SE 1/4 Sect. 8 Tp. 18 R. 22, south and east.

**349. WILLIAMS, Owen**
April 16, 1827, 4 miles WNW Campbellton, Jackson Co. SW 1/4 Sect. 28 Tp. 7 R. 12, north and west.

**392. WILLIAMS, Owen**
May 5, 1827, 3 miles NW Campbellton, Jackson Co. NW 1/4 Sect. 33 Tp. 7 R. 12, north and west.

**7982. WILLIAMS, Owen**
June 1, 1839, 3 miles E by N Graceville, Jackson Co. E 1/2 NW 1/4 Sect. 32 Tp. 7 R. 12, north and west.

**8995. WILLIAMS, Rebecca Emeline**
Nov. 23, 1846, 2 miles NW San Helena, Leon Co. SW 1/4 NW 1/4 Sect. 18 Tp. 1 R. 1, north and west.

**5599. WILLIAMS, Robert M.**
April 18, 1836, 7 1/4 miles NW Bradfordville, Leon Co. W 1/2 SW 1/4 Sect. 2 Tp. 2 R. 1, north and east.

**920. WILLIAMS, Robert W.**
Jan. 17, 1827, 6 miles SSE Quincy, Gadsden Co. E 1/2 NW 1/4 Sect. 35 Tp. 2 R. 3, north and west.

**921. WILLIAMS, Robert W.**
Jan. 17, 1827, 7 miles SE Quincy, Gadsden Co. W 1/2 NW 1/4 Sect. 35 Tp. 2 R. 3, north and west.

**996. WILLIAMS, Robert W.**
Jan. 22, 1827, 4 miles WNW Midway, Gadsden Co. W 1/2 SW 1/4 Sect. 35 Tp. 2 R. 3, north and west.

**1325. WILLIAMS, Robert W.**
May 5, 1827, 4 miles SSE Quincy, Gadsden Co. W 1/2 NE 1/4 Sect. 33 Tp. 2 R. 3, north and west.

**1866. WILLIAMS, Robert W.**
(of Fla.) June 6, 1827, just S Mear's Spur, Gadsden Co. SE 1/4 Sect. 12 Tp. 3 R. 6, north and west. 159.56 acres.

**2661. WILLIAMS, Robert W.**
Jan. 23, 1829, just N Sawdust, Gadsden Co. Lot No. 8 Fractional Sect. 21 Tp. 2 R. 4, north and west.

**3054. WILLIAMS, Robert W.**
Sept. 21, 1829, 5 miles SSW Chattahoochee, Jackson Co. NE 1/4 Sect. 25 Tp. 3 R. 7, north and west.

**3056. WILLIAMS, Robert W.**
Sept. 21, 1829, c. 4 1/2 miles SSW Chattahoochee, Jackson Co. Lot No. 3 Sect. 24 Tp. 3 R. 7, north and west.

**3057. WILLIAMS, Robert W.**
Sept. 21, 1829, 5 miles S by W Chattahoochee, Jackson Co. NW 1/4 Sect. 30 Tp. 3 R. 6, north and west.

**8870. WILLIAMS, Robert W.**
Jan. 3, 1846, 1/4 mile NNW Centerville, Leon Co. NW 1/4 NW 1/4 Sect. 24 Tp. 2 R. 1, north and east.

**8929. WILLIAMS, Robert W.**
Mar. 20, 1846, 3 miles SSW Felkel, Leon Co. SW 1/4 NW 1/4 Sect. 7 Tp. 2 R. 2, north and east.
See **Robert JAMIESON, #1453-56**

**3192. WILLIAMS, Thomas**
Dec. 30, 1829, 2 miles WSW Alma, Leon Co. E 1/2 NE 1/4 Sect. 4 Tp. 2 R. 4, north and east.

**253. WILLIAMS, Wm. Donald**
Dec. 30, 1826, 12 miles NE Chipley, Jackson Co. E 1/2 NW 1/4 Sect. 34 Tp. 7 R. 12, north and west.

**2558. WILLIAMS, William**
Dec. 2, 1828, at Jamieson, Gadsden Co. E 1/2 NW 1/4 Sect. 7 Tp. 3 R. 2, north and west.

**2559. WILLIAMS, William**
Dec. 2, 1828, at Jamieson, Gadsden Co. W 1/2 NE 1/4 Sect. 7 Tp. 3 R. 2, north and west.

**3797. WILLIAMS, William**
Dec. 15, 1830, 2 1/2 miles W by N Alma, Leon Co. E 1/2 SW 1/4 Sect. 28 Tp. 3 R. 4, north and east.

**6777. WILLIAMS, William**
Feb. 7, 1837, 4 miles SE Century, Santa Rosa Co. SW 1/4 NE 1/4 Sect. 23 Tp. 5 R. 30, north and west. East of Escambia River.

**WILLIAMS, Wm. see Dennis ADAMS**

**4577. WILLIAMS, William S.**
May 20, 1834, 1/4 mile NNE Florence, Jackson Co. SW 1/4 SE 1/4 Sect. 36 Tp. 3 R. 3, north and west.

**150. WILLIAMSON, Charles**
(Per **J. W. KEITH**) Of Ga. Dec. 28, 1826, 4 miles N Cottondale, Jackson Co. SW 1/4 Sect. 11 Tp. 5 R. 11, north and west. Transferred Dec. 29, 1826, to **John CLARK**.

**254. WILLIAMSON, Charles**
Dec. 30, 1826, 4 miles N Marianna, Jackson Co. SW 1/4 Sect. 15 Tp. 5 R. 10, north and west.

**1397. WILLIAMSON, Charles**
(of Ga.) May 21, 1827, 3 miles NE Quincy, Gadsden Co. E 1/2 SW 1/4 Sect. 28 Tp. 3 R. 3, north and west.

**1398. WILLIAMSON, Charles**
(of Ga.) May 21, 1827, 3 miles NE Quincy, Gadsden Co. E 1/2 SE 1/4 Sect. 29 Tp. 3 R. 3, north and west.

**1399. WILLIAMSON, Charles**
(of Ga.) May 21, 1827, 3 miles NNE Quincy, Gadsden Co. W 1/2 SW 1/4 Sect. 28 Tp. 3 R. 3, north and west.

**1436. WILLIAMSON, Charles**
May 22, 1827, 3 miles SW Sawdust, Gadsden Co. Lot No. 2 Sect. 31 Tp. 2 R. 4, north and west.

**1480. WILLIAMSON, Charles**
May 23, 1827, 2 1/2 miles SW Mear's Spur, Gadsden Co. E 1/2 SW 1/4 Sect. 23 Tp. 3 R. 6, north and west.

**1481. WILLIAMSON, Charles**
(DUP) May 23, 1827, 3 miles SW Mears Spur, Gadsden Co. W 1/2 SW 1/4 Sect. 23 Tp. 3 R. 6, north and west.

**1482. WILLIAMSON, Charles**
May 23, 1827, 2 miles SSE Mears Spur, Gadsden Co. E 1/2 SE 1/4 Sect. 22 Tp. 3 R. 6, north and west.

**1483. WILLIAMSON, Charles**
(DUP) May 23, 1827, 2 miles SSW Mears Spur, Gadsden Co. W 1/2 SE 1/4 Sect. 22 Tp. 3 R. 6, north and west. **1484. WILLIAMSON, Charles**
(DUP) May 23, 1827, 1 mile WNW Mears Spur, Gadsden Co. W 1/2 SE 1/4 Sect. 12 Tp. 3 R. 6, north and west.

**1485. WILLIAMSON, Charles**
May 23, 1827, 1/2 mile NW Mears Spur, Gadsden Co. E 1/2 SW 1/4 Sect. 12 Tp. 3 R. 6, north and west.

**1486. WILLIAMSON, Charles**
May 23, 1827, 1 mile NW Mears Spur, Gadsden Co. W 1/2 SW 1/4 Sect. 12 Tp. 3 R. 6, north and west.

**1487. WILLIAMSON, Charles**
May 23, 1827, 1 1/2 miles NW Mears Spur, Gadsden Co. W 1/2 NW 1/4 Sect. 12 Tp. 3 R. 6, north and west.

**1488. WILLIAMSON, Charles**
May 23, 1827, 3/4 mile NW Mears Spur, Gadsden Co. E 1/2 NW 1/4 Sect. 12 Tp. 3 R. 6, north and west.

**1489. WILLIAMSON, Charles**
(DUP) May 23, 1827, 1 mile NNW Mears Spur, Gadsden Co. W 1/2 NE 1/4 Sect. 12 Tp. 3 R. 6, north and west.

**1500. WILLIAMSON, Charles**
May 23, 1827, 1 mile N Mears Spur, Gadsden Co. E 1/2 NE 1/4 Sect. 12 Tp. 3 R. 6, north and west.

**1501. WILLIAMSON, Charles**
(DUP) May 23, 1827, 2 miles WNW Mears Spur, Gadsden Co. W 1/2 NE 1/4 Sect. 11 Tp. 3 R. 6, north and west.

**1502. WILLIAMSON, Charles**
May 23, 1827, 1 1/2 miles NW Mears Spur, Gadsden Co. E 1/2 NE 1/4 Sect. 11 Tp. 3 R. 6, north and west.

**1503. WILLIAMSON, Charles**
May 23, 1827, 4 miles WNW Mears Spur, Gadsden Co. W 1/2 NW 1/4 Sect. 9 Tp. 3 R. 6, north and west.

**1504. WILLIAMSON, Charles**
May 23, 1827, 2 1/2 miles NW Mears Spur, Gadsden Co. E 1/2 SE 1/4 Sect. 3 Tp. 3 R. 6, north and west.

**1505. WILLLIAMSON, Charles**
(DUP) May 23, 1827, 3 miles NW Mears Spur, Gadsden Co. E 1/2 NE 1/4 Sect. 3 Tp. 3 R. 6, north and west.

**1506. WILLIAMSON, Charles**
(DUP) May 23, 1827, 1 1/2 miles NW Mears Spur, Gadsden Co. W 1/2 SE 1/4 Sect. 2 Tp. 3 R. 6, north and west.

**1507. WILLIAMSON, Charles**
May 23, 1827, 2 miles NW Mears Spur, Gadsden Co. E 1/2 SW 1/4 Sect. 2 Tp. 3 R. 6, north and west. Transferred to **John McCULLOCH**, May 23, 1827.

**1508. WILLIAMSON, Charles**
(DUP) May 23, 1827, 2 1/2 miles NW Mears Spur, Gadsden Co. W 1/2 SW 1/4 Sect. 2 Tp. 3 R. 6, north and west. Transferred to **John McCULLOCH**, June 4, 1827.

**1509. WILLIAMSON, Charles**
May 23, 1827, 1 mile ENE Mears Spur, Gadsden Co. E 1/2 SW 1/4 Sect. 8 Tp. 3 R. 5, north and west.

**1510. WILLIAMSON, Charles**
(DUP) May 23, 1827, 1 mile ENE Mears Spur, Gadsden Co. W 1/2 SW 1/4 Sect. 8 Tp. 3 R. 5, north and west.

**1511. WILLIAMSON, Charles**
May 23, 1827, 1 mile ENE Mears Spur, Gadsden Co. E 1/2 SE 1/4 Sect. 7 Tp. 3 R. 5, north and west.

**1512. WILLIAMSON, Charles**
(DUP) May 23, 1827, 1/2 mile NW Mears Spur, Gadsden Co. W 1/2 SE 1/4 Sect. 7 Tp. 3 R. 5, north and west.

**1513. WILLIAMSON, Charles**
(DUP) May 23, 1827, 1 1/2 miles ESE Hermitage, Gadsden Co. E 1/2 NE 1/4 Sect. 3 Tp. 3 R. 5, north and west.

**1514. WILLIAMSON, Charles**
May 23, 1827, 2 1/2 miles E by S Hermitage, Gadsden Co. W 1/2 NE 1/4 Sect. 2 Tp. 3 R. 5, north and west.

**1515. WILLIAMSON, Charles**
(DUP) May 23, 1827, 2 1/2 miles E by S Hermitage, Gadsden Co. E 1/2 NE 1/4 Sect. 2 Tp. 3 R. 5, north and west.

**1516. WILLIAMSON, Charles**
May 23, 1827, 3 miles E by S Hermitage, Gadsden Co. W 1/2 NW 1/4 Sect. 1 Tp. 3 R. 5, north and west.

**1524. WILLIAMSON Charles**
May 24, 1827, at Simsville, Jackson Co. W 1/2 SW 1/4 Sect. 7 Tp. 3 R. 9, north and west.

**1525. WILLIAMSON, Charles**
May 24, 1827, 3 1/2 miles ENE Simsville, Jackson Co. E 1/2 SW 1/4 Sect. 7 Tp. 3 R. 9, north and west.

**1526. WILLIAMSON, Charles**
May 24, 1827, 1 mile NE Simsville, Jackson Co. W 1/2 NW 1/4 Sect. 8 Tp. 3 R. 9, north and west.

**1527. WILLIAMSON, Charles**
May 24, 1827, 1 1/2 miles S Simsville, Jackson Co. W 1/2 NW 1/4 Sect. 17 Tp. 3 R. 9, north and west.

**1528. WILLIAMSON, Charles**
(DUP) May 24, 1827, 1 mile W Rock Creek, Jackson Co. W 1/2 NE 1/4 Sect. 19 Tp. 3 R. 9, north and west.

**1529. WILLIAMSON, Charles**
(DUP) May 24, 1827, 1/2 mile W Rock Creek, Jackson Co. E 1/2 NW 1/4 Sect. 19 Tp. 3 R. 9, north and west.

**1530. WILLIAMSON, Charles**
May 24, 1827, 1 1/2 miles W Rock Creek, Jackson Co. W 1/2 NW 1/4 Sect. 19 Tp. 3 R. 9, north and west.

**1532. WILLIAMSON, Charles**
May 24, 1827, 2 miles NNW Rock Creek, Jackson Co. E 1/2 NE 1/4 Sect. 12 Tp. 3 R. 10, north and west.

**1533. WILLIAMSON, Charles**
May 24, 1827, 3 miles E Marianna, Jackson Co. W 1/2 NE 1/4 Sect. 6 Tp. 4 R. 9, north and west.

**1534. WILLIAMSON, Charles**
May 24, 1827, 1/2 mile S Simsville, Jackson Co. W 1/2 NE 1/4 Sect. 12 Tp. 3 R. 10, north and west.

**1535. WILLIAMSON, Charles**
May 24, 1827, 1 mile Simsville, Jackson Co. E 1/2 NW 1/4 Sect. 12 Tp. 3 R. 10, north and west.

**1536. WILLIAMSON, Charles**
May 24, 1827, 1 1/4 miles W Simsville, Jackson Co. W 1/2 NW 1/4 Sect. 12 Tp. 3 R. 10, north and west.

**1537. WILLIAMSON, Charles**
(DUP) May 24, 1827, 1 1/4 miles W Simsville, Jackson Co. W 1/2 SW 1/4 Sect. 12 Tp. 3 R. 10, north and west.

**1538. WILLIAMSON, Charles**
(DUP) May 24, 1827, 1 mile W Simsville, Jackson Co. E 1/2 SW 1/4 Sect. 12 Tp. 3 R. 10, north and west.

**1539. WILLIAMSON, Charles**
(DUP) May 24, 1827, 1 mile W Simsville, Jackson Co. W 1/2 SE 1/4 Sect. 12 Tp. 3 R. 10, north and west.

**1540. WILLIAMSON, Charles**
May 24, 1827, 1/2 mile SW Simsville,

Jackson Co. E 1/2 NE 1/4 Sect. 13 Tp. 3 R. 10, north and west.

**1541. WILLIAMSON, Charles**
May 24, 1827, 3/4 mile SW Simsville, Jackson Co. W 1/2 NE 1/4 Sect. 13 Tp. 3 R. 10, north and west.

**1542. WILLIAMSON, Charles**
May 24, 1827, 1 mile WSW Simsville, Jackson Co. E 1/2 NW 1/4 Sect. 13 Tp. 3 R. 10, north and west.

**1543. WILLIAMSON, Charles**
May 24, 1827, 1 1/2 miles WSW Simsville, Jackson Co. W 1/2 SW 1/4 Sect. 13 Tp. 3 R. 10, north and west.

**1555. WILLIAMSON, Charles**
May 25, 1827, 1/2 mile NW Kynesville, Jackson Co. E 1/2 NW 1/4 Sect. 9 Tp. 4 R. 11, north and west.

**1556. WILLIAMSON, Charles**
(DUP) May 25, 1827, 1/2 mile SW Kynesville, Jackson Co. E 1/2 NE 1/4 Sect. 17 Tp. 4 R. 11, north and west.

**1557. WILLIAMSON, Charles**
(DUP) May 25, 1827, 1/2 mile NW Kynesville, Jackson Co. W 1/2 NW 1/4 Sect. 9 Tp. 4 R. 11, north and west.

**1558. WILLIAMSON, Charles**
(DUP) May 25, 1827, at Kynesville, Jackson Co. E 1/2 SW 1/4 Sect. 9 Tp. 4 R. 11, north and west.

**1559. WILLIAMSON, Charles**
May 25, 1827, at Kynesville, Jackson Co. W 1/2 NE 1/4 Sect. 9 Tp. 4 R. 11, north and west.

**1561. WILLIAMSON, Charles**
May 25, 1827, 3 1/2 miles WNW Simsville, Jackson Co. E 1/2 SW 1/4 Sect. 3 Tp. 5 R. 10, north and west.

**1562. WILLIAMSON, Charles**
(DUP) May 25, 1827, 1 mile E Marianna, Jackson Co. E 1/2 SW 1/4 Sect. 2 Tp. 4 R. 10, north and west.

**1563. WILLIAMSON, Charles**
May 25, 1827, 1/2 mile E Marianna, Jackson Co. W 1/2 SW 1/4 Sect. 2 Tp. 4 R. 10, north and west.

**1564. WILLIAMSON, Charles**
May 25, 1827, at Marianna, Jackson Co. E 1/2 SE 1/4 Sect. 3 Tp. 4 R. 10, north and west.

**1565. WILLIAMSON, Charles**
May 25, 1827, 5 1/2 miles W Greenwood, Jackson Co. E 1/2 NE 1/4 Sect. 5 Tp. 5 R, 10, north and west.

**1566. WILLIAMSON, Charles.**
May 25, 1827, 3 1/2 miles SW Greenwood, Jackson Co. W 1/2 SW 1/4 Sect. 11 Tp. 5 R. 10, north and west.

**1567. WILLIAMSON, Charles**
(DUP) May 25, 1827, 3 1/2 miles SW Greenwood, Jackson Co. E 1/2 SW 1/4 Sect. 11 Tp. 5 R. 10, north and west. **1568. WILLIAMSON, Charles**
(DUP) May 25, 1827, 3 1/2 miles SW Greenwood, Jackson Co. W 1/2 SE 1/4 Sect. 11 Tp. 5 R, 10, north and west.

**1568. WILLIAMSON, Charles**

**1626. WILLIAMSON, Charles**
May 28, 1827, 7 miles NW Monticello, Jefferson Co. Lot No. 5 Fractional Sect. 7 Tp. 2 R. 4, north and west.

**1628. WILLIAMSON, Charles**
May 28, 1827, 5 miles NW Monticello, Jefferson Co. Lot No. 3 Fractional Sect. 14 Tp. 2 R. 4, north and west.

**1635. WILLIAMSON, Charles**
May 28, 1827, 2 miles WNW Monticello, Jefferson Co. Lot No. 2 Fractional Sect. 23 Tp. 2 R. 4, north and west.

**1636. WILLIAMSON, Charles**
May 28, 1827, 2 miles WNW Monticello, Jefferson Co. Lot No. 3 Fractional Sect. 23 Tp. 2 R. 4, north and west.

**ˎ1637. WILLIAMSON, Charles**
(DUP) May 28, 1827, 3 1/2 miles W Monticello, Jefferson Co. Lot No. 1 Fractional Sect. 27 Tp. 2 R. 4, north and east.

**1638. WILLIAMSON, Charles**
May 28, 1827, 3 1/2 miles W Monticello, Jefferson Co. Lot No. 2 Fractional Sect. 27 Tp. 2 R. 4, north and east.

**1639. WILLIAMSON, Charles**
(DUP) May 28, 1827, 4 miles WNW Monticello, Jefferson Co. Lot No. 1 Fractional Sect. 23 Tp. 2 R. 4, north and east.

**1642. WILLIAMSON, Charles**
May 28, 1827, 6 miles W by S Monticello, Jefferson Co. Lot No. 3 Sect. 31 Tp. 2 R. 4, north and east.

**1643. WILLIAMSON, Charles**
May 28, 1827, 6 miles W by S Monticello, Jefferson Co. Lot No. 2 Sect. 31 Tp. 2 R. 4, north and east.

**1645. WILLIAMSON, Charles**
(DUP) May 28, 1827, 7 miles W by S

Monticello, Jefferson Co. Lot No. 2 Sect. 30 Tp. 2 R. 4, north and east.

**1646. WILLIAMSON, Charles**
(DUP) May 28, 1827, 7 miles W by S Monticello, Jefferson Co. Lot No. 1 Sect. 30 Tp. 2 R. 4, north and east.

**1650. WILLIAMSON, Charles**
May 29, 1827, 12 miles NNW Haywood, Jackson Co. Lot No. 1 Fractional Sect. 11 Tp. 7 R. 8, north and west.

**1651. WILLIAMSON, Charles**
May 29, 1827, 11 miles NNW Haywood, Jackson Co. E 1/2 NE 1/4 Sect. 15 Tp. 7 R. 8, north and west.

**1653. WILLIAMSON, Charles**
(DUP) May 29, 1827, 12 1/2 miles NNW Haywood, Jackson Co. (in Alabama) E 1/2 SE 1/4 Sect. 15 Tp. 7 R. 8, north and west.

**1654. WILLIAMSON, Charles**
(DUP) May 29, 1827, 13 miles NNW Haywood, Jackson Co. (in Alabama) W 1/2 NE 1/4 Sect. 17 Tp. 7 R. 8, north and west.

**1656. WILLIAMSON, Charles**
May 29, 1827, 12 miles NNW Haywood, Jackson Co. (in Alabama) Lot No. 2 Fractional Sect. 23 Tp. 7 R. 8, north and west. 82.50 acres.

**1657. WILLIAMSON, Charles**
May 29, 1827, 11 miles NNW Haywood, Jackson Co. Lot No. 1 Fractional Sect. 26 Tp. 7 R. 8, north and west. 97 acres.

**1660. WILLIAMSON, Charles**
May 29, 1827, 9 miles NNW Haywood, Jackson Co. Lot No. 1 Sect. 36 Tp. 7 R. 8, north and west. 123.50 acres.

**1665. WILLIAMSON, Charles**
May 30, 1827, 3 miles WNW Greenwood, Jackson Co. W 1/2 SW 1/4 Sect. 26 Tp. 6 R. 10, north and west.

**1666. WILLIAMSON, Charles**
May 30, 1827, 3 miles WNW Greenwood, Jackson Co. E 1/2 NE 1/4 Sect. 27 Tp. 6 R. 10, north and west.

**1667. WILLIAMSON, Charles**
May 30, 1827, 6 miles W Greenwood, Jackson Co. W 1/2 SE 1/4 Sect. 31 Tp. 6 R. 10, north and west.

**1668. WILLIAMSON, Charles**
May 30, 1827, 5 miles W Greenwood, Jackson Co. W 1/2 SE 1/4 Sect. 32 Tp. 6 R. 10, north and west.

**1669. WILLIAMSON, Charles**
(DUP) May 30, 1827, 4 1/2 miles W Greenwood, Jackson Co. E 1/2 SE 1/4 Sect. 32 Tp. 6 R. 10, north and west.

**1670. WILLIAMSON, Charles**
(DUP) May 30, 1827, 4 miles W Greenwood, Jackson Co. W 1/2 SW 1/4 Sect. 33 Tp. 6 R. 10, north and west.

**1671. WILLIAMSON, Charles**
May 30, 1827, 4 miles W Greenwood, Jackson Co. E 1/2 SW 1/4 Sect. 33 Tp. 6 R. 10, north and west.

**1672. WILLIAMSON, Charles**
(DUP) May 30, 1827, 5 miles ESE Campbellton, Jackson Co. E 1/2 NW 1/4 Sect. 10 Tp. 6 R. 11, north and west.

**1673. WILLIAMSON, Charles**
May 30, 1827, 1 1/2 miles NE Jacob, Jackson Co. E 1/2 SW 1/4 Sect. 7 Tp. 6 R. 11, north and west.

**1674. WILLIAMSON, Charles**
May 30, 1827, 1 1/2 miles NE Jacob, Jackson Co. W 1/2 SE 1/4 Sect. 7 Tp. 6 R. 11, north and west.

**1675. WILLIAMSON, Charles**
May 30, 1827, 2 miles ENE Jacob, Jackson Co. E 1/2 SE 1/4 Sect. 7 Tp. 6 R. 11, north and west.

**1676. WILLIAMSON, Charles**
(DUP) May 30, 1827, 6 miles E Jacob, Jackson Co. E 1/2 SE 1/4 Sect. 14 Tp. 6 R. 11, north and west.

**1677. WILLIAMSON, Charles**
May 30, 1827, 6 miles E Jacob, Jackson Co. W 1/2 NW 1/4 Sect. 13 Tp. 6 R. 11, north and west.

**1678. WILLIAMSON, Charles**
May 30, 1827, 6 miles E Jacob, Jackson Co. W 1/2 SW 1/4 Sect. 13 Tp. 6 R. 11, north and west.

**1679. WILLIAMSON, Charles**
May 30, 1827, 6 miles E Jacob, Jackson Co. W 1/2 SE 1/4 Sect. 14 Tp. 6 R. 11, north and west.

**1680. WILLIAMSON, Charles**
May 30, 1827, 3 1/2 miles E by S Jacob, Jackson Co. E 1/2 NW 1/4 Sect. 21 Tp. 6 R. 11, north and west.

**1681. WILLIAMSON, Charles**
(DUP) May 30, 1827, 4 miles E Welchton, Jackson Co. W 1/2 SW 1/4

Sect. 27 Tp. 6 R. 11, north and west.

**1682. WILLIAMSON, Charles**
May 30, 1827, 3 miles E Jacob, Jackson Co. W 1/2 NW 1/4 Sect. 21 Tp. 6 R. 11, north and west.

**1683. WILLIAMSON, Charles**
May 30, 1827, 3 1/2 miles ESE Jacob, Jackson Co. W 1/2 SW 1/4 Sect. 21 Tp. 6 R. 11, north and west.

**1684. WILLIAMSON, Charles**
May 30, 1827, 4 miles E by S Jacob, Jackson Co. W 1/2 NW 1/4 Sect. 22 Tp. 6 R. 11, north and west.

**1685. WILLIAMSON, Charles**
(DUP) May 30, 1827, 5 miles E Welchton, Jackson Co. W 1/2 SW 1/4 Sect. 25 Tp. 6 R. 11, north and west.

**1686. WILLIAMSON, Charles**
(DUP) May 30, 1827, 4 miles E Welchton, Jackson Co. E 1/2 SE 1/4 Sect. 28 Tp. 6 R. 11, north and west.

**1687. WILLIAMSON, Charles**
May 30, 1827, 3 1/2 miles E Welchton, Jackson Co. E 1/2 NW 1/4 Sect. 35 Tp. 6 R. 11, north and west.

**1688. WILLIAMSON, Charles**
May 30, 1827, 4 miles E Welchton, Jackson Co. E 1/2 SW 1/4 Sect. 27 Tp. 6 R. 11, north and west.

**1689. WILLIAMSON, Charles**
May 30, 1827, 4 1/2 miles E Welchton, Jackson Co. E 1/2 SE 1/4 Sect. 27 Tp. 6 R. 11, north and west.

**1690. WILLIAMSON, Charles**
May 30, 1827, 3 1/2 miles E Welchton, Jackson Co. E 1/2 SW 1/4 Sect. 35 Tp. 6 R. 11, north and west.

**1691. WILLIAMSON, Charles**
May 30, 1827, 5 1/2 miles E Welchton, Jackson Co. W 1/2 SE 1/4 Sect. 35 Tp. 6 R. 11, north and west.

**1692. WILLIAMSON, Charles**
May 30, 1827, 5 1/2 miles E Welchton, Jackson Co. E 1/2 SE 1/4 Sect. 35 Tp. 6 R. 11, north and west.

**1710. WILLIAMSON, Charles**
May 31, 1827, 1/2 mile WSW Campbellton, Jackson Co. E 1/2 NE 1/4 Sect. 2 Tp. 6 R. 12, north and west.

**1711. WILLIAMSON, Charles**
May 31, 1827, 1/2 mile SWW Campbellton, Jackson Co. W 1/2 NE 1/4 Sect. 2 Tp. 6 R. 12, north and west.

**1712. WILLIAMSON, Charles**
May 31, 1827, 5 miles E by S Graceville, Jackson Co. E 1/2 NW 1/4 Sect. 5 Tp. 6 R. 12, north and west.

**1713. WILLIAMSON, Charles**
May 31, 1827, 4 miles E by S Graceville, Jackson Co. W 1/2 NW 1/4 Sect. 5 Tp. 6 R. 12, north and west.

**1714. WILLIAMSON, Charles**
(DUP) May 31, 1827, 4 miles E by S Graceville, Jackson Co. E 1/2 NE 1/4 Sect. 6 Tp. 6 R. 12, north and west.

**1715. WILLIAMSON, Charles**
(DUP) May 31, 1827, just W Jacob, Jackson Co. E 1/2 NE 1/4 Sect. 14 Tp. 6 R. 12, north and west.

**1716. WILLIAMSON, Charles**
(DUP) May 31, 1827, 1/4 mile W Jacob, Jackson Co. W 1/2 NE 1/4 Sect. 14 Tp. 6 R. 12, north and west.

**1721. WILLIAMSON, Charles**
May 31, 1827, 4 miles E Graceville, Jackson Co. E 1/2 SE 1/4 Sect. 31 Tp. 7 R. 12, north and west.

**1722. WILLIAMSON, Charles**
May 31, 1827, 4 1/2 miles E Graceville, Jackson Co. W 1/2 SW 1/4 Sect. 32 Tp. 7 R. 12, north and west.

**1723. WILLIAMSON, Charles**
(DUP) May 31, 1827, 4 miles E Graceville, Jackson Co. E 1/2 SW 1/4 Sect. 32 Tp. 7 R. 12, north and west.

**1724. WILLIAMSON, Charles**
(DUP) May 31, 1827, 6 miles E Graceville, Jackson Co. W 1/2 SW 1/4 Sect. 35 Tp. 7 R. 12, north and west.

**1725. WILLIAMSON, Charles**
(DUP) May 31, 1827, 2 miles W Campbellton, Jackson Co. E 1/2 SW 1/4 Sect. 35 Tp. 7 R. 12, north and west.

**1726. WILLIAMSON, Charles**
May 31, 1827, 1 1/2 miles W Campbellton, Jackson Co. W 1/2 SE 1/4 Sect. 35 Tp. 7 R. 12, north and west.

**1727. WILLIAMSON, Charles**
May 31, 1827, at Campbellton, Jackson Col. E 1/2 SE 1/4 Sect. 35 Tp. 7 R. 12, north and west.

**1731. WILLIAMSON, Charles**
June 1, 1827, at St. Mark's, Wakulla Co. Lot No. 1 Sect. 2 Tp. 4 R. 1, south and east.

**1733. WILLIAMSON, Charles**

(DUP) June 1, 1827, 1 mile S St. Mark's, Wakulla Co. Lot No. 2 Sect. 11 Tp. 4 R. 1, south and east.

**1734. WILLIAMSON, Charles**
(DUP) June 1, 1827, 1 mile S St. Mark's, Wakulla Co. Lot No. 3 Sect. 11 Tp. 4 R. 1, south and east.

**1735. WILLIAMSON, Charles**
(DUP) June 2, 1827, at St. Mark's Wakulla Co. Lot No. 3 Sect. 4 Tp. 4 R. 1, south and east.

**1782. WILLIAMSON, Charles**
June 5, 1827, 2 miles SW Chattahoochee, Jackson Co. SW 1/4 Sect. 1 Tp. 3 R. 6, north and west.

**1783. WILLIAMSON, Charles**
June 5, 1827, 3 1/2 miles SW Mear's Spur, Gadsden Co. E 1/2 NE 1/4 Sect. 27 Tp. 3 R. 6, north and west.

**1784. WILLIAMSON, Charles**
June 5, 1827, 4 miles SW Mear's Spur, Gadsden Co. W 1/2 SW 1/4 Sect. 26 Tp. 3 R. 6, north and west.

**1834. WILLIAMSON, Charles**
June 5, 1827, 1 mile E Chattahoochee, Gadsden Co. W 1/2 NE 1/4 Sect. 3 Tp. 3 R. 6, north and west.

**1835. WILLIAMSON, Charles**
June 5, 1827, 5 miles SSE Chattahoochee, Gadsden Co. W 1/2 NE 1/4 Sect. 27 Tp. 3 R. 6, north and west.

**1836. WILLIAMSON, Charles**
June 5, 1827, 2 miles SE Cottondale, Jackson Co. W 1/2 SE 1/4 Sect. 4 Tp. 4 R. 11, north and west.

**1837. WILLIAMSON, Charles**
June 5, 1827, 2 miles SE Cottondale, Jackson Co. E 1/2 SW 1/4 Sect. 4 Tp. 4 R. 11, north and west.

**1838. WILLIAMSON, Charles**
June 5, 1827, 1 1/2 miles S Cottondale, Jackson Co. W 1/2 SE 1/4 Sect. 5 Tp. 4 R. 11, north and west.

**1839. WILLIAMSON, Charles**
June 5, 1827, 2 miles S Cottondale, Jackson Co. E 1/2 NE 1/4 Sect. 8 Tp. 4 R. 11, north and west.

**1840. WILLIAMSON, Charles**
June 5, 1827, 3 miles SW Mear's Spur, Gadsden Co. W 1/2 NW 1/4 Sect. 26 Tp. 3 R. 6, north and west.

**1841. WILLIAMSON, Charles**
June 5, 1827, 1 mile S River Junction, Gadsden Co. W 1/2 NW 1/4 Sect. 8 Tp. 3 R. 6, north and west.

**1842. WILLIAMSON, Charles**
June 5, 1827, 4 miles SW Mear's Spur, Gadsden Co. SE 1/4 Sect. 27 Tp. 3 R. 6, north and west.

**1843. WILLIAMSON, Charles**
June 5, 1827, 1 mile E Chattahoochee, Gadsden Co. SW 1/4 Sect. 27 Tp. 3 R. 6, north and west.

**1844. WILLIAMSON, Charles**
June 5, 1827, 1 mile SW Kynesville, Jackson Co. E 1/2 SE 1/4 Sect. 8 Tp. 4 R. 11, north and west.

**1845. WILLIAMSON, Charles**
June 5, 1827, 2 miles S Welchton, Jackson Co. NE 1/4 Sect. 11 Tp. 5 R. 12, north and west.

**1846. WILLIAMSON, Charles**
June 5, 1827, 2 miles S Welchton, Jackson Co. W 1/2 NW 1/4 Sect. 12 Tp. 5 R. 12, north and west.

**1847. WILLIAMSON, Charles**
(DUP) June 5, 1827, 2 1/2 miles S by W Chattahoochee, Gadsden Co. W 1/2 NW 1/4 Sect. 17 Tp. 3 R. 6, north and west.

**1848. WILLIAMSON, Charles**
(DUP) June 5, 1827, 3 miles S by W Chattahoochee, Gadsden Co. W 1/2 SW 1/4 Sect. 17 Tp. 3 R. 6, north and west.

**1849. WILLIAMSON, Charles**
(DUP) June 5, 1827, 6 miles S Chattahoochee, Gadsden Co. W 1/2 NE 1/4 Sect. 28 Tp. 3 R. 6, north and west.

**1851. WILLIAMSON, Charles**
(DUP) June 5, 1827, 4 miles SW Chattahoochee, Gadsden Co. Sect. 18 Tp. 3 R. 6, north and west. (642.75 acres, $803.42)

**1852. WILLIAMSON, Charles**
June 5, 1827, 5 miles W Chattahoochee, Gadsden Co. W 1/2 SE 1/4 Sect. 8 Tp. 3 R. 5, north and west.

**1853. WILLIAMSON, Charles**
(DUP) June 5, 1827, 1 1/2 miles E Welchton, Jackson Co. NE 1/4 Sect. 36 Tp. 6 R. 11, north and west.

**1854. WILLIAMSON, Charles**
(DUP) June 6, 1827, 3 1/2 miles SSW Greenwood, Jackson Co. E 1/2 SE 1/4 Sect. 11 Tp. 5 R. 10, north and west.

**WILLIAMSON, Chas.** see **Robert Jameson, Jr. #1624 & 1625**

See **ROBERT JAMIESON, #1700-1704**
See **C. L. MATHEWS, #1551**

**95. WILLIAMSON, David Blake**
Dec. 24, 1844, 2 3/4 miles SE LaCrosse, Alachua Co. SW 1/4 SE 1/4 Sect. 1 Tp. 8 R. 19, south and east.

**96. WILLIAMSON, David Blake**
Dec. 24, 1844, 3 miles SE LaCrosse, Alachua Co. NW 1/4 NE 1/4 Sect. 12 Tp. 8 R. 19, south and east.

**2090. WILLIAMSON, David Blake**
Aug. 22, 1853, 3 miles NE Hague, Alachua Co. SE 1/4 NE 1/4 Sect. 14 Tp. 8 R. 19, south and east. Patent delivered Nov. 12, 1856.

**7138. WILLIAMSON, John**
Dec. 13, 1837, 1 1/4 miles SW Chipola, Calhoun Co. SW 1/4 Sect. 4 Tp. 1 R. 9, north and west.

**7139. WILLIAMSON, John**
Dec. 13, 1837, 2 miles SW Chipola, Calhoun Co. W 1/2 SE 1/4 Sect. 5 Tp. 1 R. 9, north and west.

**7438. WILLIAMSON, John**
April 5, 1838, 3 miles WSW Chipola, Calhoun Co. NE 1/4 and E 1/2 NW 1/4 Sect. 5 Tp. 1 R. 9, north and west.

**7466. WILLIAMSON, John**
May 9, 1838, 2 miles SSW Chipola, Calhoun Co. E 1/2 SE 1/4 Sect. 5 Tp. 1 R. 9, north and west.

**80. WILLIAMSON, Nathan**
Nov. 29, 1826, 2 miles E Chipola Big Sprg., Jackson Co. NE 1/4 Sect. 32 Tp. 5 R. 9, north and west. Indorsed by **W. T. KILBEE** for **Nathan WILLIAMSON**, June 11, 1827.

**245. WILLIAMSON, Nathan**
Dec. 30, 1826, 7 miles NE Cottondale, Jackson Co. NE 1/4 Sect. 22 Tp. 5 R. 10, north and west. Transferred from **N. WILLIAMSON** to **Jacob ROBINSON**, Jan. 1, 1827. Transferred from **Jacob ROBINSON** to **George PAYTHROP**, Feb. 14, 1827.

**246. WILLIAMSON, Nathan**
Dec. 30, 1826, 6 miles NE Marianna, Jackson Co. NW 1/4 Sect. 33 Tp. 5 R. 9, north and west. Transfers: **N. WILLIAMSON** to **W. T. KILBEE** on June 10, 1827.

**247. WILLIAMSON, Nathan**
Dec. 30, 1826, 7 miles SE Greenwood, Jackson Co. SE 1/4 Sect. 32 Tp. 5 R. 9, north and west. Transfers: **Nathan WILLIAMSON** to **W. T. KILBEE**, June 10, 1827.

**248. WILLIAMSON, Nathan**
Dec. 30, 1826, 7 miles SE Greenwood, Jackson Co. SW 1/4 Sect. 33 Tp. 5 R. 9, north and west. Transfers: **Nathan WILLIAMSON** to **W. T. KILBEE**, June 11, 1827.

**282. WILLIAMSON, Nathan**
Jan. 1, 1827, 4 miles N Marianna, Jackson Co. NE 1/4 Sect. 22 Tp. 5 R. 10, north and west. Transfers: **Nathan WILLIAMSON** to **Major George POYTHROP**, Feb. 1, 1827.

**2233. WILLIS, Byrd C.**
Jan. 22, 1828, at Rose, Jefferson Co. SE 1/4 Sect. 17 Tp. 1 R. 3, south and east.

**37. WILLIS, David**
Nov. 6, 1826, c. 4 miles W Quincy, Gadsden Co. SE 1/4 Sect. 1 Tp. 2 R. 4, north and west.

**3058. WILLIS, David**
Sept. 21, 1829, 1 1/2 miles SSW Lake Jackson Station, Leon Co. W 1/2 NE 1/4 Sect. 12 Tp. 1 R. 2, north and west.

**181. WILLIS, Edgerton**
Dec. 29, 1826, 2 miles W Jamieson Station, Gadsden Co. NW 1/4 Sect. 9 Tp. 3 R. 3, north and west. Transferred to **S. O. M. A. ARMISTEAD**, Jan. 1, 1827.

**8180. WILLIS, Edgerton**
(No date) 1 mile SSW Lake Jackson (town), Leon Co. SE 1/4 SW 1/4 Sect. 7 Tp. 1 R. 1, north and west. Lost receipt sworn before **James WILLIS**, J. P. of Leon Co.

**8785. WILLIS, Edgerton**
June 6, 1845, 1 mile S Lake Jackson (town), Leon Co. SW 1/4 NE 1/4 Sect. 7 Tp. 1 R. 1, north and west.

**3194. WILLIS, George**
Dec. 30, 1829, 3 miles W by N Stephensville, Taylor Co. W 1/2 SW 1/4 Sect. 15 Tp. 9 R. 9, south and east.

**4403. WILLIS, George**
Aug. 27, 1833, 2 1/2 miles W by S Felkel, Leon Co. NE 1/4 SE 1/4 Sect. 1 Tp. 2 R. 2, north and east.

**4953. WILLIS, George**
April 29, 1835, Note: Lot No. 1 Sect.

38 Tp. 2 R. 30, south and west. According to sectional map there are only 36 sections to the township, and therefore, the above locations would be in the middle of Pensacola Bay, Escambia Co., unless the system of marking off townships in 1835 in the above county differed radically from that of the present.

**5248. WILLIS, George**
Nov. 5, 1835, 1 mile NE West Pensacola, Escambia Co. Lot No. 6 Fractional Sect. 15 Tp. 2 R. 30, south and west.

**5624. WILLIS, George**
April 26, 1836, 2 miles E West Pensacola, Escambia Co. Lot No. 6 Fractional Sect. 15 Tp. 2 R. 30, south and west.

**5718. WILLIS, George**
June 23, 1836, 2 miles SW Camp Walton, Okaloosa Co. Fractional Sect. 22 Tp. 2 R. 24, south and west.

**5718. WILLIS, George**
June 23, 1836, 1 1/2 miles S Camp Walton, Okaloosa Co. Fractional Sect. 23 Tp. 2 R. 24, south and west.

**7951. WILLIS, George E.**
May 7, 1839, 1 mile SW Goulding, Escambia Co. S 1/2 Lot No. 2 Sect. 15 Tp. 2 R. 30, south and west.

**WILLIS, Gissett see Redden W. PARRAMORE, #4902**

**170. WILLIS, James**
Dec. 29, 1826, 2 miles NE Quincy, Gadsden Co. E 1/2 NE 1/4 Sect. 14 Tp. 3 R. 3, north and west.

**5876. WILLIS, James**
Oct. 1, 1836, 1/4 mile W Lake Jackson, Leon Co. Lot No. 8 Fractional Sect. 1 Tp. 1 R. 2, north and west.

**5562. WILLIS, Jesse H.**
Mar. 28, 1836, at Cape San Blas, 1 mile SE San Blas Lighthouse, Gulf Co. Fractional Sect. 5 Tp. 10 R. 11, south and west.

**5563. WILLIS, Jesse H.**
Mar. 28, 1836, at Cape San Blas, 3/4 mile SE San Blas Lighthouse, Gulf Co. Fractional Sect. 4 Tp. 10 R. 11, south and west.

**6409. WILLIS, Jesse H.**
Jan. 10, 1837, 3 miles NE Lutterloh, "Gray Place, Leon Co. NE 1/4 Sect. 23 Tp. 1 R. 1, south and east.

**7360. WILLIS, Jesse H.**
Feb. 27, 1838, 3 1/2 miles N by E Marianna, Jackson Co. SW 1/4 Sect. 27 Tp. 5 R. 10, north and west.
See **Redden W. PARRAMORE**

**4170. WILLIS, Jessee M.**
Feb. 18, 1856, 1 mile SE Hodgson, Levy Co. SE 1/4 NE 1/4 Sect. 32 Tp. 12 R. 19, south and east. Patent delivered Mar. 23, 1858.

**4171. WILLIS, Jessee M.**
Feb. 18, 1856, 1 1/4 miles SE Hodgson, Levy Co. W 1/2 SE 1/4 Sect. 32 Tp. 12 R. 19, south and east. Patent delivered Mar. 23, 1858.

**3506. WILLIS, Jonathan**
May 6, 1830, 4 1/2 miles NNW Bradfordville, Leon Co. E 1/2 NE 1/4 Sect. 1 Tp. 2 R. 1, north and east.

**4307. WILLIS, Jonathan**
Feb. 9, 1833, 2 1/2 miles W Felkel, Leon Co. W 1/2 NW 1/4 Sect. 1 Tp. 2 R. 2, north and east.

**5480. WILLIS, Jonathan**
Feb. 19, 1836, 1 3/4 miles SSW Felkel, Leon Co. NE 1/4 SW 1/4 Sect. 6 Tp. 2 R. 2, north and east.

**1849. WILLIS, Thomas C.**
May 5, 1853, 5 miles W Claymo, Bradford Co. NW 1/4 NW 1/4 Sect. 2 Tp. 7 R. 19, south and east.

**WILSON, Benj. see James B. COLE, #601**

**9626. WILSON, Elizabeth Ann**
Oct. 19, 1891, 5 miles W Greensboro, Gadsden Co. NE 1/4 SE 1/4 Sect. 10 Tp. 2N R. 6W.

**1995. WILSON, Henry**
July 30, 1853, 2 3/4 miles SSW Worthinton Post Office, Alachua Co. E 1/2 NE 1/4 Sect. 2 Tp. 7 R. 17, south and east. Patent delivered Mar. 6, 1870.

**5121. WILSON, Henry**
Oct. 22, 1859, 3 miles SW Lulu, Columbia Co. W 1/2 SE 1/4 Sect. 6 Tp. 5 R. 18, south and east.

**5943. WILSON, Henry**
Oct. 31, 1836, 5 miles W by N Fort Barrancas, Escambia Co. W 1/2 SW 1/4 Sect. 1 Tp. 3 R. 32, south and west.

**5944. WILSON, Henry**
Oct. 31, 1836, 6 miles W by N Fort Barrancas, Escambia Co. Lot No. 4

Fractional Sect. 2 Tp. 3 R. 32, south and west.

**2546. WILSON, James**
Nov. 16, 1828, 1 mile E Roy, Gadsden Co. W 1/2 NW 1/4 Sect. 7 Tp. 2 R. 6, north and west.

**2547. WILSON, James**
Nov. 16, 1828, 1 1/2 miles SE Roy, Gadsden Co. W 1/2 SW 1/4 Sect. 7 Tp. 2 R. 6, north and west.

**3616. WILSON, James**
Sept. 19, 1830, 1/2 mile E Roy, Liberty Co. E 1/2 NE 1/4 Sect. 12 Tp. 2 R. 7, north and west.

**1802. WILSON, Jas. I.**
June 5, 1827, 2 miles S by W Quincy, Gadsden Co. E 1/2 SE 1/4 Sect. 13 Tp. 2 R. 4, north and west.

**1467. WILSON, James J.**
(DUP) May 22, 1827, 2 miles S Quincy, Gadsden Co. E 1/2 NE 1/4 Sect. 13 Tp. 2 R. 4, north and west.

**2459. WILSON, John T. J.**
Aug. 19, 1828, 2 miles E Roy, Gadsden Co. E 1/2 SE 1/4 Sect. 6 Tp. 2 R. 6, north and west.

**2461. WILSON, John T. J.**
Aug. 19, 1828, 2 miles SE Roy, Gadsden Co. E 1/2 SE 1/4 Sect. 7 Tp. 2 R. 6, north and west.

**2462. WILSON, John T. J.**
Aug. 19, 1828, 1 mile E Roy, Gadsden Co. W 1/2 SW 1/4 Sect. 8 Tp. 2 R. 6, north and west.

**3075. WILSON, John T. J.**
Oct. 1, 1829, 2 miles S Ocheesee, Calhoun Co. W 1/2 NE 1/4 Sect. 10 Tp. 2 R. 7, north and west.

**3621. WILSON, John T. J.**
Sept. 30, 1830, 5 miles S by W Chattahoochee, Gadsden Co. E 1/2 NW 1/4 Sect. 29 Tp. 3 R. 6, north and west.

**3962. WILSON, John T. J.**
May 10, 1831, 5 miles S Chattahoochee, Gadsden Co. W 1/2 NW 1/4 Sect. 28 Tp. 3 R. 6, north and west.

**7160. WILSON, John T. J.**
Dec. 20, 1837, 4 miles N by W Malone, Jackson Co. E 1/2 SW 1/4 Sect. 28 Tp. 7 R. 10, north and west.

**WILSON, J. F. I. see Romeo LEWIS, #2671**

**2703. WILSON, Mary A.**
Feb. 2, 1829, 5 miles NE Rockbluff, Gadsden Co. W 1/2 SE 1/4 Sect. 8 Tp. 2 R. 6, north and west.

**2704. WILSON, Mary A.**
Feb. 2, 1829, 5 miles NE Rockbluff, Gadsden Co. W 1/2 SE 1/4 Sect. 8 Tp. 2 R. 6, north and west.

**5032. WILSON, William H.**
May 30, 1859, 2 1/2 miles SW Cooper, Columbia Co. E 1/2 Set. 4 Tp. 5 R. 15, south and east.

**4604. WIMBERLEY, Isaac**
Aug. 9, 1834, 2 1/2 miles NNE Marianna, Jackson Co. NE 1/4 SW 1/4 Sect. 25 Tp. 5 R. 10, north and west.

**8605. WIMBERLEY, Isaac**
Oct. 2, 1843, 4 miles W Dellwood, Jackson Co. SW 1/4 SW 1/4 Sect. 22 Tp. 5 R. 9, north and west.

**512. WINDHAM, Benjamin**
May 2, 1831, 5 miles NW Ashville, Jefferson Co. W 1/2 NW 1/4 Sect. 26 Tp. 3 R. 6, north and west.

**8578. WINDOM, Benjamin**
Feb. 13, 1843, 1 1/4 miles N by E Ocheesee, Calhoun Co. W 1/2 NW 1/4 Sect. 26 Tp. 3 R. 7, north and east.

**4189. WINGIT, William J.**
Feb. 22, 1856, 4 1/2 miles NNW Providence, Columbia Co. NE 1/4 SW 1/4 Sect. 31 Tp. 5 R. 17, south and east.

**4190. WINGIT, William J.**
Feb. 22, 1856, 5 miles NNW Providence, Columbia Co. NW 1/4 NW 1/4 Sect. 6 Tp. 6 R. 17, south and east.

**2774. WIRICK, Adam**
March 6, 1829, 2 miles SE Monticello, Jefferson Co. W 1/2 SE 1/4 Sect. 32 Tp. 2 R. 5, north and east.

**2775. WIRICK, Adam**
March 6, 1829, 1/2 mile S Monticello, Jefferson Co. W 1/2 NW 1/4 Sect. 32 Tp. 2 R. 5, north and east.

**3469. WIRICK, Adam**
March 31, 1830, 1/2 mile NW Capitola, Leon Co. W 1/2 SE 1/4 Sect. 24 Tp. 1 R. 2, north and east.

**3606. WIRICK, Adam**
Sept. 9, 1830, 1/2 mile SSW Monticello, Jefferson Co. NE 1/4 Sect. 31 Tp. 2 R. 5, north and east. Paid with Scrip Cert. No. 160 and 162, issued to **Alex'r**

MACOMB and dated May 30, 1829. "Jefferson City Lands."

**3114. WIRT, William**
Nov. 9, 1829, 2 miles E Braswell Station, Jefferson Co. W 1/2 SW 1/4 Sect. 14 Tp. 1 R. 4, north and east.

**137. WISTER, Elias**
Dec. 26, 1826, 2 miles S Mt. Pleasant Station, Gadsden Co. SW 1/4 Sect. 25 Tp. 3 R. 4, north and west. Transferred to **Aquila BRUTON** April 1927. **Jas. J. WILLIAMS** and **Daniel BUIE**, witnesses.

**153. WITHERS, John**
(DUP) Dec. 28, 1826, at Darsey Post Office, Gadsden Co. SW 1/4 Sect. 7 Tp. 3 R. 2, north and west. Transferred to **Dennis ADAMS**, Dec. 28, 1826, by **John WEATHERS(WITHERS?)**. Transferred to **William WILLIAMS**, Nov. 29, 1828, by **Dennis ADAMS**.

**1725. WITT, David**
Feb. 22, 1853, 1 1/2 miles E Mason, Columbia Co. SE 1/4 NW 1/4 Sect. 26 Tp. 5 R. 17, south and east.

**4081. WITTE, Andrew J.**
Jan. 10, 1856, at Mason, Columbia Co. NW 1/4 SW 1/4 Sect. 23 and NE 1/4 SE 1/4 Sect. 22 Tp. 5 R. 17, south and east. Patent delivered July 28, 1867.

**6489. WOLFE, William**
Jan. 18, 1837, 1/2 mile SE Centerville, Leon Co. SE 1/4 SW 1/4 Sect. 19 Tp. 2 R. 2, north and east.

**70. WOMACK, David**
Nov. 23, 1826, 3 miles S Quincy, Gadsden Co. E 1/2 NW 1/4 Sect. 24 Tp. 2 R. 3, north and west.

**3187. WOMACK, Heney M.**
Dec. 28, 1829, 3 miles SSE Florence, Gadsden Co. W 1/2 NW 1/4 Sect. 18 Tp. 2 R. 2, north and west.

**5265. WOMBLE, Henry**
Nov. 18, 1835, 2 1/2 miles SE by E Dills, Jefferson Co. SE 1/4 SW 1/4 Sect. 2 Tp. 2 R. 6, north and east.

**8575. WOOD, Andrew J.**
Jan. 7, 1843, 1 3/4 miles N by W Cox, Calhoun Co. E 1/2 NE 1/4 Sect. 6 Tp. 2 R. 9, north and west.

**3991. WOOD, Igdaliah(?)**
June 24, 1831, 4 1/2 miles ESE Chattahoochee, Gadsden Co. E 1/2 SW 1/4 Sect. 7 Tp. 3 R. 5, north and west.

**2213. WOOD, Sam'l D.**
(of Fla.) Jan. 9, 1828, a mile SE Chaires, Leon Co. E 1/2 NW 1/4 Sect. 36 Tp. 1 R. 2, north and east.

**6069. WOOD, Silas**
Oct. 27, 1837, 3 miles SSW Chipola, Calhoun Co. E 1/2 SW 1/4 Sect. 5 Tp. 1 R. 9, south and west.

**8355. WOOD, Silas**
June 18, 1840, 4 miles SW Bristol, Liberty Co. Lots No. 1, 2, and 3 Sect. 15 Tp. 1 R. 8, south and west.

**908. WOODBERRY, Collin**
Jan. 17, 1827, 5 miles SSE Quincy, Gadsden Co. E 1/2 SW 1/4 Sect. 29 Tp. 2 R. 3, north and west. Transferred Jan. 25, 1827, to **Thos. A. STRAIN**. Transferred Dec. 27, 1829, to **Wm. HELMS**.

**6920. WOODS, Willis A.**
March 17, 1837, 3 miles NW Dills, Jefferson Co. S 1/2 NW 1/4 Sect. 26 Tp. 3 R. 5, north and east.

**6921. WOODS, Willis A.**
Mar. 17, 1837, 3 miles NNW Dills, Jefferson Co. W 1/2 NE 1/4 Sect. 26 Tp. 3 R. 5, north and east.

**4442. WOOLF, Daniel**
Oct. 23, 1833, 1 1/4 miles NNE Monticello, Jefferson Co. SW 1/4 NE 1/4 Sect. 21 Tp. 2 R. 5, north and east.

**4443. WOOLF, Daniel**
Oct. 23, 1833, 1 mile NNE Monticello, Jefferson Co. NE 1/4 SW 1/4 Sect. 21 Tp. 2 R. 5, north and east.

**10. WOOTEN, Collin**
Sept. 1, 1826, near Quincy, Gadsden Co. SW 1/4 Sect. 26 Tp. 3 R. 4, north and west. Rec'd $200.31 1/4 for 160.25 acres. **R. K. CALL**, Receiver.

**81. WOOTEN, Collin**
Nov. 29, 1826, 2 miles SE Gretha Post Office, Gadsden Co. SE 1/4 Sect. 24 Tp. 3 R. 4, north and west.

**9. WOOTEN, J. J. A.**
Sept. 1, 1826, near Quincy, Gadsden Co. NW 1/4 Sect. 26 Tp. 3 R. 4, north and west. Rec'd $200.31 1/4 for 160. 25 acres. **R. K. CALL**, Receiver.

**1885. WOOTEN, John**
June 9, 1827, 6 miles SE Quincy, Gadsden Co. E 1/2 SE 1/4 Sect. 22

Tp. 2 R. 3, north and west.

**7637. WOOTEN, John**
Sept. 11, 1838, 2 miles SE Fincher, Leon Co. SE 1/4 SE 1/4 Sect. 19 Tp. 3 R. 4, north and east. This receipt is a duplicate. The original having been burnt in a fire which destroyed the house of owner. This receipt being in the nature of a deposition to that effect and sworn to before Honorable **R. W. ANDREWS**, Reg. for Land Office at Tallahassee. House was destroyed in 1839, and deposition made on Jan. 2, 1850.

**8810. WOOTEN, John**
Sept 11, 1845, 1 mile SE Chattahoochee, Gadsden Co. NE 1/4 SE 1/4 Sect. 4 Tp. 3 R. 6, north and west.

**8811. WOOTEN, John**
Sept. 11, 1845, 1 1/4 miles SE Chattahoochee, Gadsden Co. NW 1/4 SW 1/4 Sect. 3 Tp. 3 R. 6, north and west.

**8840. WOOTEN, John**
Nov. 17, 1845, 3/4 mile SE Chattahoochee, Gadsden Co. W 1/2 SE 1/4 Sect. 4 Tp. 3 R. 6, north and west.

**12. WOOTEN, Paschal H.**
Sept. 1, 1826, near Quincy, Gadsden Co. SE 1/4 Sect. 22 Tp. 3 R. 4, north and west. Rec'd $200.38 3/4 for 160.31 acres. **R. K. CALL**, Register.

**889. WORDEHOFFE, Antonie**
June 23, 1851, 2 miles S Oneco, Manatee Co. SE 1/4 SE 1/4 Sect. 25 Tp. 34 R. 17, south and east. On back of receipt was printed: "Returned Dec. 16, 1861, **A. WORDEHOFFE.**

**324. WORREL, Joseph W.**
Mar. 23, 1827, 8 miles W Greenwood, Jackson Co. NE 1/4 Sect. 32 Tp. 6 R. 11, north and west.

**5195. WORTHINGTON, Frederick**
Oct. 8, 1835, 3 1/2 miles SE Jumper, Gadsden Co. NW 1/4 SE 1/4 Sect. 34 Tp. 2 R. 5, north and west.

**2728. WRIGHT, Arthur I. T.**
(and **James W. CATHEY**) May 2, 1854, at Watertown, Columbia Co. SW 1/4 SW 1/4 Sect. 27 Tp. 3 R. 17, south and east. Patent delivered Dec. 1, 1869.

**2729. WRIGHT, Arthur I. T.**
(and **James W. CATHEY**) May 2, 1854, 1/4 mile NW Watertown, Columbia Co., NW 1/4 NW 1/4 Sect. 34 Tp. 3 R. 17, south and east. Patent delivered Dec. 1, 1869.

**645. WRIGHT, Arthur J. T.**
July 23, 1847, 1 mile NW Lake City, Columbia Co. NE 1/4 SW 1/4 Sect. 13 Tp. 3 R. 16, south and east. Patent delivered May 1, 1854.

**1231. WRIGHT, Levi**
Mar. 3, 1852, 3 1/4 miles NNW Watertown, Columbia Co. SE 1/4 SW 1/4 Sect. 17 Tp. 3 R. 16, south and east. Patent delivered Nov. 11, 1856.

**1184. WRIGHT, Thomas**
(DUP) March 2, 1827, 2 miles SW Waukenah, Jefferson Co. E 1/2 SE 1/4 Sect. 8 Tp. 1 R. 4, south and east.

**1220. WRIGHT, Thomas**
(DUP) Mar. 20, 1827, 2 miles E Lloyd, Jefferson Co. E 1/2 NW 1/4 Sect. 13 Tp. 1 R. 3, south and east.

**1259. WRIGHT, Thomas**
(DUP) April 9, 1827, 2 miles SW Waukenah, Jefferson Co. SW 1/4 Sect. 9 Tp. 1 R. 4, south and east.

**7855. WRIGHT, William A. J.**
Feb. 6, 1839, 3 miles SSE Havana, Gadsden Co. NW 1/4 SE 1/4 Sect. 11 Tp. 2 R. 2, north and west.

**2875. WYATT, Wm.**
July 6, 1829, just E Ocheesee, Calhoun Co. Lot No. 5 Sect. 20 Tp. 2 R. 7, north and west. Transferred July 28, 1829, to Seaton **GRANTHAM, G. W. WARD**, Reg.

**6917. WYCHE, George**
March 15, 1837, 3 miles NW Cherry Lake Post Office, Madison Co. E 1/2 NE 1/4 Sect. 1 Tp. 2 R. 8, north and east.

**7991. WYCHE, George**
June 17, 1839, 1/4 mile E Hamburg, Madison Co. SW 1/4 SE 1/4 Sect. 14 Tp. 2 R. 8, north and east.

**7992. WYCHE, George**
June 17, 1839, 3 1/4 miles E by N Bond, Madison Co. NW 1/4 NE 1/4 Sect. 1 Tp. 2 R. 8, north and east.

**7645. WYCHE, John S.**
Sept. 18, 1838, 2 3/4 miles W by E Hamburg, Madison Co. SW 1/4 SW 1/4 Sect. 18 Tp. 2 R. 9, north and east.

**8083. WYCHE, William**
Sept. 19, 1839, 1/4 mile E Hamburg,

Madison Co. NE 1/4 SW 1/4 Sect. 14 Tp. 2 R. 8, north and east.

**1623. WYNN, John L.**
Jan. 7, 1853, 4 1/2 miles NNW Dukes, Union Co. N 1/2 Lot No. 4 Sect. 7 Tp. 6 R. 20, south and east. Transferred to **Wm. F. HUNT**, of Granville District, S. C. Nov. 26, 1853. Patent delivered Aug. 5, 1857.

\* Y \*

**566. YEARLY, Jacob**
May 16, 1835, 1 mile N Lamont, Jefferson Co. NE 1/4 SW 1/4 Sect. 15 Tp. 1 R. 5, south and east. Transferred to **June R. BEAZLEY**, Jan. 17, 1837.

**5791. YEARTY, William**
July 3, 1836, 4 miles SE Jasper, Hamilton Co. E 1/2 SE 1/4 Sect. 14 Tp. 1 R. 14, south and east.

**7287. YEARTY, William**
Feb. 1, 1828, 2 miles W Genoa, Hamilton Co. SW 1/4 NE 1/4 Sect. 14 Tp. 1 R. 14, south and east.

**6430. YOEMANS, James**
Jan. 5, 1837, 1 mile E Alma, Jefferson Co. Lot No. 6 Fractional Sect. 25 Tp. 3 R. 4, north and east.

**2540. YON, Benjamin**
Nov. 11, 1828, 4 miles NE Quincy, Gadsden Co. W 1/2 NE 1/4 Sect. 20 Tp. 3 R. 3, north and west.

**29. YON, Jesse**
Nov. 1, 1826, at Florence, Gadsden Co. NE 1/4 Sect. 5 Tp. 2 R. 3, north and west.

**2041. YON, Jesse**
Aug. 22, 1827, 2 miles ENE Quincy, Gadsden Co. W 1/2 NE 1/4 Sect. 4 Tp. 2 R. 3, north and west.

**2179. YON, Jesse**
(of Fla.) Dec. 28, 1827, 2 miles ENE Quincy, Gadsden Co. E 1/2 NE 1/4 Sect. 4 Tp. 2 R. 3, north and west.

**2468. YON, Jesse**
Aug. 25, 1828, 1 1/2 miles ENE Quincy, Gadsden Co. W 1/2 NW 1/4 Sect. 4 Tp. 2 R. 3, north and west.

**2697. YON, Jesse**
Jan. 20, 1829, 1/4 mile N Steaphead, Gadsden Co. W 1/2 NE 1/4 Sect. 17 Tp. 2 R. 6, north and west.

**2662. YON, Jesse**
(Jipie?) Jan. 23, 1829, 1/2 mile E Steaphead, Gadeden Co. E 1/2 SE 1/4 Sect. 17 Tp. 2 R. 6, north and west.

**2663. YON, Jesse**
Jan. 23, 1829, 3 miles S Quincy, Gadsden Co. E 1/2 NE 1/4 Sect. 30 Tp. 2 R. 3, north and west.

**2726. YON, Jesse**
Feb. 11, 1829, 4 miles W Greensboro, Gadsden Co. E 1/2 NE 1/4 Sect. 10 Tp. 2 R. 6, north and west.

**2727. YON, Jesse**
Feb. 11, 1829, 4 miles W Greensboro, Gadsden Co. W 1/2 NW 1/4 Sect. 11 Tp. 2 R. 6, north and west.

**3250. YON, Jesse**
Feb. 4, 1830, 2 1/2 miles WNW Roy, Liberty Co. Lot No.7 Fractional Sect. 3 Tp. 2 R. 7, north and west.

**8613. YON, Jesse**
Nov. 6, 1843, 6 miles SE Sharpstown, Calhoun Co. Lot No. 1 and W 1/2 NW 1/4 Sect. 33 Tp. 1 R. 8, south and west.

YON, Jesse see **Romeo LEWIS, #2681**

**8522. YON, Terrell H.**
Jan. 27, 1842, 5 miles NNE Greensboro, Gadsden Co. SW 1/4 SE 1/4 Sect. 34 Tp. 3 R. 6, north and west.

**8614. YON, Terrell H.**
Nov. 6, 1843, 4 3/4 miles SE Sharpstown, Gadsden Co. Lot No. 1 Sect. 4 and W 1/2 NE 1/4 Sect. 5 Tp. 2 R. 8, south and west.

**2454. YONG, Henry F.**
Aug. 12, 1828, 3 miles ESE Sawdust, Gadsden Co. E 1/2 SE 1/4 Sect. 25 Tp. 2 R. 4, north and west.

**3159. YONGE, Philip**
Dec. 10, 1829, 1 1/2 miles NW Rock Bluff, Liberty Co. NW 1/4 Sect. 22 Tp. 2 R. 7, north and west.

**6501. YOUMANS, Absalom**
Jan. 10, 1837, 2 1/2 miles ESE Moseley Hall, Madison Co. NW 1/4 SE 1/4 and SE 1/4 NW 1/4 Sect. 35 Tp. 1 R. 8, south and east.

**6502. YOUMANS, Absalom**
Jan. 10, 1837, 1 mile ESE Moseley Hall, Madison Co. E 1/2 SW 1/4 Sect. 35 Tp. 1 R. 8, south and east.

**7050. YOUMANS, Absalom**
Sept. 28, 1837, 1 1/4 miles SW Waco, Madison Co. SE 1/4 SW 1/4 Sect. 26 Tp. 1 R. 8, south and east.

**7688. YOUMANS, Absalom**
Oct. 27, 1838, 3 1/2 miles SE Moseley Hall, Madison Co. E 1/2 SE 1/4 Sect. 35 Tp. 1 R. 8, south and east.

**3975. YOUNG, Andrew**
May 27, 1831, 4 miles NW Cottondale, Jackson Co. W 1/2 NW 1/4 Sect. 13 Tp. 5 R. 12, north and west.

**5421. YOUNG, Andrew**
Jan. 22, 1836, 4 miles NNW Jacob, Jackson Co. NE 1/4 NE 1/4 Sect. 9 Tp. 6 R. 12, north and west.

**5422. YOUNG, Andrew**
Jan. 22, 1836, 3 3/4 miles NNW Jacob, Jackson Co. NW 1/4 NE 1/4 Sect. 9 Tp. 6 R. 12, north and west.

**6498. YOUNG, Andrew**
Jan. 19, 1837, 4 miles NNW Cottondale, Jackson Co. W 1/2 SE 1/4 Sect. 12 Tp. 5 R. 12, north and west.

**6520. YOUNG, Andrew**
Jan. 11, 1837, 2 miles W by S Campbellton, Jackson Co. W 1/2 NW 1/4 Sect. 2 Tp. 6 R. 12, north and west.

**6596. YOUNG, Andrew**
Jan. 19, 1837, 3 miles SW Campbellton, Jackson Co. SE 1/4 NE 1/4 Sect. 9 Tp. 6 R. 12, north and west.

**6597. YOUNG, Andrew**
Jan. 19, 1837, 4 miles NW Cottondale, Jackson Co. W 1/2 SE 1/4 Sect. 11 Tp. 5 R. 12, north and west.

**6612. YOUNG, Andrew**
Jan. 20, 1837, 2 miles WNW Welchton, Jackson Co. W 1/2 NE 1/4 Sect. 26 Tp. 6 R. 12, north and west.

**6642. YOUNG, Andrew**
Jan. 24, 1837, 3 miles S by E Welchton, Jackson Co. E 1/2 SE 1/4 Sect. 12 Tp. 5 R. 12, north and west.

**6681. YOUNG, Andrew**
Jan. 27, 1837, 5 miles NNW Cottondale, Jackson Co. E 1/2 NE 1/4 Sect. 13 Tp. 5 R. 12, north and west.

**6732. YOUNG, Andrew**
Feb. 3, 1837, 2 miles WNW Jacob, Jackson Co. W 1/2 SW 1/4 Sect. 10 Tp. 6 R. 12, north and west.

**7119. YOUNG, Andrew**
Dec. 2, 1837, 3 miles SW Campbellton, Jackson Co. E 1/2 SE 1/4 SW 1/4 Sect. 9 Tp. 6 R. 12, north and west.

**184. YOUNG, David**
Dec. 29, 1826, 5 miles N Quincy, Gadsden Co. E 1/2 SE 1/4 Sect. 12 Tp. 3 R. 3, north and west.

**6267. YOUNG, George**
Dec. 31, 1836, 1 mile N Lake Jackson Co. E 1/2 SE 1/4 Sect. 30 Tp. 2 R. 1, north and west.

**8074. YOUNG, George**
Sept. 18, 1839, 1 mile N by W Lake Jackson Co. E 1/2 SW 1/4 Sect. 30 Tp. 2 R. 1, north and west.

**8826. YOUNG, George**
Oct. 25, 1845, 1 1/4 miles N by W Lake Jackson (town), Leon Co. NE 1/4 NW 1/4 Sect. 31 Tp. 2 R. 1, north and west. **8334. YOUNG, John**
June 5, 1840, 2 1/2 miles SW Dills, Jefferson Co. NE 1/4 Sect. 15 Tp. 2 R. 5, north and east.

**2936. YOUNG, William**
(Of Scriven Co., Ga.) Oct. 4, 1854, 1 1/4 miles N by E Wilcox Junction, Gilchrist Co. NW 1/4 Sect. 8 Tp. 10 R. 14, south and east. Patent delivered May 28, 1869.

**YOUNG see ORMAN & YOUNG**

**138. YOULEE, Darice Levy**
Mar. 4, 1847, 4 1/4 miles E Homasassa, Citrus Co. Lot No. 6 Sect. 29 Tp. 19 R. 17, south and east.

**140. YULEE, Darice Levy**
Mar. 4, 1847, 4 miles E Homasassa, Citrus Co. Lot No. 7 and SE 1/4 1/4 Sect. 29 Tp. 19 R. 17, south and east.

**2772. YULEE, David L.**
June 14, 1854, Joe's Island, Sam's Bay, St. Martin's Keys, Gulf of Mexico, Citrus Co. Lot No. 5 (Joe's Island) Sect. 34 Tp. 19 R. 16, south and east.

# * Z *

ZEIGHER, Nathaniel G. see Daniel J. BRUTON

ZEIGLER, J. J. see William C. CROOM

**8567. ZIPPERER, John L.**
July 1, 1840, 2 miles N Westlake, Hamilton Co. NW 1/4 NE 1/4 Sect. 33 Tp. 2 R. 12, north and east.

**7870. ZIPPERER, John M.**
Feb. 14, 1839, 1/2 mile SW Octahatchee, Gadsden Co. SE 1/4 NE 1/4 and NE 1/4 SE 1/4 Sect. 15 Tp. 2 R. 11, north and east.

**7871. ZIPPERER, John M.**
Feb. 14, 1839, 1/4 mile SW Octahatchee, Gadsden Co. SW 1/4 SE 1/4 Sect. 15 Tp. 2 R. 11, north and east.

ZIPPERER, Solomon see LIPPERER, Solomon #170

ZIPPERERE, Solomon see TIPPERERE, Solomon #451